Professional Visual Basic .NET Transactions

Matthew Bortniker
James Conard

Wrox Press Ltd. ®

Professional Visual Basic .NET Transactions

Published by Wrox Press Ltd,
Arden House, 1102 Warwick Road, Acocks Green,
Birmingham, B27 6BH, UK
Printed in the United States
ISBN 1-861005-95-4

Trademark Acknowledgements

Credits

Authors
Matthew Bortniker
James Conard

Additional Material
Brian Francis
Kent Tegels

Technical Reviewers
Jonathan Allen
Martin Beaulieu
Deepu Bhatia
Cristian Darie
Robin Dewson
Damien Foggon
Mark Horner
David Schultz
Carvin Wilson

Comissioning Editors
Catherine Alexander
Kate Hall

Technical Editors
Catherine Alexander
Helen Callaghan

Project Manager
Christianne Bailey

Author Agents
Avril Corbin
Laura Jones
Cilmara Lion

Project Administrators
Rob Hesketh
Chandima Nethesinghe

Managing Editors
Sarah Drew
Louay Fatoohi

Production Coordinator
Natalie O'Donnell

Index
John Collin

Proof Readers
Fiona Berryman
Chris Smith

Cover
Chris Morris

About the Authors

Matthew Bortniker

Matthew Bortniker has been in the computer field since 1982. Currently he is an independent consultant for local businesses in the Washington DC area and for the US Government. Currently his main tasks include migrating client-server applications to enterprise-wide systems written entirely in Visual Basic .NET and utilizing Oracle and Microsoft technologies.

James Conard

James M. Conard (MCT, MCSD, MCSE) is an independent developer, trainer, and author residing in the Southeastern United States. He specializes in Commerce Server, BizTalk Server, SQL Server, COM+, MSMQ, Web Services, and related Microsoft .NET technologies and has co-authored several books for Wrox Press on these subjects. James frequently teaches and mentors other developers on .NET technologies and consults organizations on how to leverage these technologies to solve real-world business problems. Lately James has been focusing on advanced business-to-business e-commerce solutions that enable organizations to integrate with their trading partners.

Acknowledgements

I would like to thank my wife for her encouragement and patience for the last three months. It's been a hectic year thus far, with a newborn baby (London Reed) in the house and my commitments to work and this book. However, Amanda has managed to keep the house, our new family, and life's everyday issues on track so I could remain focused on the goal at hand.

I would also like to thank everyone at Wrox for remaining committed to this book. It's been a challenging project, but the Wrox team has really managed it well. A special thanks to Cil Lion, Christianne Bailey, Cath Alexander, and Helen Callaghan for allowing me to participate in this book and ensuring its success. I apologize for any scheduling inconveniences I may have caused with my delays. I look forward to participating with all of you on future projects.

I would like to thank my parents who taught me the value of hard work and persistence. Finally, most importantly, I would like to thank the Lord Jesus Christ for the fulfillment of his promises.

"*If any of you lack wisdom, let him ask of God, that giveth to all men liberally, and upbraideth not; and it shall be given him.*" – James 1:5

Pro Visual Basic .NET Transactions

Table of Contents

Pro Visual Basic .NET Transactions

Introduction

Who is this Book for?

This book is written for anyone who is interested in working with transactions using Visual Basic .NET. This book can benefit intermediate-level programmers who are familiar with Visual Basic .NET, and who want to learn to incorporate transactions into their applications. It is also suitable for experienced Visual Basic 6.0 developers who have previously worked with MTS and COM+ services and want to understand how transactions are implemented in the .NET world.

Although this book will try to cover the basic concepts for many existing technologies, it is expected that the reader has already become reasonably familiar with Visual Basic .NET, SQL Server, ASP, HTML, and XML. If you are interested in learning about .NET in general, or Visual Basic .NET in particular, you may wish to consult the following books from Wrox Press:

- *Professional .NET Framework*, ISBN 1-861005-56-3
- *Professional VB.NET*, ISBN 1-861004-97-4

What's Covered in this Book?

Chapter 1, *Laying the Foundations – Transactions, Data Access, and Application Architectures*, introduces transactions, what they are and how they work. It also covers application architecture and introduces technologies for accessing data. After all, in order to work with data, we must first be able to access it.

Chapter 2, *Data access Using Visual Basic .NET*, introduces ADO.NET, and discusses how it differs from ADO. It also introduces XML as ADO.NET can use this to ensure the efficient transfer of data to any application on any platform.

Chapter 3, *SQL Server and Visual Basic .NET*, looks at SQL Server and the SQL language. It examines stored procedures, how transactions work in SQL Server, and how to create transactional stored procedures.

Chapter 4, *The Client Using ASP.NET*, focuses on Web Forms utilizing ASP.NET. As the previous chapter dealt with data tiers, this examines presentation (user) services. It begins by introducing ASP.NET and Web Forms, and then covers HTML server controls and web server controls. From there, it looks at data binding, and displaying data using the `Repeater`, the `DataList`, and the `DataGrid` controls. These data displays can be formatted utilizing various templates.

Chapter 5, *Web Services, SOAP, and Visual Basic .NET*, shows how to create and implement Web Services, as well as how to utilize them for transactions. It also features a detailed look at SOAP and the technologies available for implementing security with Web Services.

Chapter 6, *Distributed Applications Using Visual Basic .NET and COM+*, discusses the concepts of distributed transactions and how we can utilize COM+ from Visual Basic .NET to develop distributed, transactional components. In this chapter, we'll drill down on some of the technologies discussed in Chapter 1 in further detail.

Chapter 7, *Interoperability*, builds upon the concepts introduced in Chapter 6, and delves into a powerful feature of the .NET Framework called COM Interoperability, which provides two-way integration support for utilizing .NET components and applications in conjunction with COM-based components and applications.

Chapter 8, *.NET Remoting and Components*, shows you how to remote your .NET assemblies across different machines to create fully distributed .NET applications using .NET Remoting, the replacement for DCOM.

Chapter 9, *Debugging and Troubleshooting*, looks at various techniques for debugging and troubleshooting application and system problems. It starts by reviewing the basics of the `Try...Catch...Finally` structure for handling exceptions, and then moves on to review the various properties and methods of the `Exception` class, trapping errors between managed and unmanaged code, logging errors, how to write exceptions to trace files, and how to test for application performance.

Chapter 10, *Case Study: IBuyAdventure.NET 2.0*, applies the concepts and technologies we've learned in the previous chapters into a complete, distributed transaction-processing system. The main goal of the case study is to show how an organization might create a robust, scalable, and high performance transactional processing application utilizing the .NET Framework and related .NET technologies. In addition to demonstrating best practices for transaction processing, this case study will also demonstrates the utilization of several key .NET technologies including: IIS, COM+, SQL Server 2000, ADO.NET, ASP.NET Web Forms, ASP.NET Web Services, XML data processing, and new features available to Visual Basic .NET, such as structured exception handling, inheritance, shared methods, and method overloading and overrides.

What do I Need to Use this Book

All you'll need is a PC running:

- Windows 2000
- Visual Studio .NET Professional edition (or higher versions)
- SQL Server 2000
- IIS
- Internet Explorer 5.5 or greater

Conventions

We have used a number of different styles of text and layout in the book to help differentiate between the different kinds of information. Here are examples of the styles that we use and an explanation of what they mean.

Bullets appear indented, with each new bullet marked as follows:

- **Important words** are in a bold type font
- Words that appear on the screen in menus like the File or Window are in a similar font to the one that you see on screen
- Keys that you press on the keyboard, like *Ctrl* and *Enter*, are in italics
- If you see something like `Object`, you'll know that it's a filename, object name, function name, or other code word

Code in a gray box shows new, important, pertinent code:

```
Dim objMyClass as New MyClass("Hello World")

Debug.WriteLine(objMyClass.ToString)
```

Sometimes you'll see code in a mixture of styles, like this:

```
Dim objVar as Object

objVar = Me

CType(objVar, Form).Text = "New Dialog Title Text"
```

The code on a white background is code that we've already looked at and that we don't wish to examine further.

Advice, hints, and background information come in an italicized, indented font like this.

> **Important pieces of information come in boxes like this.**

Customer Support

We always value hearing from our readers, and we want to know what you think about this book: what you liked, what you didn't like, and what you think we can do better next time. You can send us your comments, either by returning the reply card in the back of the book, or by e-mail to feedback@wrox.com. Please be sure to mention the book title in your message.

How to Download the Sample Code for the Book

When you visit the Wrox site, http://www.wrox.com/, simply locate the title through our Search facility or by using one of the title lists. Click on Download in the Code column, or on Download Code on the book's detail page.

The files that are available for download from our site have been archived using WinZip. When you have saved the attachments to a folder on your hard drive, you need to extract the files using a de-compression program such as WinZip or PKUnzip. When you extract the files, the code is usually extracted into chapter folders. When you start the extraction process, ensure that your software (WinZip, PKUnzip, etc.) is set to use folder names.

Errata

We've made every effort to make sure that there are no errors in the text or in the code. However, no one is perfect and mistakes do occur. If you find an error in one of our books, like a spelling mistake or a faulty piece of code, we would be very grateful for feedback. By sending in errata, you may save another reader hours of frustration and, of course, you will be helping us to provide even higher quality information. Simply e-mail the information to support@wrox.com. Your information will be checked and, if correct, posted on the errata page for that title or used in subsequent editions of the book.

To find errata on the web site, go to http://www.wrox.com/ and simply locate the title through our Advanced Search or title list. Click on the Book Errata link, which is below the cover graphic on the book's detail page.

E-mail Support

If you wish to directly query a problem in the book with an expert who knows the book in detail, then e-mail support@wrox.com with the following information:

- The **title of the book**, **last four digits of the ISBN**, and **page number** of the problem in the Subject field
- Your **name**, **contact information**, and the **problem** in the body of the message

We *won't* send you junk mail. We need the details to save your time and ours. When you send an e-mail message, it will go through the following chain of support:

- Customer Support – Your message is delivered to our customer support staff who are the first people to read it. They have files on the most frequently asked questions and will answer anything general about the book or the web site immediately.
- Editorial – Deeper queries are forwarded to the technical editor responsible for that book. They have experience with the programming language or particular product, and are able to answer detailed technical questions on the subject.
- The Authors – Finally, in the unlikely event that the editor cannot answer your problem, he or she will forward the request to the author. We do try to protect the author from any distractions to their writing; however, we are quite happy to forward specific requests to them. All Wrox authors help with the support on their books. They will e-mail the customer and the editor with their response and, again, all readers should benefit.

The Wrox Support process can only offer support to issues that are directly pertinent to the content of our published title. Support for questions that fall outside of the scope of normal book support is provided via the community lists of our http://p2p.wrox.com/ forum.

p2p.wrox.com

For author and peer discussion, join the P2P mailing lists. Our unique system provides **programmer to programmer™** contact on mailing lists, forums, and newsgroups, all in addition to our one-to-one e-mail support system. If you post a query to P2P, you can be confident that the many Wrox authors and other industry experts who are present on our mailing lists are examining it. At p2p.wrox.com, you will find a number of different lists that will help you, not only while you read this book, but also as you develop your own applications. Particularly appropriate to this book are the pro_vb, pro_vb_dotnet, and vb_dotnet lists.

To subscribe to a mailing list, just follow these steps:

1. Go to http://p2p.wrox.com/
2. Choose the appropriate category from the left menu bar
3. Click on the mailing list you wish to join
4. Follow the instructions to subscribe and fill in your e-mail address and password
5. Reply to the confirmation e-mail you receive
6. Use the subscription manager to join more lists and set your e-mail preferences

Why This System Offers the Best Support

You can choose to join the mailing lists or you can receive them as a weekly digest. If you don't have the time, or facility, to receive the mailing list, then you can search our online archives. Junk and spam mails are deleted, and your own e-mail address is protected by the unique Lyris system. Queries about joining or leaving lists, and any other general queries about lists, should be sent to listsupport@p2p.wrox.com.

Pro Visual Basic .NET Transactions

1

Laying the Foundation – Transactions, Data Access, and Application Architectures

This chapter introduces transactions, what they are, and how they work. We will look at the four essential properties of transactions. Furthermore, we will learn about simple transactions that utilize only one data store, and complex transactions that involve manipulating data over two or more databases.

The second part of this chapter will cover application architecture and introduce technologies for accessing data. After all, in order to work with data, we must be able to first access it. We will also learn about the previous architectures and technologies that have led to the evolution of the .NET Framework.

You may be wondering why it is necessary to learn about older application architectures and technologies. The answer is simple. Although the .NET Framework is unlike anything you have worked with before, many of the architectural principles are still valid with the .NET way of doing things, and this familiarity with the past will help your learning curve.

This chapter lays the foundation for the rest of the book. Most of the concepts introduced in this chapter will be built upon throughout the rest of this book. As we work our way through this book, we will see that the .NET Framework is actually comprised of numerous technologies such as ADO.NET, ASP.NET, as well as the new **Common Language Runtime** (**CLR**), which can be thought of as a substitute for COM+ services. By combining all these technologies together, the application developer has the ability to execute transactions in a variety of ways, as we will learn in this book. As .NET offers so many new technologies, it is essential that we talk about each so you will be comfortable in deciding the best methods to use in order to design and implement your own transactional applications.

After completing this chapter, you will be able to answer the following questions:

- What is a transaction?
- What does ACID have to do with transactions?
- What are distributed transactions?
- What is Two-Phase Commit Protocol?
- Why do we still need COM+ for distributed transactions?
- What does .NET offer?

Introduction to Transactions

The first recorded use for the word **transaction** occurred in Roman civil law around 1460, which was used to define an adjustment for a dispute. Transaction was borrowed directly from the word *transactionem*, which means "an agreement or accomplishment". It was not until another 200 years or so later that the word transaction evolved to reflect a sense of business.

Actually, transactions have existed since man has roamed the earth. Before we look at a current day definition of transactions, let's travel back in time to some 2 million years ago and visit the early founder of the fictional Grog Company. Grog's first business transaction was with a local clansman named Borg. Borg had a wonderful collection of beads that Grog admired. At the same time, Borg admired Grog's collection of seashells. Grog offered to trade Borg five seashells for five beads. Borg accepted, and the trade was made. This simple exchange of goods is a transaction.

Grog in good faith gave Borg 5 seashells. However, Borg decided to see what would happen by withholding the delivery of beads to Grog and not keeping his end of the bargain. Grog hit Borg on the head with a woolly mammoth task and then took the seashells back, thus the transaction failed.

Although Borg had a headache, he was a quick learner and apologized to Grog. This time, Borg gave Grog the five beads in return for five seashells and the transaction was completed.

Now that we have seen a simple transaction, let's return back to our present time and review what we just saw.

Transactions in programming terms are very similar in concept to the transactions we witnessed with Grog and Borg. They also apply in current everyday events, such as purchasing food from the store or transferring money to your bank account.

A transaction is a set of processes that are bound as one. If any process in the set fails, the transaction fails, and all processes are restored to their original state. However, if all processes in the set are successful, then the transaction is successful, and all processes are commited.

To help reinforce this, let's take a look at a more modern example:

Suppose an individual walks up to an ATM (Automated Teller Machine) and attempts to transfer $500 from their savings account to their checking account. In order for this transfer of funds to occur, two actions must occur. $500 must be debited (removed) from savings and $500 must be credited (deposited) into the checking account. Sounds easy enough; such transfers happen all the time. But what would happen if there was not enough money in the savings account? If there are not enough funds in the savings account, then the transaction would fail.

Now that we know what a transaction is, let's look at the requirements each one must meet.

ACID Properties

We already defined that a transaction is an action, or a series of actions, that transforms a system from one consistent state to another. Every transaction must meet the following four essential requirements, known collectively as the **ACID** properties:

- Atomicity
- Consistency
- Isolation
- Durability

Atomicity

Atomicity refers to the all-or-nothing proposition of a transaction. Once a transaction is started, it will either commit or abort.

A transaction must execute either completely or not at all. When a transaction meets these requirements, it is said to be **atomic**. If a transaction is aborted or if it fails, everything should consistently revert back to the original state before the transaction started. For example, when Borg withheld his beads from Grog, Grog took back his seashells. This transaction was completely aborted. In other words, one did not get something for nothing. When Grog and Borg traded as agreed, the transaction was executed completely. The same goes with our ATM example. If there was enough money in the savings account (and there were no hardware failures!) the transaction was completed, otherwise it would be completely aborted. Hence, both of these transactions exhibit atomicity – all-or-nothing.

Although this all-or-nothing scenario is usually the first action that comes to mind when discussing transaction processing, it is important to keep in mind that the atomicity property is only one of the four required ACID properties a transaction must exhibit. With this in mind, let's take a look at **consistency**.

Consistency

Consistency means that every process that makes up a transaction cannot break any business rules or semantics specified by the environment.

In simpler terms, the business logic for Grog's transaction needs to be consistent with every transaction Grog executes. What this means is, when Grog agreed to trade five beads for five seashells, Grog did in fact receive five beads. At the same time, he gave Borg five seashells. The business logic in Grog's time was very simple: "x something" for "y something". Although this business logic is very simple, it shows that even 2 million years ago, transactions maintained consistency.

Consistency requires that changes made as a result of a transaction do not violate the integrity of the data. For example, in our ATM banking transaction scenario, after the transfer of $500 dollars from an individual's savings account to their checking account, both accounts have to reflect the transfer. Individual operations within a transaction may leave the data in an inconsistent state, because the transaction is about transforming data from one consistent state to another, but once the transaction is committed, a transaction must guarantee the consistency and integrity of the data in all the data sources affected.

Again, in our ATM banking scenario, both accounts are in a consistent state before the transfer. During the transfer, money is first withdrawn from the savings account. At this point the data is in an inconsistent state. $500 has been withdrawn as part of the transfer and has not been accounted for in another account. However, the transaction is not yet complete. The same $500 is then deposited into the checking account. This operation effectively completes the transaction and both accounts are returned to a consistent state.

Remember, a transaction is not responsible for enforcing data integrity, but instead a transaction is only responsible for ensuring that data is returned to a consistent state after the transaction is either committed or aborted. The burden of understanding data integrity rules and possibly writing code to enforce them usually falls on the shoulders of the developer who is creating business components, so be prepared.

Transactions must also maintain data consistency and integrity when multiple concurrent users are accessing and modifying the same data, a concept that goes hand in hand with the next ACID property, referred to as **isolation**.

Isolation

All of the operations performed in a transaction must be isolated from operations performed by other transactions.

This property is sometimes referred to as **serializability** because, in order to prevent one transaction's operations from interfering with another's, requests must be serialized or sequenced so that only one request for the same data is serviced at a time.

Let's consider isolation in our ATM banking transaction scenario. At the exact time an individual is transferring $500 dollars from the savings account to the checking account, their significant other, who is standing at another ATM machine, decides to withdraw $100 from the same checking account. If one transaction is performed before the other, and the transactions are serialized, there will not be a problem. However, if the withdrawal of $100 from the checking account occurs during the $500 transfer, the balance of the checking account will appear to be inconsistent. To the individual transferring the $500 from the savings to the checking account, it would appear that the checking account was short $100, but to the other person withdrawing $100 from the checking account, the balance would appear as though it had gained $400. If concurrent transactions could modify the same data at the same time, rollbacks would produce inconsistent results.

Isolation not only guarantees that multiple transactions cannot modify the same data at the same time, but isolation also guarantees that changes caused by one transaction's operations will not be seen by another transaction until the changes are either committed or aborted. Concurrent transactions will be unaware of each other's partial and inconsistent changes. This means that all requests to modify data that is already involved in the transaction are blocked until the transaction completes. Most data sources such as SQL Server and other RDBMS implement isolation through the use of **locks**. Individual data items or sets of data are locked from concurrent access if they are involved in a transaction.

Durability

Durability simply ensures that once the transaction is committed, the results of the transaction will be persisted even if there is any type of system failure immediately following the transaction's completion.

In our ATM banking transaction scenario, what if there is a power outage for the ATM machine in which the individual is performing the $500 transfer? If the $500 had already been deposited back into the checking account to complete the transaction, the power outage at the same ATM machine would not affect the resulting account balances. On the other hand, if the power outage happened during the transfer, any operations already performed would be rolled back, as part of the transaction's atomicity property. When referring to durability, we simply mean that all data has been written to permanent storage and can be recovered.

In summary, all of these related properties of a transaction are simply about ensuring data involved in the transaction is managed correctly from the time a transaction begins until after a transaction is either committed or aborted.

Overall, transactions are pretty simplistic when all data modifications are performed against a single data source. However, distributed transactions that modify data stored in multiple numbers and types of data sources that may be spread across any number of machines, are much more complex. The commit and abort behavior of a transaction can no longer be handled by the data source itself but instead must be coordinated across these different data sources for each transaction. We will learn more about distributed transactions later in this chapter. In the meantime, it's important to keep in mind that these four ACID properties apply to all types of transactions, no matter what different types of data sources are involved in the transaction, and how many there are.

Database Transactions

Let's apply Grog's transaction to a modern database transaction using SQL. In SQL, transaction management uses the command, `BEGIN TRANSACTION` to mark the beginning of the transaction. If the transaction successfully completes, the `COMMIT TRANSACTION` command makes all actions in the transaction permanent. In the transaction example, this is when Grog gives five seashells in return for five beads from Borg. However, in the event that the transaction fails, such as when Borg decided to renege on his side of the deal, a `ROLLBACK TRANSACTION` is used to return everything back to the original state. A transaction that has been rolled backed appears as if nothing ever happened.

Let's look at how we would go about representing Grog's transaction in terms of a database using SQL code:

Don't worry if you don't understand everything in the code snip. It is only meant to demonstrate the principles we have discussed, and we'll be taking a detailed look at SQL transactions in a later chapter.

```
BEGIN TRANSACTION

INSERT TradeSeashells (TransactionNo, CustName, Quantity)
     VALUES (01, "Borg", 5)

IF @@error ! = 0
BEGIN
     ROLLBACK TRANSACTION
     RETURN -1
END

UPDATE TradeSeashellsQuantity
     SET ShellsInStock = ShellsInStock - 5
     WHERE TransactionNo = 01

IF @@error !=0
BEGIN
     ROLLBACK TRANSACTION
     RETURN -1
END

INSERT AquireBeads (TransactionNo, CustName, Quantity)
     VALUES (01,"Grog", 5)

IF @@error ! = 0
BEGIN
     ROLLBACK TRANSACTION
     RETURN -1
END

UPDATE AquireBeadsQuantity
     SET BeadsInStock = BeadsInStock + 5
WHERE TransactionNo = 01

IF @@error ! = 0
BEGIN
```

```
        ROLLBACK TRANSACTION
        RETURN -1
    END

    COMMIT TRANSACTION
```

SQL and Stored Procedures

SQL is a non-procedural language in contrast to programming languages such as Visual Basic .NET. What this means is SQL tells the database system what is being requested, not how to retrieve it. How the data is retrieved or manipulated is left for the database system to interpret.

A transaction is an operation or a series of operations that change data from one consistent state to another. MS SQL Server allows the developer/administrator to implement transactions through SQL statements (referred T-SQL) or through stored procedures. Basically, stored procedures consist of one or more SQL statements. The previous example of Grog's transaction consists of numerous SQL statements working together in order to make up one transaction.

Regardless of whether a transaction is executed via stored procedures or through a programming language such as VB.NET, most modern day database systems (such as MS SQL Server and Oracle) manage transactional processing for us. Such transactions are referred to as **explicit database transactions** because we are relying on the database to manage the outcome of the transaction. For example, when a transaction is in progress, MS SQL Server internally keeps track of all the changes made during the transaction process. However, changes are not permanent. If any error occurs, SQL Server knows how to put things back to the original state – the transaction is aborted. On the other hand, if all is OK, then SQL Server makes all changes permanent – the transaction is committed.

Distributed Transactions

As business requirements increase and applications become more complex, it is becoming increasingly common to need to access multiple databases, often at different locations. For instance, suppose we have a transaction that requires data changes to occur in two separate databases and still requires that all the properties of the ACID test be met. Basic transaction management using MS SQL Server will not suffice. There is no way to ensure that if one database server fails, the other has not already committed and become permanent. In other words, there is no way to guarantee atomicity without a way to coordinate multiple transaction processes occurring at multiple locations. As you will soon see, this is why COM+ is required.

Two-Phase Commit (2PC)

Let's take another look at the SQL code for Grog's transaction. Recall that two parts of this transaction must complete for a commit to occur – an `INSERT` and `UPDATE` is required for changes to Grog's seashell inventory, and another `INSERT` and `UPDATE` is required for Grog's bead inventory. Although being able to delete (`INSERT`) items from their respective inventories is also necessary.

Suppose Grog used MS SQL Server to record changes to his seashell inventory and Oracle to record changes to his bead inventory. What if the server where Oracle resides goes down? How can we guarantee atomicity? The solution comes from a protocol called two-phase commit, and it is coordinated by **Microsoft Distributed Transaction Coordinator** (**MS DTC**).

MS DTC is integrated into MS SQL Server. MS DTC verifies all processes are ready and able to commit.

Let's explore MS DTC a little closer and see how it works. In order for two-phase commit protocol to be coordinated, each data source in the transaction must have MS DTC installed. For these installations, the main coordinator is always going to be where the transaction originates. This main coordinator is referred to as the **Commit Coordinator** and is responsible for ensuring that the transaction either commits or aborts on all servers that are involved with the transaction. It is also the responsibility of the commit coordinator to report back to the client application on whether it has successfully committed or rolled back the transaction:

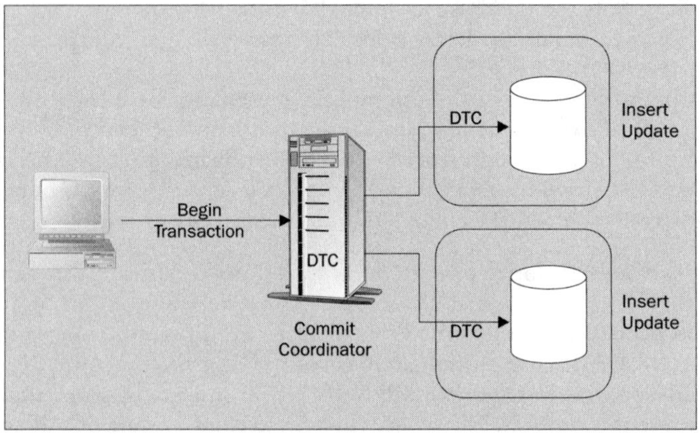

Grog's transaction requires changing data in one database to reflect his inventory of seashells. His transaction also requires changing data in another database, to reflect his inventory of beads.

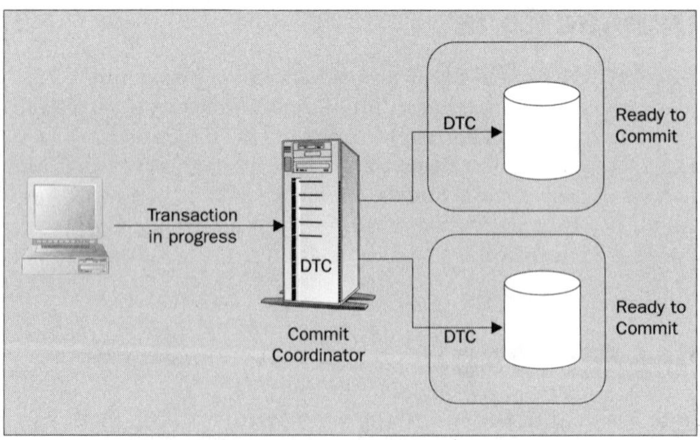

The commit coordinator is notified on the transaction's status.

If the commit coordinator receives a "ready to commit" return from each data source, the transaction is committed. However, if one failure is received from any of the data sources that will be affected, the commit coordinator will issue a roll back and notify the client application.

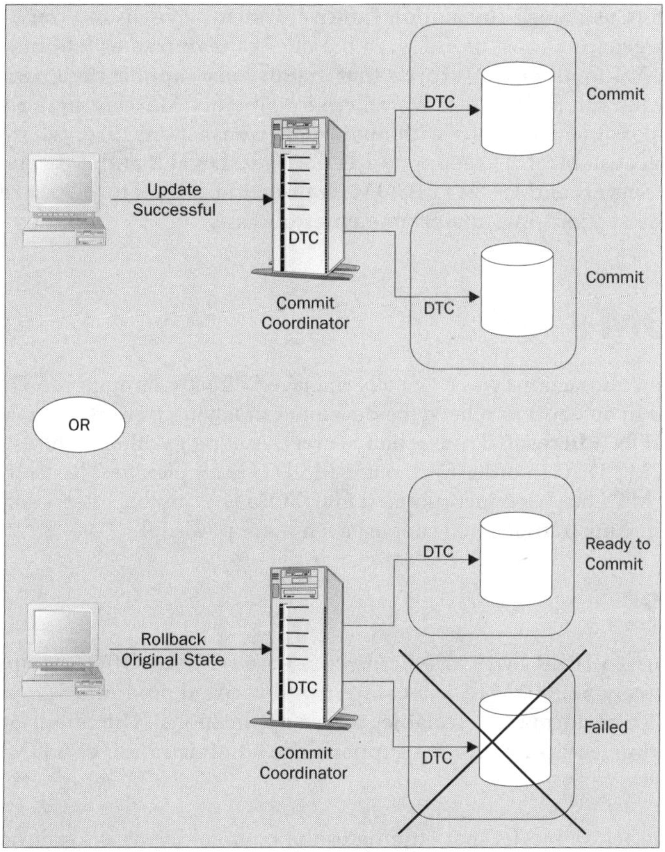

Transaction Protocols

With the advent of COM+, the developer is not tied down to working only with transactions utilizing MS Windows platforms. Let's look at a few types of protocol that COM+ supports for transaction support within different environments:

- **OLE transactions** is Microsoft's protocol definition that allows applications to communicate with MS DTC. More specifically, OLE transactions is an object-oriented protocol based on COM+ that is used for transaction management.
- **XA** is a different two-phase protocol that is common in the UNIX database world. The X/Open Distributed Transaction Processing (DTP) group has defined the XA standard, which is similar to OLE transactions. Perhaps the key point with XA is that it's not object-oriented.
- **Transaction Internet Protocol (TIP)** is a transaction protocol. The DTC can provide direct support for communicating with resource managers using TIP.

- IBM's **CICS** (**Customer Information Control System**). We visited transactions dating back to early man. Perhaps almost as old were the days of mainframes (although still in use and not at all inferior). It should be no surprise that mainframes support their own unique transaction protocols. After all, mainframes were here long before MS Windows running on PCs came about. It is possible to interact with mainframe transactions through MS DTC. How is this possible? Because MS DTC supports LU 6.2 Sync Level 2 and it can interact with HIS (Host Integration Server) and COMTI (COM Transaction Integrator). As a result, COM+ can distribute transactions into mainframe environments.

MTS and COM+

Support for distributed transactions was originally managed directly through MS DTC, but the DTC proved difficult to work with. In an effort to relieve the developer of having to work directly with MS DTC, Microsoft provided **MTS** (**Microsoft Transaction Server**). Among its other features, MTS was designed to automatically invoke MS DTC in order to alleviate MS DTC complexities. Recently, COM+ was introduced with Windows 2000. MTS has been incorporated into COM+. With this integration, the MTS environment is further refined, thus making transactional support even more powerful.

What is MTS?

Originally code-named VIPER in 1996, Microsoft released a Back Office component called MTS and sold it for approximately $2000. MTS is a component-based model for developing, deploying, and managing secure, high performance, scalable, robust applications. The important key fact to understand is that MTS is a runtime environment that supports the administration of COM components in an *n*-tiered environment.

MTS provides a transaction model that eliminates the complex transaction-processing code required for distributed transactions coordinated by MS DTC. This transactional model *transparently* merges distributed transactions with COM components.

MTS transactions are implemented through the use of **declarative attributes** that are specified *externally* to a component's implementation. All you have to do is configure your component's **transaction support** using the MTS Explorer and modify the components to vote on the transaction outcome.

MTS automatically handles the rest of the complex and redundant details of beginning and aborting transactions by interfacing with the MS DTC on behalf of your component, based on the component's transaction support. Any operations your component performs against resources will automatically be performed within a distributed transaction. Components can optionally control the transaction's lifetime through the use of such methods.

But that's not all. MTS extends transactions beyond what's possible with the simplistic SQL `BEGIN TRANSACTION` and `COMMIT TRANSACTION` statements. MTS allows transactions to seamlessly span multiple objects in the same activity. By simply changing a component's transaction support level, an MTS object can execute its own transaction or it can be composed or combined with other MTS objects as part of a larger transaction. MTS will automatically synchronize commit/abort behavior across multiple objects. Multi-object transactions allow MTS components to be utilized much more flexibly, and it enhances MTS component reuse without requiring code changes.

As with most technologies, there are disadvantages as well. Debugging MTS components can be horribly difficult. Another major drawback is that thread pooling was not possible with VB COM components that were hosted in MTS.

What is COM+?

When talking about COM+, typically we are also referring to MTS. In simple terms, COM+ is the replacement technology for COM and MTS. In other words, COM+ is the combination of **COM** (**Component Object Model**) and MTS into one enhanced package of services that are integrated into the Windows 2000 and XP operating systems. By combining COM and MTS, a developer can seamlessly utilize numerous features such as:

- Automatic transactions
- Role-based security
- Synchronization
- Instantiating objects

Let's briefly look at these major features:

Automatic Transactions

Essentially, when working with transactions, COM+ provides a mechanism that ensures data remains **atomic** – this means that if an error occurs within a transaction, COM+ can automatically rollback the transaction. If no errors occur, COM+ can automatically commit the transaction.

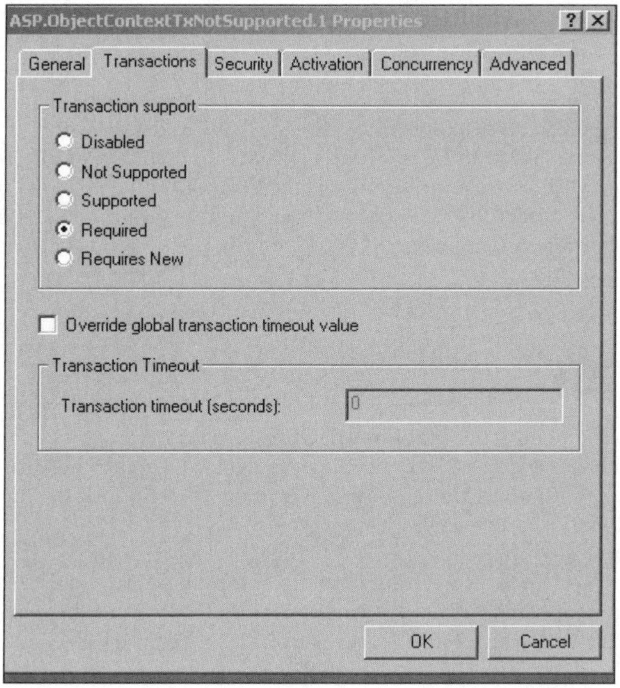

Automatic transaction committal and rollback for COM+ components can be administered from the Component Services snap-in.

In order to implement automatic transactions, the developer must initiate automatic committal and rollback from the COM+ Catalog. This can be administered from the Component Services that is a snap-in to the **MMC** (**Microsoft Management Console**). You will learn about this in detail in Chapter 6, *Distributed Applications* using Visual Basic .NET and COM+.

You have just learned about automatic transactions, but it is important to realize that distributed transactions can be processed manually. When we refer to manual transactions, we mean that a transaction can be controlled without any automatic enlistment and coordination between data stores.

Role-Based Security

Although this book is about transactions, it is important to understand security in relation to them. Transactions need to be protected from unauthorized use. If you have worked with MTS, you should know that the developer and/or administrator could set security all the way down to the interface level. COM+ has added security features that now let you set security roles at the method level. This is very powerful indeed, and will be discussed in more detail later in the book.

Synchronization

Imagine several people (while thinking of threads) all trying to use the same PC (resource) at the same time. If there is no resource management, each person will be stepping over the other. The bottom line is each job they do will be messed up. This is maybe not the best analogy, but it can be applied to objects that must perform precise operations on different threads. MTS provided the capability to lock a resource when a component wanted to make use of it. With COM+, things were greatly enhanced by not only locking a resource, but by being able to completely lock a component in order to prevent the same instance from being accessed by another thread at the same time.

Instantiating Objects

In order to instantiate an object utilizing MTS, the application developer had to incorporate additional code that would send a request to MTS in order to create an instance of the (requested) component. COM+ eliminated the need for this additional code. With COM+, all that is needed to instantiate a component is to create an object just like any ordinary (non-transactional) object. Additionally, when a request appears to instantiate a component, COM+ automatically checks the object's requirements and provides the appropriate runtime.

COM+ and .NET

Up to this point, we have been talking about MS SQL Server, stored procedures, and transactions utilizing COM+. At the same time, .NET provides new ways of handling simple transactions (which I will talk about shortly). With all of these choices, you may be wondering which should be used. This is a good question without an easy answer.

Perhaps you are concerned about the rumors for the eventual demise of COM+. First, it is important to realize that .NET fully supports COM+. As a matter of fact, Microsoft has enhanced COM+ in its XP operating systems and is still adding new features to its next release.

Even with .NET's enhanced capabilities, it's unrealistic to believe that the old technologies will be tossed aside for new. There is too much invested in software utilizing ADO, MTS, and COM+, as well as others. The important thing to keep in mind is that .NET can coexist with these legacy technologies. Simply, the .NET Framework accommodates, COM, COM+, and ADO.

Furthermore, support for transactional processing continues with Microsoft's .NET environment. In the next chapter you will learn how **simple transactions** can be handled using ADO.NET.

As previously mentioned, the .NET environment not only fully supports COM+; it must rely on COM+ for complex distributed two-phase commit transactions. Additionally, in order to build large enterprise distributed applications that incorporate **object pooling** and **just in time activation**, COM+ is still required. Simply, the .NET environment makes it easy to utilize COM+ services.

Application Architecture

An enterprise application can be, and usually is, an interchangeable term for a distributed application. However, these two terms do not always mean the same thing. In actuality, enterprise applications are simply large-scale, complex business applications; while distributed applications are separated into logical areas, typically across two or more machines – hence distributed. Furthermore, an enterprise application may not necessarily be distributed, and may, for example, reside on a mainframe.

Let's briefly look at the different types of application architectures, as they will be the basis for your next .NET application.

Client/Server Architecture

You may be familiar with the typical two-tier client/server architecture. In a nutshell, this architecture typically has a user's PC for the client (front end) and a network server that contains the database (back end). Logic is divided between these two physical locations. Usually the client contains most of the business logic, although with the advent of stored procedures, SQL language routines allow business logic to be stored and executed on the database server.

The two-tier scenario works very well when you have a small business that only uses or needs a single data source. However, the goal of most businesses is to grow, and so, hopefully, will the database and its requirements.

A common problem with traditional two-tier applications is that established database connections were kept open for the duration of the application's session. This meant that database connections were not efficiently used.

Business rules will also change. Whenever this happens, the application must be rebuilt and redistributed to each PC. Having to rebuild and redistribute applications make for a high cost of maintenance. As you can see, using stored procedures is the best method, as you'll only need to make these changes on the server. Of course, you will need to keep the stored procedure name(s) the same.

But what if your business merges with another company that has a two-tier system similar to yours? Suppose the other company is using a different database system such as Oracle. MS SQL Server does have remote stored procedures, but they are proprietary. In other words, Microsoft's remote stored procedures only work with Microsoft's SQL Server. Thus Microsoft's remote stored procedures are useless when you need information from the Oracle database.

You can implement another set of stored procedures on the Oracle server, but now you have two different sets of stored procedures at two different locations.

As you can see, the two-tier client/server is not easily scalable, and so it becomes less useful as the company starts to grow.

Three-Tier Architecture

Due to the limitations of the two-tier client/server architecture, distributed applications are often divided up into three or more logical tiers or sections. Components in each of these tiers perform a specific role – in a three-tier application, there's a **User Services** (Presentation) tier, a **Business Services** tier, and a **Data Services** tier.

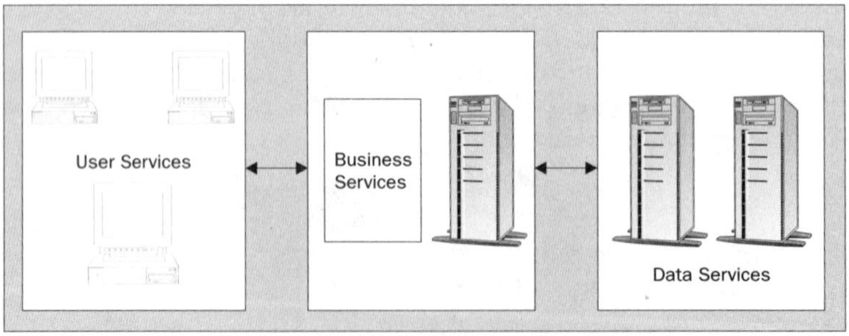

Although represented as three separate tiers, it is important to understand that the different tiers do not have to be separate. Although, all three tiers can reside on one machine, it serves little purpose other than in a development environment.

The main distinction between three-tier architecture and the two-tier client/server architecture is that, with a three-tier architecture, the evolving business logic is separated from the user interface and the data source.

Breaking up monolithic applications into these separate tiers or sections can increase the scalability and reduce the complexity of the overall application. We can develop loosely coupled systems that are not dependent on one database, or one type of user interface. All this results in applications that can meet the growing needs and dynamic nature of today's business. Developers can specialize in designing and developing a specific tier or tiers. However, everything comes with a price and it is worth remembering that the more tiers an application has, the more additional support and development staff it needs.

Windows DNA

Windows DNA (Distributed iNternet Applications) provides a programming design philosophy that application developers could follow when designing multi-tiered (*n*-tier), distributed enterprise applications using the Microsoft Windows operating system and related software products. As you can see from the picture below, there are a lot of technologies available from which you can pick and chose what you need to meet your development objectives.

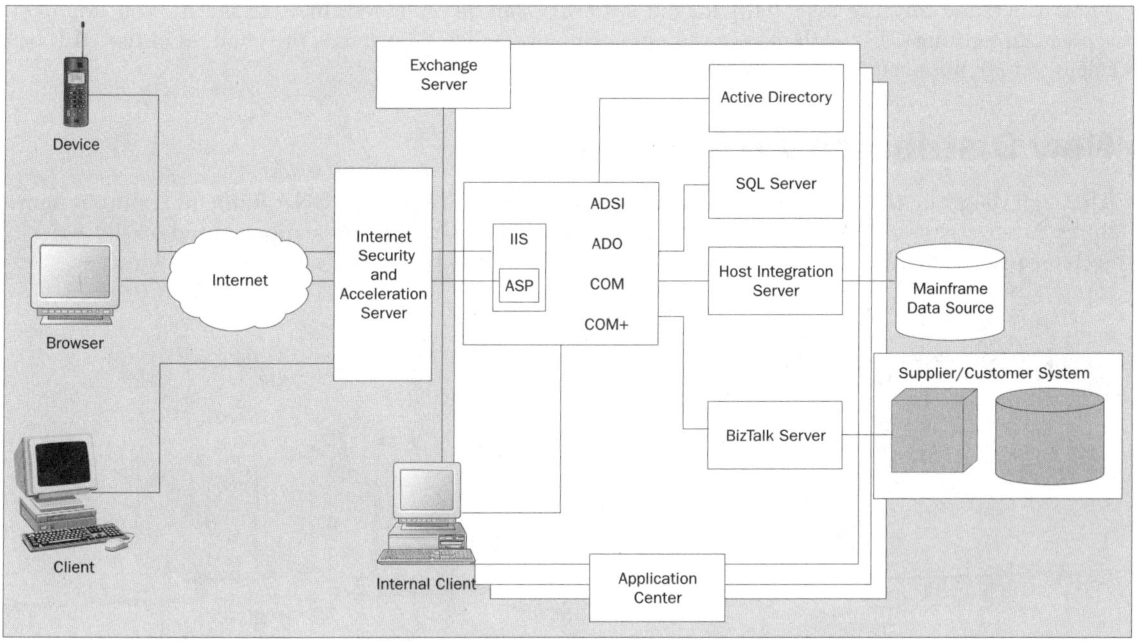

However, this programming philosophy is based on the COM (it facilitates COM+) and Win32 API.

Perhaps the biggest drawback with Windows DNA is it is difficult to implement. COM and Win32 API utilize proprietary protocols and languages. Of course the new trend is standardization across platforms, which is also a major goal of the .NET Framework.

Windows DNA indirectly has many more issues, such as the interruption of Enterprise 24X7 applications during software updates. Because DNA is heavily centered with COM/COM+, in order to make any software changes, it is necessary to halt any servers where the original software resides, install any software updates, and possibly reboot the server in order for the changes to take effect. Such a scenario is difficult enough on development machines, but what about critical systems that must remain running 24/7? As I will explain shortly, .NET provides an elegant solution.

The reason the DNA programming model typically requires a system to be halted when a component is replaced is due to the way COM manages components such as DLLs. DLLs are loaded into memory when called and they are essentially locked until they can be unloaded. In other words, you cannot replace an existing DLL while it is in memory. However, in 24/7 systems, the chances of the DLL being released may not occur without halting the system.

A New Distributed Architecture

Although the principles of *n*-tier architecture are a part of the Windows DNA model it is not the same thing. *N*-tier architecture is alive and well. As a matter of fact, .NET applications based on the *n*-tier architecture are much easier to incorporate. The difference is how .NET components interact – essentially making things easier to work with.

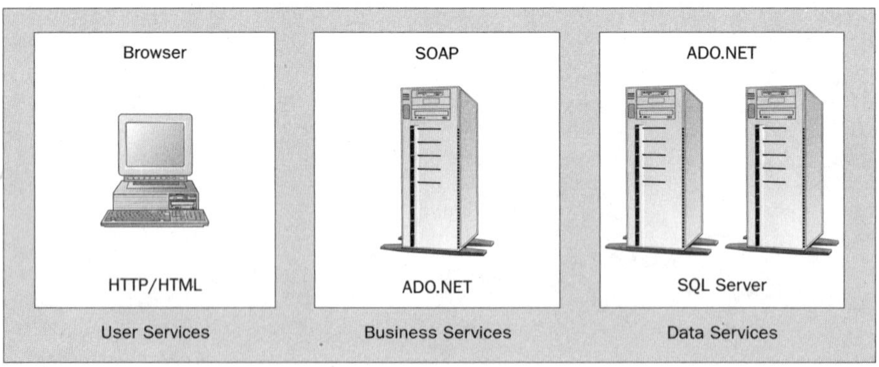

Designing distributed applications with the .NET Framework incorporates the basic principles of the *n*-tier architecture.

As you can see, the basic three-tier architecture is an important model that lays the foundation for more complex enterprise-wide applications. Let's keep moving forward and learn about the new programming model, .NET applications. As you work through this book, you will learn that with the .NET Framework, applications can utilize several development tools to create secure, robust, scalable, high performance, enterprise-wide applications. .NET makes *n*-tier applications much easier to design and implement.

.NET Distribution

The .NET Framework provides a much more elegant way of distributing components. Components can actually be replaced as simply as using an XCOPY while the application is running, as opposed to having to halt a server and possibly reboot the system. The reason new components can be distributed so easily is due to the way the **Common Runtime Library (CLR)** manages .NET code. Components no longer need to be assigned GUIDs, nor do they need to be registered into the registry. Instead, .NET components are managed through embedded identifiers that are created during compilation and travel with the component when distributed. We will return to the CLR shortly.

.NET: A New Way to Program

When referring to .NET, I am actually referring to the .NET Framework. The .NET Framework is a near seamless combination of technologies such as ASP.NET and ADO.NET that integrate with other technologies such as XML, SOAP, COM+, and of course, object-oriented programming languages such as Visual Basic .NET (yes, Visual Basic .NET is fully object-oriented language), C#, and C++.

Although you should be familiar with the .NET Framework, as it is a prerequisite for this book, let's briefly look at its major components.

> *If you feel you need a comprehensive review of .NET, Wrox Press provides* Professional VB.NET *(ISBN 1-861004-97-4).*

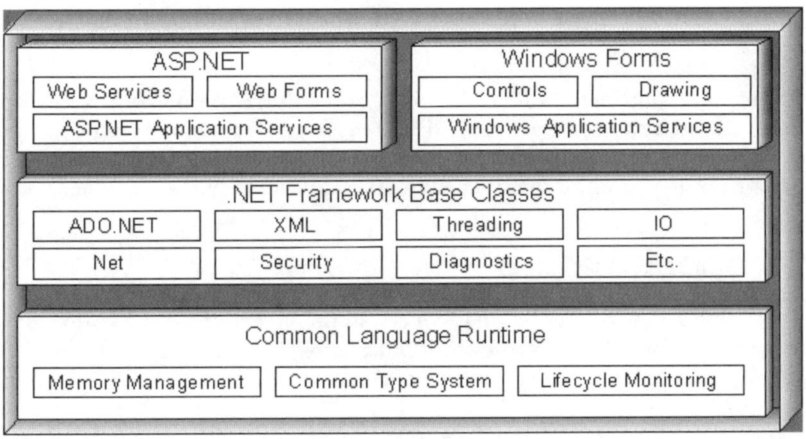

By looking at the diagram, we can see that the .NET Framework is essentially comprised of three distinct sections:

- Application Development Tools
- Base Class Libraries
- Common Language Runtime

The **Application Development Tools** contains development technologies such as ASP.NET, Web Services, and Windows Forms (also referred to as WinForms).

To describe ASP.NET would take a complete book of its own. Basically, ASP.NET provides a new approach for web development. It provides numerous tools and functionalities, such as additional language support and the ability to incorporate WebForms and Web Services. In a nutshell, you can think of ASP.NET as an enhanced technology for easily creating static and dynamic content for the Web.

Windows Forms provides the necessary form controls to create traditional looking GUI applications. If you are used to programming in Visual Basic 6, then you are familiar with the ActiveX Controls such as text boxes, datagrids, buttons, menus, toolbars, etc., so you should have no problem feeling at home with Windows Forms controls. They look the same, but the underlying workings are very different, as they are managed through the CLR as opposed to requiring COM+ services. The thing that makes Windows Forms exciting is that GUI interfaces can now easily be created for web applications.

The **Base Class Libraries** are a set of comprehensive, object-oriented classes that are available for application development.

> *Don't be surprised that the size of this library is extremely large. As a result, it will take some time to become acquainted with.*

For example, some of the types of class libraries included are:

- `System.Collections` – these classes are for working with collections and lists.
- `System.Threading` – these are classes that assist in efficiently writing multi-threaded applications.
- `System.IO` – this provides a set of classes for working with files and other stream types.
- `System.Security` – these classes are used for services such as permissions and authentication.

The **Common Language Runtime** (**CLR**) is the heart of the .NET Framework. It is responsible for managing code that targets the runtime. The CLR is responsible for providing core services within the .NET Framework, such as memory management, thread management, and remoting. Furthermore, it oversees the responsibility for enforcing security and code accuracy during execution time.

.NET: Not a Specification

First and foremost, .NET is a framework that covers all the layers of software development, above the operating system. It provides the richest level of integration amongst presentation technologies, component technologies, and data technolgies ever seen on a Microsoft, or perhaps any, platform.

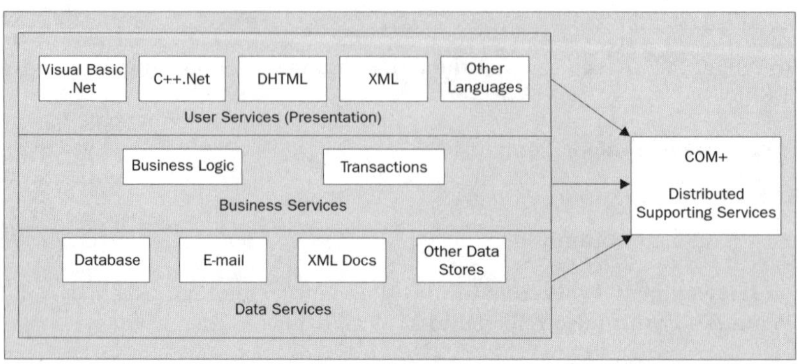

The above diagram shows the same *n*-tier structure as provided with Windows DNA. The major difference is that the .NET Framework does not utilize COM+ directly. In other words, .NET components can communicate with each other without the need for COM/COM+. However, do not think that .NET's CLR replaces COM, MTS, and COM+ Runtimes. Instead, the CLR works side-by-side with COM+. Simply, the .NET Framework fully supports COM+ services, as well as relies on COM+ for complex, distributed transactions, object pooling, and **just-in-time (JIT)** activation. You will learn more about this in Chapters 6 and 7.

As you work your way through this book, you will begin to realize how many of the .NET technologies for data access and transactions show similar ities to Visual Basic technologies. This helps the Visual Basic programmer's learning curve. At the same time, there are many radical changes that will take some getting used to. So before we continue learning about the .NET Framework, let's briefly review some important Visual Basic technologies for getting to our data upon which the .NET Framework was built.

Before ActiveX Data Objects

ODBC

Before ADO came into being, ODBC was the primary method for accessing data from a database. There is no doubt that ODBC has been a tried and true friend to the application developer for a long time. In fact, ODBC is based on international standards. As a result ODBC has been accepted among most relational database vendors. ODBC can still be used to access almost every type of relational database management system in use today.

If ODBC is such a widely used technology, why not continue to use it? There are two major reasons why ODBC is an inferior technology for data access in today's applications. First, ODBC provides access to relational databases that understand SQL. Because ODBC only understands SQL processing, it must treat all data as relational and this is where the problem arises. The new trend for data storage is non-relational (such as e-mail, faxes, and web documents), so ODBC is less suitable when it comes to new application design.

The second major reason for not staying with ODBC is due to its requirements for low-level programming. ODBC requires numerous complex API functions that are often difficult to work with.

Because of ODBC's complexity, Microsoft implemented its first data access model called **Data Access Objects (DAO)**.

DAO

DAO was designed specifically for Visual Basic and was meant to work with local databases such as MS Access. In addition to DAO's inability to access non-relational data, the main limiting feature was the fact that it was primarily intended for local database access. Yes, DAO could be used to access relational databases on a server; however, it proved to suffer in performance when not being used for its intended use – the local relational database.

Along Came RDO

The next evolution of data access technologies was **Remote Data Objects (RDO)**. RDO was a short-lived technology for accessing relational data. The big improvement RDO provided over DAO was it was designed for client/server applications. In other words, a client application could fairly easily be programmed to use RDO to access data from MS SQL Server over a network.

The big reason RDO did not last very long was due to emerging Internet technologies that required data access. For example, Microsoft had in place ASP 1.0 (Active Server Pages). However, ASP 1.0 could only work with active scripting such as VBScript. The problem was RDO technology did not provide a way to satisfactorily allow for data access from a web browser to the ASP page or the database server. Also, RDO did not offer any facility for the use of disconnected Resultsets. Additionally, RDO did not provide any way to marshall Resultsets over firewalls.

With the need to access data stores via the Internet, Microsoft quickly replaced RDO with **ActiveX Data Objects (ADO)**.

ADO

Although ADO 1.0 was a step in the right direction, it had a serious limitation for Internet applications. ADO 1.0 did not provide an answer for disconnected data. In other words, ADO 1.0 did a fine job by allowing a web application to connect to a database; however, with ADO 1.0 there was no real way of working with a disconnected Recordset. More specifically, with ADO 1.0, an application tended to first establish a connection to the data store so the user could work with the data. Once the user had done what they needed to, such as edit, update, or simply view the data, then the database connection could be closed and the connection destroyed. If the user wanted to work with more data, then another connection had to be established; there was no easy way or quick way to reconnect back to the data being worked with.

The ramifications of such a process should be clear. First, you have a continuous connection while working with data. Numerous connections to the database server take up finite resources. Secondly, establishing a connection and closing it also take resources. Although, ADO was moving in the right direction, it still had serious drawbacks.

ADO 2.0 brought some significant changes to the disconnected database issue. Now ADO had the capabilities to connect to a data store, retrieve the data you wanted to work with and then immediately disconnect from the data store. As soon as the data was manipulated, a connection back to the data store could easily be implemented and any data changes could be sent to the database. The major drawback to this approach was the lack of a method to store relationships and other details about the data. Simply, you could only store rowsets that contained values.

Additionally, this technique was satisfactory for a client/server application, but still did not offer the best efficiency via the Internet. However, ADO 2.0 also provided another technology called **RDS (Remote Data Services)** that allowed one to cash data into an IE web browser.

RDS is based on a client-side architecture and is capable of delivering a disconnected (stateless) Recordset from a database server, and sending the data to a web browser. This means that large amounts of data, such as Recordsets retrieved from a database, can be cached at the client machine. Performance is increased, because multiple records can be pulled from cached information without having to send out a new request to the server and have the information re-posted at the client's browser. Additionally, multiple records can be manipulated while still on the client machine, and then sent for processing as one batch, again providing immediate responses.

As good as RDS sounds, it has many drawbacks. First, RDS only works with Microsoft Internet browsers (4.0 and higher). Another issue is its difficulty to program with. However, the biggest drawback that kept RDS from becoming popular is severe security issues.

OLE DB and UDA

In 1996, **UDA** (**Universal Data Access**) became the latest approach for a better solution to deal with modern data-centric applications. UDA is an architecture that incorporates many different data access technologies together in order to provide access to virtually any type of data source.

OLE DB (**Object Linking and Embedding Database**) soon became Microsoft's top technology for attempting to provide Universal Data Access to virtually all types of relational and non-relational data stores. OLE DB became referred to as the glue that binds the UDA architecture together.

OLE DB is a set of COM components that expose certain interfaces. These COM interfaces permit data access in such a way that the client application never realizes nor cares what type of data source it's connected to. Through COM interfaces, data providers can supply various levels of support for data stores. Because OLE DB is essentially a part of COM, a client is capable of querying the Query-Interface method in order to see if a specific feature is available or supported on a machine or data store.

In a nutshell, OLE DB can be broken down into three entities – Data Consumers, Service Components, and Data Providers. Each of these entities is comprised of a set of COM components.

The **Data Consumers** are simply thought of as being any application or component that utilizes OLE DB data through OLE DB or ADO.

Service Components on the other hand can be thought of as components that allow the standard functionality for data providers to be extended or enhanced. Simply, service components are nothing more than components that consume and produce OLE DB data.

You can think of **Data Providers** as the components that represent data sources. OLE DB data providers expose all types of data through the same standard OLE DB interfaces, allowing consumers access in a standard way.

Data – No Longer Just Relational

Many of you are used to working with relational data through enterprise applications utilizing database systems, such as MS SQL Server, Oracle, DB2, and perhaps MS Access. What is interesting about data stores today is how they have started evolving into different types of data stores. For example, apart from the common types of relational data housed in relational databases, documents containing data such as e-mail, faxes, word processing documents, spreadsheets, XML, and web documents have found their way into our lives. More and more applications, as well as technologies, are being developed to tap into these essential data sources.

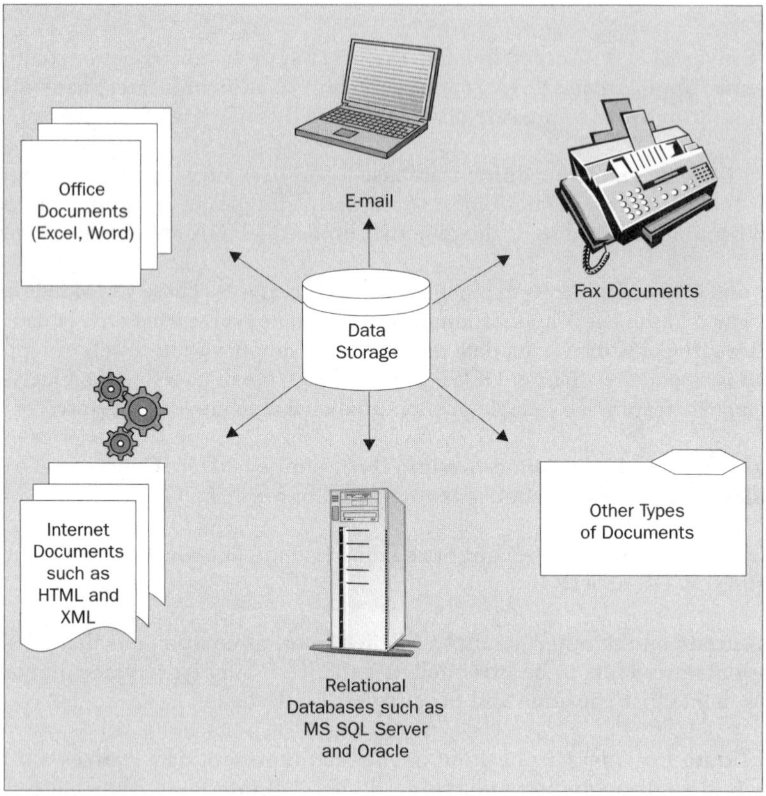

Data stores are moving away from the traditional centralized relational database model.

Introducing ADO.NET

We just looked at the evolution of data access (DAO, RDO, ADO) and we have briefly discussed how data stores have moved away from centralized relational databases such as MS SQL Server and Oracle. In actuality, it's not only the data stores that have evolved, but also the applications themselves. In order to accommodate these distributed data stores, it has been necessary to change the way applications are designed. In other words, today's applications are moving toward a distributed environment as well. ADO has been an excellent technology to the application developer when it comes to applications based on the client/server architecture; however, the new trend points to disconnected data across the Web.

ADO.NET has been designed to address the demands and needs of today's application developer by providing a new model capable of offering disconnected data. Furthermore, ADO.NET provides common data representation with the ability to combine data from numerous data types and data sources, as well as provide optimized services for interacting with databases. No doubt you will find that ADO.NET is very powerful.

ADO.NET is comprised of a set of classes designed for data access services. With these classes the application developer can access not only traditional data stores such as relational databases, but also ADO.NET can convert just about any type of data accessed from a data store into XML form. By being able to convert data feeds into XML, data can easily be transferred across the Internet. You will learn about working with XML and ADO.NET in the next chapter.

One major difference you should be aware of is that ADO.NET does not actually utilize COM/COM+ services, (neither do any of the .NET Framework components). Instead of utilizing COM/COM+ within the .NET Framework, the CLR (Common Language Runtime) handles communication between components. However, the .NET Framework is designed to co-exist with COM/COM+. In fact, complex, distributed transactions that occur across multiple databases must use COM+. The .NET Framework provides the tools to allow for interoperability between .NET and COM+ components as you will see in Chapter 6.

ADO.NET & Disconnected Data

Earlier in this chapter we talked about the typical client/server architecture (two-tier) where the client communicated directly to the data store, such as with MS SQL Server or Oracle relational databases. The problems with this architecture are many – such as the lack of scalability and the need to update each client PC when new software is released. This technology works very well as long as the hardware can manage the number of users connecting at one time. However, with the advent of the Internet, two-tier client/server technology fails due to the requirements of a continuous connection to the data store.

We tend to imply the failure is due to the various architectures (such as two-tier client/server), when it's not actually the architecture itself. Actually it is the inability of the previous data access technologies to adequately provide the disconnectivity that ADO.NET now provides.

When referring to the Internet, we may as well associate it with the term "disconnected" because of the nature of HTTP. In other words, when dealing with data and content over the Internet, a connection between a client and a server exists only during the transfer of data.

The ramifications of accessing data via HTTP should start to become apparent. Connections to the server are not kept open after a web page has been loaded. Furthermore once data has been requested, the connection is terminated. This scenario becomes even more difficult as we move away from client/server applications to *n*-tier applications. When working with *n*-tier applications we are now concerned with passing data between numerous tiers each time a client makes a request for some type of data.

It has been estimated that more than 35% of the personal computers sold to corporations are laptops. With mobile technology gaining such momentum, it becomes necessary to be able to work with data while being in a disconnected environment. Simply, we need a way to access and download data, disconnect from the data store (possibly terminate our connection to the Internet), work with and manipulate the data, and later reconnect and send the new data back to the data store.

This again brings us back to ADO.NET, which is the foundation for data access within the .NET Framework. ADO.NET is a technology that provides an easy way to incorporate data access methods that are capable of taking data from the data source and immediately disconnecting from the data store, while making the retrieved data usable for data manipulation back at the client. Furthermore, when the user has completed manipulating the data, ADO.NET provides the means for a quick connection back to the data store, where the client data can quickly be updated, and then for releasing the connection.

Managed Code & Common Language Runtime

Before .NET, you probably had never heard about managed and unmanaged code. With .NET, we now have a distinction. Managed code is unique to the .NET Framework. Basically managed code is code that targets the CLR (Common Language Runtime). For example, managed code includes memory management, security management, code verification, as well as several other system services.

As an example, ADO is not a part of the .NET Framework, thus it is considered unmanaged code. As a result OLE DB providers for ADO cannot be used with .NET. On the other hand, ADO.NET is managed code, as it is part of the .NET Framework. You will learn more about ADO.NET in the next chapter.

ASP.NET

If you are familiar with transactions over the Web, you probably are familiar with **ASP** (**Active Server Pages**). Active Server Pages require some type of script such as VBScript or JavaScript (Microsoft's version of JavaScript is JScript) in order to send and retrieve data from a data store. Scripting languages basically are simplified programming languages designed to perform specialized or limited tasks. Scripting languages do not have as much functionality as full languages such as Visual Basic, C++, and C#. If you have not used a scripting language before, you may have lucked out because .NET makes things better, as you will discover shortly.

Script languages are often not easy to work with, and, if inertwined among HTML, they can be very difficult and some what chaotic to read. The .NET Framework is designed to eliminate this. How is this accomplished? First, we no longer need to worry about the various scripting languages because .NET allows us to write in formal languages such as Visual Basic .NET or C#. Now that we can write web applications using a formal language, Visual Basic programmers can take advantage of server controls such as the DataGrid. Furthermore, we can easily bind data through data controls.

ASP.NET is completely object-oriented. This means that object-oriented programming (OOP) concepts such as encapsulation, polymorphism, inheritance, and overloading are available with ASP.NET. Furthermore ASP.NET has been designed to run side by side with standard ASP in order to keep compatibility among both new and old technologies. In other words, you can install both ASP and ASP.NET on the same server. Microsoft's goal is to allow both ASP and ASP.NET to reside together without complications. In most cases there are no problems. However, it should be pointed out that complications may arise because ASP and ASP.NET cannot share session objects. What this means is a web application can only operate using only ASP entirely, or ASP.NET entirely.

In order to separate the two, ASP.NET uses a new file extension: `.aspx`.

There are many more exciting features regarding ASP.NET, many of which you will learn about in Chapter 4.

XML Data

XML seems to be the latest buzzword but with good reason. It's a self-describing, text-based file format that is used to describe data. **XML** stands for **eXtensible Markup Language** and has become the new standard way for exchanging and representing structured documents. Like HTML, XML is a markup language; however, the term "extensible" means we can take XML much further than the limitations of HTML. With XML, the developer can create and add their own custom tags that can be applied into an orderly and easy to read structure. Furthermore, XML can be transported around implemented security specifically designed for the Internet.

Although XML has been around for several years, it was not until the release of ADO 2.1 that there was any support for XML. Actually, XML support was referred to as MSXML because Microsoft was the first to implement a version of XML. At the time, XML was not fully specified through the W3C.

You can find further information about XML at: http://www.w3.org/.

XML is ideal for passing information between application tiers, especially presentation (user services) and business tiers. Of course, XML can also be passed to a variety of data stores.

XML plays a very important role within the .NET Framework. One example is Web Services, which utilize XML for interfacing with remote objects. Also, earlier in this chapter we talked about ADO.NET and its reliance on XML for remote representation of data. With ADO.NET, data can be converted to XML, where it can be manipulated and then converted back to the original type of data. ADO.NET and XML make a great team. You will learn about working with XML and ADO.NET in the next chapter.

Although XML tends to be data-heavy because it includes the tags with the data, etc., in addition to requiring parsing, the bottom line is that XML is simple, effective, and easy to implement, and is a core technology within the .NET Framework.

SOAP

SOAP (**Simple Object Access Protocol**) is a lightweight XML messaging protocol that is used for the exchange of information in a decentralized distributed environment. Simply, SOAP is an Internet protocol that provides a means for invoking methods and functions on remote servers, remote services, remote components, as well as remote objects.

As you will already have deduced, SOAP is designed around (perhaps) the most prominent Internet protocols, HTTP and the most prominaent data format, XML. The purpose of its design was to develop a universal protocol capable of communicating with any component, regardless of the language it was written (such as VB6, Visual Basic.NET, C++, C#, COBOL), or the platform the component resides. We will return to SOAP in Chapter 5.

Web Services

Web Services are another key feature of the .NET Framework and can be exposed through ASP.NET, as well as through Windows applications. Web Services are programmable components that provide functionality that is accessible to any number of systems accessing the Internet. In other words, Web Services provide a means to develop integrated and distributed applications by combining local and remote resources across the Internet. Using HTTP as a transport protocol, calls can be transported from one web site to another. Furthermore SOAP can be used to represent the call payload. The beauty of .NET is that Web Services can be easily exposed and consumed. As a matter of fact, regardless of where interacting components are located, they can interact as if they were located on the same server.

You will learn to write and work with Web Services in Chapter 5.

Summary

This chapter served as an introduction to transactions and the technologies for working with them. First, we talked about what transactions actually are. Next, we looked at each property specified by ACID – Atomicity, Consistency, Isolation, and Durability. We also took a look at distributed transactions and learned about the two-phase commit protocol.

Next we reviewed the different types of application architectures. We first looked at the common client/server architecture and then looked at distributed *n*-tier architecture. You also learned why Windows DNA model has fallen out of favor due to its many shortcomings. Yet the principles of *n*-tier development that Windows DNA harbors are still a solid foundation within the .NET philosophy.

We also took a look at the major components making up the .NET Framework, such as ADO.NET, ASP.NET, and the CLR.

We touched on how XML is tied into the .NET Framework and we also had a cursory look at SOAP (Simple Object Access Protocol). SOAP is a major player for working with distributed components over the Internet.

We wrapped up this chapter with Web Services, where we discussed the possibility that with the .NET Framework, components can interact across the Internet as easily as if they were located on the same server.

Pro Visual Basic .NET Transactions

2

Data Access Using Visual Basic .NET

Before we can begin working with transactions, we must first be able to access the data. To do this, I will begin this chapter with an introduction to ADO.NET, because it is .NET's core technology for accessing data. Although there are some similarities between ADO and ADO.NET, ADO.NET is very different. After completing this chapter, you should have a good grasp of this technology. The good news is that once you understand ADO.NET, you will find it easy to work with and easy to implement.

The second part of this chapter is about XML. XML also is a core technology that has been incorporated within the .NET Framework. Using XML, ADO.NET can ensure the efficient transfer of data to any application on any platform.

> *As a friendly note: it is not the intention of this book to cover all of ADO.NET and XML. You will learn about the basics of ADO.NET and XML use within the .NET Framework, so you can apply the basic concepts to work with transactional applications in the upcoming chapters. You should already possess a working knowledge of XML. Wrox Press has some excellent books specific to ADO.NET and XML such as Professional ADO.NET (Wrox Press, ISBN 1-861005-27-X) and Professional XML for .NET Developers (Wrox Press, ISBN 1-861005-31-8).*

After completing this chapter, you should be able to answer the following questions:

- What is ADO.NET?
- How are ADO and ADO.NET similar? How are they different?
- What managed providers are available with ADO.NET?

- Which namespaces can be used for data access?
- What are `DataSets` and how can you implement them?
- What are `DataReaders`?
- How does XML fit within the ADO.NET architecture?
- How can you query XML data?
- How can you modify XML data?

ADO.NET: An Introduction

ADO.NET is a new generation of ADO. It provides a complete restructuring of the data access model. However, ADO.NET was not designed to create havoc among programmers by forcing them to learn an entirely new object model. On the contrary, the goal of ADO.NET is to remain as similar to ADO as possible, while at the same time fixing many of the inherent problems ADO presents. As a result of the reengineering of ADO, there are some changes in its handling of data access, but it retains some familiarity to help the application developer.

Some of the major changes include:

- `DataSet` is used instead of a record set
- `DataReader` can be used to read/display data as a read-only, forward cursor
- The `DataSet` can utilize multiple tables in a disconnected environment
- ADO.NET can utilize optimistic concurrency, thus eliminating the need to lock database resources
- XML has become the fundamental method for exchanging data

We will learn about each of these and more, so let's get started by learning about the namespaces used for data management.

Namespaces

One important aspect of the .NET Framework is the need to explicitly specify the appropriate namespace in order to utilize a particular set of class libraries for data management. When dealing with relational data, we are concerned with the classes found within the `System.Data` namespace. For example, if we want to utilize a managed provider for SQL Server, we need to provide the namespace `System.Data.SqlClient`.

Of course, the beauty of the ADO.NET Framework is that it does not restrict us only to relational data. We can also utilize XML data. For example, if we want to work with the XML classes for querying XML documents, we would provide the namespace `System.Xml.Xpath`. XML namespaces are accessed from `System.Xml`.

How do you know what namespace you need to specify? Hopefully, the table at the end of this section will help to guide you. At the same time, if you forget to specify a namespace, there are a few ways of finding out. If you are working with Visual Studio .NET, you will know immediately due to the enhanced IntelliSense.

If you are working with ASP pages, say on NotePad, you should be well aware that you are greeted with a rather helpful error (for the most part, more meaningful than the errors produced with standard ASP) when you try and execute the page.

Once you become familiar with the .NET Framework and data management, knowing what namespaces to use will become second nature. For the most part, we will be concerned with the namespaces shown in the following two tables.

System.Data

`System.Data` contains classes used for relational data issues such as connecting to a relational database, accessing relational data, and the manipulation of relational data:

Namespace for **System.Data**	Description
`System.Data`	The `System.Data` namespace contains the objects necessary to access and store relational data. Note that these objects are independent of the way relational data is accessed as well as the source type.
`System.Data.Common`	Typically, you do not need to import this namespace. The .NET providers utilize classes under this namespace. This namespace contains the base classes used by other objects, such as those found in `System.Data.SqlClient` and `System.Data.OleDb`.
`System.Data.OleDb`	Contains the classes used to connect to a data source through an OLE-DB provider.
`System.Data.SqlClient`	Contains the classes used to connect to a data source through the TDS (Tabular Data Stream) interface of Microsoft SQL Server 7.0 or later.
`System.Data.SqlType`	Contains classes that are SQL Server specific. They are used for implementation of data types stored in SQL Server relational databases. In other words, when working with SQL Server databases, using `SqlType` can avoid type conversion errors due to data types from one database being different from .NET's standard data types.

System.Xml

`System.Xml` contains classes used to work with XML such as reading, writing, and querying XML documents as well as transforming XML into other formats:

Namespace for `System.Xml`	Description
`System.Xml`	In order to create, read, write, store, and manipulate XML documents that meet the specifications provided by the W3C, we access the necessary objects by importing the `System.Xml` namespace.
`System.Xml.Schema`	This namespace contains the objects necessary for the creation, storage, and operation with XML schemas, and the nodes they contain.
`System.Xml.Serialization`	This namespace provides the necessary objects used to convert XML documents to and from other formats, such as SOAP, for transferring to disk or across the wire.
`System.Xml.Xpath`	The classes necessary for implementing reading, writing, storing, and querying XML documents utilizing a XPath-based document object are contained within the `System.Xml.Xpath` namespace. Note that this namespace also includes two objects used to represent XPath expressions, `XpathDocument` and `XpathNavigator`.
`System.Xml.Xsl`	Contains the objects necessary to transform XML into other formats utilizing XSL or XSLT stylesheets. `XslTransform` is the main object.

ADO.NET Components

In order to understand the numerous objects that make up ADO.NET classes, the best way to get a grasp of them is to break things down piece by piece. ADO.NET can be thought of as two separate core parts; **managed providers**, and the `DataSet`.

Managed providers are used to connect to a database, execute commands, and retrieve results from the database. The results can be placed in a `DataSet` object, which is a client-side container of one or more interrelated tables, regardless of their data source.

Managed Providers

In order to connect to a database, as well as for retrieving database results and executing database commands utilizing .NET, we need to use what are called managed providers (also commonly referred to as **data providers**). Currently Microsoft has given us two managed providers, SQL and OLE DB, but more are on the way and it is expected other third party vendors will soon follow suit. The good news is the syntax is very similar between providers, so if you learn one, you will easily be able to implement the other.

SQL Server Managed Provider

The SQL managed provider is designed only for accessing Microsoft SQL Server and provides all the necessary methods for seamless communication with a `DataSet` and SQL Server. Microsoft boasts that because the SQL managed provider does not utilize a COM-based OLE DB provider, performance is greatly enhanced. How is this possible? By utilizing a protocol called **tabular data stream**. This protocol is managed via the CLR (Common Language Runtime), thus it does not require COM/COM+ in order to communicate with SQL Server.

When specifying that you are using a SQL managed provider within a connection string, you use `SqlConnection`.

OLE DB Managed Provider

.NET's OLE DB managed providers are similar to ADO's OLE DB providers, which essentially permitted the client application to have transparent data access to virtually any type of data store. In other words, a client application can access data in such a way that the client never realizes, nor cares, what type of data source it's connected to.

ADO's OLE DB's success was due to its ties with COM/COM+. In actuality, OLE DB is a set of COM components. Through COM interfaces, .NET OLE DB managed providers can supply various levels of support for just about any type of data store, as with ADO. In other words, the .NET OLE DB managed provider utilizes native OLE DB through COM interfaces in order to access a data source.

OLE DB Provider Names

Provider Name	Provider Description
`Microsoft.Jet.OLEDB.4.0`	Jet OLE DB for Microsoft Access
`MSDAORA`	Used for accessing Oracle databases via OLE DB
`SQLOLEDB` (See Note Below)	Used to connect to MS SQL Server via OLE DB

SQL Server can also be accessed utilizing the OLE DB Provider. Nevertheless, it is recommended for maximum efficiency that SQL Server Provider be used. True, both providers can be managed through the CLR and both have native code components; however efficiency is gained by using SQL Server Provider because you do not need to go through the OLE DB layer in order to get to SQL Server. If you are using earlier versions than SQL Server 7.0, you should use OLE DB.

We can divide a managed provider, whether it is for SQL Server or OLE DB, into four separate objects:

- `Connection`
- `Command`
- `DataReader`
- `DataAdapter`

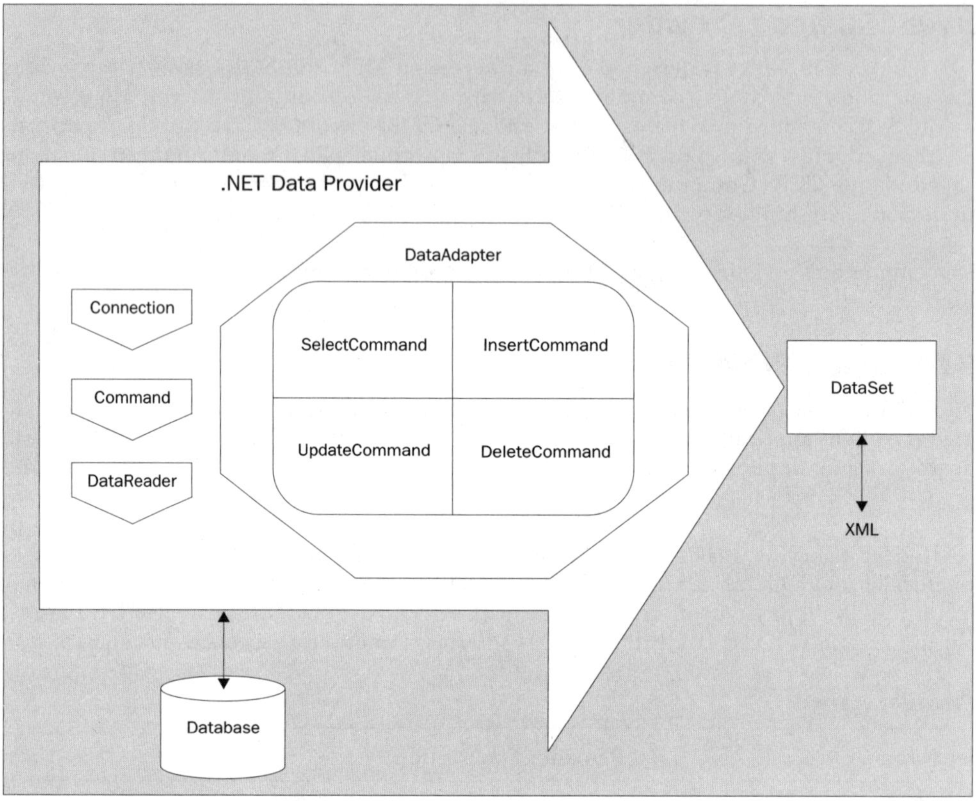

Connection Object

The `Connection` object is used to establish a session (physical) connection to a data source.

When working with the managed provider for SQL Server, we specify the `Connection` object as `SqlConnection`. Conversely, when we use the OLE DB providers, we specify the `Connection` object as `OleDbConnection`.

The following table represents the common methods typically used for the `Connection` object (for both managed providers – SQL and OLE DB):

Method	Method Description
`Open()`	Used to open a connection to a data source.
`Close()`	Used to close a connection to a data source.
`BeginTransaction()`	Used to start a transaction. When a transaction begins, a `SqlTransaction` or `OleTransaction` is returned that can be used for committing or aborting the transaction.

Command Object

The Command object is used to issue commands intended to execute against a data source. For example, a command can be any type of SQL statement (or a stored procedure), such as SELECT, INSERT, or UPDATE.

> **Note that the Command object is optional, as there are other techniques we can utilize for querying and manipulating data, as you will soon discover.**

When working with the managed provider for SQL Server, we specify a Command object as SqlCommand.

When working with the OLE DB providers, you specify the Command object as OleDbCommand.

The following table represents the common methods typically used for the Command object (for both managed providers – SQL and OLE DB):

Method	Method Description
ExecuteNonQuery()	This method executes a SQL statement that does not return any data. Instead, an integer is returned that indicates the number of rows the query affected.
ExecuteReader()	When a command is issued to execute a SQL query, the ExecuteReader() method is used to fill the reader with the data (returned from the command).

DataReader Object

Recall from Chapter 1, that I stressed that one of ADO's major deficiencies is its lack of a disconnected record set. And although ADO.NET solves this problem through the use of DataSets, there will still be times when we may wish to work with data without needing to provide a disconnected environment. For example, we may only want to work with a few records, or perhaps we may wish to access only a few selected columns from a table. Another good use for the DataReader is to bind it with a data source. This is referred to as **data binding** and you will have a chance to try it out in the next chapter.

The DataReader is essentially the same as a forward-only, read-only record set (a fire hose cursor). The DataReader stores a data stream from a data store to be used within a query operation.

When working with the managed provider for SQL Server, we specify the DataReader object as SqlDataReader.

When working with the OLE DB providers, we specify the DataReader object as OleDbDataReader.

DataAdapter Object

The DataAdapter's primary job is to pull and push data between a DataSet and a data source. When I say data is pulled, I am referring to data being moved from a data source and moved into the DataSet. The DataAdapter can also take data and move it out in the form of XML.

Remember that a DataSet resides in memory and a data store is permanent. Thus, the DataAdapter serves as an intermediary, or bridge, between the two.

DataReader and SQL Server Managed Provider Example

In this project you will connect to SQL Server using the managed provider for SQL Server and you will implement the `DataReader` object by filling a list box with the first and last names from the `employees` table located in the `Northwind` sample database. Because we do not need to store any data in memory for this project, we do not utilize the `DataSet`. The `DataSet` object will be covered later in this chapter.

For this example, we have shown the code download folder, `VBNETTrans`, as being in the root directory of `C:`. You can of course put this folder wherever you like, but remember to alter any code accordingly.

> **SQL Server (version 7 or 2000) is recommended for the projects in this book. However, if you do not have SQL Server, you can easily modify the projects in this book to accommodate other databases including MS Access. Use the `System.Data.OleDb` namespace in place of `System.Data.SqlClient` and use the appropriate OLE DB objects in place of SQL Server objects.**

Open Visual Studio .NET and start a new Visual Basic project, selecting Windows Application under the second pane labeled Templates. Also change the project name to DataReader_Project1:

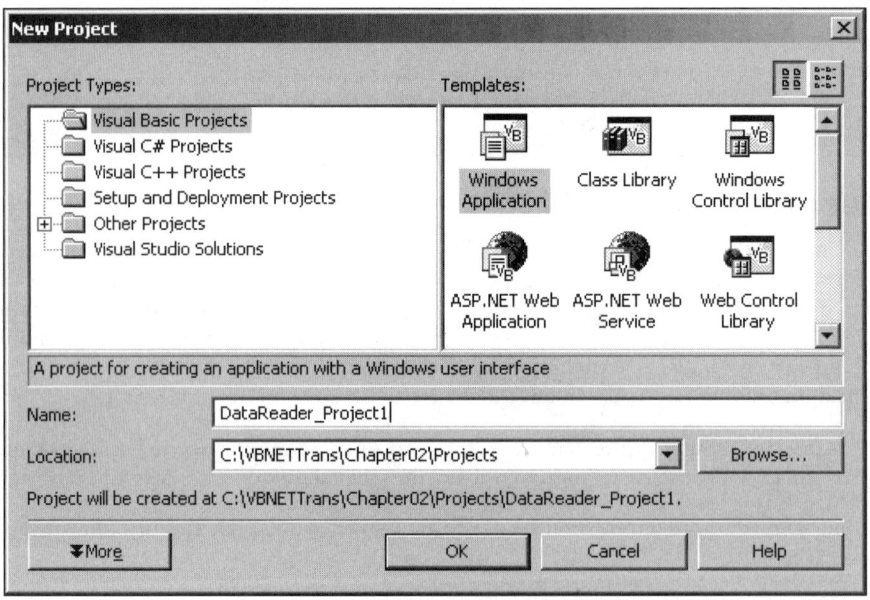

Before we start with our code, let's look at the design of our form. From the Toolbox, select the tab labeled Windows Form. Drag a List Box and Button control on to the form as shown:

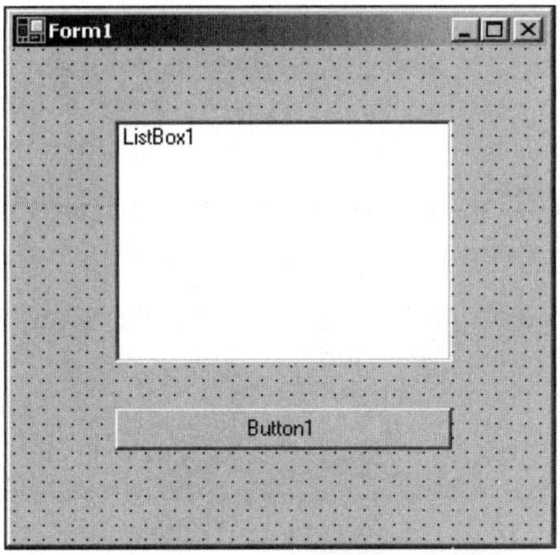

Type in the following namespaces before the `Forms Declarations` (at the top of the code window):

```
Imports System.Data
Imports System.Data.SQLClient
```

Locate the `Button1_Click()` method and enter the following highlighted code:

```
    Private Sub Button1_Click(ByVal sender As Object, ByVal e As System.EventArgs)
        Handles Button1.Click
        'Be sure to substitute the Data Source with the name of your SQL Server
        '                       the User ID with your user name
        '                       the PWD with your pass word

        Dim myConnString As String = "Data Source=HELENCA;" & _
            "initial catalog=Northwind;User ID=sa;PWD="
        Dim mySQLQuery As String = "SELECT FirstName, LastName FROM Employees"
        Dim mySQLConnection As New SqlConnection(myConnString)
        Dim mySQLCommand As New SqlCommand(mySQLQuery, mySQLConnection)
        Dim mySQLReader As SqlDataReader
        Try
            mySQLConnection.Open()
            mySQLReader = mySQLCommand.ExecuteReader()

            While mySQLReader.Read()
                ListBox1.Items.Add(mySQLReader("firstname") + " " +
                    mySQLReader("lastname"))
            End While
        Catch mySQLReaderException As Exception
            MessageBox.Show(mySQLReaderException.ToString())
        Finally

            If mySQLConnection.State = ConnectionState.Open Then
                mySQLConnection.Close()
                mySQLReader.Close()
            End If
```

```
        End Try

    End Sub
```

Note that, for cosmetic purposes, I have renamed the `Text` property of **Button1** to **Get Names**, although this change is not necessary.

You are now ready to test this application. Select **Debug | Start** from the menu bar in Visual Studio .NET. Doing this will first build the project and alert you to any build problems. If everything parses without errors, it will execute the application.

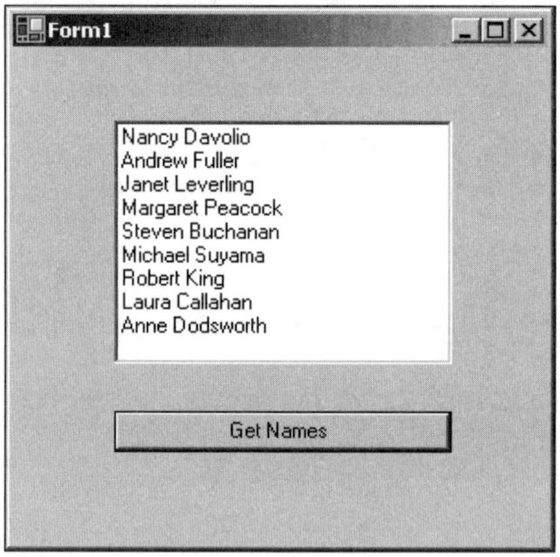

By clicking the button (**Get Names**), you should see the list box filled with names originating from the `Employees` table in the `Northwind` database.

To recap all that has happened here, we first started off by adding the namespaces `System.Data` and `System.Data.SQLClient` to utilize the data management classes for SQL Server.

Next, we established a database connection using a `SqlConnection` object, and then issued a SQL command to the database. In this example, we requested (using a SQL statement) the first and last names from the `Employees` table.

We then loaded the `DataReader` with table data from SQL Server and iterated through the records as forward only and read-only to populate the list box.

If an error occurs within the `Try` block, the next block of code labeled `Catch` is invoked. In other words, if an error occurs, the `Catch` block should be designed to handle the error. In this application, we take any errors that occur and pass it as a string to be displayed to the user in the form of a `MessageBox`.

If no errors occur within the `Try` block of code, the `Catch` block will be skipped and code execution will resume after the `End Try` (assuming there is more code to execute).

Often there is an optional block that can occur right after `Catch` and just before `End Try`, called `Finally`. If there is a `Finally` block of code, execution will resume here, regardless of whether an error occurred during the `Catch` block. The `Finally` block comes in very handy for cleanup code such as closing objects and perhaps to take some other action such as writing to a log file. That is why code is executed even if an error is handled during the `Catch` block. In this example, we use the `Finally` block to close our connection and the `DataReader`.

As a note regarding cleanup code, thanks to .NET's garbage collection, simply closing the connection will close the `DataReader`. However, it is still good practice to explicitly close any object that is no longer required as we have in this code example.

DataSet Object

If you are familiar with ADO, you know that record sets provide methods used to pull information in order to retrieve and display rows (records) from a database. One of the major drawbacks of an ADO record set is the inability to retrieve multiple sets of data at one time. Furthermore, record sets do not provide any relational information or constraints about the data it contains.

Within ADO.NET comes the introduction of a new object called the `DataSet`. In simple terms, the `DataSet` provides a collection of tables, including the relationships between them, and any constraint information that may exist. Furthermore, the `DataSet` stores all this information in memory. Basically, what you get is a miniature relational database stored in memory.

The `DataSet` is typically used with relational data, but it does not have to be. You can use a `DataSet` with XML (which may or may not contain relational data) or just about any other type of data you can imagine.

If you look hard enough, you can see the writing is on the wall. Being able to copy relational data from multiple tables and placing it in memory provides the solution to disconnected data – something ADO just cannot compete with. True ADO was capable of many of these things. But the bottom line is ADO.NET does all of this more efficiently.

Concurrency Issues

We now know we can store representations of miniature relational databases in our own `DataSets`, that allow us to do whatever we want with the data. But what happens when two or more people take some data, manipulate it, and then send it back to the data source to be updated? For example, suppose two users take the CEO's employee information and alter his title, each specifying a different title. What is likely to happen? With ADO.NET running the show, two possible things may happen, both resulting in the last person being the loser.

The scenario just discussed is referred to as **concurrency**. Concurrency comes in two flavors, pessimistic and optimistic.

Pessimistic Concurrency and Locking

Pessimistic concurrency is based on using locks. Simply, when a user is accessing data from a relational data source, a lock is placed in order to keep anyone else from accessing the same data while it is being used. As soon as the first user is finished, the lock is removed and another user can work with the same data. Getting back to the previous scenario, where two people try to update the same data at the same time – when using pessimistic concurrency the first person to update wins by being able to complete their transaction, while the other user simply is locked out from accessing it until the first user is finished. Typically, pessimistic concurrency is commonly used when using an ADO.NET command to modify data.

Optimistic Concurrency and Locking

The other type of concurrency is optimistic. Optimistic concurrency also uses locks, but instead of applying locks the moment a record is edited, locks are only placed when a record is actually updated.

Optimistic concurrency monitors and keeps track of all original data. This means that if two users retrieve the same data into a `DataSet` and one makes a change to the CEO's title, while another tries to change the CEO's title and submits it for updating, the last user's transaction will be aborted. I know that this is as clear as mud. But if you hang on a little longer, this will clear itself up.

Optimistic concurrency acts as a watchdog for data. Remember, when using a `DataSet`, for example, we are retrieving data that potentially gets outdated because data in a `DataSet` is merely a copy in a disconnected environment. In other words, the `DataSet` can act totally independently of the data source from which it was filled. When a user submits changes back to a data source, the data is compared with the original data at the data source. In other words, a copy of the original data residing at the data source is compared with the data originally stored within the `DataSet`. If both sets of data match, the new changes submitted will be accepted. However, if some of the data is old, and the same record has already been modified since the second user tried to make changes based on the data captured originally, then the changes will be rejected, as the user no longer has a valid copy of the data. The only way the user can make a change is to grab a current version of the data and try again.

The stage when locks are applied is what differentiates optimistic from pessimistic locking. In pessimistic locking, the locks are applied the moment a record is edited. With optimistic locking, locks are applied when the record is actually updated.

As you have probably surmised, both pessimistic and optimistic concurrencies involve a lot of work. The beauty of ADO.NET is that it not only handles both types of concurrency for us, it automatically applies the proper type for the right job. When working with `DataSets`, ADO.NET implements optimistic concurrency, and it implements pessimistic concurrency when using an ADO.NET command to modify data.

Common DataSet Methods

The following table represents the common methods typically used for the `DataSet` object (for both managed providers – SQL and OLE DB):

Method	Method Description
`AcceptChanges()`	This method is used to commit all changes made to the `DataSet` since it was last loaded, or if the `AcceptChanges()` method has been executed, since the last time `AcceptChanges()` was executed.
`Clear()`	If you want to remove all the data stored in `DataSet`, this is the method to use. Note that instead of using the `Clear()` method, it is more effective to destroy the object and then create a new `DataSet`.
`GetChanges()`	The `GetChanges()` method is used to return a `DataSet` that contains all of the changes it has undergone since it was loaded, or if the `AcceptChanges()` method has been executed, since the last time `AcceptChanges()` was executed.
`GetXml()`	The contents of an XML document used to represent data in a `DataSet` are returned in the form of a string.
`GetXmlSchema()`	The contents of an XML Schema used to represent data in a `DataSet` are returned in the form of a string.
`HasChanges()`	`HasChanges()` is used to indicate whether any data changes have been made within a `DataSet` since it was loaded, or if the `AcceptChanges()` method has been executed, since the last time `AcceptChanges()` was executed.
`Merge()`	You can take the entire contents (tables, relations, constraint information) from one `DataSet` and merge all of it into another `DataSet` by utilizing the `Merge()` method. Didn't I say `DataSets` have some powerful methods?
`ReadXml()`	Takes an XML document and reads it into the `DataSet`.
`ReadXmlSchema()`	Takes XML schema and reads it into the `DataSet`.
`RejectChanges()`	You can undo all the changes made to a `DataSet` up to the point of the last commitment of data. In other words, you can reject all the changes to a `DataSet` since it was first loaded, or if the method `AcceptChanges()` has been executed, up to the point of its last execution.
`WriteXml()`	This method is used to write an XML document representing the data and the schema in the `DataSet` to a disk file, a "reader/writer" object or stream.
`WriteXmlSchema()`	This method is used to write an XML schema representing the data in the `DataSet` to a disk file, a "reader/writer" object or stream.

DataSet Architecture

Now that we have a general idea about what a DataSet is, let's dig a little deeper and look at its architecture.

Before we can start using a DataSet, we must first create it:

```
Dim MyDataSet as NEW DataSet
```

Once we have a DataSet created, we can put some interesting things into it. For example, we can place any type of data we want into a DataSet:

- We can place multiple tables in it, regardless of whether they are relational or not.
- When dealing with relational data, we can even place relationships and constraints into a DataSet.
- We can place XML data into a DataSet.

In a nutshell, we can place just about any type of data imaginable into a DataSet. Pretty cool, huh?

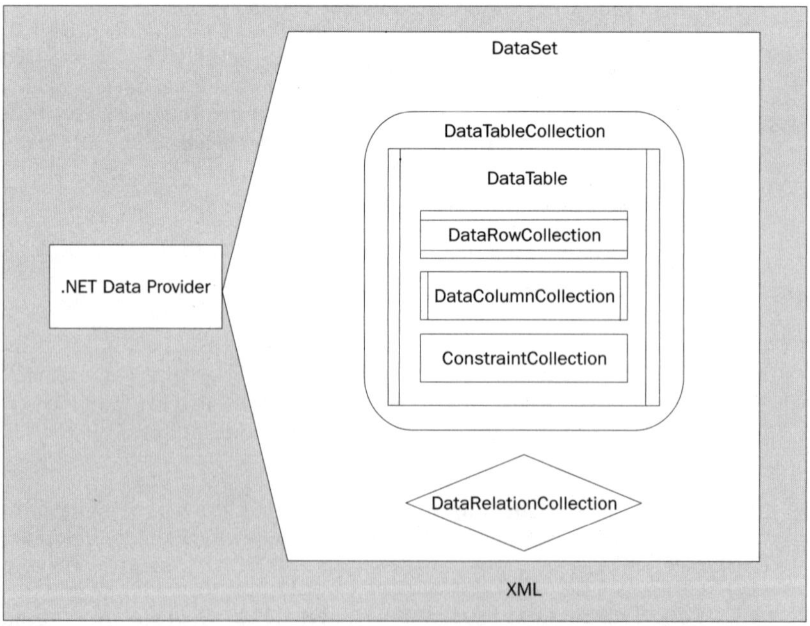

Take a look at the DataSet diagram. Notice that a DataTable object is inside the DataTableCollection. A DataTable represents a single table from a database. Because a DataSet allows us to have multiple tables, we have a larger container, the DataTableCollection. Simply, the DataTableCollection holds all the DataTables being stored in the DataSet.

Within the DataTable there are three more objects, the DataRowCollection, the DataColumnCollection, and the ConstraintCollection. For now, let's put these on hold and take a look at the DataRelationCollection.

The DataRelationCollection object provides the functionality for navigating between any tables that have defined relationships. Actually, within the DataRelationCollection, there is a DataRelations object. The DataRelations object is where the information pertaining to the actual relationships between tables is located. As you may suspect, relationship information includes the name of the relationship, and the relationships between primary and foreign keys.

Another cool feature of the DataSet is it allows you to create your own relationships among objects. Furthermore, we can define how a relationship is related. For example, suppose we have two DataTable objects. Remember that a DataTable represents one table in a database. One DataTable holds only the model names for motorcycles, and the other DataTable holds only the model names of automobiles. We can create a relationship between these two tables as *motor vehicles.* Now we can run a query – an update or an insert – within our DataSet specifying the relationship of *motor vehicles.*

With all this said, suppose we try to add a glider to our *motor vehicles* relationship. ADO.NET monitors all key constraints to ensure that any changes to a DataTable will not violate a relationship with another related table. Trying to add glider to one of the DataTables would cause a relationship violation, thus it would be rejected. However, we could add another DataTable for non-motorized vehicles and create a relationship among motorcycles, automobiles, and gliders by defining a relationship as *transportation vehicles.*

Earlier I had you put DataTables and DataRows on hold. Now it's time to take a look at them.

How the DataTable Works

As part of the DataTable there are two objects, the DataRow and RowState. The DataRow object is used to represent one row of data within the DataTable, while the RowState object is responsible for keeping track of the condition of each DataRow in a DataTable. What this means is that the DataTable (through the use of the RowState object) must keep track of three copies of each row of data (represented in the DataRow), the original state of each row, the current state of each row, and the proposed state of each row.

For clarity, the original RowState reflects the original values in a DataRow before being modified. The current RowState reflects the newly changed values in a DataRow. The proposed RowState is a little different; basically it reflects multiple row changes.

The proposed RowState is based on several methods that allow you to edit and manipulate values within multiple rows, without making any changes permanent. Furthermore, data can be manipulated among multiple rows without applying validation rules. This can come in handy when working with a lot of data in an "if-try" scenario to see how things may look. The important thing to realize is that just because you can put in any type of data without any constraints, changes will be discarded if you try to make permanent changes that don't conform to the constraint rules.

In order to enter the edit mode, we use the BeginEdit() method. In order to keep the changes, we call the AcceptChanges() method or simply call EndEdit(). Of course, you can cancel any changes as well while in edit mode. Immediately upon exiting the edit mode, all validation rules are applied.

As you can see, there is a lot a DataSet can offer. We have already looked at the common methods the DataSet provides. Let's now take a look at the common methods for the DataTable, DataRowCollection, and the DataRow.

The following table shows the common methods provided by the `DataTable` object:

Method	Description
`NewRow()`	This method is used to create a new table row.
`Select()`	The select method is used to create subsets of rows. It returns the set of rows that match the filter.

The following table shows the common methods provided by the `DataRowCollecton` object:

Method	Description
`Add()`	Adds a new row to the table created with the `NewRow()` method of the `DataTable`
`Find()`	This method is used to return a specified data row by specifying a primary key value
`Item()`	With the item method, you can retrieve a `DataRow` within a collection by specifying the name of the row or its index in the collection
`Remove()`	Removes the specified `DataRow` object from the table
`RemoveAt()`	Removes a row from a table specified by its index position

The following table shows the common methods provided by the `DataRow` object:

Method	Description
`BeginEdit()`	Begins the edit mode for a particular row. While in edit mode, constraint rules are not in effect, but if an entry is entered that violates the column rules, the change will be aborted upon exiting edit mode.
`CancelEdit()`	This method can be used to cancel a row change made while in edit mode.
`EndEdit()`	This method takes you out of edit mode.
`Delete()`	The `Delete()` method does not actually remove the row from a table. Instead, it places a marker by a row indicating it has been deleted. In order for the row to be physically removed, an update or `AcceptChanges()` must be executed.
`GetColumnsInError()`	This method will return an array reflecting errors for columns.
`GetColumnsError()`	This method is used to return an error status for a specified column.

DataSet Example

Earlier we tried accessing SQL Server using the `DataReader`, now let's access the same database and table utilizing a `DataSet`.

You can modify the code from the last project by deleting all the code under the `Button1_Click` event or start from scratch and create a new Visual Basic Project. Select **Windows Application** under the second pane labeled **Templates**. Also you may want to give this project a name, such as `DataSet_Project2`, so you can easily identify the project for later use.

Before entering any code, go to **Form Design** and drag a list box and a button from the ToolBox as in the previous example. For cosmetic purposes, you may want to change the `Text` property for the button to **Get Names**.

As with the previous project, we need the same namespaces under the forms declarations:

```
Imports System.Data
Imports System.Data.SqlClient
```

Locate the `Button1_Click()` method and enter the following:

```
    Private Sub Button1_Click(ByVal sender As Object, ByVal e As System.EventArgs)
        Handles Button1.Click
'Be sure to substitute the Data Source with the name of your SQL Server
'                        the User ID with your user name
'                        the PWD with your pass word

Dim mySQLConnection As New SqlConnection("Data Source=LocalHost;" & _
    "initial catalog=Northwind;User ID=sa;PWD=")
Dim mySQLDataAdapter As New SqlDataAdapter()
Dim myDataSet As DataSet = New DataSet()

    Try
        mySQLConnection.Open()
        mySQLDataAdapter = New SqlDataAdapter("Select Firstname, " & _
              "LastName from employees", mySQLConnection)

        mySQLDataAdapter.Fill(myDataSet, "Employees")

        Dim rowEmployee As System.Data.DataRow
        For Each rowEmployee In myDataSet.Tables("Employees").Rows
            ListBox1.Items.Add(rowEmployee("FirstName") + " " + _
                                   rowEmployee("LastName"))
        Next

    Catch myException As Exception
        MessageBox.Show(myException.ToString())
    Finally
        If mySQLConnection.State = ConnectionState.Open Then
            mySQLConnection.Close()
        End If
        If Not myDataSet Is Nothing Then
            myDataSet = Nothing
        End If
    End Try
End Sub
```

You are now ready to test this application. Select Debug | Start from the menu bar in Visual Studio .NET:

Notice that the results are identical to the previous project utilizing the `DataReader`. However, as you should be aware, the internals are very different. Let's take a look at how this example works.

As with the previous example, we first started by adding the namespace `System.Data.SqlClient` to utilize the data management classes for SQL Server.

Next, we established a database connection using a `SqlConnection` object and then issuing a SQL command to the database in order to retrieve the requested table into the `DataSet`.

Once the table had been retrieved, we iterated through the records row by row in order to populate the list box.

If any errors occur, execution will resume with our error handler located at the `Catch` block. In other words, if an error occurs anywhere within the `Try` block, it will be handled at the `Catch` block where it will be reported to the user via a `MessageBox`.

Regardless of whether an error occurs, or if the `Try` block executes properly, we placed our cleanup code in the `Finally` block. More specifically, we closed the database connection and the `DataSet`.

Updating Data Using ADO.NET

When all you need to perform is a simple transaction (that only needs to change data at one data source), ADO.NET provides a quick and simple solution. All we need is a SQL statement and the `Command` object in which to execute it.

We have already used both the ADO.NET `Command` and a `SqlDataReader` separately in previous projects. Because this project utilizes both, the code for this project should seem very familiar to you. Start a new project (choose Windows Application), or you can modify the existing project utilizing the `SqlDataReader`. Name the project `CommandUpdate` and add a list box and button to the form, as we have in our previous examples. For cosmetic reasons, you may want to change the button's `Text` property to `Employee Update`.

Type in the following namespaces under the form's **Declarations**:

```
Imports System.Data
Imports System.Data.SqlClient
```

Create a private function as shown. Because we need to create a connection for the update and another to query the results, we can place a single connection string under the public class `Form1`:

```
Public Class Form1
    Inherits System.Windows.Forms.Form

    Dim mySqlConnection As New SqlConnection("Data Source=localhost;" & _
    "initial catalog=Northwind;User ID=sa;PWD=")

Private Function MyDataReader() As SqlDataReader

    Dim mySqlCommand As New SqlCommand("Select * from Employees", _
        mySqlConnection)
    Dim MySqlReader As SqlDataReader

    Try
        ListBox1.Items.Clear()
        mySqlConnection.Open()
        MySqlReader = mySqlCommand.ExecuteReader()

        Do While (MySqlReader.Read())
            ListBox1.Items.Add(MySqlReader("firstname") + "  " + _
                                   MySqlReader("lastName"))
        Loop
    Catch ReaderException As Exception

        MessageBox.Show(ReaderException.ToString())

    Finally
        MySqlReader.Close()
        mySqlConnection.Close()
    End Try
End Function
```

Locate the `Button1_Click()` method and enter the following:

```
    Private Sub Button1_Click(ByVal sender As Object, ByVal e As System.EventArgs)
        Handles Button1.Click
Dim mySqlCommand As New SqlCommand("Update Employees Set" & _
    " FirstName = 'Susan' where FirstName = 'Andrew' And " & _
    "LastName = 'Fuller'", mySqlConnection)

Try
    mySqlConnection.Open()
    mySqlCommand.ExecuteNonQuery()
Catch myException As Exception
    MessageBox.Show(myException.ToString())
```

```
Finally

    If (mySqlConnection.State = ConnectionState.Open) Then
        mySqlConnection.Close()
    End If
End Try

MyDataReader()
End Sub
```

Finally, create the following under the `Form1` class:

```
        Me.ResumeLayout(False)

    End Sub

#End Region
Private Sub Form1_Click(ByVal sender As System.Object, ByVal e As
    System.EventArgs) Handles MyBase.Click
        MyDataReader()
End Sub
```

You are ready to test this application. When the application first opens, click anywhere on the form. This will populate the list box. Pay attention to the second name. You should see it says Andrew Fuller. This name is provided as a sample in the `Employees` table within the `Northwind` database accompanying SQL Server:

Next, click the button and notice that Andrew Fuller has been replaced with Susan Fuller:

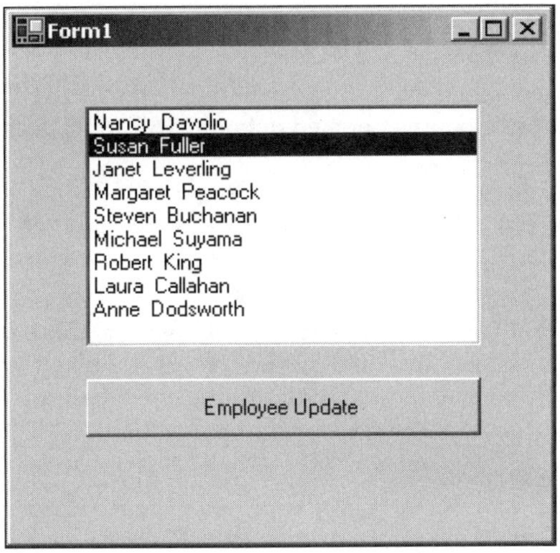

We created a private function called `MyDataReader`. Essentially, we used the same code for the `DataReader` except we created its own function. This way we can call this function when the form first loads, and directly after we execute our update in order to refresh the list box. When we worked with the `DataReader`, we used the `SqlCommand` to load it.

We created the `SqlCommand` and then loaded the `DataReader` by executing the `SqlCommand`.

We can also use the `SqlCommand` object for manipulating our data. You should recall that the `DataReader` is read-only, meaning you can only read data and not manipulate data from a `DataReader`. As a result, we need to execute a SQL statement utilizing the `SqlCommand`. In this project we created a `SqlCommand` that executes an `UPDATE` statement:

In this example, we hard-coded an `UPDATE` statement that looks for the conditions (specified by the `WHERE` clause) `FirstName` equalling `'Andrew'` and the `LastName` equalling `'Fuller'`. When these conditions were found all such occurrences for the `FirstName` of `'Andrew'` were changed to `'Susan'`. With this database, it only occurs once, but it could have involved numerous changes. Of course, we could have easily incorporated an `INSERT` or a `DELETE` statement using the same techniques.

Now that everything is declared, we execute the `UPDATE` command with the method `ExecuteNonQuery()`.

The `ExecuteNonQuery()` method is used to execute our SQL `UPDATE` statement. It should be noted that the `ExecuteNonQuery()` does not return any data (although it can return an integer value that indicates the number of rows the query affected). Because data is not returned, we will use the `DataReader` to retrieve our changes. Simply, we call the `DataReader` function:

```
MyDataReader()
```

so we can view our changes via a list box.

In case you were wondering if you can use a data grid in this example, the answer is no. The reason for this is you cannot bind a `DataReader` to a data grid so you will have to use a dataset instead.

Updating Data Using a DataSet

In the previous project you have seen how you can manipulate data using the Command statement and a SQL statement. Although the previous example updated only one row, the purpose of the SQL statement:

```
UPDATE Employees SET FirstName = 'Susan' WHERE FirstName = 'Andrew' AND LastName =
'Fuller'
```

had the potential to update multiple rows if the conditions of the WHERE clause had been met. As you can see, using a SQL statement can be very beneficial. However, there may be times when we want to have more control over each record. By utilizing the DataRow object, we can take full control by manipulating data in a specified row. For example, suppose we had the following records:

Row Number	First Name	Middle Initial	Last Name
1	Andrew	T	Fuller
2	Andrew	L	Fuller
3	Dori	C	Fuller

If we used the previous SQL statement, the first two records would be updated because both records have the same first and last name, thus meeting the requirements of the WHERE clause. However, we may only be interested in altering the second row displaying:

2	Andrew	L	Fuller

By selecting the specific row (using the DataRow) from a specific table (using the DataTable) we want to modify, we can selectively update the second row without touching the first row.

XML and the .NET Framework

XML plays a very important role within the .NET Framework. XML is ideal for passing information between application tiers, especially presentation (user services) and business tiers. Of course, XML can also be passed to a variety of data stores.

ADO.NET relies on XML for remote representation of data. With ADO.NET, data can be converted to XML where it can then be manipulated and then converted back to the original type of data. Together, ADO.NET and XML make a great team. Furthermore, you will learn in Chapter 5 about Web Services that utilize XML for interfacing with remote objects.

XML and the DataSet

ADO.NET and XML work together in unison like two wheels on a bicycle. The `DataSet` includes native support for XML formatted data. If you recall the table (in this chapter) labeled `Namespaces`, we have a specific set of XML classes that can be accessed. For example, we can access various methods that will allow a `DataSet` to read and write XML. Furthermore, you can populate a `DataSet` from any XML source, regardless of whether it is from a file or an XML stream. Conversely, a `DataSet` is capable of saving compliant XML data (schema included) regardless of where the original data came from. With all this in mind, it makes sense to say that XML is excellent for transferring data in a disconnected fashion among application tiers; all this is easily accomplished due to the `DataSet`'s native serialization being XML.

XML Objects

The .NET Framework provides numerous XML objects that provide extended features such as reading, writing, serialization, storing, manipulation, and querying. Equally important is the fact the XML classes utilized within the .NET Framework have been fully designed based on W3C standards such as the DOM Level2 Core, XPath 1.0, XSLT 1.0, and XML Schemas (XSD).

For example, by taking these XML objects and merging them with ADO.NET, we can create applications capable of retrieving relational datasets and transverse it across the **DOM (Document Object Model)**. We can also navigate and query XML using XPath and we can utilize XSLT in order to serialize XML into another format. Furthermore, `DataSets` can be serialized to Documents or Streams by taking advantage of XML Schemas. This is powerful stuff!

We will look at many of these available objects in this chapter, as well as other chapters (such as Chapter 4 on ASP.NET) to see how XML can be utilized within data intense applications.

XmlReaders and XmlWriters

There are two abstract classes within the .NET Framework that serve as the foundation for XML use, the `XmlReader` and the `XmlWriter`. Both of these abstract classes define the functionality that all derived classes must support. For example, an `XmlReader` can be implemented to `XmlTextReader` and `XmlNodeReader`, while `XmlWriter` can be broken down into `XmlTextWriter` and `XmlNodeWriter`.

In a nutshell, you can think of the `XmlTextReader` and the `XmlTextWriter` as tools for reading and writing to text-based streams, while the `XmlNodeReader` and the `XmlNodeWriter` are tools for working with DOM trees within memory.

There is one other reader worth mentioning, the `XmlValidatingReader`, which is used to validate XML against a **Document Type Definition (DTD)** or schema. Let's move on to the next section, where we take a detailed look at `XmlReaders` and `XmlWriters`.

XmlReader

When using XmlReader you have a way to read raw contents from any XML file. You can think of the XmlReader object as being similar to the DataReader object where both provide forward-only data access in a simple, and efficient manner. Where a DataReader provides a fast way to access data without the heavy overhead of a DataSet, the XmlReader provides a fast way to access XML without the heavy overhead of utilizing the DOM. Furthermore, with well-defined methods; XmlReaders tend to hide the complexities of working with data. This is something the application developer will greatly appreciate.

Speaking of forward-only data access, the XmlReader is very similar to a record set cursor that is forward only and read-only (often referred to as a fire-hose) because it allows a consumer to retrieve records one at a time from beginning to end.

The following table describes the common methods available to the XmlReader object:

Method	Description
Read()	The Read() method is used to read a node into a reader. When there are no more nodes that can be read, a value of False will be returned.
ReadInnerXml()	The contents of the current node, including all markup and the text of child nodes, can be read and returned as a string.
ReadString()	Returns the string value of the current node.
GetAttribute()	Returns the value of a specified attribute from the current node in the reader.
GetRemainder()	Reads and returns the remaining XML in the source document as a string.
MoveToXXX()	Moves the position of reader.
Skip()	Skips the current node or element in the reader and moves to the next node or element respectively.
Close()	This method is used to close the disk file or stream as well as release any references being held.

XmlReader Example

Before we start working with any of the XmlReaders, we need an XML file to work with. Open NotePad or any XML editor and enter the following code (this file is also provided in the code download for this chapter as Employees.xml):

```
<?xml version="1.0"?>

<Employee>
  <EmployeeInfo>
    <EmployeeFName>Shirley</EmployeeFName>
    <EmployeeLName>Doe1</EmployeeLName>
    <EmployeeId>123</EmployeeId>
    <Department>HR</Department>
  </EmployeeInfo>
```

```
    <EmployeeInfo>
      <EmployeeFName>Natalia</EmployeeFName>
      <EmployeeLName>Doe1</EmployeeLName>
      <EmployeeId>456</EmployeeId>
      <Department>Accounting</Department>
    </EmployeeInfo>

    <EmployeeInfo>
      <EmployeeFName>Ernest</EmployeeFName>
      <EmployeeLName>NoName1</EmployeeLName>
      <EmployeeId>789</EmployeeId>
      <Department>IT</Department>
    </EmployeeInfo>

    <EmployeeInfo>
      <EmployeeFName>Jeff</EmployeeFName>
      <EmployeeLName>NoName2</EmployeeLName>
      <EmployeeId>1010</EmployeeId>
      <Department>HR</Department>
    </EmployeeInfo>

  </Employee>
```

Now save your file as `Employees.xml`.

Next, we want to test our XML document to ensure it is well formed. To do this is easy. Because IE 5 and greater has an XML parser built-in, you simply open the XML document from IE (5 or greater) or from another XML parser. If you typed in everything properly, you should see something similar to the following screenshot:

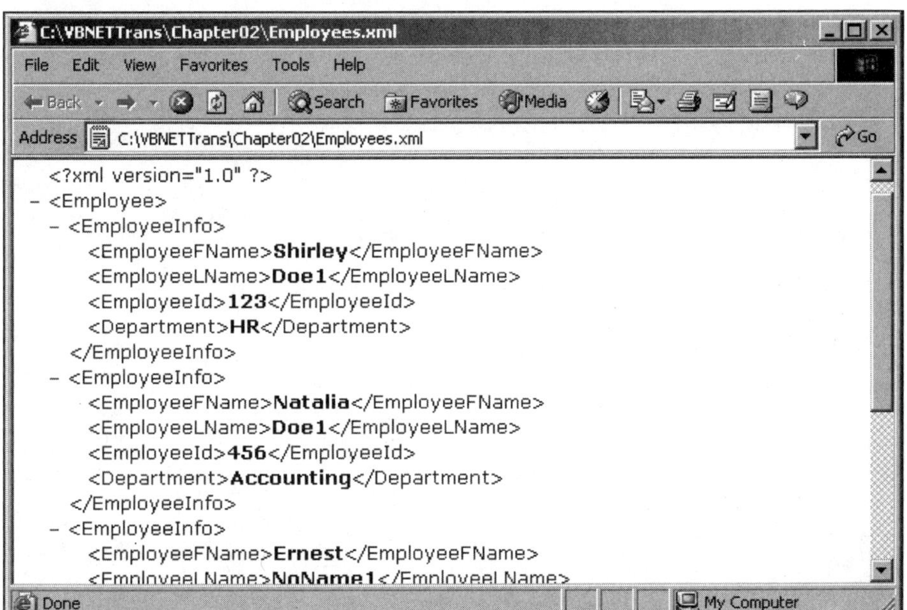

Now that we have an XML file to work with, let's go back and start a new Visual Basic .NET application. Name your project `XMLTextReader`.

Go to the Form Design. From the Toolbox, drag a list box and a button control onto the form as shown below:

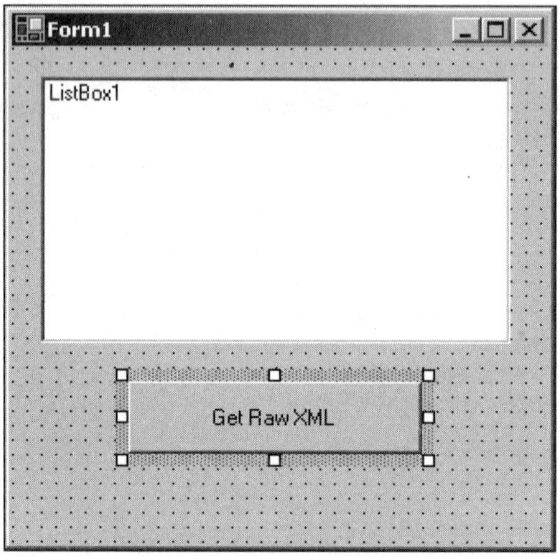

Type in the following namespace under the form's Declarations:

```
Imports System.Xml
```

Locate the `Button1_Click()` method and enter the following:

```
    Private Sub Button1_Click(ByVal sender As Object, ByVal e As System.EventArgs)
        Handles Button1.Click
    Dim reader As System.Xml.XmlTextReader = Nothing

    Try
        reader = New Xml.XmlTextReader("c:\VBNETTrans\Chapter02\Employees.xml")

        While reader.Read()

            ListBox1.Items.Add(reader.Name & reader.Value)
        End While


    Catch ReaderException As Exception
        MessageBox.Show(ReaderException.ToString() + " ")
    Finally
        If Not (reader Is Nothing) Then
            reader.Close()
        End If
    End Try
End Sub
```

Now that you have entered all the necessary code, run it. After the application opens, click the button:

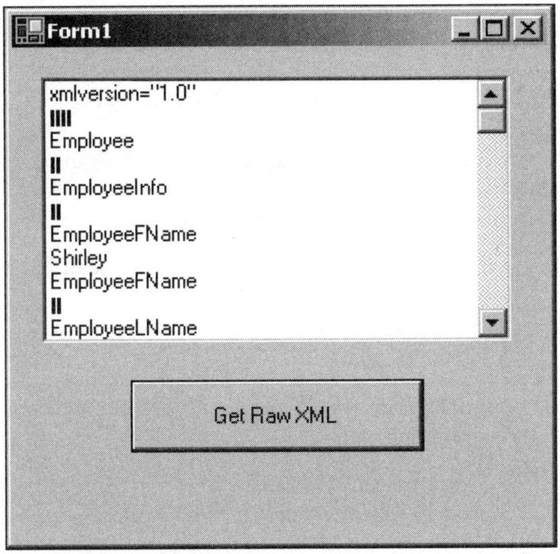

We started by adding the namespace `System.Xml` to utilize the XML classes.

Next, we created and loaded an `XmlTextReader`. Note that instead of providing a connection string to a database, we simply provide a path location to the XML file source:

```
Dim reader As System.Xml.XmlTextReader = Nothing

Try
    reader = New Xml.XmlTextReader("C:\VBNETTrans\Chapter02\Employees.xml")
```

Now that the reader is loaded, we simply iterated through the records row by row to populate the list box. The `XmlReader` is similar to the `DataReader` in that records are streamed row-by-row in a forward-only manner.

We checked for errors and then cleaned-up by closing the `XmlReader`.

Before we move on to `XmlWriters`, let's briefly detour to the `XmlValidatingReader` object.

XmlValidatingReader

The .NET Framework provides a means to validate XML against either a DTD (Document Type Definition) or a schema. This is accomplished using the `XmlValidatingReader` object. You can create the `XmlValidatingReader` to validate from a variety of XML sources such as from a stream, string, or even from an existing `XmlTextReader` or `XmlNodeReader`.

Once the `XmlValidatingReader` has been created, it can be used just like any other `XmlReader`. However, if an XML source does not correspond to its DTD or schema, an error will be raised.

XmlTextWriter

We have just seen how we can read an existing XML document, but there will be times when we wish to programmatically create a new XML document. This can be accomplished with the `XmlTextWriter`. With the `XmlTextWriter`, creating new documents is just as easy as reading XML files utilizing an `XmlTextReader`. Basically, it is used for writing character stream output and supports numerous output streams such as files, URIs, and streams. One of the things that make the `XmlTextWriter` so easy to work with is that it can easily be configured. For example, you can specify whether you want to implement namespace support. You can also specify the type of formatting, such as quote characters and indentation.

The following table describes the most common methods that are available with the `XmlTextWriter` object:

Method	Description
`WriteStartDocument()`	Begins a new XML document by writing the XML declaration to the output.
`WriteEndDocument()`	Upon completing the XML document, you use `WriteEndDocument()` to indicate the end of the XML document. Closing the document with this method closes all elements that have not been closed.
`WriteStartElement()`	By specifying an element, you can use this method to write an opening tag.
`WriteEndElement()`	Just as you use `WriteStartElement()` to open a tag, you use `WriteEndElement` to close the tag.
`Close()`	This method is used to close the file or stream, as well as releasing any references held to the `TextWriter`.

XmlTextWriter Example

Start a new Visual Basic .NET application. Name your project `XmlTextWriter`.

Go to the Form Design and drag a button control on to it as shown:

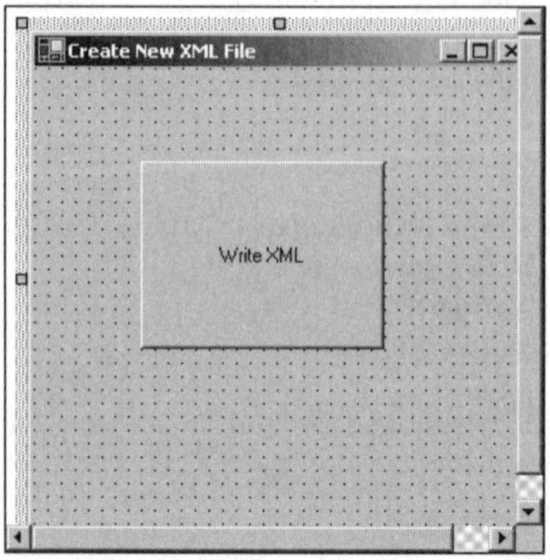

For cosmetic purposes, change the `Text` property of the form to Create New XML file and change the button's `Text` property to Write XML.

Type in the following namespace under the form's Declarations:

```
Imports System.Xml
```

Locate the `Button1_Click()` method and enter the following:

```
    Private Sub Button1_Click(ByVal sender As Object, ByVal e As System.EventArgs)
        Handles Button1.Click
Dim XmlWriter As System.Xml.XmlTextWriter

        Try

            XmlWriter = New
                Xml.XmlTextWriter("c:\VBNETTrans\Chapter02\Employees2.xml",
                Nothing)

            XmlWriter.WriteStartDocument()
            XmlWriter.Formatting = Formatting.Indented
            XmlWriter.Indentation = 3
            XmlWriter.WriteStartElement("Employees")

            XmlWriter.WriteStartElement("Employee1")
            XmlWriter.WriteElementString("EmployeeFName", "Tanya")
            XmlWriter.WriteElementString("EmployeeLName", "Doggy")
            XmlWriter.WriteElementString("EmployeeId", "8877")
            XmlWriter.WriteElementString("Department", "CEO")
            XmlWriter.WriteEndElement()

            XmlWriter.WriteStartElement("Employee2")
            XmlWriter.WriteElementString("EmployeeFName", "Shakespear")
            XmlWriter.WriteElementString("EmployeeLName", "Bigdog")
            XmlWriter.WriteElementString("EmployeeId", "8878")
            XmlWriter.WriteElementString("Department", "VP")
            XmlWriter.WriteEndElement()

            XmlWriter.WriteStartElement("Employee3")
            XmlWriter.WriteElementString("EmployeeFName", "Muppet")
            XmlWriter.WriteElementString("EmployeeLName", "Littledog")
            XmlWriter.WriteElementString("EmployeeId", "8879")
            XmlWriter.WriteElementString("Department", "CFO")
            XmlWriter.WriteEndElement()

            XmlWriter.WriteEndElement()
            XmlWriter.WriteEndDocument()
            XmlWriter.Flush()
            MessageBox.Show("File Created")
        Catch ReaderException As Exception
            MessageBox.Show(ReaderException.ToString() + " ")
        Finally
            If Not (XmlWriter Is Nothing) Then
```

```
                    XmlWriter.Close()
                End If

            End Try
    End Sub
```

Now that you have entered all the necessary code, run it. After the application opens, click the button, and then exit the application.

Look at the specified directory to find the file you just created. In this example, I indicated `C:\VBNETTrans\Chapter02\Employees2.xml`. Try opening the file with Internet Explorer to view the generated code. Your XML file should look similar to the following screenshot:

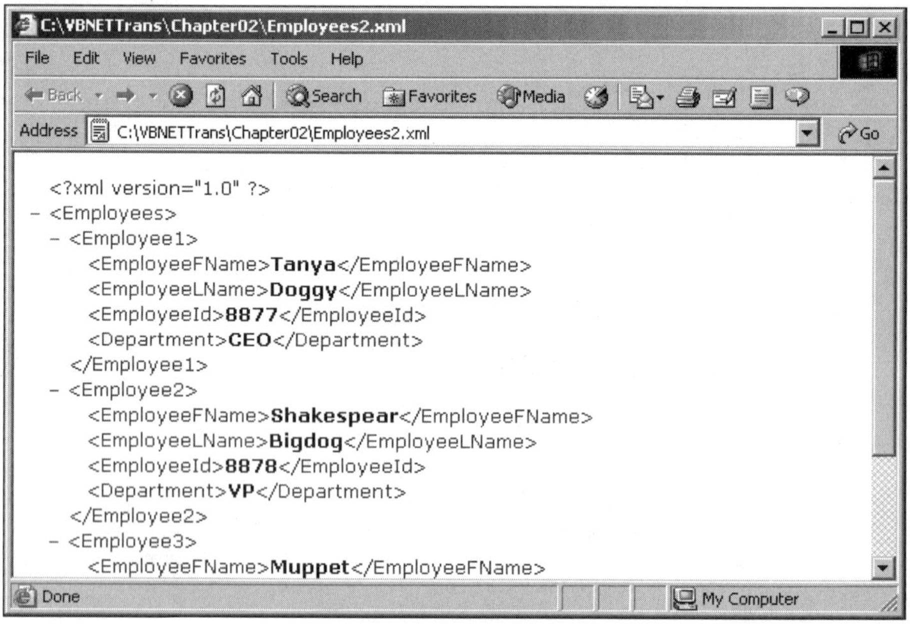

Again, because we are working with XML, we need to use the `System.Xml` namespace in order to access the XML classes.

Next, we created an `XmlTextWriter` and instructed the writer where to write the file to, and what to name the file. This project is designed to show you how to programmatically create a new XML document utilizing the `XmlTextWriter`. It's important to realize that this application will rewrite all the contents of any existing files with the same name. This can be useful, as well as potentially dangerous if you rewrite a file you intended on keeping. We will talk about this shortly.

Once the `XmlTextWriter` has been instantiated, you can start using the various write methods to design the XML document. We started with the method `WriteStartDocument()`.

`WriteStartDocument()` specifies where the XML document begins. We also indicated the beginning of each element by using `WriteStartElement()`. For example, we created an XML element called `Employees` by specifying:

```
XmlWriter.WriteStartElement("Employees")
```

In between elements, we utilized the method `WriteElementString()` in order to create the various tags and place the values for each. After tags and data for the specified element had been completed, we used the `XmlEndElement()` method to close the element.

After all the elements for the XML document had been specified, and closed, we closed the document using the `WriteEndDocument()` method.

Now that we have closed the document (using `WriteEndDocument()`), we use the `Flush()` method to take the information between `WriteBeginDocument()` and `WriteEndDocument()` and send it out to the file name at the location we specified earlier. In other words, the `flush()` method removes (flushes) whatever is in the buffer into the underlying stream. In this case, the XML document is written to a new file called `employees2.xml`.

Now that the new XML document has been created, we close the `XmlWriter`.

It should become obvious that we could have utilized the `XmlTextWriter` in a similar fashion as we did with the `DataTextReader`. In other words, we could have loaded an existing XML file into an `XmlTextReader` to view the file, and then make modifications as deemed necessary by writing a new file. Suppose you have a file called `Employees1.xml` and you are interested in adding another name to the file. Simply specifying the same file name is equivalent to performing an update to a database. The old XML file will be overwritten with a new XML file containing the new changes. However, because the XML file may be thought of as an original document, perhaps a web page, where we want to keep the original information intact, we can write to a new file such as `Employees2.xml` and use the new file elsewhere.

Now we have learned about `XmlReaders` and `XmlWriters`, let's move on and take a look at how we can access the XML Document Object Model (DOM) using Visual Basic .NET.

XML Document Object Model

The previous `XmlReaders` and `XmlWriters` we discussed are designed for quick lightweight access to XML data, while the implementation of the DOM (Document Object Model) produces large amounts of overhead. If this is the case, why bother with something that creates a lot of overhead? The answer is simple, the need for more functionality. In many cases, using `XmlReaders` and `XmlWriters` are very efficient, but they are designed as lightweight objects, meaning that they do not provide all the functionality that the DOM can give us. For example, relational data is not adequately represented through the `XmlReader`. However, we can access the `XmlDataDocument` within the DOM object to use all the relational functionality specified by W3C for DOM Level 2.

> *To learn more about the work of the World Wide Web Consortium, visit* http://www.w3.org/.

The following table shows the common methods for the `XmlDocument` object.

> *Note: The standard DOM Level 2 is implemented through the* `XmlDocument` *object.*

Method	Description
`CreateXXX()`	This method can be used to create a node, attribute, element, comments, and CDATA sections. For example, you can use this method to create an element by using `CreateElement()`. Other create methods exist such as `CreateTextNode()` and `CreateComment()`.
`CloneNode()`	With the `CloneNode()` method, you can copy a node.
`GetElementById()`	By specifying an element's `ID` attribute, you can return the specified element.
`GetElementsByTagName()`	Instead of specifying an element's `ID` attribute, which only returns one element, you can return a node containing all the elements by specifying the element's name.

XmlDataDocument

The `XmlDataDocument` extends the functionality of the `XmlDocument` by being able to represent relational data. In actuality, you can use the same methods and properties that are available to the `XmlDocument`. In other words, if you have an application utilizing the `XmlDocument` object, you can replace it with the `XmlDataDocument` without making any other changes.

The `XmlDataDocument` is similar to the `DataSet` in the fashion that both objects essentially act as a bridge between XML and ADO.NET. Both objects can easily be converted from one to another, making the integration of XML and ADO.NET virtually seamless.

XPathDocument and XPathNavigator

The `XPathDocument` is similar to the `XmlDocument`, except that the `XPathDocument` is lightweight and thus offers faster performance. Furthermore, the `XpathDocument` object does XML document processing using XSLT. On the other hand, the `XmlDocument` provides more features resulting in powerful capabilities, but surrenders the fast performance of a lightweight object (as with the `XPathNavigator`).

Actually, the only public method the `XPathDocument` provides for us is the `CreateNavigator()` that is designed exclusively to work with the `XPathNavigator` object.

By creating an `XpathNavigator`, you can then use its methods, designed for efficiently moving around an XML source. In other words, the `XpathNavigator` essentially provides a cursor model to traverse around an XML source.

The following table provides the most common methods for the `XPathNavigator`:

Method	Description
`GetAttribute()`	The value of a specified attribute from the current node in the navigator is returned using `GetAttribute()`.
`IsSamePosition()`	To determine if two navigators are residing at the same location within an XML document, we can use the `IsSamePosition()` method.

Method	Description
MoveToXXX()	The MoveToXXX() allows you to navigate from the current navigator position to a specified position. For example, to move the navigator from its current position to the root, we can use MoveToRoot(). Other positions include MoveToFirst(), MoveToParent(), MoveToChild(), amongst others.
Select()	Using Select() returns a node list that contains a collection of nodes matching the specified XPath expression. Note that the node list that is returned is referred to as an XPathIterator.
SelectAncestors()	The SelectAncestors() method is used to return a node list containing a collection of all ancestor nodes within the XML document that match a specific type or match a specific name. Note that the node list that is returned is referred to as an XPathIterator.
SelectChildren()	The SelectChildren() method is used to return a node list containing a collection of all child nodes within the XML document that match a specific type or match a specific name. Note that the node list that is returned is referred to as an XPathIterator.
SelectDescendants()	The SelectDescendants() method is used to return a node list containing a collection of all descendant nodes, within the XML document, that match a specific type or match a specific name. Note that the node list that is returned is referred to as an XPathIterator.

How to Query XML Data

In this exercise, we are going to use the XPathNavigator to query an XML file.

Start a new Visual Basic .NET application and name your project XPathQuery.

Go to the Form Design and drag a button, list box, and a text box onto the form:

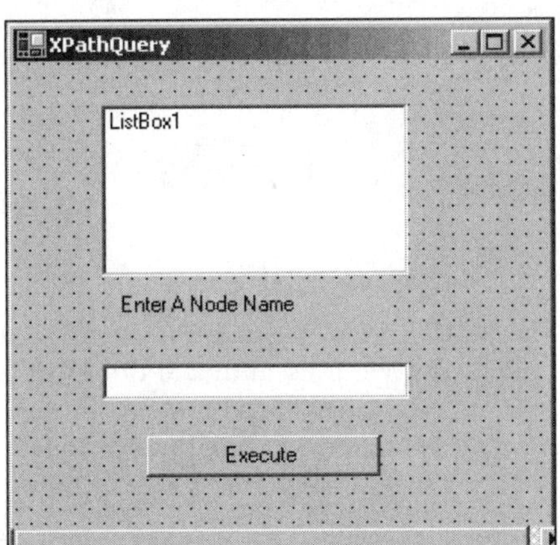

For cosmetic purposes, change the `Text` property of the form to XPathQuery, change the button's text to Execute, and add a label displaying Enter A Node Name.

Type in the following namespaces under the form's Declarations:

```
Imports System.Xml
Imports System.Xml.XPath
```

Locate the `Button1_Click()` method and enter the following:

```
Private Sub Button1_Click(ByVal sender As Object, ByVal e As System.EventArgs)
        Handles Button1.Click
ListBox1.Items.Clear()

Dim myXMLDocument As New XPathDocument("C:\VBNETTrans\Chapter02\Employees.xml")
Dim myNavigator As XPathNavigator = myXMLDocument.CreateNavigator()
Dim query As String = "descendant::" & TextBox1.Text
Dim myXPNIterator As XPathNodeIterator = myNavigator.Select(query)

Do While myXPNIterator.MoveNext()
    ListBox1.Items.Add(myXPNIterator.Current.Value)
Loop
End Sub
```

Run the application and when it opens, type in the name of a node found in the document we created earlier called `Employees.xml`. Note that node names are case sensitive. For example, the following screenshot shows the queried results for the node named `EmployeeFName`:

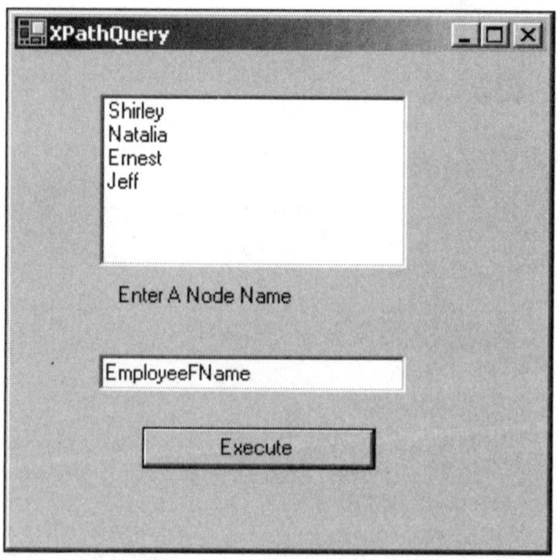

Because we are working with the XML system classes, we specified the `System.Xml` namespace, and because XPath has its own set of classes, we must indicate the `System.Xml.XPath` namespace.

We created an `XPathDocument` and specified the document's location. Next, we created the navigator and issued a query string:

```
Dim query As String = "descendant:: " & TextBox1.Text
Dim myXPNIterator As XPathNodeIterator = myNavigator.Select(query)
```

The query string takes the name of the node supplied by the user from the text box and then executes a query using the `Select` method. Using the `Select()` method returns the node list referred to the `XpathIterator`, and it contains a collection of the nodes that matched the specified expression.

Now that the node list has been returned, we iterate through the list one by one in order to populate the list box:

```
Do While myXPNIterator.MoveNext()
    ListBox1.Items.Add(strResults + myXPNIterator.Current.Value)
Loop
```

How to Modify XML Data

For our last example in this chapter, we are going to modify some of the data in our existing XML file we created earlier. After the data has been modified, we will write it out to a new file, although we can just as easily write the changes back to the original file.

Start a new Visual Basic .NET application. Name your project `ModifyXMLData`.

Go to the Form Design and drag a button control on to it:

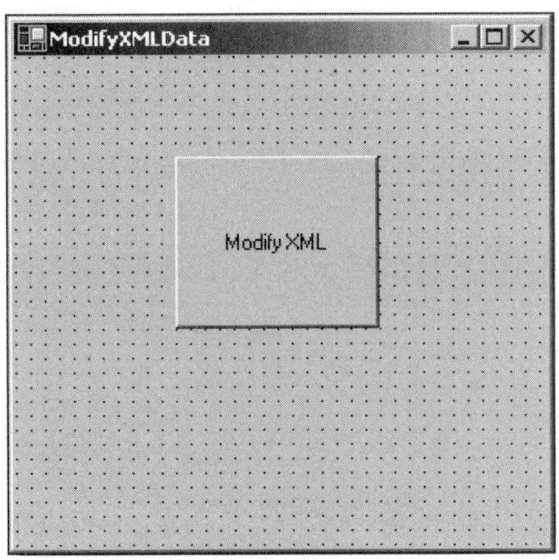

Change the form's `Text` property to Modify XML Data and change the button's `Text` property to Modify XML.

Type in the following namespace under the form's Declarations:

```
Imports System.Xml
```

Locate the `Button1_Click()` method and enter the following:

```
Private Sub Button1_Click(ByVal sender As Object, ByVal e As System.EventArgs)
        Handles Button1.Click
Dim MyDocument As New XmlDataDocument()
MyDocument.Load("C:\VBNETTrans\Chapter02\Employees.XML")
Dim MyNode As XmlNode
MyNode = MyDocument.DocumentElement

Try

    Dim My2ndNode As XmlNode
    Dim MyNodePriceText As XmlNode
    For Each MyNode In MyNode.ChildNodes
        For Each My2ndNode In MyNode.ChildNodes
            If My2ndNode.Name = "Department" And _
               My2ndNode.InnerXml = "HR" Then
                Dim strDepartment As String = "CEO"
                My2ndNode.InnerXml = strDepartment
            End If
        Next
    Next

    MyDocument.Save("C:\VBNETTrans\Chapter02\Employees3.XML")

Catch XMLException As Exception
    MessageBox.Show(XMLException.ToString())
    End
Finally
    MessageBox.Show("Operation Completed")
End Try
End Sub
```

Run the application and click the button. When the operation completes, a message box alerts you to this. Click OK and close the application:

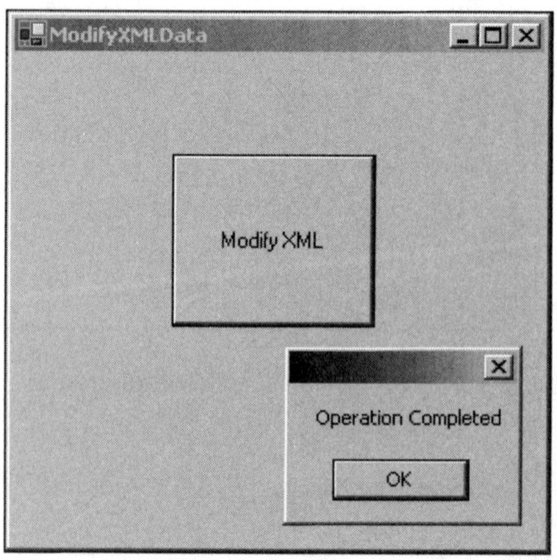

Now we need to open the new XML file titled `Employees3.xml`. Open the file using either WordPad or IE. It should look similar to the following screenshot:

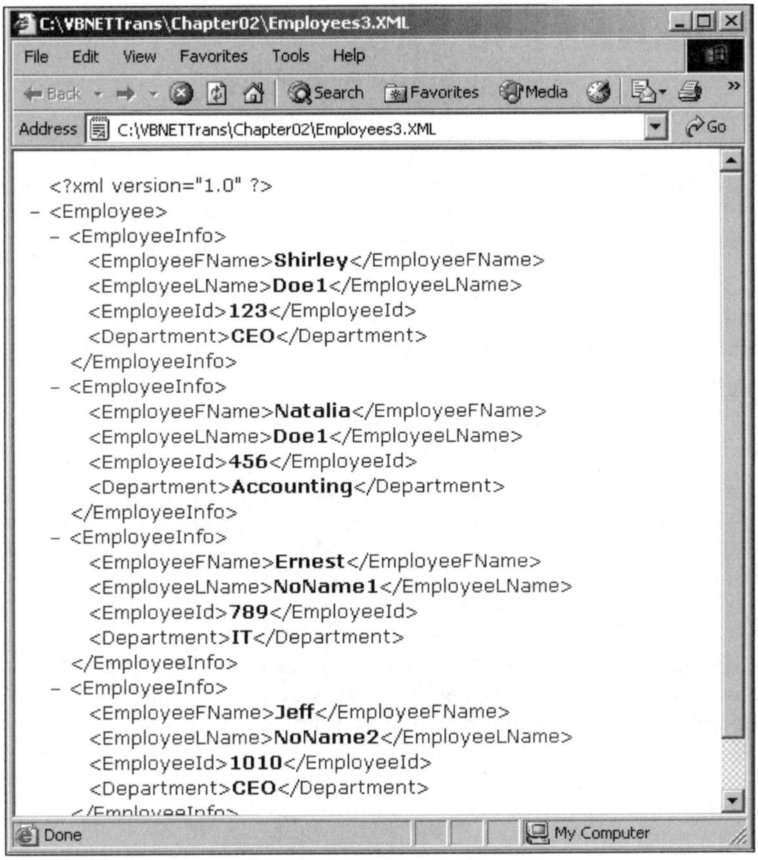

If you look at the top and bottom entries for Department, you will see that both have been modified from HR to CEO. Not a bad promotion!

We began this project by specifying the `System.Xml` namespace in order to work with XML classes. We then went on to the `Button1_Click()` method, declaring an `XmlDocument` and specifying the location of the XML file to be modified.

Using a nested `For Each` loop, we created the conditions to traverse each child node within the XML documents looking for the node name `Department` and the XML data `HR` that is associated with the node `Department`. Simply, we specified that for each occurrence of this condition, we would replace the data `HR` with `CEO`.

After each child node for `Department` had been iterated through, we saved the documents to a new file name, although we could have written over the original file, so it can continually be used as the original data source (as we do with a traditional database).

Recap of ADO.NET and XML

We have covered a lot of material in this chapter, so let's quickly review the major highlights of ADO.NET and XML.

- We learned that the `DataSet` lets us work with data in a disconnected environment, and it is capable of containing multiple tables regardless of the data source. Furthermore, the `DataSet` can also contain relationship and constraint information. In a nutshell, a `DataSet` is capable of representing an entire database in memory.
- With the help of ADO.NET, `DataSet`'s concurrency issues are automatically handled through optimistic concurrency, thus minimizing the need for locking data resources.
- Data no longer needs to be converted to data types, as was required when working with various data sources and ADO. Instead, ADO.NET utilizes XML. Because XML is text-based, data type conversions are not required.
- Because ADO.NET uses XML, XML can be utilized to easily transport data from any data source, regardless of where it is located without having to deal with Internet security such as firewalls. Because of the text-based nature of XML, it is considered relatively harmless, so it can easily pass through systems without any problem.

> **We will build upon these concepts in the next chapter where we will work with simple transactions using ASP.NET. In Chapter 3, *SQL Server and Visual Basic .NET*, we will work exclusively with transactions utilizing SQL and stored procedures.**

Summary

We have worked through the basics for several different ways of accessing and managing data. As you progress through the rest of this book, you will have the chance to work with many of these techniques in more complicated applications. The important thing to keep in mind with this chapter is that it's not exclusive to ADO.NET. All the concepts within this chapter can be applied to ASP.NET as well. We will see these concepts used in Chapter 4.

We began this chapter with a short introduction to ADO.NET, what it is, and what it's about. We looked at a short comparison between ADO and ADO.NET, and then moved on to learning about the required namespaces for using a particular set of data management class libraries.

Next, we looked at the main components of ADO.NET, and then moved on to learn about ADO.NET managed providers.

We also looked at `DataSets`, `DataSet` architecture, and concurrency issues. We also tried several hands-on projects where we worked with `DataSets` and learned how the `DataAdapter` is used as a bridge between the `DataSet` and a data source.

After working with the `DataSet`, we moved onto XML. We learned about ADO.NET and XML, as well as how to work with XML through the DOM. This chapter ended with a hands-on exercise where we manipulated XML data from an existing XML document.

3

SQL Server and Visual Basic .NET

This chapter focuses on issues relating to data services. Although the examples in this book relate directly to MS SQL Server, most of the information applies equally to other relational database management systems (RDBMS), such as Oracle and Sybase. As a matter of fact, Visual Basic .NET (ADO.NET) code designed and optimised for SQL Server can be easily transformed to support Oracle, DB2 or other RDBMS (the classes found in `System.Data.SqlClient` are very similar to the ones in `System.Data.OleDb`).

I'm not going to tell you how to use SQL Server: it's important for you to learn and understand how to use the database you choose for your data services in your applications. What I am going to do is present you with some database theory to help you better understand and handle your transactions.

> *If you want to learn more about SQL Server then have a look at* Professional SQL Server 2000 Programming *(1-861004-48-6) or* Beginning SQL Server 2000 Programming *(1-861005-23-7), both from Wrox Press.*

After completing this chapter, you should be able to answer the following questions:

- What is a stored procedure?
- What is the difference between an in-line SQL statement and a stored procedure?
- What is a savepoint and how do you use it in a transaction?
- How does a connection-based transaction differ from a database transaction?

Why SQL Server?

SQL Server is being used as the primary example in this book, but don't get the idea that it's your only option. There are many other RDBMS choices available including Oracle, and DB2.

SQL Server 7 and SQL Server 2000 are the recommended versions for the examples in this book.

I've picked SQL Server because it integrates well with the .NET Framework, and as you learned in the last chapter, Microsoft has supplied its own managed provider, specifically designed to improve efficiency when integrating with .NET and MS SQL Server.

Additionally, Microsoft SQL Server is a high performance and scalable relational database management system. It can utilize multi-processor technology without the need for complex server reconfiguration. The ability to execute a single transaction across multiple processors not only adds to SQL Server's scalability; it can greatly enhance performance and throughput.

SQL Statements

SQL stands for **Structured Query Language**. SQL is an industry-standard language designed to create, manipulate, maintain, and query relational databases.

IBM is credited with the development of Structured English QUEry Language (SEQUEL). It was not until later (exactly when is the question) that SEQUEL started being referred to as simply Structured Query Language (SQL).

SQL is a non-procedural language in contrast to programming languages such as Visual Basic .NET and Visual C++ .NET. What this means is that SQL tells the database system what is being requested, not how to retrieve it. How the data is retrieved or manipulated is left for the database system to interpret.

There are several dialects of SQL, although most are based around the **American National Standards Institute** (**ANSI**) standard. Currently the ANSI standard for SQL is referred to as SQL-92. The important thing is most RDBMS, with their dialects of SQL, usually follow ANSI SQL-92 standards. MS SQL Server, Oracle, DB2, Sybase, all follow the ANSI standard.

Most database systems provide extended capabilities to the ANSI compliant SQL. For example, MS SQL Server uses T-SQL (Transact-Structured Query Language) while Oracle's extended SQL is called PL/SQL (Procedural Language/Structured Query Language). Both build upon the SQL basis and offer performance enhancements.

Be aware, however, that when using these extended capabilities you'll sometimes have to choose between performance and portability to other RDBMS systems using other forms of SQL.

Stored Procedures

Stored procedures are interesting creatures, as application developers typically either like to use them or they don't. They are database objects that contain executable SQL statements that are capable of performing against other databases or even servers. Microsoft often refers to these executable SQL statements as T-SQL. As we have just discussed, T-SQL is not just a query language, it actually extends the capabilities of SQL, with features such as procedural functionality, and the ability to pass parameters, as well as return values.

> **T-SQL is Microsoft's version of SQL. When writing stored procedures for MS SQL Server, you are actually writing them with T-SQL.**

Stored procedures control the flow of processing through logical routines. Such logic can include the use of conditions and loops. Furthermore, they can utilize multiple SQL statements as well as numerous predefined and custom functions.

Perhaps the number one reason for using stored procedures is they greatly increase application performance. Stored procedures are directly parsed at the SQL Server, while T-SQL that is compiled within the application (called in-line) must first be passed to SQL Server before it can then be parsed.

Another major feature of stored procedures is code reuse. You can have multiple applications execute the same stored procedure(s) over and over. To build onto this, SQL Server utilizes execution plans (see next section). Execution plans make it possible for stored procedures to be executed more quickly and efficiently on subsequent use, by eliminating the need to re-compile the same SQL statement over and over again.

SQL Server Execution Plan

Although this section is specific to MS SQL Server, most major relational database systems, including Oracle and Sybase, utilize similar concepts.

Within memory, there is an allocated area called the **procedure cache**. This cache dynamically fluctuates in size depending on how SQL Server is currently being utilized. For example, there are other items SQL Server also needs to keep in memory. Depending on total resources, as well as what is currently being processed, different allocated memory structures will grow or decrease, in response to the current state of the system.

SQL Server utilizes an execution plan to efficiently process reoccurring SQL statements. When you run a query, SQL Server parses your query into its component parts and sends it to the query optimiser. The query optimiser figures out the best way to run the query to balance fast results with minimum impact to other users. This is the execution plan, which can be viewed by choosing the Show Execution Plan option in Query Analyser.

Every time a SQL statement is executed in SQL Server, the relational engine searches through the procedure cache to see if an execution plan already exists for the current SQL statement. SQL Server uses a complex, yet efficient, algorithm for locating existing execution plans. If an execution plan is located for the current SQL statement, SQL Server makes use of it. Being able to reuse an execution plan means that the SQL statement does not need to be recompiled, making the execution of the same SQL statement very efficient, as well as saving resources. Of course, if a plan does not exist for a particular SQL statement, SQL Server will create a new execution plan. As before, once this plan has been created, any subsequent SQL statements will now execute from the procedure cache without having to be recompiled.

When an execution plan is created, it remains in the procedure cache as long as the SQL statement is utilized. How can we tell how long this is? Within each execution plan there is internal information that keeps track of the cost factor for the SQL statement. The cost factor reflects how much resources are required for a particular SQL statement to compile. Simply put, both the query plan and execution content keep track of the cost factor within their data structures. There is also an age field within both the query plan and execution content. So whenever the execution plan is referenced, the age field is incremented by the formula:

```
(Cost factor X amount query plan referenced) = age
```

Suppose you have a query plan with a cost factor of 2 and it is referenced 4 times, to get the age you multiply the cost factor by the number of times the query plan has been referenced. Here we have an age of 8. But hold on, there's more!

There is a process that periodically scans the procedure cache. This process is referred to as the **lazywriter**. Every time the lazywriter scans the procedure cache, the age for each query plan is reduced by one increment. Looking back at the previous example, if we have an age factor of 8 and it sits idle without being accessed anymore, it can be scanned 8 times before reaching the value of zero. But don't jump to any conclusions and think it is all over for the execution plan! Not yet anyway. Before an execution plan is actually de-allocated, three conditions must exist:

- The age field must be at zero.
- It is not currently being referenced by a connection.
- The memory manager needs to free up memory because all memory resources are currently being utilized.

If all three of these conditions are met, then the execution plan will be de-allocated.

You may be wondering what the consequences are of having numerous unique SQL statements as opposed to having the same queries execute. Two major things occur. First, if there are numerous unique SQL statements, then you risk bogging down system resources, because of having to constantly create new execution plans instead of being able to reuse existing ones. This is certainly something you should keep in mind when designing a new application.

The second thing is that older, unused execution plans may be flushed from memory as previously described. Although, the procedure cache is dynamic, there is only so much memory available to a system. If you have numerous unique SQL statements, and the procedure cache needs to free up space, it is possible that an older existing plan will no longer exist the next time an identical SQL statement is executed. So instead of being able to utilize the procedure cache, it will have to recreate a new execution plan.

It's important to realize, that if you do have an application that utilizes numerous unique SQL statements, having one or two statements in the procedure cache really will not make much difference. It's best to design applications that utilize identical SQL statements as much as possible. As stored procedures can accept parameters, they can be created to be very flexible. Instead of creating many stored procedures with similar functionality, you can create a single stored procedure that accepts parameters and acts according to those parameters. This is another way of reducing the number of execution plans SQL Server has to create and store in memory. As you should see, stored procedures can be very efficient.

In-Line SQL Statements

The term **in-line SQL statements** (often referred to as embedded SQL) is used to refer to SQL statements that are hard-coded within your application. This means that the SQL statements within the application code are compiled with the application. As with stored procedures, when designing applications that utilize only SQL Server, we are actually writing our in-line statements utilizing T-SQL. However, we can use generic SQL if other databases are also being used.

There are times when using in-line SQL statements may make sense. For example, you can design a form that allows a user to choose the columns to query on. Thus it makes sense to design a dynamic query string into the application's code. Furthermore, no one can see or change the SQL statement because it is compiled within the program. Of course, there are also drawbacks when using in-line SQL statements. For example, the very fact you have to compile in-line statements with your code makes it difficult to change them if the need arises. This would involve changing the SQL statement to reflect the new changes, recompiling the code, and possibly redistributing clients to each user if you are following the client-server architecture. If you are using *n*-tier architecture, you only need to change the components containing in-line SQL statements; however, recompiling of the component is still required. As you can see, deciding whether to use in-line statements or stored procedures should depend on what is considered appropriate for the given circumstances.

Let's contrast in-line SQL statements with stored procedures:

- You only need to change the stored procedures located at the SQL Server. If there are multiple databases and servers involved, you need to make the appropriate changes at each location. The main advantage is no recompilation of code is required. Being able to change stored procedures at the database makes them immediately available to all clients.
- However, in-line SQL statements may become an important consideration when applications are designed to be database independent. For example, SQL Server stored procedures are capable of returning resultsets, while the same procedures may not be directly portable to Oracle in a straightforward manner.

Maximizing In-Line SQL Statements

As previously mentioned, there are times when using in-line statements makes sense. Depending on how your SQL statements are being utilized, there may be a few things you can do to help maximize their efficiency. For example, if you are executing the same SQL statements over and over, you can take advantage of the `Prepare` property of the ADO .NET `Command` object.

The `Prepare` property instructs SQL Server to compile all SQL statements first before executing them. A temporary stored procedure is created for the statement, which remains within the database for as long as the connection that was used when issuing the statement remains. This indeed slows the first execution of each SQL statement, but all subsequent executions will be from SQL Server's procedure cache, just as if they were compiled SQL procedures. This will not be as efficient as executing stored procedures, because the client still needs to transmit the information to SQL Server. Nevertheless, performance is still greatly enhanced.

> **Note that if you are using in-line statements that involve one-time execution, the `Prepare` property will be of no use.**

The `Prepare` property is Boolean. In order to have SQL Server compile the statements and then place them into the procedure cache for subsequent executions, set the property to `True`. (The default is `False`.) Also, it may seem obvious, but be sure to include the `Prepare` property before executing the `Command` object:

```
MyCommand.Text = "Insert Employees (LastName) Values('Bortniker')"
MyCommand.Prepared = True
MyCommand.ExecuteNonQuery
```

T-SQL and SQL Server

Because SQL Server has its own transaction manager, SQL Server is able to commit, abort, and rollback transactional data as necessary. SQL Server's transaction manager utilizes keywords such as `BEGIN`, `COMMIT`, and `ROLLBACK` to identify and manage transactions. In other words, SQL Server is responsible for ensuring that each of the ACID properties is enforced for transactions in a client-server environment.

> **Although SQL is not case sensitive, it is good practice to write your code consistently for ease of reading.**

The following code snippet is an example of T-SQL. Although it contains multiple SQL statements, it is only one transaction. The transaction is explicitly framed by `BEGIN TRANSACTION`, and either `COMMIT TRANSACTION` or `ROLLBACK TRANSACTION`. In this example, if both SQL statements complete, both are committed. However, if one statement fails, all work in this transaction is reversed (rolled back). Simply, everything is returned to its original state as if nothing had ever happened.

```
BEGIN TRANSACTION Customer

INSERT INTO NewCustomer (CusNo, LastName,AdType )
VALUES ('MO1', 'Muppett', 05)

If @@ERROR ! = 0
BEGIN
    ROLLBACK TRANSACTION Customer
    RETURN
END
```

```
UPDATE MailingListTotals
    SET CustomerTotals  = CustomerTotals + 1
    WHERE AdType = 05

IF @@ERROR ! =0
BEGIN
    ROLLBACK TRANSACTION Customer
    RETURN
END

COMMIT TRANSACTION Customer
```

Let's look at this code a little more closely. The first line is `BEGIN TRANSACTION Customer`. This tells the transaction manager in SQL Server that this is the beginning of a transaction, and that the name of the transaction is `Customer`. Following `BEGIN TRANSACTION Customer` is a SQL statement that adds a new customer to the `NewCustomer` database table. In the event that something goes wrong, as defined by @@ERROR, the `ROLLBACK TRANSACTION` statement tells the transaction manager to reverse the course of action. Otherwise, the transaction will continue with the next SQL statement (if any).

At this point is important to stress the `RETURN` statement. If you comment out the `RETURN` statement and an error occurs, it will hit the `ROLLBACK TRANSACTION`, but the transaction execution will still continue. An explicit `RETURN` is required to terminate the transaction immediately an error occurs.

In this example, the second SQL statement performs an update to the `MailingListTotals` table. Once again, the work is verified. If no error occurred (all work performed was successful) the transaction will continue with the next item to be processed.

This step-by-step process of "do work" and "verify work" will continue until the transaction ends. There are two ways that the transaction manager knows whether a transaction has completed. First, when a `ROLLBACK TRANSACTION` occurs, the transaction is considered complete. Once an error occurs, all statements in the transaction are aborted and everything is returned to the previous original state.

Note: As a transaction occurs, every change is recorded into a transaction log (often called a trans log). In the event the transaction needs to be rolled back, the transaction log is used to restore the database back to its original state.

The second method occurs when the transaction comes to the final statement, `COMMIT TRANSACTION`. This tells the transaction manager that everything completed successfully and that all changes in the database are to be made permanently – they are committed.

One thing to note is that this is *not* a distributed transaction (a transaction that involves more than one database). Even though multiple tables are modified, it's only affecting one database on one data source. You will work with distributed transactions in Chapter 6.

The `@@` that precedes some types of name denotes a SQL Server ***global variable****. For example, `@@ERROR` is a global variable that contains the status of the last statement.*

Save Transaction

There may be times when you prefer to have a transaction commit partial results in the event of an error as opposed to a total rollback of the entire transaction. We can mark a **savepoint** to which a transaction can return if a portion of the transaction fails or is cancelled. To do this, we use the following syntax:

```
SAVE TRANSACTION savepoint_name
```

For example, suppose we have a two-part stored procedure that is used to insert data into two separate tables. The first portion inserts rows into a table named `Food` and the second portion of the stored procedure inserts data into a table named `Dogs`. A savepoint occurs after the first three inserts into the `Food` table. Note the `savepoint_name` in this example is `insert_food`:

```
BEGIN TRANSACTION table_insert
INSERT INTO Food (FoodID,FoodDesc) VALUES (1,'Crunchy Cereal')
          IF @@ERROR <>0
  BEGIN
    ROLLBACK TRANSACTION table_insert
        RETURN
  END

INSERT INTO Food (FoodID,FoodDesc) VALUES (2,'Table Scraps')
          IF @@ERROR <>0
  BEGIN
    ROLLBACK TRANSACTION table_insert
        RETURN
  END

INSERT INTO Food (FoodID,FoodDesc) VALUES (3,'Dog Biscuits')
          IF @@ERROR <>0
  BEGIN
    ROLLBACK TRANSACTION table_insert
        RETURN
  END

SAVE TRANSACTION insert_food

INSERT INTO Dogs (Breed,FoodPref) VALUES ('German Shepherd',1)
  IF @@ERROR <>0
  BEGIN
    ROLLBACK TRANSACTION insert_food
        RETURN
  END

INSERT INTO Dogs (Breed,FoodPref) VALUES ('Maltese',2)
  IF @@ERROR <>0
  BEGIN
    ROLLBACK TRANSACTION insert_food
        RETURN
  END

INSERT INTO Dogs (Breed,FoodPref) VALUES ('Yorkshire Terrier',3)
```

```
IF @@ERROR <>0
  BEGIN
    ROLLBACK TRANSACTION insert_food
        RETURN
  END

COMMIT TRANSACTION tables_insert
```

In our example, we have a savepoint marked after the first batch of SQL statements that insert into the `Food` table. If all the SQL statements for the `Food` table complete successfully, but there is an error in the next batch of SQL statements for the inserts into the `Dogs` table, we will retain the first batch of SQL statements even if the second batch of SQL statements failed. In this scenario, the transaction is rolled back to the savepoint.

There can be multiple savepoints within a transaction, but an important thing to understand about working with savepoints is that if a transaction is rolled back to a savepoint, there must be a continuation in the code with a `COMMIT` or `ROLLBACK` statement, as demonstrated in the previous code example. Another important thing to keep in mind about the usage of savepoints is they must be very clearly defined, as a transaction will commit until the last savepoint, even though the transaction may not have completed as a whole. This occurs only if we rollback the transaction to the last savepoint, by specifying that savepoint's name. For clarity, if you give a blanket rollback transaction statement without using a savepoint name, the entire transaction will get rolled back.

It is also important to understand that after a `ROLLBACK` occurs, all savepoints are cleared. This means that you cannot `ROLL BACK` to a previous savepoint, and then `ROLL BACK` to another savepoint. However, once you roll back to a savepoint, the transaction is not completed. Therefore, you can create new savepoints and roll back to these savepoints, complete some other work (or fixes) and then usefully `COMMIT` the transaction.

Creating the Tables

Now that we have talked about SQL and stored procedures, let's lay the groundwork for the projects in this chapter, as well as the next chapter.

You will need to create a database with the system you are using and name it `Wrox`. We are simply going to create two new tables within the `Wrox` database. The two tables we want to create are called `Dogs` and `Food`.

When working with SQL Server, there are several ways that we can create our tables. If you feel you do not need a review of writing statements that are executed within Query Analyzer, which we will look at shortly, then you may simply create the database and tables shown below easily and quickly using Enterprise Manager.

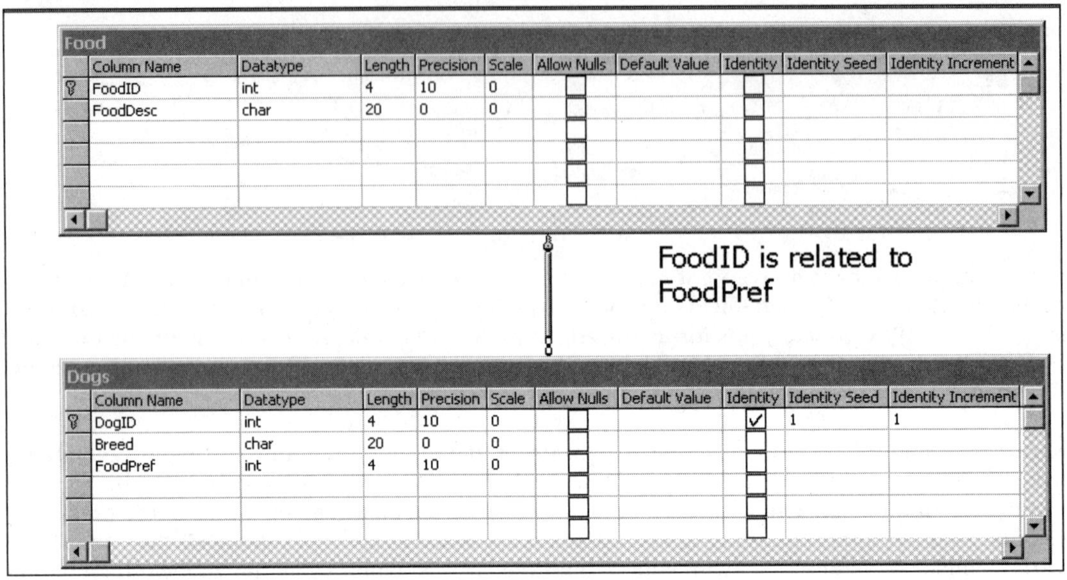

Let's now see how we would create our tables using SQL statements executed through the Query Analyzer tool.

There are a number of ways to open Query Analyzer. From Enterprise Manager, you can select the **Tools** menu and then select **SQL Query Analyzer**. You can also open Query Analyzer by going through the shortcuts (that point to `isqlw.exe`) from the **Programs** menu.

From Query Analyzer, make sure you have selected the `Wrox` database and type in the following scripts (these scripts are available in the code download for this chapter in `VBNETTrans/Chapter03/CreateTables.txt`):

```
/****** Object:  Table [dbo].[Dogs]    Script Date: 2/3/2002 1:40:36 PM ******/
IF EXISTS (SELECT * FROM sysobjects WHERE id = object_id(N'[dbo].[Dogs]') AND
OBJECTPROPERTY(id, N'IsUserTable') = 1)
DROP TABLE [dbo].[Dogs]
GO
```

```
/****** Object:  Table [dbo].[Food]    Script Date: 2/3/2002 1:40:36 PM ******/
IF EXISTS (SELECT * FROM sysobjects WHERE id = object_id(N'[dbo].[Food]') AND
OBJECTPROPERTY(id, N'IsUserTable') = 1)
DROP TABLE [dbo].[Food]
GO
```

```
/****** Object:  Table [dbo].[Food]    Script Date: 2/3/2002 1:40:37 PM ******/
CREATE TABLE [dbo].[Food] (
      [FoodID] [int] NOT NULL,
      [FoodDesc] [char] (20) NOT NULL
)
GO
```

```
/****** Object:  Table [dbo].[Dogs]    Script Date: 2/3/2002 1:40:37 PM ******/
CREATE TABLE [dbo].[Dogs] (
      [DogID] [int] IDENTITY (1, 1) NOT NULL,
      [Breed] [char] (20) NOT NULL,
      [FoodPref] [int] NOT NULL
)
GO
```

```
ALTER TABLE [dbo].[Food] WITH NOCHECK ADD
      CONSTRAINT [FoodID] PRIMARY KEY CLUSTERED
      (
            [FoodID]
      )  ON [PRIMARY]
GO
```

```
ALTER TABLE [dbo].[Dogs] WITH NOCHECK ADD
      CONSTRAINT [PK_DogID] PRIMARY KEY CLUSTERED
      (
            [DogID]
      )  ON [PRIMARY]
GO
```

```
ALTER TABLE [dbo].[Dogs] ADD
      CONSTRAINT [FK_Dogs_Food] FOREIGN KEY
      (
            [FoodPref]
      ) REFERENCES [dbo].[Food] (
            [FoodID]
      )
GO
```

Execute the statement using the green arrow icon, or press *F5*:

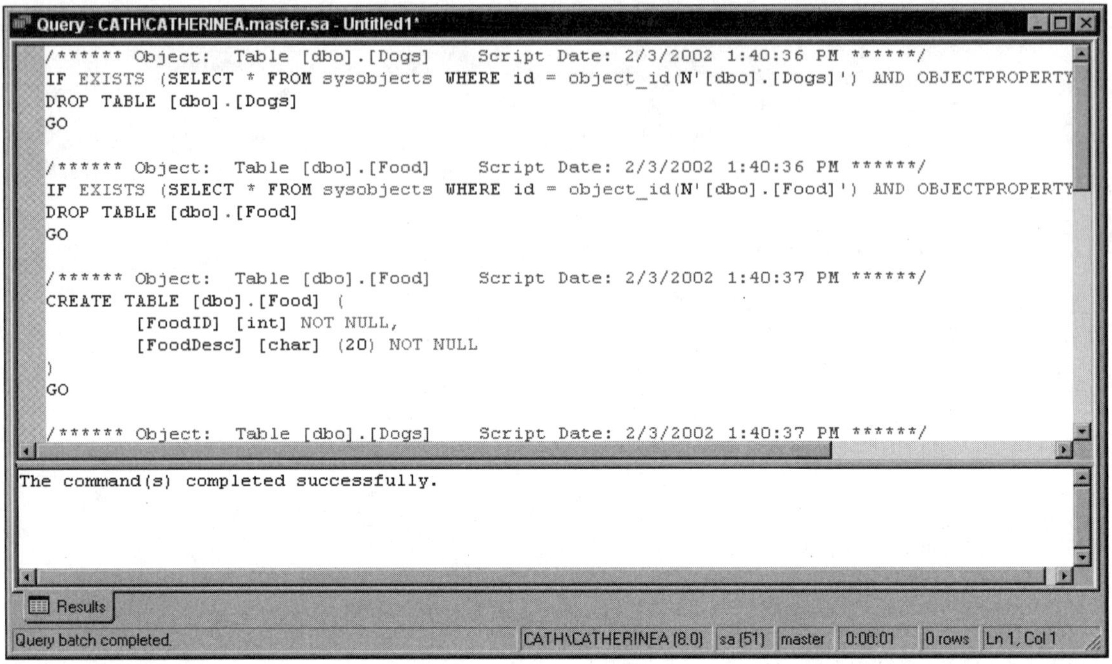

After execution, you should receive the message The command(s) completed successfully in the message pane of Query Analyzer.

Let's look at the syntax for the `Dogs` table.

We start off by defining a name for the table followed by an opening parenthesis:

```
CREATE TABLE [dbo].[Dogs](
```

The next part of the statement simply describes the columns we want to create. In both tables we created, we provided the name of the column, the data type we want to use, and whether it can contain `NULL` values.

```
[DogID] [int] IDENTITY (1, 1) NOT NULL,
[Breed] [char] (20) NOT NULL,
[FoodPref] [int] NOT NULL
```

Notice the keyword `IDENTITY` after the data type `int`. Using `IDENTITY` makes the column generate values that uniquely identify each row. By indicating `(1, 1)`, we are specifying that the first unique number start with the number `1`, and increment each new row by one. Note that this statement actually continues on the next line. A comma must come at the end of each complete parameter.

We then alter the table to provide the constraint information. First we are creating a primary key for this table. This shows us what we are creating (a constraint), the name of the constraint, the type of constraint (`PRIMARY KEY`), and the column the constraint applies to.

```
CONSTRAINT [PK_DogID] PRIMARY KEY CLUSTERED,
(
          [DogID]
    )  ON [PRIMARY]
```

We then similarly create a foreign key, which references the `FoodID` column of the `Food` table.

After all the column information has been added, we use a closing parenthesis.

Creating the Transactional Stored Procedure

Now that we have created the tables for the projects in this chapter, we are going to create a stored procedure that will be used to populate the tables. We are also going to create a stored procedure, so we can quickly and easily clean out the tables and recreate them, so that we can use the same tables for other examples. Let's start with the stored procedure titled `Insert_Dog_Food`.

In Query Analyzer, make sure you have selected the `Wrox` database and type in the following code (this stored procedure is available in the code download for this chapter in `VBNETTrans/Chapter03/Insert_Dog_Food.txt`:

```
CREATE PROCEDURE Insert_Dog_Food
AS

BEGIN TRANSACTION Tables_Insert
INSERT INTO Food (FoodID,FoodDesc) VALUES (1,'Crunchy Cereal')
IF @@ERROR <>0
  BEGIN
    PRINT 'TRANSACTION ROLLED BACK'
    ROLLBACK TRANSACTION Tables_Insert
    RETURN
  END

INSERT INTO Food (FoodID,FoodDesc) VALUES (2,'Table Scraps')
IF @@ERROR <>0
  BEGIN
    PRINT 'TRANSACTION ROLLED BACK'
    ROLLBACK TRANSACTION Tables_Insert
    RETURN
  END

INSERT INTO Food (FoodID,FoodDesc) VALUES (3,'Dog Biscuits')
IF @@ERROR <>0
  BEGIN
    PRINT 'TRANSACTION ROLLED BACK'
    ROLLBACK TRANSACTION Tables_Insert
    RETURN
  END

INSERT INTO Dogs (Breed,FoodPref) VALUES ('German Shepherd',1)
IF @@ERROR <>0
```

```
  BEGIN
    PRINT 'TRANSACTION ROLLED BACK'
    ROLLBACK TRANSACTION Tables_Insert
    RETURN
  END

INSERT INTO Dogs (Breed,FoodPref) VALUES ('Maltese',2)
IF @@ERROR <>0
  BEGIN
    PRINT 'TRANSACTION ROLLED BACK'
    ROLLBACK TRANSACTION Tables_Insert
    RETURN
  END

INSERT INTO Dogs (Breed,FoodPref) VALUES ('Yorkshire Terrier',3)
IF @@ERROR <>0
  BEGIN
    PRINT 'TRANSACTION ROLLED BACK'
    ROLLBACK TRANSACTION Tables_Insert
    RETURN
  END

PRINT 'TRANSACTION COMMITED'
COMMIT TRANSACTION Tables_Insert
```

Execute the statement using the green arrow icon, or press *F5*. After executing notice the message located at the lower pane of Query Analyzer. It should display:

The command(s) completed successfully.

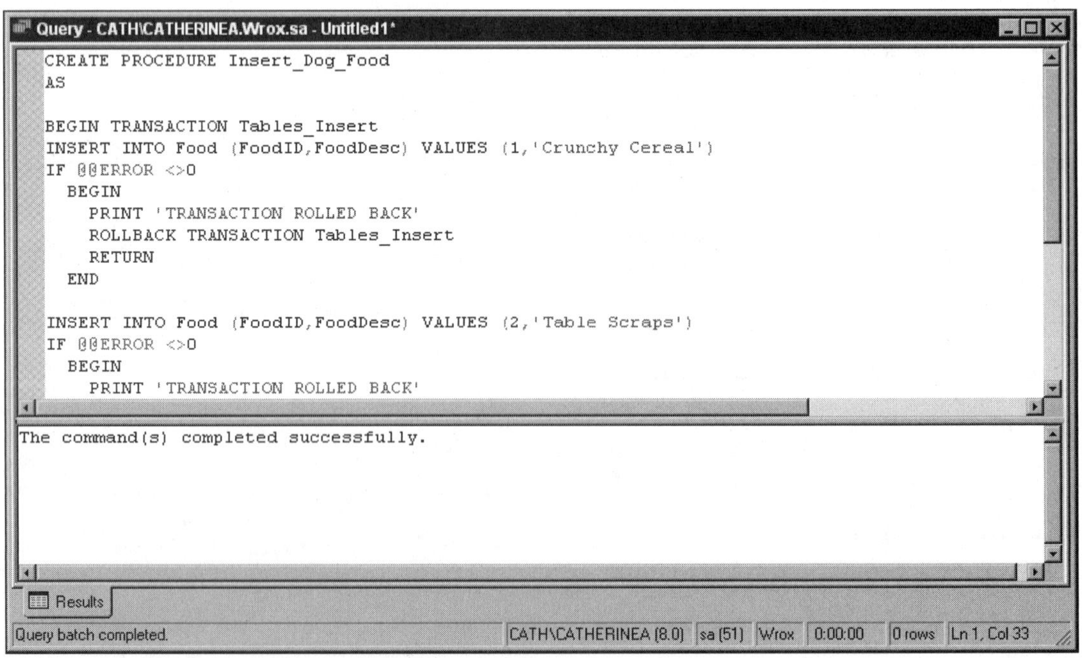

We will be populating our tables using different techniques (that you will learn over the next few chapters). Every time we execute our stored procedure, we append the data over. But, by repeatedly executing these stored procedures, we run into primary key issues due to successive execution attempts to duplicate the data. As we want to experiment in different way with our tables over the next few chapters, we will need to create a stored procedure to delete the tables and recreate them, ready to be repopulated.

Again using Query Analyzer, clear the previous statement, then enter the following code, and execute the statement using the green arrow icon, or press *F5*. The procedure below is available in the code download for this chapter in `VBNETTrans/Chapter03/CleanUp.txt`.

Notice the message located at the lower pane of Query Analyzer. Once again, upon execution, it should indicate that The command(s) completed successfully.

```
CREATE PROCEDURE CleanUp
AS

BEGIN TRANSACTION Tables_Delete

DROP TABLE Dogs

IF @@ERROR <>0
  BEGIN
    PRINT 'TRANSACTION ROLLED BACK'
    ROLLBACK TRANSACTION Tables_Delete
    RETURN
  END

DROP TABLE Food

IF @@ERROR <>0
  BEGIN
    PRINT 'TRANSACTION ROLLED BACK'

    ROLLBACK TRANSACTION Tables_Delete
    RETURN
  END

PRINT 'TRANSACTION COMMITED'
COMMIT TRANSACTION Tables_Delete
```

Let's quickly test our stored procedures. Start a new query from Query Analyzer and type in the name of the stored procedure: `Insert_Dog_Food` and execute it either by using the green arrow icon, or press *F5*.

You should see the following results:

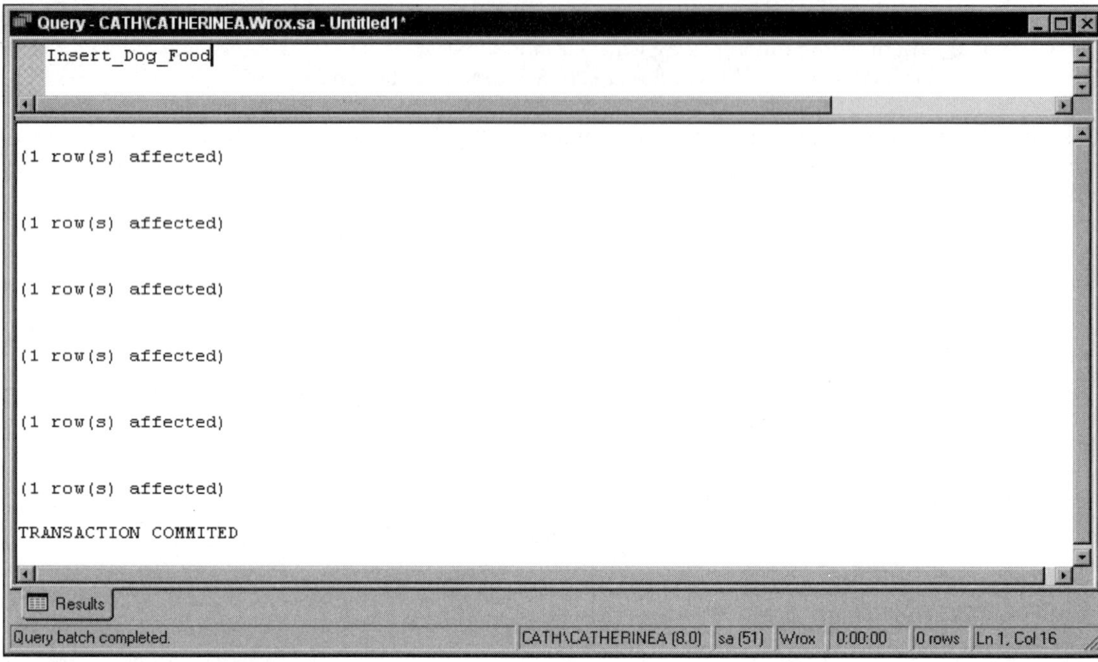

Go ahead and execute `SELECT * FROM Dogs` so you can see the data that has been added. Now try the same thing, this time using the stored procedure called `CleanUp` (this is included in the file `ResetTables.txt`, which starts the `CleanUp` stored procedure and then recreates the tables. Make sure you clear the previous statement first. This time you should see that the **Messages** pane indicates:

```
(3 row(s) affected)
(3 row(s) affected)
Transaction Commited
```

You may be wondering why you had to clear the statement `Insert_Dog_Food` before executing the `ResetTables.txt` script. Feel free to try it!

To execute these two statements individually one after the other, you must use the command `GO` between each statement. It's important to understand that `GO` is not a T-SQL statement. It's a command that is used to separate T-SQL statements (stored procedures included), so they are not treated as a single entity. More specifically, `GO` is used to define the end of a batch of work. In other words, it splits a script up into multiple batches.

Note that all statements since the beginning of the script or the last GO statement (whichever is nearest) are compiled into one execution plan and sent to the server independently of any other batches.

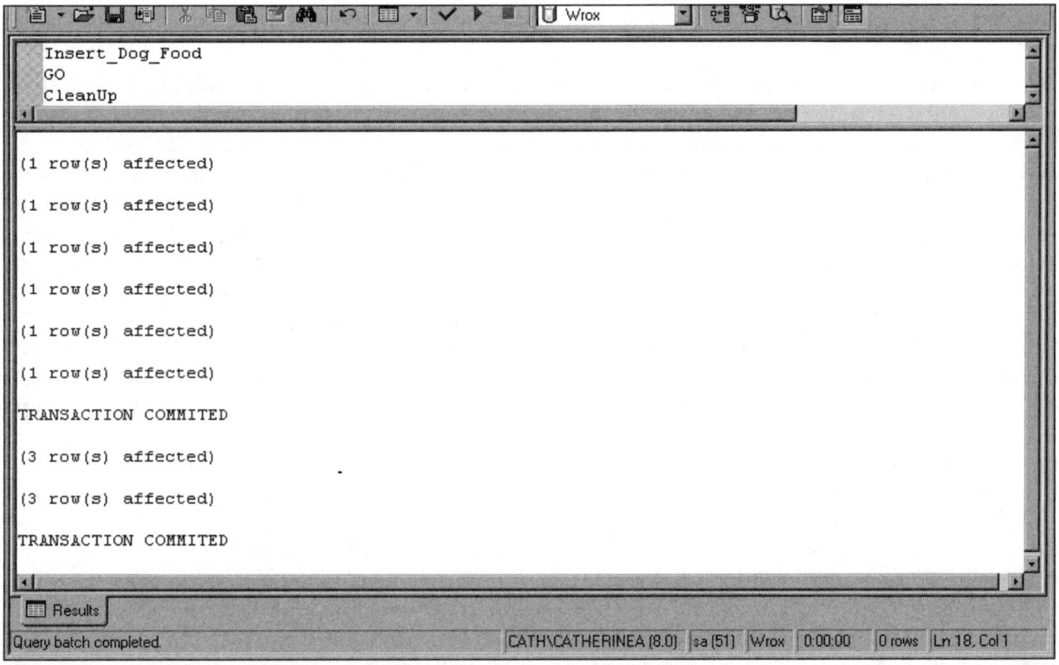

Transaction Architecture

SQL automatically commits or rolls back after each `UPDATE`, `INSERT`, or `DELETE` operation is completed. In other words, if an explicit transaction does not exist, each SQL statement becomes its own transaction. This is referred to as an **automatic transaction** because each SQL statement is committed after it has been completed, without the need to explicitly specify a `ROLLBACK` and/or a `COMMIT` command. For example, in the previous chapter we used ADO.NET to manipulate SQL data. We did not specify any `ROLLBACK` or `COMMIT` statements, yet each statement was automatically committed upon the successful completion of the transaction or rolled back if an error occurred.

Before we start working with transactions, it seems fitting to look at the (generalized) steps it takes for a transaction to complete. Obviously some assumptions must be taken in to account, such as the transaction is the only one executing at the time and that transactions have the proper error handling in place.

- The database is in a consistent state before a transaction begins.
- The start of a transaction is signaled through an application either explicitly or automatically.
- Modifications to data are performed one table at a time. The database is temporarily in an inconsistent state while modifications are performed.
- If an error occurs, all modifications are rolled back to the consistent state as before the transaction was attempted.
- If no errors occur, the database is returned to a consistent state.
- The transaction is committed, making the data changes permanent.

Using Transactions

In the previous chapter, we used ADO.NET to connect to SQL Server. We even had a few hands-on projects where we manipulated data within SQL Server. However, it is important to understand that individually manipulating data using automatic transactions does not constitute a transactional procedure. Just because we used SQL Server as our database, SQL Server will not automatically treat two related transactions as an all-or-nothing procedure unless explicitly told to. For example, in the previous chapter we changed the name in the `Employee` table from Andrew Fuller to Susan Fuller. This change constitutes an automatic transaction. If something were to go wrong, SQL Server would not have accepted this change.

However, suppose we made a batch of three updates to occur at once within the table. What if the first two updates were successful and the last update were to fail? If we had not specified within this batch of updates that these three are to be treated as one transaction, we would have ended up with two updates and one failure. Perhaps in this scenario, this would not be horrible. But consider the bank example from Chapter 1, where money was transferred from one account to another. Suppose this time, money was successfully taken out of your savings account but the entry failed when trying to post it to your checking account. I don't know about you, but I would not be very happy!

Recall the ACID rules, particularly that atomicity refers to the all-or-nothing proposition of a transaction. Simply, a transaction will either commit everything within the transaction, or it will abort everything within the transaction. If we have transactional processing in place, you don't need to worry if a part of the transaction fails, because we have specified we want an all-or-nothing scenario to occur. So either our money is successfully transferred from the savings account and credited to our checking account, or the transaction will be aborted and rolled back to the original state as if nothing had ever happened.

The grouping of one or more SQL statements surrounded by explicitly assigning transaction delimiters such as: `BEGIN`, `ROLLBACK`, and `COMMIT` are referred to as an explicit transaction.

Note that for compatibility with other major RDBMS systems, SQL Server supports the notion of implicit transactions. Implicit transactions do not require a `BEGIN TRANSACTION` statement. Instead they start automatically with your first statement, and only end when a `COMMIT` or `ROLLBACK` statement is issued. Otherwise, as we stated earlier, SQL Server treats each SQL statement as a separate transaction. By default the `IMPLICIT_TRANSACTIONS` option is turned off, and you need to turn it on by using the command `SET IMPLICIT_TRANSACTIONS ON`. Note that this will only affect the current connection. However, using this option can lead to transactions being open for a long time, and hence cause problems with the database becoming more and more locked up, and therefore it is not really recommended.

Database Transactions

There are two transactional techniques used to manipulate data. You can make your transactions be database transactions or you can rely on connection-based transactions. We will look at connection-based transactions later in the chapter, but first let's examine database transactions.

Database transactions use specific statements such as stored procedures in order to control the transaction. Let's look at an example.

Before entering any code, open Query Analyzer, and execute the `ResetTables` script to make sure there is no data in our two tables.

Start a new Visual Basic .NET project and select **Windows Application** under the pane labeled **Templates**. Also change the project name to `Transactions_Database`.

Before entering any code, go to **Form Design** and drag a button control from the Toolbox onto the form. For cosmetic purposes, you may want to change the `Text` property of the button to **Insert Rows**.

As with the previous projects, we need the same namespaces under the form's declarations:

```
Imports System.Data
Imports System.Data.SqlClient
```

Locate the `Button1_Click()` method and enter the following:

```
Private Sub Button1_Click(ByVal sender As System.Object, ByVal e As
System.EventArgs) Handles Button1.Click

Const SP As String = "Insert_Dog_Food"

        Dim MySqlConnection As New SqlConnection("Data Source=localhost; initial
catalog=Wrox;User ID=sa;PWD=")

        Dim MySqlCommand As New SqlCommand(SP, MySqlConnection)
        Dim RowsAffected As Integer

        MySqlCommand.CommandType = CommandType.StoredProcedure

        Try
            MySqlConnection.Open()
            RowsAffected = MySqlCommand.ExecuteNonQuery()
            MessageBox.Show(RowsAffected & " " & "Row(s) Inserted")
        Catch StoredProcedure_Error As Exception
            MessageBox.Show(StoredProcedure_Error.ToString())
        Finally
            MySqlConnection.Close()

        End Try
End Sub
```

Start the application; when the form opens, click the button to insert the data.

You should receive a message box indicating six rows have been inserted.

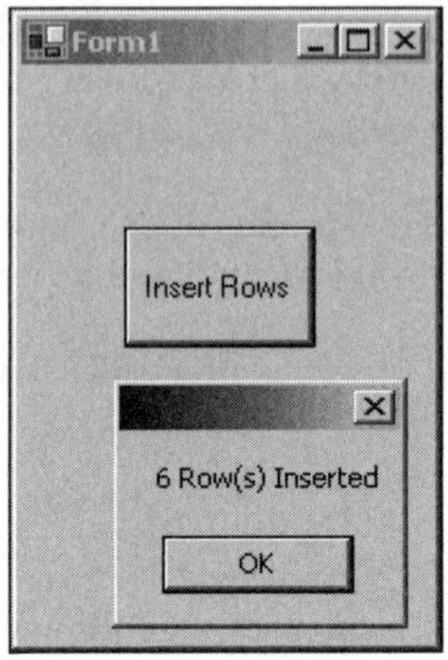

As you can see, it is very easy to execute a stored procedure using Visual Basic .NET. The namespaces `System.Data` and `System.Data.SqlClient` are the same as used with other projects utilizing SQL Server.

Under the `Button1_Click()` method, we declared a string and assigned it the value of the stored procedures name:

```
Const SP As String = "Insert_Dog_Food"
```

We follow this with the `Connection` and `Command` object, as we have done in previous projects. However, because we are executing a stored procedure, we need to set the `CommandType` of the `Command` object. The `CommandType` is used to indicate that a stored procedure is to be executed:

```
MySqlCommand.CommandType = CommandType.StoredProcedure
```

The final step involves opening a database connection and executing our stored procedure.

Using Parameters

Earlier in this chapter it was mentioned that T-SQL is unlike procedural languages because T-SQL tells the database what is being requested, not how to retrieve it. What T-SQL has in common with procedural languages is it can accept and return **parameters** as well as return values.

With stored procedures, you can have any combination of input and output parameters, or you don't have to have any at all. With an input parameter, you can pass data to a stored procedure in a similar manner to passing data from a function or procedure in other programming languages such as Visual Basic .NET. By using a stored procedure's output parameter, you can pass data back to the caller.

Of course, as you have seen with the previous stored procedures in this chapter, stored procedures do not require any parameters at all.

When working with stored procedures we often use a return value to indicate how the procedure performed. More specifically, we use this to see whether the stored procedure execution completed or aborted. By default, the return value for a stored procedure is zero, which indicates that it completed successfully. However, you can set the return value to be any integer in the range of –2,147,483,648 through 2,147,483,648. Typically you would want to keep zero as the return value indicating a successful completion, while a non-zero would indicate a problem. Thus you can use a specific integer value (as long as it is in the range previously mentioned and follows MS standards) to indicate a type of problem.

Using Parameters with Visual Basic .NET

Of course the purpose of using parameters with stored procedures is to be able to pass it a dynamic value, such as from a client application. In our case, we want to pass parameter values using Visual Basic .NET. As it happens, ADO.NET provides a parameters collection for us to use.

The `Parameter` object provides numerous properties, such as the name of the parameter, its data type information, column information, and, of course, the parameter's value. The following table briefly describes the available properties that can be used:

Property	Description
`DbType`	States a data type from the `SqlDbType` or `OleDbtype` enumeration.
`Direction`	Used to indicate the parameter direction. See the direction table below.
`IsNullable`	If a parameter can accept `NULLs`, you set the Boolean `IsNullable` to `True`.
`OleDbType` / `SqlDbType`	This it the data type, and it is selected from the `SqlDbType` or `OleDbType` enumeration. There are 24 data types for `SqlDbType` and 40 data types for `OleDbType`.
`ParameterName`	States the name for the parameter.
`Precision`	Used to indicate the amount of digits a value is to be resolved.
`Scale`	Used to indicate how many decimal places a value is to be resolved.
`Size`	Used to indicate the size of an integer.
`SourceColumn`	This property is used to specify the column name in a table where the parameter value will be obtained.
`SourceVersion`	States a value from the `DataRowVersion` indicating the version. Enumerations include `Default`, `Original`, `Current`, and `Proposed`.
`Value`	This is an assigned value given to a parameter.

The parameter directions come in four varieties:

Direction	Description
`Input`	Represents a passed value.
`InputOutput`	Represents a value that can be passed as well as returned.
`Output`	Represents a returned value.
`ReturnValue`	Represents a returned value without a name or parameter.

Now that we have looked at parameters from the point of view of stored procedures and from Visual Basic .NET, let's go on to the next project that makes uses of several of these properties.

Using Parameters Example

In this project we will pass two parameters from the client to indicate the values for an `INSERT` statement into the `Dogs` table.

From the Query Analyzer, make sure you have selected the `Wrox` database and type in the following code. After executing the stored procedure, notice the message located at the lower pane of Query Analyzer to be sure it completes successfully (this procedure is available as a text file (`Param_Insert.txt` in the code download for this chapter):

```
CREATE PROCEDURE Param_Insert
   @Breed char(20),
   @Food integer

AS

BEGIN TRANSACTION Ins_Dogs

INSERT INTO Dogs
     (Breed,  FoodPref)
 VALUES (@Breed, @Food)

IF @@ERROR <> 0
   BEGIN
   ROLLBACK TRANSACTION Ins_Dogs
      RETURN
   END

COMMIT TRANSACTION Ins_Dogs
```

Now that you have completed the stored procedure, let's create the application. Start a new Visual Basic .NET project and select **Windows Application** under the pane labeled **Templates**. Also change the project name to `Transaction_Parameters`.

Before entering any code, go to the form design and drag a button, two text boxes, and two labels from the Toolbox onto the form as shown below. Change the properties for the labels. Also, for cosmetic purposes, you may want to change the `Text` property for the button to **Insert Rows**:

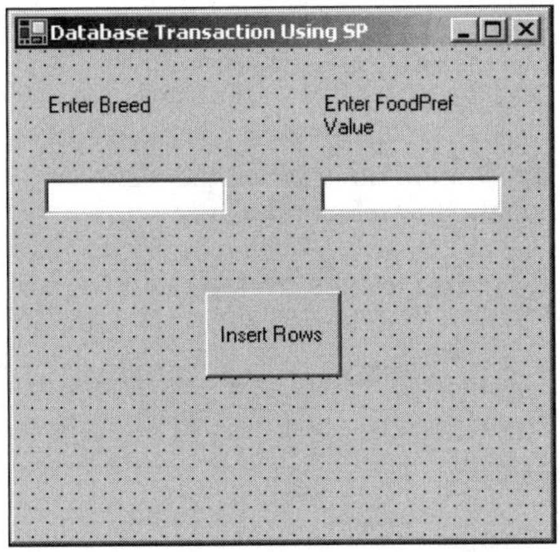

As with the previous projects, we need the same namespaces under the form's declarations:

```
Imports System.Data
Imports System.Data.SqlClient
```

Locate the `Button1_Click()` method and enter the following:

```
Private Sub Button1_Click(ByVal sender As System.Object, ByVal e As
System.EventArgs) Handles Button1.Click
```

```
Dim SP As String = "Param_Insert"
Dim MySqlConnection As New SqlConnection("Data Source=localhost;" & _
    "initial catalog=Wrox;User ID=sa;PWD=")
Dim MySqlCommand As New SqlCommand(SP, MySqlConnection)
Dim I As Integer

MySqlCommand.CommandType = CommandType.StoredProcedure


Dim MyParameter As SqlParameter
MyParameter = MySqlCommand.Parameters.Add("@Breed", SqlDbType.Char, 20)
MyParameter.Direction = ParameterDirection.Input
MyParameter.Value = TextBox1.Text

MyParameter = MySqlCommand.Parameters.Add("@Food", SqlDbType.Int)
MyParameter.Direction = ParameterDirection.Input
MyParameter.Value = Val(TextBox2.Text)


Try
    MySqlConnection.Open()
    I = MySqlCommand.ExecuteNonQuery()
Catch StoredProcedure_Project As Exception
    MessageBox.Show(StoredProcedure_Project.ToString())
End Try
```

```
    MySqlConnection.Close()
    MessageBox.Show(I & " " & "Row(s) Inserted")
    End Sub
```

OK, you are ready to test this application now. When the form opens, enter a breed of dog and a food preference value, then click the button to insert the data:

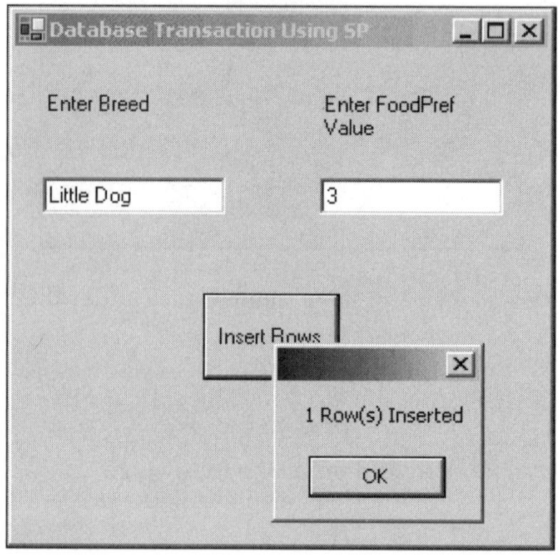

This project is identical to the previous project where we executed a stored procedure, except we added the use of a `Parameter` object.

Directly after the `CommandType`, we declared a parameter as a `SqlParameter`:

```
Dim MyParameter As SqlParameter
```

Next, we make use of the `Parameters` collection. First, we start off with the `Add()` method. This creates a new parameter, adds it to the `Parameters` collection, and returns a reference to it. Notice we first provide the name of the parameter including the `@` sign. This is new with ADO.NET. Previous versions of ADO only used the parameter name without the `@` sign. Following the parameter name is the SQL data type. The numeric `20` indicates the `char` data type can be up to 20 characters:

```
MyParameter = MySqlCommand.Parameters.Add("@Breed", SqlDbType.Char, 20)
```

For the second parameter we did not specify a size, as it is not necessary to do this when using numeric types. When using numeric data types, the size is automatically defaulted:

```
MyParameter = MySqlCommand.Parameters.Add("@Food", SqlDbType.Int)
```

We also specified the parameter `Direction`. Because we are taking a value from the client and sending it to the stored procedure, we indicate it by using the `Direction` of `Input`:

```
MyParameter.Direction = ParameterDirection.Input
```

Finally, here is the parameter `Value`. We simply assign the value for the parameter by taking user input in the form of a textbox:

```
MyParameter.Value = TextBox1.Text
```

Connection-Based Transactions

As stated earlier, we have two transactional techniques we can use to manipulate our data – database transactions or connection-based transactions.

Database transactions are the type of transactions discussed so far in this chapter. **Connection-based transactions** involve utilizing the ADO.NET `Command` object to explicitly control the transaction. An important differentiation between database transactions and connection-based transactions is that connection-based transactions manage the execution of transactions outside the database. Database transactions such as stored procedures execute within the database itself.

As previously mentioned, connection-based transactions involve utilizing the ADO.NET `Command` object to execute a SQL statement or stored procedure. When using the `Command` object to execute SQL statements, the execution and management of the transaction occur outside of the database.

You can perform transacted data manipulations using both the `SqlConnection` object and the `OleDbConnection` object.

In order to begin a transaction, you need to call the `BeginTransaction()` method from the current `Connection` object. When this occurs, a `Transaction` object is returned where you can enroll any `Command` objects you want to be included as part of the transaction.

After the `Command` objects have been successfully executed, you call the `Commit()` method. This officially ends the transaction and makes all database changes final. You also want to make sure to utilize the `Rollback` method in case of errors. As with the `ROLLBACK` keyword used with stored procedures, this method restores the database back to its original state before the transaction occurred.

Connection-Based Transactions Example

This project will manually enroll several `Command` objects in order to execute a transaction comprising a series of `INSERT` statements into the `Dogs` table and the `Food` table.

Before entering any code, open Query Analyzer and execute the `ResetTables.txt` script so we can insert new data.

Start a new Visual Basic .NET project and select Windows Application under the pane labeled Templates. Also change the project name to `Transactions_Connection`, and add a button to the form.

As with the previous projects, we need the same namespaces under the form's declarations:

```
Imports System.Data
Imports System.Data.SqlClient
```

Locate the `Button1_Click()` method and enter the following:

```
Private Sub Button1_Click(ByVal sender As System.Object, ByVal e As
System.EventArgs) Handles Button1.Click

        Dim I As Integer
        Dim SqlDog(5) As String

        SqlDog(0) = "INSERT INTO Food (FoodID,FoodDesc) VALUES (1,'Crunchy
            Cereal')"
        SqlDog(1) = "INSERT INTO Food (FoodID,FoodDesc) VALUES (2,'Table Scraps')"
        SqlDog(2) = "INSERT INTO Food (FoodID,FoodDesc) VALUES (3,'Dog Biscuits')"
        SqlDog(3) = "INSERT INTO Dogs (Breed,FoodPref) VALUES ('German
            Shepherd',1)"
        SqlDog(4) = "INSERT INTO Dogs (Breed,FoodPref) VALUES ('Maltese',1)"
        SqlDog(5) = "INSERT INTO Dogs (Breed,FoodPref) VALUES ('Yorkshire
            Terrier',1)"

        'Be sure to change your connection string to reflect your environment
        Dim MySqlConnection As New SqlConnection("Data Source=localhost;" & _
            "initial catalog=Wrox;User ID=sa;PWD=")

        Dim MySqlCommand As New SqlCommand()
        Dim MySqlTransaction As SqlTransaction


        Try
            MySqlConnection.Open()
            MySqlTransaction = MySqlConnection.BeginTransaction
            MySqlCommand.Connection = MySqlConnection
            MySqlCommand.CommandType = CommandType.Text
            MySqlCommand.Transaction = MySqlTransaction

            Dim x As Integer = 0
            For x = 0 To 5
                MySqlCommand.CommandText = SqlDog(x)
                I = I + MySqlCommand.ExecuteNonQuery()
            Next

        Catch TransactionException As Exception
            MySqlTransaction.Rollback()
            MessageBox.Show(TransactionException.ToString())
            Exit Sub
        End Try


        MySqlTransaction.Commit()
        MessageBox.Show(I & " " & "Row(s) Inserted")
        MySqlTransaction = Nothing

        MySqlConnection.Close()
My Sub
```

Start the project. When the form opens, click the button to insert the data. A message box should indicate that 1 row was updated.

As for importing namespaces, we still use the `System.Data` and the `System.Data.SqlClient`.

Under the `Button1_Click()` method, things are a little different from the other projects. First, we declared an array so we can efficiently loop through the six SQL statements.

Next we created the `Connection` and `Command` objects, as we have in previous projects. However, this time we created a variable to hold the `Transaction` object.

```
Dim MySqlTransaction As SqlTransaction
```

Now we are ready to start the transaction. First, we open the `Connection` and then explicitly start the transaction with the `BeginTransaction()` method:

```
MySqlConnection.Open()
MySqlTransaction = MySqlConnection.BeginTransaction
```

Next we assign the `Connection` object to the `Connection` property. We also need to indicate that we are using SQL statements. To do this we set the `CommandType` to `Text`. Although obvious, I'll mention it anyway; you need to attach the current transaction to the `Command` object:

```
MySqlCommand.Connection = MySqlConnection
MySqlCommand.CommandType = CommandType.Text
MySqlCommand.Transaction = MySqlTransaction
```

Finally, we are ready to execute each SQL statement in the array by looping through each of the array's elements:

```
    Dim x As Integer = 0
    For x = 0 To 5
        MySqlCommand.CommandText = SqlDog(x)
        I = I + MySqlCommand.ExecuteNonQuery()
    Next
```

Summary

We started this chapter by looking at the SQL language, and SQL statements written in the T-SQL language used by Microsoft's SQL Server. We then moved on to examine stored procedures, and how execution plans are used to make them run more efficiently and effectively. Next, we considered in-line SQL statements, how to maximise these using the `Prepare` property, and how they compared to stored procedures, and some advantages of each.

We then took a look at transactions in SQL Server, and how they are managed. We also examined savepoints, so that we could commit part of the transaction rather than rolling all the way back to the beginning.

Next we created the tables that we will be using for the examples in this chapter and later in the book, using either Query Analyser or Enterprise Manager. We then looked at creating transactional stored procedures, and how to use transactions. We also discussed automatic and implicit transactions.

We finished by studying database transactions and connection-based transactions, how they differ, and examples of their usage.

Pro Visual Basic .NET Transactions

4

ASP.NET

The first chapter dealt with data tiers, now it's time to develop ways to present the data. Because the trend is for applications via the Web, we will explore ASP.NET. ASP.NET is an integral part of the .NET Framework. This chapter deals with the presentation (user) services. Simply, in order to work with our data, we need some type of user interface. Because .NET is designed with the Internet in mind, we are going to concentrate on Web Forms utilizing ASP.NET.

> *Note that it is beyond the scope of this book to teach ASP.NET. Most of the applications in this book require a working knowledge of ASP.NET. Although I will cover some fundamental concepts, most concepts will be based on working with data. For more information about ASP.NET I suggest* Professional ASP.NET 1.0 Special Edition *(ISBN: 1-861007-03-5) from Wrox Press, and* ASPToday *(http://www.asptoday.com), Wrox's codesource for ASP and .NET applications.*

After completing this chapter you should be able to answer the following questions:

- What are Web Forms and how are they processed?
- What are Server Controls?
- How do Web Forms handle events?
- How well does data binding work with Web Forms?
- How are templates used to format data?
- Do validation controls make coding easier?
- Can you use validation controls with bound controls, such as the `DataGrid` control?

Introduction to ASP.NET

If you have worked with transactions over the Web, you probably are familiar with traditional **ASP (Active Server Pages)**. Active Server Pages require some type of script such as VBScript or JScript in order to send and retrieve data from a data store. ASP.NET changes the way scripting is handled. In other words, much of the script we used in traditional ASP pages has been reduced because ASP.NET lets us use fully developed languages such as Visual Basic .NET, C++ .NET, and C#. This makes programming data-intense applications much easier and more efficient because you can now design interactive web pages (referred to as Web Forms) that closely resemble common Win32 applications.

Furthermore, ASP.NET is completely object-oriented. This means that object-oriented programming concepts such as encapsulation, polymorphism, inheritance, abstraction and overloading are available within ASP.NET.

Because businesses have already invested a lot of money, manpower, and resources in developing with ASP, ASP.NET maintains compatibility by being able to run side by side with traditional ASP pages. In other words, you can install both ASP and ASP.NET on the same server without any complications. In order to separate the two, ASP.NET uses a new file extension `.aspx`.

Web Forms

If you have worked with forms using traditional ASP, you will appreciate the power of Web Forms. Web Forms are the new generation of web development technology that allows you to create programmable web pages. Web Forms are built seamlessly into the Visual Studio .NET IDE. What makes Web Forms so powerful is that application logic can be implemented through the server and displayed to the user regardless of the browser they are using.

As with Windows Forms, Web Forms offer great flexibility through the use of drag and drop controls. In the case of Web Forms, these drag and drop controls are called **server controls**. Server controls are reusable interface elements that are used to construct a Web Form's user interface (UI). What makes this exciting is that server controls can use the server to dynamically generate web pages. What this means is that Web Forms are created on the server and then sent to the browser.

The whole principle behind Web Forms is simplified web application development. In addition to server controls, Web Forms provide:

- Easier separation of HTML and application logic
- Advanced Event-based programming
- Compiled code
- Easier application development with enhanced tools when utilizing the Visual Studio .NET IDE

Note that Web Forms are still retrieved by client browsers through HTTP requests. After receiving a request to a Web Form, the web server automatically renders a correct, browser-compliant HTML page, which is sent back to the client. Although Web Forms can be programmed in any Common Language Runtime-supported language, they can run in any browser.

When working with Web Forms, we once again are working with classes. More specifically we are working with the `Page` class.

```
Public Class WebForm1
    Inherits System.Web.UI.Page
```

Web Forms allow for a complete separation between the visual content of the page and the logic behind the User Interface. Developers that have used RAD tools in the past, such as with Visual Basic, will find this separation natural and easy to understand.

The visual content consists of an HTML page that acts as a container for text and server controls. The interface logic of the Web Form consists of the code that supports and interacts with the User Interface, which as you already know, can be written in any CLR-supported language.

Writing ASP Code

One of the most frustrating, as well as confusing, aspects of traditional ASP pages is the intermingling of HTML and script code. As you will see shortly, the ASP.NET team at Microsoft has done an excellent job of separating the two in order to make reading and writing code easier.

When writing ASP.NET code, you will typically have the HTML layout and the Visual Basic .NET logic saved in separate files, because this is the way Visual Studio .NET works. But if you are a die-hard web developer, you may prefer using a text editor such as Notepad, in order to write both the HTML and the Visual Basic code in a single file, as shown below:

```
<%@ page language="vb" %>

<script runat="server">
     Sub Click_MyButton(ByVal myObject As Object, ByVal e As EventArgs)
        Response.Write("Welcome " & MyASPTextBox.Text)
             End Sub
</script>

<html>
   <body>
      <form id="Form1" method="post" runat="server">
<asp:Label id="MyASPLabel" Text="Enter your name" Runat="server" />
<asp:Button ID="MyASPButton" Text="Submit Name" OnClick="Click_MyButton"
                   Runat="server"  />
<asp:TextBox id="MyASPTextBox" runat="server" />
     </form>
  </body>
</html>
```

If you use Visual Studio .NET, two separate files are utilized. One file with the `.aspx` extension handles all the HTML elements. A second accompanying page is set aside for the Visual Basic .NET code logic, which is defined in an `.aspx.vb` file. We can see how these work together in the diagram below. Although you had the ability to use include files and other techniques to separate your code with traditional ASP pages, you will find that using Visual Studio .NET makes seperating your code a breeze. You will see how this looks in the forthcoming project.

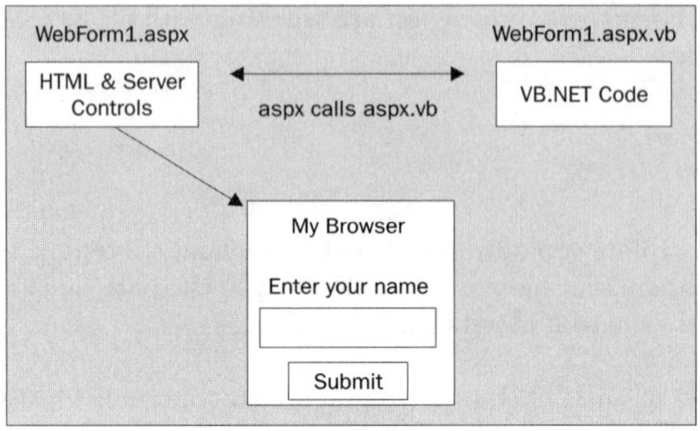

Handling State

If you have programmed traditional ASP pages, you are well aware that when a form is filled out and submitted, then the same page is returned to the user, typically the form fields will be empty. This occurs because the web itself is **stateless**; meaning that information does not persist from web page to web page. Not having data persist can often be troublesome to the application developer. For example, when working with form validation, maintaining state makes it easier to return to the page, so that the user can make any necessary corrections without losing the data they correctly entered. It is true, the developer can utilize several techniques to get around these problems, but it often requires a lot of extra programming.

> *The .NET Framework essentially provides three options for retaining state between roundtrips: the* `ViewState` *property, the* `StateBag` *class, and session/application objects. We won't discuss all of these in this chapter, as we are just providing an overview.*

ASP.NET changes the way state is handled between round trips to the server. Instead of the application developer having to create a routine to maintain page state, ASP.NET can automatically handle state by outputting hidden HTML form fields. These hidden HTML form fields are created when you specify the form to run at the server as shown below:

```
<form  id="Form1" method="post" runat="server" />
```

Hidden HTML form fields are automatically created by ASP.NET to maintain state.

ViewState

Let's take a closer look at the `ViewState` property, which is new to ASP.NET. As we shall see shortly, `ViewState` takes advantage of the hidden form fields that developers have been using manually for years and automates the process.

As we have hinted at above, one of the goals of maintaining state in a server is to persist its properties across postback events.

> *A postback event is fired when a Web Form posts or sends data back to itself, as in our example above where a user fills out a form and then has the same page returned to them.*

Each control that runs at the server has a property referred to as ViewState, which is inherited from the base Control class. This property is an instance of the StateBag class and stores the values of a server control's properties during a postback. In other words, the values of each page and control are saved prior to the page being processed. The values are saved in the page as a hidden field called _VIEWSTATE.

In the screenshot below showing hidden fields you see _VIEWSTATE highlighted.

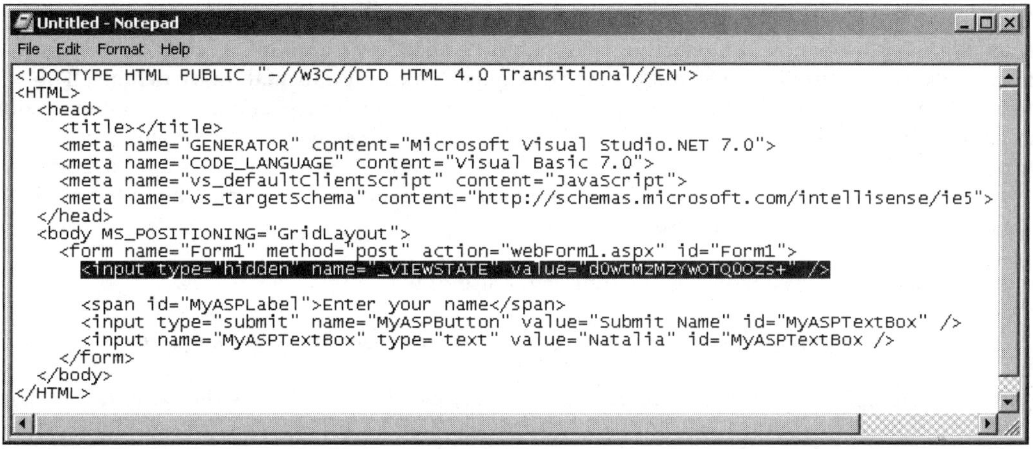


```
<!DOCTYPE HTML PUBLIC "-//W3C//DTD HTML 4.0 Transitional//EN">
<HTML>
  <head>
    <title></title>
    <meta name="GENERATOR" content="Microsoft Visual Studio.NET 7.0">
    <meta name="CODE_LANGUAGE" content="Visual Basic 7.0">
    <meta name="vs_defaultClientScript" content="JavaScript">
    <meta name="vs_targetSchema" content="http://schemas.microsoft.com/intellisense/ie5">
  </head>
  <body MS_POSITIONING="GridLayout">
    <form name="Form1" method="post" action="webForm1.aspx" id="Form1">
      <input type="hidden" name="_VIEWSTATE" value="dOwtMzMzYwOTQOOzs+" />

      <span id="MyASPLabel">Enter your name</span>
      <input type="submit" name="MyASPButton" value="Submit Name" id="MyASPTextBox" />
      <input name="MyASPTextBox" type="text" value="Natalia" id="MyASPTextBox />
    </form>
  </body>
</HTML>
```

When the page is posted back to the server, the information is read from the _VIEWSTATE, and the control's properties are restored.

> **The term ViewState is sometimes used to describe how a form or control looks at a given time. For instance, we could say that if the user were to return to the same Web Form at a later time, the ViewState for the fields would be blank, unless we were to write extra routines to maintain state.**

Notice that all the data under ViewState is encrypted. What's interesting is that this encrypted data contains all the information about the controls and any data associated with it. How do you enable ViewState? You don't do anything; ViewState is enabled by default for all server controls. However, as an application developer you need to keep in mind that having ViewState enabled can deteriorate performance, particularly with pages that contain numerous controls, as all control information and the data associated with each control is commonly transmitted to the server and then back to the client again.

Turning ViewState off for a particular page can be accomplished in two ways:

- You can disable ViewState at the page level by setting EnableViewState to False at the page directive:

  ```
  <%@ Page EnableViewState="false" %>
  ```

  By disabling ViewState at the page level, no controls on the page will be maintained.

- You can disable `ViewState` at the control level. In other words, you can disable `ViewState` for one control and leave it enabled for another control on the same page. This is accomplished by setting the `EnableViewState` parameter to `False` within the control declaration, as shown:

```
<asp: ListBox id="myListBox" EnableViewState="false" runat="server" />
```

Another important issue to keep in mind is portable devices such as PDAs. Devices of this nature are not capable in either bandwidth or memory of handling such large amounts of data, so there will be times when you want to disable `ViewState`. So why is `ViewState` turned on by default? The advantages tend to out-weigh the disadvantages. The primary advantage is that page state is maintained within the page residing at the client and not at the server. This relieves server resources while putting a minimal burden on the client. Think about it, each client connecting to your web application maintains its own state, as opposed to the server maintaining state for every client connecting to the application. Not a bad way to manage system resources!

Another advantage that is becoming apparent is the use of web farms.

Web farms are two or more servers working together that are designed to handle a web site.

In this situation, a request from a client does not need to continuously utilize the same server. Because `ViewState` reflects the information for each control within a Web Form, any server that is a part of a web farm can pick up from where the other server left off.

Now the question is, how do you know if you should deactivate `ViewState` within a page? Well, it's a judgment call. However, knowing who is going to use the application and how the application is going to be used is your first step. Under normal circumstances, I suggest leaving `ViewState` alone. For example, suppose you have a bound `DataGrid`, and it is bound only during the first page load and not during each postback. In order for the page to reflect current changes after a postback, you need to add code in order to maintain the values. For example, you could bind the `DataGrid` to reload the data after each trip from the server, but constantly requesting information from the server or data source is also a costly process. Nevertheless, if you plan for your web applications to work with portable devices, then you may have little choice but to deactivate `ViewState`.

Server Controls

Server controls run at the server. As profound as this statement sounds, it is important to understand that a lot of behind-the-scenes activity occurs within Web Forms. Server controls are key players in ASP.NET. What makes server controls so different from HTML form elements is that controls exhibit properties, events, and methods, and they even manage state for us. The ramifications of this should appear obvious; you can control their behavior.

There are many server controls available to the application developer. For the most part, server controls can be separated into two types, **HTML server controls** and **web server controls**.

HTML Server Controls

HTML server controls are defined within the `System.Web.UI.HtmlControls` namespace. HTML server controls, or simply HTML controls, are very similar to HTML elements you have worked with before. For all practical purposes, they are the same. However, instead of these elements being client-side, they are server-side. These server controls generate HTML that is sent to the browser. So when a client calls a particular ASP.NET page, HTML code is generated at the server, and then sent to the client. In different terms, the object of elements such as textboxes, radio buttons, etc., are created on the server and displayed on the web page. You may be wondering why Microsoft would want a technology that will take a performance hit. Perhaps the best reason is having all your logic written in the language of choice and executed on the server, allowing any browser, regardless of the platform, to be able to access the .NET web page.

It is important to realize HTML controls are not intended as a complete replacement for the standard HTML elements. First, HTML controls are essentially designed to provide an easy and quick way to convert legacy web pages to fit within the ASP.NET framework. Basically, HTML controls are nothing more than wrappers that fit around HTML tags. As a matter of fact, all you need to do to change an HTML element to an HTML control is to simply add `runat="server"` as shown:

```
<input type = "TextBox" id="TextBox1" Text="MyTextBox1" runat="server" />
```

The second reason HTML controls are not meant to completely replace standard HTML elements is server controls versus HTML elements do take a performance hit. So if you don't need any server code behind an HMTL server control, there is no real reason to use them.

Data Binding

Many of you are familiar with the binding of Visual Basic (pre-.NET) controls to a data source such as to MS Access, SQL Server or even Oracle. Data binding worked very well with the common client-server applications. The problem is data binding does not work in a disconnected environment such as the Internet.

Interestingly, Microsoft tried to dance around the disconnected problem with the introduction of Internet Explorer 4.0 (IE 4). IE 4 presented the concept of **client-side data binding** through the use of several COM components. This new technology worked well. Unfortunately, it raised several security issues, and thus client-side data binding failed. If the security issues were not the reason for the demise of client-side data binding, then it would have been due to the technology being browser-specific.

Microsoft has gone back to the drawing board, and is now presenting a new technology that meets the requirements for working in disconnected environments as well as meeting security standards. This technology is a part of ASP.NET and is called **server-side data binding**.

Server-side data binding eliminates both security and browser compatibility issues because all the work is conducted at the server. In other words, web pages are created at the server including the retrieval and/or manipulation of data. After everything is processed, it is sent to the client, regardless of the browser being used. Additionally, ASP.NET provides application developers with an easy way to bind data that works well in disconnected environments such as the Internet.

In order to directly bind data to an ASP.NET control, the control must possess the `DataSource` property. Remember, data binding in ASP.NET is not like the data binding many of you are used to with traditional Visual Basic applications. The point is; data binding does not have to be to a database. You can bind to any type of data including collections such as Hash Tables (similar to VBScript Dictionary objects) and Array Lists. Furthermore, you can indirectly bind a control that does not possess a `DataSource` property. This can be accomplished by embedding a control that supports data binding inside a control that does not support data binding. For example, you can bind data to a HyperLink control in order to allow a drill-down type of scenario. You will see how this works later in this chapter.

The following chart shows the available controls that can be used with ASP.NET data binding:

Control	ASP.NET Syntax Description
`ListBox`	`<asp:ListBox runat="server" />`
`DropDown`	`<asp:DropDownList runat="server" />`
`CheckBox`	`<asp:CheckBoxList runat="server" />`
`RadioButton`	`<asp:RadioButtonList runat="server" />`
`Repeater`	`<asp:Repeater runat="server" />`
`DataList`	`<asp:DataList runat="server" />`
`DataGrid`	`<asp:DataGrid runat="server" />`

List Controls

When working with web applications, particularly when working with automatic transactions the three most utilized web server controls will be:

- `Repeater` control
- `DataList` control
- `DataGrid` control

By far, these data-binding controls are the most complicated of all the controls. All three of these controls are capable of taking collections of data and automatically looping through the data. Although each provides different features, they all eliminate a lot of code that was necessary when displaying the contents of Recordsets using traditional ASP page technology. Let's look at each in detail:

Repeater Control

Although the `Repeater` control does not provide a means to manipulate data, it is still a handy control for transactional applications because it provides a vast array of customizable features for displaying read-only data from any type of data source. In other words, even though the `Repeater` control is not used in regard to transactions, it can be a good tool to allow a user to easily view data that has just been manipulated.

Although the `Repeater` control has the least functionality of the three list controls, it may at first appear difficult to work with because it lacks a predefined display. At the same time, not having a predefined display provides the developer with a lot of flexibility about how data will be shown to the user.

> **The most important thing to keep in mind is that the `Repeater` control cannot be used to modify data; it is designed only to display data.**

Because the `Repeater` control does not default to any type of display, data formatting must be specified through the use of templates. There are five different templates that can be used to format the appearance. However, you must make use of the `ItemTemplate`, otherwise the `Repeater` control will not render anything for you to see. The other four templates are optional.

The `Repeater` control can utilize five different templates:

- `HeaderTemplate`: Anything placed within the `HeaderTemplate` is rendered only once at the top of the display. In other words, it will not repeat itself. This is typically used to display titles and column names.
- `ItemTemplate`: As previously mentioned, this template is required in order to render data output. The reason for this is that the `Repeater` control is basically a control that loops through data. The `ItemTemplate` allows you to display data on a row-by-row basis.
- `SeparatorTemplate`: You can separate each row by placing spaces, paragraph breaks, underlines, or even images by utilizing this template.
- `AlternatingItemTemplate`: This template is particularly handy when you are displaying numerous rows of data as well as displaying numerous columns of data. By alternating different display styles, such as alternating colors, rows of data are easier to read and follow.
- `FooterTemplate`: As with the `HeaderTemplate`, anything placed within the `FooterTemplate` is rendered only once at the end of the display. In other words, it will not repeat itself.

I feel the best way for you to get a feel of the power and flexibility of the `Repeater` control is to experience it directly. So let's jump right in with a project.

Using the Repeater Control in ASP.NET

Note that the tables and data used in this project are the same that we created in the previous chapter. To refresh this database, run the `ResetTables2.txt` script provided in the code download, which will rebuild and repopulate the database.

Open Visual Studio .NET, start a new project and select ASP.NET Web Application under the second pane labeled Templates. Also change the project name to Repeater:

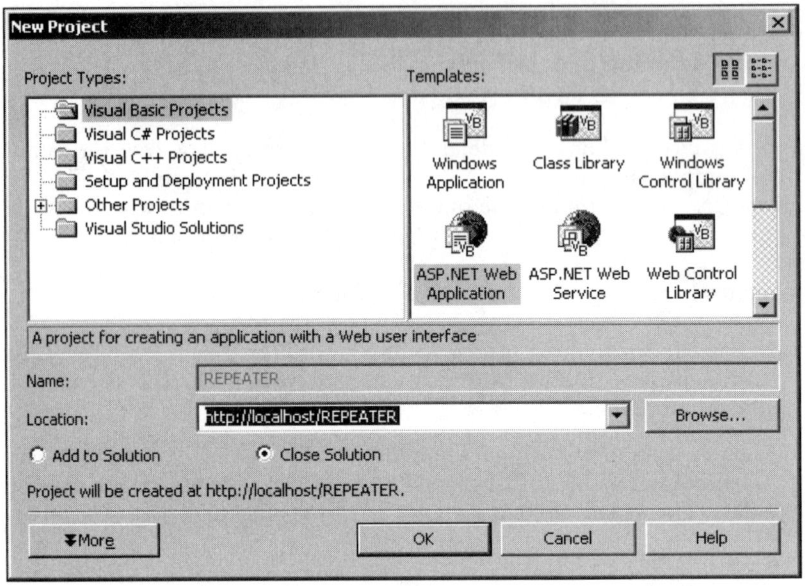

Because Visual Studio .NET uses two separate files, `.aspx` for HTML and `aspx.vb` for Visual Basic .NET code, you will want to enter the HTML code portions first, otherwise you will not receive the support of IntelliSense when working with the Visual Basic .NET code.

If you have not worked much with ASP.NET pages, it may seem a little confusing as to where to enter your code when starting a new project. As soon as you have created a new ASP.NET application you will see a layout similar to this:

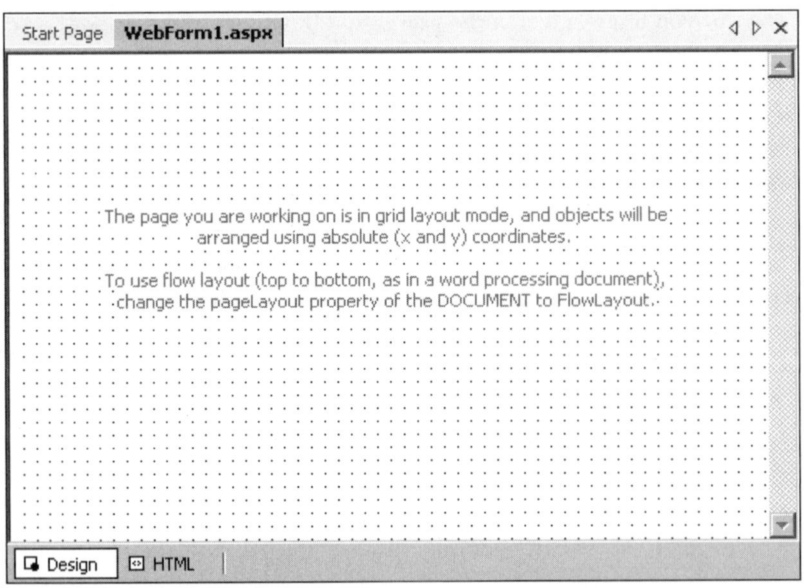

If you look towards the upper left you will see a tab labeled WebForm1.aspx*. This is the work area for your HTML code. Keep in mind that there is no tab (at the present moment) for your Visual Basic .NET code. We will come back to this after we enter the HTML code. Also notice that the above screenshot is in design mode. If you look toward the bottom left, you will see two tabs, one for Design and the other for HTML. Select the HTML tab and enter the following code between the form tags:

```
...
</head>
  <body MS_POSITIONING="GridLayout">
    <form id="Form1" method="post" runat="server">
      <asp:repeater id="MyRepeater" runat="server">
        <HeaderTemplate>
          <table>
            <tr>
              <td bgcolor="Olive" width="200">
                <b>Dog ID</b>
              </td>
              <td bgcolor="Olive" width="200">
                <b>Breed</b>
              </td>
              <td bgcolor="Olive" width="200">
                <b>Food Preference</b>
              </td>
            </tr>
          </table>
        </HeaderTemplate>

        <ItemTemplate>
          <table>
            <tr>
              <td width="200">
                <%# Container.DataItem("DogID")%>
              </td>
              <td width="200">
                <%# Container.DataItem("Breed")%>
              </td>
              <td width="200">
                <%# Container.DataItem("FoodDesc")%>
              </td>
            </tr>
          </table>
        </ItemTemplate>
      </asp:repeater>
    </form>
  </body>
</html>
```

Now that you have entered the HTML portion for this project, we want to get back into design mode. From HTML design mode, double-click anywhere in the work area. This will take you into the familiar Visual Basic .NET work area. Also notice from the next screenshot that a tab was added for the `aspx.vb`. Now you can quickly tab between the two:

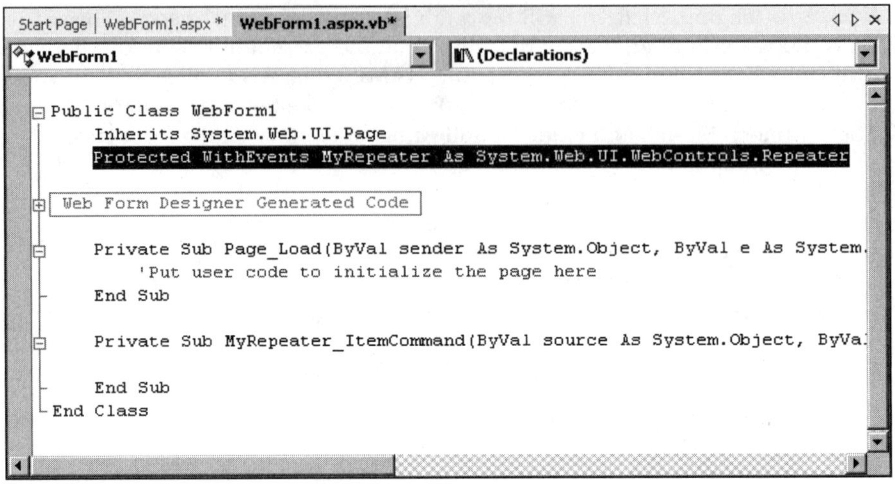

Notice the highlighted line. This was added for you when you entered the `repeater` tags:

```
<asp:repeater id="MyRepeater" runat="server"> </asp:repeater>
```

If you have not already opened the `aspx.vb` work area, do it now and enter the following namespaces under the forms declarations:

```
Imports System.Data
Imports System.Data.SqlClient
```

Locate the `Page_Load()` method and enter the following:

```
Private Sub Page_Load(ByVal sender As System.Object, ByVal e As System.EventArgs)
    Handles MyBase.Load
        'Put user code to initialize the page here
        Dim objConn As New SqlConnection()
        Dim objDataAdapter As New SqlDataAdapter()
        Dim objDataset As New DataSet()

        Dim strSQL As String

        'Set the connection string and open the connection
        objConn.ConnectionString = "Data Source=localhost;initial
            catalog=Wrox;User ID=sa;PWD=;"
        objConn.Open()

        'Use the adapter to retrieve the data and fill the dataset
        strSQL = "SELECT DogID,Breed,FoodDesc FROM Dogs,Food WHERE FoodPref =
            FoodID"
        objDataAdapter.SelectCommand() = New SqlCommand(strSQL, objConn)
        objDataAdapter.Fill(objDataset, "Dogs")

        'Set the datasource of the repeater and bind the data
```

```
        MyRepeater.DataSource = objDataset.Tables("Dogs").DefaultView
        MyRepeater.DataBind()

        objConn = Nothing
        objDataAdapter = Nothing
        objDataset = Nothing
    End Sub
```

Run the project, your results should appear similar to the following screenshot:

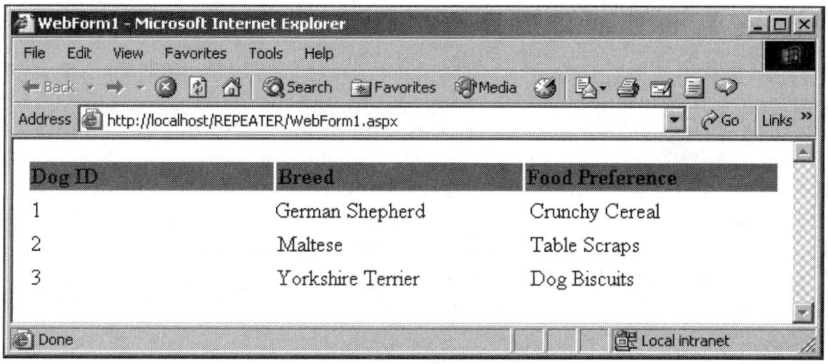

Because the `Repeater` control does not have a default display, we had to create our own by utilizing the available templates.

Starting with the HTML side – the `.aspx` file, we began our project with the `Repeater` control definition by using the `<asp:Repeater>` tag. Next, we added templates for header and item templates. The header template is fairly straightforward HTML; all we did was describe how we wanted the header (title bar) for the columns to be labeled and utilized a table to separate the columns. The Item template is also fairly straightforward, except we make use of the `<%# %>` tags. At first you may think these are code-rendering blocks. In actuality, they are expressions used for data binding. Looking at the code, you can see that we bound data for each item representing a column in the database (`DogID`, `Breed`, and `FoodDesc`) by referencing a row as a `DataItem` object within the `Repeater` control's container:

```
<ItemTemplate>
   <table>
      <tr>
         <td width="200">
            <%# Container.DataItem("DogID")%>
         </td>
         <td width="200">
            <%# Container.DataItem("Breed")%>
         </td>
         <td width="200">
            <%# Container.DataItem("FoodDesc")%>
         </td>
      </tr>
   </table>
</ItemTemplate>
```

The Visual Basic .NET code is similar to the other projects you have done in the previous chapters. We made use of the namespace for SQL Server:

```
Imports System.Data.SqlClient
```

We established a connection to the Wrox database in SQL Server and then filled a DataSet with the database information. The one item that is different is that we bind the repeater to the Dogs table.

```
MyRepeater.DataSource = objDataSet.Tables("Dogs").DefaultView
MyRepeater.DataBind()
```

I previously mentioned that the Repeater control allows us to customize the layout of our data through the use of templates. For example, instead of laying out data in the traditional table form as we have, we can lay out our data with alternating colored lines, separating lines, and even numbered lists.

So far we have only worked with the HeaderTemplate and the ItemTemplate, but you'll recall that there are three other templates that are available for formatting our data within the Repeater control. You can add other templates to achieve a different look. For example, we can use the SeparatorTemplate to add a horizontal line:

```
<SeparatorTemplate>
<HR>
</SeparatorTemplate>
```

I like adding the SeparatorTemplate immediately after the tag because I can quickly change the line colors or other parameters:

```
<asp:repeater id="MyRepeater" runat="server">

   <SeparatorTemplate>
<HR>
</SeparatorTemplate>
```

However, remember the nice thing about these templates is they don't have to be in a particular order. Although one should try to keep things listed in a structured order for ease of code reading.

OK, you can insert an <HR> tag as shown below to create the same effect.

```
     </Table>
   <HR color="olive">
</ItemTemplate>
```

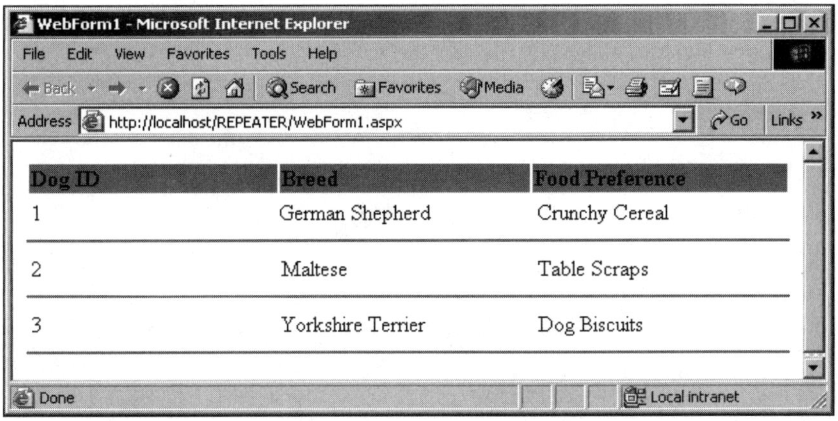

You can also use the separator control for inserting images by using the following syntax:

```
<SeparatorTemplate>
    <table>
        <tr>
            <td>
                <img scr="Images/BlueSeparator.gif">
            </td>
        </tr>
    </table>
</SeparatorTemplate>
```

Let's go back to our HTML code and add the following templates. Also be sure to remove the `<HR>` tag and add back in the `<SeparatorTemplate>` if you tried the previous example so we can easily distinguish the results. Now all you have to do is add the following templates directly after the closing tag for easy code reading:

```
</ItemTemplate>
<AlternatingItemTemplate>
    <table>
        <tr bgcolor="LightBlue">
            <td width="200">
                <%# Container.DataItem("DogID")%>
            </td>
            <td width="200">
                <%# Container.DataItem("Breed")%>
            </td>
            <td width="200">
                <%# Container.DataItem("FoodDesc")%>
            </td>
        </tr>
    </table>
</AlternatingItemTemplate>

<FooterTemplate>
    <table>
```

```
        <tr>
            <td>
                End of File
            </td>
        </tr>
    </table>
</FooterTemplate>
</asp:repeater>
```

Now run the project; your browser should display results similar to the following screenshot:

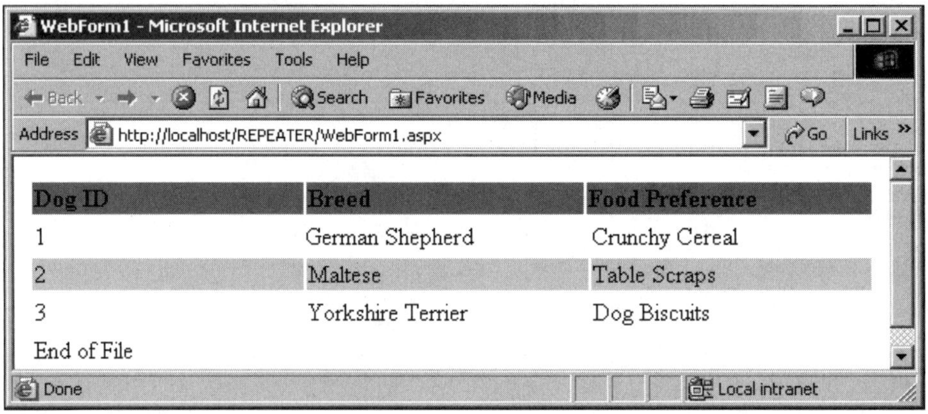

DataList Control

The `DataList` control is similar to the `Repeater` control as it also lacks a predefined display, but the DataList control provides functionality for data manipulation by user interaction. Because the `DataList` provides the ability to manipulate data, there is another template you need to learn about. It is referred to as the `EditItemTemplate` and it is used to create the form layout when placing the control into edit mode. For example, you have seen how the previous templates are used to format the way data is presented on the form. The `EditItemTemplate` is no different; it is used to display data so it can easily be manipulated. This will become clear when you try the next project.

Manipulating Data with the DataList

Start a new ASP.NET Web Application and name the project DataListEdit. Again, let's start by entering HTML code (between the <form> </form> tags) first:

```
<form id="Form1" method="post" runat="server">
<asp:datalist id="MyDataList" Runat="server" onEditCommand="MyDataList_Edit"
    onUpdateCommand="MyDataList_Update" onCancelCommand="MyDataList_Cancel"
    DataKeyfield="DogID" RepeatDirection="Vertical">
  <HeaderTemplate>
    <table>
      <tr>
        <th>
          <font color="Olive" size="14">Dogs Table</font>
        </th>
      </tr>
```

```
      </table>
    </HeaderTemplate>
    <ItemTemplate>
      <asp:LinkButton text="Edit" CommandName="Edit" Runat="server"
          ID="Linkbutton1" />
      <%# Container.DataItem( "Breed" )%>
    </ItemTemplate>
    <EditItemTemplate>
      <table border="1">
        <tr>
          <th bgcolor="Olive"> Breed </th>
          <th bgcolor="Olive"> Food Pref </th>
        </tr>
        <tr>
        <td>
          <asp:TextBox ID="Breed" Text='<%# Container.DataItem("Breed") %>'
              Runat="server" />
        </td>
        <td>
          <asp:TextBox ID="FoodPref" Text='<%# Container.DataItem( "FoodPref") %>'
              Runat="server" />
        </td>
        <td>
          <asp:button text="Update" CommandName="Update" runat="server"
              ID="Button1" />
        </td>
        <td>
          <asp:Button Text="Cancel" CommandName="Cancel" Runat="server"
              ID="Button2" />
        </td>
        </tr>
      </table>
     </EditItemTemplate>
     <SeparatorTemplate>
       <hr>
     </SeparatorTemplate>
   </asp:datalist>
   <br>
   <br>
 </form>
```

Now that the HTML part of this project is complete, let's add the following Visual Basic .NET code to the declarations:

```
 Imports System.Data
 Imports System.Data.SqlClient
```

Locate the `Page_Load()` method and enter the following:

```
     Private Sub Page_Load(ByVal sender As System.Object, ByVal e As
         System.EventArgs) Handles MyBase.Load
         'Put user code to initialize the page here
         If Not Page.IsPostBack Then
```

```
            Bind_MyDataList()
        End If

    End Sub
```

Because we need to open a connection twice, let's add our connection string under the public class:

```
Public Class WebForm1
    Inherits System.Web.UI.Page
Dim mySQLConnection As New SqlConnection("Data Source=LocalHost;" & _
      "initial catalog=Wrox;User ID=sa;PWD=")
```

Create the following sub procedures:

```
Public Class WebForm1
    Inherits System.Web.UI.Page
    Dim mySQLConnection As New SqlConnection("Data Source=LocalHost;" & _
          "initial catalog=Wrox;User ID=sa;PWD=")
    Protected WithEvents MyDataList As System.Web.UI.WebControls.DataList
    Sub Bind_MyDataList()
        Dim mySQLConnection As New SqlConnection("Data Source=LocalHost;" & _
            "initial catalog=Wrox;User ID=sa;PWD=")
        Dim mySqlCommand As New SqlCommand("SELECT * FROM Dogs", mySQLConnection)
        mySQLConnection.Open()

        MyDataList.DataSource = mySqlCommand.ExecuteReader
        MyDataList.DataBind()
        mySQLConnection.Close()
    End Sub

    Sub MyDataList_Edit(ByVal MyObject As Object, ByVal e As
        DataListCommandEventArgs)
        MyDataList.EditItemIndex = e.Item.ItemIndex
        Bind_MyDataList()
    End Sub

    Sub MyDataList_Cancel(ByVal MyObject As Object, ByVal e As _
        DataListCommandEventArgs)
        MyDataList.EditItemIndex = -1
        Bind_MyDataList()
    End Sub

    Sub MyDataList_Update(ByVal MyObject As Object, ByVal e As _
        DataListCommandEventArgs)
        Dim mySQLConnection As New SqlConnection("Data Source=LocalHost;" & _
            "initial catalog=Wrox;User ID=sa;PWD=")
        Dim mySQLString As String
        Dim mySqlCommand As New SqlCommand()
        mySQLString = "UPDATE Dogs SET Breed=@breed,FoodPref=@FoodPref WHERE " & _
                      "DogID=@DogID"

        mySqlCommand = New SqlCommand(mySQLString, mySQLConnection)
```

```
        With mySqlCommand
            .Parameters.Add(New SqlParameter("@breed", SqlDbType.Char, 20))
            .Parameters("@breed").Value = CType(e.Item.FindControl("breed"), _
                                                TextBox).Text

            .Parameters.Add(New SqlParameter("@FoodPref", SqlDbType.Int))
            .Parameters("@FoodPref").Value = _
                            CType(e.Item.FindControl("FoodPref"), TextBox).Text

            .Parameters.Add(New SqlParameter("@DogID", SqlDbType.VarChar, 5))
            .Parameters("@DogID").Value = _
                            MyDataList.DataKeys.Item(e.Item.ItemIndex)
        End With

        mySQLConnection.Open()
        mySqlCommand.ExecuteNonQuery()

        mySQLConnection.Close()
        MyDataList.EditItemIndex = -1
        Bind_MyDataList()
    End Sub

#Region " Web Form Designer Generated Code "
```

OK, you are now ready to run the project. When the form opens, click one of the edit links. Two text boxes appear allowing the user to change the breed and/or food preference.

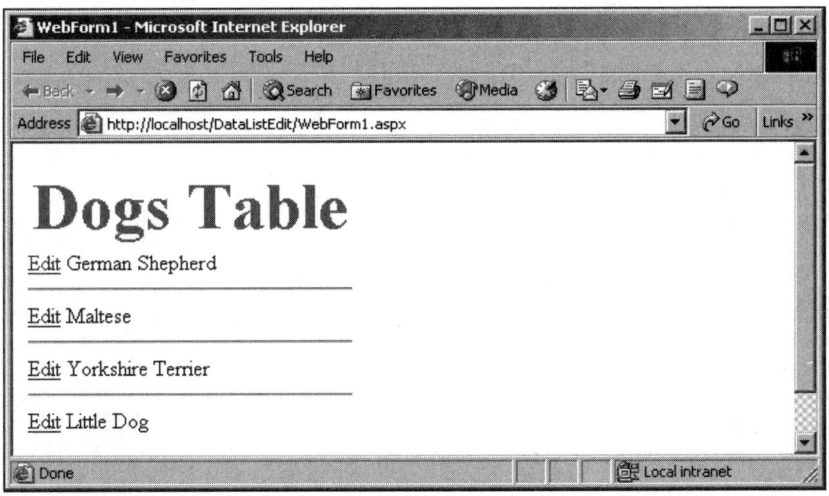

After modifying your changes, select either **Update** to post the new data to SQL Server or select **Cancel** to return to the original form.

Because we are updating one row at a time, we are letting SQL Server handle these transactions for us. In other words, SQL Server is automatically committing each update on an individual basis without having to specify a `COMMIT` statement. At the same time, if an error occurs with the update, SQL Server will automatically abort and roll back the transaction for us. You may recall from the last chapter that these types of transactions are referred to as automatic transactions.

At this point, you may be concerned that there is no form validation. Don't worry, you will learn about ASP.NET's new validation controls later in this chapter. In the meantime, be sure to enter only correct data!

The HTML portion for the DataList is very similar to the Repeater control as both utilize templates to display the data. In other words, the DataList like the Repeater Control lacks a default display, thus they both require the ItemTemplate as a minimum. The major difference between these two controls is the Repeater can only display data, while the DataList can allow for data manipulation. When manipulating data via DataList, we are in fact executing automatic transactions where each update constitutes an individual transaction.

The DataList utilizes event bubbling in order to allow us to edit, update, and cancel our data manipulations. **Event bubbling** can be described as server controls that are capable of containing other controls as children of the parent control. What this means is that children controls are not capable of raising their own events. However, you can wrap an event using the container and then pass it as a Command event.

The DataList provides five events that can be used, although this project only utilizes three methods: CancelCommand(), EditCommand(), and UpdateCommand(), that are associated with sub procedures in our Visual Basic .NET code. The other two events are ItemCommand and DeleteCommand. Perhaps obvious by, the ItemCommand raises an event that is not captured by any of the other four methods: EditCommand(), UpdateCommand(), CancelCommand(), or DeleteCommand().

These events are raised by events from the DataList control. For example, the EditCommand event is raised, which utilizes a property set to Edit:

```
<asp:datalist id="MyDataList" Runat="server"
   onEditCommand="MyDataList_Edit"
   onUpdateCommand="MyDataList_Update"
   onCancelCommand="MyDataList_Cancel"
   onDataKeyfield="DogID" RepeatDirection="Vertical" >
```

Jumping to our Visual Basic .NET code, we associate the EditCommand with the sub procedure MyDataList_Edit:

```
Sub MyDataList_Edit(ByVal MyObject As Object, ByVal e As DataListCommandEventArgs)
  MyDataList.EditItemIndex = e.Item.ItemIndex
  Bind_MyDataList()
End Sub
```

When the user selects the Edit link from their browser, a Click event is first initiated. It is the Click event that raises the Command event within the DataList control, which in turn raises the associated sub procedure for MyDataList_Edit.

Note that the associated Edit link resides within the ItemTemplate:

```
<ItemTemplate>
<asp:LinkButton text="Edit" CommandName="Edit" Runat="server" />
```

Now that we have jumped around between HTML and Visual Basic .NET code and looked at how the associated DataList events and sub procedures are utilized, let's go back to the beginning of our Visual Basic .NET code for a more compete explanation.

Under the Page_Load() method, we use the page property IsPostBack. Every time we click a link such as the Edit, Update, or Cancel from the DataList, a post is triggered, resulting in a round trip to the server and back to the browser. As a result of this round trip, the Page_Load() method executes for each trip. If you recall our earlier discussion about ViewState, it is inefficient to keep sending data back and forth to the server. Additionally, executing code repeatedly on an unneeded basis is also tough on resources. By utilizing the IsPostBack property, we can ensure that code is not re-executed after the first time it has been loaded as shown below:

```
If Not Page.IsPostBack Then
    Bind_MyDataList()
End If
```

Instead of placing our database code and binding instructions within the Page_Load(), we simply place it in a separate routine. This way we can call it only during the initial page load or by calling it explicitly when we need to re-execute this code as we do within our other sub procedures.

```
    Sub Bind_MyDataList()
        Dim mySQLConnection As New SqlConnection("Data Source=LocalHost;" & _
            "initial catalog=Wrox;User ID=sa;PWD=")
        Dim mySqlCommand As New SqlCommand("SELECT * FROM Dogs", mySQLConnection)
        mySQLConnection.Open()

        MyDataList.DataSource = mySqlCommand.ExecuteReader
        MyDataList.DataBind()
        mySQLConnection.Close()
    End Sub
```

In our example, we make use of the IsPostBack property because we need to call the Bind_MyDataList() every time we raise an event. If we did not check for the IsPostBack condition, we would end up executing the Bind_MyDataList() method twice for every round trip made. Obviously this is something we don't want happening.

One more important sub procedure to look at is MyDataList_Update as this procedure is complex compared to the other sub procedures. Although complex, it should look familiar to you, as we make use of SQL parameters as previously done in the last chapter.

First we start off with a new SQLConnection to SQL Server:

```
    Sub MyDataList_Update(ByVal MyObject As Object, ByVal e As _
        DataListCommandEventArgs)
        Dim mySQLConnection As New SqlConnection("Data Source=LocalHost;" & _
            "initial catalog=Wrox;User ID=sa;PWD=")
```

In order to execute an update, we need to use an instance of the SQLCommand class. Notice (below) we are using parameters for DogID, Breed, and FoodPref in the SQL statement:

```
Dim mySQLString As String
Dim mySqlCommand As New SqlCommand()
mySQLString = "UPDATE Dogs SET Breed=@breed,FoodPref=@FoodPref WHERE " & _
              "DogID=@DogID"
mySqlCommand = New SqlCommand(mySQLString, mySQLConnection)
```

We simply pass parameters from the textboxes to our SQL statement. We make use of the `FindControl` method to retrieve the values from the corresponding textboxes. For example, data from the textbox `breed` (see HTML code) and the textbox `FoodPref`, is retrieved by the `FindControl` method and passed to the respective parameters `@breed` and `@FoodPref`.

```
      With mySqlCommand
          .Parameters.Add(New SqlParameter("@breed", SqlDbType.Char, 20))
          .Parameters("@breed").Value = CType(e.Item.FindControl("breed"), _
                                                              TextBox).Text

          .Parameters.Add(New SqlParameter("@FoodPref", SqlDbType.Int))
          .Parameters("@FoodPref").Value = _
                         CType(e.Item.FindControl("FoodPref"), TextBox).Text
```

In order to correctly identify the database row to be updated, you need to retrieve the primary key from the record you want to update. Thus you need to retrieve the primary key (`DogID`) for the record to update from the `DataKeys` collection.

```
          .Parameters.Add(New SqlParameter("@DogID", SqlDbType.VarChar, 5))
          .Parameters("@DogID").Value = _
                         MyDataList.DataKeys.Item(e.Item.ItemIndex)
      End With
```

The final step is to open the SQL connection and execute our `UPDATE` statement:

```
      mySQLConnection.Open()
      mySqlCommand.ExecuteNonQuery()

      mySQLConnection.Close()
      MyDataList.EditItemIndex = -1
      Bind_MyDataList()
  End Sub
```

DataGrid Control

Unlike the `DataList` control, the `DataGrid` control displays data within columns as well as allowing for the manipulation of data. This is very similar to the `DataGrid` control in previous versions of Visual Basic, except we have a very easy way to implement it within a Web Form, in addtion to some handy enhancements. For example, we can easily validate data being entered by the user. I will talk more about this shortly.

The `DataGrid` provides the most flexibility, as well as the most functionality, out of the three data controls. Although the `DataGrid` can utilize each of the templates used with the `Repeater` and `DataList` for formatting data, the `DataGrid` has a default display for data. To best understand the major features, let's jump into another project.

Manipulating Data with the DataGrid

Start a new ASP.NET Web Application and name the project DataGridEdit. Again, let's start by entering HTML code (between the form tags) first:

```
...
<form id="Form1" method="post" runat="server">
<asp:DataGrid ID="MyDataGrid" AutoGenerateColumns="False"
   GridLines="Both" HeaderStyle-BackColor="LightBlue"
   AlternatingItemStyle-BackColor="LightYellow"
   DataKeyField="DogID"
   onEditCommand="MyDataGrid_Edit"
   onCancelCommand="MyDataGrid_Cancel"
   onUpdateCommand="MyDataGrid_Update"
   Runat="server">

  <Columns>
    <asp:EditCommandColumn EditText="Edit" CancelText="Cancel"
                           UpdateText="Update" />
    <asp:BoundColumn HeaderText="Dog ID" DataField="DogID" ReadOnly="True" />
    <asp:BoundColumn HeaderText="Breed of Dog" DataField="Breed" />
    <asp:BoundColumn HeaderText="Food Preference" DataField="FoodPref" />
    <asp:BoundColumn HeaderText="Food Description" DataField="FoodDesc"
                     ReadOnly="True"/>
  </Columns>
</asp:DataGrid>
</form>
```

Add the following Visual Basic .NET namespaces to the declarations:

```
Imports System.Data
Imports System.Data.SqlClient
```

Locate the `Page_Load()` method and enter the following:

```
    Private Sub Page_Load(ByVal sender As System.Object, ByVal e As
        System.EventArgs) Handles MyBase.Load
        'Put user code to initialize the page here
        If Not Page.IsPostBack Then
            Bind_MyDataGrid()
        End If
    End Sub
```

Add your connection string under the public class `WebForm1`:

```
Public Class WebForm1
    Inherits System.Web.UI.Page
    Protected WithEvents MyDataGrid As System.Web.UI.WebControls.DataGrid
    Dim mySQLConnection As New SqlConnection("Data Source=LocalHost;" & _
          "initial catalog=Wrox;User ID=sa;PWD=")
```

```
#Region " Web Form Designer Generated Code "
...
```

Create the following sub procedures within the class:

```
...
  "initial catalog=Wrox;User ID=sa;PWD=")

Sub Bind_MyDataGrid()
    Dim mySQLConnection As New SqlConnection("Data Source=LocalHost;" & _
        "initial catalog=Wrox;User ID=sa;PWD=")
    Dim mySqlCommand As New SqlCommand("SELECT DogID,Breed,FoodPref,FoodDesc "
        & _
        "FROM Dogs,Food WHERE FoodPref=FoodID", mySQLConnection)
    mySQLConnection.Open()
    MyDataGrid.DataSource = mySqlCommand.ExecuteReader
    MyDataGrid.DataBind()
    mySQLConnection.Close()
End Sub

Sub MyDataGrid_Edit(ByVal MyObject As Object, ByVal e As
    DataGridCommandEventArgs)
    MyDataGrid.EditItemIndex = e.Item.ItemIndex
    Bind_MyDataGrid()
End Sub

Sub MyDataGrid_Cancel(ByVal MyObject As Object, ByVal e As _
    DataGridCommandEventArgs)
    MyDataGrid.EditItemIndex = -1
    Bind_MyDataGrid()
End Sub

Sub MyDataGrid_Update(ByVal MyObject As Object, ByVal e As _
    DataGridCommandEventArgs)

    Dim Breed As TextBox
    Dim FoodPref As TextBox
    Breed = e.Item.Cells(2).Controls(0)
    FoodPref = e.Item.Cells(3).Controls(0)


    Dim mySQLString As String
    Dim mySqlCommand As New SqlCommand()
    mySQLString = "UPDATE Dogs SET Breed=@breed,FoodPref=@FoodPref WHERE " & _
                  "DogID=@DogID"

    mySqlCommand = New SqlCommand(mySQLString, mySQLConnection)
    mySqlCommand.Parameters.Add(New SqlParameter("@Breed", SqlDbType.Char,
        20))
    mySqlCommand.Parameters("@Breed").Value = Breed.Text

    mySqlCommand.Parameters.Add(New SqlParameter("@FoodPref", SqlDbType.Int))
    mySqlCommand.Parameters("@FoodPref").Value = FoodPref.Text
```

```
        mySqlCommand.Parameters.Add(New SqlParameter("@DogID", SqlDbType.VarChar,
            5))
        mySqlCommand.Parameters("@DogID").Value = _
                    MyDataGrid.DataKeys.Item(e.Item.ItemIndex)

        mySQLConnection.Open()
        mySqlCommand.ExecuteNonQuery()

        mySQLConnection.Close()
        MyDataGrid.EditItemIndex = -1
        Bind_MyDataGrid()
    End Sub
```

```
#Region " Web Form Designer Generated Code "
...
```

Build and start the application. When the form opens, click one of the edit links. Two textboxes appear allowing the user to change the breed and/or food preference. Try changing the food description. After clicking the update, notice that the Food Description also reflects the new changes:

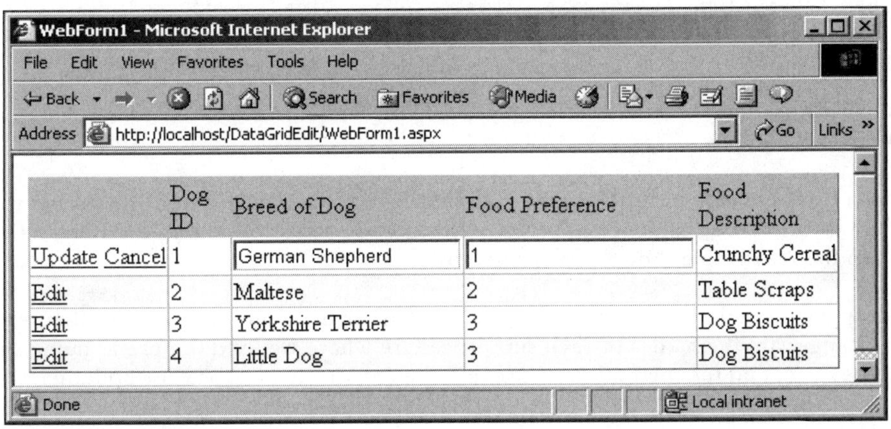

The Visual Basic .NET code is virtually the same as with the `DataList`. We utilize sub procedures to correspond with the `DataGrid`'s `Command` events. Like the `DataList`, the `DataGrid` is capable of using the same five events: `ItemCommand` (not used in this project), `EditCommand`, `UpdateCommand`, `DeleteCommand` (not used in this project), and the `CancelCommand`.

Before moving to the next block of code, notice the `AutoGenerateColumns="False"`.

```
<asp:DataGrid ID="MyDataGrid" AutoGenerateColumns="False"
```

I previously mentioned that the `DataGrid`, by default, will display columns for us. However, for our project, we want to have control over what we display, so we need to override the default. Thus we set the `AutoGenerateColumns` to `False`.

Also notice we can specify to have our header row as well as data rows display alternating colors by using the HeaderStyle-BackColor (for the header) and AlternatingItemStyle (for data rows.) This is one method to add a little cosmetics to the data layout, as well as help make rows easier to read:

```
GridLines="Both"
HeaderStyle-BackColor="LightBlue"
AlternatingItemStyle-BackColor="LightYellow"
DataKeyField="DogID"
onEditCommand="MyDataGrid_Edit"
onCancelCommand="MyDataGrid_Cancel"
onUpdateCommand="MyDataGrid_Update"
Runat="server">
```

You can add virtually any column you want to the DataGrid, even columns from another table. As a matter of fact, this is just what we did in this project. Below is the code where we used the Columns collection:

```
  <Columns>
    <asp:EditCommandColumn EditText="Edit" CancelText="Cancel"
         UpdateText="Update" />
    <asp:BoundColumn HeaderText="Dog ID" DataField="DogID" ReadOnly="True" />
    <asp:BoundColumn HeaderText="Breed of Dog" DataField="Breed" />
    <asp:BoundColumn HeaderText="Food Preference" DataField="FoodPref" />
    <asp:BoundColumn HeaderText="Food Description" DataField="FoodDesc"
         ReadOnly="True" />
  </Columns>
</asp:DataGrid>
```

As you can see, we have bound each of the columns we want to display. In this case, we want to show all the columns for the Dog table (DogID, Breed, and FoodPref), as well as the related field to FoodPref in the Food table (Food Description).

As previously mentioned, the Visual Basic .NET code is virtually the same as with the DataList. The two major changes are the names of each sub procedure where we used the prefix name DataGrid in place of DataList, and the method for retrieving the data from a textbox for updating:

```
Sub MyDataGrid_Update(ByVal MyObject As Object, ByVal e As _
    DataGridCommandEventArgs)

    Dim Breed As TextBox
    Dim FoodPref As TextBox
    Breed = e.Item.Cells(2).Controls(0)
    FoodPref = e.Item.Cells(3).Controls(0)
```

In the above code snippet notice the statement: Breed=e.Item.Cells(2).Controls(0). What we are doing here is accessing the cells collection from the items that are contained in the DataGridCommandEventArgs object. By specifying the cell index being edited, we can pass the information from the textbox to the variable, in this case the variable breed. Let's look at this a little more closely as this may come across as confusing.

If you look at the DataGrid, you see that the first column displays the Edit links, the second column displays the DogID, the third displays the breed of dog, fourth displays food preference, and the fifth column displays the food description. The way this works is that data from the textbox Breed is retrieved from the third cell of the DataGrid, however, the cell index is actually 2, while the fourth column reflecting FoodPref has a cell index of 3.

Now that you have a good grasp for using the Repeater, DataList, and DataGrid controls, let's move on and learn how we can validate user input.

Validating User Input

If someone were to ask me what is the most tedious task there is when developing web applications relying on user data, I would say validating user input. But thanks to ASP.NET, the tedious task has greatly been reduced through **ASP.NET validation controls**. The provided validation controls make available to the application developer a set of common constraints. For example, using the RangeValidator control, we can verify that a certain value entered is within the range 1 through 10.

Aside from the common validation controls, there is a custom-defined control (CustomValidator) that allows the application developer to create their own validation logic.

Another cool feature about the common and custom validator controls is that you can tailor the error messages that are displayed to the user.

The following table shows the type of validation controls available with ASP.NET:

Control Type	Description
<ASP:CompareValidator>	This validator allows you to compare different inputs on the same page. For example, if you have an input field for the first name and another input field for the last name, you can compare the two fields to ensure they have different data. In other words, you could prevent a user from entering their first name in both fields.
<ASP:CustomValidator>	When the above validating controls are not satisfactory for your validation needs, you can create your own custom validation controls using the CustomValidator control. Essentially, the CustomValidator serves as an empty container for your custom logic.
<ASP:RangeValidator>	Used to require a specific range to be entered. For example, if the range is set to allow numbers 1-3, only those numbers will be accepted. At the same time, this example disallows any non-numeric items as well. This saves you a lot of extra coding.

Control Type	Description
<ASP:RegularExpressionValidator>	Used to validate complex strings and enforce formats to be strictly followed. For example, you can use this validator to force a phone number to be entered using only three characters for the prefix, and four characters for the body.
<ASP:RequiredFieldValidator>	Used to require input from the user.
<ASP:ValidationSummary>	This control is used to output a summary of all validation errors occurring on a page.

When recording user data, particularly when the user needs to supply input for a parameter such as to a stored procedure, it is essential that we make sure data is entered and is entered correctly. Let's look in detail to see how the different ASP.NET validating controls work:

RequiredFieldValidator

Before we worry about whether the correct data is inputted by the user, we need to make sure that data is in fact entered. In other words, we need an easy way to verify if something has been entered into a control such as a textbox. For example, suppose we have a Web Form that requires input for the user's phone number. By using the `<ASP:RequiredFieldValidator>`, we can ensure that user input for phone number (`txtPhone`) is entered before sending to the database:

Note that the following example is a rudementery in scope for implementing the `RequiredFieldValidator`. In applications supporting globalizaiton and localization, such strings would need to be internationalized.

```
<input type="text" id="txtOfficePhone" size="12" runat="server">

<asp:RequiredFieldValidator runat="server" id="reqOfficePhone"
     ControlToValidate="txtOfficePhone"
     Display="Dynamic">
ErrorMessage="Please enter your Office Phone Number." />
```

Note that an alternate way of writing validation is to sandwich the error message between the beginning and ending validator tags:

```
<input type="text" id="txtOfficePhone" size="12" runat="server">

<asp:RequiredFieldValidator runat="server" id="reqOfficePhone"
     ControlToValidate="txtOfficePhone"
     Display="Dynamic">
Please enter your Office Phone Number
</asp:RequiredFieldValidator>
```

CompareValidator

Now that we know something will be entered into the phone number textbox, we can utilize other validation controls such as the `CompareValidator`. For example, with the `CompareValidator`, you can validate to ensure two fields on the Web Form are identical, or you can validate to ensure that both fields are different. Suppose we have two fields on the Web Form, one for work phone and the other for home phone. We can validate against both fields to check that both phone numbers are the same (which doesn't make much sense in this example) or we can validate against both numbers to make sure they are different. The following example shows how to validate that both Web Form fields are different:

```
<input type="text" id="txtOfficePhone" size="12" runat="server">
<input type="text" id="txtHomePhone" size="12" runat="server">

<asp:ComparValidator runat="server" id="CompEquality"
   ControlToValidate="txtOfficePhone"
   ControlToCompare="txtHomePhone"
   Type="string"
   operator="NotEqual"
   ErrorMessage="Office Phone and WorkPhone cannot be the same." />
```

Notice that this example uses `operator="NotEqual"`. If we wanted to check that both Web Form fields were the same, all you need to do is change `NotEqual` with `Equal`:

```
Operator="Equal"
```

We have just looked at the `NotEqual` and `Equal` operators. Are there more operators available for this control? As a matter of fact, there are a total of seven operators (including `NotEqual` and `Equal`) that can be utilized:

- `Equal`
- `NotEqual`
- `GreaterThan`
- `GreaterThanEqual`
- `LessThan`
- `LessThanEqual`
- `DataTypeCheck`

The `DataTypeCheck` is used to validate whether data is of a specific type such as an integer, string, etc.

Just as there are several operators for us to utilize, there are also several types for us to use:

- `Date`
- `String`
- `Integer`
- `Double`
- `Currency`

RangeValidator

Another handy validator is called the RangeValidator. With the RangeValidator, you can check to verify data falls within certain ranges. Although this validator may not be usable with our phone number example, it is great for other situations such as validating an age category. For example, suppose you have a Web Form that breaks down age by category. Category 1 covers ages 1-15 years of age. Category 2 covers ages 16-50 and category 3 covers ages 51 and above.

The following code snippet shows how we can require it to accept values ranging from 1-15. The first line defines our textbox with the id = textAgeCatagory1:

```
<input type="text" id="txtAgeCatagory1" size="12" runat="server">
```

Next, we specify txtAgeCatagory1 for the ControlToValidate. Additionally, we specify the type and set the minimum and maximum values as shown below:

```
<asp:RangeValidator runat="server" id="RangeAgeCat1"
   ControlToValidate="txtAgeCategory1"
   MinimumValue="1" MaximumValue="15"
   Type="Interger"
   ErrorMessage="Age for this category must range between 1 and 15" />
```

RegularExpressionValidator

By utilizing the RegularExpressionValidator, you can validate complex text (string) values. Going back to our phone number example, we can validate the prefix and the body of the phone number:

```
<asp:RegularExpressionValidator runat="server"
    ControlToValidate="tblPhone"
     ValidationExpression=[0-9]{3}-[0-9]{4}
     ErrorMessage="That is not a valid phone" />
```

CustomValidator

There is no doubt that the previous validation controls do a great job for most common types of input validation. Nevertheless, there will be times when these controls just can't check what we need. This is where the CustomValidator comes into play. With the CustomValidator, you are provided with an empty container, the framework. It is up to you to design the routine needed to meet your requirements. In a way, designing your own custom routine is similar to traditional ASP page validation, except you have a container to house your code. For example, let's go back to our phone number example:

The first block of code shown below is our CustomValidator. Here we call the sub procedure MyCustomPhoneValidator to check to see if the phone number entered from the textbox named textPhoneNumber is 12 digits long:

```
<asp:CustomValidator runat="server"
   OnServerValidate="MyCustomPhoneValidator"
   Display="Dynamic"
   ControltoValidate="textPhoneNumber"
   ErrorMessage="The phone number must be 12 digits long" />
```

If the phone number is less than 12 digits or greater than 12 digits, an error is raised telling the user The phone number must be 12 digits long:

```
Sub MyCustomPhoneValidator(MyObject as Object, arg as ServerValidateEventArgs)
   If len(args.Value) <>12 then
      args.IsValid = False
   Else
      Args.IsValid = True
   End IfEnd Sub
```

Using Validation with the DataGrid

For our last project in this chapter, let's add a few validation controls so we can check user input within a bound DataGrid. When using the validation controls, we need to change the way we originally bound information to the DataGrid. As a result, you will want to create a new ASP.NET Web application and enter the following HTML code between the form tags:

```
...
<form id="Form1" method="post" runat="server">
  <asp:DataGrid ID="MyDataGrid" width="200" cellpadding="3"
      AutoGenerateColumns="False" GridLines="Both" HeaderStyle-
      BackColor="LightBlue" AlternatingItemStyle-BackColor="LightYellow"
      DataKeyField="DogID" OnEditCommand="MyDataGrid_Edit"
      OnCancelCommand="MyDataGrid_Cancel" OnUpdateCommand="MyDataGrid_Update"
      Runat="server">

    <Columns>
      <asp:EditCommandColumn EditText="Edit" CancelText="Cancel"
          UpdateText="Update" />
        <asp:TemplateColumn HeaderText='Dog ID <%#DataField="DogID"%>'>
          <ItemTemplate>
            <%# Container.DataItem( "DogID" )%>
          </ItemTemplate>
        </asp:TemplateColumn>
        <asp:TemplateColumn HeaderText='Breed <%#DataField="Breed"%>'>
          <ItemTemplate>
            <%# Container.DataItem( "Breed" )%>
          </ItemTemplate>
          <EditItemTemplate>
            <asp:TextBox ID="Breed" Text='<%# Container.DataItem("Breed")%>'
                Runat="server" />
            <asp:RequiredFieldValidator ControlToValidate="Breed"
                Display="Dynamic" Runat="server"   ID="Requiredfieldvalidator1">
                  Breed requires an entry.
            </asp:RequiredFieldValidator>
          </EditItemTemplate>
        </asp:TemplateColumn>
        <asp:TemplateColumn HeaderText='Food Pref <%#DataField="FoodPref"%>'>
          <ItemTemplate>
            <%# Container.DataItem( "FoodPref" )%>
          </ItemTemplate>
          <EditItemTemplate>
```

```
            <asp:TextBox ID="FoodPref" Text='<%# Container.DataItem("FoodPref")%>'
                Runat="server" />
            <asp:RequiredFieldValidator ControlToValidate="FoodPref"
                Display="Dynamic" Runat="server" ID="Requiredfieldvalidator2">
                  Food Pref requires an entry.
            </asp:RequiredFieldValidator>
            <asp:RangeValidator ControlToValidate="FoodPref" Display="Dynamic"
                MinimumValue="1" MaximumValue="6" Runat="server"
                ID="RequiredRangeValidator1">
                  Food Pref requires an entry between 1-6.
            </asp:RangeValidator>
          </EditItemTemplate>
        </asp:TemplateColumn>
        <asp:TemplateColumn HeaderText='Food Description
            <%#DataField="FoodDesc"%>'>
          <ItemTemplate>
            <%# Container.DataItem( "FoodDesc" )%>
          </ItemTemplate>
        </asp:TemplateColumn>
      </Columns>
    </asp:DataGrid>
```

Add the following Visual Basic .NET code to the declarations:

```
Imports System.Data
Imports System.Data.SqlClient
```

Locate the `Page_Load()` method and enter the following:

```
    Private Sub Page_Load(ByVal sender As System.Object, ByVal e As
        System.EventArgs) Handles MyBase.Load
        'Put user code to initialize the page here
        If Not Page.IsPostBack Then
            Bind_MyDataGrid()
        End If
    End Sub
```

Create the following sub procedures:

```
Public Class WebForm1
    Inherits System.Web.UI.Page
    Protected WithEvents MyDataGrid As System.Web.UI.WebControls.DataGrid
    Sub Bind_MyDataGrid()
        Dim mySQLConnection As New SqlConnection("Data Source=LocalHost;" & _
            "initial catalog=Wrox;User ID=sa;PWD=")

        Dim mySqlCommand As New SqlCommand("SELECT DogID,Breed,FoodPref,FoodDesc "
            & _
            "FROM Dogs,Food WHERE FoodID=FoodPref", mySQLConnection)
        mySQLConnection.Open()
        MyDataGrid.DataSource = mySqlCommand.ExecuteReader
        MyDataGrid.DataBind()
```

```
        mySQLConnection.Close()
    End Sub

    Sub MyDataGrid_Edit(ByVal MyObject As Object, ByVal e As
        DataGridCommandEventArgs)
        MyDataGrid.EditItemIndex = e.Item.ItemIndex
        Bind_MyDataGrid()
    End Sub

    Sub MyDataGrid_Cancel(ByVal MyObject As Object, ByVal e As _
        DataGridCommandEventArgs)
        MyDataGrid.EditItemIndex = -1
        Bind_MyDataGrid()
    End Sub

    Sub MyDataGrid_Update(ByVal MyObject As Object, ByVal e As _
        DataGridCommandEventArgs)

        Dim Breed As TextBox
        Dim FoodPref As TextBox
        Breed = e.Item.FindControl("Breed")
        FoodPref = e.Item.FindControl("FoodPref")

        Dim mySQLConnection As New SqlConnection("Data Source=LocalHost;" & _
            "initial catalog=Wrox;User ID=sa;PWD=")
        Dim mySQLString As String
        Dim mySqlCommand As New SqlCommand()
        mySQLString = "UPDATE Dogs SET Breed=@breed,FoodPref=@FoodPref WHERE " & _
                      "DogID=@DogID"

        mySqlCommand = New SqlCommand(mySQLString, mySQLConnection)
        mySqlCommand.Parameters.Add(New SqlParameter("@Breed", SqlDbType.Char,
            20))
        mySqlCommand.Parameters("@Breed").Value = Breed.Text

        mySqlCommand.Parameters.Add(New SqlParameter("@FoodPref", SqlDbType.Int))
        mySqlCommand.Parameters("@FoodPref").Value = FoodPref.Text

        mySqlCommand.Parameters.Add(New SqlParameter("@DogID", SqlDbType.VarChar,
            5))
        mySqlCommand.Parameters("@DogID").Value = _
                     MyDataGrid.DataKeys.Item(e.Item.ItemIndex)

        mySQLConnection.Open()
        mySqlCommand.ExecuteNonQuery()

        mySQLConnection.Close()
        MyDataGrid.EditItemIndex = -1
        Bind_MyDataGrid()
    End Sub
```

Start the project. When the form opens, click one of the Edit links. Try entering a blank (NULL) into one of the textboxes. Also try entering either a character or a number out of the range from 1 to 6:

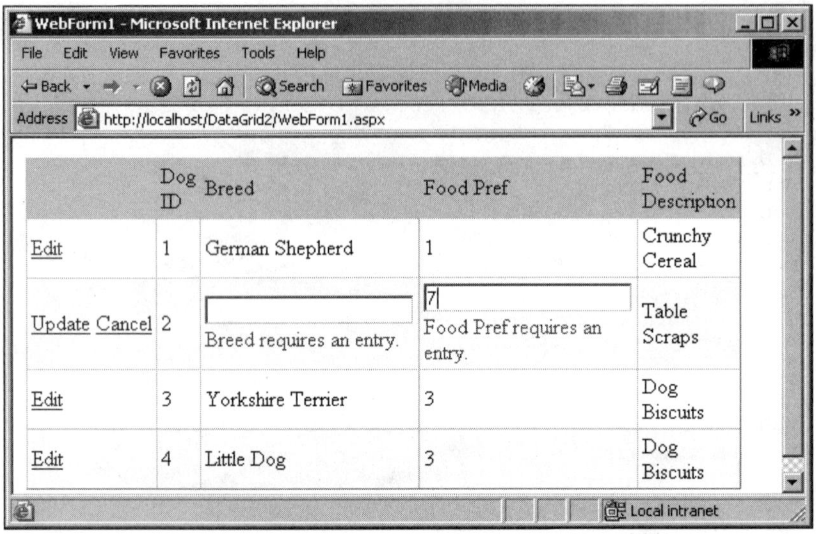

You may be surprised to see that the way we used the DataGrid in this project is considerably different from the DataGrid in the previous project. The good news is the Visual Basic .NET code is the same as in the other DataGrid project. However, the HTML in this project is considerably different. This is because we need to use validation controls to check user input. However, if you recall the last project, we utilized BoundColumn. The problem with using BoundColumn is the inability to slip in validation controls for these columns. However, we have no problem adding one or more validation controls if we don't use BoundColumn, but instead use TemplateColumn. Furthermore, you can include the ItemTemplate as well as the EditItemTemplate within the TemplateColumn. Thus we can achieve the full flexibility of an editable DataGrid as well as user validation. Let's briefly look at what we did:

Looking at the first block of code, you can see how we utilized the TemplateColumn.

First we specified our columns and headers for DogID and Breed as shown:

```
<asp:TemplateColumn HeaderText='Dog ID <%#DataField="DogID"%>'>
  <ItemTemplate>
    <%# Container.DataItem( "DogID" )%>
  </ItemTemplate>
</asp:TemplateColumn>
<asp:TemplateColumn HeaderText='Breed <%#DataField="Breed"%>'>
  <ItemTemplate>
    <%# Container.DataItem( "Breed" )%>
  </ItemTemplate>
```

Next we use the EditItemTemplate to create our textbox. The following code snippet shows this for Breed:

```
  <EditItemTemplate>
    <asp:TextBox ID="Breed" Text='<%# Container.DataItem("Breed")%>'
        Runat="server" />
    <asp:RequiredFieldValidator ControlToValidate="Breed" Display="Dynamic"
        Runat="server" ID="Requiredfieldvalidator1">
```

We are only checking to see if there is anything entered into the breed textbox. This is accomplished by using the RequiredFieldValidator:

```
            <asp:RequiredFieldValidator ControlToValidate="Breed"
                Display="Dynamic" Runat="server"   ID="Requiredfieldvalidator1">
                  Breed requires an entry.
            </asp:RequiredFieldValidator>
          </EditItemTemplate>
        </asp:TemplateColumn>
```

One important thing to understand is that typically templates can be entered in any order, however, for readability and continuity it makes sense to keep things in an easy to read order. Now that we have specified our validation for the textbox Breed, we move on to the next column Food Pref. First we specify the column and header information and then we introduce two validation controls for the textbox FoodPref. In the following code snip you can see that we are validating for an empty textbox using the RequiredFieldValidator and validating a range between 1-6 using the RangeValidator:

```
        <asp:TemplateColumn HeaderText='Food Pref <%#DataField="FoodPref"%>'>
          <ItemTemplate>
            <%# Container.DataItem( "FoodPref" )%>
          </ItemTemplate>
          <EditItemTemplate>
            <asp:TextBox ID="FoodPref" Text='<%# Container.DataItem("FoodPref")%>'
                Runat="server" />
            <asp:RequiredFieldValidator ControlToValidate="FoodPref"
                Display="Dynamic" Runat="server" ID="Requiredfieldvalidator2">
                  Food Pref requires an entry.
            </asp:RequiredFieldValidator>
            <asp:RangeValidator ControlToValidate="FoodPref" Display="Dynamic"
                MinimumValue="1" MaximumValue="6" Runat="server"
                ID="RequiredRangeValidator1">
                  Food Pref requires an entry between 1-6.
            </asp:RangeValidator>
          </EditItemTemplate>
        </asp:TemplateColumn>
        <asp:TemplateColumn HeaderText='Food Description
             <%#DataField="FoodDesc"%>'>
          <ItemTemplate>
            <%# Container.DataItem( "FoodDesc" )%>
          </ItemTemplate>
        </asp:TemplateColumn>
      </Columns>
    </asp:DataGrid>
```

As a note about using both the RequiredFieldValidator and the RangeValidator in the manner we have in this project: If you try to send a NULL value by deleting any entries out of the FoodPref textbox, the RequiredFieldValidator will give you a message telling you that FoodPref requires an entry as you would expect. But what if we took out this validator entirely and then tried to send a NULL value? In this case the RangeValidator would prevent you from submitting the NULL because you have explicitly defined that only values 1-6 are acceptable. Thus instead of receiving a message that FoodPref requires an entry, the user would receive a message that FoodPref requires an entry between 1 and 6.

Turning Validation Off

Usually when I develop a web application, I like to add my validation controls last. The reason is having a lot of constraints in place while testing code logic (other than restraints) can become burdensome. For example, if I have a Web Form that has 15 fields and I am trying to work exclusively with one or two fields for the time being, having constraints in place prematurely means I have to enter proper data for the entire form, as opposed to concentrating only on the fields I am interested in. Of course, you can comment out your constraints, but there is an easier way. All we have to do is make use of the `Enabled` property. The `Enabled` property is Boolean in nature, and by default it is set to `True`, meaning the validation is on (it will run). To turn a validator off, all you need to do is to set the property to `False`.

```
<input type="text" id="txtOfficePhone" size="12" runat="server">

<asp:RequiredFieldValidator runat="server" id="reqOfficePhone"
     ControlToValidate="txtOfficePhone"
     Display="Dynamic">
     ErrorMessage="Please enter your Office Phone Number."
     Enabled="false" />
```

Validation and Browser Compatibility

Although the problem of older browser compatibility is beginning to diminish as more and more people are updating their browsers to later versions, there are still a few browsers around that cannot support ASP.NET's validation controls. There are two ways to handle this:

- Require the user to upgrade their browser to a conforming browser
- Enter a statement to ignore ASP.NET validation controls by setting the `ClientTarget` property directive to `downlevel`:

```
<%Page Language="VB" ClientTarget="downlevel" %>
```

Both choices have their pros and cons.

The first one is commonly done. Many web sites clearly state that "X" browser is required to view the site. However, forcing a user to comply with the web site places a large burden on them. Aside from possibly not wanting to use a different browser or browser version, it may be possible they cannot change browser, for reasons such as company restrictions.

The second one will indeed allow you to use an older browser to surf your web site, however, there is a potential danger. Setting the `ClientTarget` to `downlevel` disables DHTML events (such as client-side validation). However, by turning off DHTML events, it also means that other advanced features such as **CSS (Cascading Style Sheets)** and its attributes will not function. The good news is that the most recent browsers are capable of handling ASP.NET's validation controls. Such browsers include:

- IE Version 4.0 and later for Windows and Macintosh
- Netscape Navigator Version 4.0 and later for Windows and Macintosh
- Opera 3.61 (Beta) and later for Windows
- Opera 5.0 (Technology Preview 2.278) and later for Macintosh

Summary

This chapter was designed to show you how to display data from SQL Server and execute automatic transactions utilizing the `DataList` and the `DataGrid` controls.

We started this chapter with an introduction to ASP.NET and Web Forms. You learned how ASP.NET pages typically separate the visual HTML code from the logic code. You also learned how Web Forms are processed.

Next you learned about HTML server controls and web server controls. From there, we took a look at data binding and concentrated how to displaying data using the `Repeater`, the `DataList`, and the `DataGrid` controls. Here you learned about formatting data displays by utilizing various templates.

Finally, you learned about validation and how to implement it within web applications that require user input.

5

Web Services, SOAP, and Visual Basic .NET

There is a lot of hype over Web Services and with good reason. Web Services provide an easy way to connect numerous different applications, on different Operating Systems, and written in different languages through loose coupling as opposed to being tightly integrated within an application. Web Services are easy to create and implement. As a matter of fact, creating Web Services is no more complex than writing a typical .NET class. Furthermore, Web Services are based on open standards, thus they are more easily used across different computing platforms. And if these reasons are not good enough for you now, perhaps you will be swayed by the time you complete this chapter. Here you will learn how to create and implement Web Services, as well as learn to utilize them for transactions.

After completing this chapter, you should be able to answer the following questions:

- What are Web Services?
- How can Web Services be used in .NET applications?
- What types of security can be implemented when using Web Services?
- Can Web Services be transactional?
- What is SOAP and how does it fit in with Web Services?

Web Services – Introduction

A Web Service is a programmable entity that provides functionality through the use of Internet standards, such as XML or HTTP. Web Services are designed to perform some type of work over a computer network like the Internet. More specifically, for our purposes, Web Services are executable applications comprised of one or more .NET classes that provide functions and methods accessible via HTTP methods or by the Simple Object Access Protocol. A good way to describe Web Services is to correlate them with business components in an n-tier type/distributed environment.

Actually, Web Services are short for **XML Web Services**. The reason for this is that XML is the encoding mechanism Web Services use to communicate information.

Perhaps the most obvious characteristic of Web Services is that they do not have what we've come to expect from typical user interfaces. Instead, they provide the means for program-to-program communication across the network typically using HTTP or **SOAP** (the **Simple Object Access Protocol**) as the protocol. Because Web Services are based on open standards, cross platform interoperation can be more easily achieved. Furthermore, Web Services exhibit the "black box" features of components, where functionality is hidden behind an interface. The bottom line is that a Web Service exhibits many of the same features as COM components, except Web Services are easily accessible over the Internet via standardized protocols such as HTTP and SOAP. Additionally, Web Services are based on open standards whereas COM components are based on proprietary standards.

Another characteristic of Web Services is they are identified with `.asmx` for the file extension. Web Services are stored as plain text files, just as ASP.NET pages are.

Now that we know what Web Services are, the next question is why use Web Services? Some key reasons include:

- Web Services work like components in that they encapsulate data and business logic and abstract them into properties and methods.
- Web Services function in a cross-platform way and are capable of combining functionality, both directly and indirectly. They allow processes to work together with applications regardless of their location, and yet perform as if all actions were taking place on the local host. Web Services make distributed computing over the Internet an achievable reality.
- Web Services are easy to implement. A lot goes on in the background with Web Services. The good thing is that most of it is automatically taken care of for us. There is no doubt that understanding the working of Web Services is more complicated than using them.

Web Services are relatively new. They have only been around since the unveiling of the SOAP (version 1.0) toolkit, when Microsoft presented it to the public in the fall of 1999. This was an important step for the .NET technology because many of its concepts rely on SOAP for distributed communication. Microsoft revealed the SOAP protocol as open source. Furthermore, Microsoft submitted its SOAP specification to the W3C shortly after its release.

Because of SOAP's potential, IBM and Lotus quickly joined a group team with Microsoft to develop SOAP 1.1. Shortly after, SUN announced they would support SOAP. Today, there are many other companies that are supporting the SOAP protocol. You will learn about SOAP in detail later in this chapter. For now, it's important to understand that SOAP was originally developed to handle **Remote Procedure Calls** (**RPC**) over the Internet using HTTP and XML. RPC is one way to invoke and communicate with a process running on a different computer using messages binary-formatted according to vendor-specific standards. However, equally important, SOAP is not limited to RPCs.

Technically, Web Services are not strictly limited to .NET-enabled Windows-based servers. Using the SOAP toolkit with Visual Basic 6.0, it is reasonably easy to write a Web Service hosted on Windows NT 4 Server and Internet Information Server 4 (with Service Pack 6 installed). But don't limit your Web Services vision to just Windows platforms because Web Services can be written for and operate equally well on other platforms. This time it looks like we really do have an accepted cross platform technology. You could easily have a Windows Form-based application invoke services on a remote web server running Apache or have an GNOME-based application invoke a .NET-based Web Service. The differences between these systems are not important. Each client sends a SOAP message to request action of the Web Service, which does the actual work.

Web Service Protocols

There are three protocols that are available for accessing Web Services: HTTP-GET, HTTP-POST, and SOAP. Both HTTP-GET and HTTP-POST are primarily used for backwards compatibility with systems that cannot use SOAP directly.

By HTTP-GET and HTTP-POST, we mean that we can issue HTTP-GET or POST commands to the Web Server hosting the Web Service and get back an XML document for the response. For example, suppose we have a simple Web Service that takes two integers and returns the sum. If that Web Service were hosted on the local computer, you could use Internet Explorer or Netscape Navigator to browse to:

http://localhost/AddTwoIntegers/AddTwoIntegers.asmx/AddTwoIntegers?A=5&B=3

and get back a result like:

```
<?xml version="1.0" encoding="utf-8" ?>
<int xmlns="http://5954.tegels.org/">8</int>
```

As you probably already know, this is actually issuing an HTTP-GET command to the URL for this document. HTTP-GET commands send the parameters for a Web Service as part of the URL. HTTP-POSTs do not, however. HTTP-POST places the parameters for a request in the message body instead. As complicated as that sounds, it's very easy to demonstrate. Issuing an HTTP-POST request formatted as:

```
POST /AddTwoIntegers/AddTwoIntegers.asmx/AddTwoIntegers HTTP/1.1
Host: localhost
Content-Type: application/x-www-form-urlencoded
Content-Length: 7

A=5&B=3
```

results in the same XML response. HTTP-GET is supported because that is the most primitive, most supported HTTP method. HTTP-POST methods allow for considerably more data to be sent to the server, including a Web Service.

SOAP

In this section, we will provide a brief overview of SOAP so you understand how it helps Web Services function. There's much more to it than we'll cover here. If you need to know more about SOAP, we think you'll find the specification will answer all of your questions.

You can view the SOAP specification at http://www.w3.org/TR/SOAP/

It happens to be that the default communication protocol for Web Services is SOAP. Essentially, SOAP is a simple protocol used in distributed environments for exchanging messages. These messages are written in XML and are used to relay information as opposed to using an HTTP request message.

What makes SOAP exciting is that it is a widely accepted protocol capable of communicating with components over the Internet, regardless of the components' languages or platforms they reside on. This sounds a lot like the goals of COM/DCOM. The problem with COM is it is a proprietary technology.

DCOM (Distributed Component Object Model) is a mere extension to the Component Object Model (COM). In fact it's often described as "COM with a long wire". Typically, COM is thought of being implemented on the same machine, while DCOM can communicate across multiple network transport protocols and different operating systems.

SOAP is designed with simplicity in mind, as well as platform independence. As a result, SOAP does not exhibit many of the rich features found with DCOM. For example, DCOM manages object identity through the use of `CLSIDs` (Class IDs) and `ProgIDs` (Program IDs). This is a handy feature because it enables us to precisely identify the object to call. Additionally, the client manages the lifetime of a DCOM object through the `IUnknown` interface. Furthermore, DCOM is more efficient at transferring information. There is little doubt that XML can be very wordy. As a result, it can take a lot of XML data to convey a small amount of data.

SOAP on the other hand forfeits these rich features of DCOM in the name of simplicity and ease of use and greater interoperability. It does not rely on object identity to manipulate the lifetimes of objects. All SOAP will do is allow a call to timeout.

At first interpretation, SOAP may not seem very effective at all, as it does not have the efficiency or features of DCOM. However, the fact that SOAP is such a minimal protocol actually gives us some powerful features, such as the ease of use, and the ability to pass through firewalls. DCOM, as efficient and feature rich as it is, is difficult to configure and administer. Furthermore, DCOM does not easily pass through firewalls. Allowing DCOM to function through a firewall requires exposure of security-sensitive TCP/IP ports. This is commonly strongly discouraged by firewall administrators. SOAP, on the other hand, easily transverses firewalls because it is effectively well understood and reasonably secure HTTP. This allows us to use all of our favourite tools to shape and manage that network traffic as well.

Let's briefly recap the pros and cons of COM/DCOM and SOAP:

DCOM

Pros:

- Uses object identification
- Manages the lifetime of objects
- Better network performance – transmits binary data as opposed to wordy XML

Cons:

- Proprietary technology – not universally accepted
- Difficult to configure
- Difficult to administer
- Requires potentially risky ports to be opened in order to pass through firewalls

SOAP

Pros:

- Cross platform and cross language
- Easy to use
- Can pass through firewalls – does not require assigned ports

Cons:

- Lacks the rich features DCOM exhibits
- Not as efficient because SOAP requires wordy XML translations

> **A Web Service can be considered as an object's method that is exposed via a SOAP interface. Other SOAP enabled applications on the Web can take advantage of that message by calling this service.**

All in all, SOAP's ease of use and its universal acceptance make it the protocol of choice for communication with objects across the Internet.

How Web Services Work

Although Web Services are easy to work with, particularly when working with Visual Studio .NET IDE, there is a lot of activity that occurs behind the scenes. Let's take a look at how a typical Web Service behaves when it is called upon by a client:

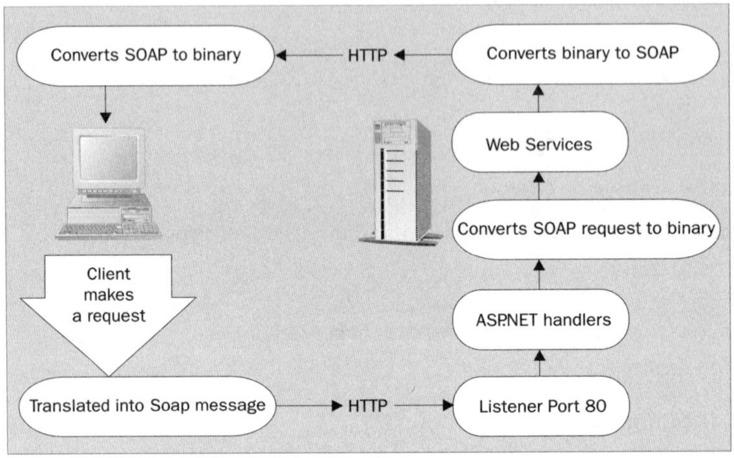

Looking at the diagram, you can see that the consumer (client) invokes a request where binary information is translated into a SOAP message. In order to translate the binary information into a text-format SOAP message, a **proxy class** is generated at the client. This proxy class is responsible for describing the details about itself. More specifically, the proxy class is in a dialect of XML referred to as **WSDL** (**Web Services Description Language**) – more about WSDL later – and describes things such as how data types will be represented, the arguments for methods being offered, etc.

Next, the SOAP message is passed to the Web Service via HTTP. Also notice the listener at the Web Service side. IIS essentially listens for Web Service requests using **TCP** (**Transmission Control Protocol**) port 80. Port 80 is the standard port for HTTP communications regarding web sites. When the listener receives a request, IIS will direct the request to ASP.NET handlers. These handlers are responsible for locating the Web Service.

Once the appropriate Web Service has been located, the SOAP request is converted back to binary form. The Web Service will take the binary request and begin its processing.

After processing, the results are passed in binary form to ASP.NET, where it will be converted back into a SOAP message and sent back to the consumer. When the consumer receives the SOAP message, ASP.NET creates a proxy class, as previously described, in order to convert the SOAP message back to binary form. Once back in binary form, the client application is able to utilize the information in order to satisfy the original request.

More simply put, the process works like this:

- At runtime, the client program creates the proxy object
- Then the client invokes a method on the proxy
- The proxy changes the call to XML over HTTP and sends it over the Internet to the server
- The server responds to the HTTP request with the required results
- The proxy receives the results in XML over HTTP and converts it into the method's return value
- Client receives the return value from the proxy

Web Services Description Language

In a nutshell, **WSDL** is nothing more than an XML document that describes how a Web Service is used, where the Web Service resides, and how the message is being exchanged. WSDL is conceptually similar to IDL (Interface Definition Language) used with other object-oriented languages such as C++ (Visual Basic 6 automatically took care of IDL behind the scenes) for describing objects, interfaces, and methods. IDL allows for a certainly level of interoperation between objects using Component Object Model (COM). The main difference with WSDL is that it is XML based and is used to describe six elements that are defined and used by the SOAP protocol:

- `types` – this section is actually an XML schema used to define the message section.
- `message` – this required portion of WSDL is used to characterize the format used by messages. Simply, a Web Service may be characterized as a one-way message or, more commonly, it may exhibit two-way messaging – a response and a request message. The `message` section is responsible for describing the format for how a Web Service will accept messages and, if applicable, what the format will be for responding. One thing to be aware of is that there will always be at least one message section for requesting. A Web Service does not have to respond back to a client.
- `portType` – because a Web Service can utilize other Web Services, it is necessary to describe each response and/or request message (previously described in the `message` section) for all the available Web Services.
- `binding` – this section is used to describe the format of the message. Typically, this will be used to describe the schema for the message XML message body. Each available method or function will have a `binding` definition – more or less the signature of each exposed method.
- `port` – the `port` section describes the URL-based location of each available method or function that is available for the Web Service.
- `service` – the last section found in a WSDL document is `service` and it simply portrays the name of the Web Service being described.

Because WSDL is very wordy, it can easily take up several pages to describe a Web Service. To reserve space, we will view WSDL for the following Web Service:

```
<WebMethod()>Public Function MyDog() As String
    MyDog = "My Dog likes chrunchy cerial"
End Function
```

We will cover how to create a Visual Basic .NET Web Service project in a following section. However, if you want to start now, simply follow these steps:

- Launch Visual Studio .NET
- Create a new project using the **Web Service** template and call it `DogFood`
- Add the previous example function to the `Service1.asmx` file and save it

```
' WEB SERVICE EXAMPLE
' The HelloWorld() example service returns the string Hello World.
```

```
' To build, uncomment the following lines then save and build the project.
' To test this web service, ensure that the .asmx file is the start page
' and press F5.
'
<WebMethod()> Public Function MyDog() As String
   MyDog = "My Dog likes chrunchy cerial"
End Function
```

- Right-click on the `Service1.asmx` file, then select View in browser
- Follow the link at the top of the rendered page by clicking on Service Description

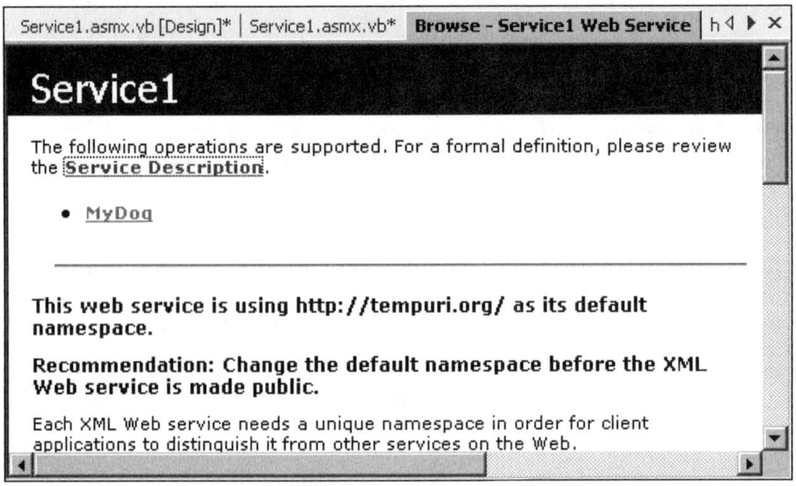

The resulting WSDL is used to describe this simple Web Service! Be sure to look for the six elements previously described – `types`, `message`, `portType`, `binding`, `port`, and `service`.

> **Note you will learn how to view WSDL when you create a Web Service in the next project.**

```
<?xml version="1.0" encoding="utf-8" ?>
<definitions xmlns:s="http://www.w3.org/2001/XMLSchema"
             xmlns:http="http://schemas.xmlsoap.org/wsdl/http/"
             xmlns:mime="http://schemas.xmlsoap.org/wsdl/mime/"
             xmlns:tm="http://microsoft.com/wsdl/mime/textMatching/"
             xmlns:soap="http://schemas.xmlsoap.org/wsdl/soap/"
             xmlns:soapenc="http://schemas.xmlsoap.org/soap/encoding/"
             xmlns:s0="http://localhost/WebService2"
             targetNamespace="http://LocalHost/WebService2/"
             xmlns="http://schemas.xmlsoap.org/wsdl/">
  <types>
    <s:schema attributeFormDefault="qualified" elementFormDefault="qualified"
              targetNamespace="http://LocalHost/WebService2">
      <s:element name="MyDog">
        <s:complexType />
      </s:element>
```

```
         <s:element name="MyDogResponse">
            <s:complexType>
               <s:sequence>
                  <s:element minOccurs="1" maxOccurs="1" name="MyDogResult"
                             nillable="true" type="s:string" />
               </s:sequence>
            </s:complexType>
         </s:element>
         <s:element name="string" nillable="true" type="s:string" />
      </s:schema>
   </types>
   <message name="MyDogSoapIn">
      <part name="parameters" element="s0:MyDog" />
   </message>
   <message name="MyDogSoapOut">
      <part name="parameters" element="s0:MyDogResponse" />
   </message>
   <message name="MyDogHttpGetIn" />
   <message name="MyDogHttpGetOut">
      <part name="Body" element="s0:string" />
   </message>
   <message name="MyDogHttpPostIn" />
   <message name="MyDogHttpPostOut">
      <part name="Body" element="s0:string" />
   </message>
   <portType name="Service1Soap">
      <operation name="MyDog">
         <input message="s0:MyDogSoapIn" />
         <output message="s0:MyDogSoapOut" />
      </operation>
   </portType>
   <portType name="Service1HttpGet">
      <operation name="MyDog">
         <input message="s0:MyDogHttpGetIn" />
         <output message="s0:MyDogHttpGetOut" />
      </operation>
   </portType>
   <portType name="Service1HttpPost">
      <operation name="MyDog">
         <input message="s0:MyDogHttpPostIn" />
         <output message="s0:MyDogHttpPostOut" />
      </operation>
   </portType>
   <binding name="Service1Soap" type="s0:Service1Soap">
      <soap:binding transport="http://schemas.xmlsoap.org/soap/http"
                    style="document" />
      <operation name="MyDog">
         <soap:operation soapAction="http://tempuri.org/MyDog" style="document" />
         <input>
            <soap:body use="literal" />
         </input>
         <output>
            <soap:body use="literal" />
         </output>
```

```
      </operation>
   </binding>
   <binding name="Service1HttpGet" type="s0:Service1HttpGet">
      <http:binding verb="GET" />
      <operation name="MyDog">
         <http:operation location="/MyDog" />
         <input>
            <http:urlEncoded />
         </input>
         <output>
            <mime:mimeXml part="Body" />
         </output>
      </operation>
   </binding>
   <binding name="Service1HttpPost" type="s0:Service1HttpPost">
      <http:binding verb="POST" />
      <operation name="MyDog">
         <http:operation location="/MyDog" />
         <input>
            <mime:content type="application/x-www-form-urlencoded" />
         </input>
         <output>
            <mime:mimeXml part="Body" />
         </output>
      </operation>
   </binding>
   <service name="Service1">
      <port name="Service1Soap" binding="s0:Service1Soap">
         <soap:address location="http://localhost/WebService2/Service1.asmx" />
      </port>
      <port name="Service1HttpGet" binding="s0:Service1HttpGet">
         <http:address location="http://localhost/WebService2/Service1.asmx" />
      </port>
      <port name="Service1HttpPost" binding="s0:Service1HttpPost">
         <http:address location="http://localhost/WebService2/Service1.asmx" />
      </port>
   </service>
</definitions>
```

The good news is you don't have to be a wizard with XML or WSDL to accomplish this, as Visual Studio .NET will do most of the work for you. However, you can learn a fair amount about how a Web Service works by studying its WDSL file.

Creating the Service

Start a New | Project and select ASP.NET Web Service from the New Project screen. Name the project MyWebService:

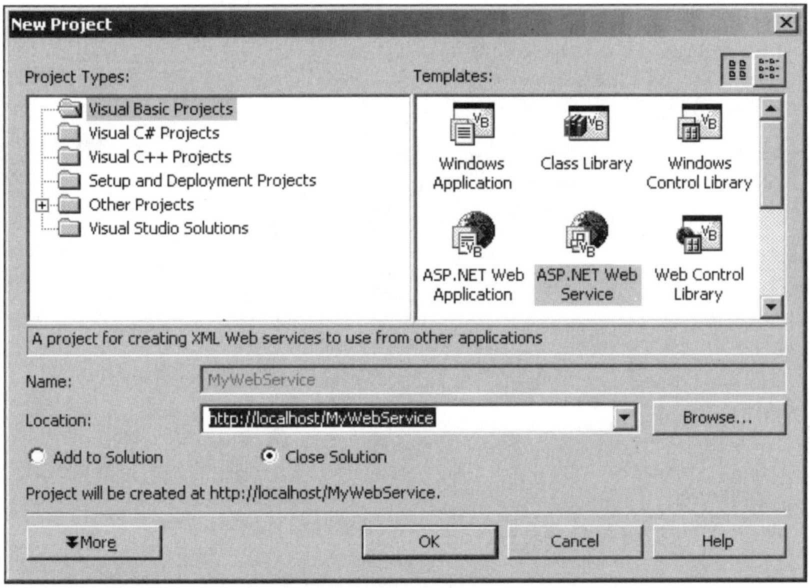

Add the following namespace:

```
Imports System.Data.SqlClient
```

If not already here, add <WebService()>at the beginning of the Public Class as shown below. (<WebService()> is a method attribute that tells the .NET runtime that the following function will be exposed as a part of our Web Service. Any function you want exposed must have this attribute prefixed.)

```
<WebService()> Public Class Service3
    Inherits System.Web.Services.WebService
```

Note the Public Class Service3. The number you have after the service may be different or not exist at all. In this example, the 3 shows up because I specified this number after the Public Class to help distinguish between different services I have available on my test platform.

Directly under the Web Service class declaration, add a connection string:

```
Public Class Service3
    Inherits System.Web.Services.WebService

    Private mySQLConnection As New SqlConnection("Data Source=LocalHost;" & _
        "initial catalog=Wrox;User ID=sa;PWD=")
```

Next, add the following directly under the Visual Studio .NET Web Service Designer generated code:

```
    ' WEB SERVICE EXAMPLE
    ' The HelloWorld() example service returns the string Hello World.
    ' To build, uncomment the following lines then save and build the project.
    ' To test this web service, ensure that the .asmx file is the start page
    ' and press F5.
```

```
<WebMethod()> Public Function ShowSQL(ByVal DogsTable As String) As DataSet
     Dim myDataAdapter As SqlDataAdapter
     Dim myDataSet As New DataSet()
     Dim MySQLString As String

     MySQLString = "SELECT DogID,Breed,FoodPref,FoodDesc " & _
                   "FROM Dogs,Food WHERE FoodPref=FoodID"
     myDataAdapter = New SqlDataAdapter(MySQLString, mySQLConnection)
     myDataAdapter.Fill(myDataSet, "Dogs")
     Return myDataSet
End Function

<WebMethod()> Public Function UpdateSQL(ByVal UpdateFoodPref As String, _
                                        ByVal MyDogID As String)

     UpdateDatabase(UpdateFoodPref, MyDogID)

End Function

Private Sub UpdateDatabase(ByVal UpdateFoodPref As String, _
                           ByVal MyDogID As String)

     Dim mySqlCommand As New SqlCommand("UPDATE Dogs SET FoodPref = '" + _
         UpdateFoodPref + "' WHERE DogID='" + MyDogID + "'", mySQLConnection)

     mySQLConnection.Open()
     mySqlCommand.ExecuteNonQuery()
     mySQLConnection.Close()

End Sub
```

Looking over the code, you should notice that this project is no different from any other Visual Basic .NET class, except that the Web Service inherits from the `System.Web.Services` (added by default courtesy of Visual Studio .NET). We added the attribute `<WebMethod()>` to the `Public Function` in this project to let .NET know that we want this function to be able to be accessed across the Internet utilizing SOAP. What actually happens is .NET adds information regarding the method or function to the SOAP contract.

As you can see, creating a Web Service is no more difficult than creating a typical Visual Basic .NET class. Let's move on to the next section and test our Web Service.

Testing the Web Service

Now that we have created a Web Service, we need to test it. First you need to run the Service by selecting Debug from the main menu bar, and then selecting Start or pressing *F5*, as you have for all other projects. Wait for the browser to open and display the Web Service information as depicted below:

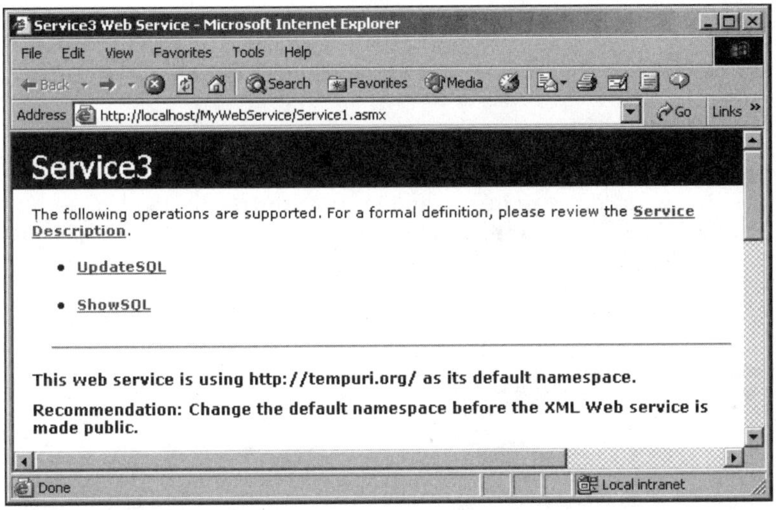

Why is this page complaining about the "default namespace?" **By default, Visual Studio .NET generates a namespace to be used in the response. That namespace – http://tempuri.org/ – works until you try to combine results from multiple Web Services with matching entities. Each Web Service should, therefore, return a namespace unique to the service provider. One of the best ideas I've seen to this end is to use a URL to where additional documentation about the service can be found. This is particularly important if you are sending DataSets via a Web Service and need to describe what data is actually being returned.**

Let's start off by taking a look at this service in action. Click on the link for UpdateSQL.

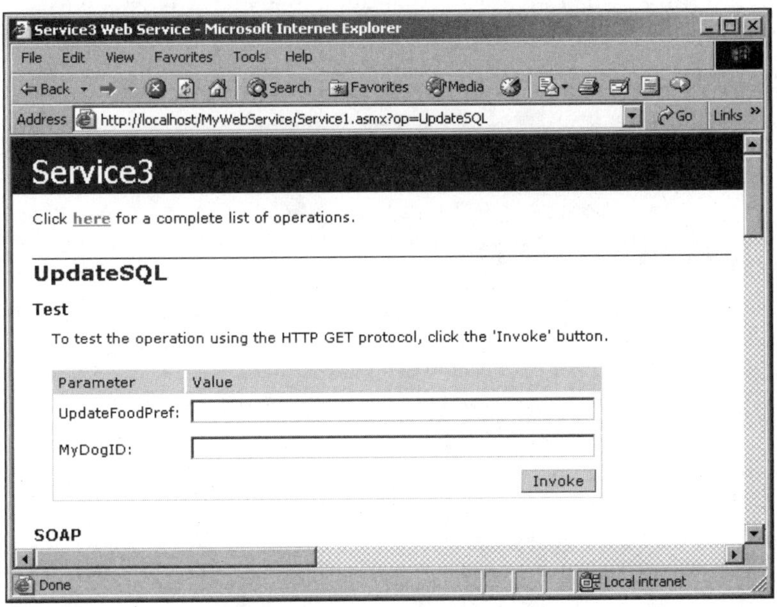

Before we do anything with the displayed Service, first open the Query Analyzer from SQL and execute the following in the Wrox database:

```
SELECT * FROM Dogs
```

Make a note of one of the DogIDs and the FoodPref number. Now go back to your browser and change the number in the UpdateFoodPref and indicate the record to change with MyDogID. For example, if the original data for UpdateFoodPref was 3 and 1 for MyDogID, change the 3 to 2, and indicate the record to change by entering 1.

If things work properly, you should get a new browser window with the following:

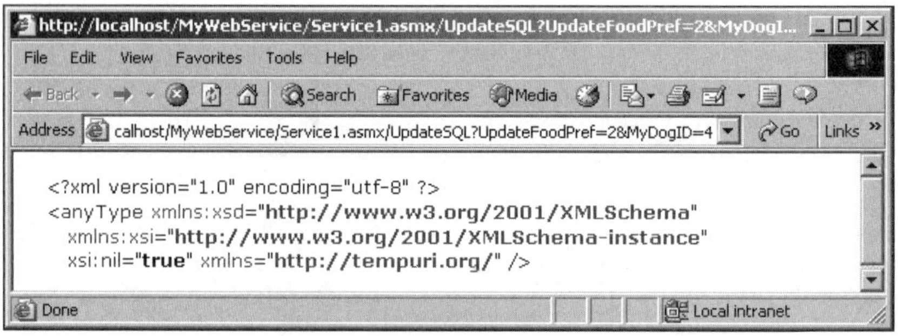

As verification, open Query Analyzer and select the items for the Dogs table. You should see the data has changed.

Selecting the Invoke button causes the browser to initiate an HTTP-POST to the Web Service. A HTTP-POST is used because SOAP is not needed here. In this test environment, we don't need to actually implement SOAP, because we are testing the service locally, so a simple command sent by HTTP is quite satisfactory. However, when we use an application to invoke a Web Service, SOAP will be the default protocol.

After the Web Service finishes the execution of the method, an XML formatted message will be returned and displayed in the browser. This message is similar to the message a requesting application would receive and utilize as appropriate.

Consuming a Web Service

There are two major steps for consuming Web Services: **discovery** and **proxy**. Briefly, discovery is how an application locates methods and functions available from a particular Web Service. Proxy on the other hand is how the Web Service will describe the specific details about itself such as the arguments for the methods it offers and how data types will be represented. Let's take a closer look at each of these two steps.

Discovery

Discovery is the process of acquiring information from SOAP's contract in order to find out (discover) the available methods, functions, and data formats the Web Service has to offer. Technically, discovery is an optional process because it can be incorporated with the creation of a proxy class. This is accomplished by adding a web reference using Visual Studio .NET. By adding a web reference, Visual Studio .NET acquires the SOAP contract from the Web Service. I will talk about this in more detail shortly.

What's interesting is SOAP's discovery is capable of reporting information back to the client about Web Services in the form of a dialog. In other words, as SOAP discovers information, it is relayed back to the client, while the client can take the relayed information and utilize the appropriate methods or functions disclosed through discovery.

When you create a Web Service using Visual Studio .NET there is a file with the extension `.disco` that is automatically created for you. This "disco" file, which stands for **Discovery of Web Services**, acts as a pointer to the location to the Web Service.

One problem you may encounter with "disco" is if you don't know where the location of a "disco" document resides, you may be out of luck. To help keep this type of problem at bay, Microsoft, in conjunction with Ariba, set out to create a repository where businesses can publicly describe their Web Services. The joint project for creating these repositories is referred to as the **UDDI project**. UDDI is very similar to DNS servers. UDDI stands for **Universal Description, Discovery and Integration** and its purpose is to define how businesses can describe and publish Web Services. More specifically, its purpose is to act as a Web-based directory for Web Services. The project is designed to provide a directory described in XML, not too different from using a search engine such as Google to display documents available at a web site.

> **For more information about the UDDI project, check out www.uddi.org.**

Currently the project is still young so it has a way to go. Nevertheless, there are more than 160 companies that have joined the project. Given time, UDDI may become the standard for locating Web Services. You will have the opportunity to view a Microsoft sample UDDI project when we add a Web Service in the next project.

Proxy Class

There's more to just having a client and a Web Service talk back and forth in the form of XML. A Web Service needs a way to describe the specific details of things, such as the arguments for the methods it offers and how data types will be represented. Creating a **proxy class** is easy when using Visual Studio .NET because it creates it automatically for you. All you need to do is to add a reference for the Web Service to the application. This is very similar to adding COM object type libraries by adding a reference using Visual Basic 6. The major difference is SOAP is based on a WSDL. More specifically, when you add a reference for the Web Service, Visual Studio .NET retrieves a copy of the SOAP contract and uses that to build a proxy as needed. A SOAP contract depicts the Web Service's interface using WSDL to describe the protocols supported by the Web Service. During runtime, Visual Studio .NET automatically creates the proxy class at the client machine.

Creating the Proxy

Create a new ASP.NET Web Application. Call it MyWebApplication. The first thing we need to do is to add a reference to a Web Service. Recall in our previous discussion that adding Web Services is very similar to adding COM object type libraries by adding a reference using Visual Basic 6. Begin by selecting Project from the main menu bar. From the drop-down menu, select Add Web Reference. A popup dialog should open as shown below:

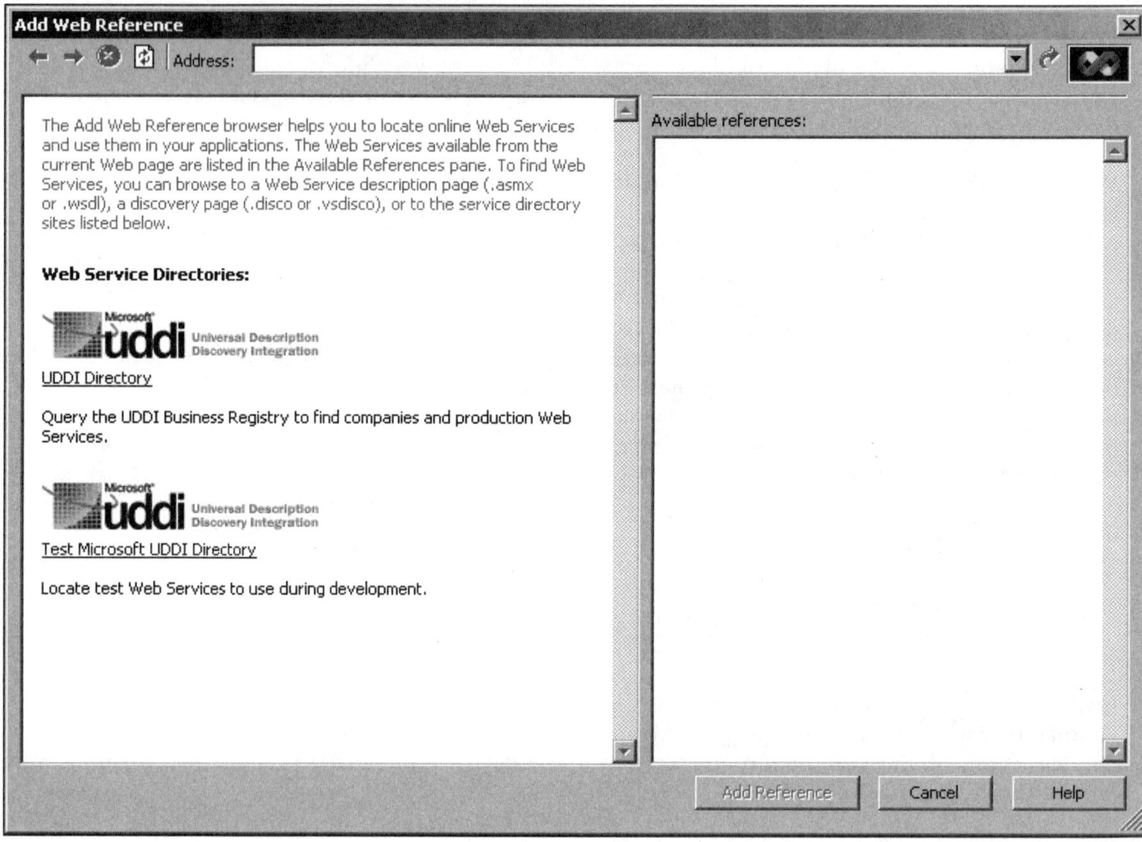

Let's study this dialog. First notice the Address line at the top. This area is similar to the text area for a URL in a web browser. If you know the location of a remote Web Service, you can simply type in the appropriate URL address.

Next, look at the UDDI links in the left pane. Recall the UDDI project used to define how businesses can describe and publish Web Services. More specifically, its purpose is to serve as a Web-based repository for Web Services. If you are curious, select the first link labeled Microsoft UDDI Directory. Next, enter the letter I into the textbox labeled Business name:

Entering a business name and submitting a search is similar to using a common search engine such as Google. In our case we are not sure what businesses are available, so we are searching all businesses that begin with the letter "I". You should receive similar results as shown below:

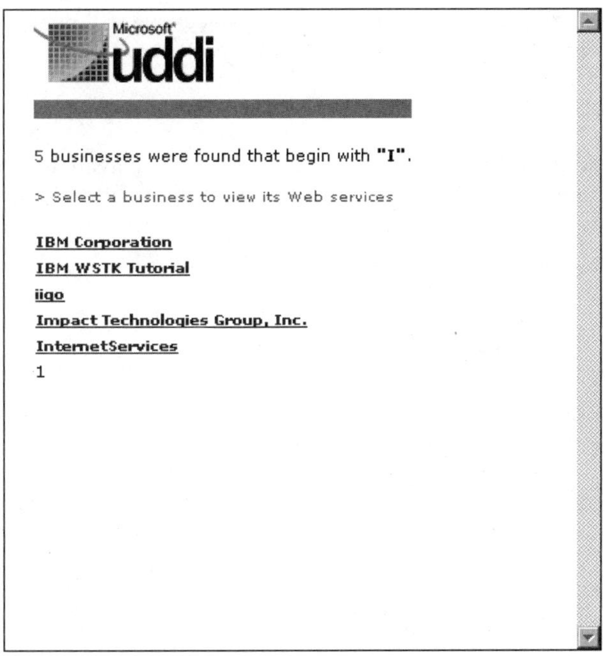

Select one of the items on the list. Notice below, I have selected IBM WSTK Tutorial. By selecting the desired business, the available public Web Services are listed. Simply clicking the address for the Web Service will add the reference for you:

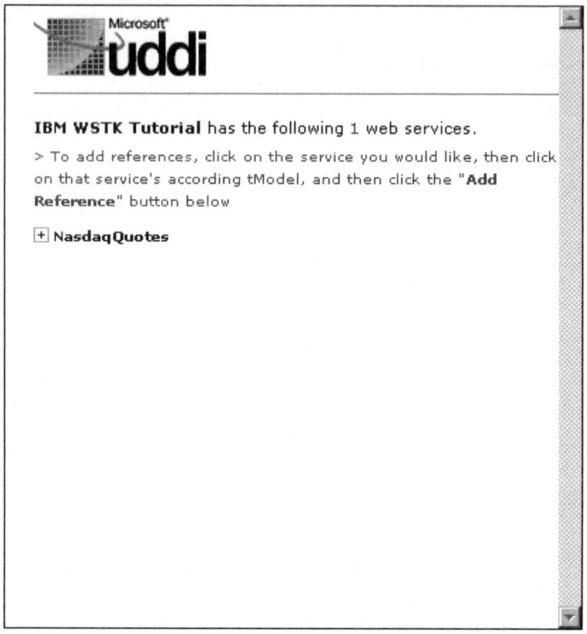

Now that we have taken a detour, let's get back to our project. we still need to add a Web reference to our project. For this project, you need to locate the Web Service:

http://localhost/MyWebService/Service1.asmx

and select the link. Looking at the next screenshot, notice that the available Web Services on the local server are listed in the right pane. Now click the Add Reference button located at the bottom of the dialog. That's all there is to it; the references have been added.

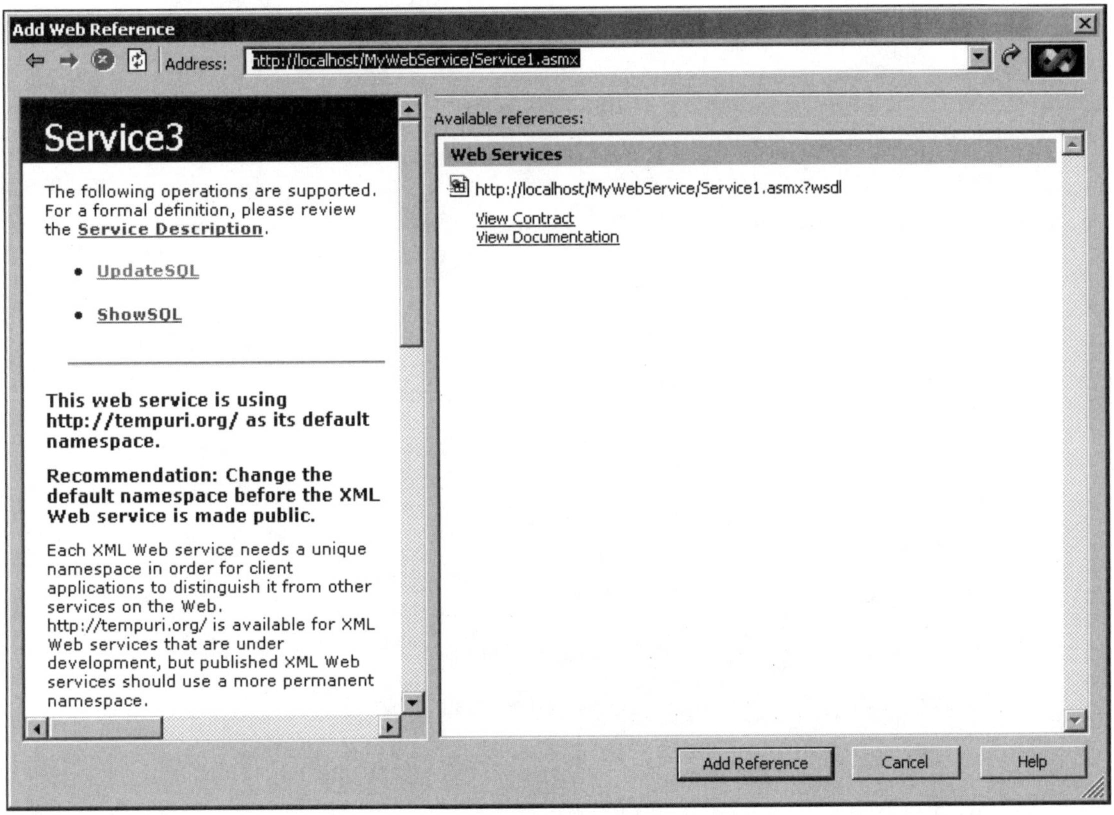

Now that we have added a reference for our Web Service, let's get back to building our project. From Design Mode, open the Toolbox and drag a DataGrid, two labels, two textboxes, and a button onto the form as shown below:

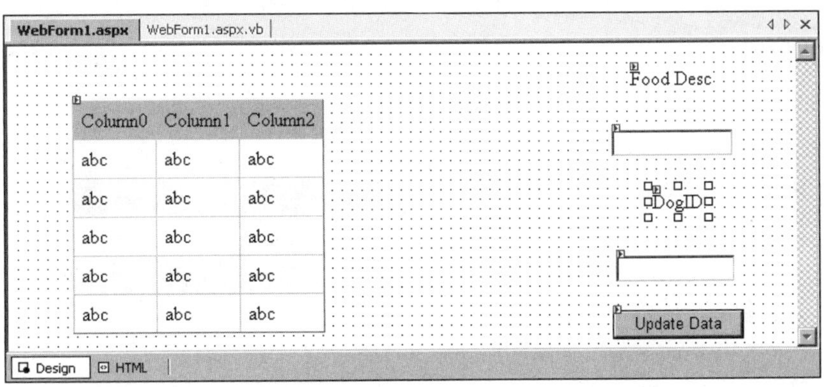

Leave the DataGrid's ID as `DataGrid1`. However, to give our application a nicer look than the default, set the following properties as shown below either by using the `Properties` box in Visual Studio .NET or programmatically through HTML code as we have done in the previous chapter:

```
<asp:DataGrid id="DataGrid1"
style="Z-INDEX: 101; LEFT: 53px; POSITION: absolute; TOP: 45px" runat="server"
HeaderStyle-Backcolor="LightBlue"
AlternatingItemStyle-BackColor="LightYellow"
CellPadding="6">
</asp:DataGrid>
```

Go to the Visual Basic .NET code area (`WebForm1.aspx.vb`) and create the following subroutine:

```
Public Class WebForm1
    Inherits System.Web.UI.Page
    Protected WithEvents DataGrid1 As System.Web.UI.WebControls.DataGrid
    Protected WithEvents TextBox1 As System.Web.UI.WebControls.TextBox
    Protected WithEvents TextBox2 As System.Web.UI.WebControls.TextBox
    Protected WithEvents Button1 As System.Web.UI.WebControls.Button
    Protected WithEvents Label1 As System.Web.UI.WebControls.Label
    Protected WithEvents Label2 As System.Web.UI.WebControls.Label


Sub ViewSQL()
    Dim MyDataSet As DataSet
    If Not Page.IsValid Then Exit Sub

    Dim MyWebService As New localhost.Service3()
    MyDataSet = MyWebService.ShowSQL(True)
    DataGrid1.DataSource = MyDataSet.Tables("Dogs")
    DataGrid1.DataBind()
End Sub
```

Next, locate the `Page_Load` event and add the following:

```
    Private Sub Page_Load(ByVal sender As System.Object, ByVal e As
        System.EventArgs) Handles MyBase.Load
        'Put user code to initialize the page here
        Call ViewSQL()
    End Sub
```

Now locate the `Button_Click` event and add the following code:

```
    Private Sub Button1_Click(ByVal sender As Object, ByVal e As System.EventArgs)
        Handles Button1.Click
        Dim MyString As String
        Dim MyWebService As New localhost.Service3()

        Dim a As String
        Dim b As String
        a = TextBox1.Text
        b = TextBox2.Text

        MyString = MyWebService.UpdateSQL(b, a)

        Call ViewSQL()
    End Sub
```

After all our code is entered, you are ready to test the application in conjunction with the Web Service we previously created. Build the application. When the browser opens, select a row to change by inputting a `DogID` to indicate which row to change, and then enter a different number from what is indicated for `FoodPref`. Finally, click the button labeled **Update Data**:

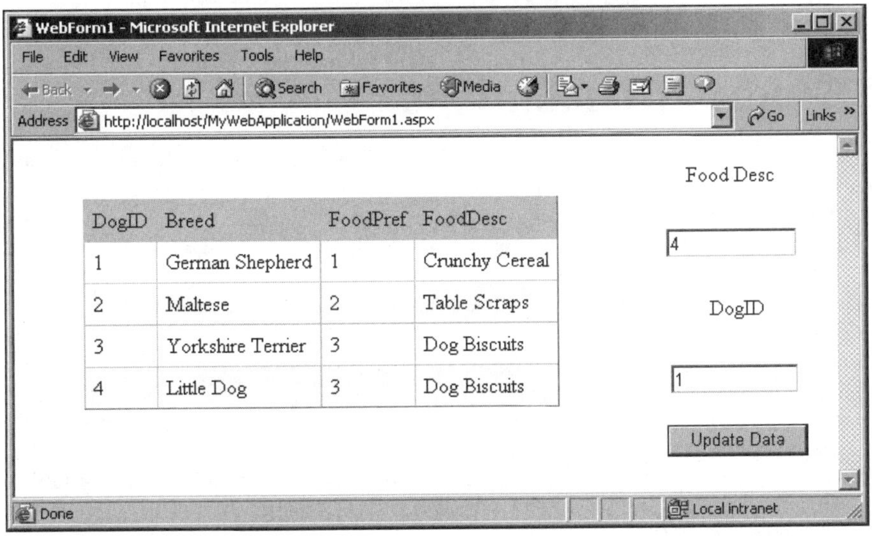

Also notice when the data is updated, our original data can still be seen within the two textboxes. This is due to ASP.NET view state being turned on by default – recall this from our discussion in the previous chapter.

This project, in conjunction with the Web Service, makes a good example of how distributed components work together to establish *n*-tier architectures. The Web Services act as business components that separate our business logic from the presentation logic – namely the client. Business logic in this example includes the `SELECT` statement for the DataSet, the connection string, and the SQL for the update. Furthermore, we could have easily added other Web Services from different locations to perform other tasks. The key issue here is the complete black box functionality that is provided by our Web Service. Furthermore, if we need to modify the SQL statements, we can make the change in one location without affecting each client.

> **Note: If you are familiar with COM, you will know that COM interfaces are immutable. In other words, the contract between a COM component and a consumer component must not be broken by altering an interface. Web Services are very similar in this aspect. The good news is you don't have as many headaches as you did with COM. You can indeed make major changes within a Web Service. If you do make such changes, you need to reinstall the affected Web Services reference at the client application. Because we are no longer using COM interfaces, but using SOAP to remotely communicate, updating the Web Service at the client is much easier because you no longer have to deal with Class ID and immutable interfaces.**

The code used for the client application is straightforward. As a matter of fact, you can't tell that this code is any different from any other application that utilizes class development. There are no special namespaces needed or any other types of specialized statements.

The first part of this application uses a data-bound grid where we allow the Web Service to pass a DataSet.

The second part of this application involves taking user input to indicate which row of data we want to change and the actual change itself. When the user clicks the Update Data button, the user data is passed to the Web Service, where it takes the data and performs a database update.

Using Windows Applications

Using Windows applications as opposed to ASP.NET pages can be very efficient over a corporate Intranet because Windows applications run on the client machine. As a result, server load is greatly reduced. Additionally, Windows applications can create a richer user environment including sophisticated graphics (without needing to worry as much about network bandwidth).

Web Services are just as easy to use in Windows Applications as they are in Web Applications. You still need to add a web reference to your application just as we did with our ASP.NET application. Let's try a project where we use a Web Service to execute a stored procedure.

As with the previous project, we start by creating a Web Service. Here we will utilize the stored procedure `ParamInsert` we created in the previous chapter. Recall this stored procedure was designed to pass parameters to the client so we could insert a new row of data into the `Dogs` table.

Creating the Web Service

Start a new project and select ASP.NET Web Service from the New Project screen. Name the project `MyNewWebService`.

Add the following namespace:

```
Imports System.Data.SqlClient
```

Next, create the two functions as described below:

```
<WebMethod()> Public Function UpdateDatabase(ByVal Breed As String, _
                                            ByVal FoodPref As String)
   Dim mySqlConnection As New SqlConnection("Data Source=LocalHost;" & _
       "initial catalog=Wrox;User ID=sa;PWD=")
   Dim mySQLCommand As SqlCommand = New SqlCommand("Param_Insert",
       mySqlConnection)
   Dim mySQLParameter As SqlParameter
   mySQLCommand.CommandType = CommandType.StoredProcedure
   mySQLParameter = mySQLCommand.Parameters.Add("@Breed", SqlDbType.Char)
   mySQLParameter.Direction = ParameterDirection.Input
   mySQLParameter.Value = Breed

   mySQLParameter = mySQLCommand.Parameters.Add("@Food", SqlDbType.Char)
   mySQLParameter.Direction = ParameterDirection.Input
   mySQLParameter.Value = FoodPref
```

```
        mySQLCommand.Connection.Open()
        mySQLCommand.ExecuteNonQuery()
        mySqlConnection.Close()

    End Function

    <WebMethod()> Public Function ShowSQL(ByVal DogsTable As String) As DataSet
        Dim myDataAdapter As SqlDataAdapter
        Dim myDataSet As New DataSet()
        Dim mySQLConnection As New SqlConnection("Data Source=LocalHost;" & _
            "initial catalog=Wrox;User ID=sa;PWD=")
        Dim MySQLString As String
        MySQLString = ("Select * from dogs")
        myDataAdapter = New SqlDataAdapter(MySQLString, mySQLConnection)
        myDataAdapter.Fill(myDataSet, "Dogs")
        Return myDataSet
    End Function
```

Build the Web Service by selecting Debug from the main menu bar, and then selecting Start or press *F5*. Be sure to test the service as described earlier in this chapter.

The code for this project should look remarkably similar to the project in the previous chapter that utilized the stored procedure called `Param_Insert`. As a matter of fact, the code is identical, except we had to add `<WebMethod()>`in front of our public functions. The other difference is the namespace `Imports System.Web.Services` is automatically added for us by Visual Studio .NET when we specified to create a Web Service.

Creating the Client

Start a new Windows Application and name it `WinApp4WebService`. Save this to `C:\VBNETTrans\Chapter05\Projects`, or you may use the project already created in the downloadable code for this chapter.

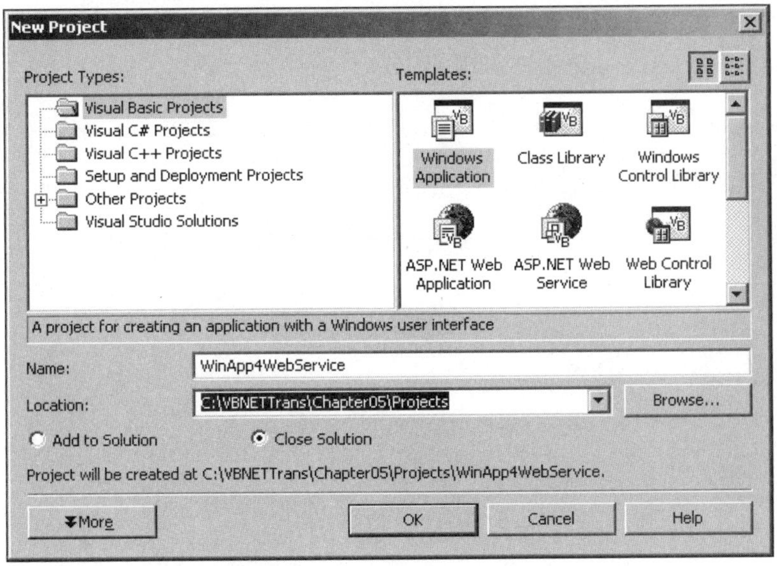

Go to Design View. From the toolbox, drag a DataGrid, two labels, two textboxes, and a button onto the form. Change the properties as shown below. Keep the default name for the DataGrid as `DataGrid1`.

Don't forget to add a Web Reference to your Web Reference to the Web Service we created earlier (`http://localhost/MyNewWebService/Service.asmx`) before continuing.

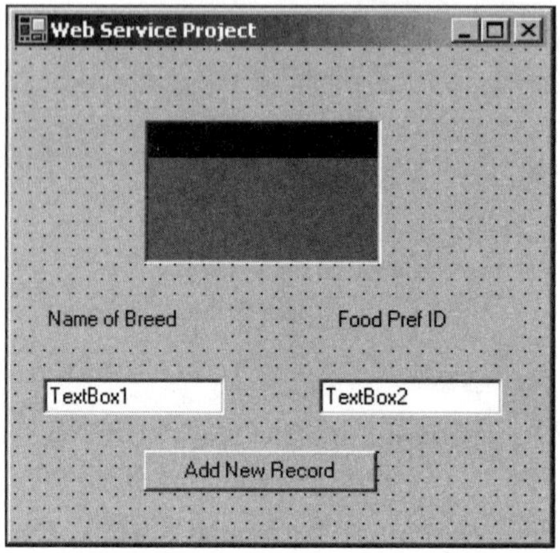

Switch to the code work area and create a subroutine as shown:

```
Public Class Form1
    Inherits System.Windows.Forms.Form
    Sub ShowSQL()
        Dim MyDataSet As DataSet

        Dim MyWebService As New localhost.MyNewWebService()
        MyDataSet = MyWebService.ShowSQL(True)
        DataGrid1.DataSource = MyDataSet.Tables("Dogs").DefaultView

    End Sub
```

Locate `Button1_Click` and add the following code:

```
    Private Sub Button1_Click(ByVal sender As System.Object, ByVal e As
        System.EventArgs) Handles Button1.Click
        Dim MyString As String

        Dim MyWebService As New localhost.MyNewWebService()

        Dim a As String
        Dim b As String
        a = TextBox1.Text
        b = TextBox2.Text

        MyString = MyWebService.UpdateDatabase(a, b)

        ShowSQL()

    End Sub
```

Locate `Form1_Load` and add:

```
Private Sub Form1_Load(ByVal sender As System.Object, ByVal e As
    System.EventArgs) Handles MyBase.Load
    ShowSQL()
End Sub
```

Select **Debug** from the main menu bar and then select **Start** or press *F5*.

This code is identical to the client we used in our ASP.NET project earlier in this chapter, with the exception that we don't use the statement `DataGrid1.DataBind()` as required with the ASP.NET project.

Again, all we are doing is passing user input as parameters for the stored procedure from `textbox1` and `textbox2` in order to insert a new row of data into the database. Didn't I say Web Services were easy to build and work with?

Synchronous Versus Asynchronous

One caveat to using Web Services is that it can take a considerable amount of time before a Web Server returns a request. The primary reason for delays is network traffic issues that we have no control over, and the translation processes that occur with SOAP. Recall that the SOAP client converts the binary invocation request into a SOAP message and is then reconverted back to a binary format at the SOAP server. Once the Web Service does its thing, such as process database manipulations or other calculations, the results are again converted to a SOAP message and passed back so that the SOAP client can convert the response back to binary. What this boils down to is a time-consuming translation process. Matters are complicated by the amount of Web Service processing that may be required. Don't forget, you are not just translating SOAP information; you are using Web Services to do things. Typically this will involve a lot of processing, especially when databases are involved. For example, suppose we have an e-commerce site where you can pay bills. You can use Web Services to validate your bank information. Before money can be wired from your account to another account, it is necessary to validate this information with the bank accounts that are involved. Obviously this may take some time.

When designing applications that consume Web Services, there are two approaches to handling long response time, one is to use asynchronous calls and the other is to use synchronous calls. An application making an **asynchronous call** to a Web Service is permitted to continue processing while waiting for a return response from the Web Service. The other approach, a **synchronous call**, halts other application activity until a response is received from the Web Service.

The dilemma an application developer has is to decide which method to use. At first, one may say go with asynchronous calls all the time. Going back to the online bill payment example, allowing the user to add new creditors for payment while previously entered data is verified makes it easier for the user. Instead of having to wait for each item to be validated at one time, which potentially may take a long time because it is likely the financial information may be dispersed, thus it will not reside at one location. In this example, asynchronous calls make total sense.

Aside from long processing bottlenecks that potentially can occur with synchronous calls, you should also consider other side effects. For instance, if your Web Service requires heavy IO, such as back and forth to a database, you can potentially stall what is referred to as an **ASP.NET worker thread**. An ASP.NET worker thread is a thread that executes ASP.NET code in a separate process (worker process) other than the process used by IIS. There is a finite amount of threads available for ASP.NET to use, like CPU cycles, memory accesses and such. If an ASP.NET worker thread becomes blocked, it can no longer service other requests. As a result, pending requests begin to backlog in the queue. Obviously this is not a desirable situation to achieve. The backlogging of requests not only reduces efficiency, it affects the overall scalability of the application and system the Web Service resides on.

When using asynchronous calls, you are actually creating special events referred to as asynchronous events. By using asynchronous events, you can free up other threads that are not currently being used by ASP.NET. Thus when one thread is blocked, you can continue processing by utilizing these asynchronous events.

In typical enterprise applications, the usage of asynchronous SOAP calls far outweighs the benefits of synchronous SOAP calls. For example, how do we recover from a server crash while a synchronous SOAP call is being processed? There's no way for the server to find out what SOAP calls failed to complete. On the other end, clients wait endlessly without getting the expected response. In asynchronous SOAP calls, an incoming request is immediately logged, preferably in a database, and an acknowledgement is issued to the client. That way the client is made aware that the server hosting the web service has received the request and is processing it. Once the request has been processed, a SOAP response is sent back to the client with the results. Although web services may sound trivial at first, they need to be designed to be fault tolerant and robust. In an enterprise environment, that is a basic necessity.

But don't just use asynchronous calls for the sake of doing it; there are times when synchronous calls make more sense. For example, suppose an e-commerce site lets you download information only after you have paid for it. Obviously, you don't want the customers to start downloading material until the payment transactions have been completed. In this case it makes sense to use synchronous calls.

Finally, when making a decision which to use, you ultimately must realize that designing and coding Web Services to utilize asynchronous calls is more complex using synchronous calls.

> **If you need to learn more about asynchronous Web Service programming, see *Professional C# Web Services: Building .NET Web Services with ASP .NET and .NET Remoting* (ISBN 1-861004-39-7).**

Web Service and ASP.NET Security

Unfortunately Web Services, as with anything else, raise security issues that must be taken into account. There are two major areas of concern. One major issue is that of **interception**. SOAP messages can potentially expose personal information such as credit card numbers, passwords, and other private information. Another major issue simply is unauthorized use of Web Services.

> **Note: Because Web Services are not much different from an ASP.NET page, both can utilize most of same security techniques. As a matter of fact, most of the security concepts presented here are a part of the ASP.NET framework.**

It is true that because SOAP can freely travel in and out of firewalls, there potentially can be security concerns. However, SOAP does not carry any more security risks than HTTP does. While you have to be careful about using plain packets, you can implement SSL and HTTPS. Furthermore, because SOAP is nothing more than a payload that can be carried with HTTP, you can invoke Windows NT/2000 and XP, to use HTTP authentication using Windows Integrated authentication.

One important thing to keep in mind about implementing SSL is that it is much slower than HTTP, because SSL requires communication processing at both ends. Special hardware can be installed to offset this effect. However, if critical data is being transmitted, it's my opinion that using SSL is worth taking a performance hit, as opposed to exposing sensitive data to others.

In addition to SSL, there are other security technologies that can be implemented, such as SOAP header authentication, forms authentication, and Windows authentication.

SOAP Headers

SOAP headers usually contain data relating to method invocation. However, the header may be used for authentication purposes as well. The SOAP specification does not lay down a strict rule about this. We can pass authentication credentials utilizing the SOAP header. The web method unwraps the credentials and validates it. For public web services, this approach sounds to be the most logical route.

Microsoft is promoting **Web Services Security Language (WS-Security)** as a standard approach SOAP header-based authentication. This standard offers great promise as a way to authenticate and encrypt data within SOAP messages. The practical downside of this is, at least for now, utilizing it in a .NET-based Web Service involves a significant amount "working-around" what Visual Studio .NET does for you – far more than is appropriate to cover here. So .NET does make it rather easy to write a Web Service that "just works". But it also shields you from and abstracts the SOAP messaging involved to the point where trying to modify it can lead to considerable frustration.

> **For a very practical and pragmatic look at SOAP-based security, read *Real SOAP Security* by Microsoft's Matt Powel in the MSDN library (http://msdn.microsoft.com/library/en-us/dn_voices_webservice/html/service11212001.asp).**

Forms Authentication

With **forms authentication**, you can have an HTML form request user validation directly from the user. User input would be validated from a data store such as a database, text file, or even a cookie stored at the client. This type of web security is common with many applications where a user is first redirected to an authentication form before being able to enter the web site.

However, there is a caveat you must be aware of when using form validation in conjunction with Web Services. In order to accept form validation via a Web Service, ASP.NET will redirect requests to an HTML form login page. At first this scenario may not sound like a big deal, but it is. The problem is SOAP at the web proxy expects a response. When jumping to an HTML form, the response does not occur. The work around for this occurs on the client side. The first step in that code is to create an instance of the `NetworkCredentials` class, then the `.Credentials` property of the Web Service Proxy can be set to this object.

Windows Authentication

Another security technology available is to use **Windows authentication**. This type of security involves authenticating using **Windows NTLM** (sometimes called **Challenge Response**) or Kerberos against a Windows domain authority such as the Security Accounts Manager. There is little doubt that this type of security is very good. Both NTLM and Kerberos use a hash algorithm to code and decode the user's credentials. The key point to be aware of is that the user's password is not transmitted across the network during authentication. The problem with this is that Windows authentication is only practical for corporate intranets, because it is based on existing Windows users and user groups, and requires the IE browser. It simply is not practical to have an administrator create new users for every new user that wants to access a public web site. Also, Windows NTLM and Kerberos do not transverse smoothly through most proxy servers and firewalls.

Implementing Windows authentication involves two steps, first you need to configure IIS to accept Windows authentication, and then you need to alert the Web Service that we are validating user information by adding some code. Let's take a look at the process:

Setting Up IIS

I am going to describe the process of implementing Windows authentication. However, I will not be implementing it with our projects in this book. Don't let this prevent you from trying it with your projects, but for ease of use, be sure to return security back to anonymous authentication.

As previously mentioned, you first need to configure IIS to use Windows authentication. This is accomplished through the Internet Services Manager utility that can be accessed from the Administrative tools under Programs using the Start menu. You can also use the Microsoft Management Console (MMC) and add the snap-in for Internet Information Services to access this utility.

From the left pane locate the web site. In the screenshot below, I am using Default Web Site. Click the + to open the folder, and locate the Web Service you wish to enforce Windows authentication on. Notice in the example below, I have selected MyWebService:

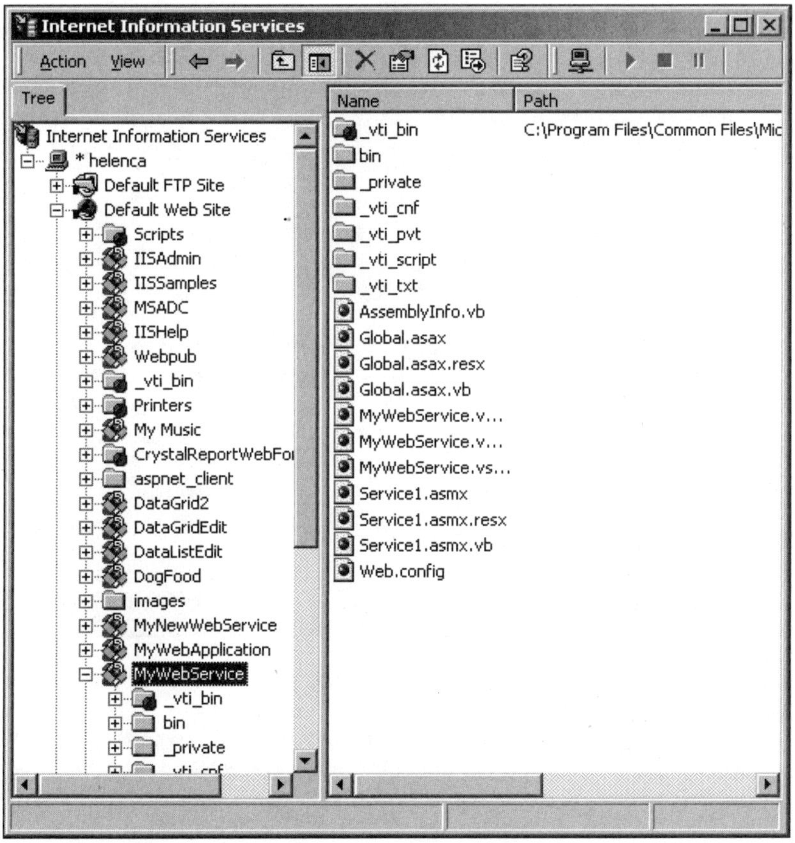

After selecting the Web Service, right-click your mouse and from the popup menu select Properties. When the Web Service's Properties dialog appears, select the center tab, Directory Security, as shown below, and then select the Edit... button:

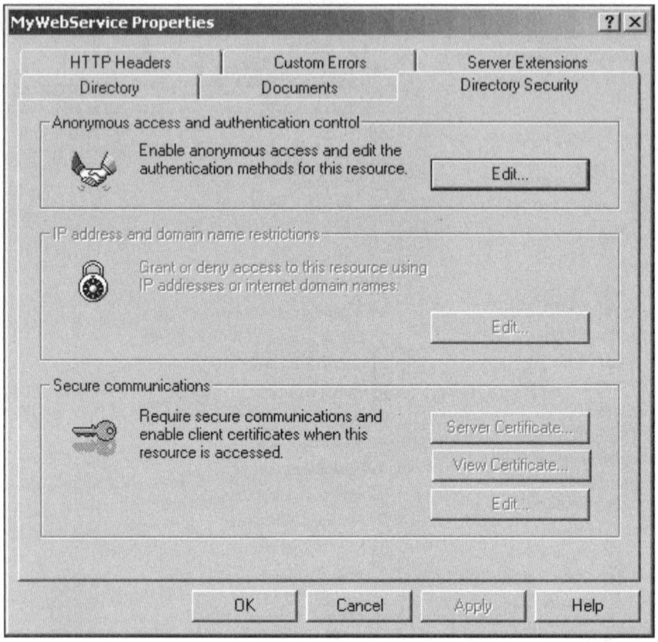

After selecting the Edit… button, a dialog called Authentication Methods appears. Notice that the check box labeled Anonymous access is checked by default. This allows the Web Service to be accessed without requiring the client application to provide any user credentials to the IIS server. Simply, the Web Service will work for anyone in the same manner we have worked with Web Services in this chapter. Actually what is happening is instead of supplying user credentials, an anonymous set of credentials is being passed to IIS every time you access a Web Service.

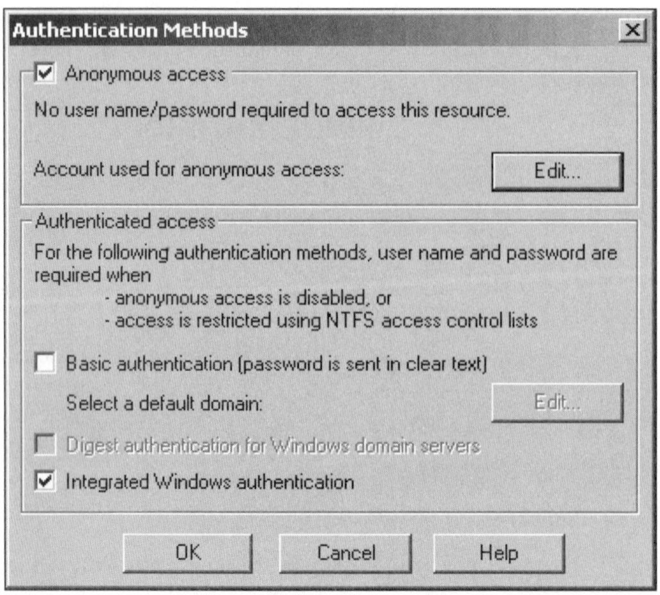

You can view the anonymous account by selecting the Edit... button. The Anonymous User Account typically has the prefix IUSER_ followed by the computer name. In the next example, you see HELENCA, which is the name of my test machine. The grayed out password field is filled with asterisks to conceal the password.

Going back to the Authentication Methods dialogue, if you uncheck Anonymous access, and leave the Integrated Windows authentication box checked (it is by default), then IIS will require NTLM authentication.

The second part of setting up Windows authentication is to have the client appropriately respond to the Web Service with the proper user credentials. This can be accomplished by changing the `Web.config` file authentication mode to reflect `Windows` as shown in the following code snippet (if it is not already in this mode):

```
<system.web>
...
   <authentication mode="Windows" />
...
</system.web>
```

Transactions and Web Services

Much of the printed text about transactions and Web Services basically says they don't mix. In other words, Web Services are not suitable for transactions. The biggest argument against Web Services and transactions is based on the thought that if a connection is dropped in the middle of a transaction, a lock on the database would occur without any way of correcting the problem unless the database is smart enough to close "timed-out" locks.

Regardless of what the critics say, I am going to go out on a limb and say that Web Services and transactions can coexist in a happy relationship. Web Services are not much different from ASP.NET pages and, with good application design, have little trouble executing transactions. The key to using Web Services and transactions is proper application design. In this chapter, we worked with automatic transactions where SQL Server automatically commits or aborts a single SQL statement. Simply, if everything goes well, the transaction commits. If something goes wrong, it aborts. Additionally, we created a Web Service that executes a stored procedure. Again, we have built in the necessary events to make sure either everything in our stored procedure executes, or nothing executes.

Along the lines of concern is what do you do if a Web Service is not available. There are several options an application developer can undertake. The easy way to handle non-available Web Services is to return an error message to the user. However, when dealing with critical conditions such as transactions, it may make more sense to have the application automatically switch to a backup Web Service located at a different server.

The bottom line is, with proper application design, all we need to be concerned with is that the request makes it to the server to execute. From there, we sit back and let our transactions process. If the request never makes it to the server, again, we have nothing to worry about – the transaction never occurs. With good application design, we can check to see if our message was received or not and notify the user.

In the next chapter, we are going to take a look at distributed transactions where two different databases are manipulated in order to complete one transaction. Obviously there is more we need to do to ensure that both databases are either committed or aborted together. Furthermore, I will show you how to safely incorporate a distributed transaction via Web Services.

Web Services Based on Transactions

So far, we've seen how to write a simple Web Service, and in this section, I will show you how to write a Web Service that actually participates in a transaction. We'll visit this very important concept extensively in the case study as well. For now, let's see how we can use SQL Database Transactions within a Web Service. We'll start by looking at a simple component that can be used in any style of .NET application (WebForm, Windows Form or Service.) We'll then use a Web Services "wrapper" to expose that functionality on the network. Finally, we'll look at a short testing program that puts our Web Service through its paces.

For this example, we're going to use the Northwinds' `Shippers` table. We're going to write a simple component that acts as a read and write cache of that data. Ideally, then Northwinds could use this Web Service as part of any solution that needs to access the `Shippers` information.

NwtShippersComponent

Today, most developers are familiar with the concept of a component. They are, more or less, reusable blocks of functionality that one can use to make programming simpler, make better use of abstraction and encapsulation and provide for "loose-coupling" of system elements. Our component does four things:

- Defines a `Shipper` class, used for defining our cached data
- Manages all of the database access functions between our Web Service and the database
- Provides a cache of existing data in memory to save database server resources
- Allows for the adding, updating and removal items both from the cache and database

With that in mind, let's look at the code for this. If you want to code along, launch Visual Studio .NET, then create a `Blank Solution` at `C:\VBNETTrans\Chapter05\Projects` and name it `NWTSolution`. Alternatively, you can open the solution provided in the code download for this chapter. Then, add a Visual Basic.NET class library project to that solution. Call this new project `NwtShipperComponent`, and then rename `Class1.vb` to "`ShipperComponent.vb`."

Now insert the following code into that file.

The file starts by enforcing good coding practices and importing the namespaces we will be using.

```
REM Require strong data type and
REM require explicit castings of types
Option Explicit On
Option Strict On

REM Import any namespaces will be using
REM Data and Data.SqlClient for database access
REM XML for serialization of Shippers
REM Collections for Sorted List containers
Imports System.Data
Imports System.Data.SqlClient
Imports System.Xml
Imports System.Collections
```

Next, the file defines two interfaces that our classes will support. We do this here simply to make changing the internal class structures as needed easier in the future. This is good practice for components that you expect to be used in a number of applications, where maintaining a consistent set of class attributes is important, but you want and need the flexibility to make changes.

```
#Region "Interface Definitions"
Public Interface IShipper
  Property ShipperID() As Integer
  Property CompanyName() As String
  Property Phone() As String
  Property IsChanged() As Boolean
  Property IsNew() As Boolean
  Property IsDeleted() As Boolean
  ReadOnly Property Version() As String
End Interface

Public Interface IShipperComponent
  Sub Load()
  Sub Save()
  Function AddShipper(ByVal CompanyName As String, ByVal Phone As String) As
String
  Function UpdateShipper(ByVal ShipperID As Integer, ByVal CompanyName As String,
ByVal Phone As String) As String
  Sub DeleteShipperByID(ByVal ShipperID As Integer)
  Function GetShipperList() As DataSet
  Function GetShipperIDByName(ByVal Name As String) As String
  Function GetShipperByShipperID(ByVal ShipperID As Integer) As Shipper
  Function GetShipperXMLByShipperID(ByVal ShipperID As Integer) As
XmlDocumentFragment
End Interface
#End Region
```

Next up, we have the `Shipper` class. This provides a template for future shipper objects. It also has a method that returns the current values of the object as an XML Document element. This allows the object to be serialized (expressed as text) in a SOAP response message.

```
REM The Shipper class provides a template for
REM Shipper objects and for serialization.
#Region "Shipper Class"
Public Class Shipper
  Implements IShipper

  REM Class member fields
  REM encapsulated into this class
  Private mShipperID As Integer
  Private mCompanyName As String
  Private mPhone As String
  Private mIsChanged As Boolean
  Private mIsDeleted As Boolean
  Private mIsNew As Boolean
  Private Const mVersion As String = "1.0.0"
```

You might find yourself wondering why this next property is here. Because we aren't using "Strong" components, if we want to provide information about what version of the class is being used, we need to provide that information manually. Versioning of components can be helpful in tracking down problems.

```
#Region "Class Properties"
  Public ReadOnly Property Version() As String Implements IShipper.Version
    Get
      Return mVersion
    End Get
  End Property

  Public Property ShipperID() As Integer Implements IShipper.ShipperID
    Get
      Return mShipperID
    End Get
    Set(ByVal Value As Integer)
      mShipperID = Value
      mIsChanged = True
    End Set
  End Property

  Public Property CompanyName() As String Implements IShipper.CompanyName
    Get
      Return mCompanyName
    End Get
    Set(ByVal Value As String)
      mCompanyName = Value
      mIsChanged = True
    End Set
  End Property

  Public Property Phone() As String Implements IShipper.Phone
    Get
```

```
      Return mPhone
    End Get
    Set(ByVal Value As String)
      mPhone = Value
      mIsChanged = True
    End Set
  End Property
```

We also have a number of cache state properties for this class.

```
  Friend Property IsChanged() As Boolean Implements IShipper.IsChanged
    Get
      Return mIsChanged
    End Get
    Set(ByVal value As Boolean)
      mIsChanged = value
    End Set
  End Property

  Friend Property IsNew() As Boolean Implements IShipper.IsNew
    Get
      Return mIsNew
    End Get
    Set(ByVal Value As Boolean)
      mIsNew = Value
    End Set
  End Property

  Friend Property IsDeleted() As Boolean Implements IShipper.IsDeleted
    Get
      Return mIsDeleted
    End Get
    Set(ByVal Value As Boolean)
      mIsDeleted = Value
    End Set
  End Property
#End Region
```

Finally, we have our method that provides an XML document fragment that can be used to serialize this class.

```
#Region "Class Methods"
  REM Provides for serialization of a shipper
  REM by returning the shipper's properties
  REM as an XML Document Element
  Public Function GetXML() As XmlDocumentFragment
    Dim doc As New XmlDocument()
    Dim root, elem As XmlElement
    Dim atr As XmlAttribute
    Dim xdf As XmlDocumentFragment
```

```
        REM Create a root element to work with
        REM then add elements to that with the
        REM properties of the Shipper.
        root = doc.CreateElement("shipper")
```

Note that those items that are properties of the class are treated as subelements, while metadata about the data instance is expounded as attributes on the root node. This is consistent with how ADO.NET describes data in a **DataSet** in XML.

```
        atr = doc.CreateAttribute("version")
        atr.Value = mVersion
        root.Attributes.Append(atr)
        atr = doc.CreateAttribute("isNew")
        atr.Value = mIsNew.ToString()
        root.Attributes.Append(atr)
        atr = doc.CreateAttribute("isChanged")
        atr.Value = mIsChanged.ToString()
        root.Attributes.Append(atr)
        atr = doc.CreateAttribute("isDeleted")
        atr.Value = mIsDeleted.ToString
        root.Attributes.Append(atr)
```

Finally, we just add the properties as elements.

```
        elem = doc.CreateElement("shipperID")
        elem.InnerText = ShipperID.ToString()
        root.AppendChild(elem)
        elem = doc.CreateElement("companyName")
        elem.InnerText = CompanyName.ToString()
        root.AppendChild(elem)
        elem = doc.CreateElement("phoneNumber")
        elem.InnerText = Phone.ToString()
        root.AppendChild(elem)

        REM Create a document fragment
        REM so the Shipper data can be
        REM embedded into another XML document
        REM then populate the fragment
        REM with the completed Shipper element
        xdf = doc.CreateDocumentFragment()
        xdf.AppendChild(root)
        Return xdf

    End Function
  #End Region
```

Next, we have our class constructors.

Why two different constructors? One of the more annoying things about the .NET Web Service implementation is that any class you intend to be used as the return type of a Web Method must have a "default constructor" with a parameter-less signature.

```
#Region "Constructor"
  REM Added to make the web service happy
  Public Sub New()
    mShipperID = 0
    mCompanyName = ""
    mPhone = ""
    mIsChanged = False
    mIsNew = False
    mIsDeleted = False

  End Sub

  Public Sub New(ByVal ShipperID As Integer, ByVal CompanyName As String, _
  ByVal Phone As String)

    mShipperID = ShipperID
    mCompanyName = CompanyName
    mPhone = Phone
    mIsChanged = False
    mIsNew = True
    mIsDeleted = False

  End Sub
#End Region
End Class
#End Region
```

Now that we have a class for the `Shipper` data, let's look at the class we will use to access and cache instances of that class.

```
REM The ShipperComponent class provides
REM a cache of ShipperObjects and methods
REM for updating and saving objects in the
REM cache from the database
#Region "ShipperComponent Class"
Public Class ShipperComponent
  Implements IShipperComponent
```

This class shares the following objects between all of its functions and subroutines.

```
#Region "Module Level Shared Objects"
  REM mSqlConnStr is the connection string to the database,
  REM mShipperCollection is the cache of Shipper objects,
  REM mConn is the connection to the database,
  REM mTransaction is the current transaction scope for
  REM the active database connection.
```

```
    REM mLastLoaded and mLastSaved represent the Date and Time
    REM the data was last loaded from and saved back to the database
    Private mSqlConnStr As String
    Private mShipperCollection As SortedList
    Private mConn As SqlConnection
    Private mTransaction As SqlTransaction
    Private mLastLoaded As DateTime
    Private mLastSaved As DateTime
    Private Const mVersion As String = "1.0.0"
    Private Const SHIPPERIDCOLUMN As Integer = 0
    Private Const COMPANYNAMECOLUMN As Integer = 1
    Private Const PHONECOLUMN As Integer = 2
  #End Region
```

Next, we have the few class properties.

```
  #Region "Class Properties"
    Public ReadOnly Property LastLoaded() As DateTime
      Get
        Return mLastLoaded
      End Get
    End Property

    Public ReadOnly Property LastSaved() As DateTime
      Get
        Return mLastSaved
      End Get
    End Property

    Public ReadOnly Property Version() As String
      Get
        Return mVersion
      End Get
    End Property

  #End Region
```

We do have a few functions that are just used within this class. The first of these makes sure a string value is in proper form to use in a SQL statement, while the second gives a quick way to execute a SQL command without returning any **ResultSets**.

```
  #Region "Private Utility Functions"
    REM This function trims off excess white space,
    REM makes single-quotes 'safe' for SQL statements
    REM and wraps the value in single quotes.
    Private Function PrepareForSql(ByVal Str As String) As String
      Dim SqlStr As String = Str

      SqlStr.Trim()
      SqlStr.Replace("'", "''")
      SqlStr = "'" & SqlStr & "'"
```

```
      Return SqlStr
    End Function

    REM Provides one-off execution of an SQL Statement
    REM Useful for cleaning out test data
    Public Sub SqlExc(ByVal SqlConnStr As String, ByVal Stmt As String)
      Dim Conn As New SqlConnection(SqlConnStr)
      Dim Cmd As New SqlCommand(Stmt, Conn)

      Try
        Conn.Open()
        Cmd.ExecuteNonQuery()
      Catch SqlExc As SqlException
        Throw SqlExc
      Catch Exc As Exception
        Throw Exc
      Finally
        Conn.Close()
      End Try
    End Sub
  #End Region
```

The next batch of functions and subroutines are what we use to get data to and from the database. These functions are fairly spartan by design. They make sure of connections and commands, rather than `DataAdapters`, because of the relatively simple nature of the data.

You might wonder a bit about `ExecuteStatement()` – how does it use transactions? It doesn't, but the functions and subroutines that call this function will have already opened a connection to the database and set the transaction level as appropriate. This allows us to execute several statements, and then commit the next change only if everything succeeds.

```
  #Region "Private Data Access Functions"
    REM Executes a given SQL statement
    REM against the database with the option
    REM of returning a scalar result.
    REM Assumes that connection is open and
    REM transaction level is set.
    Private Function ExecuteStatement(ByVal Stmt As String, _
    ByVal ExecScalar As Boolean) As Object
      Dim Cmd As SqlCommand
      Dim RetVal As New Object()

      Try
        Cmd = New SqlCommand(Stmt, mConn, mTransaction)
        If ExecScalar Then
          RetVal = Cmd.ExecuteScalar()
          Return RetVal
        Else
          Cmd.ExecuteNonQuery()
          Return Nothing
        End If
      Catch SqlExc As SqlException
```

```
      Throw SqlExc
    Catch Exc As Exception
      Throw Exc
    Finally
      Cmd.Cancel()
    End Try
  End Function
```

The next function simply loads the Shippers table into the cache. It doesn't use transactions as it's simply reading data from the table.

> **We're using embedded SQL statements here rather than Stored Procedures simply to avoid having that layer of complexity in the text. Ideally, Stored Procedures should be used instead as they offer the best performance and encapsulation of code.**

```
  REM Loads the database from the database
  REM and return a SortedList appropriate for
  REM populating the cache
  Private Function SelectFromDB() As SortedList
    Dim Cmd As SqlCommand
    Dim DR As SqlDataReader
    Dim ShipperInfo As Shipper
    Dim Col As New SortedList()

    Try
      Cmd = New SqlCommand("SET NOCOUNT ON;" & _
       "SELECT ShipperID,CompanyName,Phone FROM Shippers ORDER BY ShipperID;", _
       mConn)
      DR = Cmd.ExecuteReader()
      While DR.Read
        ShipperInfo = New Shipper(DR.GetInt32(SHIPPERIDCOLUMN), _
         DR.GetString(COMPANYNAMECOLUMN), _
         DR.GetString(PHONECOLUMN))
        ShipperInfo.IsNew = False
        Col.Add(ShipperInfo.CompanyName, ShipperInfo)
      End While
      Return Col
    Catch SqlExc As SqlException
      Throw SqlExc
    Catch Exc As Exception
      Throw Exc
    End Try
  End Function
```

Since we allow changes and deletions to the cached data, we'd better allow for those changes to be effected on the data in database. The next set of subroutines and functions do just that.

```
  REM Updates a single Shipper record in the database
  REM based on the values provided
  Private Sub UpdateDB(ByVal ShipperInfo As Shipper)
```

```
    Try
      ExecuteStatement("SET NOCOUNT ON; UPDATE Shippers SET CompanyName = " & _
       PrepareForSql(ShipperInfo.CompanyName) & ", Phone = " & _
       PrepareForSql(ShipperInfo.Phone) & _
       " WHERE ShipperID = " & ShipperInfo.ShipperID, False)
    Catch SqlExc As SqlException
      Throw SqlExc
    Catch Exc As Exception
      Throw Exc
    End Try
  End Sub

  REM Inserts a single, new Shipper record in the database
  REM based on the values provided
  Private Function InsertIntoDB(ByVal ShipperInfo As Shipper) As Shipper
    Dim NewID As Integer

    Try
      REM When the database actually inserts the
      REM Shipper into the database, it may generate a
      REM different ShipperID for it. We'll use
      REM an execute scalar to get that value
      REM then update the Shipper returned with it.
      NewID = Convert.ToInt32( _
       ExecuteStatement("SET NOCOUNT ON; " & _
       "INSERT INTO Shippers(CompanyName,Phone) VALUES (" & _
       PrepareForSql(ShipperInfo.CompanyName) & _
       "," & PrepareForSql(ShipperInfo.Phone) & "); " & _
       "SELECT @@IDENTITY FROM Shippers;", True))
      ShipperInfo.ShipperID = NewID
      Return ShipperInfo

    Catch SqlExc As SqlException
      Throw SqlExc
    Catch Exc As Exception
      Throw Exc
    End Try
  End Function

  REM Removes a shipper from the database based
  REM on the ShipperID provided.
  Private Sub DeleteFromDB(ByVal ShipperInfo As Shipper)
    Try
      ExecuteStatement("SET NOCOUNT ON;" & _
       "DELETE FROM Shippers WHERE ShipperID = " & _
       ShipperInfo.ShipperID.ToString(), False)
    Catch SqlExc As SqlException
      Throw SqlExc
    Catch Exc As Exception
      Throw Exc
    End Try
  End Sub
#End Region
```

With the ability to load, update and save data on the database taken care of, we need to offer the same at the cache level. That's what the next batch of functions and subroutines do. They start off with a method to populate the cache from the database.

```
#Region "Public Class Methods"

  REM Loads the database from the server
  REM and puts the results into the cache
  Public Sub Load() Implements IShipperComponent.Load
    Try
      mConn.Open()
      mShipperCollection = SelectFromDB()
      mLastLoaded = Now()
      mConn.Close()
    Catch SqlExc As SqlException
      Throw SqlExc
    Catch Exc As Exception
      Throw Exc
    End Try
  End Sub
```

Our `Save()` subroutine processes each of the objects in the cache, creating, updating or removing them from the cache and database as appropriate.

```
  REM Saves the cached database back
  REM to the database using a single
  REM transaction so that if any update fails,
  REM the whole update fails.
  Public Sub Save() Implements IShipperComponent.Save
    Dim ShipperInfo As Shipper
    Dim NewShipperID, OldShipperID As Integer
    Dim Index As Integer = 0

    Try
      REM Open the database and start
      REM a new transaction scope
      mConn.Open()
```

So far, so good, but here's the interesting part. Once our connection is opened, we can start a transaction that all of our changes will be controlled by. If all of the changes work, we can commit the data to the database – otherwise we can roll back these changes as if they were never made. Although we are making each `UPDATE`, `INSERT` or `DELETE` independently, they will all either commit or roll back if they don't all succeed.

```
      mTransaction = mConn.BeginTransaction

      REM Examine each of the cached objects
      REM and take the appropriate insert, update or
      REM delete action.
      While (Index < mShipperCollection.Count)

        REM Get the Shipper at the current Index...
```

```
        ShipperInfo = CType(mShipperCollection.GetByIndex(Index), Shipper)

        REM Delete from the database and cache if
        REM marked for deletion. Clear the IsChanged and
        REM IsNew flags to prevent additional processing.
        If ShipperInfo.IsDeleted Then
          DeleteFromDB(ShipperInfo)
          mShipperCollection.Remove(ShipperInfo.CompanyName)
          ShipperInfo.IsChanged = False
          ShipperInfo.IsNew = False
        End If

        REM Update this Shipper in the database.
        REM Clear any flags, indicating that this
        REM Shipper is 'in-sync' with the database.
        REM Must remove from cache, set flags, then add back.
        If ShipperInfo.IsChanged Then
          UpdateDB(ShipperInfo)
          Index = mShipperCollection.IndexOfKey(ShipperInfo.CompanyName)
          ShipperInfo.IsChanged = False
          ShipperInfo.IsDeleted = False
          ShipperInfo.IsNew = False
          mShipperCollection.SetByIndex(Index, ShipperInfo)
        End If

        REM Add this Shipper to the database
        REM Clear any flags, indicating that this
        REM Shipper is 'in-sync' with the database.
        REM Must remove from cache, set flags, then add back.
        If ShipperInfo.IsNew Then
          ShipperInfo = InsertIntoDB(ShipperInfo)
          Index = mShipperCollection.IndexOfKey(ShipperInfo.CompanyName)
          ShipperInfo.IsChanged = False
          ShipperInfo.IsDeleted = False
          ShipperInfo.IsNew = False
          mShipperCollection.SetByIndex(Index, ShipperInfo)
        End If

        REM get the cached Shipper
        Index += 1
      End While
```

If no exceptions are thrown and we've updated all of the changed records, we can let the transaction commit.

```
      REM If we survived this far,
      REM we can commit the transaction
      REM and actually save the data.
      mTransaction.Commit()
      mLastSaved = Now()
```

Otherwise, we need to roll back all of the changes.

```
      REM If any errors occur, rollback
      REM all of our attempted changes
      REM so the database isn't corrupted.
    Catch SqlExc As SqlException
      mTransaction.Rollback()
      Throw SqlExc
    Catch Exc As Exception
      mTransaction.Rollback()
      Throw Exc
    Finally
      REM close the database to
      REM free up its resources
      If mConn.State <> ConnectionState.Closed Then
        mConn.Close()
      End If
    End Try
  End Sub
```

The next function allows us to add a new shipper to the cache.

```
  REM Adds a new Shipper to the cache
  REM (will be written back to the database when
  REM the save method is called.)
  REM Returns the temporary ShipperID
  Public Function AddShipper(ByVal CompanyName As String, ByVal Phone As String)
As String Implements IShipperComponent.AddShipper
    Dim NewShipper, LastShipper As Shipper
    Dim Index, NewShipperID As Integer

    REM Need to find a suitable ID for this shipper
    REM so assume that it can be one greater than
    REM the current maximum ID.
    NewShipperID = -1
    For Index = 0 To mShipperCollection.Count - 1
      LastShipper = CType(mShipperCollection.GetByIndex(Index), Shipper)
      If LastShipper.ShipperID > NewShipperID Then
        NewShipperID = LastShipper.ShipperID
      End If
    Next
    NewShipperID = NewShipperID + 1

    REM Create a new shipper and add
    REM add it to the cache
    NewShipper = New Shipper(NewShipperID, CompanyName, Phone)
    mShipperCollection.Add(NewShipper.CompanyName, NewShipper)

    Return NewShipper.ShipperID.ToString
  End Function
```

We have a similar function for updating a cached `Shipper` as well.

```
  REM Updates a Shipper in the cache.
  REM Returns the ShipperID of the updated Shipper
  Public Function UpdateShipper(ByVal ShipperID As Integer, _
  ByVal CompanyName As String, ByVal Phone As String) As String Implements
IShipperComponent.UpdateShipper
    Dim ShipperInfo As Shipper
    Dim Found As Boolean = False
    Dim Index As Integer

    REM Finds the physical position in the cache
    REM of the Shipper indicated and removes it.
    For Index = 0 To mShipperCollection.Count - 1
      ShipperInfo = CType(mShipperCollection.GetByIndex(Index), Shipper)
      If ShipperInfo.ShipperID = ShipperID Then
        mShipperCollection.RemoveAt(Index)
        Exit For
      End If
    Next

    REM Create a new Shipper and update
    REM its flags as appropriate.
    ShipperInfo = New Shipper(ShipperID, CompanyName, Phone)
    ShipperInfo.IsChanged = True
    ShipperInfo.IsNew = False
    ShipperInfo.IsDeleted = False

    REM Put the updated shipper into the cache
    mShipperCollection.Add(ShipperInfo.CompanyName, ShipperInfo)

    Return ShipperInfo.ShipperID.ToString
  End Function
```

And a way to delete shippers:

```
  REM Mark Shipper as being deleted in the cache
  REM but don't delete it from the database until
  REM the save method is called.
  Public Sub DeleteShipperByID(ByVal ShipperID As Integer) Implements
IShipperComponent.DeleteShipperByID
    Dim Index As Integer
    Dim ShipperInfo As Shipper

    REM Find this Shipper and set its
    REM deleted flag to true
    For Index = 0 To mShipperCollection.Count - 1
      ShipperInfo = CType(mShipperCollection.GetByIndex(Index), Shipper)
      If ShipperInfo.ShipperID = ShipperID Then
        ShipperInfo.IsDeleted = True
        mShipperCollection.SetByIndex(Index, ShipperInfo)
        Exit For
      End If
    Next
  End Sub
```

All of that's well and good, but of course, the applications consuming this service will actually need some way to get at the data. We'll start by offering them a DataSet with one DataTable, listing all of the non-deleted shippers in the cache.

```
REM Returns a constructed DataSet with
REM a single table, the Shippers.
Public Function GetShipperList() As DataSet Implements
IShipperComponent.GetShipperList
  Dim Dr As DataRow
  Dim ShipperInfo As Shipper

  REM Ready a DataSet and Data table for use
  Dim Ds As New DataSet("Shippers")
  Dim Dt As New DataTable("Shipper")

  REM Create the Database Table with
  REM the appropriate columns and types.
  Dt.Columns.Add("ShipperID", GetType(Integer))
  Dt.Columns.Add("CompanyName", GetType(String))
  Dt.Columns.Add("Phone", GetType(String))

  REM Create a DataRow for each of the
  REM not-deleted Shippers and then add them
  REM to the DataTable
  For Each ShipperInfo In mShipperCollection.Values
    If Not ShipperInfo.IsDeleted Then
      Dr = Dt.NewRow()
      Dr("ShipperID") = ShipperInfo.ShipperID
      Dr("CompanyName") = ShipperInfo.CompanyName
      Dr("Phone") = ShipperInfo.Phone
      Dt.Rows.Add(Dr)
    End If
  Next

  REM Add the DataTable to the DataSet
  Ds.Tables.Add(Dt)

  Return Ds
End Function
```

We'll also allow the consumer to look up the ShipperID for a given Shipper, based on their name.

```
REM Returns the ShipperID for a given Shipper's Company Name
Public Function GetShipperIDByName(ByVal Name As String) As String Implements
IShipperComponent.GetShipperIDByName
  Dim ShipperInfo As Shipper

  ShipperInfo = CType(mShipperCollection(Name), Shipper)
  Return ShipperInfo.ShipperID.ToString()
End Function
```

We can also provide a complete Shipper object if the ShipperID is provided.

```
    REM Returns a Shipper given its ShipperID
    Public Function GetShipperByShipperID(ByVal ShipperID As Integer) As Shipper
  Implements IShipperComponent.GetShipperByShipperID
      Dim ShipperInfo As Shipper

      For Each ShipperInfo In mShipperCollection.Values
        If ShipperInfo.ShipperID = ShipperID Then
          Return ShipperInfo
        End If
      Next
      Return Nothing
    End Function
```

It's good for .NET-based applications that we can return an instance of the `Shipper` class directly to them via the previous function. But what about non-.NET consumers – they can't access the Assembly or CLR to know how a shipper is internally structured. For these clients, we need to return the `Shipper` information as something they can understand. Chances are that XML will fit that need.

```
    REM Returns a serialized version of a given Shipper
    Public Function GetShipperXMLByShipperID(ByVal ShipperID As Integer) As
  XmlDocumentFragment Implements IShipperComponent.GetShipperXMLByShipperID
      Dim ShipperInfo As Shipper

      For Each ShipperInfo In mShipperCollection.Values
        If ShipperInfo.ShipperID = ShipperID Then
          Return ShipperInfo.GetXML()
        End If
      Next
      Return Nothing
    End Function
  #End Region
```

Finally we have the class constructor. This one is rather busy, because it also automatically loads the data into the cache.

```
  #Region "Constructor"

    REM Creates an instance of ShipperSupport class.
    REM The Database connection string must be provided.
    REM If AutoLoad is true, the cache of Shippers is
    REM loaded immediately.
    Public Sub New(ByVal SqlConnStr As String, ByVal AutoLoad As Boolean)

      If SqlConnStr.Length = 0 Then
        Throw New ArgumentException("The SQL Connection String cannot be left
            blank.", _
         "SqlConnStr")
      End If
      mSqlConnStr = SqlConnStr

      If AutoLoad Then
```

```
        Try
          mConn = New SqlConnection(mSqlConnStr)
          Load()
        Catch SqlExc As SqlException
          Throw SqlExc
        Catch Exc As Exception
          Throw Exc
        End Try
      End If

    End Sub
  #End Region
  End Class
  #End Region
```

Go ahead and build this class now. Granted, you can't use it just yet, but it's a good time to stop and check for typos and other bugs.

Let's make our component class actually useful in a Web Service. Add a new project to the current solution. Use the Visual Basic .NET Web Service Template for this project. Name this `NwtShipper`. Set this as your new Start Up Project, and then rename `Service1.asmx` to `NwtShipper.asmx`.

Next, add a project reference to the `NwtShipperComponent` project to this project (right-click on **References**, click on the **Projects** tab, select the only project shown, click **Select**, click **OK**).

We'll start this code review by tweaking `global.asax`. Open that and go to the code view. Find the `Application_Start` event handler and add the following code to it.

```
Sub Application_Start(ByVal sender As Object, ByVal e As EventArgs)
    ' Fires when the application is started
    Try
        Application.Add("ShipperService", _
         New NwtShipperComponent.ShipperComponent( _
         "Password=;Persist Security Info=True;User ID=sa;Initial
              Catalog=Northwind;Data Source=127.0.0.1;", True))
    Catch Exc As Exception
        Throw Exc
    End Try

End Sub
```

Remember that you will need to change the connection string actual parameter to point to your database and supply it with the appropriate credentials.

This simple statement is rather powerful. What we're doing here is creating an instance of the component, and storing it in the block memory servicing all requests made for the service – this means all requests will be looking at the same data, without multiple connections to the database server or different caches.

Now, open the NwtShipper.asmx file and go to its code view. Remember the old saying about the three virtues of programmers being "laziness, impatience and hubris?" Well, the component class we've just finished can certainly help me be lazy as you're about to see – I hardly had to do any work with it. It's just going to be a wrapper around the public methods of that class. It's also helping me be impatient, because I was able to go from a component based on .NET interfaces to a Web Service based on XML interfaces in virtually no time flat. It's even something I can be proud of. Here's the code, then, and again, it starts by declaring that we want to use good coding practices and import and define the appropriate namespaces.

```
Option Explicit On
Option Strict On

Imports System.Web.Services
Imports System.Xml

Namespace NwtShippers
```

Next, we have the bit of code that makes this class available to the ASP.NET runtime as a Web Service.

```
  <WebService(Namespace:="http://webservices.northwindtraders.com/docs/shippers/")>
Public Class NwtShippersService
        Inherits System.Web.Services.WebService
```

You may be thinking to yourself that we've used an odd namespace for the Web Service. In practice, I've started using the URL to where developers could find additional documentation about the service at here instead. It's just a convenient thing to do.

```
        Private mShipperService As NwtShipperComponent.ShipperComponent
        Private mSqlConnStr As String

#Region " Web Services Designer Generated Code "

        Public Sub New()
            MyBase.New()

            'This call is required by the Web Services Designer.
            InitializeComponent()
```

Once the class underlying the service is initialised, we can fetch the instance of our component from the application and use it throughout the service.

```
            REM Fetch the instance of ShipperService from the Application space
            mShipperService = CType(Application("ShipperService"),
                NwtShipperComponent.ShipperComponent)
            If mShipperService Is Nothing Then
                Throw New ApplicationException("Cannot get an instance of
                    ShipperService.")
            End If
```

```
        End Sub

        'Required by the Web Services Designer
        Private components As System.ComponentModel.IContainer

        'NOTE: The following procedure is required by the Web Services Designer
        'It can be modified using the Web Services Designer.
        'Do not modify it using the code editor.
        <System.Diagnostics.DebuggerStepThrough()> Private Sub
        InitializeComponent()
            components = New System.ComponentModel.Container()
        End Sub

        Protected Overloads Overrides Sub Dispose(ByVal disposing As Boolean)
            'CODEGEN: This procedure is required by the Web Services Designer
            'Do not modify it using the code editor.
            If disposing Then
                If Not (components Is Nothing) Then
                    components.Dispose()
                End If
            End If
            MyBase.Dispose(disposing)
        End Sub

    #End Region
```

Now, we have the wrappers. Each public method of our component is exposed as a Web Service simply by calling from it a function with the `WebMethod` attribute. Hence, all of our useful functionality is "wrapped up and ready to serve the Web".

```
        <WebMethod()> Public Sub Load()
            mShipperService.Load()
        End Sub

        <WebMethod()> Public Sub Save()
            mShipperService.Save()
        End Sub

        <WebMethod()> Public Function AddShipper(ByVal CompanyName As String,
            ByVal Phone As String) As String
            Return mShipperService.AddShipper(CompanyName, Phone)
        End Function

        <WebMethod()> Public Function UpdateShipper(ByVal ShipperID As Integer,
        ByVal CompanyName As String, ByVal Phone As String) As String
            Return mShipperService.UpdateShipper(ShipperID, CompanyName, Phone)
        End Function

        <WebMethod()> Public Sub DeleteShipperByID(ByVal ShipperID As Integer)
            mShipperService.DeleteShipperByID(ShipperID)

        End Sub
```

```
        <WebMethod()> Public Function GetShipperList() As DataSet
            Return mShipperService.GetShipperList()
        End Function

        <WebMethod()> Public Function GetShipperIDByName(ByVal Name As String) As
        String
            Return mShipperService.GetShipperIDByName(Name)
        End Function

        <WebMethod()> Public Function GetShipperByShipperID(ByVal ShipperID As
        Integer) As NwtShipperComponent.Shipper
            Return mShipperService.GetShipperByShipperID(ShipperID)
        End Function

        <WebMethod()> Public Function GetShipperXMLByShipperID(ByVal ShipperID As
        Integer) As XmlDocumentFragment
            Return mShipperService.GetShipperXMLByShipperID(ShipperID)
        End Function

    End Class
End Namespace
```

And that's all it takes to expose a component as a Web Service. Now would be a good time to save all open files and build the project. You could just "build and browse" it to test the various methods. To make sure it works and to complete our example, let's look at a little Visual Basic .NET testing application that will make use of this service.

Close the current solution and start a new one based on the Visual Basic .NET Console Application. Call this project `Tester`. Alternatively, reconfigure the project of this name included in the code download for this chapter. When ready, add a Web Reference to the service we've just reviewed to that project. Rename the Web Reference to `NwtShipper`. Then launch Query Analyzer, connect to your database, and select the Northwind database. In the query window enter:

```
SELECT * FROM Shippers ORDER BY ShipperID
```

We'll be toggling between Visual Studio.NET and Query Analyzer as we go along now. Although I want you to type in this whole program first, I'm going to review its runtime behavior in-line. Once you have the code typed in, press *F10* to step through the code line by line to see how it works.

Edit the Visual Basic file in this project and enter the following text.

```
Module Tester

  Sub Main()
```

The next statement creates a local reference to the Web Service for use.

```
    Dim MyTester As New NwtShipper.NwtShippersService()
    Dim MyID As Integer
```

At this point, all of the existing data is already loaded into the cache, so let's add a test item.

```
REM Add a test company
Console.WriteLine("Adding Test Company")
MyTester.AddShipper("A Test Shipping Company", "(800) 555-1212")
Console.WriteLine(MyTester.GetShipperList().GetXml())
```

You'll see the console window display something like this...

```
Adding Test Company
<Shippers>
  <Shipper>
    <ShipperID>4</ShipperID>
    <CompanyName>A Test Shipping Company</CompanyName>
    <Phone>(800) 555-1212</Phone>
  </Shipper>
  <Shipper>
    <ShipperID>3</ShipperID>
    <CompanyName>Federal Shipping</CompanyName>
    <Phone>(503) 555-9931</Phone>
  </Shipper>
  <Shipper>
    <ShipperID>1</ShipperID>
    <CompanyName>Speedy Express</CompanyName>
    <Phone>(503) 555-9831</Phone>
  </Shipper>
  <Shipper>
    <ShipperID>2</ShipperID>
    <CompanyName>United Package</CompanyName>
    <Phone>(503) 555-3199</Phone>
  </Shipper>
</Shippers>
```

... if you are stepping through the code. We know our test item is in the cache. Notice the position of the test record in the XML stream.

Now toggle over to Query Analyzer and execute the query. Notice that new `Shipper` isn't in the base yet.

```
REM Use QueryAnalyzer to see that it's not in the DB yet...
Console.WriteLine("SELECT * FROM SHIPPERS ORDER BY SHIPPERID")

REM Save back
MyTester.Save()
```

Re-run the query and see that we have saved the new `Shipper`.

```
REM Use QueryAnalyzer to see that it's in the DB
Console.WriteLine("SELECT * FROM SHIPPERS ORDER BY SHIPPERID")

REM Update the name of the test company
MyID = MyTester.GetShipperIDByName("A Test Shipping Company")
```

We can now see what ShipperID SQL Server actually assigns to the new Shipper quite easily. With that information, we can change the name of the shipper.

```
        Console.WriteLine("Test Company ID is " & MyID.ToString())
        MyTester.UpdateShipper(MyID, "Test Express, Inc.", "(800) 555-1212")
        Console.WriteLine(MyTester.GetShipperList().GetXml())
```

Looking at the console output, the cache has been updated.

```
        REM Use QueryAnalyzer to see that it's not in the DB yet...
        Console.WriteLine("SELECT * FROM SHIPPERS ORDER BY SHIPPERID")
```

But the database hasn't until we execute the next statement.

```
        MyTester.Save()

        REM And now it is updated...
        Console.WriteLine("SELECT * FROM SHIPPERS ORDER BY SHIPPERID")
```

Re-run the query in Query Analyzer. Sure enough, we're updated.

```
        REM Show the XML version of just that Shipper
        Console.WriteLine(MyTester.GetShipperXMLByShipperID(MyID).OuterXml)

        REM Delete the test shipper
        MyTester.DeleteShipperByID(MyID)
```

Re-run the query in Query Analyzer. It still has the updated information...

```
        REM Use QueryAnalyzer to see that it's still in the DB yet...
        Console.WriteLine("SELECT * FROM SHIPPERS ORDER BY SHIPPERID")

        REM ...but it's not in the cache
        Console.WriteLine(MyTester.GetShipperList().GetXml())
```

But it's not in cache. To get it out of the database, we can just call the Save() web method again.

```
        REM Okay, save the list
        MyTester.Save()

        REM Use QueryAnalyzer to see that it's gone...
        Console.WriteLine("SELECT * FROM SHIPPERS ORDER BY SHIPPERID")
        Console.ReadLine()

    End Sub

End Module
```

Summary

In this chapter we learned about Web Services. We started this chapter with an introduction to Web Services, what they are, and what they are used for.

Next, we learned about the different protocols available for web servers – namely, HTTP-GET, HTTP-POST, and SOAP. Because the default protocol for Web Services is SOAP, we took a detailed look at SOAP and how it works.

As Web Services can cause security issues, we took a fairly detailed look at several technologies available for implementing security.

We looked at the implications of using transactions in conjunction with Web Services, and implemented a solution for using a transactional Web Service.

Finally we ended this chapter with a discussion about the pros and cons of using transactional Web Services.

Pro Visual Basic .NET Transactions

6

Distributed Applications Using Visual Basic .NET and COM+

As business applications are transformed from separate islands of information into tightly integrated enterprise systems, it has become increasingly common for an application to need to access and manipulate data stored in multiple data stores, often located in diverse locations. Suppose we have a transaction that must update data stored in two separate databases residing on two different servers, and we still require that all the properties of the ACID test be met. Basic transaction management using ADO.NET or Transaction SQL will not suffice.

When using ADO.NET or basic T-SQL transactions, there is no way to ensure that if one database server fails, the other has not already committed and become permanent. In other words, these technologies do not provide the ability to guarantee the atomicity of a transaction that spans multiple data stores, located on separate machines. Distributed transactions are transactions that can span multiple data stores, possibly located on different machines and diverse platforms.

Over the past several years, Microsoft has released several technologies to facilitate the development of distributed, transaction-processing systems. Some of these technologies include the **Microsoft Distributed Transaction Coordinator (MS DTC)**, **Microsoft Transaction Server (MTS)**, and **Windows Component Services (COM+)**. Microsoft Transaction Server originally introduced a transaction model that was designed to simplify the development of component-based, distributed transaction processing systems. As the successor to MTS, COM+ enhanced and extended MTS' powerful transaction model to provide even more flexibility and simplicity. Both of these technologies rely upon the transaction coordination functionality of MS DTC to support distributed transactions.

In this chapter we will discuss the concepts of distributed transactions and learn how we can utilize COM+ from Visual Basic.NET to develop distributed, transactional components. We briefly discussed some of these technologies in Chapter 1, so in this chapter we'll drill down on these technologies in further detail. Specifically, in this chapter we will:

- Outline the basic concepts of Distributed Transactions
- Discuss the behavior and functionality of COM+
- Learn how to utilize COM+ Transactions
- Compare and contrast techniques for voting on the transaction outcome
- Learn how to develop .NET `ServicedComponents`
- Analyze the life cycle of a COM+ Transaction
- Develop and test a transactional .NET `ServicedComponent`

Distributed Transactions

A distributed transaction is essentially a transaction that modifies data stored in two or more data stores. In addition to the requirements of local transactions, distributed transactions have the additional responsibilities of coordinating a transaction with diverse data stores, and potentially managing the success or failure of a transaction across physical machine boundaries. For example, using distributed transactions an application could insert a record into a SQL Server database, send a message using MSMQ, and update data in an Oracle database, all within the same transaction. If any of these operations were to fail for any reason, then the entire transaction would be rolled back by communicating with each data store.

Distributed transactions are executed and managed by several types of software components that collectively form a **distributed transaction processing system**. A distributed transaction processing system is an environment that processes and carries out the commitment or rollback of a distributed transaction, and consists of the following three types of participants:

- **Transactional Application**
  A transactional application is simply any application, component, or service that initiates and controls the transaction. A transactional application interacts with the transaction manager, specifically the **Coordinating Transaction Manager**, to start and commit or abort the transaction.

- **Resource Managers**
  A resource manager is a system service, such as a database management system (DBMS), that manages durable resources in a distributed transaction. Some of the existing resource managers that can participate in a distributed transaction coordinated by MS DTC include: Microsoft SQL Server, Microsoft Message Queue (MSMQ), Oracle, Sybase, Informix, IBM DB2, and Ingres.

- **Transaction Managers**
  With local transactions which only affect a single data store, the data store itself is responsible for coordinating the commitment and rollback of a transaction. However, because distributed transactions involve multiple data stores, it is necessary to offload these tasks to a separate service called a transaction manager. A transaction manager is a service that resides between the transaction application and the resource managers.

A transaction manager typically executes on each machine hosting a resource manager. This transaction manager is appropriately called the **local transaction manager** or the **participating transaction manager**. The participating transaction manager is responsible for interacting with the resource manager directly.

One transaction manager is assigned the special role of acting as the **Coordinating Transaction Manager**. The coordinating transaction manager is responsible for coordinating the entire life cycle of a transaction by interacting with each participating transaction manager involved in the transaction. It is also the responsibility of the coordinating transaction manager to report back to the client application whether it has successfully committed or rolled back the transaction.

Microsoft's transaction manager is named the **Microsoft Distributed Transaction Coordinator** (**MS DTC**). MS DTC is a Windows service that's included with several Microsoft Products. When asked to commit a transaction, MS DTC, acting as the coordinating transaction manager, executes a process called the two-phase commit protocol to coordinate the transaction outcome with all of the involved resource managers through each local transaction manager. We'll step through the two-phase commit protocol later in this chapter.

The following diagram illustrates the participants in a distributed transaction processing system. In this situation, all three resource managers are running on separate machines, and each resource manager is assigned its own local instance of MS DTC, which acts as the participating transaction manager. The coordinating transaction manager resides on the same machine as the transactional application.

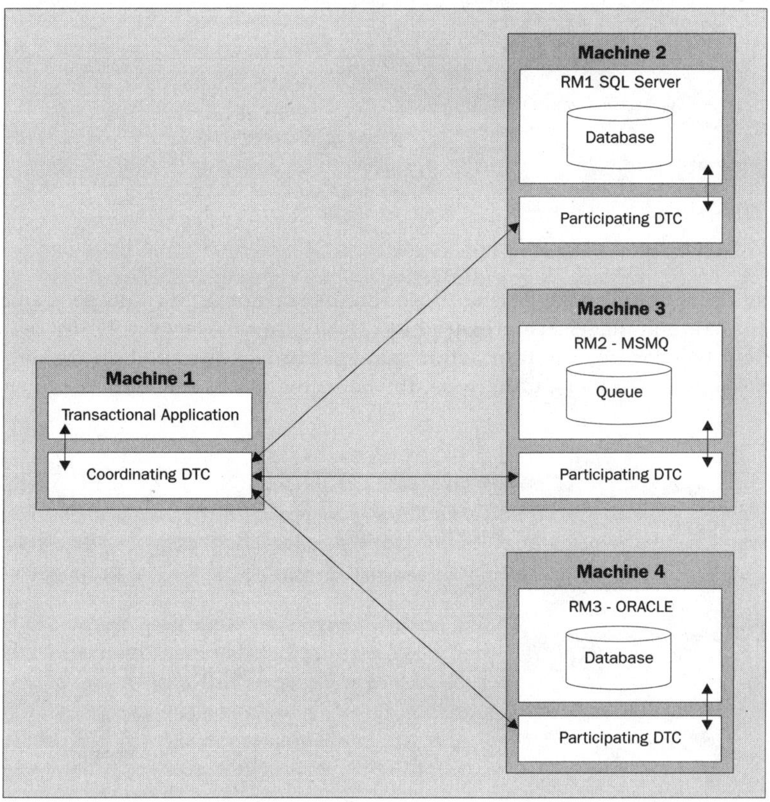

MS DTC

MS DTC is a Windows service that coordinates distributed transactions that span multiple resource managers. MS DTC was first integrated into SQL Server, and is now directly or indirectly utilized by a number of products, including COM+, Microsoft Message Queue Server, Host Integration Server, and Microsoft BizTalk Server. MS DTC is available for virtually all of the Microsoft Windows products including Windows NT, 2000, and XP.

As I mentioned, MS DTC executes a two-phase commit protocol when the transactional application instructs MS DTC to commit the distributed transaction. The two-phase commit protocol (2PC) is designed to guarantee the atomicity (all or nothing behavior) of a distributed transaction even if the resource manager becomes unavailable. Let's briefly walk through the steps of the two-phase commit protocol.

The Two-Phase Commit with MS DTC

The first phase in a 2PC is known as the *Prepare* phase. During this stage, the coordinating transaction manager sends out an "Are You Prepared?" request to each participating transaction manager, which then forwards the request to each resource manager:

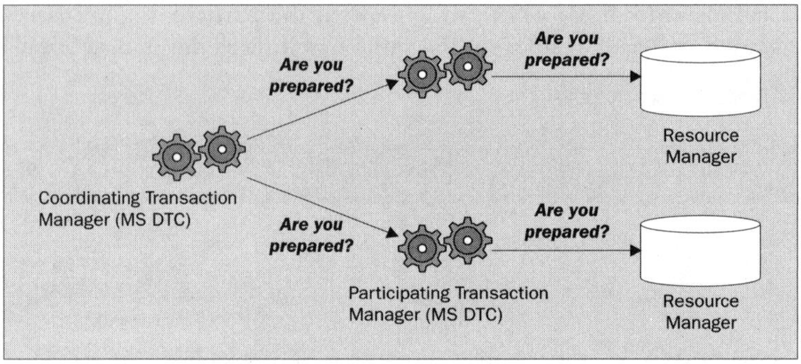

The coordinating transaction manager is notified whether or not each resource manager and participating transaction manager are prepared to commit the transaction. If any resource manager is not prepared, then the coordinating transaction manager broadcasts an abort message to all of the participating transaction managers. Otherwise, the coordinating transaction manager begins the second phase of the 2PC.

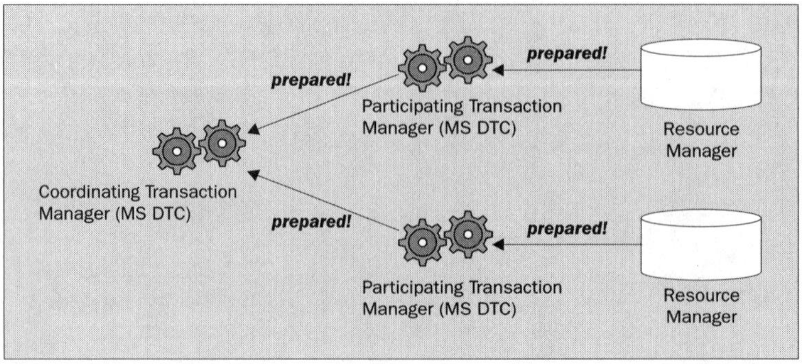

The second phase of the two-phase commit protocol is the *Commit* phase. If the commit coordinator receives an "I'm Prepared" response from each participating transaction manager and resource manager, the coordinating transaction manager attempts to commit the transaction by sending a "Commit" command to each participating transaction manager:

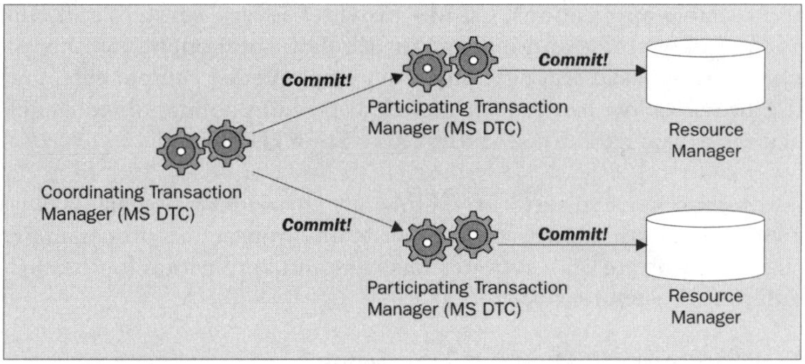

As each resource manager commits its part of the transaction, it sends a "Committed" response to the local participating transaction manager, which forwards the response to the coordinating transaction manager. However, if one "failure" is received from any resource manager that is to be affected, the coordinating transaction manager will issue a rollback and notify the client application.

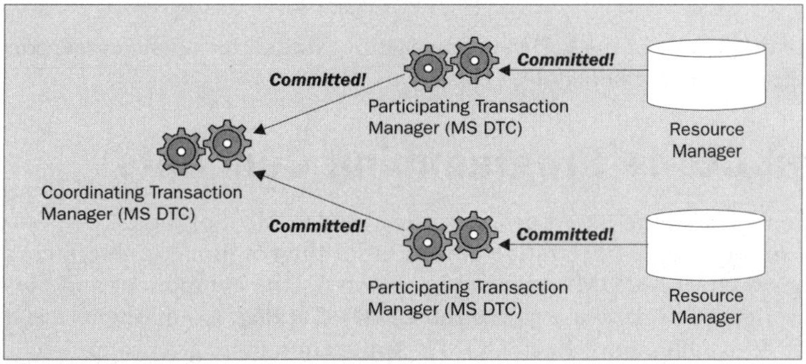

Distributed Transactions Using MS DTC

MS DTC supports resource managers that implement either the OLE Transaction or X/Open XA standard communication protocols. OLE Transactions is Microsoft's standard programming interface for developing transactional applications and transactional resource managers. OLE Transactions consists of several COM-based interfaces implemented by the DTC proxy DLL (`MSDTCPRX.dll`). By programming against these interfaces, an application can be designed to utilize the distributed transaction support of MS DTC. Resource managers also communicate with MS DTC through these interfaces implemented by the DTC proxy. Several resource managers, including Microsoft SQL Server and Microsoft Message Queue, utilize OLE Transactions. X/Open XA is a standard programming interface supported by several resource managers, including Oracle, IBM DB2, Informix, Sybase, and Ingres.

Although it is possible to develop a distributed transaction processing system using MS DTC by programming against the OLE Transactions interfaces, it is very difficult. MS DTC requires developers to write a significant amount of code in order to utilize MS DTC directly. Thankfully, COM+ provides us with an alternative for developing distributed, transaction processing systems that support MS DTC.

Introducing COM+

Simply stated, COM+ is a runtime environment for distributed components. The primary goal of COM+ is to simplify the development, management, and deployment of components used to compose mission-critical and scalable applications. COM+ provides several services and administrative tools that enable developers to rapidly create and manage distributed, component-based applications. Some of these services include: **role-based security, object pooling, queued components**, and **loosely coupled events**. COM+ also provides low-level services such as thread pooling, object synchronization, and an object management technique called **just-in-time activation (JIT)**.

In addition to these comprehensive services, COM+ also provides a powerful transaction model based on MS DTC that virtually eliminates the need to write any transaction processing code. These services enable developers to concentrate on a system's business and application logic instead of implementing common, middle-tier infrastructure.

COM+ is actually the successor to Microsoft Transaction Server product available on Windows NT 4.0, and is currently available in two different versions. At the time of this writing, COM+ 1.0 is currently available on the Windows 2000 platform, and the latest version, COM+ 1.5, is available on Windows XP. When released, the upcoming .NET Server product family will most likely include COM+ version 1.5. COM+ 1.5 provides support for additional features such as Windows services, Web Services, and multiple configurations of a single component.

Before we discuss the details of the COM+ Transaction Model, let's first review some of the fundamental programming concepts of COM+.

Fundamental COM+ Programming Concepts

COM+ is based on an attribute-based programming model. Most of the COM+ services can be implemented by simply setting declarative attributes for the component, interface, or method. When a component is registered with COM+, the configuration for the component and the services it utilizes are stored in a configuration database called the **COM+ Catalog**. Components are organized into logical groups called **COM+ Applications**. Each COM+ Application manages group-level configuration settings such as the activation, which determines if its components execute in-process or out-of-process. Developers or administrators can optionally modify the configuration of a component after it has been registered using the Component Services Administration tool provided by COM+. When a component is instantiated, COM+ automatically retrieves the configuration stored for the component and its application from the COM+ Catalog and initializes the configured services for the new object.

However, just before creating the new object, COM+ creates what's known as a *context* for the object. The context is responsible for storing metadata information for the COM+ object. Some of this information includes the configuration for the object that was stored in the COM+ Catalog, the security information for the caller, and values used to track the status of the object.

This information includes the configuration for the object that was read out of the COM+ Catalog, as well as values that track the status of the object. At runtime an object running within COM+ can interact with its context to influence or control its behaviour and control the services it utilizes.

The following diagram illustrates the relationship between a COM+ object, its context, and the COM+ Catalog.

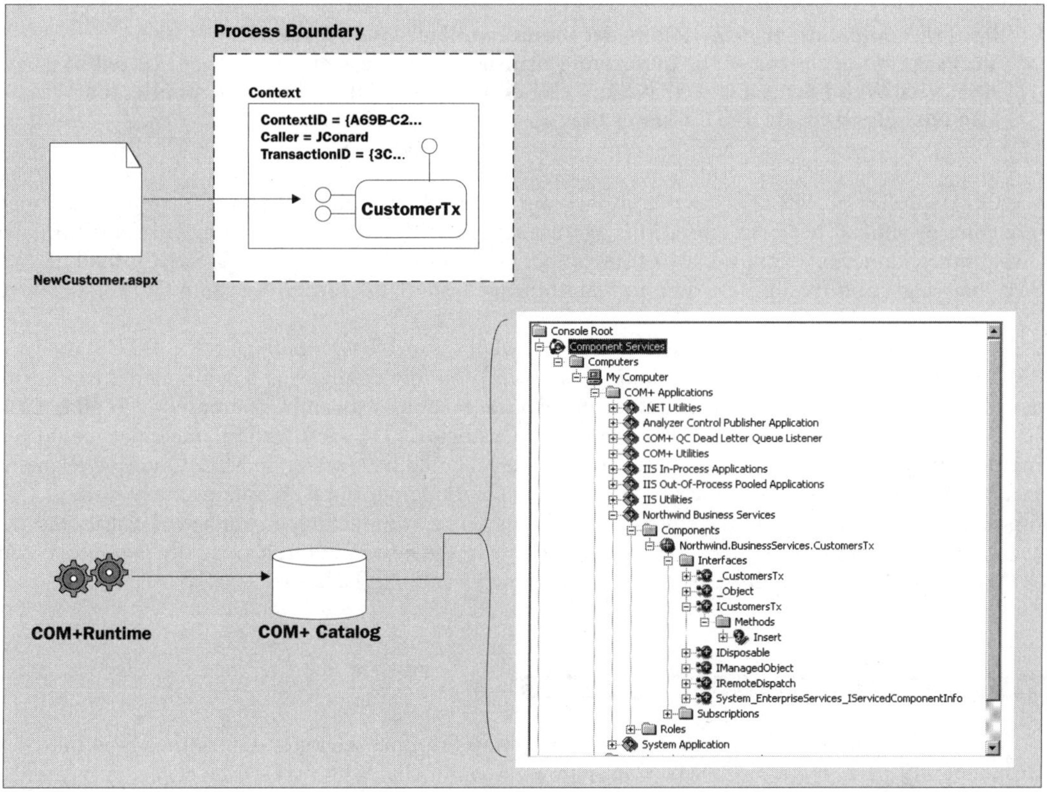

Later in this chapter we'll discuss more about these fundamental COM+ concepts, and how they apply to COM+ Transactions.

The COM+ Transaction Model

As I mentioned earlier, the COM+ transaction model eliminates the complex transaction-processing code required for distributed transactions coordinated by MS DTC. But what's even more significant, is that the COM+ transaction model merges the benefits of distributed transactions with component-based programming.

COM+ transactions, sometimes called **declarative transactions** or **automatic transactions,** are implemented through the use of declarative attributes. As a developer you can simply configure a **Transaction Support Attribute (TSA)** for your component either by applying .NET attributes on your class definitions, or by using the Component Services Explorer administration tool. At runtime the TSA is used by COM+ to determine the transactional behaviour of the component and automatically manage the transaction boundaries. COM+ automatically handles the complex details of beginning and committing or aborting transactions by interacting with MS DTC on behalf of your component, based on the component's configured Transaction Support Attribute. Any operations your component performs against resource managers will automatically be performed within a distributed transaction. Components can also optionally vote on the outcome of the transaction to influence COM+'s decision to commit or abort the transaction. This is very different to the manual transaction models provided by ADO.NET and T-SQL, which require you to explicitly control the transaction boundaries by manually starting and committing or aborting a transaction.

Does this automatic transaction model sound familiar? Well it should. COM+ Transactions are actually the underlying transaction processing technology utilized by ASP.NET Web Forms and ASP.NET Web Services. As we'll see in just a minute, it's also possible to create .NET Classes that leverage COM+ Transactions.

Since COM+ relies on MS DTC as the underlying transaction manager to coordinate transactions, a single component can perform operations against several different types of data sources within a single COM+ transaction. For example, a COM+ object could modify data in a SQL Server database, send an MSMQ message, and manipulate data in a mainframe system, all within the same COM+ transaction.

COM+ also extends distributed transactions beyond what's possible when utilizing MS DTC directly. COM+ allows transactions to seamlessly span multiple objects. By simply configuring a component's transaction support level, a COM+ object can execute in its own transaction or it can be composed with other COM+ objects as part of a larger transaction. For example, in a single COM+ transaction, one object could manipulate data in a SQL Server database, another object could be sending an MSMQ message, and a third object could insert data into an Oracle database. By segmenting out these operations into separate components we can simplify management and facilitate reuse, while taking advantage of distributed transactions coordinated by MS DTC. As we'll examine in the next chapter, it's actually possible to compose a COM+ transaction with both Visual Basic 6 components and .NET classes.

Transaction Support Levels

As I mentioned, each COM+ component's Transaction Support attribute determines how the component will participate in COM+ transactions. Specifically, when a COM+ object is created, COM+ examines the object's transaction support and determines whether or not the creator is running within an existing transaction. Based on these two pieces of information, the COM+ run-time will either activate the object within the creator's transaction, a new transaction created specially for the object, or no transaction at all. Every COM+ object is either activated with a transaction or without one. Consequently, COM+ components that will utilize transactions are often referred to as **transactional components** and components that will not participate in transactions are typically called **non-transactional components**.

There are five possible settings for the COM+ Transaction Support Attribute:

- `Disabled`
  When a component's transaction support is set to `Disabled`, COM+ will completely ignore the component's transactional requirements and create instances in the most efficient way possible. COM+ will first attempt to activate the object within the creator's context. However, if the creator's context is unavailable or incompatible due to the configuration of other services, the object will be activated within a new context. Since the object may or may not inherit the creator's context, the object may or may not share the creator's transaction. Because of this variable behavior, I recommend avoiding this setting and choosing one of the other four settings in order to explicitly control the transactional behavior of a component.

- `Not Supported`
  When a component's transaction support is set to `Not Supported`, instances of the component will *never* participate in a transaction, regardless of the transactional behavior of the creator. This setting is designed for COM+ components that do not access resource managers and do not need to control the outcome of a COM+ transaction, or for components that utilize manual transactions through ADO.NET or Transact SQL (T-SQL). An object with the transaction support of `Not Supported` will *always* be activated within a new context. This is different from the `Disabled` attribute, which means that the object might share the context and the transaction of the creator.

- `Supported`
  When a component's transaction support is set to `Supported`, instances of the component can participate within an existing transaction. However, a transaction is not required by the component and it can execute without one. If the creator is running within a transaction, then instances of a component configured with a TSA of `Supported` will automatically be created within the creator's transaction. Otherwise, the new object will not execute within a transaction.

  Unlike the transaction support attribute of `Disabled`, instances of a component configured as `Supported` will always be activated within their own context. This setting is typically used for components that don't perform transactional operations, but need to be able to vote on the outcome of a transaction.

- `Required`
  When a component's transaction support is set to `Required`, instances will *always* execute within a transaction. COM+ will enlist the new object in the creator's transaction if one exists, or in a new transaction created specifically for the object. Either way, the new component instance will *always* execute within a transaction. This setting is typically used for any component that should always leverage the COM+ transaction services.

- `Requires New`
  When a component's transaction support is set to `Requires New`, instances will always be activated within a new component, and will *always* be instantiated inside of a *new* transaction created specially for this object, regardless of whether it was created by an object within an existing transaction or not.

  This setting is designed for components that must perform work within a transaction, but their work must be kept separate from all other transactions. When you use this setting, the COM+ object never runs inside the scope of the creator's transaction. Instead, COM+ creates a new transaction that is completely independent of the creator's transaction. The creator's transaction may commit while this object aborts, or vice versa. This behavior of COM+ is different from the behavior of nested or chained transactions supported by some transaction monitors and resource managers. With nested transactions, a parent-child relationship between transactions is maintained, and committing or aborting a parent transaction causes the same results for all child transactions. COM+ does not support nested transactions. Consequently, any transactions created by a transactional object execute completely independently of the creator.

The following table summarizes the differences between the possible values for the Transaction Support Attribute. Be sure to note the footnotes below the table, which clarify the conditional scenarios.

Attribute Value	New Transaction	Client's Transaction	Root of Transaction
`Disabled`	Never	If the creator has a transaction	Never
`Not Supported`	Never	Never	Never
`Supported`	Never	If the creator has a transaction	Never
`Required`	If the creator does not have a transaction	If the creator has a transaction	If the creator does not have a transaction
`Requires New`	Always	Never	Always

> **The Just-in-time (JIT) Activation and Synchronization services are required by COM+ Transactions. Consequently, these services will automatically be enabled for any COM+ Components configured with a TSA other than `Disabled`.**

Serviced Components

Although COM+ is tightly coupled to the COM programming model, the .NET Framework has built in facilities for creating components that can execute in COM+, and take advantage of COM+ services, including transaction services. .NET classes that are designed to execute in COM+ are called **Serviced Components**.

`ServicedComponents` are special .NET classes that inherit directly or indirectly from the `ServicedComponent` base class defined in the `System.EnterpriseServices` namespace. The `System.EnterpriseServices` namespace also defines several .NET attributes that can be applied in code to a `ServicedComponent` 's class declaration, method declaration, or at the assembly level. These attributes are used to indicate how the component should be configured in COM+ and specify which services it will utilize. When a .NET assembly containing `ServicedComponents` is registered with COM+, the values of the attributes applied in code are read from the metadata in the assembly and the component is configured in the COM+ Catalog accordingly.

Creating Transactional ServicedComponents

In order to create a .NET `ServicedComponent` that utilizes COM+ Transaction Services you must perform the following five tasks:

1. **Create a .NET class that inherits from the `ServicedComponent` base class**
As we have just seen, .NET classes that wish to utilize COM+ services, including transactions, must derive either directly or indirectly from `System.EnterpriseServices.ServicedComponent` base class.

2. **Apply the `TransactionAttribute` .NET attribute to the class declaration**
To utilize COM+ Transactions, a `ServicedComponent` must specify its transaction support level. The `TransactionAttribute` .NET attribute defined in the `System.EnterpriseServices` namespace can be applied to the class declaration for a .NET `ServicedComponent` to specify the `ServicedComponent` 's transaction support attribute, and the isolation level and timeout for the transaction. The possible values for the `TransactionAttribute` are the same values we just discussed for the TSA. The fully typed name for this .NET attribute class is `System.EnterpriseServices.TransactionAttribute`, although you can use `Transaction` or `TransactionAttribute` interchangeably.

3. **Apply assembly-level .NET attributes to specify the COM+ application configuration**
In addition to the class-level `TransactionAttribute` attribute, the `System.EnterpriseServices` namespace also defines several assembly-level attributes that are used to specify information for the COM+ Application that will be created during registration to host the `ServicedComponents` in the assembly. Some of these attributes include the `ApplicationNameAttribute`, which is used to specify the name of the COM+ application that should be created, the `ApplicationActivationAttribute` which specifies whether the components in the COM+ Application will execute in-process or out-of-process to the creator, and the `ApplicationAccessControlAttribute` which specifies the security configuration for the COM+ Application.

4. **Create a strong name**
A **strong name** is a set of information embedded in the assembly's metadata that is used to uniquely identify an assembly. This information includes the text name of the assembly, its version number, a public key and digital signature. An assembly must be signed with a strong name before it is created in order to register the assembly and its `ServicedComponents` with COM+.

   To sign an assembly with a strong name, you must first generate a public and private key pair using a command-line utility, included with the .NET Framework SDK and Visual Studio .NET, called the Strong Name Tool (`Sn.exe`). The Strong Name Tool can create and save a key pair to a file, which can then be specified using the assembly-level `AssemblyKeyFile` attribute in the code for a `ServicedComponent`.

5. **Register the component in the COM+ Catalog**
Finally, after the assembly containing the .NET `ServicedComponents` has been created, it must be registered with COM+ before it can be used. There are actually a couple of different ways to register `ServicedComponents`. We'll talk about each of these techniques later in this chapter. For now it's important to understand what happens when a .NET assembly containing `ServicedComponents` is registered. The values for the attributes specified in code are read from the assembly's metadata. This information is used to create or find and configure a COM+ application and configure each of the .NET `ServicedComponents` in the COM+ Catalog. This information includes the Transaction Support Level specified for the .NET Class using the `TransactionAttribute`.

For example, the following code defines a .NET `ServicedComponent` named `CustomersTx` that is configured with a transaction support level of `Required`. Notice that we import a reference to the `System.EnterpriseServices` namespace, and our class inherits from the `ServicedComponent` base class.

```
'Import namespaces containing commonly used types
Imports System.EnterpriseServices

<Transaction(TransactionOption.Required)> _
Public Class CustomersTx

    'Inherit from the System.EnterpriseServices.ServicedComponent class to allow
    '...this component to utilize COM+ services
    Inherits ServicedComponent


    Public Sub InsertCustomer()
        '
    End Sub
End Class
```

After a serviced component is registered, clients can create instances of the component the way they create instances of any other component. For example, the following code creates a new instance of the .NET `ServicedComponent` that we just defined by using the `New` keyword in Visual Basic .NET:

```
Dim objCustomersTx As New CustomersTx ()
```

If the tasks required to create a transactional .NET `ServicedComponent` sound complex, don't worry. We'll walk through each of these steps when we create a transactional `ServicedComponent` later in this chapter. Technically, by simply creating a .NET `ServicedComponent` and applying the `Transaction` attribute, a .NET class will fully support transactions. However, in order to best take advantage of the COM+ Automatic Transaction model and maximize performance and scalability, it is important to understand the lifetime of a COM+ transaction.

Life Cycle of a COM+ Transaction

The lifetime of a COM+ automatic transaction is similar to the life cycle of any transaction. The transaction must begin, perform some work, and complete by either committing or aborting. However, the life cycle of a COM+ transaction is much more involved than a manual transaction with ADO.NET or T-SQL, because of all the work COM+ must do behind the scenes to support the automatic transaction model. Thankfully, COM+ abstracts us from most of the details of a transaction's lifetime. However, by understanding what happens behind the scenes in a COM+ transaction, we can effectively design components around the transaction, and optimise the performance and scalability of COM+ Transactions.

The life cycle of a COM+ Transaction consists of four complex stages. These stages are:

1. Starting the transaction
2. Enlisting connections to transactional resource managers

3. Accessing and manipulating data within the transaction

4. Completing the transaction and determining the outcome

Let's discover what happens during each of these stages – for both single and multi-object COM+ transactions.

> **Although the techniques for creating transactional COM+ components have changed with .NET, the fundamental COM+ transaction model – and the lifecycle of a COM+ transaction – has not. Consequently, if you are already familiar with the concepts of COM+ transactions, then you may find it beneficial to skip ahead to the comprehensive code sample in this chapter.**

Starting a Transaction

As we discussed earlier, with the COM+ transaction model, a component does not explicitly start a COM+ Transaction. Instead, COM+ automatically creates a new COM+ transaction in one of two scenarios:

- A component with a transaction support of `Required` is instantiated by a non-transactional client
- A component with a transaction support of `Requires New` is instantiated by *any* client

A COM+ transaction is composed of two parts: a **logical transaction** and a **physical transaction**.

A logical transaction, also known as a **transaction stream**, is a logical collection or grouping of objects that share a physical transaction. A physical transaction, on the other hand, is the underlying MS DTC transaction that coordinates commit and abort behaviour with resource managers using two-phase commit protocol. When the physical transaction is created by COM+, it is created with the isolation level and the transaction timeout interval specified for the root object in the COM+ Catalog. COM+ completely abstracts objects from the underlying physical transaction and instead allows us to manage the transaction through the logical transaction stream and each object's context. It is important to note that there is always a one-to-one relationship of transaction streams to physical transactions, although, as we'll discuss in the following section, a logical transaction can be composed of several COM+ objects.

The following diagram illustrates the process creation of a COM+ transaction. Let's briefly discuss the sequence of events illustrated in this diagram:

1. When COM+ receives a request to instantiate a component, the COM+ runtime retrieves the configuration for the component out of the COM+ Catalog.

2. If the component has a transaction support attribute of any value other than `Disabled`, then COM+ always creates a new context before creating the object.

3. COM+ instructs the MS DTC to begin a new physical transaction. When MS DTC creates a new transaction, it also creates a new GUID value called the `TransactionID`, which is used to identify the physical transaction.

4. The `TransactionID` is stored in the COM+ object's context, so COM+ can correlate an object with its underlying MS DTC transaction. COM+ also creates the logical transaction at this time.

5. COM+ creates an instance of the requested component and assigns the object to the new context. Finally, the new object and the transaction are created and the object can then begin processing method calls.

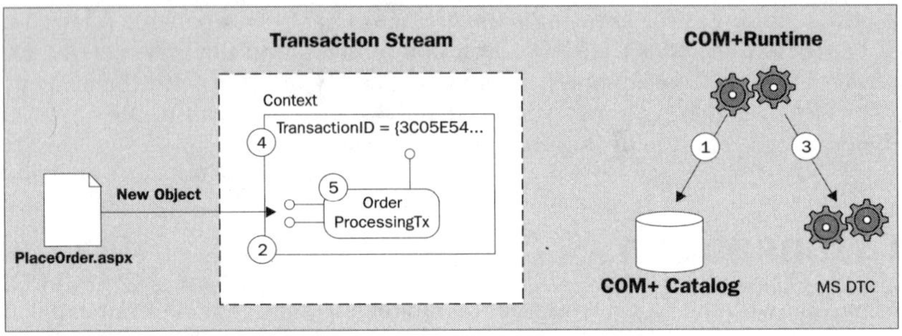

Creating Subordinate Objects

The first object created within a transaction stream is called the **root** of the transaction. Every COM+ transaction has only one root object. The root of the transaction can optionally add or *enlist* other COM+ objects in the same logical transaction by instantiating COM+ components that have a TSA of either `Required` or `Supported`. These additional objects are called **interior** objects or **subordinate** objects. When an object is created in the same transaction, COM+ automatically replicates or **propagates** the `TransactionID` from the root object's context to the new object's context, so COM+ can maintain the association between all objects in the transaction.

For example, in the following diagram the `OrderProcessingTx` component is the root of the transaction. When the `OrderProcessingTx` component instantiates the `OrderDetailsTx` component, which is configured with a TSA of `Required`, COM+ automatically propagates the transaction information to the new object's context, and the new object then becomes part of the same transaction stream as the creator. This process is repeated for each COM+ component instantiated by the root of the transaction.

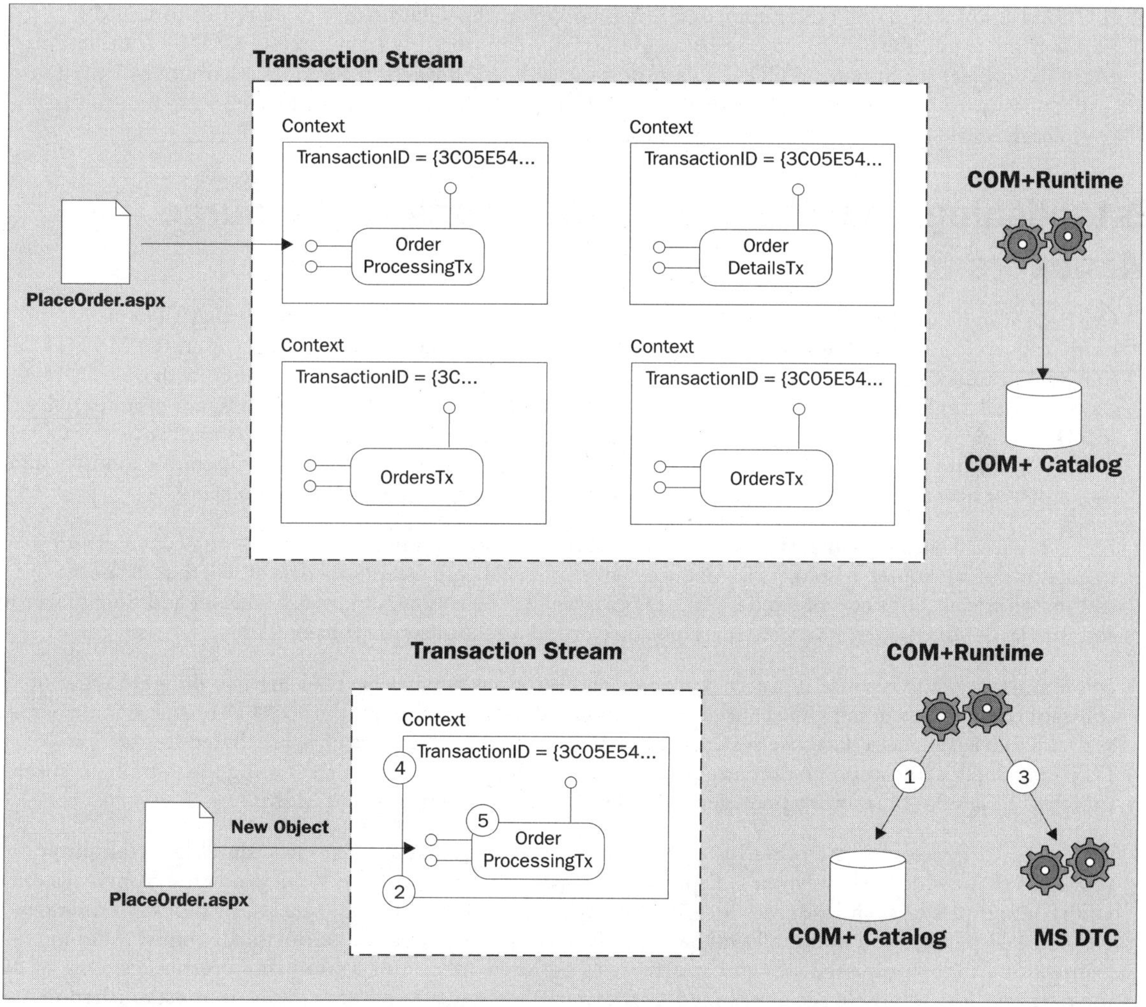

For these new objects to be enlisted in the creator's COM+ transaction they must also be created in the same ***activity***. Basically, an activity is a logical grouping of objects used at runtime by COM+ to manage and coordinate multi-user concurrency, synchronization and threads. In Microsoft Transaction Server the root object in a transaction had to create subordinate objects using a special method named `CreateInstance()`, in order for the new object to belong in the same activity and transaction of the caller. Since COM+ has integrated the MTS and COM programming models, the `CreateInstance()` method is no longer required and Visual Basic 6.0 components can create sub-objects using the `CreateObject()` function.

However, Visual Basic 6 still suffers from one peculiar issue. If a COM+ Component developed using Visual Basic 6 creates an instance of another component located in the same DLL by using the `New` keyword, then the Visual Basic runtime would create the instance of the component instead of COM+. Consequently, the new object would not have a context and could not take advantage of COM+ services including transaction support. In .NET, subordinate objects can be created using the `New` keyword, just as you instantiate any .NET class.

A COM+ transaction can never span activities; however, the relationship of activities to COM+ transactions is not always one-to-one. A single activity can possibly have several COM+ transactions. If a COM+ Object instantiates a COM+ Component with a Transaction Support Attribute of `Requires New`, the new object will be in the same activity but in a different COM+ transaction – one that is completely independent of the creator's transaction.

Establishing and Enlisting Connections to Resource Managers

Once the transaction is started by the creation of the root object, COM+ must ensure that all data modification operations performed by the object against data sources are performed within the MS DTC (physical) transaction. Each connection to each data source must be *enlisted* or registered with the MS DTC transaction. By enlisting a connection, all operations performed through the connection are monitored by the MS DTC and are protected by a transaction. Although the entire enlistment process is performed by COM+ behind the scenes for each connection established within a transactional object, it's imperative to understand the details of how this important step in an automatic transaction's lifetime is accomplished.

As we discussed earlier in this chapter, transactional applications (in this case COM+ objects) read and write to data through resource managers (RMs). Resource managers are essentially data stores that support distributed transactions coordinated by MS DTC. The COM+ transaction model adds an additional layer of software to the distributed transaction architecture called a **resource dispenser (RD)**.

It is important not to confuse resource managers and resource dispensers. They are two different types of software components in the COM+ transaction model that serve different purposes. A resource manager is a system service, such as a database system, that manages durable resources in a distributed transaction. MS DTC coordinates transaction commitment and rollback with resource managers using the two-phase commit protocol. Examples of resource managers include: SQL Server, Oracle, and MSMQ.

A resource dispenser, on the other hand, is an in-process DLL that manages non-durable or temporary resources that reside in the resource dispenser's memory and do not need to be protected from a system failure. Examples of such resources include network connections, threads, objects, or blocks of memory. Resource dispensers can optionally manage pools of reusable resources, automatically enlist them in transactions and expose methods and interfaces to perform operations against these resources. One of the most common nondurable resources managed by a resource dispenser are connections established to a resource manager.

Don't let the terminology "resource dispensers" confuse you. A resource dispenser is simply a role assigned to software components that are positioned between a COM+ object and a resource. Many resource dispensers also provide components that can be used outside of the COM+ environment. The COM+ Shared Property Manager, which we'll discuss in a moment, is an example of such a resource dispenser.

Some of the most commonly used resource dispensers include:

1. **COM+ Shared Property Manager (SPM, pronounced "spam")**
   The COM+ Shared Property Manager allows multiple objects running in COM+ to share data and memory within a process. This can be helpful because data is stored in memory globally for the process, so it is persisted beyond the lifetime of a single object. Even though the SPM is a resource dispenser, it does not participate in transactions. The SPM is accessible in a .NET `ServicedComponent` through the `System.EnterpriseServices.SharedPropertyGroupManager` class.

2. **Microsoft Message Queue Server (MSMQ)**
   MSMQ includes a resource dispenser for enlisting MSMQ queues in distributed transactions.

3. **OLE DB Service Component**
   OLE DB Service Component is a resource dispenser for OLE DB sessions, being the low-level object that represents an OLE DB connection to a data store. The OLE DB Service Component is responsible for enlisting connections when using ADO or ADO.NET, and also the OLE DB Managed Provider with a transactional-aware OLE DB Data Provider.

4. **SQL Server Managed Provider**
   The SQL Server Managed Provider itself behaves as a resource manager by enlisting connections to a data store within a transaction.

If you need a component that can efficiently manage a custom resource for your COM+ components, you could develop a custom COM+ resource dispenser. However, you should be warned that developing a resource dispenser is much more difficult than developing COM+ components, because a resource dispenser must be multi-threaded and thread-safe. Due to these requirements, we could not develop custom COM+ resource dispensers using Visual Basic 6.

However, COM+ provides an alternative, called **compensating resource managers**, which can be developed from any .NET or COM compliant language. CRMs provide the ability for transactional objects to access custom resources (durable or non-durable) within a transaction without the need for a complex resource dispenser and resource manager pair.

It is important to understand that not all resource dispensers have a corresponding data source that acts as a resource manager. Remember, the qualification for a data source being considered a resource manager is that the data source supports distributed transactions. The Shared Property Manager is responsible for managing memory, a non-transactional resource, in a COM+ process. Unlike other resource dispensers which can only be accessed indirectly through component layers, the Shared Property Manager exposes a set of classes, defined in the `System.EnterpriseServices` namespace, that allows `ServicedComponents` to directly invoke methods to receive requested functionality.

In addition to creating and managing resources, some resource dispensers optionally provide the following functionality:

- **Resource Pooling**
  Resource pooling provides an efficient way of reusing non-durable resources by providing a COM+ object with a recycled resource instead of creating a new one. After a COM+ object is through with the resource, it is placed back into the pool where it is made available for immediate reuse by the same or another COM+ object. As I mentioned, connections to data sources (resource managers) are one of the most commonly used non-durable resources. Creating and destroying a connection to a resource manager is an expensive process. To efficiently provide COM+ objects with data source connections, both the SQL Managed Provider and the OLE DB Service Component provide resource pooling of connections to resource managers.

- **Transaction Enlistment**
  Transaction Enlistment is the process of associating or **enlisting** a connection to a resource manager with the MS DTC (physical) transaction. Once this transaction enlistment is completed, all work performed by the COM+ object through that connection will be monitored by MS DTC and be protected within a distributed transaction. All operations will be performed as a single unit of work and the transaction as a whole will be required to conform to the ACID properties (Atomicity, Consistency, Isolation and Durability).

  When the logical transaction completes, MS DTC can then execute the two-phase commit protocol with all the participating resource managers. It is important to note that the transaction enlistment is totally optional. It is the resource dispenser's decision whether or not to enlist the resource in the current transaction. Currently, the SQL Server managed provider, the OLE DB Service Component, and MSMQ, amongst others, all support transaction enlistment. A resource dispenser that provides transaction enlistment is sometimes called a transactional resource dispenser. Transaction enlistment plays a significant role in COM+ transactions because it abstracts the component developer from this repetitive task.

Transaction Enlistment Process

The following diagram illustrates the complex process performed by the **resource dispenser manager (DispMan)** when a transactional COM+ object attempts to establish a connection to a SQL Server database using the SQL Server Managed Provider. DispMan is responsible for providing resource pooling for the resource dispensers and managing the enlistment process.

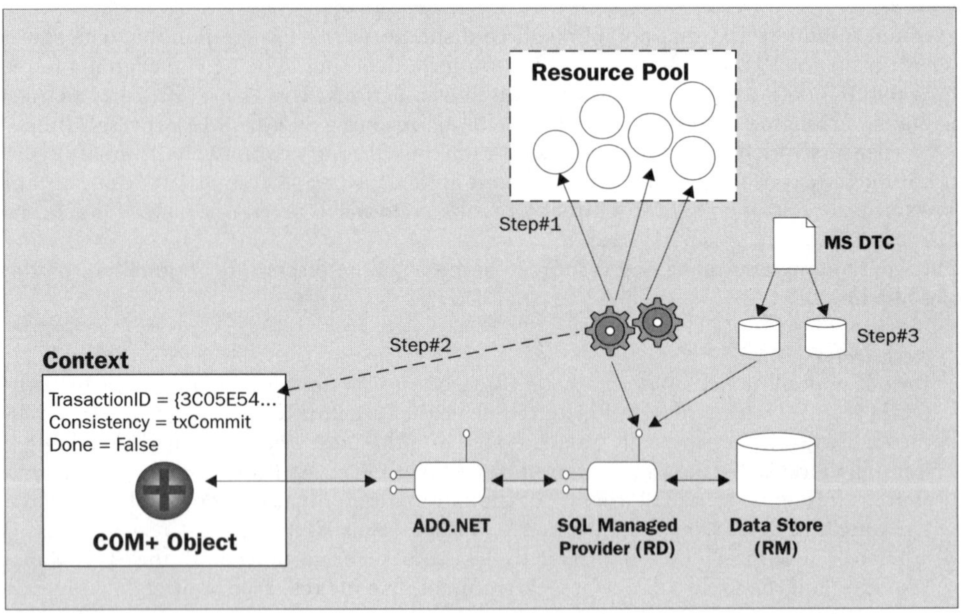

1. When a resource dispenser receives a request for a resource, in this case a new connection to the database, the resource dispenser manager (DispMan) either reuses an existing resource from a pool or requests the resource dispenser to create a new one.

2. After DispMan has allocated a resource, it determines if the resource is transactional and attempts to obtain the current transaction information (`TransactionID`) for the calling COM+ object from object's context. If no transaction information is available, DispMan assumes that the object is non-transactional and simply returns the resource back to the resource dispenser, which in turn gives the resource to the COM+ object. However, if DispMan does obtain the transaction information, it passes the information to the resource dispenser.

3. The resource dispenser then automatically forwards the transaction information and the resource to the MS DTC, where it is enlisted with the physical transaction. Finally the resource is returned to the resource dispenser and eventually to the calling COM+ object where it can be utilized.

This entire process occurs every time a transaction COM+ object opens a connection to a data source. Thankfully, COM+ does an excellent job of hiding components from these complex details of distributed transactions. In fact, our only responsibility at this stage of a transaction's lifetime is to establish a connection to a data source in our .NET `ServicedComponent` just as we do normally using ADO.NET or ADO. COM+. The dispenser manager and the resource dispensers are responsible for performing the complex tasks of resource pooling and transaction enlistment.

Accessing and Manipulating Data

After connections have been established to the data store(s) and enlisted in the transaction, a transactional COM+ object can begin performing operations against resource managers just as it normally would. All of the work performed by the transactional object through an enlisted connection will be performed with the protection of a distributed transaction coordinated by MS DTC. MS DTC automatically keeps track of the operations performed by the objects in the logical transaction, and ensures that they are performed as part of the physical transaction.

When a resource manager receives and processes operations against its data, it takes certain measures to ensure that the transaction meets the ACID requirements. Most resource managers implement a logging mechanism to provide the ability to roll back uncommitted changes to satisfy the atomicity requirement. Logging mechanisms also allow a resource manager to ensure the durability of a transaction by being able to reapply or recover changes should an unforeseen problem occur. Locks are typically used to isolate a transaction's changes from affecting other transactions against the same resource manager. To ensure consistency, resource managers usually define special mechanisms or rules to protect the integrity of data.

Completing the Transaction and Determining the Outcome

After the objects within a COM+ transaction have completed their work, the transaction must complete. Remember, according to the ACID transaction processing rules, every transaction has a start and an end, and can only execute exactly once. In order to completely understand when a COM+ transaction ends and how COM+ determines the outcome of a transaction, we need to first discuss some of the underlying details of how COM+ tracks the status of a transaction.

As we learned earlier, a transactional COM+ object's context contains a GUID value called a TransactionID, which is used to associate multiple objects within a transaction and link the COM+ logical transaction to the underlying physical transaction managed by MS DTC. However, this is not the only information that is stored in an object's context. A transactional object's context also contains two other important pieces of information that are used to know when to complete a transaction and whether or not the transaction should be committed or aborted. These two pieces of information are:

- Done **Bit**
  The Done bit is a Boolean value that indicates whether or not the object should be deactivated. A value of True indicates that the object has completed its work and can be deactivated, while a value of False indicates that the object is not ready to be deactivated. The Done bit defaults to False. The value of the Done bit is not inspected by COM+ until a method call completes. As a result, the value of the Done bit can be changed any number of times, but its value is only meaningful after method calls. The Done bit is actually provided by Just-in-time (JIT) Activation, another COM+ service required by COM+ Transactions. Consequently, it is used the same way with non-transactional components that support JIT activation. When an object is created, the Done bit is initially set to False.

- Consistency **Bit**
  The Consistency bit, sometimes called the "Happy Bit", is a Boolean value that indicates whether or not the object is happy with its work and whether the COM+ object votes to commit or abort the transaction. A value of True indicates the object wants to attempt to commit the transaction and a value of False indicates the object wants to abort the transaction. The value of the Consistency Bit is only evaluated by COM+ after the object is deactivated (Done bit is set to True). As a result, the value of the Consistency Bit can be changed repeatedly, even over the course of multiple method calls, because only the last value of the Consistency bit, before the object is deactivated, is used to determine the transaction's outcome. COM+ initializes the Consistency bit with a default value of True – meaning that COM+ assumes the transaction should commit.

In addition to the Consistency and Done bits, COM+ also maintains a single global flag for each transaction called the Transaction Abort flag or sometimes called the Doomed flag. The Transaction Abort flag is used to store the overall status of the transaction. When the root of the transaction is deactivated (the Done bit is set to True for the root object's context), the transaction completes and COM+ evaluates the Transaction Abort flag in the transaction stream to determine the transaction outcome. If the Transaction Abort Flag is set to False, the default value, COM+ will commit the transaction. However, if the Transaction Abort flag is set to True, COM+ will instruct MS DTC to abort the transaction.

In either of these situations, COM+ instructs MS DTC to either commit or abort the underlying physical transaction. MS DTC is then responsible for coordinating the commitment or rollback of the distributed transaction with all enlisted resource managers through the use of the two-phase commit protocol.

It's important to understand that the Transaction Abort flag is a *global* flag used by COM+ to manage the status of the transaction. The value of the Transaction Abort flag, and thus the outcome of the transaction, is determined by the consistency of the individual objects within the transaction. When a transactional object is deactivated (Done bit is set to True), COM+ evaluates the value of the Consistency bit for the object. If the Consistency bit is set to False, then COM+ will set the Transaction Abort flag to True, indicating that the transaction is doomed to fail. No matter what any other objects in the transaction do, the Transaction Abort flag's value cannot be changed.

Consequently, the decision to attempt to commit a transaction is actually a unanimous decision. If all objects in the transaction vote to attempt to commit the transaction by setting the `Consistency` bit of their context to `True`, then the Transaction Abort flag will remain set to `True` and all operations performed within the transaction will attempt to be permanently committed. However, if any object within the transaction votes to abort the transaction by setting the `Consistency` bit of their context to `False`, then the Transaction Abort flag will be set to `False` and all the operations performed within the transaction will be rolled back.

The following table summarizes the outcome of a COM+ Transaction as a result of the combination of values for the `Done` and `Consistency` bits.

Done	**Consistency**	**Result**
`True`	`True`	COM+ and MS DTC will attempt to commit the transaction
`True`	`False`	COM+ and MS DTC will abort the transaction
`False`	`True`	The transaction will not be committed or aborted until the root object is deactivated (`Done` Bit is set to `True`)
`False`	`False`	The transaction will not be committed or aborted until the root object is deactivated (`Done` Bit is set to `True`)

The following diagram illustrates the completion of a COM+ transaction consisting of a single object. In this situation, the `Done` and `Consistency` bits have been set to true in the object's context and the Transaction Abort flag is set to `False`. As a result, COM+ will instruct MS DTC to commit the transaction identified by the `TransactionID`, also stored in the object's context. Finally, MS DTC will execute the two-phase commit protocol, to notify all of the enlisted resource managers to commit the transaction.

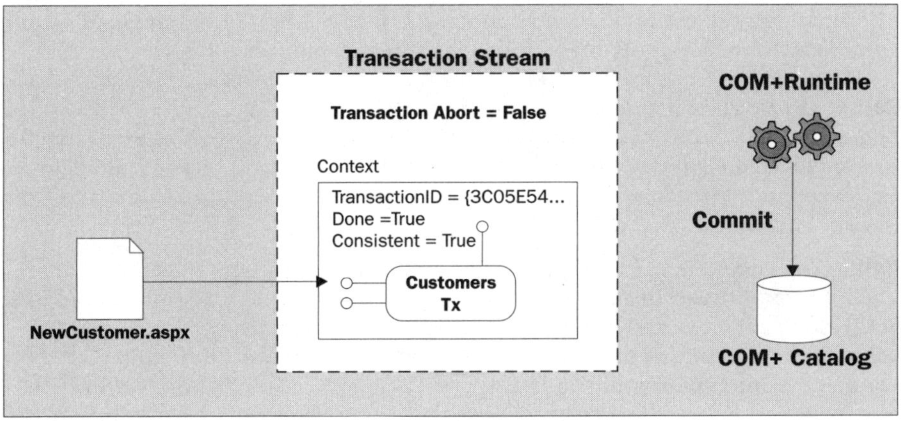

The following diagram demonstrates a COM+ Transactions scenario involving multiple objects within a single transaction. In this example, one of the objects votes to abort the transaction by setting the `Consistency` bit to `False` and deactivating. Since a single object voted to abort transaction the Transaction Abort flag has been set, the COM+ runtime will instruct MS DTC to abort the entire distributed transaction when the root object deactivates.

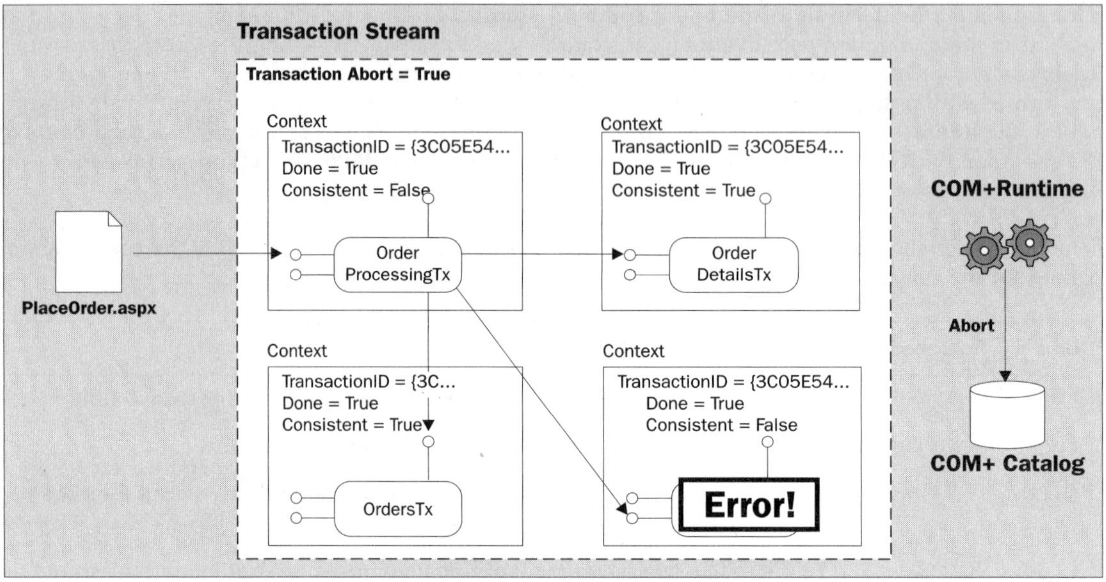

Now that we understand when a COM+ Transaction completes and how COM+ determines the transaction outcome through the use of the Transaction Abort flag and the `Done` and `Consistency` bits, let's discuss how we control the outcome of a transaction.

Controlling the Transaction Outcome

To maximize performance and scalability, a transactional .NET `ServicedComponent`, especially the root object, should vote on the transaction outcome and deactivate as soon as possible. A .NET `ServicedComponent` can manipulate the `Done` and `Consistency` bits to explicitly control the outcome of a transaction, using any of the following three techniques:

- **Calling the `ContextUtil` methods**
  The `System.EnterpriseServices.ContextUtil` class provides shared methods that can be used to set the values of both the `Consistency` and `Done` bits with a single method call. These methods are named `SetComplete()`, `SetAbort()`, `EnableCommit()`, and `DisableCommit()`.

- **Calling the `ContextUtil` properties**
  The `ContextUtil` class also provides two shared properties that can be used to set the values of the `Consistency` and `Done` bits independently. These properties, named `DeactivateOnReturn` and `MyTransactionVote`, can also be used to read the values of the `Done` and `Consistency` bits.

- **Applying the `AutoComplete` attribute**
  The `System.EnterpriseServices.AutoComplete` attribute can be applied to a method signature, so COM+ will automatically vote to commit the transaction if the method completes successfully, or vote to abort the transaction if the method throws an exception. COM+ casts these votes by setting the `Done` and `Consistency` bits to the appropriate values.

While most of the time you will want to explicitly complete a transaction and control its outcome using one of these three techniques, you also should be aware that COM+ would inadvertently complete a transaction in two additional situations:

- **Transaction Timeout**
  A transaction can end if there is no activity within the transaction for more than the configured transaction timeout value. When a transaction exceeds its configured time out interval, the objects in the transaction will be deactivated and the transaction will automatically abort. The default timeout value is 60 seconds. The machine-level transaction timeout value can be changed from the Options tab of the Computer Properties dialog window in Component Services. A specific transaction timeout can also be specified as a parameter of the `TransactionAttribute` .NET Attribute used to specify the classes transaction support attribute. If you are debugging transactional COM+ objects, you will definitely want to increase the transaction timeout from the 60 second default so that you will have enough time to step through a method call on an COM+ object without the transaction automatically aborting.
- **Client releases all references to the root of the transaction**
  When the client releases the last reference to the root object, the root object deactivates and COM+ *implicitly* attempts to commit the transaction. Implicit transaction commitments should be avoided whenever possible because they introduce several problems.

One problem with implicit commitments is that the client cannot be notified of the transaction outcome. When a root object explicitly sets the `Done` and `Consistency` bits, COM+ attempts to commit the transaction prior to returning control to the caller. If an error occurred while committing the transaction, COM+ simply raises an error message to the client. This allows the client application to gracefully deal with the problem and possibly try the transaction again. However, with implicit commitment the client is no longer connected to the root object and it consequently cannot receive error messages if the transaction cannot be committed. The client is totally unaware of the transaction outcome.

Implicit transaction commitments also leave a transaction alive longer than necessary. While a transaction is alive it is holding precious locks to resources to ensure the isolation requirement of the ACID properties. Consequently, an open, inactive transaction could be blocking other transactions from performing operations on the same resource. This could create a performance bottleneck and severely limit an application's scalability. A much better approach is to explicitly commit or abort the transaction as soon as possible using one of the three techniques we just discussed. Let's discuss each of these three techniques for explicitly voting on the outcome of a COM+ transaction, starting with the `ContextUtil` methods.

ContextUtil Methods

The shared methods of the `System.EnterpriseServices.ContextUtil` class can be used to control a COM+ transaction's outcome programmatically by simultaneously setting both the `Consistency` bit and the `Done` bit with a single method call. Since there are four possible combinations of values between the `Consistency` bit and the `Done` bit, there are four corresponding methods defined by the `ContextUtil` class. These four methods are:

- `SetComplete()`
- `SetAbort()`
- `EnableCommit()`
- `DisableCommit()`

Each of these ContextUtil methods maps to a unique combination of values for the Consistency and Done bits, as outlined in the following table:

ContextUtil Method	Done	Consistency
SetComplete()	True	True
SetAbort()	True	False
EnableCommit()	False	True
DisableCommit()	False	False

Let's discuss each of these methods in further detail.

SetComplete()

The SetComplete() method notifies COM+ that the object has completed its work successfully, so it can now be deactivated and the transactional operations it performed can be committed. Calling the SetComplete() method effectively forces an object to deactivate and votes to commit the transaction by setting both the Done and Consistency bits to True. When SetComplete() is called on the root object, COM+ will check the value of the Transaction Abort flag to determine the outcome of the transaction. However, it's important to understand that calling the SetComplete() method in the root object does not guarantee that the transaction will be committed. If any subordinate object in the transaction deactivated with the Consistency bit set to False, then COM+ will instruct MS DTC to abort the transaction.

SetAbort()

The SetAbort() method notifies COM+ that the object was unsuccessful in completing its work and it wants to abort the transaction. The SetAbort() method effectively sets the Consistency bit to False and the Done bit to True – indicating that the object has completed, but it is unhappy with the outcome. If one or more objects in the transaction call the SetAbort() method, then the entire transaction will be aborted and all of the work performed in the transaction will be rolled back. In fact, calling the SetAbort() method in any object in the transaction guarantees that the transaction will not commit and will never be able to commit because COM+ will set the Transaction Abort flag for the transaction to True. However, COM+ does not instruct MS DTC to abort the transaction until the root object calls the SetAbort() method, or deactivates in any other way with the Consistency bit set to False.

EnableCommit()

The EnableCommit() method notifies COM+ that the object is consistent and the transaction can be committed at any time, but the object is not complete and does currently not want to deactivate. It's important to understand that EnableCommit() does not force a transaction to commit. By calling this method, an object is effectively saying, "I'm able to commit at any time, but I don't want to yet." The EnableCommit() method accomplishes this by setting the Consistency bit to True and the Done bit to False. This is actually the default state of an object when it is first activated in a transaction.

DisableCommit()

The `DisableCommit()` method is exactly the opposite of the `EnableCommit()` method. The `DisableCommit()` method notifies COM+ that the object's work is not finished and the transaction cannot currently be committed, so it does not want to be deactivated at this time. By calling the `DisableCommit()` method, an object is effectively saying "I'm not able to commit at this time, because I'm not done yet". `DisableCommit()` sets both the `Consistency` and `Done` bits of the object's context to `False`. After calling `DisableCommit()`, COM+ will not implicitly commit the transaction, but instead implicitly abort the transaction if the client releases the reference to the root object prior to the object indicating that it has completed.

The `EnableCommit()` and `DisableCommit()` are used with transactional objects whose work needs to span multiple method or property calls. Since these methods set the `Done` bit to `False`, they prevent the object from deactivating and losing its state. The `EnableCommit()` and `DisableCommit()` are most often used with property-based objects. If you design your `ServicedComponents` to be stateless, you will most likely not need to use these methods.

SetComplete() and SetAbort() Example

The following code example demonstrates how to call the `SetComplete()` and `SetAbort()` methods in a .NET `ServicedComponent` to control the outcome of the transaction:

```
'Import namespaces containing commonly used types
Imports System.EnterpriseServices


<Transaction(TransactionOption.Required)> _
Public Class CustomersTx
    'Inherit from the System.EnterpriseServices.ServicedComponent class to allow
    '...this component to utilize COM+ services
    Inherits ServicedComponent

    Public Sub InsertCustomer()

        Try

                 '***Do Some Work Here***


            'We successfully completed our processing, so tell COM+ that this
object votes
            '...to commit the transaction and deactivate.
            ContextUtil.SetComplete()


        Catch excp As system.Exception
            'An exception occured creating the order.

            'Tell COM+ that this object votes to abort the transaction and
deactivate
            ContextUtil.SetAbort()

            'Throw the exception to the caller of this method
```

```
                Throw excp
            End Try
        End Sub
    End Class
```

Notice that this code example catches exceptions and throws them up the call stack to the immediate caller after calling the `SetAbort()` method. If a subordinate object within a transaction causes the transaction to abort, but does not indicate that it did so to the parent object, then the parent has no way of knowing that the transaction is doomed to fail. Consequently, the parent object will unnecessarily continue its tasks until it completes. A better approach is to always throw exceptions in a .NET `ServicedComponent` when forcing the transaction to abort, so that the parent object can catch the exception and suspend further processing.

ContextUtil Properties

The methods of the `SetComplete()`, `SetAbort()`, `EnableCommit()`, and `DisableCommit()` methods of the `ContextUtil` class set the values of the `Done` and `Consistency` bits as a group. However, the `ContextUtil` class also provides two properties that allow you to set and retrieve the values of the `Done` and `Consistency` bits independently. These properties are:

- `MyTransactionVote`

  The `MyTransactionVote` shared property of the `ContextUtil` class can be used to retrieve or set the value of the consistent bit stored in an object's context. Remember, the value of the consistent bit is not evaluated by COM+ until the object deactivates by setting the `Done` bit to `False`. The `MyTransactionVote` property defaults to consistent.

- `DeactivateOnReturn`

  The `DeactivateOnReturn` shared property of the `ContextUtil` class can be used to retrieve or set the value of the `Done` bit stored in an object's context. If a method of the root object completes with the `Done` bit set to `True`, then COM+ will attempt to commit or abort the transaction depending on the value of the `Consistency` bit. Initially, the value of this property is set to `False`.

The `MyTransactionVote` and `DeactivateOnReturn` properties are essentially equivalent to the methods of the `ContextUtil`. For example, instead of calling the `SetComplete()` method, an object could set the `MyTransactionVote` property to Consistent (`True`) and the `DeactivateOnReturn` property to `True`. Since both the methods and properties can be used to accomplish the same results, it doesn't really matter which technique is used. However, most developers prefer to use the `SetComplete()`, `SetAbort()`, `EnableCommit()`, and `EnableAbort()` shared methods of the `ContextUtil` class instead of the equivalent set of property calls because they only require one line of code and they are more familiar techniques. These methods have been provided in one form or another since Microsoft Transaction Server.

The following table compares the combination of values for the `MyTransactionVote` and `DeactivateOnReturn` properties to the individual methods defined by the `System.EnterpriseServices`:

Property Combination	Equivalent Method
MyTransactionVote = Commit DeactivateOnReturn = True	SetComplete()
MyTransactionVote = Abort DeactivateOnReturn = True	SetAbort()
MyTransactionVote = Commit DeactivateOnReturn = False	EnableCommit()
MyTransactionVote = Abort DeactivateOnReturn = False	DisableCommit()

The following code example shows how to use the properties of the `ContextUtil` class to produce the same results as the `SetComplete()` and `SetAbort()` methods in our previous example:

```
'Import namespaces containing commonly used types
Imports System.EnterpriseServices


<Transaction(TransactionOption.Required)> _
Public Class CustomersTx
    'Inherit from the System.EnterpriseServices.ServicedComponent class to allow
    '...this component to utilize COM+ services
    Inherits ServicedComponent

    Public Sub InsertCustomer()

        Try

            'We successfully completed our processing, so tell COM+ that this
object votes
            '...to commit the transaction and deactivate.
            ContextUtil.MyTransactionVote = TransactionVote.Commit
            ContextUtil.DeactivateOnReturn = True

        Catch excp As system.Exception
            'An exception occured creating the order.

            'Tell COM+ that this object votes to abort the transaction and
deactivate
            ContextUtil.MyTransactionVote = TransactionVote.Abort
            ContextUtil.DeactivateOnReturn = True

            'Throw the exception to the caller of this method
            Throw excp
        End Try
    End Sub
End Class
```

Although the `MyTransactionVote` and `DeactivateOnReturn` properties can be used to accomplish the same results as the methods of the `ContextUtil` class, there are some slight differences that you should be aware of before using these properties.

Specifically, if a COM+ object is not running within a transaction then the attempts to retrieve or set the value of the `MyTransactionVote` property will throw an exception. Likewise, if the COM+ object is not configured to support Just-in-time Activation (JIT), attempts to retrieve or set the value of the `DeactivateOnReturn` property will also throw an exception.

The `MyTransactionVote` and `DeactivateOnReturn` properties also provide the ability to read the current values of the `Done` and `Consistency` bits, which is not possible using the methods of the `ContextUtil` class.

AutoComplete Attribute

The `System.EnterpriseServices.AutoComplete` attribute is a .NET method-level attribute that causes COM+ to automatically cast a vote on the outcome of a transaction based on the success or failure of a method. If a method with the `AutoComplete` attribute completes successfully, the `Consistency` bit will be set to `True` and the `Done` bit will automatically be set to `True`, effectively causing the same result as calling the `SetComplete()` method. However, if the method throws an exception, then the `Consistency` bit will be set to `False` and the `Done` bit will be set to `True`, which is the same behaviour as calling the `SetAbort()` method.

Many developers prefer to use the `AutoComplete` attribute instead of manually calling the methods or setting the properties of the `ContextUtil` class because it requires less code. However, utilizing the `AutoComplete` attribute may require more up front time to properly design your components around the transaction. The following code example uses the `AutoComplete` attribute on our method declaration, instead of calling the methods or properties of the `ContextUtil` class as we have in the past couple of examples:

```
'Import namespaces containing commonly used types
Imports System.EnterpriseServices


<Transaction(TransactionOption.Required), _
  AutoComplete()> _
Public Class CustomersTx
    'Inherit from the System.EnterpriseServices.ServicedComponent class to allow
    '...this component to utilize COM+ services
    Inherits ServicedComponent

    Public Sub InsertCustomer()

        Try

        Catch excp As system.Exception
            'An exception occured creating the order.

            'Throw the exception to the caller of this method, which will cause
            '...the transaction to automatically abort.
            Throw excp
        End Try
    End Sub
End Class
```

Transaction Lifetime Summary

Although the entire life cycle of a COM+ transaction may sound complex and somewhat overwhelming, it's important to remember that the only requirement for a .NET `ServicedComponent` to participate in transactions is that they are configured with the appropriate transaction support attribute. To maximize performance of COM+ transactions, you should also explicitly complete the transaction and vote on its outcome. While some of these concepts may be a little confusing to understand right now, the better you understand what happens behind the scenes in a COM+ transaction, the better you can effectively utilize COM+ transactions when developing .NET `ServicedComponents`.

Single Transactional Component Example

To best learn how to create, deploy, and test .NET classes that take advantage of COM+ transactions, let's walk through a detailed example. In this example, we'll create a transactional .NET `ServicedComponent` called `CustomersTx` that provides the ability to insert `Customer` records into the Northwind SQL Server 2000 database. The behaviour and functionality of the component is intentionally simplistic so we can focus on the key concepts and issues regarding transactional .NET `ServicedComponents`.

During this example, we will perform the following tasks:

1. Create the `Northwind.BusinessServices.CustomersTx` .NET `ServicedComponent`
2. Create the project and solution using Visual Studio .NET
3. Implement the `CustomersTx` class
4. Specify the COM+ configuration through attributes
5. Sign the assembly with a shared name
6. Register the .NET class with COM+
7. Create a test application

> **The entire `CustomersTx`.NET class, Visual Studio .NET project files, and the test application can be downloaded from Wrox Press' Programmer-to-Programmer site located at http://www.wrox.com/.**

Create the NorthwindBS Project

If you decide to use the code from the downloadable code for this chapter, you will need to set up a Virtual Directory in IIS to run the test example. Let's quickly set this up now, so it doesn't get in the way.

Save the download code to your computer – in the example, it is saved to `C:\VBNETTrans\Chapter06\`. The download contains both the `NorthwindBS` project and the `NorthwindWeb` application. We are going to create a virtual directory for the web application now. Open Administrative Tools from the Control Panel and from there, click on Internet Services Manager.

Right-click on Default Web Site, and then select New. Virtual Directory is the first choice offered, so click on that, as shown below:

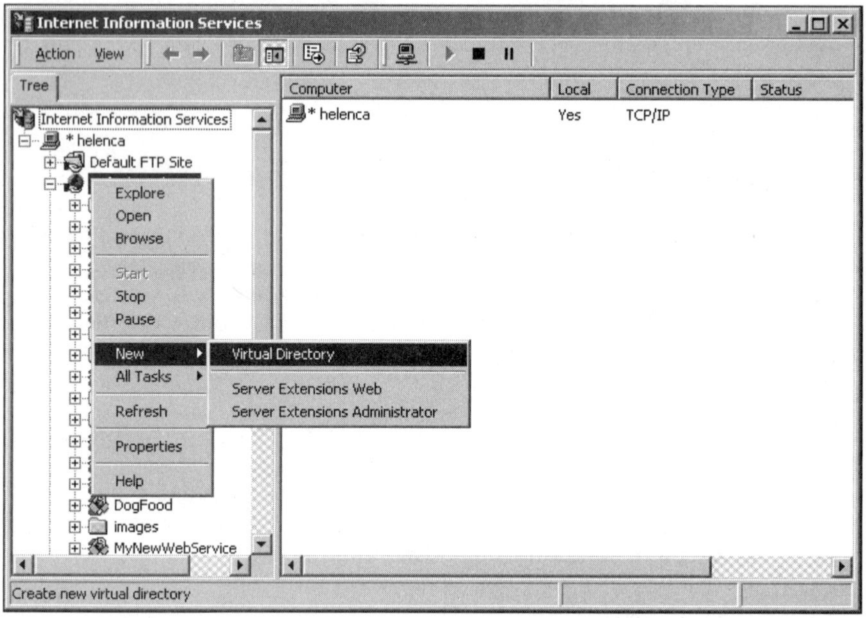

This should open the Virtual Directory Wizard. Click past the introductory screen and when asked for an alias, type in `NorthwindWeb`.

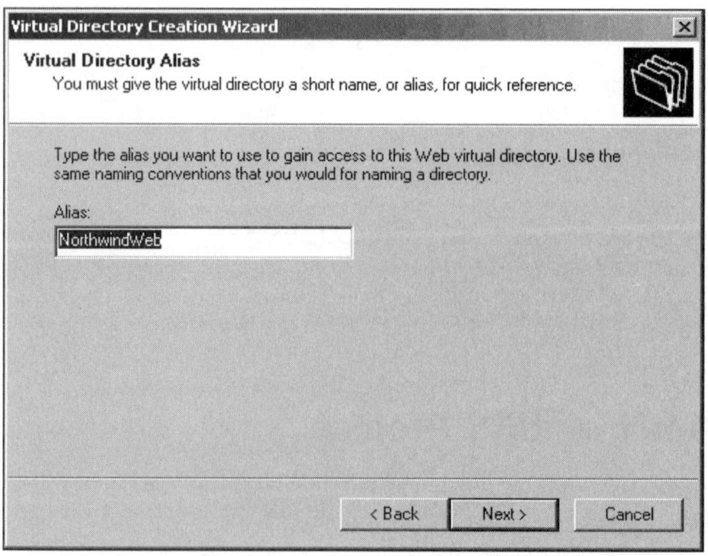

Next, you will be asked to browse through to the directory you wish to make a virtual directory. In our case this is `C:\VBNETTrans\Chapter06\NorthwindWeb`.

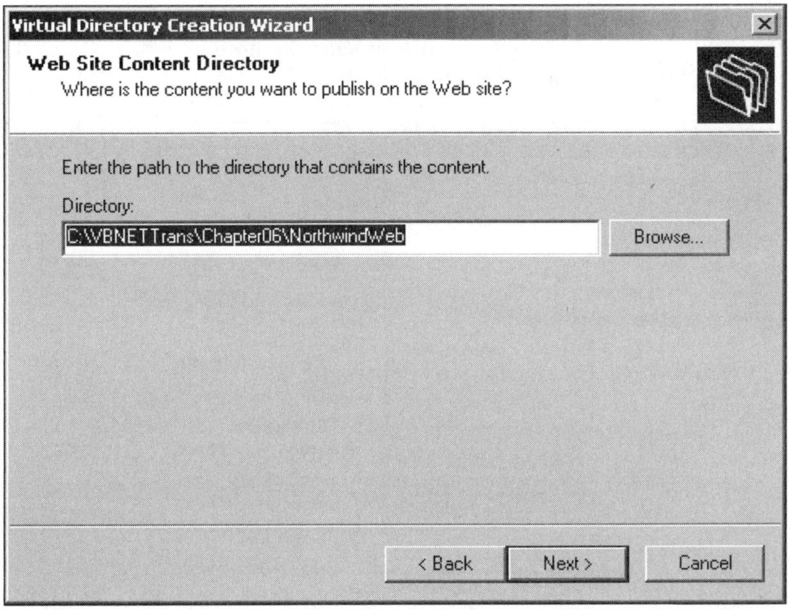

Accept the default permissions on the next screen:

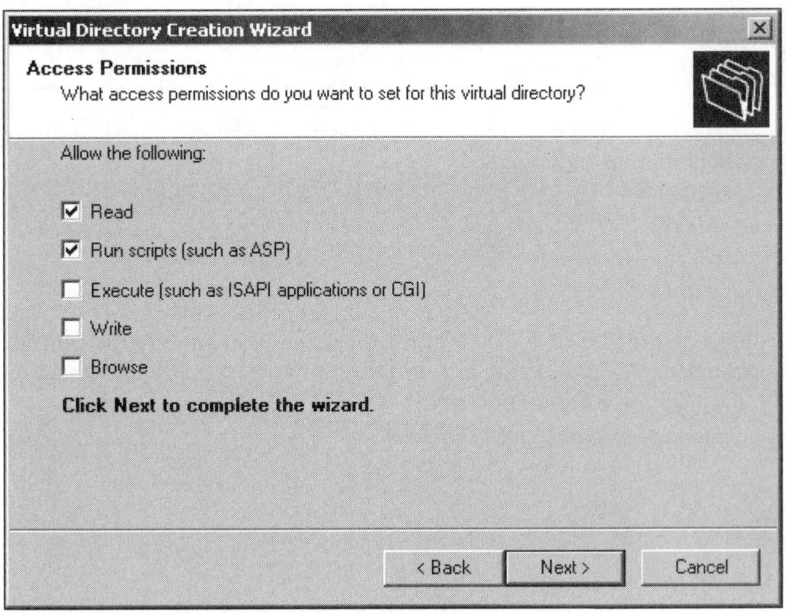

And then click **Finish**. `NorthwindWeb` is now accessible to your application via localhost. If you look in Internet Services Manager, you will see an icon for this application.

To begin this example, using Visual Studio .NET, let's create a new class library project named `NorthwindBS` (Northwind Business Services) and specify a name for the solution of "Northwind". If you're not using Visual Studio .NET, that's fine. We're not going to use any development features of the .NET Framework that are specific to Visual Studio .NET and can't also be performed manually using a source code editor. Where necessary, we will also specifically note how to perform the equivalent tasks using the Visual Basic .NET command line compiler.

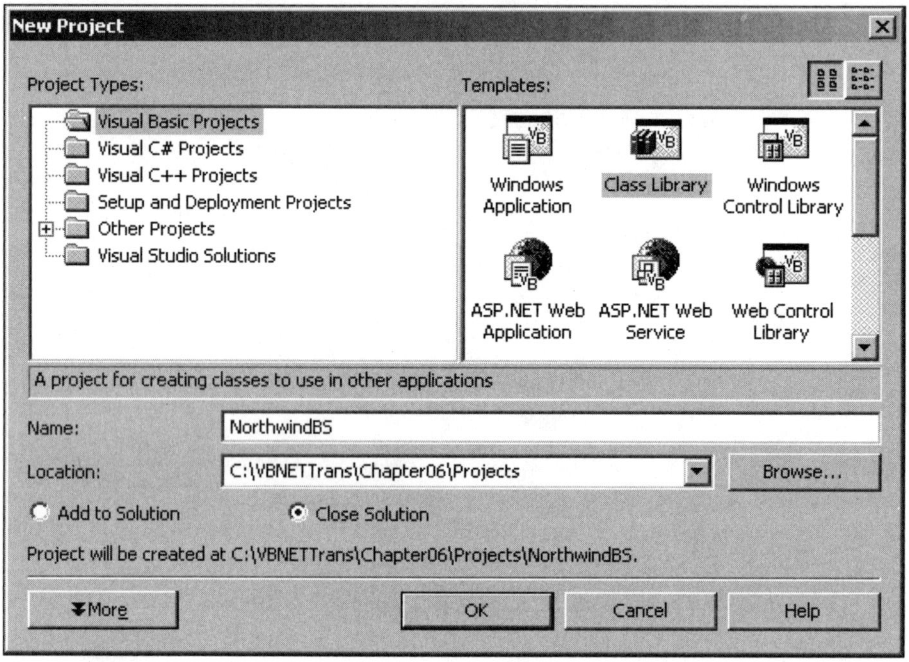

By default, a single class file named `Class1.vb` will be contained in your class library project. It will contain just the class definition statements.

```
Public Class Class1

End Class
```

Rename the included `Class1.vb` file to `CustomersTx.vb`. Now modify the source code to assign the class a name of `CustomersTx` and define it in the `Northwind.BusinessServices` namespace.

```
Namespace Northwind.BusinessServices
    Public Class CustomersTx

    End Class
End Namespace
```

As we mentioned earlier in this chapter, .NET classes that want to take advantage of COM+ services such as declarative transactions must inherit from the `System.EnterpriseServices.ServicedComponent` class.

Before we can modify our `CustomersTx` class to inherit from the `ServicedComponent` class, we must first add a reference to the assembly `System.EnterpriseServices.dll` containing the necessary types for utilizing COM+. In Visual Studio .NET, right-click on the **References** folder under the `NorthwindBS` project and select **Add Reference**. If you're using the command-line compiler for Visual Basic .NET, you can skip this process and instead we'll reference to this assembly when we compile and build our `ServicedComponent`.

When the **Add Reference** dialog window is displayed, select `System.EnterpriseServices` from the assembly list on the **.NET** tab, press the `Select` button to add it to the list of selected components, and click the **OK** button to add the reference to our project and close the dialog.

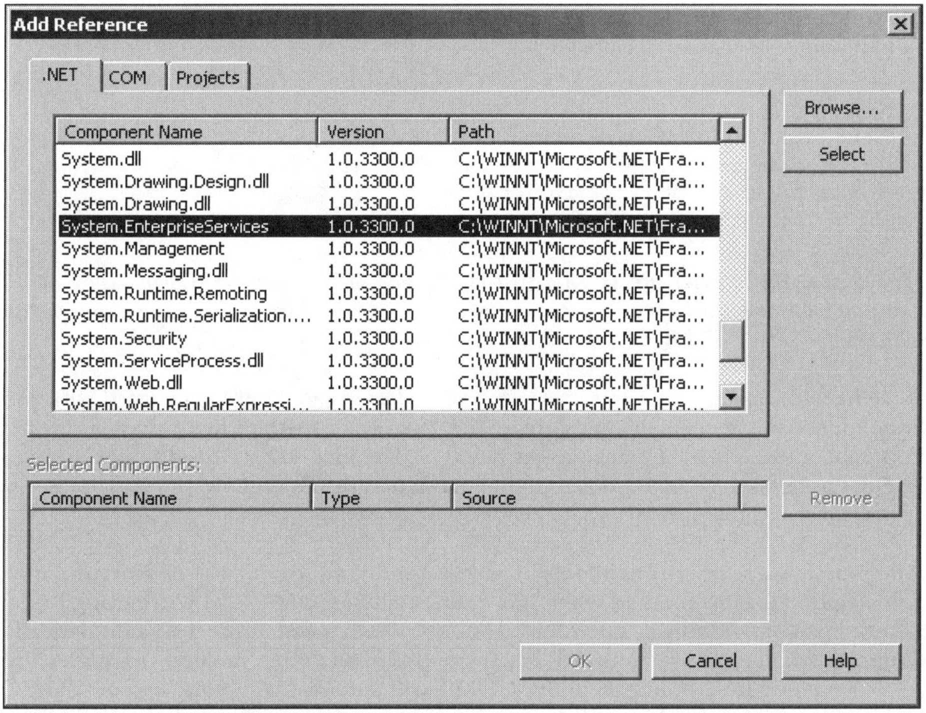

Now let's modify our `CustomersTx` class to import the `System.EnterpriseServices` namespace and inherit from the `ServicedComponent` defined in this namespace. We'll also import the `System.Data` and `System.Data.SqlClient` namespaces to simplify the data access code in this source file:

```
Imports System.Data
Imports System.Data.SqlClient
Imports System.EnterpriseServices

Namespace Northwind.BusinessServices
    Public Class CustomersTx
        Inherits ServicedComponent

    End Class
End Namespace
```

Now we'll see the real power of COM+ transactions! As we discussed earlier, .NET ServicedComponents that wish to participate in COM+ transactions need to simply declare their support level using the Transaction Support attribute. This attribute can be set by assigning the .NET System.EnterpriseServices.TransactionAttribute to a class definition. The following code uses the Transaction attribute to specify that our CustomersTx component always requires a transaction.

We have also set some other attributes defined in the System.EnterpriseServices namespace to control the configuration of our CustomersTx class in COM+. Specifically, we provided a description for this class and explicitly set the Synchronization and JustInTime activation attributes. If you remember our earlier discussion, you'll recall that the Synchronization and JustInTimeActivation COM+ services are required by COM+ Transactions. Consequently, these services do not need to be explicitly enabled for a ServicedComponent with a transaction support attribute of anything other than disabled.

```
<Description("Contains methods for inserting Customers in Northwind."), _
    Transaction(TransactionOption.Required), _
    Synchronization(SynchronizationOption.Required), _
    JustInTimeActivation(True)> _
Public Class CustomersTx
```

NOTE: Visual Studio .NET provides a class template named Transactional Component that contains the class definition for a new transactional ServicedComponent. This class template is available for both Visual Basic .NET and C#.

Now that we have the skeleton for our CustomersTx class created, let's get started with some of the implementation details. Specifically, let's create the Insert() method that inserts a record into the Customers table using the data passed as parameters. The first task we need to perform when implementing the Insert() method is to define its signature. The following code defines our Insert() method and the parameters it accepts.

In this code sample we're also using the System.EnterpriseServices.DescriptionAttribute to specify a description for this method when it is configured in COM+, and we're using the System.EnterpriseServices.AutoCompleteAttribute so COM+ will automatically attempt vote to commit a running transaction and deactivate this object if the method completes successfully. If the Insert() method throws an exception, COM+ will automatically vote to abort the COM+ transaction because this method is configured with the AutoComplete attribute. We'll discuss this attribute in more detail a little later in this chapter.

```
<Description("Creates a new customer record in the Northwind system."), _
    AutoComplete()> _
        Public Sub Insert(ByVal strCustomerID As String, _
            ByVal strCompanyName As String, _
            ByVal strContactName As String, _
            ByVal strContactTitle As String, _
            ByVal strAddress As String, _
            ByVal strCity As String, _
            ByVal strRegion As String, _
            ByVal strPostalCode As String, _
            ByVal strCountry As String, _
            ByVal strPhone As String, _
            ByVal strFax As String) Implements ICustomersTx.Insert
```

Finally, we need to specify that the `Insert()` method we've implemented is actually an implementation of the `Insert()` method defined by the `ICustomersTx` public interface. Simply add the statement `Implements ICustomerTx.Insert` after the method signature definition.

Implement the code to use the classes provided by ADO.NET, in order to establish a connection to the Northwind SQL Server 2000 database. Now, we execute a dynamic SQL statement to insert a record into the `Customers` table using the parameters to this method as parameters to our SQL `INSERT` statement. In this situation we're hard-coding the connection information for the Northwind database for simplicity. In a production application we would want to store the connection information in a configuration file. Notice that we execute the `SqlCommand()` object for our `INSERT` statement by calling the `ExecuteNonQuery()` method, since we're not trying to retrieve a result set:

```
        Try

            'Declare and initialize our local variables
            Dim sqlconNorthwind As New
                System.Data.SqlClient.SqlConnection()
            Dim sqlcmdInsertCustomer As New
                System.Data.SqlClient.SqlCommand()


            'Set the Connection String and establish a
            'connection to the Northwind SQL Server 2000
            'database
            sqlconNorthwind.ConnectionString = _
                "data source=(local);initial
                    catalog=northwind;password=;user id=sa;"
            sqlconNorthwind.Open()

            'Assign the SQLConnection object to our SQLCommand
            'object
            sqlcmdInsertCustomer.Connection = sqlconNorthwind

            'Assign a SQL Insert statement for the Customers
            'table to our new SQLCommand object
            sqlcmdInsertCustomer.CommandText = _
                "INSERT INTO Customers(CustomerID, CompanyName,
                ContactName, ContactTitle, Address" & _
                ", City, Region, PostalCode, Country, Phone,
                Fax) VALUES (@CustomerID, @CompanyNa" & _
                "me, @ContactName, @ContactTitle, @Address,
                @City, @Region, @PostalCode, @Country" & _
                ", @Phone, @Fax)"

            'Create and set the values of the parameters for
            'our SQLCommand to the values of the parameters
            'passed to this method
            With sqlcmdInsertCustomer.Parameters
                .Add(New SqlParameter("@CustomerID",
                    strCustomerID))
                .Add(New SqlParameter("@CompanyName",
                    strCompanyName))
```

```
                .Add(New SqlParameter("@ContactName",
                    strContactName))
                .Add(New SqlParameter("@ContactTitle",
                    strContactTitle))
                .Add(New SqlParameter("@Address", strAddress))
                .Add(New SqlParameter("@City", strCity))
                .Add(New SqlParameter("@Region", strRegion))
                .Add(New SqlParameter("@PostalCode",
                    strPostalCode))
                .Add(New SqlParameter("@Country", strCountry))
                .Add(New SqlParameter("@Phone", strPhone))
                .Add(New SqlParameter("@Fax", strFax))
            End With

            'Execute the Insert statement to insert a new
            'Customer record
            sqlcmdInsertCustomer.ExecuteNonQuery()

            'Close our SQLConnection to the Northwind SQL
            'Server 2000 database
            sqlconNorthwind.Close()
```

After we have inserted a record in the `Customers` table using ADO.NET classes, we should tell COM+ that this method has completed its processing successfully and, consequently, this object votes to commit the running transaction and the object can now be deactivated. There are a variety of techniques for voting on transaction outcome, but in this situation we decided to call the `SetComplete()` method of the `System.EnterpriseServices.ContextUtil` class. If the exception occurred during the execution of our `INSERT` statement, then the exception will be trapped in our `Catch` handler and we'll call the `SetAbort()` method of the `ContextUtil` class to vote to abort the transaction and deactivate our object. We'll also throw the exception up the call stack to the immediate caller so they are aware that the `InsertCustomer()` method encountered a problem during the transaction.

```
            'We successfully inserted the Customer record, so
            'tell COM+ that this object votes to commit the
            'transaction and deactivate.
            'NOTE:  This is not necessary when using the
            'AutoComplete attribute
            ContextUtil.SetComplete()

        Catch excp As System.Exception
            'An exception occurred inserting a Customer record.

            'Tell COM+ that this object votes to abort the
            'transaction and deactivate

            'NOTE:  This is not necessary when using the
            'AutoComplete attribute
            ContextUtil.SetAbort()

            'Throw the exception to the caller of this method
            Throw excp
        End Try
    End Sub
```

It's important to note that in this situation we didn't actually need to call the ContextUtil object's SetComplete() and SetAbort() methods explicitly, because we configured the CustomersTx component with the AutoComplete attribute. However, I wanted to demonstrate another technique for voting on the transaction outcome.

Another alternative for controlling transaction outcome is provided by the MyTransactionVote and DeactivateOnReturn properties of the ContextUtil class. These properties allow you to write (or read) the transaction vote and deactivation values for the object independently, without setting them both together – as the SetComplete() and SetAbort() methods behave. Finally, the EnableCommit() and DisableCommit() methods of the ContextUtil class also set the transaction vote and deactivation values for an object together with one statement, but in different combinations from the SetComplete() and SetAbort() methods.

That's all the code that is needed for controlling the outcome of a COM+ transaction. Notice that we didn't need to explicitly start the transaction, because COM+ automatically creates a distributed transaction behind the scenes based on the value of the Transaction Support Attribute configured for our CustomersTx component.

Implement a Public Interface

In order to utilize method-level attributes for a .NET ServicedComponent, it is necessary to define a public interface for the methods exposed by the component. If a .NET ServicedComponent does not implement a public interface and its expose its methods and properties through it, then the interface and associated methods will not be registered within COM+. The component will be configured correctly and is accessible without a public interface, however; interface and method-level attributes, such as the AutoComplete attribute, will not be configured.

> NOTE: **If you do not define a public interface and expose methods defined by a public interface in your .NET ServicedComponents, you may receive the following error when invoking the methods contained in the component:**
>
> **Method-level role based security requires an interface definition for class method.**

To define a public interface for our CustomersTx component, simply navigate to the section of the source file just below the declaration of the namespace but before the class declaration and add the following ICustomersTx Interface definition. Notice that the Insert() method in this interface has exactly the same signature as the Insert() method we've already implemented for the CustomersTx component:

```
Namespace Northwind.BusinessServices

    'Define a public interface containing the signatures for
    'members of this class
    '
    'NOTE:  It is necessary to define a public interface with the
    'signatures for methods that utilize COM+ method-level
    'attributes. Otherwise the interface and methods will not be
    'displayed and configured in COM+, although the component will
    'be configured.
    Public Interface ICustomersTx
```

```
        Sub Insert(ByVal strCustomerID As String, _
                   ByVal strCompanyName As String, _
                   ByVal strContactName As String, _
                   ByVal strContactTitle As String, _
                   ByVal strAddress As String, _
                   ByVal strCity As String, _
                   ByVal strRegion As String, _
                   ByVal strPostalCode As String, _
                   ByVal strCountry As String, _
                   ByVal strPhone As String, _
                   ByVal strFax As String)
    End Interface
```

Next we need to modify the CustomersTx class to implement the new ICustomersTx interface. Simply insert an Implements statement below the CustomersTx class declaration:

```
    Public Class CustomersTx
        'Inherit from the
        'System.EnterpriseServices.ServicedComponent class to allow
        'this component to utilize COM+ services
        Inherits ServicedComponent

        'Implement the ICustomersTx interface and its members
        Implements ICustomersTx
```

Set the COM+ Application Attributes in our Assembly

In order for our component to successfully register with COM+, it is necessary to also use assembly-level attributes to specify information for the COM+ application that is to contain the ServicedComponents. Some of these attributes include System.EnterpriseServices.ApplicationNameAttribute, which is used to specify the name of the COM+ application, and System.EnterpriseServices.ApplicationActivationAttribute, which is used to specify whether the application should be configured to execute in the process of the creator (Library) or in a separate process (Server).

An AssemblyInfo.vb file is automatically included with every Visual Basic .NET project created using Visual Studio .NET. By convention, this file is used to define assembly-level attributes, although assembly-level attributes can be specified in any source file in the project. Let's open the AssemblyInfo.vb file for our NorthwindBS project and add the necessary code to apply the assembly-level attributes for the COM+ Application. If you're not using Visual Studio .NET, you can simply create a source file and include all of the following code.

First, let's add the Imports statement for the System.EnterpriseServices namespace to the top of the AssemblyInfo.vb source file:

```
Imports System.Reflection
Imports System.Runtime.InteropServices
Imports System.EnterpriseServices

' General Information about an assembly is controlled through the following
' set of attributes. Change these attribute values to modify the information
```

```
' associated with an assembly.

' Review the values of the assembly attributes

<Assembly: AssemblyTitle("")>
<Assembly: AssemblyDescription("")>
<Assembly: AssemblyCompany("")>
<Assembly: AssemblyProduct("")>
<Assembly: AssemblyCopyright("")>
<Assembly: AssemblyTrademark("")>
<Assembly: CLSCompliant(True)>

'The following GUID is for the ID of the typelib if this project is exposed to COM
<Assembly: Guid("20C32037-8736-475C-9592-66EDC306A236")>

' Version information for an assembly consists of the following four values:
'
'      Major Version
'      Minor Version
'      Build Number
'      Revision
'
' You can specify all the values or you can default the Build and Revision Numbers
' by using the '*' as shown below:

<Assembly: AssemblyVersion("1.0.*")>
```

Now let's append the following code to specify the configuration for the COM+ application containing our `CustomersTx` .NET `ServicedComponent`:

```
'--------------------------------------------------------------------------------
'Use attributes defined in the System.EnterpriseServices namespaces to 'specify
the configuration for the COM+ Application that is created when the
'ServicedComponents in this assembly are registered in COM+.
'--------------------------------------------------------------------------------

'Specify the name of the COM+ Application to create
<Assembly: ApplicationName("Northwind Business Services")>

'Specify the Activation attribute for the COM+ Application. Possible values
'include:
'   Library : ServicedComponents run in the creator's process
'   Server : ServicedComponents run in a system process, dllhost.exe
<Assembly: ApplicationActivation(ActivationOption.Library)>

'Disable call authentication in the COM+ application that will contain the
'ServicedComponents in this assembly to avoid an 'Access Denied' exception.
<Assembly: ApplicationAccessControl(Value:=False,
Authentication:=AuthenticationOption.None)>
```

Create a Strong Name and Sign the Assembly

Now that we've written the implementation code for our `CustomersTx` .NET `ServicedComponent`, we need to perform some other tasks before building the project. The first thing we need to do is to create a **strong name** and assign it to our project. As we discussed earlier, a strong name is a cryptographic signature that provides name uniqueness for the compiled assembly. Assemblies containing .NET `ServicedComponents`, as well as shared assemblies that are to be installed in the .NET **Global Assembly Cache (GAC)**, must have a strong name.

> **NOTE: If you do not create a strong name and use it to sign the assembly, your project will still compile and build successfully. However, when you attempt to register the assembly or instantiate one of its classes, you will receive an unavoidable run-time error indicating that the assembly must be signed with a strong name.**

This is what happens when you try to register an assembly without using a strong name:

```
C:\>regsvcs C:\TransactionClass\bin\TransactionClass.dll
RegSvcs - .NET Services Installation Utility Version 1.0.2914.16
Copyright (C) Microsoft Corp. 2000-2001. All rights reserved.

The following installation error occurred:
1: The assembly 'C:\TransactionClass\bin\TransactionClass.dll' does not have a
strong name.

C:\>
```

The **Strong Name tool** (`Sn.exe`) is a console or command-line application included with the .NET Framework SDK for creating shared names. The Shared Name tool can perform several tasks related to creating and managing shared names; however, for our example components we simply need to use the shared name tool to generate a new shared name key pair, and store it in a file that we can associate with our source code. Such a project is called a **shared name key file**.

To generate a new shared name key file, execute the Strong Name tool, located in the .NET Framework SDK directory, and pass the `-k` switch along with the desired path and filename of the shared name key file with the following parameters. The `-k` switch instructs the Strong Name tool to create a new shared name key and write it to the specified file. For example, the following command will create a new shared name key file named `NorthwindBS.snk`, located in my project directory for the `NorthwindBS` project. Please note, the path to the Strong Name tool on your machine may vary based on the operating system, the installation of Visual Studio .NET, or the version of the .NET Framework.

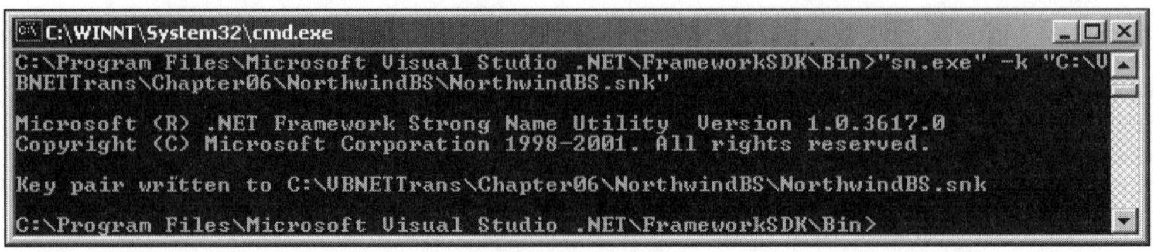

Note: the extension `.snk` *stands for Strong Name Key*

After creating the shared name key file, we need to use it to sign the assembly created by compiling our project. If you are using Visual Studio .NET, add the `NorthwindBS.snk` file to the `NorthwindBS` project by right-clicking on the project and selecting **Add Existing Item**.

Note: It is not absolutely necessary to add the shared name key file to your Visual Studio .NET project; however, it can be more convenient because the shared name key file can be managed with the other project files and stored in source control.

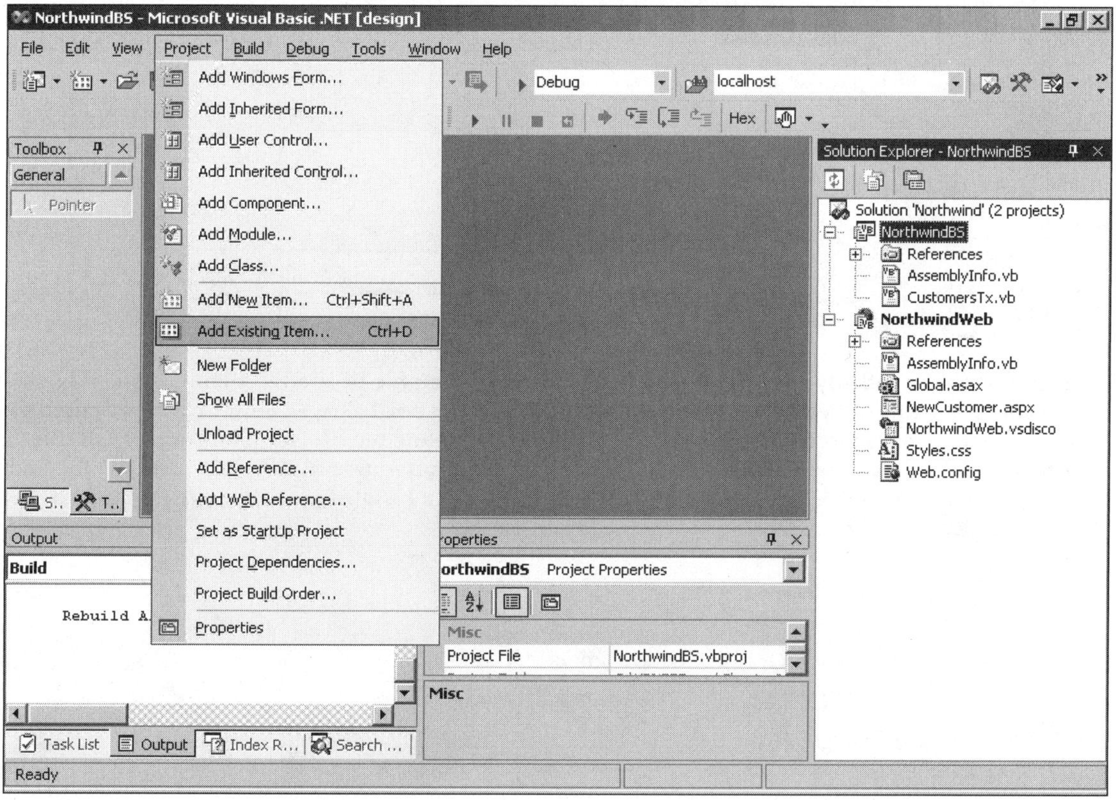

From the **Add Existing Item** dialog window, browse to the `NorthwindBS.snk` file we created using the Shared Name utility and add it to the project.

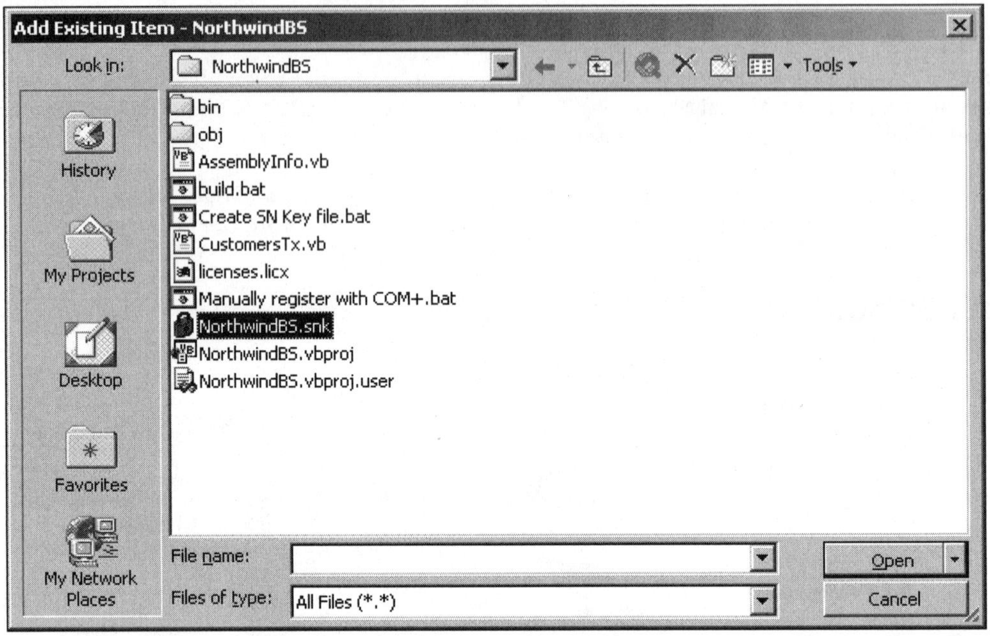

Finally, we must explicitly specify that the `NorthwindBS.snk` file be used to sign the assembly created when compiling this project. The `System.Reflection.AssemblyKeyFileAttribute` is used to specify the path to a shared name key file to use when compiling the project. The code to call this attribute should already be included in the `AssemblyInfo.vb` source file. Simply open the file and modify the line containing a reference to the `AssemblyKeyFile` attribute to specify the path to the `NorthwindBS.snk` file:

```
<Assembly: AssemblyVersion("1.0.*")>

'Use the System.Reflection.AssemblyKeyFile attribute to sign this assembly
'...with our shared-name key file
'
'NOTE:  The path is relative to the output directory for the compiled assembly
<Assembly: AssemblyKeyFile("..\..\NorthwindBS.snk")>

'-----------------------------------------------------------------------------
'Use attributes defined in the System.EnterpriseServices namespaces to
```

The path that must be specified for `AssemblyKeyFile` attribute is relative to the output directory for the assembly. If your build configuration has been customized, then it may be necessary to modify this path. If the path to the shared name key file is not correct, you will receive the following compile error:

```
Error creating assembly manifest: Error reading key file '..\NorthwindBS.snk' --
The system cannot find the file specified.
```

Change Project Properties

If you're using Visual Studio .NET, there's one last issue we should address before building our project. By default, Visual Studio .NET assigns the project name as the top-level namespace for types contained in the project. Consequently, our `CustomersTx` class would have a fully-qualified type name of `NorthwindBS.Northwind.BusinessServices.CustomersTx`. `NorthwindBS` is added by Visual Studio .NET and `Northwind.BusinessServices` is the namespace we specified in the `CustomersTx.vb` source file.

We can disable this behavior in Visual Studio .NET by clearing the value for the Root Namespace property in the `NorthwindBS` project properties dialog. In the **Project Properties** dialog window, navigate to **Common Properties/General** and clear the value in the **Root Namespace** field.

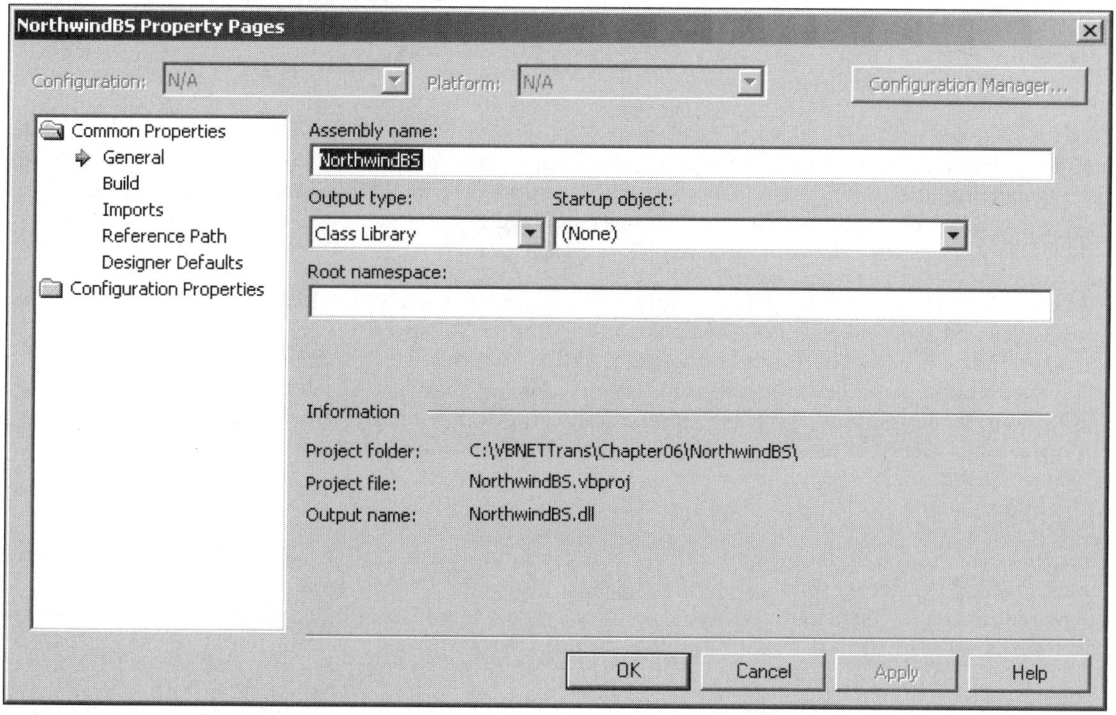

Build the Project/Source Files

Finally, we're ready to compile and build our `NorthwindBS` project. If you're using Visual Studio .NET, simply select **Build Solution** or one of the other build options from the **Build** menu. The build output should be a single assembly named `NorthwindBS.dll`.

If you're using the Visual Basic .NET compiler from the command line, the following command will compile and build the `NorthwindBS.dll` assembly. Notice that we've referenced to the `System.EnterpriseServices.dll` using the `/r` switch. Also remember that `AssemblyInfo.vb` will instruct the program to look for the `NorthwindsBS.snk` file in a different relative directory. Be sure to alter `AssemblyInfo.vb` so that it reflects the correct relative path information, or you will generate an error.

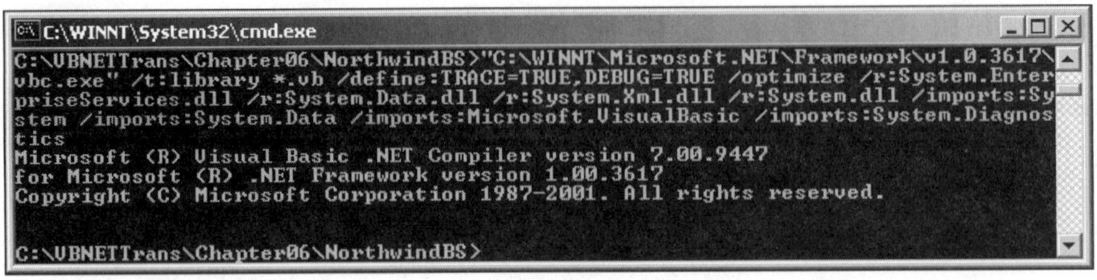

Registration

Before .NET `ServicedComponents` can be instantiated by a client application or component, they must first be registered with COM+. There are actually two techniques that can be used to register assemblies containing .NET `ServicedComponents` with COM+. These techniques are called "lazy registration" and manual registration.

Lazy registration is a technique that was designed to facilitate .NET's "zero-touch" or "x-copy" deployment model with .NET `ServicedComponents`. Lazy registration doesn't actually require a component developer or system administrator to do anything to register components with COM+. With lazy registration, .NET automatically registers an assembly and all of its contained `ServicedComponents` the first time an instance of the `ServicedComponent` in the assembly is created.

When a new version of the .NET assembly replaces an older version, the .NET Framework, specifically the `RegistrationHelper` and `RegistrationHelperTx` classes in the `System.EnterpriseServices` namespace, will automatically register and utilize the newer version. The information contained in the assembly's metadata or manifest is used to properly configure the COM+ application and the COM+ component(s), interface(s), and method(s). This configuration information is stored in the assembly's metadata by utilizing the attributes defined in the `System.EnterpriseServices` namespace.

In the case of our `CustomersTx` .NET `ServicedComponent`, we utilized attributes in this namespace to specify the transactional support attribute for our component, descriptions for the component and methods, and the name, activation type, and security for the COM+ application. While at first lazy registration sounds like a great model, it is not without its faults. We'll discuss some of the challenges and workarounds with lazy registration later in this chapter.

Manual registration, on the other hand, is just as it sounds. Manual registration requires someone to manually execute a command-line utility called the .NET Services Installation Tool, formerly called the Registration Services Tool, (`regsvcs.exe`) and pass the path and filename of the assembly as a parameter. There are also additional parameters to control the behavior of the .NET Services Installation Tool with respect to the creation and updating of the COM+ application. The .NET Services Installation Tool is typically located in the version dependent .NET Framework directory, which is located at `C:\WINNT\Microsoft.NET\Framework\v1.0.3705\` on my machine at the time of this writing.

We can use either registration technique with the `NorthwindBS.dll` assembly containing our `CustomersTx` component. However, I'll go ahead and walk through the manual registration process. If you want to use the lazy registration technique, then you can skip over this task, although I would strongly encourage you to learn both techniques and utilize the best one for a particular situation. Let's execute the .NET Services Installation Tool and pass the path and filename of the `NorthwindBS.dll` assembly as a parameter. Keep in mind that the path to `regsvcs.exe` may vary in your environment, based on the version of the .NET Framework you have installed:

Note: if you want to view the available options for `RegSvcs` *or simply don't remember a particular switch, simply type* `RegSvcs` *from the command prompt to list the options as shown:*

```
C:\VBNETTrans\Chapter06\NorthwindBS>
C:\VBNETTrans\Chapter06\NorthwindBS>"C:\WINNT\Microsoft.NET\Framework\v1.0.3617\re
gsvcs.exe" "C:\VBNETTrans\Chapter06\NorthwindBS\bin\NorthwindBS.dll"
Microsoft (R) .NET Framework Services Installation Utility Version 1.0.3617.0
Copyright (C) Microsoft Corporation 1998-2001.  All rights reserved.

WARNING: The class 'Northwind.BusinessServices.CustomersTx' has no class
interface, which means that unmanaged late bound calls cannot take advantage of
AutoComplete methods.
Installed Assembly:
        Assembly: C:\VBNETTrans\Chapter06\NorthwindBS\bin\NorthwindBS.dll
        Application: Northwind Business Services
        TypeLib: c:\vbnettrans\chapter06\northwindbs\bin\NorthwindBS.tlb

C:\VBNETTrans\Chapter06\NorthwindBS>
```

It's important to watch the output returned from executing the .NET Services Installation Tool when registering `ServicedComponents`. In this situation, the .NET Services Installation Tool is raising a warning that the `CustomersTx` class will not be accessible from unmanaged code because it does not implement a public interface. We'll address this issue later in this chapter.

If we look in the directory containing the assembly `NorthwindBS.dll`, you'll notice that the `Regsvcs.exe` utility exported a type library with the same name as the assembly.

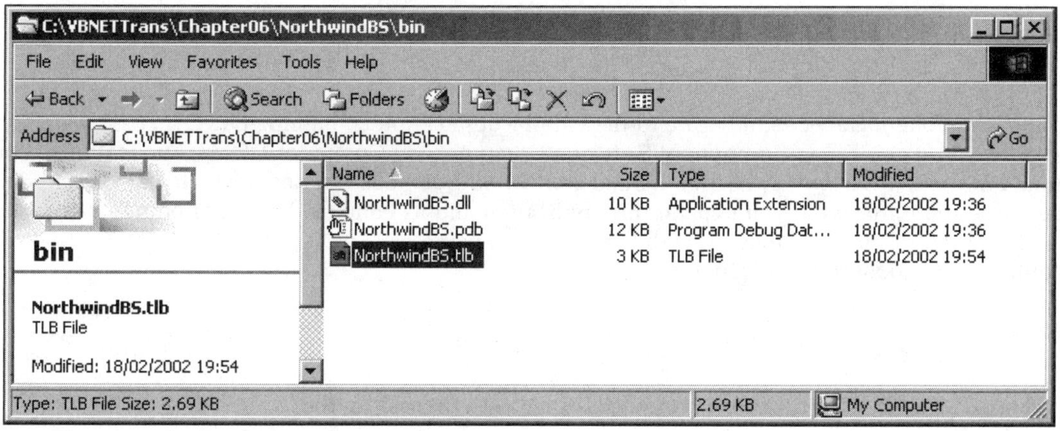

Choosing a Registration Technique

Lazy registration has a number of challenges including:

- Applications instantiating the `ServicedComponent` must be running under an account with Administrative privileges or registration will fail.

- There is the possibility of conflicts if you have multiple applications because COM+ application information is stored in the assemblies' manifests (metadata). With COM+ 1.0, only one version of a COM+ component can be registered. However, .NET supports multiple versions of the same component. Consequently, you could encounter a situation where one application is using one version of a `ServicedComponent`, while another application is using a different version of the same `ServicedComponent`. If you were using lazy registration in this situation, you could encounter conflicts because each application would cause it's own incompatible version of the `ServicedComponent` to register. To help overcome this challenge you should also configure your components in the .NET Global Assembly Cache (GAC).
- More significant performance degradation at first access.
- Registration problems will not be discovered until runtime instead of during deployment. If an error should occur during registration it can be more difficult to diagnose at runtime than during deployment.

On the other hand, manual registration breaks the xcopy deployment model provided by COM+, but chances are that it's not a significant issue because xcopy deployment is only used on the server hosting the COM+ components and not the machine(s) hosting the client application(s).

Verify Registration

No matter which registration technique you decide to utilize, it is helpful to verify that your .NET `ServicedComponents` have been successfully registered and configured in COM+. Keep in mind that if you choose to use the "lazy registration" technique, then the .NET `ServicedComponents` contained in the assembly will not be registered until the first time they are instantiated.

To verify the registration of our `CustomersTx` .NET `ServicedComponent`, let's launch the Component Services Microsoft Management Console (MMC) snap-in from Administrative Tools.

Using Component Services, navigate to the COM+ application containing our `CustomersTx` component by expanding Component Services/Computer/My Computer/COM+ Applications. You should now see a COM+ application named Northwind Business Services, which was created during the registration process. If you expand this application and its contained Components folder, you will see our `CustomersTx` component with the registered name of Northwind.BusinessServices.CustomersTx.

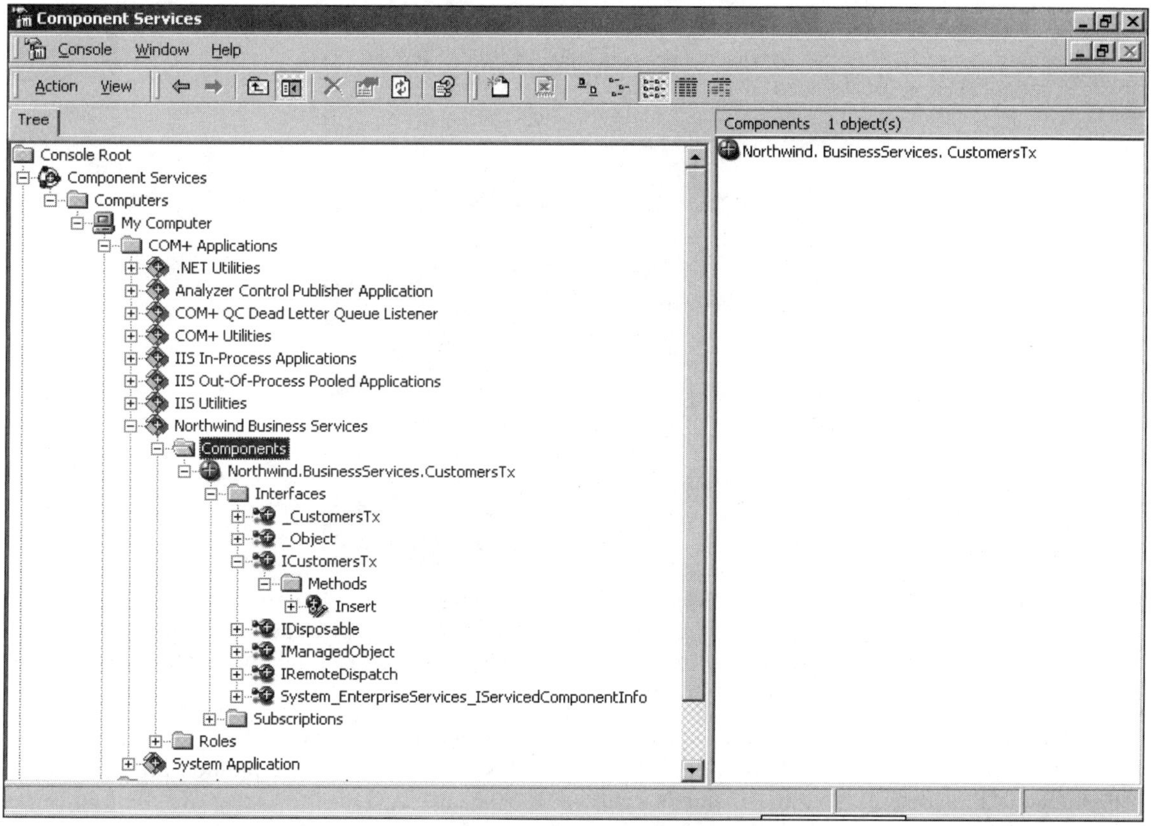

By right-clicking on the Northwind.BusinessServices.CustomersTx component and selecting Properties, Component Services will display a dialog window that will allow us to view and/or change any of the COM+ configuration settings for our `CustomersTx` component. However, keep in mind that if the component is re-registered either through lazy registration or manually, any changes to the COM+ configuration for the COM+ application, component, interfaces, or methods will be over-written by the values contained in the assembly `NorthwindBS.dll`. Consequently, permanent changes to the COM+ configuration should be performed in the source code for the assembly and component, using the .NET attributes defined in the `System.EnterpriseServices` namespace.

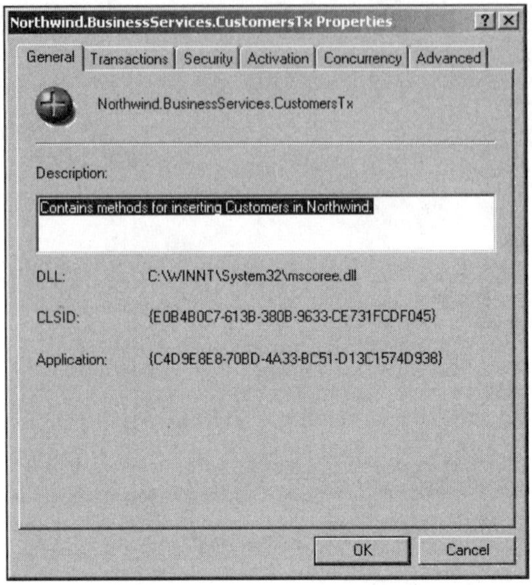

Notice that the DLL registered with COM+ for our `CustomersTx` .NET `ServicedComponent` is `MSCOREE.dll`, not the `NorthwindBS.dll` assembly. `MSCOREE.dll` provides the COM interoperability that enables .NET classes to execute within COM+. We'll talk more about COM Interoperability and this DLL in Chapter 7.

If we expand the `ICustomersTx` interface in **Component Services** and expand the methods section, we will see the `Insert()` method that we defined for this interface. From the **Method** properties dialog window for this method, we can see the description that we specified for the `Insert()` method by using the `System.EnterpriseServices.DescriptionAttribute` attribute in our `CustomersTx.vb` source file.

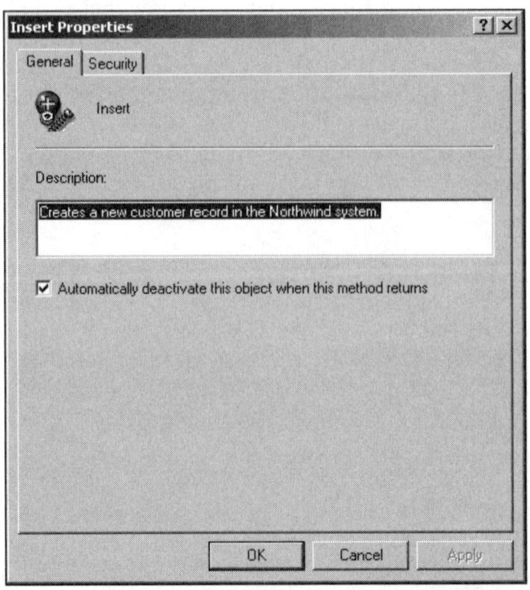

We can also see that the COM+ configuration option Automatically deactivate this object when this method returns, is configured for the `Insert()` method. This lengthy-titled attribute in the COM+ configuration is the equivalent of the `System.EnterpriseServices.AutoCompleteAttribute`. Here's the code in our `CustomersTx.vb` file that set these attributes:

```
<Description("Creates a new customer record in the Northwind system."), _
    AutoComplete()> _
Public Sub Insert(ByVal strCustomerID As String, _
                    ByVal strCompanyName As String, _
                    ByVal strContactName As String, _
                    ByVal strContactTitle As String, _
                    ByVal strAddress As String, _
                    ByVal strCity As String, _
                    ByVal strRegion As String, _
                    ByVal strPostalCode As String, _
                    ByVal strCountry As String, _
                    ByVal strPhone As String, _
                    ByVal strFax As String) Implements ICustomersTx.Insert
```

Create the Test Application

In this exercise we'll create a simple ASP.NET Web Form application to test our transactional .NET `ServicedComponent`. This application will consist of a single Web Form named `NewCustomer.aspx`, which will allow a user to insert a customer into the Northwind database. You can of course use the test application supplied with the code download, after setting up a virtual directory for it. Instructions for doing this are given at the beginning of this example.

If you wish to create this ASP.NET Web Form application yourself from scratch, right-click on the Northwind Solution from Solution Explorer and select Add->New Project. Visual Studio .NET will then display the standard create project dialog window. Select the Visual Basic Projects folder in the `Project Types` tree and then select the ASP.NET Web Application project template from the Templates list. We'll specify a virtual directory name of NorthwindWeb on the local web server for the new project.

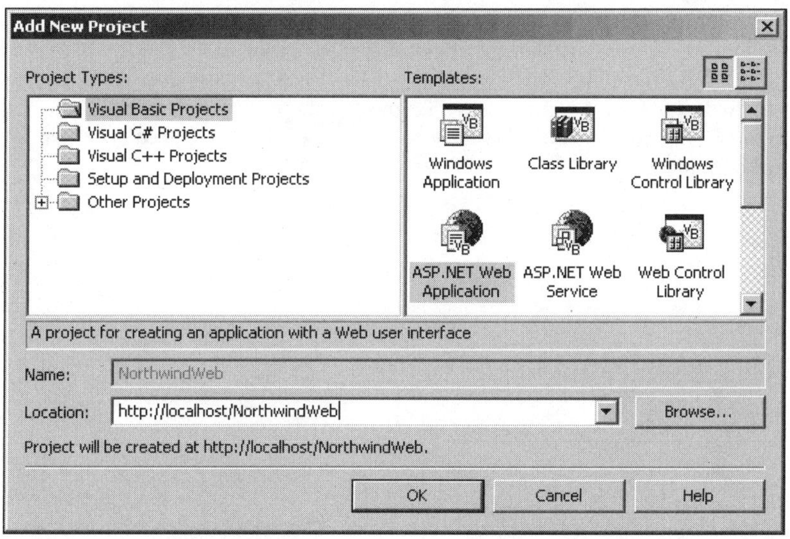

Now that the `NorthwindWeb` project has been created and added to our solution, we need to add a reference to the `NorthwindBS` project so we can utilize the `CustomersTx` .NET `ServicedComponent`. Right-click on the **References** folder in solution explorer for the new `NorthwindWeb` project and select **Add Reference** from the context menu.

In the **Add Reference** dialog window, navigate to the **Projects** tab, add the `NorthwindBS` to the selected components list, and click the **OK** button.

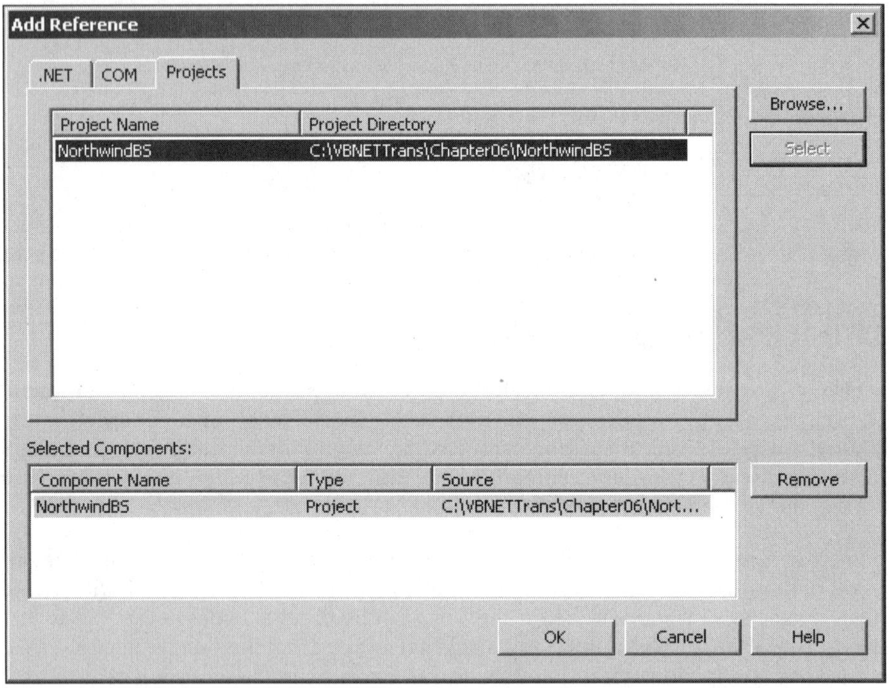

Next, we need to rename the included `WebForm1.aspx` file to `NewCustomer.aspx`, and build a simple user interface to capture the data for new customer records. Basically, this Web Form will contain several ASP.NET Textbox and Dropdown List WebControls that allow the user to enter data for a customer record. For sake of space, I won't go into the details for the WebControls and HTML formatting on this Web Form. Instead, I'll let you download the sample Web Form application along with all of the other samples.

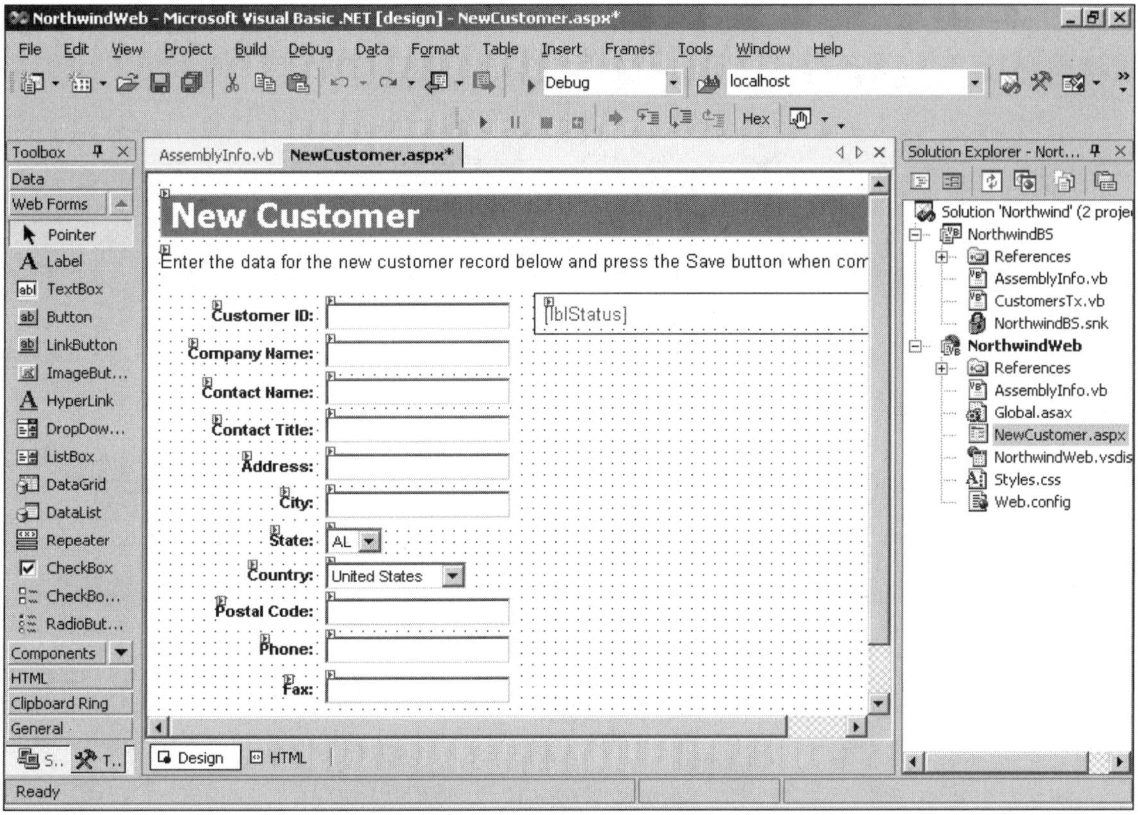

When the user clicks the Save button on this WebForm, it creates an instance of the `Northwind.BusinessServices.CustomersTx` class and invoke its `Insert()` method passing the data entered on the Web Form's fields as parameters. Here's the simple code behind the Save buttons event handler:

```
Private Sub btnSave_Click(ByVal sender As System.Object, ByVal e As
    System.EventArgs) Handles btnSave.Click

    Try
        'Create an instance of the CustomersTx .NET ServicedComponents
        Dim objCustomersTx As New
            Northwind.BusinessServices.CustomersTx()

        'Insert a new customer record by passing the values of the
        'WebControls on this page
        objCustomersTx.Insert(txtCustomerID.Text, _
                                        txtCompanyName.Text, _
                                        txtContactName.Text, _
                                        txtContactTitle.Text, _
                                        txtAddress.Text, _
                                        txtCity.Text, _
                                        lstStates.SelectedItem.Value, _
                                        txtPostalCode.Text, _
```

```
                                       lstCountries.SelectedItem.Value, _
                                       txtPhone.Text, _
                                       txtFax.Text)

                'Display a message that the record was inserted successfully
                lblStatus.Text = "Customer '" & txtCustomerID.Text & "' was
                    inserted successfully!"

            Catch excp As System.Exception
                'An unexpected Exception occured.  Display it to the user.
                lblStatus.Visible = True
                lblStatus.Text = "The following exception occured: " &
                    excp.ToString
            End Try
        End Sub
```

That's all the code that is necessary to invoke our `CustomersTx` class and perform work within a COM+ transaction! Now let's run the `NewCustomer.aspx` Web Form and insert some customer records!

If you're using Visual Studio .NET, simply select **Start** from the **Debug** window and Visual Studio.NET will automatically build both projects in the solution, and run the `NorthwindWeb` application, displaying the `NewCustomer.aspx` page in a new Internet Explorer window. It will be necessary to make the `NorthwindWeb` project the active project before using this technique to build and execute the `NewCustomer.aspx` Web Form, so right-click on it and select it as your start up project.

To create customer records in the Northwind database, simply enter the data for the customer record in the fields on the `Northwind.aspx` page and press the **Save** button. The `NewCustomer.aspx` page will then perform a post-back and execute the code behind the **Save** button's server-side event handler, which invokes the `Insert()` method on a new instance of our `CustomerTx` .NET `ServicedComponent`.

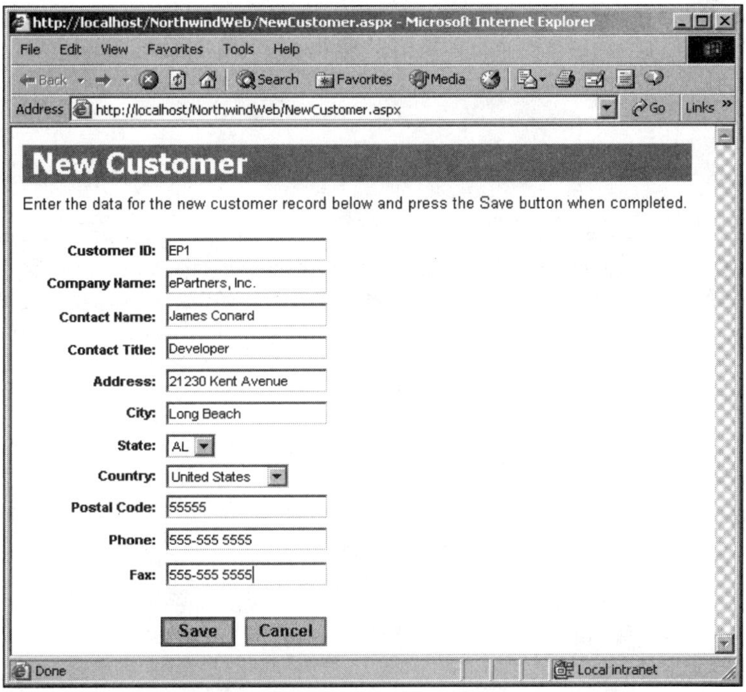

If the `Insert()` operation is successful, a friendly message is displayed on the `NewCustomer.aspx` page, as shown in the following screenshot.

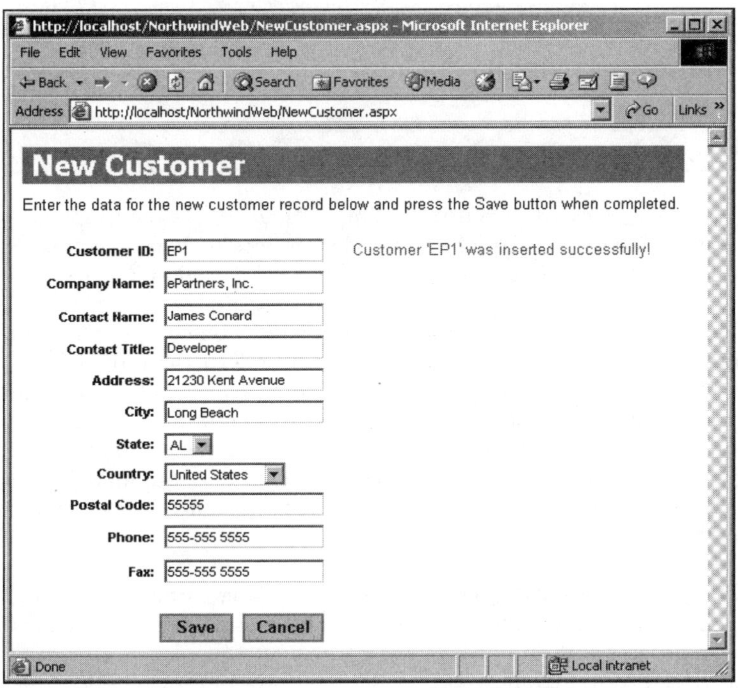

If an error occurs, the transaction will abort, all changes performed by the `CustomersTx` component will be rolled back, and an error message will be displayed on the page.

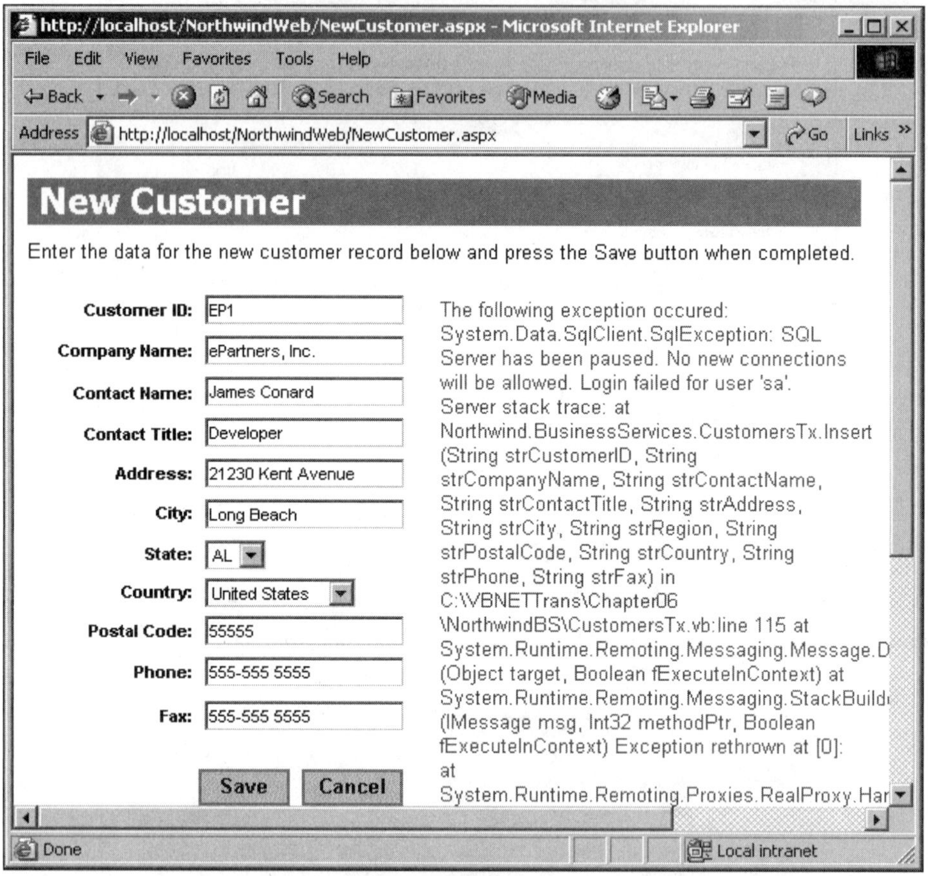

While the example that we created here is fairly simple, you can see the simplicity of the declarative transaction model provided by COM+. Other COM+ services such as object pooling, concurrency, loosely coupled events (LCE), and queued components can be used in a similar fashion.

The real advantages of COM+ transactions are evident when you compose multiple components within a single transaction and/or access multiple data stores within a single transaction. For example, suppose we decided to develop an order-processing component that facilitated the creation of orders in the Northwind database. Orders and their associated items are stored in the `Orders` and `Order Details` tables respectively. Now let's imagine that the customer placing the order has not been created in the system – so they need to be inserted when an order is placed. In addition, the distribution and fulfillment department has requested that the order be sent to their ERP system through Microsoft Message Queuing (MSMQ).

Of course all of these operations need to be performed in a single transaction, and all data changes are rolled back if anything should fail. After all, the distribution and fulfillment department wouldn't be happy if they had to process and ship orders that weren't actually placed. This realistic business problem could be solved with the following .NET `ServicedComponents`:

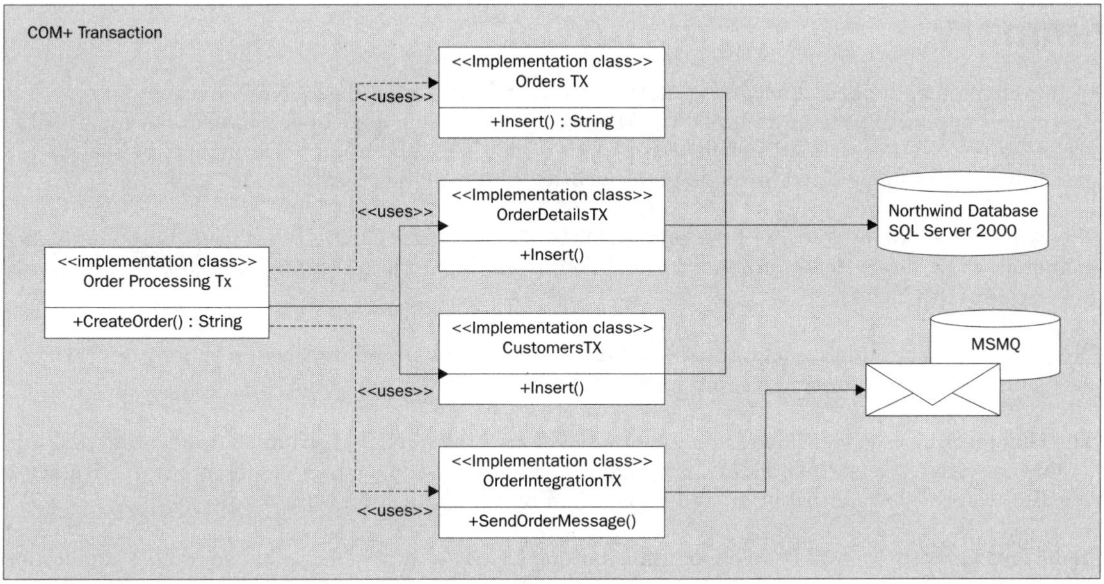

In this scenario, the `OrderProcessingTx` component provides a method named `CreateOrder()` that receives an XML-formatted string containing the order and customer data. When the `CreateOrder()` method is called, the `OrderProcessingTx` component simply parses the XML data, applies any business logic or rules, and utilizes several supporting components to perform the actual operations against the Northwind database.

The `OrdersTx` and `OrderDetailsTx` components provide insert methods to insert record(s) into the `Orders` and `Order Details` tables respectively. Since the `CustomersTx` component already provides the ability to insert `Customer` records, we can utilize the same exact component within this new transaction without any code or configuration changes if we need to create a customer record when placing an order.

Finally, the `OrderIntegrationTx` component provides a method named `SendOrderMessage()` that, when invoked, sends orders to Northwind's ERP system through MSMQ by recording the order data as an MSMQ message. Since MSMQ is a resource manager that supports distributed transactions based on MS DTC and the OLE Transactions protocol, the task of writing the message to the queue will also be performed within the COM+ transaction.

Hopefully, this scenario gives you an idea of the extensibility features provided by COM+ transactions, which are not available with local or distributed transactions as implemented by ADO, ADO.NET, or transact SQL (T-SQL). We'll discuss a similar scenario, with complete code examples, in the case study located in Chapter 10.

Summary

In this chapter we looked at accessing COM+ services from Visual Basic .NET. Because larger distributed applications tend to utilize COM+, we started this chapter by learning about the distributed architectures. We saw that a distributed application should exhibit good performance, be scalable, extensible, easily maintained, provide good security, and provide reusable code.

Next we took a look at how .NET supports COM+ services through .NET-serviced components. We examined a .NET-serviced component. We then moved on and looked at the methods and properties of the `ContextUtil` class.

We also learned about transactions using COM+. Here we explored transaction support levels and JIT Activation, and how to manage components through component services.

The chapter project gave us hands-on experience of creating a .NET distributed application that utilizes COM+ services. We learned about strong names and how to add a strong name to our .NET assembly. We also examined the distribution and registration of our application using `regsvcs`.

In the next chapter, you will learn about using existing COM+ components within your .NET applications.

7

Interoperability

In the previous chapter we learned how to develop .NET Serviced Components that take advantage of the distributed, automatic transaction model provided by MS DTC and COM+ Transaction services. After discussing all of these transaction processing technologies, as a developer I'm sure you've been thinking how you can leverage the .NET Framework and Visual Basic .NET in your organization's existing transactional applications. In this chapter we'll build upon the concepts introduced in Chapter 6 and learn about a powerful feature of the .NET Framework called **COM Interoperability**. The COM Interoperability services provide two-way integration support for utilizing .NET components and applications in conjunction with COM-based components and applications. Using COM Interoperability, organizations can leverage their existing technology investments in COM-based applications, while beginning to utilize the powerful new features and functionality of the .NET Framework. In this chapter we will:

- Define the strategies and considerations for migrating a transactional application to the .NET platform using Visual Basic .NET
- Analyze the benefits and drawbacks of each migration strategy
- Understand the role of COM Interoperability services in the .NET Framework
- Discuss the concepts of COM-Callable Wrappers and Runtime-Callable Wrappers
- Leverage tools included with the .NET Framework SDK to utilize COM Interoperability

Let's begin this chapter by first discussing some of the common techniques for migrating transactional applications to the .NET platform.

Rewrite, Upgrade, or Integrate

As you've probably learned by now, Visual Basic .NET and the .NET Framework provide a number of enhancements for developing transactional processing applications. Although the transaction processing technologies, such as ADO.NET transactions and COM+ transactions, are fundamentally equivalent to their COM counterparts, the .NET framework has a significant impact on how transaction processing applications are developed. With all of the enhancements and changes introduced with the .NET Framework, Microsoft determined that it was necessary and timely to also completely overhaul Visual Basic .NET.

Historically the Visual Basic language has carried over a number of legacy keywords and features from previous versions in order to provide backwards compatibility with existing source code. However, with Visual Basic .NET, the Visual Basic language has been modernized to be consistent with the rest of the .NET Framework and take its place in the ranks as a fully-featured object-oriented programming language. Many keywords, functions, and programming practices are no longer supported with Visual Basic .NET. As a result, it is not possible to simply migrate an existing Visual Basic application to the .NET platform by simply recompiling it, as we have done in years past when migrating to new versions of Visual Basic. Instead, the migration of an existing transaction processing application to the .NET platform and Visual Basic .NET must be carefully planned, while considering a number of factors.

When considering a migration to the .NET Framework, you should first ask yourself if you should be migrating the application at all. In some situations it may actually make sense from a business and/or technical perspective to leave your applications in Visual Basic 6.0 and utilize Visual Basic .NET for new development. Microsoft promises to continue to support Visual Basic 6.0 for several years to come. For example, if an application has a limited lifetime, or its role within an organization is nearing its end, it may not make sense to invest the time and costs of migrating the application to .NET. However, in most situations there are significant advantages to moving to Visual Basic .NET and the .NET Framework.

If you've made the decision to begin investing in the .NET platform, then you have basically three migration options:

- **Rewrite** – Design, develop, and test the application entirely from scratch, without upgrading existing code or utilizing existing COM components
- **Upgrade** – Upgrade existing Visual Basic code to the Visual Basic .NET language, either manually or using the Visual Basic .NET Upgrade Wizard, and modify the code to adjust for the differences in Visual Basic .NET and the .NET Framework
- **Interoperate (Partial Upgrade)** – Utilize the COM Interoperability features of the .NET Framework to leverage your existing code and only upgrade the portions of the application where it makes sense to do so

Unfortunately, there are no definite answers or hard rules to follow when choosing between these options. Instead, the decision you should make will vary with the individual characteristics of each application. A few of the characteristics to consider and questions to be asking when choosing a migration strategy include:

- **Application architecture** – How was the application designed? Does it consist of a single client application? Does it utilize a client-server or an n-tier architecture? Does it make use of custom COM components?

- **Quality of the existing code** – Is the code available for the existing application? What language is it written in? Does it use common programming techniques and best practices? Does it utilize object-oriented programming techniques?
- **Amount of code** – How much total code composes the application? How much code could be eliminated by using a different architecture or the features of Visual Basic .NET and the .NET Framework?
- **Performance and scalability** – Does the existing application meet the current performance and scalability requirements? Will it scale to meet the organization's demands of the next several years?
- **Security** – Does the existing application have any known security holes? Do users have concerns about privacy and protection of their data?
- **Extensibility** – How difficult is it to modify the existing application to fix a bug or add a new feature? Does the existing application require the expertise of the original developer(s)?

There are also many non-technical factors to consider when choosing a migration strategy. Some of these factors include the support, maintainability, and usability of the existing application and the need for enhancements in these areas. Perhaps one of the most critical factors to consider is the time and cost budgeted for the migration. Let's evaluate the benefits and drawbacks and tasks involved with each migration approach, while considering some of these technical and non-technical issues.

Rewrite

If the choice were given to me, I would rewrite all my applications using Visual Basic .NET. Not only would this give me a chance to incorporate those changes I have been wanting to make that I never got around to, rewriting with VB.NET will offer me the advanced features that are only available through the .NET Framework.

Furthermore, .NET is the new platform of choice. Although .NET provides excellent InterOp features for your COM components, history has shown that as legacy applications get older they tend to break. Think how many times a new version of VB, Windows, Excel, or Access has come out and you have had to make modifications to your code in order to get things working again. The bottom line is that often a complete rewriting using Visual Basic .NET is the most cost effective strategy for the long term.

Although the advantages to rewriting outweigh the disadvantages over the long run, I usually don't get what I want because the real world usually does not allow for such luxuries. Rewriting legacy code for the short term is very expensive, as it involves the starting over of the entire development cycle and this costs time, manpower, and dollars. However as previously mentioned, rewriting your code with Visual Basic .NET will pay off in the long run.

Of course one approach for migrating an application to the .NET platform is to completely rewrite it. Rewriting an application for the .NET platform will allow you to take advantage of the new features of the .NET Framework and Visual Basic .NET, and it should result in the highest performance and scalability of any of the migration techniques. Generally, rewriting should only considered an alternative when upgrading an application would be too challenging and the situation does not permit interoperability with the existing application because of performance or maintenance requirements. Rewriting is a feasible migration solution in some of the following conditions:

- The overall application architecture is the source of extensibility, maintenance, support, or functionality problems, or the application doesn't take advantage of a component-based programming model.

  Typically, architecture problems can only be resolved sufficiently with redesigning and rewriting an application.

- The application is small and the amount of code is minimal.

  Obviously, with applications that have limited amounts of code, there is less code to recreate in Visual Basic .NET than for enterprise-level applications.

- You desire to change programming languages.

  If for some reason you desire to change programming languages, perhaps because your project team is more skilled with another language, or because another language is more suited to the application's requirements, then it will not be possible to upgrade an existing application. However, you could utilize COM interoperability in this situation, to leverage your existing components from .NET, regardless of the .NET language you decided to utilize.

- The code has significant quality problems to the point that the entire application might as well be rewritten.

  Generally, if upgrading an application would involve rewriting a major portion of the code (50% or so), then it is probably beneficial to go ahead and rewrite the application so you can leverage the new features of the .NET Framework.

- The application suffers from performance and/or scalability problems.

  Performance and scalability of an application typically goes hand-in-hand with the application architecture and the quality of the code. The best way to resolve performance and scalability problems is to re-architect, and thus rewrite the application.

Although rewriting an application can have its advantages, in most situations the benefits are outweighed by the drawbacks. The primary drawbacks to rewriting an application for the .NET platform is the time and costs involved with the rewriting, as well as the complete loss of the original technology investment. Not only must all of the code be rewritten, but the application must be completely retested to ensure that it meets the requirements of the original system. For most organizations, the notion of rewriting their mission-critical, line-of-business applications is simply unrealistic. After all, most organizations and their users don't care about the underlying technology or how much easier it is to develop a transaction using Visual Basic .NET over Visual Basic 6.0, but instead they simply care whether or not the application solves their business problem and meets their requirements.

Upgrade

An alternative to completely rewriting an application for the .NET Framework is to upgrade your existing Visual Basic code to Visual Basic .NET. The Enterprise Developer and Enterprise Architect editions of Visual Studio.NET include an add-in called the Visual Basic Upgrade Wizard. When you attempt to open a Visual Basic 6.0 project file from either of these versions of Visual Studio .NET, the Visual Basic Upgrade Wizard will automatically load and guide you through a five step process of upgrading an application or component to Visual Basic .NET.

> **It is important to note that the Visual Basic Upgrade Wizard can only be used with Visual Basic 6.0 projects. If you want to upgrade from a prior version of Visual Basic, then you should first upgrade to Visual Basic 6.0 and then to Visual Basic .NET.**

However, as with most upgrade or code conversion tools, the Visual Basic Upgrade Wizard is not without its problems. Because of the significant differences between the Visual Basic 6.0 and Visual Basic .NET languages, there are typically dozens, if not hundreds, of warnings and errors generated by the Visual Basic Upgrade Wizard in response to incompatible lines of code. All of these issues must be manually resolved by the developer after running the Visual Basic Upgrade tool. Upgrading an application using this tool can represent a significant amount of painstaking code rework, depending on the type of application, the quality of the existing code, and its use of Visual Basic language features that are no longer supported with Visual Basic .NET.

Despite some of these challenges, upgrading existing code using the Visual Basic Upgrade Wizard is a reasonable migration strategy, especially with medium-size to large applications where the maximum performance, scalability, and maintainability are critical requirements. By upgrading an application instead of rewriting it, you can leverage your existing technology investments in the code, while reducing the amount of the time and costs involved when migrating to the .NET platform. After performing an upgrade, you can utilize some of the saved time and cost for leveraging some of the new features of the .NET Framework. Additionally, if you have a legacy project utilizing COM that is expected to undergo numerous changes in the future, it may be to your advantage to consider upgrading your application over to .NET beforehand.

However, you should carefully weigh the benefits and drawbacks of upgrading before simply moving forward with this migration strategy. In some situations it may make since to completely rewrite and redesign your application from the ground up to take full advantage of the .NET Framework. Even though the VB Upgrade Wizard can convert code from Visual Basic 6 to VB .NET, it cannot address fundamental architecture problems that affect the performance, scalability, and extensibility of the system. As I mentioned earlier, generally these important issues can only be resolved by re-architecting and rewriting an application.

Interoperate

For most organizations, it is simply not feasible to rewrite or upgrade an entire application to Visual Basic .NET and the .NET Framework. In these situations, the best migration strategy may be to utilize the COM Interoperability support of the .NET Framework. COM Interoperability provides a two-way integration between the managed and unmanaged code. Specifically, COM interoperability allows .NET applications to utilize COM components and COM-based applications to utilize .NET components. For example, using COM interoperability an ASP.NET WebForm could consume an existing COM component or a Visual Basic 6 application could call methods on a .NET class. The Common Language Runtime encapsulates all of the details of COM Interoperability and abstracts applications from the details of the other platform. This two-way, bidirectional integration between COM and .NET is a powerful migration technique and the key to the future success of .NET.

COM Interoperability effectively allows you to perform a partial migration to the .NET Framework, where it makes the most sense for your organization and the application at hand. Some of the benefits of this migration strategy include:

- Organizations can begin investing in the .NET platform while still leveraging existing technology investments in COM-based applications
- Developers can learn Visual Basic .NET and the features of the .NET Framework over time without sacrificing the success of the migration
- Applications can continue to use Microsoft and third-party COM components, such as ADO, without requiring developers to learn entirely new object libraries while learning how to develop code in a new language and on a new platform
- Code can be migrated to the .NET platform over time in modular and manageable pieces
- Code that does not upgrade easily or is not easy to reproduce in Visual Basic .NET and the .NET environment can remain as Visual Basic 6.0 COM components

Just as with the other migration techniques, COM Interoperability also has some drawbacks that should be carefully considered.

The primary drawback of COM interoperability is the performance overhead. To facilitate COM interoperability, the Common Language Runtime must translate method calls and marshal parameters from one data type to another when calling between the platforms. In most situations the performance degradation is minimal and probably unnoticeable. However, for some components the performance degradation can be more significant, especially those components that utilize a property-based design requiring several property or method calls to carry out an operation. In these situations, it make may more sense to rewrite or upgrade that individual component as a .NET class.

It can also be more difficult to deploy and maintain applications that utilize COM interoperability when compared to applications that have been completely upgraded or rewritten for the .NET Framework. Whether your using a COM component from .NET or a .NET component from a COM-based language, the component must first be registered, whereas applications written entirely in .NET can generally take advantage of the XCOPY deployment benefits of the framework.

Out of the three options for migrating to .NET, COM Interoperability is often the best compromise between leveraging your existing code and taking advantage of the new Visual Basic .NET and .NET Framework features. With interoperability, you can write all your new applications utilizing VB.NET, while keeping your existing COM components just as they are.

But before deciding whether COM interoperability is the right solution for your given situation, it is important to understand how COM interoperability works, the limitations with this migration strategy, and the tasks involved when using COM components from .NET or vice-versa. Let's discuss some of these topics and learn how we can leverage COM interoperability with transactional applications.

> **Although we'll discuss COM Interopability in further detail, this chapter just barely scratches the surface on this complex topic. For more detailed information about COM Interopability, I recommend the book titled *Professional Visual Basic Interoperability – COM and VB6 to .NET* (ISBN – 1-861005-65-2), also published by Wrox Press.**

COM Components

Actually there is quite a bit that goes on in the background with .NET interoperability. For example, .NET interoperability is responsible for managing between managed and unmanaged code such as:

- How interfaces are supported between early and late binding
- How objects are released – this includes marking objects for garbage collection
- How data is marshaled and translated (this process includes converting data types between managed and unmanaged data types)
- How rules are enforced regarding COM identity

You should be familiar with the basic rules for developing COM components. Nevertheless the following is a brief recap for ensuring your COM components work well with .NET interoperability:

- Be sure to explicitly release your objects. You will learn about .NET wrappers and how they affect COM objects shortly. For now understand that .NET wrappers provide the means for communication between the .NET environment and COM objects. Because .NET wrappers are managed code, even COM objects referenced by these wrappers will be cleaned up by the .NET garbage collection when the time comes, as opposed to being terminated when an COM object is de-referenced. This means that unless you explicitly free your resources, COM objects will be held until the .NET wrapper object is destroyed or terminated.
- When developing COM components with Visual Basic 6, be sure to set version compatibility to binary. Binary compatibility acts as a safety net. Instead of creating new GUIDs for each compilation, binary compatibility will only create new GUIDs when an interface is affected. Simply changing business rules will not cause a new GUID to be generated.
- Make sure you create a type library. Without a type library, .NET won't know how to call into the COM component. You may recall that type libraries are automatically incorporated into COM components (including standard DLLs, OCX, and EXEs).
- Keep the number of methods that need to be called from .NET into a COM component down. You will learn more about marshaling later in this chapter. For now, realize that calls must pass through different boundaries (.NET and COM). Crossing these boundaries takes a lot of work. As a result, the more times these boundaries need to be crossed, the more inefficiency occurs.
- Data types should be common to both .NET and COM. Common data types between .NET and COM are referred to as **Isomorphic types**. Isomorphic types do not need any kinds of conversions when crossing boundaries. We will cover these common types later in this chapter.

Marshaling

Information that is transmitted across the boundaries between two processes is referred to as **marshaling**. COM cannot communicate directly with managed code, nor can managed code communicate directly with COM. The lack of communication between COM and managed code presents some problems, however the .NET Framework does provide a solution has some performance issues, referred to as **wrappers**.

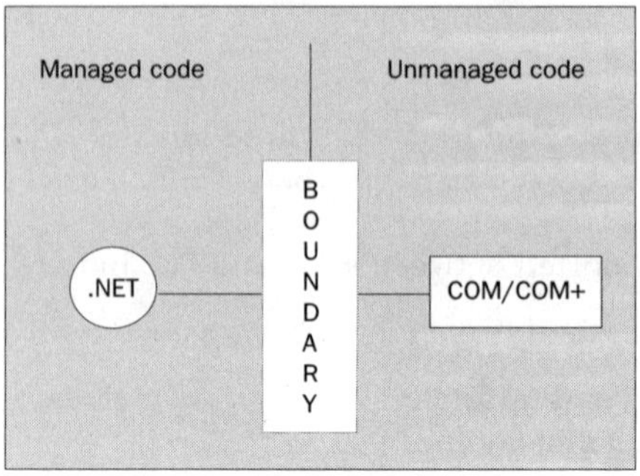

We will talk about wrappers and how they work shortly. First, let's look at data types, and how they convert between boundaries.

Marshaling Data Types

As mentioned earlier in this chapter, it is best to use **isomorphic** types as much as possible because they don't need any kind of conversions. The following table displays the isomorphic types and how they map between Visual Basic 6 and .NET:

Visual Basic 6	.NET
`Byte`	`Byte`
`Integer`	`Short`
`Long`	`Integer`
`Single`	`Single`
`Double`	`Double`
`Char`	`Char`

Dates, strings, and a few other data types are **non-isomorphic** and must be converted when crossing boundaries as listed in the following table:

Visual Basic 6	.NET
`String`	`String`
`Boolean`	`Boolean`
`Variant`	`Object`
`Date`	`Date`
`Currency`	`Decimal`
`Object`	`UnmanagedType.IUnknown`

With .NET, marshaling makes use of wrappers that make data appear as if it was native to the model in which it was called. For example, there is a **COM-Callable Wrapper (CCW)** that allows communication from a COM object to .NET, by providing a COM-like interface to the client. There is also a **Runtime-Callable Wrapper (RCW)** that allows a managed code type of interface to the client when communicating with a COM object.

As previously mentioned, using wrappers does come at a cost. Without getting into too much detail about marshaling, you need to understand that there are a series of instructions that occur for data to be transmitted across boundaries. When using wrappers to marshal this data, a lot of instructions are needed. Making a few calls across boundaries really should be of little concern. However, if your application requires numerous short functions between COM and managed code, the application will likely suffer dramatically.

The nice thing about wrappers is you don't need to concern yourself with their inner workings, as .NET handles everything for you. However, there are a few caveats about COM InterOp that you need to be aware of:

- Static members are not supported because the CCW cannot distinguish to its clients the difference between a class and an instance. Simply, COM can only utilize interfaces that are exposed.
- Another problem with COM is it cannot distinguish between public, private, or internally exposed types. As a result only public types are visible to the COM environment.
- Overloading is very common within the .NET Framework, however COM doesn't support it. As a result the .NET Framework through the help of the CCW (COM-Callable Wrapper) can provide the COM client with access to overloaded methods by generating a unique signature.
- The only constructor COM can support is a default, parameter-less constructor.

Runtime-Callable Wrapper

During run time, a run time callable wrapper (RCW) is created when a COM component is called from the .NET Framework. More specifically, COM objects are exposed via the common language runtime (CLR) through a proxy. This proxy is in fact the RCW, and its purpose is to marshal calls between the .NET application (client) and COM objects. Simply, all interaction between the COM component and .NET client code is handled through the RCW.

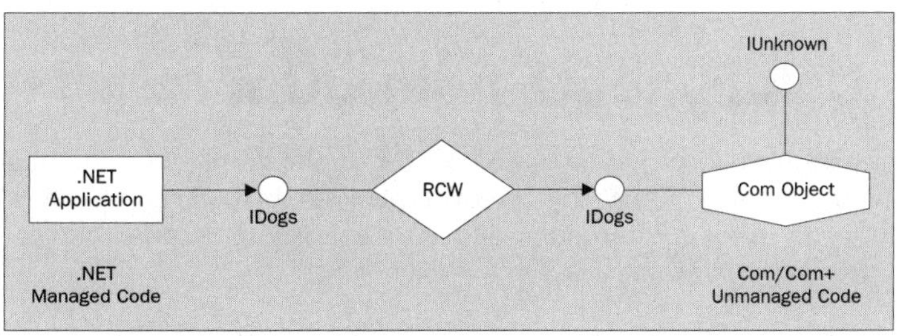

COM-Callable Wrapper

You can also call a .NET component (assembly) from COM. In this scenario, a COM callable wrapper (CCW) is created during run time, when a .NET component is called by a COM component as shown in the following diagram.

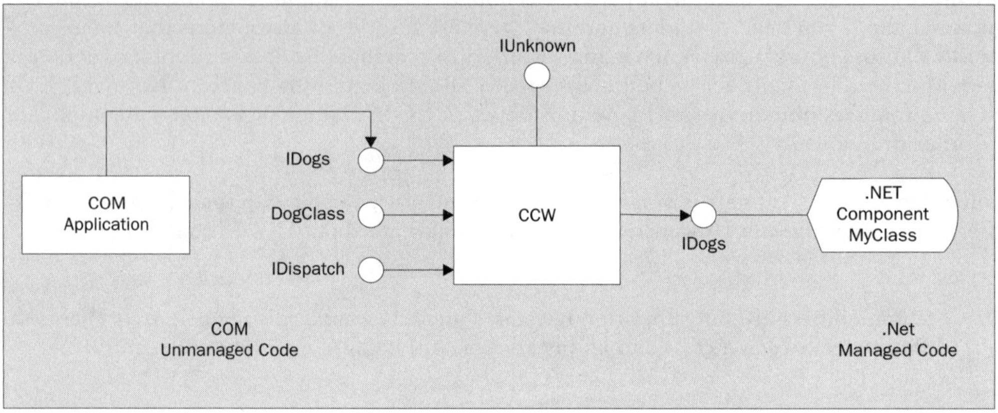

Deployment Issues

Applications that utilize COM components are a bit more difficult to distribute than .NET applications that utilize only managed code. As a matter of fact, with .NET applications you can distribute an application simply by using XCOPY. However, when COM objects come into play, we need to take a few extra steps. Simply we now have two sets of registration requirements, .NET managed code and COM's unmanaged code.

As previously mentioned, .NET code can be easily deployed; however, COM components require they be properly registered into the Windows systems registry by utilizing the `regsvr32.exe` application. In other words, each COM component must be individually registered before it can be accessed. You still may have more to do regarding COM deployment, however, unless your COM components utilize late binding. You can only create COM types via `CLSID` or `ProgID`, and you must also deploy all the InterOp assemblies that the COM components need to use.

Using .NET Components from COM

In order for a .NET assembly to be called from a COM application, you need to create a COM type assembly for the .NET assembly. Creating a COM type assembly is accomplished through a command-line utility called `Regasm.exe`. Additionally, `Regasm.exe` is also responsible for making an entry into the system registry for the type library.

The following screenshot shows the syntax for registering your .NET assemblies:

```
C:\WINNT\System32\cmd.exe
Microsoft Windows 2000 [Version 5.00.2195]
(C) Copyright 1985-2000 Microsoft Corp.

C:\WINNT\Microsoft.NET\Framework\v1.0.3617>regasm
Microsoft (R) .NET Framework Assembly Registration Utility 1.0.3617.0
Copyright (C) Microsoft Corporation 1998-2001.  All rights reserved.

Syntax: RegAsm AssemblyPath [Options]
Options:
    /unregister             Unregister types
    /tlb[:FileName]         Export the assembly to the specified type library
                            and register it
    /regfile[:FileName]     Generate a reg file with the specified name
                            instead of registering the types. This option
                            cannot be used with the /u or /tlb options
    /codebase               Set the code base in the registry
    /registered             Only refer to already registered type libraries
    /nologo                 Prevents RegAsm from displaying logo
    /silent                 Silent mode. Prevents displaying of success messages
    /verbose                Displays extra information
    /? or /help             Display this usage message

C:\WINNT\Microsoft.NET\Framework\v1.0.3617>_
```

Once the assembly has been registered and a COM type library created, you can add the type library from the Visual Basic 6 IDE references, just as you would with any other type library.

In order for the .NET assembly to interact with the COM components, you must:

- Ensure that that the .NET assembly is physically installed within the same directory as the COM application
- Load the assembly into the global assembly cache

It's important to understand the difference between working with .NET applications and working with interoperability between .NET and COM. A .NET DLL can reside in numerous different directories on the same machine without affecting the other .NET applications. COM components, on the other hand, can only reside in one directory on the machine. The COM component is located and accessed through a single entry within the system registry. What all this boils down to is that if you have more than one COM application that wants to access your .NET assembly, you must load it into the global assembly cache. Remember, your .NET assembly is viewed as a COM component because you created a COM type library for it.

Summary

In this chapter you learned about COM interoperability. We began this chapter with migration strategies including questions to determine whether you should rewrite, migrate, or integrate your code. We found that integrating COM with .NET applications (referred to as interoperability) was a good compromise between total rewrites and migrating code to the .NET application.

Next you learned about COM components. Here we reviewed the basic rules for COM components to use with your .NET applications.

We took a look at what goes on in the background between .NET and COM. More specifically, we looked at marshaling and data types – which ones easily cross boundaries as opposed to data types that need to be translated. We also learned about wrappers, such as the RCW and the CCW.

Finally, we ended this chapter with issues regarding deployment.

Pro Visual Basic .NET Transactions

8

.NET Remoting and Components

A distributed application utilizes the resources of multiple machines by separating the application processing and functionality into more manageable portions, which can then be deployed in a wide variety of physical configurations. Over the last few chapters we have talked about a number of the benefits of dividing applications up into pieces, such as reusability, scalability, and manageability.

Previously, we worked with distributed applications that utilize COM+. There is little doubt that the development of middle-tier components utilizing Visual Basic had become a standard for distributed applications. Visual Basic .NET not only maintains this legacy by following the same types of scenarios, it does it in a better way.

The purpose of this chapter is to show you how to remote your .NET assemblies across different machines to create fully distributed .NET applications using .NET Remoting, the replacement for DCOM.

In this chapter, we will look at:

- Creating distributed applications in .NET using different techniques
- How .NET Remoting works
- How to design and build remotable objects
- Configuration to support remotable objects
- Using configuration files to configure .NET Remoting

To get started, let's look at the different ways to create distributed applications using the .NET Framework.

Distributed Applications in .NET

In order to build large complex applications that will continue to run efficiently as they grow, it is usually necessary to think about distributing the processing of that application. The whole concept of component-based application architecture is to split the application up into discrete components. In most cases, these components all run on the same machine in the same process space. But when the load on the application grows, it makes sense to let other processes or machines share in the load of the application.

In the past, it had been up to the developer to provide this inter-process or inter-machine plumbing to support distributed applications. DCOM provided some of this plumbing for us in the Win32 architecture, but the developer still had to know a great deal about the pipes, the protocols and the tools to make it happen. It made the process much more difficult than single-process development, and therefore was not at the top of too many programmers' kit bags.

As with a lot of other things in the .NET Framework, the Framework handles most of the plumbing and makes building distributed applications much easier than they have been in the past. The developer can focus on building the business rules of the application and using components to effectively build their application. Then when it comes to distributing those components, they can use the features of .NET to handle all of the complexity.

There are two primary ways of building distributed applications in .NET – XML Web Services and .NET Remoting. Each of these methods has their pros and cons, and depending on your application environment, one will probably work better than the other. Let's take a look at the two different methods, and then the criteria for choosing the appropriate mechanism. There is a third method – using the `System.Net` namespace – but this pretty much defeats the purpose of letting the .NET Framework handle the majority of the plumbing for you.

Web Services

In the .NET Framework, Web Services are implemented as part of ASP.NET, which handles all the web interfaces. It allows programs to talk to each other directly over the web, using the XML Protocol (formerly known as the Simple Object Access Protocol or SOAP) standard. This capability requires very little work on the part of the developer. All that is needed is to indicate that a member should be included in the Web Services interface, and the .NET Framework takes care of the rest. This has the capacity to dramatically change the architecture of web applications, allowing services running all over the web to be integrated into one application.

It is hard to over-emphasize the potential importance of Web Services. Consider, for example, the potential for Web Services to replace packaged software. A commercial software company could produce a Web Service that, for instance, calculates sales tax for every jurisdiction in the nation. A subscription to that Web Service could be sold to any company needing to calculate sales tax. The customer company then has no need to deploy the sales tax calculator because it is just called on the web. The company producing the sales tax calculator can dynamically update it to include new rates and rules for various jurisdictions, and their customers using the Web Service don't have to do anything to get these updates.

.NET Remoting

.NET Remoting supplies the plumbing for a wide range of distributed application designs. These include Web Services, but also encompass other methods of communication. With .NET Remoting, you can provide or use services in any .NET application domain. You can use it from a console application, a Windows Form, ASP.NET, Web Services, or a traditional windows service.

Since you are still using the .NET Framework, you can take advantage of a unified type system of .NET. This is different from Web Services, which uses SOAP formatting for its types. Remoting is actually implemented by the Common Language Runtime, so it can take advantage of CLR types. You can pass objects `By Reference` using Remoting, and also have direct control over the lifetime of the remote object. The only protocol supported by Web Services is HTTP, whereas .NET Remoting can be extended to support other communication protocols.

Choosing the Right One for You

Now that we have an understanding of what .NET Remoting and XML Web Services are, the next question that comes to mind is what to use when. Both Web Services and Remoting have their specific applications where they make sense, and conversely applications where one doesn't make sense. There are four primary areas to examine when trying to choose the distributed object technology for your application.

Scalability

The scalability of a distributed application is based on the scalability of the platform that is serving the distributed objects. With XML Web Services, the objects are hosted within ASP.NET, which provides the highest degree of scalability through its scale-up or scale-out capabilities. Scale-up refers to adding more processors to a single machine to provide greater processing capability. This is referred to in some places as a Web Garden. Scale-out refers to adding more identical systems to a networked architecture and then distributing the processing across those machines using a load balancer. This is known as a Web Farm.

With .NET Remoting, we have a choice of what platform to host our distributed objects from. We listed these earlier in the chapter, but you should remember that you can use ASP.NET as a platform for hosting .NET Remoting. So in terms of scalability, the choice of the platform is more important than the choice of the plumbing technology.

Speed

Later in this chapter, we will look at the concept of channels and encoding for .NET Remoting. Basically, .NET Remoting can communicate using either the HTTP or the TCP protocol. The default data encoding for TCP is Binary, while the default for HTTP is ASCII. For the best performance, you should use the binary method of encoding. This means that for best performance using HTTP, you should select a binary encoder for the data.

Interoperability

Interoperability defines how well the distributed objects in the application can work with other applications. While Microsoft would prefer all applications to run on the Windows platform, this just isn't the case in real life. We often have to build applications that need to access data or perform operations on other non-Microsoft platforms. For this type of interoperability, .NET Remoting does not work at all – unless that other platform has a version of the .NET Framework running on it. If you need to distribute your application among disparate systems, you should use XML Web Services.

Security

The final criteria for selecting your distributed application architecture is the level of security needed. The only method that has security already built-in is to host your distributed application in IIS. While it is possible to secure the other object hosting methods, you have to do that work yourself. You can use either an ASP.NET application or a Remoting application, but the access to it must be through IIS. Also, the SOAP encoding format is text-based, making it inherently insecure, so you need to use the binary encoding format to provide security.

How .NET Remoting Works

Remoting is a new term that comes with the .NET technology. In simple terms, remoting can be thought of as a new infrastructure for building distributed applications and systems. More specifically, it is how inter-processing communication is performed within the .NET framework. Because DCOM is not utilized by .NET, a new technology had to be developed to take its place.Before you go moaning about another new technology we need to learn, let me reassure you that remoting is a better and more efficient technology than DCOM. It is true that we will have to learn some new terminology, and a few more methods, but we will be able to do the same things that we did with DCOM. As a matter of fact, .NET Remoting is the basis for Web Services that we learned about earlier in this book. With .NET Remoting, you can even expose an object to be used as a Web Service.

.NET Remoting can be used to communicate between different applications running in the CLR on different machines across a network. It can also be used to communicate between different applications running on the same machine. These applications need to be both CLR applications and running in different AppDomains on the same machine. All interaction with a remoted object is done through a proxy – even if the object is running on the same physical machine. A client cannot directly access an object running in a different AppDomain since the object only exists in the AppDomain where it is executed – not where the client is calling it from.

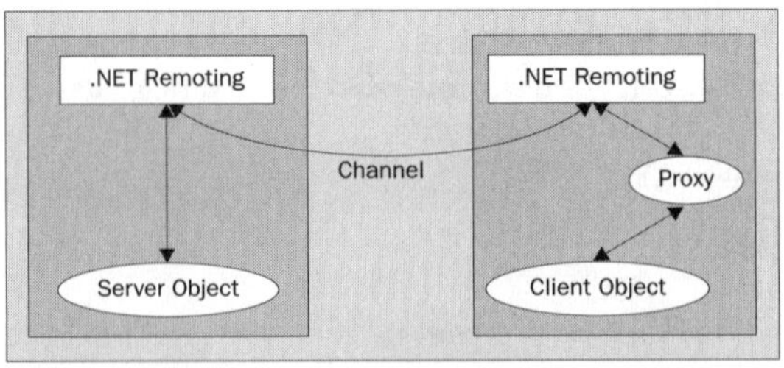

As you can see in the above diagram, the client object communicates with the server object through the .NET Remoting service and a proxy object that exists in the same AppDomain as the client object. The connection between the two AppDomain spaces is known as the **Channel**. This channel supports the communication between two AppDomain spaces on different machines, as well as on the same machine.

In order for the server object to be used by a client, it will need to be activated. There are two methods for activation: server activation and client activation. In server activation, the object on the server will be created by the server when a call for it comes in from the client. In client activation, the client must send a specific activation request to the server for the object to be activated. The reason for two different activation models deals with object state. If the client needs to control the lifetime of the object, then it needs to be the one to activate it. We will look at the activation step in more detail later in the chapter.

The first step in deploying a remote object is for it to be registered with the CLR. This somewhat goes against the concept of XCOPY deployment that the CLR is known for, but when dealing with objects outside of the AppDomain of your current application, something has to know where to find the other objects that you are looking for – and then once those objects are located, how to activate and execute them. The registration information includes the assembly, namespace, and type name of the object that you are going to activate. You also have to set the name of the endpoint at which the object can be accessed. You need to register the client channels that will be used to talk to the object. You can register more than one channel, but you must also specify the communication protocol for each channel as well.

Once you have registered the component on its various channels, these channels will start listening for a client to connect to the object. The client has to connect via the channel in order to work with the object. All that has to happen is that the client communicates via a channel that is supported by the object. The first step after connecting to the object is for the client to activate it. This can be done by calling `new`, `GetObject`, or `CreateInstance`.

After the call to activate the object, .NET Remoting passes back information to the client about how to create the proxy object. The CLR takes care of this by itself, and no call goes all the way through to the remote object. If the object is setup to be server activated, then once the client has the proxy, it can use that object to make the call to the server object. The CLR will use the appropriate channel to communicate the interactions between the proxy and the server object.

This information is passed through a `Message` object. The object is serialized and passed over the communication channel. The type of serialization is based on the channel that is being used. For the TCP channel, the object is serialized into a binary format. For HTTP, the object is serialized to text XML format. This information is then transmitted using the SOAP protocol.

At the server, the `Message` object is recreated by deserializing the data that was passed. This object then calls the server object and processes the request. The server object does its work, and then to send back a return value, the process is reversed – the `Message` object is serialized, then transmitted to the client, where it is deserialized and passed to the proxy which responds to the client.

Application Domains

In previous Windows application architectures like Win32, applications were separated from one another by process boundaries. Each application was run in a different process space to provide separation between applications. When calling between applications, you had to cross a process boundary, which meant that calls had to pass through a level of indirection like a proxy in order to call into the other process. This generally had a negative impact on performance.

Application Domains are how the .NET framework implements an application's execution of boundaries. Although Application Domains are not specific to .NET Remoting, it is important to understand that remoting becomes necessary when we need to have an object's communication cross over an application's boundary. Since .NET can have multiple application domains running in the same process, the calls between applications – while still having to go through a proxy – do not need to cross a process boundary. This ability to run multiple applications in their own domains all within the same process space make scalability that much easier to achieve, as less work is spent with process switching overhead.

.NET Remoting is the method for making calls between Application Domains. The great thing about Remoting is that the developers don't need to concern themselves with where the client and server domains are located. They could be in the same process space, different process spaces on the same system, or different systems altogether – the way that their code interacts with the remote object stays the same. .NET Remoting takes care of all the plumbing to make it work.

Remotable Objects

In our object-based applications, we are creating and destroying objects throughout the lifetime of the application. These objects are normally created within the application domain of the application making calling them from the application very straightforward. When we want an object to be called from outside its application domain, there are certain things that need to be done to make that happen. But it doesn't make sense for every object to be callable from outside the application – you need to make that determination based on your application and what the components do.

The classification of objects is relatively straightforward when it comes to remote activation. Objects are either **remotable** or **non-remotable**. If an object is non-remotable then it can only be accessed from within the application domain that it was created in. Remotable objects can be accessed from within the domain it was created in, as well as from other application domains on the same machine, or on other machines. You can either pass a proxy to the other application domain (marshal-by-reference), or you can package and pass the object itself (marshal-by-value).

Marshal-by-Reference

In a marshal-by-reference object, a proxy of the remote object is created in the application domain of the client, and the client interacts with the object through the proxy. To create a marshal-by-reference remote object, the object must be derived from `System.MarshalByRefObject`. When a client tries to create an instance of an object derived from this, then a proxy for the real object is created in the client's application domain. The .NET Remoting system will then connect this proxy to the actual remote object running in a different application domain.

One nice thing about .NET Remoting is that it is smart about what application domains the client and the server are in. If the client is running in the same application domain as where the server is going to be activated, then Remoting steps out of the way and the client and server interact directly.

Marshal-by-Value

When you design a remote object to be of type marshal-by-value, you are creating an object that will be packaged and passed to the application domain of the client. These objects are not derived from `System.MarshalByRefObject`, but rather they extend the `ISerializable` interface. When an object of this type is activated by the client, the Remoting system detects this and has the server create a new instance of the object. This object is then serialized through the `ISerializable` interface and passed from the server to the client, where it is deserialized and then executed. Once it arrives in the client's application domain for execute, Remoting steps out of the way and all calls to the object are direct.

These types of objects are used throughout the .NET Framework. We have already seen the `Message` object, which the Remoting system uses to pass data from the proxy to the server. This object is an example of a marshal-by-value object. In ASP.NET, the `DataSet` object, which is used to transfer data from a data source to an application, is also a marshal-by-value object.

Choosing the Type of Object

Now we are presented with another choice: do we create our remote object as marshal-by-reference or as marshal-by-value. Since a marshal-by-value object is actually executed within the client's application domain, the calls to the object are quite fast. If your application would be adversely affected by slower calls to specific remote objects, then it makes sense to make those objects marshal-by-value.

But since you are moving a copy of the object to your client and executing it there, there is no automatic way to communicate any state changes in that object back to the server where the object originally resided. Also, since the entire object must be marshaled and sent, the initial sending of the object to the client could take a large amount of time and bandwidth. In these cases, it makes more sense to create the object as marshal-by-reference. Every call to the object will have to marshaled, but it will remain within the server's application domain for execution.

The remainder of this chapter will look at marshal-by-reference objects, as these types of objects are the most common for .NET Remoting.

Creating a Remote Object

Now that we understand a bit about what goes into making a remote object, let's look at a quick example to create one. We won't be able to call it just yet – we will look at activation in the next step – but we can get the object ready to be called. We are going to create a very simple object to start.

Here is the source for the class that will be used to create our object:

```
imports System
imports System.Runtime.Remoting

namespace ChapterEight

  public class MyRemote
    inherits MarshalByRefObject

    public sub MyRemote()
      Console.WriteLine("MyRemote activated")
    end sub

    public function RemoteCall(name as String) as String
      Console.WriteLine("MyRemote.RemoteCall : {0}", name)
      RemoteCall = "Remote Call returns: " + name
    end function

  end class

end namespace
```

There are only two things that make this class different from any other class that you might create. And those are the two things that make this class remotable.

```
Imports System
Imports System.Runtime.Remoting
```

In order for this class to be remotable, we need to import the `System.Runtime.Remoting` namespace. This will bring in the proper Remoting interface so that we can derive our class from it.

```
public class MyRemote
  inherits MarshalByRefObject
```

The remainder of the class is straightforward except for the class definition. As we stated earlier, for any object to be remotable, it must derive from the `MarshalByRefObject` class.

Now that we have the remote object created, we should be ready to begin Remoting it. But in order for a remote object to be used, it has to be delivered by a server to a client. So we will need to create a server and a client to use our object. First, we will take a look at how to active the object so that it can be accessed remotely.

Activation

There are two types of MBR (marshal-by-reference) objects. They are differentiated by where they are activated. A server-activated object is created by the server when it is first needed. This is usually AFTER the client proxy object is created. It also saves a round-trip between the client and server that would be used just for object activation. A client-activated object is created by the server when the proxy is created on the client – usually by a call to `new` or `Activator.CreateInstance()`.

The primary reason for two methods of object activation is to allow the client to better control the state of the object. If the client needs to have state maintained on the remote object between calls, then it needs to control the lifetime of that object – hence the client should be activated on the client. This shows us that whatever side activates the object is also responsible for releasing that object as well. On the other hand, if the client needs to get a stateless object, then it can rely on server activation to provide a new instance with each call to the remote object.

On the Server

When you activate a remote object on the server, that object can be declared as either `Singleton` or `SingleCall`. A `Singleton` object will only have one instance for ALL clients that call into the object. A `Singleton` object has a specified lifetime, so it may be released by the server at a specified time. Because of this, the client is not guaranteed of always getting back the same instance – even if there is only one instance of the object running at any one time on the server.

With a `SingleCall` object, there will be a unique instance of the object provided for each call made by a client. This means that for every call into a remote object by a client, the client can be guaranteed to get a new instance of the remote object. This is the case even if the server has not yet garbage collected a previous object instance – a new instance will always be created and passed back to the client.

You can create an instance of a server-activated object in two ways. An object can be configured to be a remote object (we will look at configuration later in the chapter) and then activated by a call to `New()`. If the object is not already configured as remote, then you can use the `Activator.GetObject` method and pass in the configuration of the remote object.

```
Dim myObjRemote As objRemoteClass = CType( Activator.GetObject(_
        GetType(objRemoteClass, AssemblyName), _
          "tcp://computername:8080/objRemoteUri"), _
      objRemoteClass
   )
```

In this call (which occurs on the client), there are three parameters that we will need to set. The `objRemoteClass` is the class of the object we are creating. First, we are declaring our local object reference to be of this type. Then we are passing the type and assembly of the class to the `Activator.GetObject` method. Finally, we are casting the results of that call to the proper type through the `CType` method. We also need to declare where the remote object server lives. This is done with the second parameter to the `Activator.GetObject` method. This Uniform Resource Identifier (URI) indicates the connection type (`tcp://`), the address of the server (`computername`), the port on the server (`8080`), as well as the location of the object on the server (`objRemoteUri`).

Once we have created this object reference, we can now make calls to it as if it were local to the client. Remember that since this is a server-activated object, the object really hasn't been instantiated yet on the server. It will not be activated until the first call to the object. The client will also not need to know if this is a `Singleton` or a `SingleCall` object – that is up to the server and the way it was configured.

On the Client

A client-activated object has its lifetime controlled by the client. The object is activated on the server by an explicit call. This is different from the server-activated object, which doesn't get activated until it is first called. Each time the object is activated, a new instance will be created by the server. This means that every client will get its own instance and likewise will retain that instance until the client explicitly releases it.

When the client creates an instance of a remote object, it will get a reference to the local proxy for that object. The object has an associated lifetime lease that will determine how long the object will remain instantiated on the server. Once the lease expires, the server will query the proxy on the client to see if the object is still needed. This eliminates the need for any "keep-alive" traffic between the client and the server while the lease is still valid.

The creation of a client-activated object is very similar to the creation of server-activated object. You can either configure the object and create it with the `New()` operator, or you can use the `Activator.CreateInstance` method.

```
Dim myObjRemote As objRemoteClass = CType( Activator.CreateInstance(_
        GetType(objRemoteClass, AssemblyName), _
          "tcp://computername:8080/objRemoteUri"), _
     objRemoteClass
  )
```

This is almost exactly the same call we made to create a server-activated object. The only difference is that you are calling `CreateInstance` instead of `GetObject`. All of the parameters are the same for both calls.

Creating a Remote Server

Earlier in the chapter, we created our sample remote object. But we had no way to deliver the object to a remote client. For that, we need to create a server to deliver the object. There are two primary ways to serve a remote object. You can either write a service or application that will serve the remote object, or you can use IIS to serve the object to a client. We will first look at creating our own server application.

```
imports System
imports System.Runtime.Remoting
```

```
imports System.Runtime.Remoting.Channels
imports System.Runtime.Remoting.Channels.TCP

namespace ChapterEight

  public class MyServer
    shared sub main
      dim chan as TCPChannel
      chan = new TCPChannel(8085)
      ChannelServices.RegisterChannel(chan)
      RemotingConfiguration.RegisterWellKnownServiceType( _
        Type.GetType("ChapterEight.MyRemote, MyObject"), _
        "RemoteCall", WellKnownObjectMode.SingleCall)
      System.Console.WriteLine("ChapterEight.MyRemote Server Activated...")
      System.Console.WriteLine("Press <enter> to exit...")
      System.Console.ReadLine()
    end sub
  end class

end namespace
```

This server will deliver its remote object using the TCP channel. It will deliver the `ChapterEight.MyRemote` object that we created earlier in the chapter. The first step is to import the proper namespaces into the application.

In addition to the two namespaces that we included for the object itself, we also need to import the `System.Runtime.Remoting.Channels` and `System.Runtime.Remoting.Channels.TCP` namespaces. These will allow us to create the TCP channel that the server will use to serve the object.

> *You may need to add a reference to System.Runtime.Remoting from the Project | Add Reference... menu here.*

```
imports System
imports System.Runtime.Remoting
imports System.Runtime.Remoting.Channels
imports System.Runtime.Remoting.Channels.TCP
```

This app is a console Visual Basic .NET application, so we can do all of the work inside of the main subroutine. The first step is to create the channel that we will be using to communicate with the client. This is a TCP channel, and we pass the TCP port number `(8085)` as the parameter to the constructor for this class. Once we have created the valid channel, we will need to register it with the .NET Remoting system. This is done using the static `RegisterChannel` method of the `ChannelServices` class. The one parameter for this method is the `TCPChannel` object that we just created.

```
shared sub main
  dim chan as TCPChannel
  chan = new TCPChannel(8085)
  ChannelServices.RegisterChannel(chan)
```

Now that we have registered the communication channel, the next step is to register the actual object to be remoted with the Remoting system. To register the object, we need to call the `RegisterWellKnownServiceType` method of the `RemotingConfiguration` class. This method takes three parameters. The first is the type of the object that we will be Remoting. We will use reflection to get the type of our object. This is done by calling the `GetType` static method of the `Type` class. We will pass the namespace, class name, and assembly file name of our object to this method.

The next parameter is the Uniform Resource Identifier (URI) that will be used to identify this specific object so that clients can connect to it. This allows a single server to deliver multiple objects using the same channel and port – but each one must be at a different URI. In this example, the URI of the specific object is `"RemoteCall"` – so if this was running on a machine name `MyNetServer`, the complete URI would be `tcp://MyNetServer:8085/RemoteCall`.

```
RemotingConfiguration.RegisterWellKnownServiceType( _
  Type.GetType("ChapterEight.MyRemote, MyObject"), _
  "RemoteCall", WellKnownObjectMode.SingleCall)
```

Finally, we need to let the console executing the server application know what is going on and output some text to the screen. Since we want this application to keep running, the `ReadLine()` method will let the server keep executing until someone at the console presses the `Enter` key.

```
System.Console.WriteLine("ChapterEight.MyRemote Server Activated...")
System.Console.WriteLine("Press <enter> to exit...")
System.Console.ReadLine()
```

With our server compiled and executing, we can turn to creating a client that will access the remote object.

Creating a Client for the Remote Object

Now that we have our remote object and a server to deliver that remote object, we need to create a client to access it. This will be a console application as well. It will instantiate the remote object, execute a method of the object, and then display the results to the screen.

```
imports System
imports System.Runtime.Remoting
imports System.Runtime.Remoting.Channels
imports System.Runtime.Remoting.Channels.TCP

namespace ChapterEight

  public class MyClient

    shared sub main
      dim chan as TCPChannel
      chan = new TCPChannel()
      ChannelServices.RegisterChannel(chan)
      dim objMyRemote as Object
      objMyRemote = Activator.GetObject( _
        Type.GetType("ChapterEight.MyRemote, MyObject"), _
```

```
            "tcp://localhost:8085/RemoteCall")
        dim obj as MyRemote
        obj = CType(objMyRemote, MyRemote)
        if obj is nothing then
            System.Console.WriteLine("Could not locate server")
          else
            Console.WriteLine(obj.RemoteCall("Call from MyClient"))
          end if
      end sub

    end class
  end namespace
```

As with the server, we will need to include the namespaces that will let us work with the .NET Remoting system. These will provide us with access to the ChannelServices and Activator classes in our application.

The first step is to register the communication channel that will be used to communicate with the server. This code is similar to what was used in the server, with one difference. In the server, we defined the port that the remote object would be served over. With the client, we are just going to declare the channel now. The port will be set in the next step.

```
dim chan as TCPChannel
chan = new TCPChannel()
ChannelServices.RegisterChannel(chan)
```

The next step is to get a reference to the remote object. Since we defined this object as a SingleCall server-activated object, we will need to call the GetObject method of the Activator class. This is a static method of the class, so we don't need to create an instance of the class to call the method. There are two parameters to pass to this method.

The first parameter is a Type object that refers to the remote object. We will use Reflection to get this object. The GetType method takes the namespace.classname and the assembly name, and will return a Type instance. The second parameter is the URI of the server. This is where the port is defined, along with the specific object to access on the server.

```
dim objMyRemote as Object
objMyRemote = Activator.GetObject( _
  Type.GetType("ChapterEight.MyRemote, MyObject"), _
  "tcp://localhost:8085/RemoteCall")
```

The object that is returned from the GetObject method is of type Object. Since we will want to be able to call the appropriate methods of that object, we need to cast it to the appropriate type. This is done using the CType function, and passing the object reference as well as the classname we want to cast to.

```
dim obj as MyRemote
Obj = CType(objMyRemote, MyRemote)
```

Finally, we check to make sure that a valid object has been returned, and then we can call a method on it.

```
      if obj is nothing then
         System.Console.WriteLine("Could not locate server")
       else
         Console.WriteLine(obj.RemoteCall("Call from MyClient"))
       end if
```

To test our application, we can either copy the server exe and object assembly to another machine and execute the client locally, or we can just open up two command prompts on the same machine – run the server in one window and run the client in the other.

Next, we will look in more detail at the concept of channels and configuration.

Channels and Security

With remoting, the developer has the option of specifying the method of transport. This is often accomplished with a configuration file that resides outside of the application's code. The use of an external configuration file should seem obvious in that it allows a developer to change the transport mechanism without going into the application's code.

The transport mechanisms we are referring to here are called **channels**. In order to have our objects remotely communicate with each other, we must specify a channel in the application's remoting configuration file.

A channel is used to communicate between the different application domains that host the client and the server in the .NET Remoting scenario. The two sides of a communication channel are known as **endpoints**.

In order for a server to make itself available via a specific channel, the server must register the specific channel with the .NET Remoting service. When you create a channel to serve a remote object, you must also name that channel. This name needs to be unique within the application domain in which it exists. You can also specify a specific TCP/IP port for the server to listen on, or you can let the Remoting system select one automatically for you. Once you establish a remote object session, the .NET Remoting system takes care of ensuring that the right channel is used each time to communicate between client and server.

HTTP Channel

The `HttpChannel` is found under the namespace `System.Runtime.Remoting.Channels.Http`. The `HttpChannel` is used to transport messages using SOAP protocol. The message content is passed through the `SoapFormatter` object, where it is converted to XML text, the appropriate SOAP headers are then added, and then the message is transmitted using the HTTP protocol. You can also chose to format the message using the binary format as well, but the `HttpChannel` generally uses SOAP and XML.

TCP Channel

Similarly, the `TCPChannel` is located under the namespace `System.Runtime.Remoting.Channels.TCP`. When using the `TCPChannel`, messages between objects are converted into a binary stream, and then serialized to the target URI via the TCP protocol. As with the HTTP Channel, you can also select the message formatting type, and chose the SOAP formatter instead of the binary formatter.

Security

Since an application that uses .NET Remoting will have code executing in two application domains, and potentially on different machines, it is easy to conclude that there are a number of security issues that will need to be addressed. The two main questions that need to be answered when looking at .NET Remoting security have to do with which channels are used for communication and what methods for user authentication and authorization are used.

For the most secure Remoting option, you should chose the HTTP channel hosting inside of IIS. IIS provides the secure communication protocol using Secure Sockets Layer and the authorization using either Windows authentication or Kerberos. On the other hand, the TCP channel does not have secure communications or authorization available by default. While the developer can write these themselves, that defeats the purpose of relying on the Remoting infrastructure for the majority of the plumbing.

Configuration

Configuration allows us to declaratively set up our remote objects and servers. In our earlier examples, we set up the ports and channels programmatically. While this is more straightforward from a development standpoint, it makes it difficult to reconfigure the system after it is deployed. We can use declarative registration on the server and on the client.

Server-Side Registration

You will need to register all of your objects on the server, regardless of if they are server-activated or client-activated. The <service> element within the <application> element is where you define all of the objects that you are hosting.

```
<configuration>
  <system.runtime.remoting>
    <application name = "mylibrary">
      <service>
        <wellknown mode = "singleton" Type= "ExampleLibrary1.ExampleClass1,
       ExampleLibrary1" objectUri="ExampleLibraryEndpoint" />
        <activated type="ExampleLibrary1.ExampleClass2, ExampleLibrary1" />
      </service>
      <channels>
        <channel ref="tcp" port="8085" />
      </channels>
    </application>
  </system.runtime.remoting>
</configuration>
```

The <wellknown> tag is used to declare server-activated objects. If you recall, there are two types of server-activated objects: `Singleton` or `SingleCall`. This must be set in the configuration file with the `mode` property. The `Type` property defines the full name of the object as well as the assembly containing the object that will be made available. The `objectUri` property defines the location of the endpoint. If you are hosting your object within IIS, then the extension of the `objectUri` must be `.soap` or `.rem`.

The <activated> tag is used to declare client-activated objects. With this type, the only parameter that you have to provide is the class and the assembly that is going to be remoted.

To host your remote objects inside of IIS, you will need to add configuration information to the web.config file of the IIS application that will host your objects. There are a few differences in the configuration file when hosting in IIS. The <application> tag must not have a name attribute. The name of the remote application will be the same as the virtual IIS application that the object is hosted in.

Client-Side Registration

In addition to configuring your remote objects on the server that will be serving them, you should also configure your objects on the client as well. The configuration file is similar, in that it allows you to configure both client-activated and server-activated objects, but they are under a <client> tag rather than a <service> element.

```
<system.runtime.remoting>
  <application name = "mylibrary">
    <client url="tcp://localhost:8085/mylibrary">
      <wellknown type = "mylibrary1.myclass1, myAssembly"
        url="http://localhost/ExampleLibraryEndPoint" />
    </client>
    <channels>
      <channel ref="http" />
    </channels>
  </application>
</system.runtime.remoting>
```

The <client> element defines the URL that the remote object is being served from. This element can contain both <wellknown> and <activated> elements – <wellknown> for server-activated objects and <activated> for client-activated objects. While these child elements look similar to what we saw earlier, the allowable attributes are different when being used to define a remote object from the client side. The <wellknown> element can only contain the type, url, and displayName attributes. The displayName attribute is used by the Framework Configuration Tool, and is ignored by the Remoting system.

Channel Registration

The final configuration piece that can be set is the channel configuration. On the server side, you can declare what channels are supported and on the client side you can choose what channel to use for the remote communication. You don't necessarily have to choose a channel on the client side – you can rely on the Remoting system to choose one of the default channels – HttpChannel or TcpChannel – for you.

There are default channel templates that are in the machine.config file for both HTTP and TCP. These should be sufficient for most applications. To specify the default channels, you simply use the ref attribute of the <channel> tag.

```
...
    <channels>
      <channel ref="http" port="0" />
      <channel ref="tcp" port="8085" />
    </channels>
```

```
...
```

The format is the same for both the client registration and the server registration.

Using Configuration Files

In this example, we will take the example programs we looked at earlier, and convert them to use configuration files instead of the programmatic configuration that we used earlier. We will then take our object and host it inside of IIS as opposed to the server executable that we used earlier. The object we created stays exactly the same – it isn't even necessary to recompile it. The first file we need to change is the server application.

```
imports System
imports System.Runtime.Remoting
imports System.Runtime.Remoting.Channels
imports System.Runtime.Remoting.Channels.TCP

namespace ChapterEight

  public class ConfigServer
    shared sub main
      RemotingConfiguration.Configure("ConfigServer.exe.config")
      System.Console.WriteLine("ChapterEight.MyRemote Server Activated...")
      System.Console.WriteLine("Press <enter> to exit...")
      System.Console.ReadLine()
    end sub
  end class

end namespace
```

As you can see, we have removed a whole series of lines that were used to register the communication channel and set up the remote object.

```
      dim chan as TCPChannel
      chan = new TCPChannel(8085)
      ChannelServices.RegisterChannel(chan)
      RemotingConfiguration.RegisterWellKnownServiceType( _
        Type.GetType("ChapterEight.MyRemote, MyObject"), _
        "RemoteCall", WellKnownObjectMode.SingleCall)
```

These lines have been replaced with just one call to `RemotingConfiguration.Configure`.

```
      RemotingConfiguration.Configure("ConfigServer.exe.config")
```

But we still need to configure the channel and the object itself as we did before. It is just that this time, we will set this configuration in a configuration file. This file will be named `ConfigServer.exe.config`. There is nothing special about the name we chose for the file, except that it fits the conventions set down by Microsoft. This convention is `filename.extension.config`, where the filename and extension refer to the file you are creating the configuration for. Let's take a look at the contents of this file.

```
<configuration>
  <system.runtime.remoting>
    <application name = "ConfigServer">
      <service>
        <wellknown mode = "SingleCall"
          type = "ChapterEight.MyRemote, MyObject"
          objectUri="RemoteCall_Config" />
      </service>
      <channels>
        <channel ref="tcp" port="8085" />
      </channels>
    </application>
  </system.runtime.remoting>
</configuration>
```

The key parts to this file are the `<service>` entry and the `<channel>` entry. The `<channel>` element defines the communication channel that will be used to deliver the remote object. This replaces the `ChannelServices.RegisterChannel()` method that we saw earlier. The `<wellknown>` element under the `<service>` element defines the object to be remoted. It replaces the `RemotingConfiguration.RegisterWellKnownServiceType()` method that we used before.

The compilation and execute of the server is exactly the same. The only new requirement is that the `ConfigServer.exe.config` file needs to be in the same directory as the executable itself. Next, we can turn our attention to the modifications to the client piece.

```
imports System
imports System.Runtime.Remoting
imports System.Runtime.Remoting.Channels
imports System.Runtime.Remoting.Channels.TCP

namespace ChapterEight

  public class ConfigClient

    shared sub main
      RemotingConfiguration.Configure("ConfigClient.exe.config")
      dim obj as new MyRemote()
      if obj is nothing then
          System.Console.WriteLine("Could not locate server")
        else
          Console.WriteLine(obj.RemoteCall("Call from MyClient"))
        end if
    end sub

  end class
end namespace
```

You will see that the trend of less code through the use of configuration files continues with the client program. We have removed seven lines of code from the program.

```
dim chan as TCPChannel
chan = new TCPChannel()
```

```
ChannelServices.RegisterChannel(chan)
dim objMyRemote as Object
objMyRemote = Activator.GetObject( _
  Type.GetType("ChapterEight.MyRemote, MyObject"), _
  "tcp://localhost:8085/RemoteCall")
dim obj as MyRemote
obj = CType(objMyRemote, MyRemote)
```

These lines of code to create the channel, create a remote object, and then cast the remote object to be the proper type have been replaced by two lines of code.

```
RemotingConfiguration.Configure("ConfigClient.exe.config")
dim obj as new MyRemote()
```

The first line loads the configuration file for the client. This is the same statement we saw in the server program, but it is loading a different configuration file. In this case, the file is named `ConfigClient.exe.config`. Once the configuration file is loaded into the Remoting system, then any objects defined as remoted in the configuration file will automatically be created as remote objects. So to create an instance of one, we don't need to call `Activator.GetObject()` anymore – we can simply call `new`.

Our configuration file `ConfigClient.exe.config` looks like this:

```
<configuration>
  <system.runtime.remoting>
    <application>
      <client>
        <wellknown type="ChapterEight.MyRemote, MyObject"
          url="tcp://bfrancis:8085/RemoteCall_Config" />
      </client>
      <channels>
        <channel ref="tcp" port="8085" />
      </channels>
    </application>
  </system.runtime.remoting>
</configuration>
```

There are two key entries in this configuration file. The first is to define that the object `ChapterEight.MyRemote` found in the `MyObject` assembly is a remote object. This is done through the `<wellknown>` element. The remote object will be served from a specific URL – in this case `tcp://bfrancis:8085/RemoteCall_Config`. The second entry is to define the Remoting channel to communicate over. This is done using the `<channel>` element.

Note that in testing on a single machine – using the two command prompt windows like we showed earlier – you need to delete the `<channel>` element from the client config file. This is due to the fact that the port/ref combination for a channel can only be configured once on the same machine. In our earlier example, the `RegisterChannel` method will return the existing channel rather than creating a new duplicate one. The configuration file method does not do that.

Next, let's serve our remote object using IIS and then access it with our client. First, let's get IIS configured to serve a remote object. Here are the steps we need to follow to do that:

- Create a virtual directory (Chapter8) on your IIS Server
- Using the Microsoft Management Console, change the Authentication Methods for this virtual directory to allow Anonymous Access

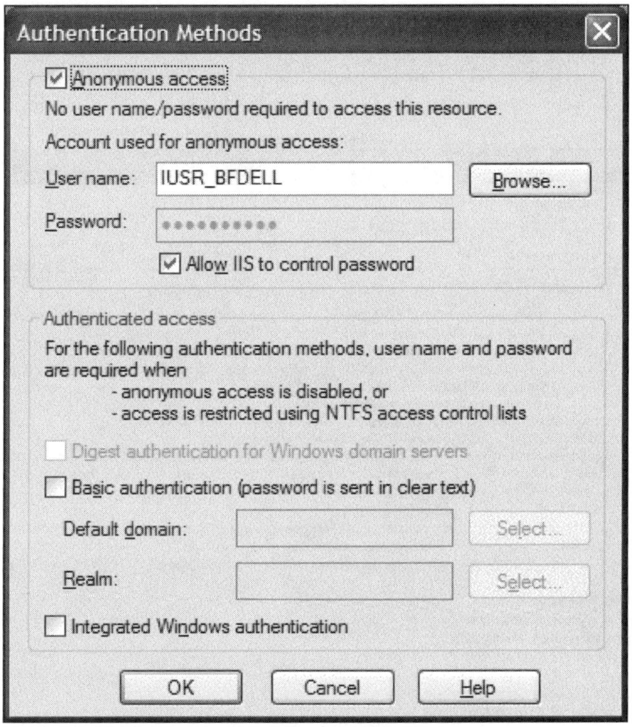

- Create a physical bin directory under the virtual directory
- Copy the `MyObject.dll` file to that directory

Now we are ready to create the Remoting configuration. This needs to go into the `web.config` file for this IIS application. It will exist in the virtual root directory for the application. The file looks like this:

```
<configuration>
  <system.runtime.remoting>
    <application>
      <service>
        <wellknown mode = "SingleCall" type = "ChapterEight.MyRemote, MyObject"
           objectUri="RemoteCall_IIS.rem" />
      </service>
      <channels>
        <channel ref="http"/>
      </channels>
    </application>
  </system.runtime.remoting>
</configuration>
```

This looks very similar to the configuration files we used earlier, except for a few changes. When hosting a remote object in IIS, the name of the application is the name of the virtual directory. Since IIS already knows this, we should not add a `name` attribute to the `<application>` element. The other difference is that the `objectUri` only needs to declare the endpoint name – the server, protocol, and virtual directory are all configured by IIS. Also, we need to put the proper file extension onto the endpoint, so that IIS knows what to do with the request when it comes in. We have named our endpoint `RemoteCall_IIS.rem`.

If we want to test to see if IIS is properly configured, we can use the Web Services Description Language query to retrieve the SOAP headers for this object. To do this, we enter the URL for the endpoint and add ?wsdl after the name. So in our example, it would look like this:

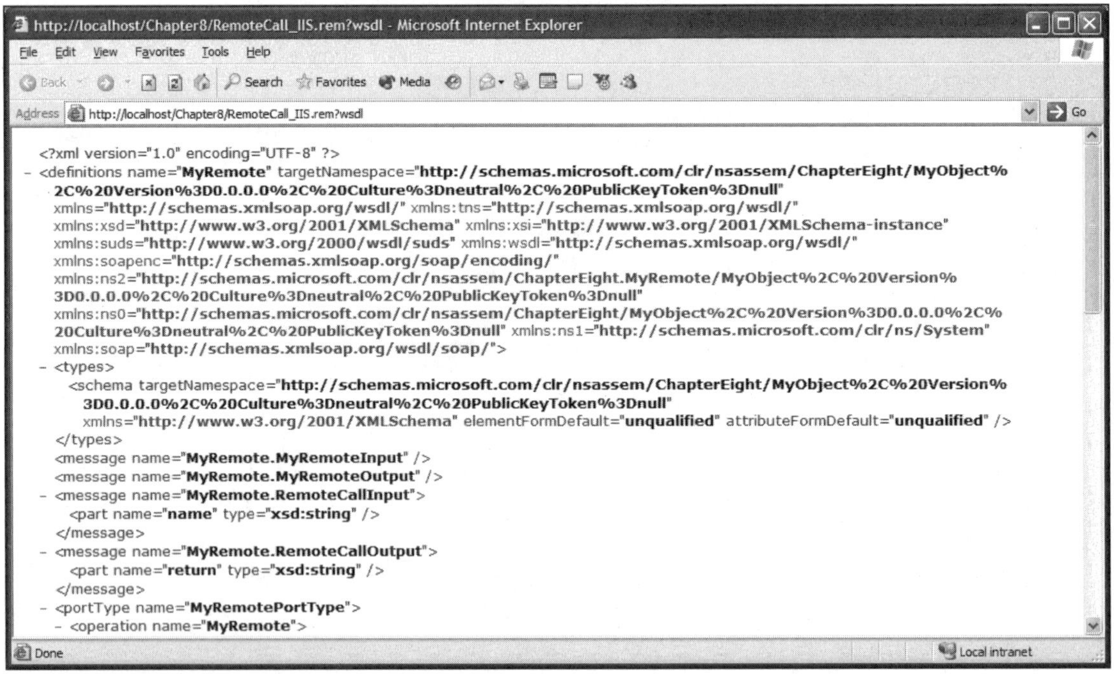

Now that the server is up and running, we can change our client program to use IIS as the remote object server. Since we just looked at how to create a client that uses an external configuration file to set up Remoting, we can use that configuration file to point the client at IIS instead of the server application that we wrote. To do this, we make the following changes to the `ConfigClient.exe.config` file.

```
<configuration>
  <system.runtime.remoting>
    <application>
      <client>
        <wellknown type="ChapterEight.MyRemote, MyObject"
          url="http://localhost/Chapter8/RemoteCall_IIS.rem" />
      </client>
      <channels>
        <channel ref="http" port="0" />
      </channels>
```

```
      </application>
    </system.runtime.remoting>
  </configuration>
```

The only changes to the file are the `url` attribute of the object declaration in the `<wellknown>` element and the `ref` attribute of the `<channel>` element. The URL needs to be changed to point to the IIS server, the proper virtual directory, and the correct endpoint with file extension. The `<channel>` element needs to be changed since we are now using the HTTP channel instead of the TCP channel.

When you run this application, you will see the same output in the command prompt window, but you will not see anything on the server, since it is handling the serving of the application behind the scenes.

Summary

In this chapter, we looked at how to remote your .NET assemblies across different machines to create fully distributed .NET applications using .NET Remoting. We saw how Remoting works, how to create objects, clients, and server, as well as how to configure it.

Specifically we looked at:

- The differences between .NET Remoting and XML Web Services, and when to choose which one
- How .NET Remoting works
- Building objects that can be remoted, servers to serve remote objects, and clients that can consume them
- How to configure the Remoting system on both the client and the server
- Using configuration files to configure .NET Remoting

Pro Visual Basic .NET Transactions

9

Debugging and Troubleshooting

Unfortunately, errors can and do happen. Although the best way to avoid the need for debugging is to write perfect code, this is never going to happen. We therefore need to be familiar with the range of tools and techniques .NET offers us, so that we can quickly and easily solve most problems that occur.

You should already be familiar with basic error handling using Visual Basic .NET, so we will only touch upon some of the basics. Instead, you will learn some techniques for using tools, such as the `Debug` and `Trace` classes that come with the .NET framework.

After completing this chapter you should be able to answer the following questions:

- How can you handle errors that occur between managed and unmanaged code?
- How can you log errors and other events?
- What is the difference between the `Debug` class and the `Trace` class?
- What techniques can you use if you do not have access to the event logs?
- How can application and system performance be tested?

Exception Handler

The `Try...Catch...Finally` block is the most essential structure for handling exceptions in Visual Basic .NET. The following is its basic structure:

- `Try` – This statement comes before a block of code that you suspect may cause an exception.
- `Catch` – This section of code is used to associate an exception handler with the code that has been placed in the `Try` block. You can place multiple `Catch` statements to handle different exceptions. However, it is important to keep the finer-grained exceptions first and then expand the granularity of the exceptions as you add more. More specifically, keep the finest grained exceptions toward the top and the broadest grained exceptions at the bottom. The reason for this is if you have a wider grained exception at the top, you run the risk of not receiving the best exception response. This is because the exceptions, like other nested conditional statements, will start with the top and work down until something happens.

  If the exception is not handled by a `Catch` statement, the code simply moves to the next statement, which is `Finally`.
- `Finally` – This block is optional. However, if there is code present, it will always execute. This is a block of code typically used for cleanup procedures such as explicitly closing objects. This block of code is executed regardless of whether an exception is generated or not. What if a procedure such as `Exit Sub` or an `Exit Try` statement is used to exit early before the `Finally` block statements? It will not matter. Simply, any code residing within the `Finally` block will be executed before exiting the procedure.
- `End Try` – This statement is used to end the `Try` exception handler.

Remember that a `Catch` catches instances of the `Exception` class. The following table lists the available properties of an `Exception` you can use into your structured `Try...Catch...Finally` error handling:

Property	Description
`InnerException`	Exceptions are frequently caught at a fairly low level in a component and then thrown back up to the calling function. As this happens, the up-level procedure may throw an exception. In this case, the first exception is nested into the `InnerException` property of the second exception. You can create a new exception that catches an earlier exception. The code that handles the second exception can make use of the additional information from the earlier exception to find out what caused the initial error, and hence it can handle the error more appropriately.
`Message`	The `Message` property is a string that contains the description of the error.
`Source`	When an error is generated, the `Source` property is used to store the name of the assembly that created the error.
`StackTrace`	The `StackTrace` property is read-only. It is used to store a stack trace in the form of a text-based string.
`TargetSite`	When an exception is thrown, a read-only string is used to store the method creating the exception.

The following table lists the available methods of an `Exception` that you can incorporate into your structured `Try...Catch...Finally` error handling:

Method	Description
`Equals()`	Used to test the equality of one exception object with another exception object.
`GetBaseException()`	Used to return the first exception in the chain.
`GetHashCode()`	Used as a hash function.
`GetObjectData()`	When serializing exception data, the `GetObjectData()` method allows you to retain the data within an `Exception` object.
`GetType()`	When an object causes an exception, the `GetType()` is used to retrieve the type of object where the exception occurred.
`ToString()`	This method simply returns exception information and stores it into a string.

Many times the error message generated by Visual Basic .NET is not the easiest to decipher, or perhaps you simply want to create an exception message to let the user know something has happened, such as "An error occurred regarding the `Shipper` table in the `Northwind` database. Please contact your system administrator." Such customizable messages can easily be replaced by Visual Basic .NET error messages through utilizing the `Throw` statement, as shown in the code snippet below:

```
Catch NorthwindDBerror as ShipperTableException

  Throw New ShipperTableException("An error occurred regarding table Shipper in
the Northwind database. Please contact your system administrator.")

End Try
```

In this case, `ShipperTableException` is derived from the `System.Exception` class.

Let's take a look at a quick example of a Visual Basic .NET console application that demonstrates what we've talked about. As we've seen in previous chapters, we'll start this class by requiring good coding practices.

```
REM Require explict data type declarations and
REM require that casts not result in losses of
REM meaning or precision
Option Explicit On
Option Strict On
```

Next we will define a class for the exceptions this application might need to throw back. This exception inherits from the `System.Exception` class and has properties for the numerator, divisor and the exception that actually occurred when attempting a calculation. It then exposes these properties. The constructor simply sets values for the encapsulated properties.

```
REM This is a custom exception class for describing
REM errors that occured when calculating.
Class CalculatorException
 Inherits Exception
 Private mNumerator As Integer
 Private mDivisor As Integer
 Private mException As Exception

 REM property exposing the error that occured
 Friend ReadOnly Property Exception() As Exception
  Get
   Return mException
  End Get
 End Property

 REM The numerator of calculation attempted
 Friend ReadOnly Property Numerator() As Integer
  Get
   Return mNumerator
  End Get
 End Property

 REM The denominator of calculation attempted
 Friend ReadOnly Property Divisor() As Integer
  Get
   Return mDivisor
  End Get
 End Property

 REM Provides a new instance of this class
 Sub New(ByVal Numerator As Integer, ByVal Divisor As Integer, _
 ByVal Message As String, ByVal SourceExc As Exception)
  MyBase.New(Message)
  mException = SourceExc
  mNumerator = Numerator
  mDivisor = Divisor
 End Sub

End Class
```

Next, we have a short class that provides for a way to divide two integers. Its sole method will either return that result or an exception – if something goes wrong.

```
REM Provides for calculations
Class Calculator
 Public Function Divide(ByVal numerator As Integer, ByVal divisor As Integer) As
Integer
  Dim CalcExc As CalculatorException

  REM Attempt the calculation
  Try
```

```
    Return CType(numerator / divisor, Integer)

   Catch exc As DivideByZeroException
    CalcExc = New CalculatorException(numerator, divisor, _
     "Divide by zero error", exc)
    Throw CalcExc
   Catch exc As OverflowException
    CalcExc = New CalculatorException(numerator, divisor, _
    "Overflow exception", exc)
    Throw CalcExc
   Catch exc As Exception
    CalcExc = New CalculatorException(numerator, divisor, _
    "Generic exception", exc)
    Throw CalcExc
   End Try
  End Function
 End Class
```

All that's left to do is actually test a calculation out.

```
 Module ExceptionExample
  Dim exc As Exception
  Sub Main()
   Dim calc As New Calculator()

   REM Set these to any values you like.
   Dim Numerator As Integer = 3
   Dim Divisor As Integer = 0

   Try
    Console.WriteLine("Dividing {0} by {1}", Numerator, Divisor)
    Console.WriteLine(calc.Divide(Numerator, Divisor))
   Catch CalcExc As CalculatorException
    Console.WriteLine("An exception occured!")
    Console.WriteLine("{0}. Numerator {1} Divisor {2}", CalcExc.Message, _
     CalcExc.Numerator, CalcExc.Divisor)
    Console.WriteLine("Additional Errors:")

    REM Now we can "walk through" any additional exceptions
    REM nested into the current one.
    exc = CalcExc.Exception
    While Not (exc Is Nothing)
     Console.WriteLine(exc.Message)
     exc = exc.InnerException
    End While
   Catch exc As Exception
   Finally
    Console.WriteLine("Calculation Complete.")
   End Try
   Console.ReadLine()
  End Sub

 End Module
```

Once you have all this code entered, start it in debug mode. As it runs you'll see how exceptions are handled and reported.

> **Surprise... it's not a divide by zero error! That's not a bug, it's a feature! This isn't a divide by zero error due to how Visual Basic .NET divides integers. Instead of returning a Divide by Zero exception, Visual Basic .NET instead attempts to return an infinitely large value, which is far greater than the `Integer` type can hold. So, the result of this calculation is an overflow instead.**

Just as there is a structured way to handle exceptions within managed code, there are ways to handle exceptions that occur between managed and unmanaged code. Let's proceed to the next section and see how this is done.

Trapping Errors – Interop Components

Traditionally, unmanaged code errors had to be handled by utilizing the return codes that could be returned by a function. However, this method often does not produce the desired results.

When an error occurs between managed and unmanaged code, Visual Basic .NET steps in by automatically populating an `Exception` object that can be passed to the client application. More specifically, when an error occurs within a COM component, the CLR will automatically take the COM `HRESULT` value relating to the occurring error, and convert it into an `Exception` object. Converting COM errors makes it possible for managed code to deal with problems in a consistent manner. As a matter of fact, for consistency, the CLR can also convert errors that occur in managed code to the appropriate `HRESULT` values for COM.

The way to trap an error when working with Interop is to add a function to your unmanaged code to handle the error for you. For example, suppose you have an unmanaged DLL that counts the number of records in a database.

If an error were to occur within our unmanaged DLL, we need to pass the `Exception` object back to the user (front-end) application as described in the following code snippet:

```
Sub InterOp()
        Dim iResult As Integer
        Dim oUnManaged As New NameOfDLL.ComponentName()
        Try
            iResult = oUnManaged.countrecords
            MessageBox.Show("Total Records = " & iResult)
        Catch InterOpError As System.Exception
            MessageBox.Show("The following error occured: " & InterOpError.Message
              & " " & InterOpError.Source)
        End Try

        oUnManaged = Nothing
```

Looking at the above example, you should see that the trick to this technique is to simply create an instance of the unmanaged component. If things work correctly, we can take the result from `iResult` and do what we need. In this example, we simply display the result to a message box. However, if an error is generated instead of producing the desired results for `iResult`, the managed code client will "catch" the error and display it using a message box at the client.

Logging Your Errors

We all strive to write bug proof applications. But let's face it; no matter how much we test and debug them, errors can popup unexpectedly. Typically, these unexpected errors surface after the application has been released. Having an unexpected error occur will leave the typical user in distress. Furthermore, getting the exact error message reported back to the programmer tends to be difficult, at best.

Perhaps one of the best tools you can use to help figure out what problems may be occurring, without having to burden the user, is to implement error logging. There are two techniques for logging, using trace files and writing to the event log.

When choosing which method to use, you need to take into account the type of operating system in use. In order to utilize event logging, you must be using Windows NT, 2000, or XP operating systems. So if you plan to support other types of operating systems, you will want to consider trace files. Trace files are simply text files accessed through a .NET interface.

Another consideration you need to take into account is the type of errors you wish to trap. Too much logging will cause a lot of unnecessary disk I/O. Additionally logs can fill up your disk space very quickly when not managed properly. Simply, too much logging will cause performance loss.

Event Log

The Event Viewer provides a list of system events in data and time order. Three types of logs can be viewed: Application, Security, and System.

- The **Application log** contains application events including those logged through Visual Basic .NET.
- The **System log** receives events generated by the operating system (NT, Windows200, & XP) system components.
- The **Security log** is for security-generated events. Although some security related events are system generated, many security-related events can be configured to generate messages to the security log.

The Event Viewer can be opened via Administrative Tools from the Programs menu, or you can run `eventvwr.exe`.

We manage the event log using the `EventLog` component that resides within the `System.Diagnostics` namespace.

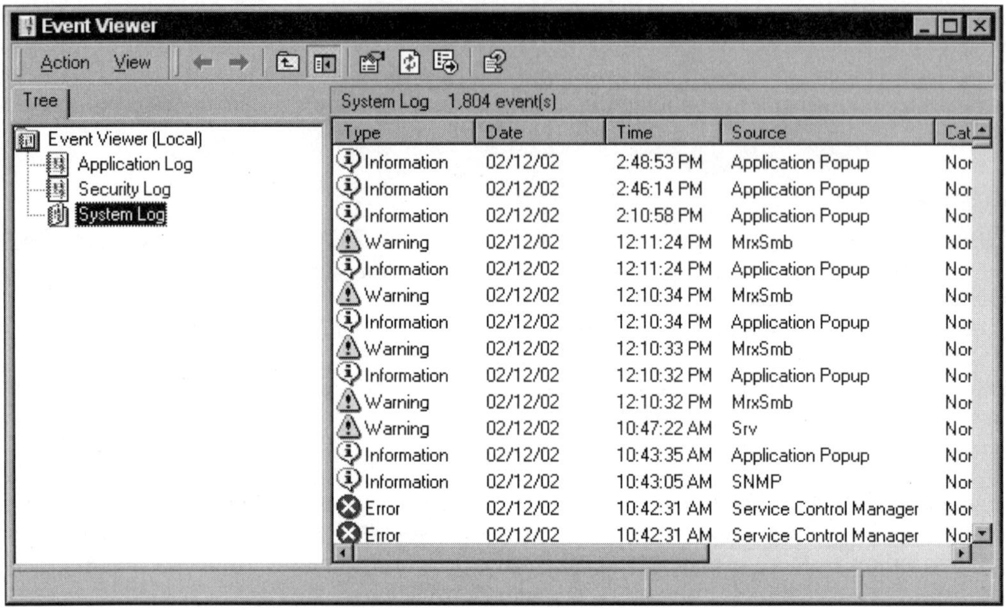

Just as there are three types of logs, there are three levels of log entries that can be recorded:

- **Information** – represented by a blue icon with the letter i in the center. Information messages inform us about major events, that don't occur very often, but tend not to be error-related.
- **Error** – represented by a red icon with an X in the center. This indicates that a significant error has occurred.
- **Warning** – represented by a yellow icon with an ! in the center. A warning message means that a potential problem may be occurring, that could develop into a more serious problem.

Additionally there is another type of entry that can be placed into the event log, referred to as audit entries.

- `SuccessAudit` – used to signal a successful login, such as a successful login to the operating system, SQL Server, or any other application that requires some kind of authentication.
- `FailureAudit` – used to signal a failed login.

Typically these audit entries are used for security type exceptions, thus they are typically recorded within the security logs.

Often we are not as concerned about the success of a login, but rather the amount of failed logins. Obviously, if the security logs start to show several failed login attempts, we have a problem that needs to be investigated. Perhaps it's only a user who forgot his/her password. A more severe scenario would be someone who does not have permission to log in, but is attempting to gain access.

Often you may want to know a little more about the message being displayed in the log window. By double-clicking a particular message displayed here, you can open a popup window that provides you with more detail about the message.

For example, the following screenshot details the information message about the event log:

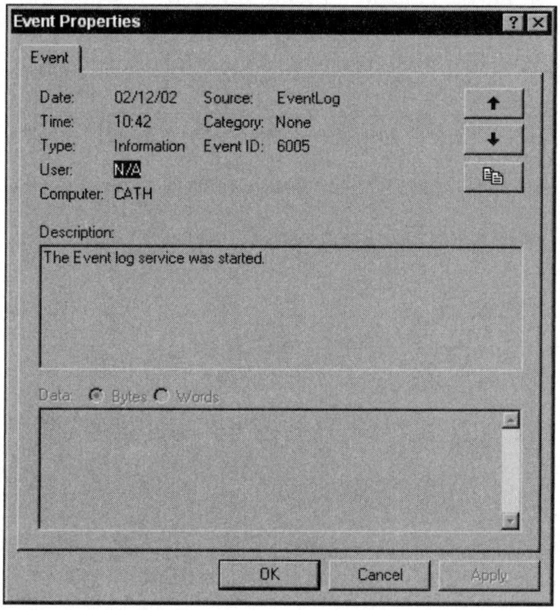

EventLog Class

In order to write messages to the event view, we need to access the `EventLog` Class. The `EventLog` class is derived from the namespace: `System.Diagnostics`.

There are two important properties for this class, `Log` and `Source`. While the `Log` property is used to specify which of the three types of logs (Application, Security, or System – System is the default if not specified) to write to, the `Source` property is used to specify the name of the event source that logs the events. Note that the source name must be unique.

While there are only a few properties to be concerned with, there are several methods of the `EventLog` class you should become familiar with.

The following are the more common methods of the `EventLog` class:

Method	Description
`CreateEventSource()`	This method is used to generate an event source to the specified log
`Delete()`	You can permanently delete an entire event log using this method
`Exists()`	This method allows you to verify whether a specific log exists
`SourceExists()`	This handy method allows you to verify whether or not a specific source already exists in a log
`WriteEntry()`	`WriteEntry()` method is simply used to write an entry to the event log

The `WriteEntry()` method is simply used to write an entry to the event log. This entry can include things such as the exception message, as well as a timestamp for when the exception occurred. Furthermore, we can indicate the type of event by specifying a value for the `EventLogEntryType`. The `EventLogEntryType` values include `Information`, `Error`, `Warning`, `SuccessAudit`, and `FailureAudit`.

Let's take a look at how you can create entries to the **Event Viewer** by trying a short hands-on project.

Writing to the Event Log

Start a new Visual Basic .NET application and place a button on the form. Add the following code to the `Button1_Click` event.

```
LogTest()
```

Add the following namespace to the declarations section:

```
Imports System.Diagnostics
```

Now you need to create a subroutine as shown:

```
Sub LogTest()
  Dim EvtLog As New System.Diagnostics.EventLog()

Try
   Throw (New Exception("Serious Problem! Can't find the specified table within
the Northwind DB."))
  Catch myObject As System.Exception

   If Not EvtLog.SourceExists("MyLogExample") Then
    EvtLog.CreateEventSource("MyLogExample", "system")
   End If

   EvtLog.Log = "system"
   EvtLog.WriteEntry("MyLogExample", myObject.Message, EventLogEntryType.Error, 0)

  End Try
 End Sub
```

After entering all your code, build your application and click the form button once. This will generate an error in the event log as shown below:

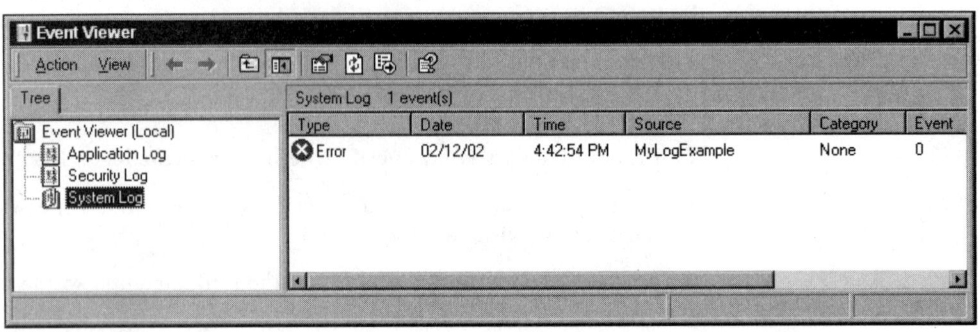

In order to receive a detailed description of the error, simply double-click the particular message (whether it be **Information**, **Warning**, or **Error**) if you want additional information. The following screenshot shows the error we generated with this project:

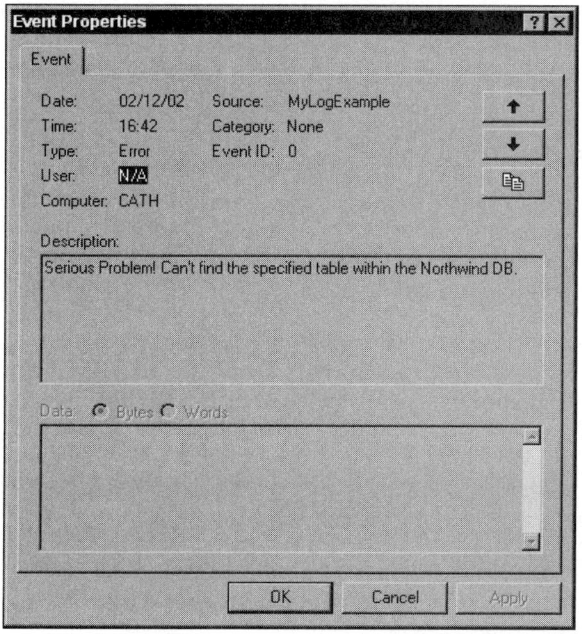

Going back to our code – because the `EventLog` class is derived from the `System.Diagnostics` namespace, we had to import it by making a declaration.

Next, we threw an exception and specified the type of message we wanted to associate with it. With `Catch`, we also specified that this exception would be created as a system exception, thus the message would be sent to the system log.

```
Try
            Throw (New Exception("Serious Problem! Can't find the specified table
within the Northwind DB."))
        Catch myObject As System.Exception
```

As previously mentioned, the `Source` property is used to specify a unique name for the event source that is used to log our events. This is accomplished with a conditional statement that makes use of the `SourceExists()` method. Recall that the `SourceExists()` method is used to verify whether or not a specific source already exists in a log. In our project, we simply used an `If` statement to verify we had a unique source name. If the source name tests to be unique, the event source is created:

```
If Not EvtLog.SourceExists("MyLogExample") Then
                EvtLog.CreateEventSource("MyLogExample", "system")
End If
```

Finally, we use the `WriteEntry()` method to write to the system log:

```
EvtLog.WriteEntry("MyLogExample", myObject.Message, EventLogEntryType.Error, 0)
```

Trace Log

As previously mentioned, depending on the platform your applications are residing on, you may not have an event log to write to. It's also possible that the developer may not have access to the event logs. In such scenarios we can write exception information to a text-based file. Furthermore, if event logs are available, they make excellent supplements by being able to supply additional details about an error, without us having to worry about overloading the event logs with detailed information.

In order to write errors and other information to a trace log, you will want to work particularly with three classes, `StreamWriter`, `Debug`, and `Trace`.

The `Debug` class allows you to send detailed information about an error after it occurs. However, in order to send any information for output, we need to use a listener. A listener is responsible for receiving, storing, and sending stored information to an output. Listeners are .NET processes that receive debug messages and persist them to a file.

The `StreamWriter` is used to open an output path to a text file, while the `Debug` class is designed to write information after an error occurs. More specifically, the `StreamWriter` object binds itself to a listener object. This allows for the output produced by the `Debug` object to be sent and written to a text-based file.

The `Trace` class is very similar to the `Debug` class. The major difference between the two is typically that you have `Debug` disabled in your releases, while the `Trace` can be enabled in pre-release testing and can then be left enabled in the released project.

The following table is a recap of the common methods in the `Debug` class:

Method	Description
`Assert()`	This method is used to test a condition to see if it is true. If the condition returns `False`, the `Assert()` method will display a message.
`Close()`	This method is used to clear (flush) the output buffer as well as closing all listeners.
`Fail()`	You can use the `Fail()` method to display a message box in the form of Abort/Retry/Ignore.
`Flush()`	This method is used to send all content residing in output buffer (flush) and write the contents to the listeners.
`Write()`	This method is used to write to the output buffer in byte increments.
`WriteLine()`	This method is used to write any characters to the current stream object that may follow a line terminator.
`WriteIf()`	This method is used to test a condition to see if it is true. If so, the messages are saved by the listener.
`WriteLineIf()`	This method is used to test a condition to see if it is true. If the condition returns `True`, all characters are written to the output buffer object that may follow a line terminator.

The `StreamWriter` class is accessed through the `System.IO` namespace. The following table shows some of the common methods in the `StreamWriter` class:

Method	Description
`Close()`	This method is used to close the `StreamWriter`. You must call this method to complete the writing of any messages to the underlying stream.
`Flush()`	This method is used to send all content to the output file.
`Write()`	This method is used to output information to the stream in bytes.
`WriteLine()`	This method is used to write any characters to the current stream object that may follow a line terminator.

Using the Debug Class

Start a new Visual Basic .NET application and add a list box, label, text box, and a button as shown below. This program will execute once. Subsequent clicks of the **Execute Query** button will fail with an exception.

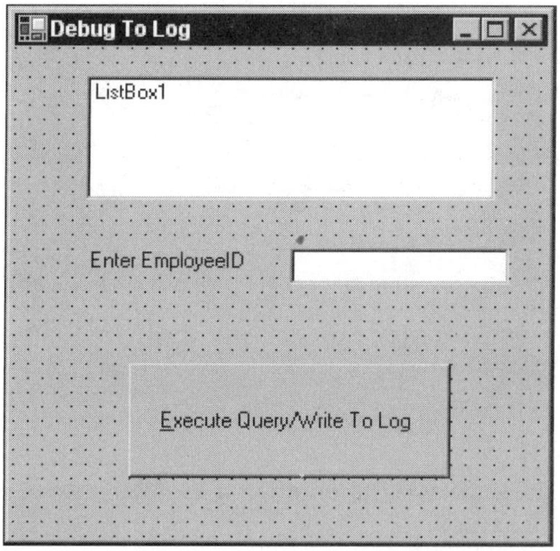

Add the following namespaces:

```
Imports System.IO
Imports System.Data.SqlClient
Imports System.Diagnostics
```

Add the following code to the `Button1_Click` event:

```
    Dim X As Integer
        X = TextBox1.Text
        DebugToTraceFileExample(X)
```

Create the following method as shown:

```
Private Sub DebugToTraceFileExample(ByVal IntEmployeeID As Integer)
        Dim MySQLReader As SqlDataReader
```

```
        Dim MySQLConnection As SqlConnection
        Dim MySQLCommand As SqlCommand

        Dim MyStreamFile As Stream = File.Create("C:\MyDebug.log")
        Dim MyTraceListener As New TextWriterTraceListener(MyStreamFile)
        Dim MyConnectionString As String
        Dim MyCommandString As String

        Debug.Listeners.Add(MyTraceListener)

        MyConnectionString =
"server=YourServerName;uid=YourUserID;pwd=YourPassword; database=Northwind"
        MyCommandString = "SELECT FirstName,LastName FROM Employees WHERE
EmployeeID =" & IntEmployeeID
        MySQLConnection = New SqlConnection(MyConnectionString)
        MySQLCommand = New SqlCommand(MyCommandString, MySQLConnection)
        MySQLCommand.Connection.Open()
        MySQLReader = MySQLCommand.ExecuteReader()

        Debug.WriteLine("The following SQL query: " & MyCommandString)
        Debug.WriteLine(" was executed at " & Now())

        Do While (MySQLReader.Read())
            ListBox1.Items.Add(MySQLReader("FirstName") + "  " +
MySQLReader("LastName"))
        Loop

        MyTraceListener.Flush()
        MyTraceListener.Close()
        MySQLConnection.Close()

    End Sub
```

Build the project and enter an `EmployeeID` number. The default `EmployeeID`s that come with the `Northwind` database range from `1-9`.

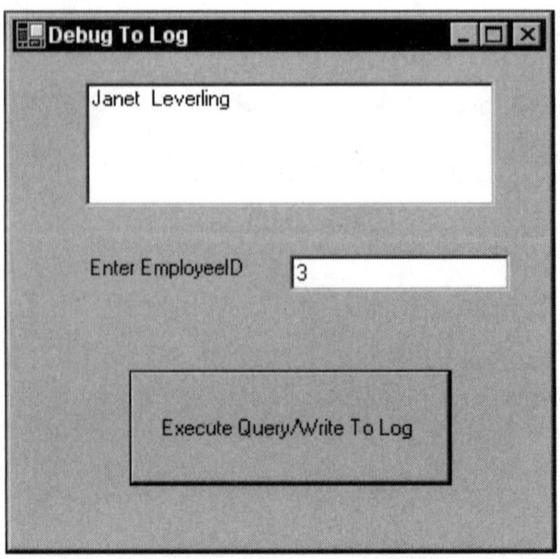

Click the form button one time, and then locate the text-based log file that was created. In this example, we named the log file `myDebug.log` and placed it into the `C:\` drive:

Open the file to view the exceptions that we have recorded:

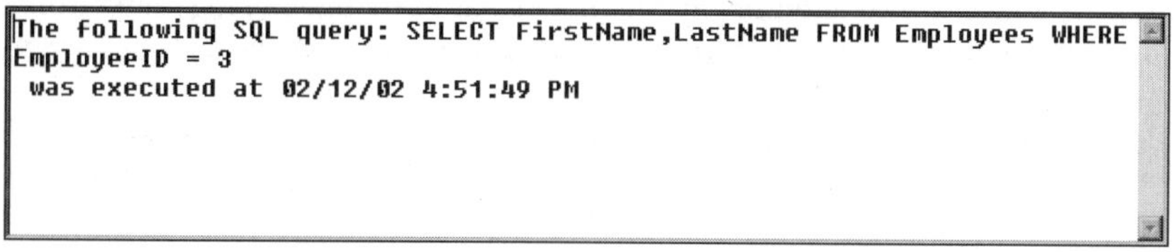
The following SQL query: SELECT FirstName,LastName FROM Employees WHERE EmployeeID = 3
 was executed at 02/12/02 4:51:49 PM

This project utilizes the `StreamWriter` object that resides within the `System.IO` namespace, thus we had to import it in our code declarations. We also imported the `System.Data.SqlClient` as we plan to access an SQL Server database.

We added the appropriate statements for creating and displaying data from the `SqlDataReader`. You should already be familiar with the `SqlDataReader`, so we will move on.

The first important step we need to take is to create a file object instance and then assign it to a stream, so it can later be written to the log file `MyDebug.log` (which will be placed into the `C:\` drive):

```
Dim MyStreamFile As Stream = File.Create("C:\MyDebug.log")
```

The next set of statements involve the listeners. At this stage, we specify the object `TextWriterTraceListener` to direct our output to the stream object `MyStreamFile`.

```
Dim MyTraceListener As New TextWriterTraceListener(MyStreamFile)
```

Now that we have a way to direct all our debugging output to a file, we add `MyTraceListener` from the `TextWriterTraceListener` to the listeners that we want to use for monitoring and debugging our output.

```
Debug.Listeners.Add(MyTraceListener)
```

After we loop through the `SqlDataReader` and populate the list box, we can now send the output from the output buffer to the writer by using the method `Flush()`. Recall that `Flush()` is used to send all content residing in the output buffer (flush) and then write the contents to the listeners:

```
Do While (MySQLReader.Read())
    ListBox1.Items.Add(MySQLReader("FirstName") + "  " +
     MySQLReader("LastName"))
Loop
MyTraceListener.Flush()
```

Now that our messages have been written to the log, we want to explicitly close any open objects. In this case, we want to close any instances of `MyTraceListener` and `MySQLConnection`.

Using the Trace Class

Earlier in this chapter, I mentioned that you could change Debug to Trace and vice versa. Just to prove the point, open the Debug class project you previously created and change all Debug class references to Trace. There are three class changes, and additionally you may want to change the log name from MyDebug.log to MyTrace.log so you can distinguish it from the output log used with the Debug class project.

```
Private Sub DebugToTraceFileExample(ByVal IntEmployeeID As Integer)
        Dim MySQLReader As SqlDataReader
        Dim MySQLConnection As SqlConnection
        Dim MySQLCommand As SqlCommand

        Dim MyStreamFile As Stream = File.Create("C:\MyTrace.log")
        Dim MyTraceListener As New TextWriterTraceListener(MyStreamFile)
        Dim MyConnectionString As String
        Dim MyCommandString As String

         Trace.Listeners.Add(MyTraceListener)

        MyConnectionString =
"server=YourServerName;uid=YourUserID;pwd=YourPassword;database=Northwind"
        MyCommandString = "SELECT FirstName,LastName FROM Employees WHERE
EmployeeID =" & IntEmployeeID
        MySQLConnection = New SqlConnection(MyConnectionString)
        MySQLCommand = New SqlCommand(MyCommandString, MySQLConnection)
        MySQLCommand.Connection.Open()
        MySQLReader = MySQLCommand.ExecuteReader()

        Trace.WriteLine("The following SQL query: " & MyCommandString)
        Trace.WriteLine(" was executed at " & Now())

        Do While (MySQLReader.Read())
            ListBox1.Items.Add(MySQLReader("FirstName") + "  " +
MySQLReader("LastName"))
        Loop

        MyTraceListener.Flush()
        MyTraceListener.Close()
        MySQLConnection.Close()

    End Sub
```

Troubleshooting

So far you have seen how to record error messages by using either the event log or a trace file. But there is more to making sure your applications work properly – we are also concerned about application performance. You can utilize the Trace class for just this purpose. The Trace class will allow you to receive pertinent information regarding an application's performance, or even the performance of a section of code in the application.

Performance

As with all trace and logging techniques, you must be careful not to degrade your application's performance by creating heavy I/O traffic to your trace files. It may sound counterproductive to have a trace determine an application's performance, while at the same time degrading that performance. Unfortunately, this is true. Using trace features to log application performance is an excellent tool, but it should only be used during development and testing. However, it is important not to confuse this issue with that of leaving trace statements active in your releases for logging unexpected events, as discussed earlier.

Tracing Performance Characteristics

For our next example, start a new Visual Basic .NET project and add a list box to the form.

Add the following namespaces:

```
Imports System.IO
Imports System.Data.SqlClient
Imports System.Diagnostics
```

Add the following under the `Form_Load` event:

```
Dim myCommand As SqlCommand
        Dim mySQLConnection As New SqlConnection("Data Source=myServerName;initial
catalog=Northwind;User ID=MyUserID;PWD=MyPassword")
        Dim mySqlCommand As New SqlCommand("SELECT FirstName, LastName FROM
Employees", mySQLConnection)
        Dim MySqlReader As SqlDataReader
        Dim myWriter As New _
            IO.StreamWriter(File.Open("C:\QueryPerformance.log",
FileMode.OpenOrCreate))

        mySQLConnection.Open()
#Const myTrace = 4
        Trace.Listeners.Add(New TextWriterTraceListener(myWriter))

#If myTrace Then
        Trace.WriteLine("Select Query Began at " & Now())
#End If
        MySqlReader = mySqlCommand.ExecuteReader() 'Load data to reader


        Do While (MySqlReader.Read()) 'populate listbox row by row
            ListBox1.Items.Add(MySqlReader("FirstName") + "  " +
MySqlReader("LastName"))
        Loop

#If myTrace Then
        Trace.WriteLine("Select Query Completed and ListBox Populated at " &
Now())
#End If
```

```
            Trace.Listeners.Clear()
            myWriter.Close()
            MySqlReader.Close()
            mySQLConnection.Close()
            myWriter = Nothing
            MySqlReader = Nothing
            mySQLConnection = Nothing
```

After entering your code, build your application. Because we have our code entered under the `Form_Load` event, we only need to start the application and then close it. Our log has been written and can be found in the `C:\` drive.

If you open the `QueryPerformance.log` file that has been created, you will see that there are no performance issues when executing this query. All processing occurred at the same measurable time down to the second. Nevertheless, the principle is here. When dealing with heavily populated databases involving millions of records, a query or transaction can take a considerable amount of time. Getting a performance estimate can help you isolate potential bottlenecks and take necessary action to increase performance.

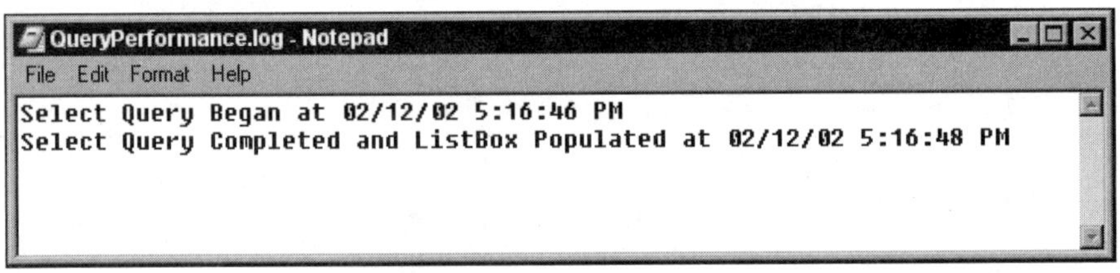

Most of this code is fairly straightforward; however, you may be wondering what the constant `myTrace` (with the value set to `4` in our example) does.

```
    #Const myTrace = 4
```

The "#" character here tells the compiler that you are defining a processing constant, not a program constant. This value will only be used in the tracing context.

There are five enumerations, ranging from `0` to `4`, that you can specify in order to trace certain characteristics.

For example, if you want to trace only error messages, you would set the value to `1`. However, if you wanted to trace error messages as well as warnings, you would set the value to `2`.

The following table describes each enumeration value:

Enumeration Value	Description
0	No traces will occur
1	Records error messages
2	Records error and warning messages

Enumeration Value	Description
3	Records error, warning, and information messages
4	Records error, warning, information, and verbose messages

It is a condition based on the value of this constant that determines whether we can write to the log or not, and the type of messages written:

```
#If myTrace Then
        Trace.WriteLine("Select Query Began at " & Now())
```

If you set the constant to a value of 0 no log will be written. However, in this project, we still create a log file if one does not already exist using:

```
            IO.StreamWriter(File.Open("C:\QueryPerformance.log",
FileMode.OpenOrCreate))
```

So if your constant is set to 0 and a log file does not exist, we simply generate an empty log file. In other words, a log file is still being created, but we do not write a message to it.

Other Tools

As an application developer, you may be asking why you should concern yourself with Windows performance. After all, isn't that the job of the network administrator? Up to a point, you're right: once your application has been distributed, it should be the Windows administrator's job to make sure the system where your application is installed is running properly.

But let's try looking at Windows system performance in another way. When you're developing applications, how do you know if your application will meet the hardware specifications of the future users of your application? It's quite possible that your development machine has more horsepower than the machine where your application will be installed. Your application may run fine on your super charged 1.2 GHz Pentium with 500 MB of RAM, but how will your application act on a lesser machine?

As a developer, it's important to think about the user. Will your application support the user's hardware? Did you ever consider the user's hardware before you started building the application? What if your application is not properly releasing instances? Your system will start to eat up valuable resources, but how will you know? During testing, your application may appear to run smoothly.

So, once you have your components debugged and everything appears to be running properly, you should test your application to match similar specifications to the user's hardware. In other words, paying attention to system performance is the second part of application development.

Windows offers a very useful tool for monitoring your Windows system called Performance Monitor.

Measuring a system can affect the measurement. It takes system resources to run diagnostic tools, and having too many diagnostic tools running will affect the outcome of the measurements you receive. A good rule of thumb is to turn monitoring off as soon as you have retrieved the information you want to see.

Performance Monitor

> **Windows NT called it Performance Monitor. With the introduction of Windows 2000 it was referred to simply as Performance.**

The **Performance Monitor** is a very robust tool that has improved its capabilities since it was first introduced with Windows NT.

With Performance Monitor, you can monitor several types of processes at the same time, as well as setting alerts and error logging. Problems are often hidden among other activities. While using the Task Manager is practical for a quick reference (particularly when monitoring CPU and memory usage), in most situations you need to rely on other tools that can provide you with a detailed report over a greater amount of time.

As an example, I was once working with a system that dropped in performance. Coincidentally, I had added a new application. I say coincidentally, because it turned out that the new application was only related to the problem and was not the actual problem. But how do you find out what's wrong? Is it a new application or is it something else?

Analyzing the graph and log files produced by Performance Monitor, I was able to see that CPU levels were moderately high; yet CPU levels were not sustained. However, memory utilization showed to be considerably high over a long duration. Additionally, the log showed that there was a lot of reading and writing going on within my hard drive. Knowing that my system performed properly before adding my application, and seeing that both memory and disk activity was high, I concluded that I needed more memory in my server. The application itself was fine, but it drew more memory resources than my test server could provide. Problem solved!

Windows Performance Monitor can be displayed by opening the Programs menu. Select Administrative Tools, followed by Performance. You can also run `perfmon.exe` from the command line.

> **Note that when you first open the Performance Monitor, it appears empty. You need to add the items you wish to monitor, as shown below. After you have configured the items to be monitored into the application, you can save your settings.**

Using Performance Monitor

Performance Monitor is not the most intuitive tool around, because it's very feature-rich. However, once configured, it can become your best friend. As a matter of fact, once configured, you can even create alerts to let you know of any problems. This takes a large burden off of the developer as well as the person administering the server.

Because the Performance Monitor offers so much, my intention is to only show you a few of the major features.

From the icon-based tool bar directly over the graph area, click the + icon. You can also place your cursor in the white space at the very bottom and right-click. From the pop-up, select Add Counters (as seen at the bottom right of the following screenshot).

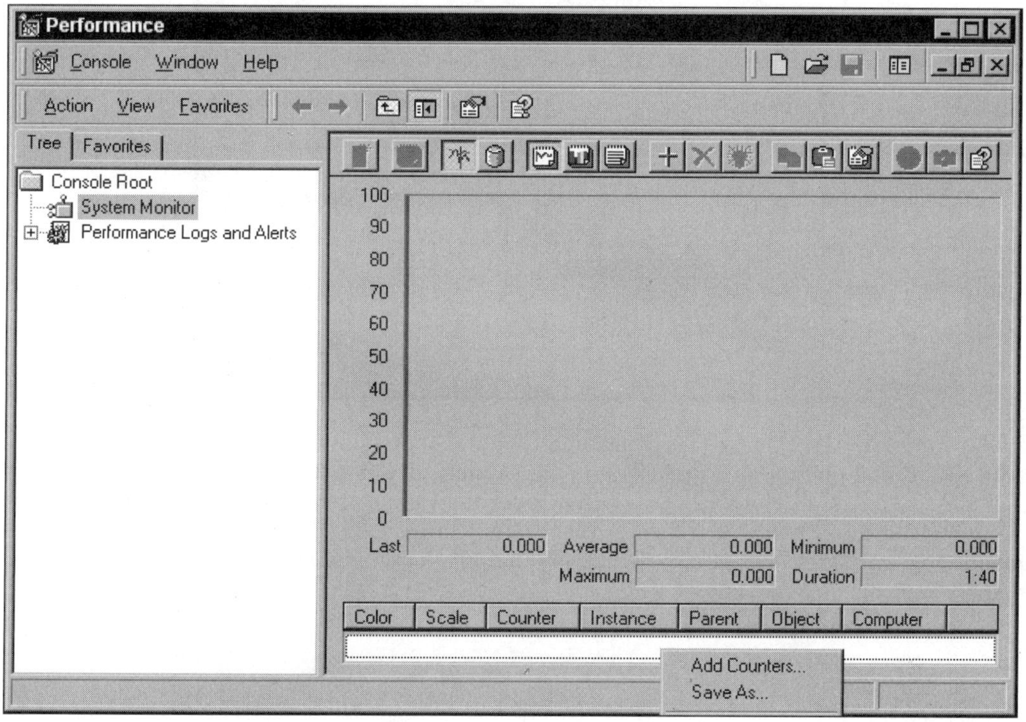

There are many pre-configured counters already available, ranging from .NET CLR Data, ASP.NET Applications, SQL Server and Web Services. Additionally, you can programmatically create your own custom counters. We will return to this shortly.

The following screenshot shows the systems processor as the Performance object and the counter being selected is the % Processor Time. You can add as many counters as you want, just keep in mind the more you add, the busier the graph becomes.

Each object counter you want to monitor is represented by an automatically designated color.

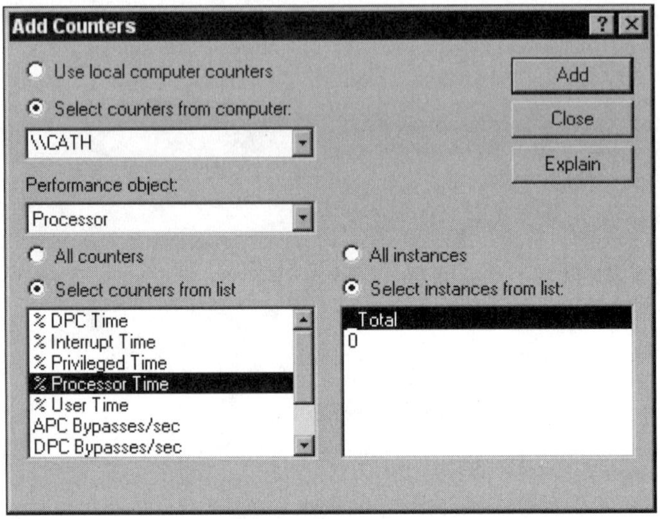

The following screenshot shows processor time with all counters selected for the ASP.NET performance counter (horizontal line at 30). I find using process time with any of the other counters to be very valuable. As a general rule of thumb, if the %Processor Time counter results in a sustained reading of 90 or above, it is likely that a processor bottleneck is occurring. If you monitor Pages/Sec and it maintains a 60 or higher, then it means that your application is probably fine, but your system may need more memory.

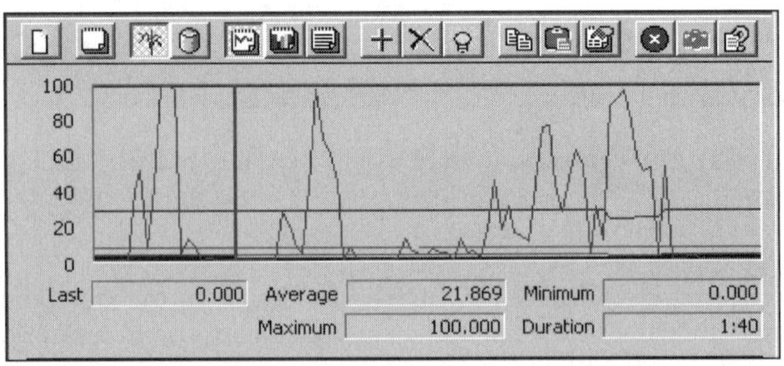

Directly below the graph is a list of the counters you are monitoring. The following screenshot shows that we have opted to monitor various errors that may occur in regard to the ASP.NET applications. By highlighting any one of the counters, we can get the actual counts as opposed to a general graphical depiction. In the following summary, I highlighted Total Errors. The results show that there have been a total of 7 errors.

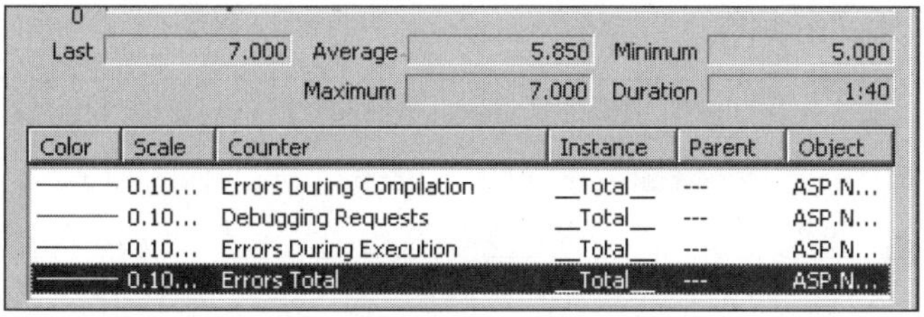

Creating Custom Counters

Although Windows and the .NET framework provide numerous categories for specific counters, the counters provided tend to be a little grainy in nature. In other words, they are only able to profile your applications on the complete scale – the entire application, not specific tracts of your code. As a result, there may be times when you wish to create your own custom counters.

Custom counters are not difficult, although there are several syntax forms because many of the methods are overloaded. Because of this, I am only going to show one example. If you want to know more, Microsoft has a fair amount of information at its web site at: http://msdn.microsoft.com/library/en-us/cpqstart/html/cpsmpnetsamples-howtodiagnostics.asp?frame=true#cpsmppcdemosample.

When creating a category, you simply utilize the `PerformanceCounterCategory` object.

There are three properties for the `PerformanceCounterCategory`:

Property	Description
`CategoryName`	Specifies the category name.
`CategoryHelp`	Provides a description that describes the category.
`MachineName`	Specifies the name of the machine where the category is installed.

There are nine methods for the `PerformanceCounterCategory`class:

Method	Description
`CounterExists()`	This method is used to verify the counter name is unique.
`Create()`	This method is used to create a category, as well as one or more counters.
`Delete()`	This method is used to delete a category, including all counters within the category. Not recommended!
`Exists()`	This method is used to verify the category name is unique.
`GetCategories()`	This method is used to return an array list of categories.
`GetCounters()`	This method is used to return an array list of counters.
`GetInstanceNames()`	This method is used to return an array list of counter instances.

Table continued on following page

Method	Description
InstanceExists()	This method is used to verify if a counter instance exists.
ReadCategory()	You can retrieve a collection of all category and instance data by utilizing this method.

As you can see there are a lot of methods. The good news is that you will typically only need to use a few of them. However, before looking at sample syntax for creating a category and counter, it's important to clarify that you cannot add new counters to existing categories. This means once a category exists, even if it is custom, you cannot modify or add a counter without first deleting the category and then recreating the category with the new counters, as well as any other existing counters. Take my word on this, this is not something you want to do and it is very risky at best. The best way to deal with this problem is simply to create a new category when creating new counters.

The easiest way to create a category and new counters is to combine your statements as the following snippet shows:

```
Dim NewCounter4CodeTest as New CounterCreatationDataCollection

NewCounter4CodeTest.Add(New CounterCreationData("MyCounter/Seconds", _
      PerformancecounterType.RateOfCountersPerSecond32)

PerformanceCounterCategory.Create("NewCategory_Name", "Counter_Name",
CounterCreationDataCollection_Name)
```

Summary

This chapter covered various techniques for debugging and troubleshooting application and system problems. We started this chapter by reviewing the basics of .NET's exception handler. Here we looked at the Try...Catch...Finally structure for handling exceptions. We then moved on and reviewed the various properties and methods of the Exception class.

Next, we talked about trapping errors between managed and unmanaged code. You saw how you could pass an error from a COM component to the client that utilizes managed code.

The next section covered logging errors. Here you learned how to use the EventLog class to record exceptions that can be viewed through the Windows Event Viewer. We also took a look at the Event Viewer with its various types of logs and levels of log entries.

After working with the EventLog class, we moved on and learned how to write exceptions to trace files. Here you learned about utilizing the StreamWriter, Debug, and Trace classes. You learned the difference between the Debug and Trace classes and you learned when to appropriately use each. We followed up with hands-on examples of each.

For the remaining parts of this chapter, you learned how to test for application performance. Here you learned about two tools. The first is to programmatically utilize the Trace class to test for application performance. The other tool comes with the various Windows operating systems and is called Performance Monitor. With Performance Monitor you learned how to set a counter in order to benchmark system resources, as well as application performance.

Pro Visual Basic .NET Transactions

10

Case Study: IBuyAdventure.NET 2.0

By now you've learned that the .NET Framework provides many different technologies for developing transactional applications. Some of these technologies we've discussed included .NET Serviced Components and COM+ transactions, ADO.NET transactions, transactional ASP.NET Web Forms, and transactional ASP.NET Web Services. Now it's time to apply some of the concepts and technologies we've learned in the previous chapters into a complete, distributed transaction-processing system!

In this chapter we will create a business-to-consumer (B2C) and business-to-business (B2B) eCommerce solution for a fictitious organization named AdventureWorks. AdventureWorks is an on-line reseller of climbing equipment or "extreme" sporting goods. The eCommerce system that we will create, called IBuyAdventure, is actually the third version of an eCommerce solution for AdventureWorks. The first version, then called AdventureWorks, was built using ASP 2.0 and included as a sample application with IIS 4.0 and the Windows NT Option Pack. The second version upgraded the system from ASP 2.0 to the .NET platform utilizing ASP.NET Web Forms. Version 2.0, called IBuyAdventure, was described in detail in the case study found in the Professional ASP.NET book. In this chapter we will enhance the IBuyAdventure system to support additional functionality such as integrating with an outside fulfillment provider, tracking and allocating inventory, and receiving orders electronically from business customers. However, we will completely rebuild the IBuyAdventure system so you don't need to be familiar with any previous versions.

We will look at the overall solution from a broad level, while focusing on the aspects of design and development that are specifically related to transactional applications on the .NET platform. In the process we will demonstrate design and development best practices for creating transactional .NET applications.

Specifically, during this chapter we will:

- Walk through the entire process of creating the IBuyAdventure system, from the solution definition and requirements analysis to implementing the code
- Discuss the business requirements that influenced the design and architecture of the new IBuyAdventure system
- Discuss each progressive stage of the design process, including the conceptual, logical, and physical design models
- Utilize the Universal Modeling Language (UML) to diagram and architect complex transactions
- Analyze the advantages and disadvantages of transactional .NET Serviced Components and transactional ASP.NET Web Forms or ASP.NET Web Services for a given scenario
- Implement both simple and complex transactions for business processes such as creating customers, processing orders, and receiving order fulfillment updates
- Learn how to optimize the database design and data access for transactional applications

The main goal of the case study is to show how an organization might create a robust, scalable, and high performance transactional processing application utilizing the .NET Framework and related .NET technologies. However, I believe that one of the most significant challenges developers are being faced with today is learning how to utilize all the new .NET technologies and legacy COM-based technologies together to compose a complete solution. In addition to demonstrating best practices for transaction processing, this case study will also demonstrate the utilization of several key .NET technologies including: IIS, COM+, SQL Server 2000, ADO.NET, ASP.NET Web Forms, ASP.NET Web Services, XML data processing, and new features available to Visual Basic .NET such as structured exception handling, inheritance, shared methods, and method overloading and overrides.

Although AdventureWorks is a fictitious organization, the design and development issues we encountered when building a new version of their transactional eCommerce solution are very real and the knowledge gained from these real-world issues can be applied to developing all types of applications on the .NET platform. Let's begin our case study by learning more about AdventureWorks and some of the business challenges they faced as a rapidly growing organization.

The entire IBuyAdventure system including the Visual Studio .NET project files, database scripts, sample data, graphics, and source files can be downloaded from Wrox Press' Programmer-to-Programmer web site at http://www.wrox.com.

Business Overview

AdventureWorks is a fictitious organization that resells outdoor adventure and "extreme" sporting products to consumers. Some of the types of products that AdventureWorks currently sells include camping equipment such as tents and sleeping bags, climbing equipment such as harnesses and backpacks, and clothing and apparel such as parkas and boots.

Over the past two years AdventureWorks has been able to organically grow from a small e-commerce startup to a recognized and respectable provider of adventure sporting equipment. AdventureWorks has been able to succeed while other online stores have failed because they provide a source for consumers to purchase specialized products that are not available in most sporting goods stores and they have gained creditability and recognition within their industry. They also credit their growth and success to their focus on providing outstanding customer service and expert advice for the products they sell.

As AdventureWorks has grown as an organization they have continually enhanced their eCommerce system. There are currently two major versions of AdventureWorks eCommerce system:

- **AdventureWorks**
  The first version of AdventureWorks eCommerce system, then simply named AdventureWorks, was developed using Active Server Pages 2.0. The AdventureWorks site featured all the basic features of a typical e-commerce system, including product viewing and selection, user registration, and a shopping basket.
- **IBuyAdventure 1.0**
  After hearing about Microsoft's new .NET strategy, framework, and tools, AdventureWorks decided to migrate the existing AdventureWorks eCommerce system to the .NET Platform and ASP.NET. The new system, named to IBuyAdventure or IBA for short, was developed for Windows 2000 Server using the .NET Framework (Beta 2), C#, and SQL Server 2000. In addition to the basic e-commerce features migrated from the AdventureWorks site, the IBuyAdventure system also featured increased scalability by intelligently managing the user's state and shopping cart.

It is not necessary to be familiar with the AdventureWorks system included with ASP 2.0 or the IBuyAdventure.NET site created in the Professional ASP.NET book. We will be covering everything necessary to build the new IBuyAdventure eCommerce system in this chapter, while focusing on the issues that are specific to transaction processing. With that said, I would recommend reading the IBuyAdventure case study in the Professional ASP.NET book if you would like to learn more about utilizing ASP.NET Web Forms to create a complete application.

> **Be sure to start your ASP.NET State Service (accessible from Administrative Tools | Services) before attempting to run this application.**

Business Challenges

So why is it necessary to create a new version of the IBuyAdventure system? As a rapidly growing organization, AdventureWorks was being faced with a number of business challenges. Some of these challenges or "growing pains" include:

Managing and Tracking Inventory

AdventureWorks does not currently have a system to manage and track inventory of the products that they sell. Therefore the existing IBuyAdventure system does not display inventory or availability information to customers. Instead customers blindly place orders for products and assume that they are immediately available. When AdventureWorks fulfills a customer's order, a shipping associate simply locates the products in the warehouse, packages the products, and fills out the necessary paperwork to ship the order. If a product is not available or there is a lower quantity available than outstanding orders for a product, then the shipping associate notifies the purchasing department that the particular product is not in stock. If a sufficient quantity of the product is not on order from the supplier, then a purchasing agent must create and place an order with the supplier. As you can probably imagine, there have been several incidents where a customer was unhappy after placing an order for a product that was backordered for several weeks.

Outsourcing Order Fulfillment

Due to some of their inventory problems and the costly expense of managing a warehouse, AdventureWorks has decided to outsource the physical task of order fulfillment to an outside fulfillment provider. After considering several potential partners, AdventureWorks decided to partner with eFulfill, a fulfillment services provider specializing in order fulfillment for e-commerce and mail order companies. In this partnership, eFulfill will be responsible for storing the physical product inventory in their warehouse and picking, packing, and shipping orders that are sent by AdventureWorks. eFulfill's order fulfillment process is paperless and entirely automated. In order to best utilize eFulfill's services and avoid manual data entry, AdventureWorks must be able to electronically send orders to eFulfill and receive fulfillment order status updates when orders are shipped.

Processing Orders From Business Customers

AdventureWorks has recently been approached by several businesses ranging from specialty sporting equipment stores to large sporting goods retailers who are interested in procuring products from AdventureWorks and reselling the products in their physical stores. Based on the projected order volume of the potential business customers, AdventureWorks estimates that this new source of orders could increase their revenue by approximately 240% or $1.8 million per year. However, in order for AdventureWorks to solidify these business relationships, they must provide the ability for the business customers to submit orders electronically from their existing electronic procurement (eProcurement) systems and through electronic marketplaces (eMarketplaces) without having to manually visit the IBuyAdventure web site. Orders from business customers should be placed against the customer's established account and invoiced to the customer instead of being billed against a credit card at the time of shipment.

AdventureWorks realized that they must address these issues in order to retain existing customers, attract new consumer and business customers, and increase profitability. AdventureWorks believed that once the necessary infrastructure is in place to overcome these challenges, they would be well positioned to proceed with the next phases of their business strategy by expanding into water sports, skiing, and snowboarding equipment. Consequently, these challenges were driving factors in AdventureWorks decision to enhance the IBuyAdventure system.

Solution Overview

As a result of their current business challenges, AdventureWorks decided to enhance and extend the functionality of their existing flagship e-commerce system. The new system, simply called IBuyAdventure version 2.0, would provide the ability to:

Maintain Inventory Information for Each Product

Although AdventureWorks will outsource the physical process of order fulfillment to eFulfill, the IBuyAdventure system must be enhanced to provide the ability to track inventory and maintain inventory levels for each product. At any given time the IBuyAdventure system must accurately reflect the physical inventory that is available in eFulfill's warehouse. When orders are placed in the system, inventory will be allocated or reserved for the products on the order. After orders are fulfilled, the inventory levels for each product will be decremented by the quantities on the order. By intelligently tracking and managing inventory levels, AdventureWorks can provide availability information to their customers and know when to re-order products from their suppliers.

Submit Orders to the Fulfillment Provider

Outsourcing a business process or a portion of a business process to another organization typically requires a certain level of business-to-business integration between the organization's enterprise systems. To outsource order fulfillment to eFulfill, AdventureWorks must send orders to eFulfill electronically. eFulfill can receive orders in a variety of data formats including electronic data interchange (EDI), comma separated values (CSV), tab-delimited, and various flavors of XML. eFulfill currently supports HTTP, HTTPS, and FTP file upload as integration protocols. The IBuyAdventure system will be enhanced to automatically send XML-formatted orders across HTTPS to eFulfill whenever a customer places an order. After an order has shipped, eFulfill will send an XML-formatted `OrderStatusUpdate` message to the IBuyAdventure system across HTTPS.

Expose Web Service for Receiving Ordering from Business Customers

To satisfy the requirements of AdventureWorks potential business customers, the IBuyAdventure system will expose an XML Web Service that will include methods for receiving orders and checking the status of existing orders. The order receiving Web Service will utilize some of the same components as the e-commerce storefront for processing orders.

In addition to these major enhancements, the IBuyAdventure 2.0 system will also include an extensible framework for processing orders. This new order processing subsystem will utilize several specialized, transactional .NET Serviced Components to perform work within a single distributed transaction and ensure the reliability of the business process.

Process Model

Due to the complexity of the IBuyAdventure 2.0 system, it was necessary to utilize a structured project process to guide the design, development, and deployment of the solution. We decided to utilize the Microsoft Solutions Framework (MSF) process model because of its wide adoption by many developers, architects, and IT specialists. MSF is a collection of concepts, models, and best practices for creating and implementing technology solutions.

The MSF Process Model for Application Development, one of the fundamental models of the Microsoft Solutions Framework, is a disciplined project process that defines the stages, milestones, and typical deliverables of an application development project. This model is essentially a guideline that specifies what activities should be performed and when they should be performed during a project. Whether you choose to utilize MSF, or some other methodology, it is absolutely critical to define and adhere to a structured project process, especially for distributed transaction processing systems because of their increased complexity.

The MSF Process Model for Application Development consists of the following four sequential stages:

- Envisioning

  During the **Envisioning** stage the vision and the requirements for the entire solution are defined and documented. The envisioning phase focuses on determining *what* business problems a solution will resolve and what functionality the solution will provide, not *how* it will function to meet the requirements. This stage is crucial to a project's success because it represents an opportunity for all project team members to agree on a shared vision for the solution and the functionality that will be included.

- Planning

  During the **Planning** stage the solution is thoroughly designed and architected, based on the requirements defined during the Envisioning stage. The Planning stage is the point in the project process when you determine *how* a solution will function. The end result of the Planning phase is typically a functional specification and a project schedule for the Developing and Stabilizing stages. The functional specification effectively serves as the guidelines or "blueprints" for the development, testing, and deployment of the solution.

- Developing

  During the **Developing** stage, the solution is simply developed and implemented according to the design and architecture defined during the Planning stage. At the completion of the Developing phase, all coding work should be concluded and the solution should be "code-complete."

- Stabilizing

  Finally, during the **Stabilizing** phase the solution is thoroughly tested and modified as necessary to address any outstanding issues. After all outstanding issues have been resolved; the solution can then be shipped and/or deployed in a production environment. Many logistic issues are also addressed during this stage including hardware and software allocation, end-user training, and ongoing support and management procedures.

I've just scratched the surface of the MSF Process Model for Application Development. Hopefully, I've provided you with enough information so you can understand how this model was utilized for the IBuyAdventure 2.0 system. In addition to the process model, the Microsoft Solutions Framework also defines additional best practices such as the team structure model, risk management, and change control procedures. Although we won't utilize them during this chapter, I would definitely recommend familiarizing yourself with these best practices so you can begin applying some of them to your projects.

> **If you would like to learn more about the MSF process model, there are several MSF-related white papers and documents available at the http://www.microsoft.com/msf.**

Defining the Requirements (Envisioning)

We have already established a high level vision for the new IBuyAdventure system, now it's time to expand on the vision we've discussed and outline the specific requirements for the new solution. The Microsoft Solutions Framework process model calls this stage of the project the "Envisioning Phase." Whatever you want to call it, requirements gathering and analysis is arguably one of the most important steps in creating an application. A clearly defined set of requirements will guide the design, development, and testing of the solution.

Typically requirements are defined after analyzing existing systems, reviewing manual processes, and interviewing potential users. However, since AdventureWorks is a fictitious organization, we have based the requirements for the IBuyAdventure 2.0 system on a standard set of features and requirements that are found in most typical e-commerce systems.

System requirements are categorized as either Functional Requirements (FRs) or Non-Functional Requirements (NFRs). Functional requirements are useable features of a system such as "User X can do Y", where non-functional requirements are system-wide capabilities or behaviors of the system such as performance, scalability, and availability. Functional requirements are typically satisfied by a particular capability of the technology solution while non-functional requirements are typically addressed by the system architecture of the solution or particular technologies that are used to compose the solution. For this case study, we'll concentrate on the functional requirements of the IBuyAdventure system.

It's important to reiterate that when defining the requirements, we're trying to explicitly list the functionality the system *should* provide, not *how* it will provide the functionality. We'll answer the questions of how the system functions to meet the requirements during the Planning stage.

Functional Requirements

IBuyAdventure was designed to meet the following functional requirements. The functional requirements that were addressed with version 1.0 of the IBuyAdventure system are also included in this list for completeness:

FR1. A consumer customer should be able to browse the IBuyAdventure product catalog by selecting a product category.

> **FR1.1.** A consumer customer should be able to browse the product catalog and view products without logging in or creating a new account.

FR1.2. The system should support an unlimited number of products and categories.

FR1.3. The system should allow a product to be associated with one or more categories.

FR2. A consumer customer should be able to search for specific products within the IBuyAdventure catalog using one of the following methods:

FR2.1. Search for products by keyword (product name or description).

FR2.2. Search for products by Item # or SKU.

FR3. A consumer customer should be able to select a product and view the detailed information for the product including:

FR3.1. Product name.

FR3.2. Product description.

FR3.3. Product picture.

FR3.4. Available inventory.

FR4. A consumer customer should be able to easily access their shopping cart at any time during the shopping session.

FR5. A consumer customer should be able to view a summary of their shopping cart's contents on every page in the system.

FR6. A consumer customer should be able to manage all aspects of their shopping cart including:

FR6.1. Selecting and adding one or more products to their virtual shopping cart for later purchase.

FR6.2. Removing items from their shopping cart.

FR6.3. Changing the quantity for each item in their shopping cart.

FR7. A consumer customer should be able to place an order to purchase the products in their virtual shopping cart.

FR7.1. The system should require the user to login or create a new customer account before placing an order.

FR7.2. A consumer customer will be required to enter credit card information each time the customer places an order.

FR7.3. The system should send an Order Confirmation e-mail to the customer after receiving and saving the order.

FR7.4. The system should display an order summary, including a list of the products on the order and the subtotal, shipping, tax, and grand totals for the order. A consumer customer should then be able to place the order or cancel the order.

FR7.5. A consumer customer should be able to cancel an order at any time before it has been submitted.

FR8. The system should calculate shipping as a base cost of $8.99, plus one dollar for each item above five.

FR9. The system should calculate sales tax for orders that ship to AdventureWorks' home state of Florida.

FR9.1. Tax should be calculated for all products and for all customers. The system does not need to support tax exempt products or customers.

FR10. A consumer customer should be able to login to the system at any time.

FR11. A consumer customer should be able to create a new customer account at any time.

FR11.1. The following information should be captured and stored with a customer account:

FR11.1.1. Contact information (First name, last name, e-mail address, etc.).

FR11.1.2. Billing address.

FR11.1.3. Shipping Address.

FR12. The system should not store credit card information with each customer's account. A consumer customer should be able view their entire past order history including the following information for each order:

FR12.1. Order Number.

FR12.2. Order Date.

FR12.3. Order Status.

FR12.4. Shipped Date.

FR12.5. Order Total.

FR13. The system should display rotating ad banners, advertising products or services available from other organization and/or products available for sale from the IBuyAdventure site.

FR14. Trusted business customers should be able to submit XML-formatted orders electronically.

FR14.1. Business customer accounts will be stored and managed the same way as consumer customer accounts, except that they should not be created from the web site.

FR14.2. The system must support receiving these orders across HTTP.

FR14.3. The order receiving functionality must be exposed as an XML Web Service supporting SOAP and HTTP.

FR15. The system should automatically send electronic orders to the fulfillment provider for processing when an order is placed.

FR15.1. The system should support receiving XML formatted order status update messages from the fulfillment provider.

FR15.2. The system should send the customer an order status update e-mail message whenever the status of an outstanding order changes.

FR16. The system should track the available inventory for each product so the inventory and availability can be displayed to the customer.

FR16.1. The system should allow customers to place orders for products even if they are not currently available.

FR17. The system should send orders to the AdventureWorks ERP system through Microsoft Message Queue when they are placed.

Planning Stage

The key to a successful solution is careful planning. In no situation is this more correct than with the complex transaction processing systems being developed today. In fact, with a fully object-oriented environment such as the .NET Framework, it has become even more critical to carefully architect and design applications to maximize performance, scalability, and reusability. The data model, the data access technology, and the user interface are just a few of the hundreds of specific design issues that must be addressed prior to development. In this section we will discuss the design considerations and decisions made during the Planning stage of the IBuyAdventure 2.0 system.

Phases of the Planning Stage

The Microsoft Solutions Framework Process Model for Application Development divides the planning stage of an application development project into the three sequential phases: the conceptual phase, the logical phase, and the physical phase. These phases are defined as follows:

Conceptual Phase

The **conceptual phase** is the first phase in the planning stage. During the conceptual phase developers or system analysts focus on analyzing the functional requirements and defining how the system will theoretically function to satisfy the requirements. This involves defining the roles of the users that will be interacting with the system and the processes or activities they can perform within the system. Although much of this information could be found from reading the functional requirements, by explicitly mapping the roles of users to their activities, it is easier to identify commonalities in the system and potential opportunities for reuse.

Logical Phase

The second phase in the planning stage is the **logical phase**. During the logical phase developers or technical architects map the activities or processes defined in the conceptual design into logical classes or components responsible for providing the required functionality. Developers typically divide the system into three or more logical segments or tiers. This type of architecture is appropriately called three-tier or *n*-tier architecture. The logical phase is also the point in the design process where the database architect designs the data model, including the data structures, data integrity rules, and data access techniques.

Physical Phase

During the final phase of the planning stage, the **physical phase**, developers and system architects focus on defining the physical and technology-specific attributes of the system. For three-tier or n-tier architectures this often involves mapping the logical tiers to the physical machines that will host the software components that compose each tier.

While the conceptual and logical design phases focus on the features and functionality of the solution, the physical phase addresses many of the non-functional requirements such as availability, security, and manageability.

UML and Visual Studio .NET Enterprise Architect Edition

Throughout this design/planning process of the IBuyAdventure 2.0, we utilized the Unified Modeling Language and Visual Studio .NET EnterpriseArchitect edition to conceptualize, architect, and design the IBuyAdventure 2.0 system. The Unified Modeling Language (UML) is a widely adopted industry standard for graphically diagramming virtually every aspect of a software systems design. It is used to create sophisticated diagrams that visually define and document the architecture, behavior, functionality, and implementation details of a software system. Some of the more common UML diagrams include: Use Case diagrams, which illustrate the roles of users and the activities they perform in the system, Class diagrams, which define the interactions and relationships between logical classes, and Component diagrams, which map the software components to a physical architecture. By documenting a software design using UML diagrams, system architects can more effectively communicate information about the design with project team members.

Visual Studio .NET Enterprise Architect edition is the newest edition in the Visual Studio product family. It provides an integrated set of design and architecture tools including a rich set of visual diagramming tools for software and database modeling. The software modeling tools combine the flexible freeform diagramming capabilities of Visio and full support for the Unified Modeling Language 1.2 specification. The database modelling tools allow architects to create entity relationship diagrams (ERDs) and perform roundtrip engineering so the actual data structure and the ERD diagram are always in sync.

The next sections of this chapter detail the conceptual, logical, and physical design phases of the IBuyAdventure 2.0 system. During these phases we will utilize Visual Studio .NET Architect Edition and the Universal Modeling Language extensively to visually illustrate the design of the new system. After the Planning stage has been completed, the development process will simply involve executing the design and architecture decisions made during this stage.

Conceptual Design

During the conceptual design phase developers or analysts concentrate on defining how the system will conceptually work to solve the requirements, without focusing on which technologies will be utilized. The conceptual design phase is an important step in a system's design that many developers and architects tend to overlook. However, the conceptual design phase can be very beneficial by helping you identify potential challenges with a solution before investing too much time in the wrong direction or with wrong technologies.

For the IBuyAdventure 2.0 system, during the conceptual design phase we analyzed the functional requirements and from these requirements we derived a set of UML Use Case diagrams. A Use Case diagram graphically define the roles of the users, called *actors*, that will be interacting with the system and the activities or ***use cases*** that they will perform. By representing the functional requirements as Use Cases, you are forced into thinking about the system from the user's perspective. Thinking of the system in terms of actors and activities also allows you to identify commonalities between different types of users and activities, and therefore identify opportunities for reuse earlier in the design.

IBuyAdventure Use Cases

After reviewing the functional requirements, it is fairly clear that the IBuyAdventure version 2.0 system will be utilized by two types of users: consumers, who select products and place orders at the IBuyAdventure web site, and business customers, who submit electronic orders from their own electronic procurement applications. As a result, during the conceptual design we defined two sets of Use Case diagrams – one for each type of customer. Let's discuss each of these Use Case Diagrams and the activities they define.

Consumer Use Cases

In the IBuyAdventure system a consumer is an individual who would visit the IBuyAdventure site to find and purchase climbing equipment and other adventure products. The following Use Case diagram illustrates the high-level activities or use cases that can be performed by a consumer customer within the IBuyAdventure system:

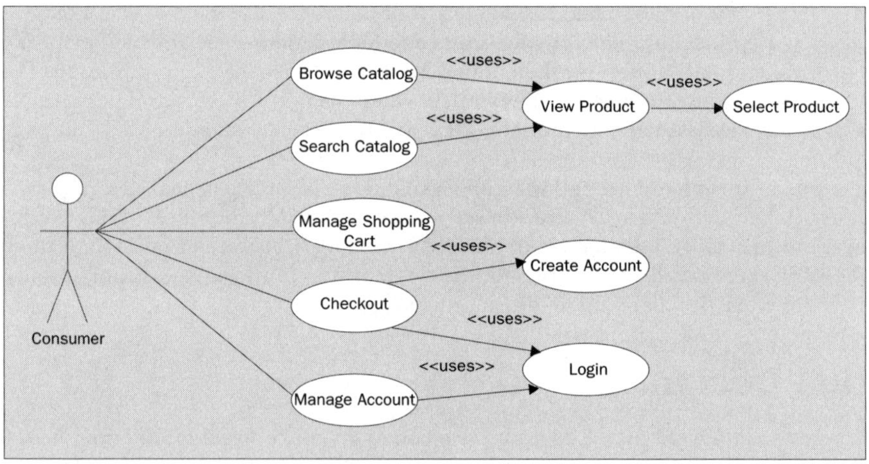

Each of the use cases illustrated in this diagram corresponds to functional requirements that we defined for consumer customers in the IBuyAdventure system. These use cases are defined as follows:

Browse Catalog

A consumer customer can view and select products by either browsing through the product catalog or searching for a specific product. When the user browses the product catalog they navigate through the hierarchy of product categories and view a list of products belonging to each category.

View Product

Once a consumer customer finds a product, either by browsing through the product catalog or by performing a search, they can view all of the information about a product including the product's name, long description, picture, and list price.

Select Product

When viewing a product, a consumer customer can select the product for purchase by adding it to their virtual shopping cart.

Search Catalog

A consumer customer can also view and select products by searching for a particular product within the product catalog. The user can entire a variety of criteria including the product name, description, or SKU number and a list of products matching the search criteria will be displayed. If no products match the customer's search criteria then a friendly warning message will be displayed.

Manage Shopping Cart

A consumer customer can view all of the items in their virtual shopping cart and delete or update the quantities for each item. When the customer removes an item or changes the quantity of an item, the system recalculates the extended price and subtotal for the order. If the customer's shopping cart is empty, they will be displayed a friendly warning message. The consumer customer can manage their shopping cart without first logging into the system because the shopping cart is not associated with a customer account.

Checkout

After reviewing and managing their shopping cart, a consumer customer can then perform the checkout process and place an order for the products they selected. If the user has not already logged into the IBuyAdventure site, they will be asked to do so or create a new account, before proceeding with the checkout process. After logging in or creating a new account, the customer will be required to enter their credit card information including their credit card number, expiration date, card type, and name on the card.

Next, the customer can review the details of their order and submit it or cancel the checkout process. When reviewing the order, the customer will be able to view all of the items on their order including the SKU, product name, description, quantity, unit price, and extended price for each item. The customer can also view the subtotal for the items and the shipping, tax, and grand totals for the order. If the customer chooses to submit the order, it will be saved in the IBuyAdventure system and the customer will be displayed a confirmation indicating that their order has been received. At this time, an Order Confirmation e-mail, containing the summary of the order, is sent to the customer's e-mail address.

Login

If a consumer customer attempts to place an order or access their past order history, they will automatically be prompted to login to the IBuyAdventure site. Users can also login at any time during their shopping session. Logging into the site involves entering the e-mail address and password combination that they specified when they created the customer account. If the customer enters the correct e-mail address and password combination, they will be redirected to the portion of the system they were attempting to access. However, if they enter an invalid combination, they will be asked to login again. If the user does not have a customer account, they can create a new one.

Create Account

If a user has not previously created a customer account, they will be required to do so before placing an order. When a user creates a customer account they must enter their name and contact information and their billing and shipping addresses. After creating a new account, the user can return to the IBuyAdventure system and login using the e-mail address and password combination they specified.

Manage Account

After logging into the IBuyAdventure system or creating a new account, the user can manage their customer account. The account management functionality in the IBuyAdventure 2.0 system is limited to viewing past order history.

Business Customer Use Cases

The activities performed by a business customer in the IBuyAdventure system are much simpler than a consumer customer. This is primarily due to the fact that business customers don't interact with the system through a user interface. Instead business customers utilize their own client applications, which integrate with the Web Services provided by the IBuyAdventure system. The following UML Use Case diagram illustrates the activities performed by a business customer in the IBuyAdventure system:

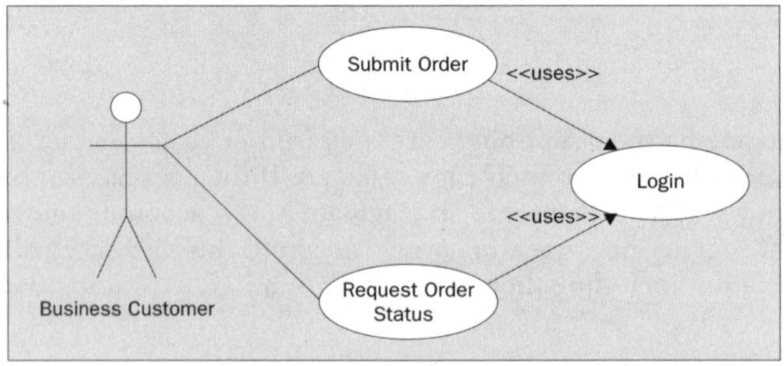

The use cases illustrated in this diagram are defined as follows:

Submit Order

The primary activity performed by a business customer involves submitting an electronic XML formatted order. The order contains the equivalent information to what is collected during the Checkout process for a consumer customer. When a business customer submits an order they also must provide their primary contact's e-mail address and password information for logging into the system.

Login

The login activity is a portion of the submit order process for a business customer. Unlike the login process for a consumer customer, the business customer login is performed without user intervention, by simply passing credential information to the Web Services that receive and process orders.

Request Order Status

After a business customer has submitted an order to the IBuyAdventure system, they can periodically request the status for the order. When a business customer requests the status for an order they are also required to provide their primary contact's e-mail address and password so they can first be authenticated.

IBuyAdventure Sequence & Activity Diagrams

After defining the activities that can be performed in the system by end users, it can be beneficial to conceptually design some of the behind-the-scenes business processes. This is especially true when designing complex, distributed transaction processing systems. UML Sequence and Activity diagrams are ideal for visually modeling complex, transactional business processes. UML Sequence diagrams illustrate the sequence of events or method calls between actors and/or classes in a system, while Activity diagrams show the workflow of tasks within an activity. Activity diagrams are typically used in conjunction with Use Case diagrams to capture the details of a particular activity.

The following UML Sequence diagram illustrates the high-level sequence of events that occur in the IBuyAdventure system during the lifetime of an order:

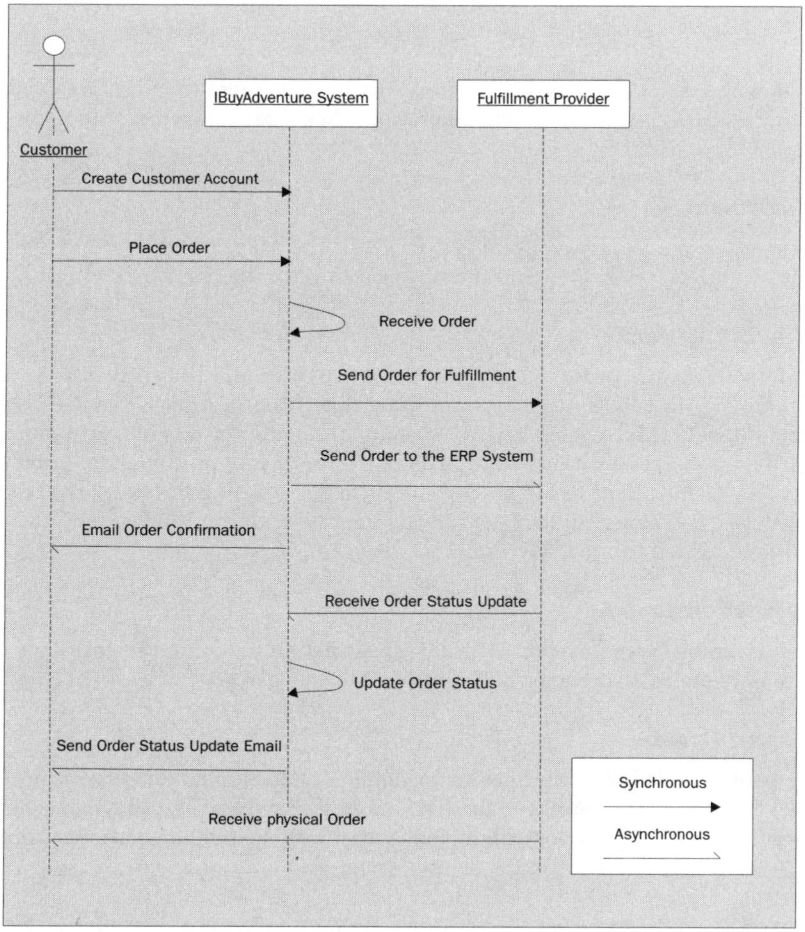

Although this diagram depicts only a single type of customer, the only differences between a consumer and business customer in this process is the first interaction.

Let's briefly discuss each of the interactions illustrated in this diagram:

Create Customer Account or Customer Login

Before they can place orders, consumer customers are required to create a customer account or login to the IBuyAdventure system using their existing customer account. From the end user's perspective, creating a new account simply involves entering their contact and address information and telling the system to save the information. Business customers do not need to create customer accounts from the system, but they will login when submitting electronic orders by providing their authentication information with an order.

Place Order

After creating an account, the customer can then place an order for the products they wish to purchase. A consumer customer places an order from the IBuyAdventure web site, while business customers submit electronic orders containing all of the order information.

Receive Order

Regardless of how the order was placed, the IBuyAdventure system then receives and processes the order. Processing an order involves several operations. We'll discuss some of these operations later in this chapter.

Send Order to Fulfillment

After saving the order, the IBuyAdventure system sends the order information to the fulfillment services provider so they can pick, pack, and ship the physical order to the customer.

Send Order to the ERP System

In addition to forwarding the order to the Fulfillment provider, the IBuyAdventure system also sends an order to AdventureWorks ERP system by submitting the order information as the body of a Microsoft Message Queue (MSMQ) Message. The ERP system automatically receives any submitted orders and imports them. The only responsibility of the IBuyAdventure system is to ensure that the order is formatted as an XML document in the proper structure and sending the order to the pre-determined queue. Send Microsoft Message Queue is used to integrate with the ERP system; this process is asynchronous, as indicated in the UML sequence diagram.

Send Order Confirmation E-mail

Next, the IBuyAdventure system sends an order confirmation e-mail to the customer who placed the order. This e-mail contains a summary of the order that was placed.

Receive Order Status Update

Sometime after receiving the order information for fulfillment, the fulfillment services provider sends an electronic Order Status Update message to the IBuyAdventure system. The IBuyAdventure system receives and processes the Order Status Update without interacting with the fulfillment services provider.

Update Order Status

The IBuyAdventure system updates the status of an order and updates inventory information when processing the Order Status Update message from the fulfillment services provider.

Send Order Status Update E-mail

The final task performed by the IBuyAdventure system during the lifetime of an order, involves sending an e-mail message to the customer. The Order Status Update e-mail message is sent immediately after the system receives an Order Status Update from the fulfillment provider. This e-mail contains information describing the latest status of the order.

Receive Physical Order

Finally, the customer receives the physical products they ordered. The physical order is sent directly from the fulfillment services provider to the end customer.

Logical Design

The next phase in the Planning stage is the logical design phase. During the logical design phase of the IBuyAdventure 2.0 system, the activities and processes identified in the conceptual design were mapped to a data model and a set of logical classes responsible for providing the desired functionality. We also defined the behaviors or methods and the attributes or properties of each class, as well as the relationships between classes.

The IBuyAdventure 2.0 system utilizes a three-tier logical architecture. Three-tier or n-tier architecture divides an application into three or more logical layers or *tiers*. The classes defined during the logical design phase were assigned to the appropriate tier, based on the type of functionality they provide. Everyone seems to have a different name for each tier in the fundamental three-tier architecture. However, for the IBuyAdventure 2.0 system, these three tiers were defined as follows:

User Services

The **User Services tier**, sometimes refered to as the **Presentation Services**, is the endpoint of the application with which the user interacts. The User Services tier typically consists of a Win32 or Browser-based Graphical User Interface (GUI) application that allows users to view, input, and manipulate data. From the user's perspective, the User Services tier *is* the entire application. However, in a three-tier or *n*-tier architecture, the User Services tier only performs user interface related tasks, such as simple data formatting and validation, while relying on the Business Services tier for executing transactions, applying business rules, and retrieving data. In the IBuyAdventure 2.0 system, the User Services tier will consist of ASP.NET Web Forms that allow consumer customers to browse and search for products, add products to their shopping basket, and place orders.

Business Services / Business Logic Layer

The Business Services tier, also referred to as the **middle tier** or the **Application Services** tier, is responsible for encapsulating transaction processing, business rules, data access, and any other core application logic. The Business Services tier efffectively serves as a bridge between the front end User Services tier and the backend Data Services and Data Store. In the IBuyAdventure 2.0 system, the Business Services tier will consist of both transactional and non-transactional .NET Serviced Components that execute within Windows Component Services (COM+). The Business Services tier will also contain ASP.NET Web Services that expose business processes, such as placing orders and checking product availability. These Web Services will be consumed by remote applications operated by AdventureWorks business customers and trading partners.

Data Services / Data Access Layer

The Data Services tier is responsible for retrieving and manipulating data stored in one or more data stores. By separating data access and manipulation into a separate logical tier, the Business Services tier is abstracted from the details of the underlying data store. The Data Services tier is typically implemented as either a layer of compiled components or data source specific interfaces such as Store Procedures, Triggers and/or Views. In the IBuyAdventure 2.0 system, the Data Services tier will be implemented as a set of stored procedures that encapsulate the SQL data access logic and return Resultsets to the Business Service components. The Business Service components will always access and manipulate data in the IBuyAdventure database through these stored procedures.

Although not generally considered a part of the three-tier architecture, the logical architecture for the IBuyAdventure system also includes the data store itself. The data store will be implemented as a SQL Server 2000 relational database named IBuyAdventure and will be responsible for data storage, retrieval, data integrity, and transaction participation.

The following diagram illustrates the logical architecture of the IBuyAdventure system and the relationship between each of these tiers:

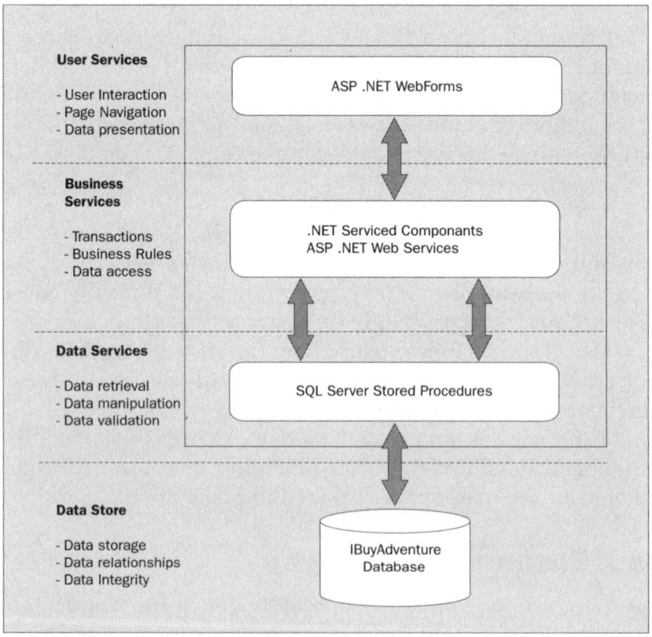

It's important to understand that the three-tier and *n*-tier application models are logical and not physical. The three tiers of the IBuyAdventure system do not necessarily correspond to separate physical machines. Instead they simply represent separate, logical sections of the application. We'll discuss the technology requirements and constraints for the physical architecture of the IBuyAdventure system during the physical design phase.

Let's continue our discussion of the IBuyAdventure 2.0 logical architecture by analyzing the design of the new data model. Once the data model has been defined, we will discuss each tier of the IBuyAdventure system architecture and the classes that compose each tier.

Data Model

The IBuyAdventure 2.0 system will utilize a single database, appropriately named IBuyAdventure, to store all of the data related to the system including the product catalog, inventory information, customer accounts, and orders. The primary goal when designing the new IBuyAdventure data model was to architect a relational database that could process transactions efficiently while remaining simplistic for application development. This goal required us to find a careful balance between database normalization, optimization, and simplicity.

The following Entity Relationship Diagram (ERD) defines the tables or **entities** in the new IBuyAdventure 2.0 database and the relationships between each table:

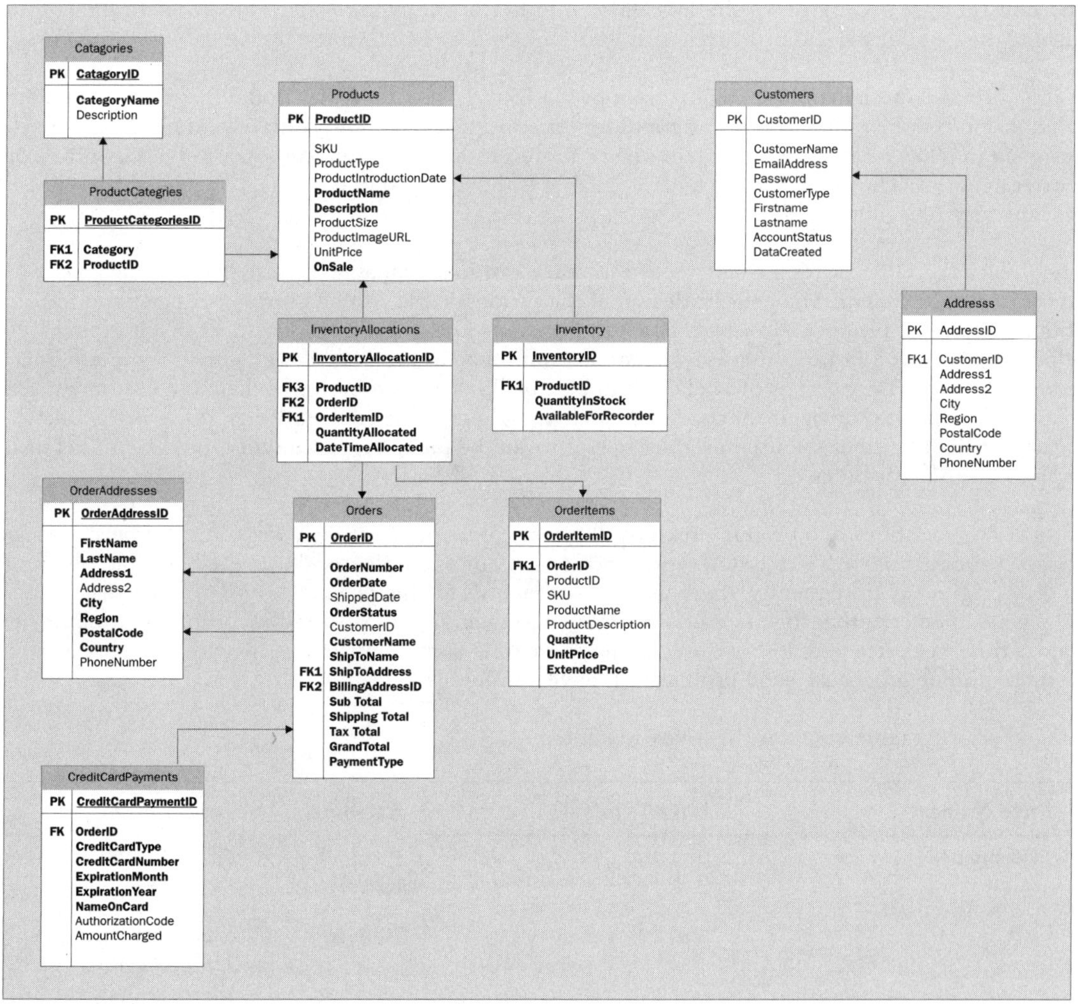

The IBuyAdventure tables can be grouped into four logical categories based on their functionality:

- ❑ Product Catalog Tables

- Customer Account Tables
- Order Processing Tables
- Inventory Management Tables

Let's discuss each of these categories and examine each of the table structures in the IBuyAdventure data model in further detail. The complete data model, including table definitions, referential integrity rules, and a set of sample data is included with the code download for this chapter.

Product Catalog Tables

The product catalog tables are responsible for storing information about the products available for sale and how they are organized within the catalog on the IBuyAdventure site. The product catalog tables include the `Products`, `Categories`, and `ProductCategories` tables.

It's important to notice in the ERD diagram of the IBuyAdventure Data Model that there isn't a direct relationship between the `Categories` and the `Products` tables. The IBuyAdventure data model was designed to allow a category to contain one or more products and for a product to belong to one or more categories. The `ProductCategories` table is the joining table in this many-to-many relationship of categories to products.

The `Products` table stores a single record for each product available for sale through the IBuyAdventure system. The generic design of the product table can be used to store general information about any type of product. However, in some situations it may be necessary to store additional information about a product that is specific to certain type of product. For example, we might decide to store and display the number of pockets with backpacks. The number of pockets is a custom attribute that doesn't apply to other products in the catalog. Although our current design does not facilitate custom attributes, other than the product size, it would be fairly easy to modify the data model design to support custom attributes.

If there are variations of a product, such as different colors or sizes, each variation will be stored as a separate product record with a different `ProductID`. For example, the "Starlight" tent can be purchased in grey or green. Consequently, there will be two records for the product – one product record for the grey version and another for the green model. Since each variant is stored as a separate product, it can have a different price and description. Furthermore, this approach reduces the risk of errors occurring during fulfillment because each product will have a different `ProductID`.

This `Products` table contains the following columns:

Field Name	Data Type	Attributes	Description
`ProductID`	`UniqueIdentifier`	Primary Key	Identifier for a product record
`SKU`	`nvarchar(10)`	Required	Stock Keeping Unit (SKU), short identifier for a product

Field Name	Data Type	Attributes	Description
`ProductType`	`nvarchar(20)`		General type of product
`ProductIntroduction Date`	`smalldatetime`		Date when the product was first introduced
`ProductName`	`nvarchar(50)`	Required	Name of the product
`Description`	`nvarchar(255)`	Required	Description of the product
`ProductSize`	`nvarchar(5)`		The size of the product, if applicable
`ProductImageURL`	`nvarchar(255)`		Filename and/or relative path to a product image file
`UnitPrice`	`money`	Required	Price for one unit of the product
`OnSale`	`bit`	Required	Flag indicating whether or not the product is on sale

The `Categories` table stores a single record for each category defined in the IBuyAdventure product catalog. This table contains the following columns:

Field Type	Data Type	Attributes	Description
`CategoryID`	`UniqueIdentifier`	Primary Key	Identifier for a category record
`CategoryName`	`nvarchar(10)`	Required	Name of the category
`Description`	`nvarchar(50)`		Description of the category

The `ProductCategories` table stores a single record for each product and category association. This table contains the following columns:

Field Type	Data Type	Attributes	Description
ProductCategoryID	UniqueIdentifier	Primary Key	Identifier for a ProductCategory record
CategoryID	UniqueIdentifier	Required: Foreign Key to Categories	The category the product is associated with
ProductID	UniqueIdentifier	Required: Foreign Key to Products	The product associated with the category

Customer Account Tables

The customer account tables are responsible for storing information for both consumer and business customers. The information stored in these tables includes basic demographic information such as the customer's name, address, and phone number, as well as login information such as the customer's user name and password. The customer account tables include the Customers and Addresses tables.

The Customers table stores a single record for each customer who has registered and can place orders through the IBuyAdventure system. This table contains the following columns:

Field Type	Data Type	Attributes	Description
CustomerID	Unique Identifier	Primary Key	Identifier for a customer record
CustomerName	nvarchar(50)	Required	First and last name of a consumer or the name of an organization for business customers
E-mailAddress	nvarchar(50)	Required	Primary e-mail address
Password	nvarchar(20)	Required	Password used for login
CustomerType	int	Required	Type of customer as either Consumer (1) or Business(2)
FirstName	nvarchar(50)	Required	First name of a consumer customer or the first name of a primary contact for a business customer
LastName	nvarchar(50)	Required	Last name of a consumer customer or the last name of a primary contact for a business customer

Field Type	Data Type	Attributes	Description
`AccountStatus`	`Int`	Required	Status of the customer's account as either active (1) or disabled (2)
`DateCreated`	`Datetime`	Required	Full date and time when the customer record was created

The `Addresses` table stores a single record for each of a customer's addresses. By separating address information from the `Customers` table into a separate table, the IBuyAdventure data model design can store multiple addresses for a single customer. Although the IBuyAdventure system does not support international orders, we purposely used generic column names and also included a column to store the country of the address:

Field Type	Data Type	Attributes	Description
`AddressID`	`Unique Identifier`	Primary Key	Identifier for an `Address` record
`CustomerID`	`Unique Identifier`	Required: Foreign Key to `Customers` table	Associates an `Address` record with a `Customer` record
`Address1`	`nvarchar(50)`	Required	First line of the address
`Address2`	`nvarchar(50)`		Second line of the address
`City`	`nvarchar(30)`	Required	City for the address
`Region`	`nvarchar(30)`	Required	State/Region for the address
`PostalCode`	`nvarchar(20)`	Required	PostalCode for the address
`Country`	`nvarchar(30)`	Required	Country name for the address
`PhoneNumber`	`nchar(15)`		Phone number associated with the address

Order Processing Tables

The order processing tables are responsible for storing all of the information for an order processed by the IBuyAdventure system. Orders originating from both consumer and business customers are stored in the same set of tables. The order processing tables include the `Orders`, `OrderItems`, `OrderAddresses`, and `CreditCardPayments` tables.

The `Orders` table stores a single record containing the general information for each order in the IBuyAdventure system. The `Orders` table can be thought of as the master or header record with all of the other order processing tables storing the child or detail records. The primary key of the `Orders` table, the `OrderID` column, is used to associate records in the other order processing tables back to the root order. The `Orders` table contains the following columns:

Field Type	Data Type	Attributes	Description
`OrderID`	`Unique Identifier`	Primary Key	Identifier for an `Order` record
`OrderNumber`	`nvarchar(40)`	Required	Formatted text and numeric identifier for an order
`OrderDate`	`datetime`	Required	Full date and time when the order was received
`ShippedDate`	`datetime`		Full date and time when the order was shipped
`OrderStatus`	`int`	Required	Status of the order as either: 1 – Received 2 – Processing 3 – Shipped
`CustomerID`	`Unique Identifier`		Identifier of the customer who placed the order
`CustomerName`	`nvarchar(50)`	Required	First and last name of a consumer or the name of an organization for business customers
`ShipToName`	`nvarchar(40)`	Required	Full name of the shipping recipient
`ShipToAddressID`	`Unique Identifier`	Required: Foreign Key to `OrderAddresses`	Identifier of the `OrderAddress` record containing the shipping address
`BillingAddress ID`	`Unique Identifier`	Required; Foreign Key to `OrderAddresses`	Identifier of the `OrderAddress` record containing the billing address

Field Type	Data Type	Attributes	Description
SubTotal	Money	Required	Subtotal of the order before shipping, handling, and tax
ShippingTotal	Money	Required	Total shipping costs
HandlingTotal	Money	Required	Total handling costs
TaxTotal	Money	Required	Total calculated tax or 0 if tax is not required
GrandTotal	Money	Required	Total including subtotal of items, shipping, handling, and tax
PaymentType	int	Required	Type of payment as either credit card (1) or on account (2)

The `OrderItems` table stores a single record for each line item on an order. Consequently, there is a one-to-many relationship between the `Orders` and `OrderItems` table on the `OrderID` column contained in both tables. The `OrderItems` table contains the following columns:

Field Type	Data Type	Attributes	Description
OrderItemID	Unique Identifier	Primary Key	Identifier for an `OrderItem` record
OrderID	Unique Identifier	Required; Foreign Key to the `Orders` table	Identifier for a `Order` record to associate an `OrderItem` with its parent `Order`
ProductID	Unique Identifier	Required	Identifier for the `Product` record that indicates which product was ordered
SKU	nvarchar(10)	Required	Short text identifier for the product that was ordered
ProductName	nvarchar(50)	Required	Name of the product that was ordered
Product Description	nvarchar(255)		Description of the product that was ordered

Table continued on following page

Field Type	Data Type	Attributes	Description
Quantity	int	Required	Quantity of the product ordered
UnitPrice	money	Required	Unit price of the product ordered
ExtendedPrice	money	Required	Extended price (Unit price * quantity) of the product ordered

The OrderAddresses table stores information for the address(s) associated with an order. There is a one-to-many relationship between the Orders and OrderAddresses tables. This relationship is implemented on the ShipToAddressID and BillToAddressID columns of the Orders table to the OrderAddressID primary key column in the OrderAddresses table.

It is very common for an order to have the same billing address and shipping address. In this situation there would only need to be a single record in the OrderAddresses table, and the record could be referenced by both the ShipToAddressID and the BillToAddressID columns of the Orders table. The OrderAddresses table contains the following columns:

Field Type	Data Type	Attributes	Description
OrderAddress ID	Unique Identifier	Primary Key	Identifier for a OrderAddress record
FirstName	nvarchar(50)	Required	First name for the address
LastName	nvarchar(50)	Required	Last name for the address
Address1	nvarchar(50)	Required	First line of the address
Address2	nvarchar(30)		Second line of the address
City	nvarchar(30)	Required	City for the address
Region	nvarchar(30)	Required	State/Region for the address
PostalCode	nvarchar(20)	Required	PostalCode for the address
Country	nvarchar(50)	Required	Country name for the address
PhoneNumber	char(15)		Phone number associated with the address

The CreditCardPayments table stores payment information for orders placed using a credit card. The credit card information is stored in a separate table instead of as columns of the Orders table because a credit card is not always used as the payment method for an order. Business customers can place an order on an account based on their available credit limit, in which case a record in the CreditCardPayments table would not be created. By separating credit card information into a separate table, the IBuyAdventure Data Model design also facilitates multiple credit cards per order, should this become a future requirement of the IBuyAdventure system. The CreditCardPayments table contains the following columns:

Field Type	Data Type	Attributes	Description
CreditCardPayment ID	Unique Identifier	Primary Key	Identifier for an CreditCardPayment record
OrderID	Unique Identifier	Primary Key: Foreign Key to Orders table	Identifier for an Order record
CreditCardType	nvarchar(30)	Required	Type of credit card
CreditCardNumber	nvarchar(20)	Required	Credit card number
ExpirationMonth	int	Required	Month the credit card expires
ExpirationYear	int	Required	Year the credit card expires
NameOnCard	nvarchar(50)	Required	Full name on the credit card
AuthorizationCode	nvarchar(50)	Required	Credit card pre-authorization code returned from authorization service
AmountCharged	money	Required	Amount charged to the credit card

Inventory Management Tables

The inventory management tables are responsible for storing data used to track and manage the product inventory. In the IBuyAdventure system, the inventory for a particular product is impacted when orders are placed and when an order is shipped by the fulfillment provider. The inventory management tables include the Inventory and InventoryAllocations tables.

The Inventory table stores a single record with the inventory information for each product available for sale in the IBuyAdventure system. The ProductID column in the Inventory table corresponds to the ProductID primary key in the Products table. The QuantityInStock column, which stores the available quantity of a product, is decremented when the fulfillment provider ships an order. Since there is a one-to-one relationship between the Products and Inventory table, we could utilize the ProductID as the primary key for the Inventory table, but we'll define a separate UniqueIdentifier key for consistency with the rest of our data model design.

The `Inventory` table contains the following columns:

Field Type	Data Type	Attributes	Description
`InventoryID`	`Unique Identifier`	Primary Key	Identifier for an `Inventory` record
`ProductID`	`Unique Identifier`	Required: Foreign Key to `Products` table	Identifier for the `Product` record that associates a product with its inventory
`QuantityInStock`	`int`	Required	The quantity available for the product
`AvailableFor Reorder`	`bit`	Required	Indicates whether the product is available for reorder

The `InventoryAllocations` table stores a single record for each line item on an order. This table is used to track the allocated or reserved inventory for outstanding orders that have not been shipped. Records are inserted into this table when the IBuyAdventure system processes orders. As orders are shipped, their corresponding records in the `InventoryAllocations` table are deleted and the `QuantityInStock` in the `Inventory` table is decremented for each product on the order. Consequently, the available inventory for a product can always be calculated by subtracting the `QuantityInStock` from the `Inventory` table for the product from the total `QuantityAllocated` in the `InventoryAllocations` table for the same product.

This table contains the following columns:

Field Name	Data Type	Attributes	Description
`InventoryAllocation ID`	`Unique Identifier`	Primary Key	Identifier for an `InventoryAllocation` record
`ProductID`	`Unique Identifier`	Required; Foreign Key to `Products` table	Identifier for the `Product` record that indicates which product inventory was allocated for
`OrderID`	`Unique Identifier`	Required: Foreign Key to `Orders` table	Identifier for the `Order` record that caused this inventory to be reserved

Field Name	Data Type	Attributes	Description
`OrderItemID`	`Unique Identifier`	Required: Foreign Key to `OrderItems` table	Identifier for the `OrderItem` record that caused this inventory to be reserved
`QuantityAllocated`	`int`	Required	The quantity that was allocated by the `Order` and `OrderItem`
`DateTimeAllocated`	`datetime`	Required	The date and time when the `InventoryAllocation` record was created

Design Issues

Now that you are familiar with the new data model for the IBuyAdventure database, let's briefly discuss some of the design decisions we made when deriving the data model and the impact of those decisions.

Managing Transactional Data

You might have noticed in the IBuyAdventure data model that some of the product and customer information is stored in two different sets of tables. Addresses, for example, are stored in both the `Addresses` and `OrderAddresses` tables. Another example is the product information found in both the `Products` and `OrderItems` tables. Although this design violates database normalization rules, it does so for a very good reason. When working with transactional data such as orders it is often necessary to store a complete snapshot of any related data at the time the transaction occurred. By storing a copy of all necessary data used within a transaction we eliminate the risk that the original data is inadvertently changed or deleted. For example, if an order simply referenced to the customer's address stored in the `Addresses` table and the customer changed their address, every order that referenced to the address would also be inadvertently changed.

In some situations we do wish to maintain values that reference to non-transactional records for reporting and historical data analysis purposes. For example, the `Orders` table contains a `CustomerID` field that stores the unique identifier of the customer who placed the order, which corresponds to the primary key of the `Customers` table. However, to avoid some of the challenges we just discussed, we are not using SQL Server's declarative referential integrity to enforce integrity for inserts and updates in these situations and the `CustomerID` field in the `Orders` table does not require a value.

Transactions and the Inventory Management Tables

In the IBuyAdventure data model, the `Inventory` and `InventoryAllocations` tables are a great example of how the impact of transactions should be carefully considered during the design of the data model. To understand how these tables work together to optimize order processing, let's briefly walk through the process in which they are used:

- Firstly, when an order is placed in the IBuyAdventure system, records are inserted into the `InventoryAllocations` table to allocate or reserve inventory for the products on the order.

- Next, when the system receives an `OrderStatusUpdate` message from the fullfilment provider indicating the order has shipped, the system decrements the `QuantityInStock` in the `Inventory` table and deletes the corresponding `InventoryAllocation` records for the same product and order.
- The available inventory for a particular product is calculated by subtracting the `QuantityInStock` value for the product record in the `Inventory` table from the total quantity allocated for the product, or the sum of the quantity allocated for the product from the `InventoryAllocations` table.

The following diagram illustrates the operations involved to the `Inventory` and `InventoryAllocations` tables for reading product inventory and executing create order and order status update transactions:

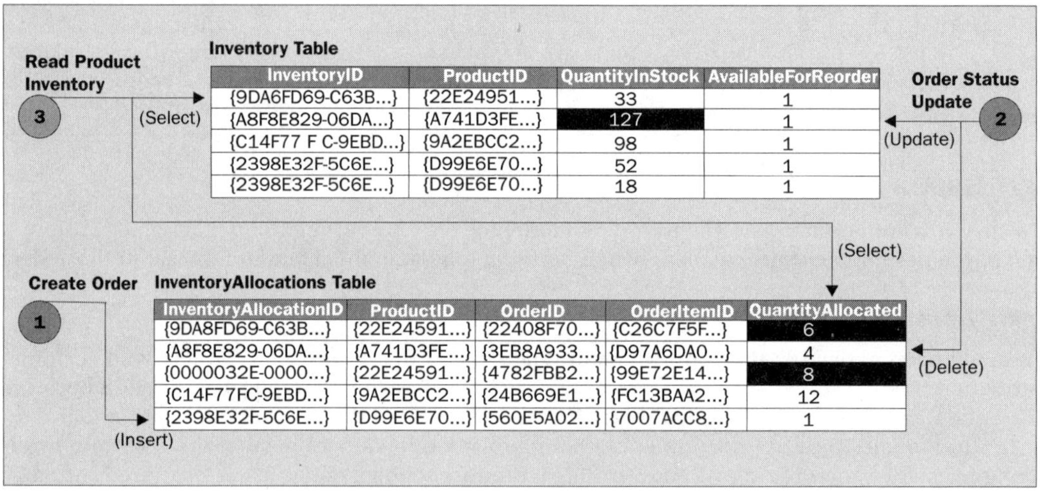

We took this approach of allocating and deallocating inventory with the `InventoryAllocations` table instead of simply decrementing the quantity in stock for each order when an order is created, because it allows the system to process far more transactions without creating a database bottleneck. Multiple create order transactions can be processed concurrently because `InventoryAllocation` records are inserted independently to reserve inventory. If we had utilized a single row to maintain the inventory level we would have created a situation where a create order transaction would hold an exclusive lock on an `Inventory` record for each product on the order. Consequently, orders containing the same products would be executed sequentially.

Since there is a one-to-one relationship between records in the `Products` table and the `Inventory` table, the fields in the `Inventory` table could have logically been included in the `Products` table, while still utilizing the allocation and deallocation technique for managing inventory. However, by separating the inventory-specific information into the separate `Inventory` table we can improve the performance of the product catalog. Product information can be retrieved without being blocked by transactions updating the `UnitsInStock` for a product when an order has shipped. Additionally, since product information does not frequently change, the data in the `Products` table can be cached by the business services or the user services tier to further optimize performance.

UniqueIdentifier Datatypes for Keys

In the IBuyAdventure data model, every table has a primary key consisting of a single `UniqueIdentifier` column. Although the integer data type would have been smaller to store and would have yielded better performance, especially in Joins, we decided to use the `UniqueIdentifier` data type for the primary key columns because it provides significant programming flexibility and extensibility. Since `UniqueIdentifiers`, also known as GUIDs, are guaranteed to always be unique, there's no need to query the database after inserting a record to determine the value of the primary key. Instead applications can simply generate a new GUID value and supply the value when inserting records. For example, when saving an order to the IBuyAdventure database, the application can generate a new GUID value for the `OrderID` and provide the value when inserting a record into the `Orders` table. Since the value is a GUID, it is guaranteed to be unique regardless of the number of concurrent transactions or any other factors, its not necessary to query the `Orders` table to get the value of the primary key. When the application inserts records into the `OrderItems` and `OrderAddresses` tables for the items and addresses on the order, the application can simply use the `OrderID` that it generated when inserting the order.

Now consider the situation where you need to change your application to take advantage of queued processing. When using `UniqueIdentifiers` as primary keys, an application can generate a new `OrderID`, write the entire order information to an MSMQ message, and continue on with its work assuming that the `Order` will be created with the new `OrderID`. However, if you were using a column with the Identity property or some other type of incremental counter, the database would have to validate its uniqueness.

Shared Services

Before we discuss each tier of the IBuyAdventure system's logical architecture, we need to define some of the common classes that are used across multiple tiers. The shared classes in the IBuyAdventure system include business objects and typed ADO.NET Datasets used to manage in-memory data, as well as re-usable utility classes that provide generic functionality that is not specific to any one tier. Typically these classes are identified when defining the classes that compose the User Services or Business Services tier. However, we'll identify and discuss the shared classes now so you are familiar with their functionality when we design the classes in the other tiers.

Business Objects

In the IBuyAdventure system we will create several business objects that represent data structures such as an `Order` or `Customer`. These business objects effectively serve as object-based wrappers on top of a data structure. They maintain data as state in instance variables and implement properties and methods for working with the data. For example, our `Order` business object encapsulates all of the data related to an order, including the order number, the order date, and the items on the order, and exposes the data through properties and methods.

Business objects are not to be confused with business services classes, which are responsible for processing transactions, applying business rules, and accessing and manipulating data in the data store through the data services tier.

By encapsulating data in business objects, we can easily pass structured data between classes and tiers. With Visual Basic .NET it is now possible to create objects that can be serialized to a data stream and passed by value across application domain, thread, process, or even machine boundaries. When an object is passed by value, an exact copy of the object and its contained data is re-created at the destination process. Objects that support serialization can also be persisted as files, stored in databases, or stored as a value in other objects such as ASP.NET's `Session` or `Application` objects. We'll discuss how to create serializable business objects and use them in this capacity a little later in this chapter.

The following UML class diagram illustrates the common business objects used in the IBuyAdventure system and the relationships between the classes:

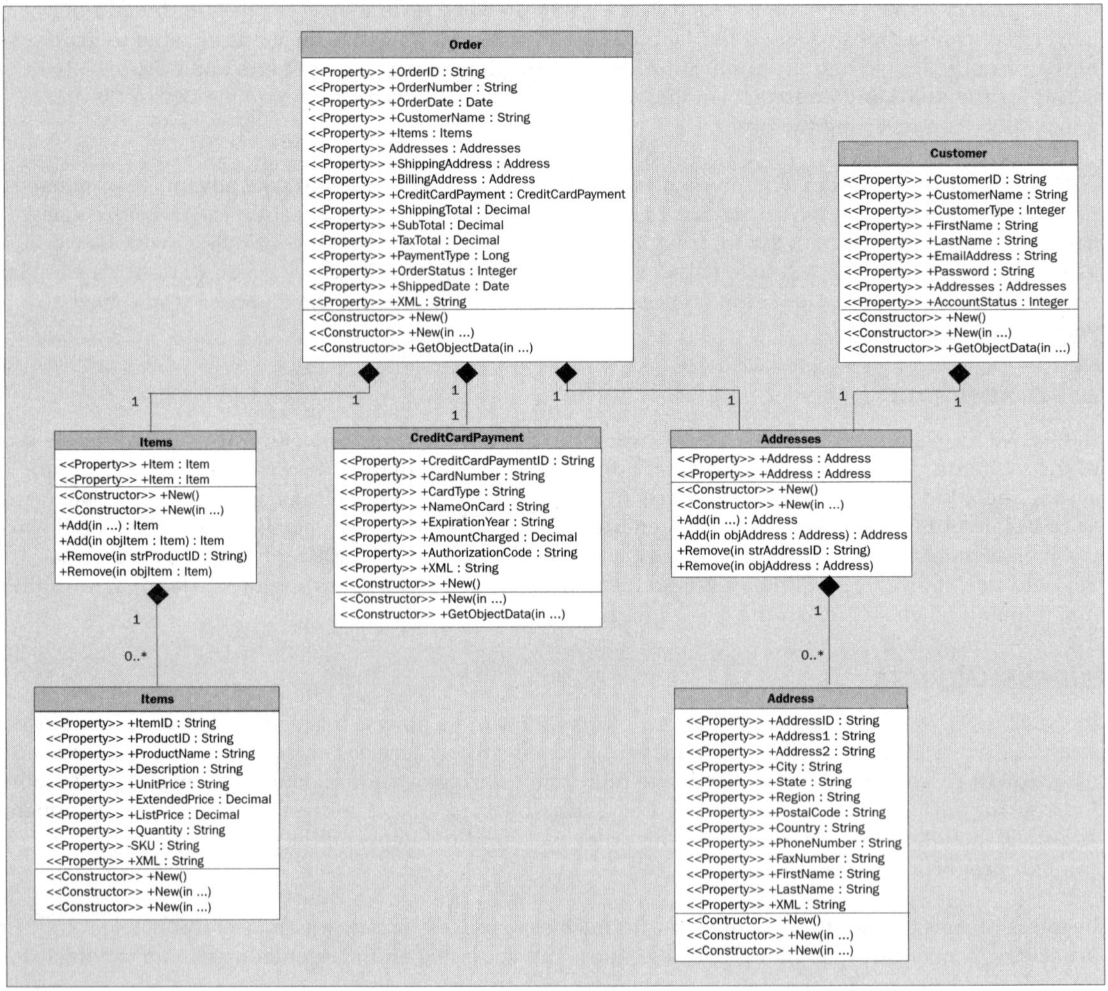

Let's discuss each of these business objects in detail, but first let's discuss a shared class that is not depicted in the above diagram, the `ExtensibleObjectBase` class.

ExtensibleObjectBase

The `ExtensibleObjectBase` class is a base class that provides common functionality for managing data, converting the object's data to XML, and supporting serialization and deserialization. It is inherited by several of the business objects including the `Customer`, `Order`, `Item`, `Address`, and `CreditCardPayment` objects. By deriving from the `ExtensibleObjectBase` class, these classes can leverage all of the functionality provided by the `ExtensibleObjectBase` class and override the methods or properties as necessary.

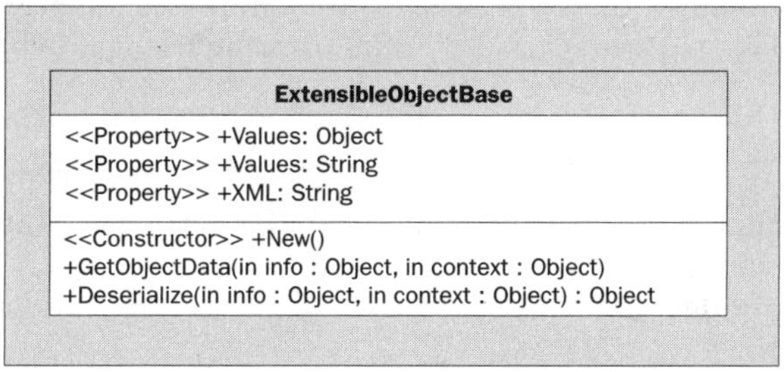

Order

As I mentioned, the `Order` class encapsulates the data related to an order in the IBuyAdventure system and provides properties and methods for managing the data. The `Order` class is actually the root in an object model consisting of several other classes including: the `Addresses`, `Address`, `Items`, and `Item` classes. The `Order` class is also used to store and manage a customer's shopping cart data. An instance of the `Order` class (representing the customer's shopping basket) is created when the user first accesses the IBuyAdventure site. As the user adds or updates items in their basket, the items are added to an `Order` object. The `Order` object is persisted between page requests in the ASP.NET `Session` object to preserve the customer's order information during their shopping session. When the customer places an order, the `Order` object is passed to an instance of the `OrderProcessingTx` class in the business services tier, which processes and saves the order using the data in the `Order` object. As you can see, the `Order` class has a significant role in the entire IBuyAdventure system.

Addresses

The `Addresses` class is responsible for maintaining a collection of `Address` objects. The `Addresses` class is used by both the `Order` class to represent the addresses associated with an order and by the `Customer` class to represent the customer's saved addresses. This `Addresses` inherits from the `System.Collections.CollectionBase` base class and provides strongly-typed methods and properties for adding and removing addresses, and referencing to individual `Address` objects in the collection.

Address

The `Address` class represents an address associated with an order or a customer. This class provides properties that can be used to get and set address fields such as the first (`Address1`) and second line (`Address2`) of the address, and the city, state or region, and postal code.

Items

The `Items` class is responsible for maintaining a collection of `Item` objects, representing the products associated with an order. This class inherits from the `System.Collections.CollectionBase` base class and provides strongly typed methods and properties for adding and removing items, and referencing to individual items in the collection.

Item

The Item class represents a product associated with an order. This class provides properties that can be used to retrieve and set information for an OrderItem, including the ProductID, ProductName, Description, UnitPrice, Quantity and ExtendedPrice.

CreditCardPayment

The CreditCardPayment class manages the credit card payment information associated with an order including the credit card number, card type, and expiration month and year. The CreditCardPayment class exposes access to this information through public properties.

Customer

The Customer class represents a consumer or business customer in the IBuyAdventure system. This class provides properties that can be used to manage all of the data for a customer account including the customer's name, e-mail address, and password. The Customer class also uses the Addresses collection class to represent the addresses associated with a customer account.

Typed Datasets

Although customer business objects simplify the management of in-memory data structures, they are not as well suited for data originating from a data store. In particular, custom business objects typically require a fair amount of code to populate with a resultset from a database query. For this reason, in the IBuyAdventure system we decided to supplement our custom business objects with **typed datasets**.

While we discussed ADO.NET and the DataSet class in Chapter 2, we didn't discuss typed datasets. Typed datasets are simply classes that inherit from and extend the standard ADO.NET dataSet base class to provide additional properties, methods, and events for the specific data structure the Dataset represents. For example, we could create a typed dataset named ProductsDataset for the Products entity in the IBuyAdventure database. The ProductsDataset would implement properties named after the columns in the Products entity, such as ProductID, ProductName, and so on. These properties could then be called by a client application or object on an instance of the ProductsDataset to get the value of a specific column, instead of using the generic collection-keyed methods of the standard ADO.NET DataSet class.

Typed datasets can simplify and improve the readability of code in consuming applications and classes when compared to the generic DataSet class. Furthermore, the extended properties, methods, and events provided by a typed dataset are strongly typed, meaning, that they are declared as a specific data type instead of the generic System.Object data type. As a result any type conversion errors are identified at compile-time instead of at run-time.

Since typed datasets inherit from the standard ADO.NET DataSet class, they take advantage of all of the features and functionality of an ADO.NET DataSet, including the ability to:

- Populate with the results from a query to a data store
- Combine data from multiple data stores and/or XML documents into a single dataset
- Create different views of data by creating in-memory relationships between tables
- Insert, update, and delete records to the in-memory tables and propagate changes to the data store
- Scroll through and manipulate records without holding locks in the data store

- Load and persist the data and/or schema in the DataSet as XML
- Pass by value across application domain, thread, processor, or machine boundaries
- Bind to Windows Form and Web Form controls

In the IBuyAdventure system we will create a typed dataset for almost all entities in the IBuyAdventure data model. Each typed dataset will contain the same fields as the corresponding table in the IBuyAdventure database. The typed datasets that we will create include:

- ProductsDataset
- CategoriesDataset
- InventoryDataset
- CustomersDataset
- AddressesDataset
- OrdersDataset
- OrderItemsDataset
- OrderAddressesDataset
- CreditCardPaymentsDataset

User Services

The User Services tier in the IBuyAdventure 2.0 system consists of ASP.NET Web Forms that allow consumer customers to perform tasks typical of a business-to-consumer e-commerce site, including the ability to browse and search for products, manage products in their shopping basket, create a new customer account, and place an order for the selected products. Although the first version of the IBuyAdventure system provided much of this same functionality, it was necessary to revise the Web Forms in the User Services tier to take advantage of the new IBuyAdventure architecture and business service components. We also made several other changes to the Web Forms including:

Code-behind Programming Model

The original version of the IBuyAdventure system that was highlighted in the Professional ASP.NET book embedded `<script runat="server">` tags and server-side code within the ASPX files which also contained the Web Form's layout. While this technique is simple and consistent with the ASP programming model, it makes it difficult to change the page layout and it limits reusability of the user interface logic. In the new IBuyAdventure system we will utilize the ASP.NET code-behind programming model to separate the layout from the user interface logic. The code-behind programming model allows you to store the page directives and page layout in the ASPX file while the server-side code is physically stored in a separate class file, called the code-behind file. The ASPX file references the code-behind file using the Inherits and CodeBehind attributes of the @Page directive. For example, the following Page directive contains an Inherits attribute with the full type name of the code-behind class and the CodeBehind attribute contains the file name of the code-behind class:

```
<%@ Page Language="vb" Inherits="IBuyAdventureWeb.NewAccount"
CodeBehind="NewAccount.aspx.vb" AutoEventWireup="false" %>
```

By using the code-behind programming model, the page layout can easily be changed without affecting the functionality or behavior of the Web Form. Consequently, HTML designers can work in conjunction with developers to create a Web Form. Once the structure and controls used by the Web Form have been defined, HTML designers can design the fonts, colors, and layout, while developers concentrate on implementing logic to retrieve and display data to the user, validate and accept input, and invoke methods of business service components to execute transactions.

The code-behind programming model also facilitates reuse of user interface logic. Since code for a Web Form is contained in a separate class, you can easily inherit from the class to create a new Web Form. With this model, it is also possible to create separate page designs that share the same code-behind class.

Session Management Using ASP.NET Session State Service

Version 1.0 of the IBuyAdventure system managed user state by manually persisting and loading the customer's basket and shopping information in the IBuyAdventure SQL Server database between page requests. While this technique effectively satisfied the requirements by allowing the application to scale across multiple web servers, it required a fair amount of code to implement. The IBuyAdventure 2.0 system will utilize the ASP.NET Session State Service for storing the user's state, including their shopping basket and customer account information, between page requests. The ASP.NET Session State Service allows state in the `Session` object to be stored in the same process as the web application, in a separate process on another machine, or within a SQL Server database between page requests. By simply configuring the ASP.NET Session State Service to store session data on another machine or in a SQL Server database, the session data will automatically be shared between web servers. Additionally, the Web Forms in the User Services tier can simply read and write values from the ASP.NET `Session` object, without having to implement additional code to load and persist state to a database.

Web Forms and User Controls

The following UML Class diagram illustrates the ASP.NET Web Forms, User Controls, and standard classes that compose the User Services tier in the new IBuyAdventure system. Although no relationships are illustrated in this diagram between the Web Forms and the User Controls, almost every Web Form in the system utilizes the Footer, Header, and Categories User Controls.

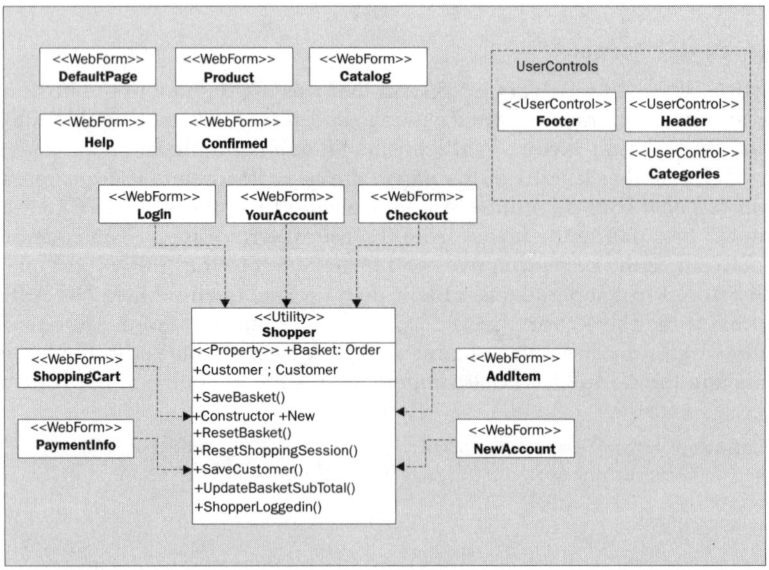

Most of the Web Forms in the IBuyAdventure system have a similar page design, which utilizes the Header, Footer, and Categories User Controls. The Web Forms do not utilize frames, although they achieve the same page design effect using HTML tables. The following diagram illustrates this common page design:

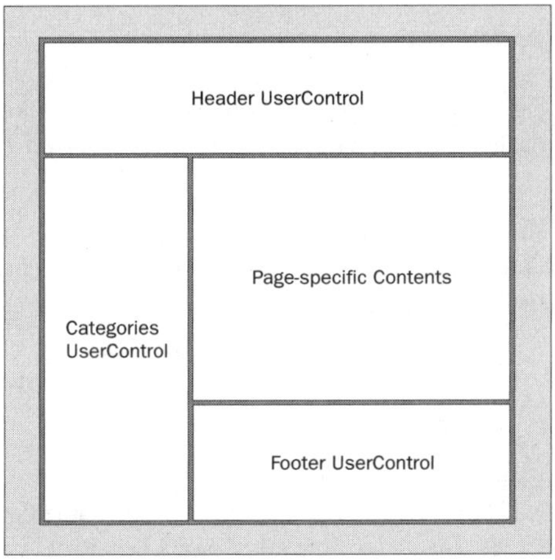

Let's discuss each of the ASP.NET Web Forms, User Controls, and utility classes that compose the User Services tier of the IBuyAdventure 2.0 system.

Shopper class

The `Shopper` class is a utility class that provides properties and methods for common operations related to a shopper, such as loading and saving the shopper's customer account information and shopping basket between page requests. This class uses the ASP.NET session state service to store and manage this data. The `ShopperUtil` class implements the following properties and methods:

- `Public Sub New(ByRef context As HttpContext)`
  This overloaded constructor receives a reference to an `System.Web.HttpContext` object as a parameter and stores the reference in a member-level variable so it can be used by the `Shopper` object for loading and persisting the user's basket and customer data to the session state.

- `Public Sub SaveBasket()`
  The `SaveBasket()` method persists the `IBuyAdventure.Common.Order` object representing the user's shopping basket to the session state, so it is available between page requests.

- `Public Sub SaveCustomer()`
  The `SaveCustomer()` method persists the `IBuyAdventure.Common.Customer` object containing the user's customer account data to the session state, so it is available between page requests.

- `Public Sub ResetBasket()`
  The `ResetBasket()` method resets the user's shopping basket by deleting it from the session state.

- `Public Sub ResetShoppingSession()`
  The `ResetShoppingSession()` method resets the user's shopping session by deleting their shopping basket and customer account information from the session state.

- `Public Property Customer() As Customer`
  The `Customer` property can be used to get or set a reference to the `IBuyAdventure.Common.Customer` object containing the user's customer account data. When this method is called, the `Customer` object will be loaded from the session state if it has not already been.

- `Public Property Basket() As Order`
  The `Customer` property can be used to get or set a reference to the `IBuyAdventure.Common.Order` object representing the user's current shopping basket. When this method is called, the `Order` object will be loaded from the session state if it has not already been.

- `Public Function ShopperLoggedIn() As Boolean`
  The `ShopperLoggedIn()` function returns a Boolean indicating whether or not the current user has logged into the IBuyAdventure site.

- `Public Function GetCustomerID() As String`
  The `GetCustomerID()` method returns the current user's `CustomerID`, which was set when the user logged in or registered with the site.

- `Public Sub UpdateBasketSubTotal()`
  The `UpdateBasketSubTotal()` method creates an instance of the `IBuyAdventure.BusinessServices.OrderCalculations` class and calls the `CalculateSubTotal()` method to update the subtotal of the user's current shopping basket.

DefaultPage Web Form

The `DefaultPage` WebForm is the start or home page in the IBuyAdventure site. This Web Form simply displays static text describing the IBuyAdventure site.

Catalog Web Form

The `Catalog` WebForm retrieves the products associated with a particular category in the IBuyAdventure system and displays the list of the products to the user. The `CategoryID` of the category whose products should be displayed is passed as a parameter to this Web Form. From the `Catalog` Web Form users can select a product to view more detailed information or add the product to their shopping basket.

Product Web Form

The `Product` Web Form is responsible for displaying the detailed information for a single product. Some of this information includes the product's SKU, name, description, picture, and available inventory. The `ProductID` of the product that should be displayed is passed as a parameter to this Web Form. After reviewing the product information, users can add the product to their shopping basket from this Web Form.

ShoppingCart Web Form

The `ShoppingCart` Web Form is responsible for displaying the contents of the user's shopping cart/basket. From this Web Form, users can change the quantities of selected items, delete items from their shopping cart, or proceed to the checkout process. When the user chooses to proceed with the checkout process they are redirected to the `Checkout` Web Form. However, if they have not yet logged into the IBuyAdventure site during the shopping session, they will be required to do so before beginning the checkout process.

AddItem Web Form

The `AddItem` Web Form is responsible for adding a product to the user's shopping basket. The `ProductID` of the product that should be added is passed as a parameter to this Web Form. The `AddItem` Web Form does not render a page, but instead redirects the user to the `ShoppingCart` Web Form where they can view the contents of their shopping cart including the new item.

Login Web Form

The `Login` Web Form allows registered users to enter their e-mail address and password to login to the IBuyAdventure site. This Web Form is loaded automatically when the user is linked to a secure Web Form in the site and they have not previously logged in. In addition to authenticating the user's e-mail address and password, behind the scenes the `Login` Web Form loads the customer account information for the user in an instance of the `Customer` class and saves the `Customer` object to the session state by calling the `SaveCustomer()` method of the `Shopper` object. After logging in, the user is automatically redirected to the Web Form they were attempting to access. If a user has not previously registered with the IBuyAdventure system, they can click on a link to the `NewAccount` Web Form where they can enter information to create a new customer account.

NewAccount Web Form

The `NewAccount` Web Form allows users to create a new customer account by entering their contact information and billing and shipping addresses. Some of the contact information collected on this Web Form includes the user's first and last name, e-mail address, and password. The information entered on this Web Form is loaded into a `Customer` object, which is passed to an instance of the `CustomersTx` business service class to create the new account. After creating the new account, the `NewAccount` Web Form saves the `Customer` object to the session state by calling the `SaveCustomer()` method of the `Shopper` object.

PaymentInfo Web Form

The `PaymentInfo` Web Form allows users to enter their credit card information when placing an order. The information collected by this Web Form is stored in the `CreditCardPayment` object managed by the `Order` object that represents the shopper's basket. After entering payment information, the user is redirected to the `Checkout` Web Form where they can complete the checkout process.

Checkout Web Form

The `Checkout` Web Form is responsible for displaying a summary of the customer's order and allowing the user to confirm or cancel the order. If the user confirms the order, then the `Order` object that represents their shopping basket is passed to an instance of the `OrderProcessingTx` business service class, which creates and processes the order. If the user chooses to cancel the order they are transferred to the `DefaultPage` Web Form. After placing an order the user is redirected to the `Confirmed` WebForm.

Confirmed Web Form

The `Confirmed` WebForm is responsible for displaying static content that thanks the user for the order and allows the user to navigate to the `YourAccount` Web Form where they can view information about their past orders.

YourAccount Web Form

The `YourAccount` Web Form is responsible for retrieving and displaying the entire IBuyAdventure order history for the customer including the `Order` number, placed date, status, shipped date, and total amount for each order. This Web Form requires the user to log into the IBuyAdventure site.

Help Web Form

The `Help` Web Form is responsible for displaying static content that describes how to place an order at the IBuyAdventure site.

Categories User Control

The `Categories` User Control is responsible for retrieving all of the product categories defined in the IBuyAdventure system and displaying each of the categories as a clickable hyperlink. When clicked, this hyperlink redirects the user to the `Catalog` Web Form where they can view all of the products belonging to the selected category.

Footer User Control

The `Footer` Web Control is responsible for displaying rotating advertisements and static content that is typically displayed at the bottom of a Web Form.

Header User Control

The `Header` Web Control is responsible for displaying the IBuyAdventure site logo, a navigation menu that allows the user to navigate through the site, and a dynamic summary of the user's shopping basket.

Business Services

The Business Services tier is arguably the most critical tier in a three-tier distributed transaction processing system. Classes that compose the business services tier are typically responsible for several crucial tasks including coordinating transactions, applying business rules, and retrieving and manipulating data. Because of their crucial role, these classes must be designed and architected carefully in order to maximize performance, scalability, reliability, extensibility, security, and maintainability of the overall application.

Design Considerations

There are a number of design decisions that must be made during the logical design phase of the business services tier, especially for a distributed transaction processing system. To add to the complexity, many of these design considerations have resulting side-effects that impact other decisions. Consequently, many of these considerations should be taken into account prior to defining the logical classes that will compose the Business Services tier. Some of the issues we considered in the IBuyAdventure system include:

- Data access technology and techniques
- Passing and returning structured data
- Transaction processing model

Let's discuss each of these topics in further detail and learn about the decisions made for the IBuyAdventure system.

Data Access Technology and Strategy

There are two major data access technologies available on the .NET platform, ADO.NET and ADO. Making the choice between these two technologies can be relatively straightforward. As we discussed in Chapter 2, ADO.NET was designed specifically for the .NET platform and it provides several advantages over ADO when developing a distributed transaction-processing application. However, choosing a technique or strategy for retrieving and manipulating data using ADO.NET can be less straightforward.

When devising a data access strategy using ADO.NET, it's important to consider the type of data store(s) you will be accessing and the extensibility and performance requirements of the system. Since the IBuyAdventure system stores data in a SQL Server database exclusively, we decided to use the SQL Server managed provider. The SQL Server managed provider consists of data access classes that are designed and optimized specifically for accessing Microsoft SQL Server 7.0 and 2000 databases. In this situation we decided to sacrifice the extensibility provided by the generic OLE DB .NET data provider in favor of the performance and programming simplicity of the SQL Server managed provider.

Passing and Returning Structured Data

Another architecture topic that's frequently debated in development circles is the issue of how business service classes should return complex data structures. On the COM platform many systems were architected to return disconnected ADO Recordsets to client applications that could then scroll though, read, and manipulate data with the convenience and simplicity of the ADO object model. Some systems utilized XML formatted strings for exchanging data between objects. Although XML formatted data benefits from platform independence, it requires developers to write a fair amount of code to read and manipulate the data. This is unless you create a custom object model on top of each XML document exchanged in a system, which many developers have done.

In the IBuyAdventure system we decided to utilize a combination of custom business objects and typed datasets, which we defined earlier, for passing data between business service objects and the user services tier. Both typed datasets and custom business objects that we defined support serialization, so they can safely be passed by value across application domain, thread, process, or even machine boundaries. Typed datasets are ideal in most situations because they can be populated with the results from a query to the data store. As a result, data doesn't have to be transformed from one data format to another. Typed datasets also provide a simplistic, but powerful object model for working with data, while providing extensive, built-in support for XML. However, I should point out that both typed and generic datasets do not provide the highest performance when working with single records or simply scrolling through data in a forward, read-only fashion. In situations where optimal performance is a critical requirement, data reader classes such as the `SqlDataReader` or `OleDbDataReader` might be a better choice. With the IBuyAdventure system we decided to use typed datasets and custom business objects because of their simplicity and flexibility.

Transaction Processing Model

Throughout this book we have discussed a number of transaction processing techniques and technologies including: Transact SQL (TSQL) transactions, ADO.NET transactions, transactional ASP.NET Web Forms, transactional ASP.NET Web Services, and transactional .NET Serviced Components. However, each of these transaction-processing technologies available on the .NET platform has both benefits and drawbacks. Needless to say, choosing the appropriate transaction model can be challenging.

Each transaction technology that we have discussed requires a trade-off between transaction performance or simplicity and extensibility. T-SQL Transactions provide the best pure performance because they are controlled by the SQL Server database engine and they are started and completed within a single roundtrip to the database. However, T-SQL Transactions require you to explicitly start and commit or abort the transaction and they can only be used with a single Microsoft SQL Server database. Like T-SQL Transactions, ADO.NET transactions also require manual control. However, an ADO.NET transaction can be performed with a single Microsoft SQL Server database, through the SQL Server managed provider or with any single OLE DB accessible data store that supports transactions, through the OLE DB .NET data provider. While ADO.NET transactions provide more flexibility and a simpler programming model than T-SQL transactions, this flexibility comes at the cost of reduced performance because transactions are controlled through the ADO.NET object model not at the database level.

Transactional ASP.NET Web Forms, ASP.NET Web Services, and .NET Serviced Components, utilize the same declarative/distributed, automatic transaction model provided by COM+. As we learned in Chapter 6, the COM+ transaction model automatically starts, commits or rolls back a transaction based on the configuration of the transaction support attribute (TSA). ASP.NET Web Forms, Web Services, and .NET Serviced Components all support the same possible TSA values, although the syntax to apply the TSA varies slightly in each environment:

Unlike T-SQL and ADO.NET Transactions whose scope is limited to a single data store, the COM+ transaction model supports distributed transactions based on MS DTC. Consequently, a COM+ transaction can span multiple data stores, called resource managers, including Microsoft SQL Server databases, MSMQ Message Queues, Oracle databases, and any other data stores that support MS DTC's OLE Transactions protocol. For example, a single COM+ transaction could insert an order into a SQL Server database, write the order to an MSMQ message, and update inventory information in an Oracle database. In addition to supporting multiple data stores, COM+ transactions can also span multiple objects. COM+ automatically orchestrates the work performed by multiple objects into a single transaction based on the component's configured transaction support attribute.

Although the COM+ transaction model is very simple and flexible, it is not without it's drawbacks. This simplicity and flexibility comes at the cost of reduced performance when compared to T-SQL or ADO.NET Transactions. TSQL and ADO.NET transactions generally yield higher performance than COM+ transactions because they are coordinated by the data source and do not have the overhead of MS DTC.

The following table summarizes the benefits and drawbacks of each of the transaction processing technologies available on the .NET platform:

Technology	Model	Scope	Performance	Extensibility
T-SQL Transactions	Manual	Local	Higher	Lower
ADO. NET Transactions	Manual	Local	Medium	Medium
COM+ Transactions (using .NET Serviced Components, ASP.NET Web Forms, or ASP.NET Web Services)	Automatic	Distributed	Lower	Higher

If optimal performance is a critical requirement, it may make sense to avoid the additional overhead and performance reduction that occurs from COM+ transactions and use either ADO.NET or T-SQL transactions. However, if you are unsure which model to choose, I would recommend to err on the side of flexibility and simplicity by utilizing the COM+ transaction model. Regardless of the transaction model you choose, you should always avoid mixing transaction models and technologies. Mixing transaction technologies such as using T-SQL transactions or ADO.NET transactions with transactional .NET Serviced Components can result in unexpected behavior and an application that's difficult to maintain and extend.

The IBuyAdventure 2.0 system will utilize the automatic transaction model provided by COM+ through .NET Serviced Components. Although the IBuyAdventure system will only be accessing a single Microsoft SQL Server database, we decided not to utilize the T-SQL or ADO.NET transactions in favor of transactional .NET Serviced Components because of the simplified programming model and extensibility provided by the COM+ declarative transaction model. The business services classes will be implemented as modular, specialized components that can easily be utilized independently or as a part of a larger, multi-object transaction. Should ordering or fulfillment processes ever need change in the IBuyAdventure system, we can easily leverage the existing .NET Serviced Components as a part of new transactions.

Components

Now that we have considered several of the important factors when designing classes for the business services tier and we have discussed some of the typical types of business services classes, let's take a look at the classes that compose this tier for the IBuyAdventure system. The following UML Class diagram illustrates the classes that compose the Business Services tier of the IBuyAdventure system, and the properties, methods, and relationships for each class. The inheritance relationship between the `System.EnterpriseServices.Serviced` Component base class and several of the business services classes have been omitted from this diagram for simplicity.

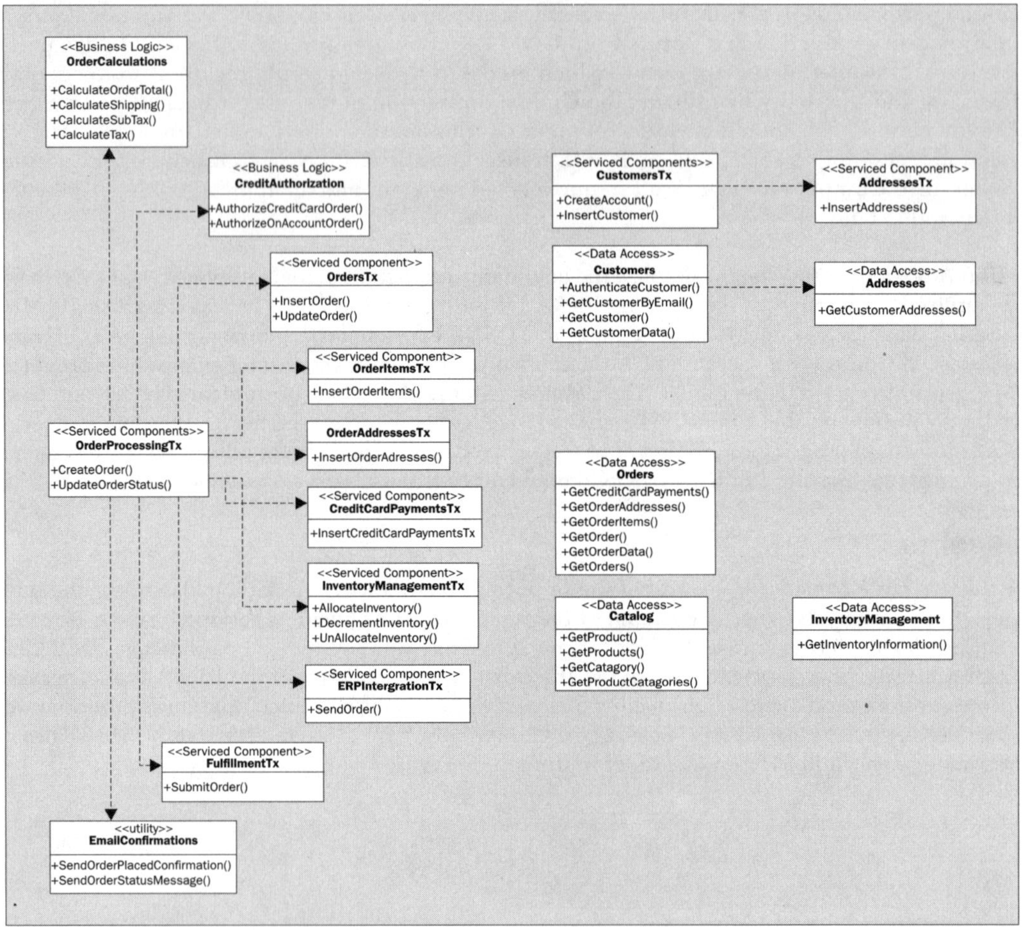

Let's define and discuss each of these business service classes in detail.

Catalog

The `Catalog` class is a data access class that provides methods for retrieving product and category records from the product catalog tables in the IBuyAdventure database. This class provides the following methods:

- `Public Function GetProduct (ByVal strProductID As String) As ProductsDataset`
  The `GetProduct()` method retrieves all of the information for the product specified by the `strProductID` parameter and returns the product data in a `ProductsDataset` object.

- `Public Function GetProducts(Byval strCategoryID As String) As ProductsDataset`
  The `GetProducts()` method retrieves all of the product records associated with the category specified by the `strCategoryID` parameter and returns the product records in a `ProductsDataset` object.

- `Public Function GetCategory(ByVal strCategoryID As String) As CategoriesDataset`
  The `GetCategory()` method retrieves a single category record specified by the `strCategoryID` parameter and returns the record in a `CategoriesDataset` object.

- `Public Function GetProductCategories() As CategoriesDataset`
  The `GetProductCategories()` method simply retrieves all of the categories defined in the IBuyAdventure database and returns them in a `CategoriesDataset` object.

CreditAuthorization

The `CreditAuthorization` class is a business rule/logic class that provides methods for authorizing the purchase amount of an order. For consumer customers, this simply involves rejecting any orders from the web site that exceed $2500. For business customers, authorizing purchases simply involves verifying the customer's account is not disabled. However, while these rules are intentionally very simplistic, the `CreditAuthorization` class could easily encapsulate additional credit validation business logic such as pre-authorizing a credit card for consumer orders, or checking the available credit line established for business customers. This class implements the following methods:

- `Public Function AuthorizeOnAccountOrder(ByVal objOrder As Order, ByVal objCustomer As Customer) As Order`

  The `AuthorizeOnAccountOrder()` method checks the account status for the customer specified by the passed `Customer` business object and throws an exception to the caller if the customer's account status is `disabled`.

- `Public Function AuthorizeCreditCardOrder(ByVal objOrder As Order, ByVal objCustomer As Customer) As Order`

  The `AuthorizeCreditCardOrder()` method checks the amount charged for the `CreditCardPayment` object associated with the passed `Order` business object and simply throws an exception to the caller if the amount exceeds $2,500 dollars.

Customers

The `Customers` class is a data access class that provides methods for retrieving information for customer accounts from the IBuyAdventure database. This class implements the following methods:

- `Public Function GetCustomer (ByVal strCustomerID As String) As CustomersDataset`
  The `GetCustomer()` method retrieves all of the data for the customer specified by the `strCustomerID` parameter and returns the customer record in a `CustomersDataset` object.

- `Public Function GetCustomerData(ByVal strCustomerID As String) As Customer`
  The `GetCustomerData()` method retrieves all of the data for the customer specified by the `strCustomerID` parameter by calling the `GetCustomer()` method. The customer data is then loaded into an instance of the `Customer` business object and returned to the caller.

- `Public Function GetCustomerByE-mail(ByVal strE-mail As String) As CustomersDataset`
  The `GetCustomerByE-mail()` method retrieves all of the data for the customer with an e-mail address matching the value specified by the `strE-mailAddress` parameter and returns the customer record in a `CustomersDataset` object.

- `Public Function AuthenticateCustomer(ByVal strE-mail As String, ByVal strPassword As String) As Customer`
  The `AuthenticateCustomer()` method calls the `GetCustomerByE-mail()` method to find a customer with an e-mail address matching the value specified by the `strE-mailAddress` parameter and compares the specified password against the password stored for the customer account. If the customer record is found and the passwords match, then the `AuthenticateCustomer()` method returns a `Customer` business object containing all of the data for the customer. However, if the customer record cannot be found or the passwords do not pass a case-sensitive comparison, then this method returns a null object reference, or nothing.

Orders

The `Orders` class is a data access class that provides methods for retrieving information for existing orders that have previously been created in the IBuyAdventure system. This class implements the following methods:

- `Public Function GetOrder(ByVal strOrderID As String) As OrdersDataset`
  The `GetOrder()` method retrieves all of the data for the order specified by the `strOrderID` parameter and returns the order record in a new `OrdersDataset` object.
- `Public Function GetOrderData(ByVal strOrderID As String) As Order`
  The `GetOrderData()` method retrieves all of the data for the order specified by the `strOrderID` parameter by calling the `GetOrder()` method. This method also calls the `GetOrderItems()`, `GetOrderAddresses()`, and `GetCreditCardPayments()` methods to retrieve all of the data associated with the specified order. All of the order data is then loaded into an instance of the `Order` business object and returned to the caller.
- `Public Function GetOrders(ByVal strCustomerID As String) As OrdersDataset`
  The `GetOrders()` method retrieves all of the orders that have been placed by the customer specified by the passed `strCustomerID` parameter. The order records are returned in a new instance of the `OrdersDataset` typed dataset class.
- `Public Function GetOrderItems(ByVal strOrderID As String) As OrdersDataset`
  The `GetOrderItems()` method retrieves all of the order line items that are associated with the existing order matching the `OrderID` specified in the `strOrderID` parameter. The order item records are returned in a new instance of the `OrderItemsDataset` typed dataset class.
- `Public Function GetOrderAddresses(ByVal strOrderID As String) As OrdersDataset`
  The `GetOrderAddresses()` method retrieves all of the order addresses that are associated with the existing order matching the `OrderID` specified in the `strOrderID` parameter. The order address records are returned in a new instance of the `OrderAddressesDataset` typed dataset class.
- `Public Function GetCreditCardPayments(ByVal strOrderID As String) As CreditCardPaymentsDataset`
  The `GetCreditCardPayments()` method retrieves the credit card payment information associated with the existing order matching the `OrderID` specified in the `strOrderID` parameter. The credit card payment information is returned in a new instance of the `OrderAddressesDataset` typed dataset class.

CustomersTx

The `CustomersTx` class is a data access class that provides methods for creating IBuyAdventure customer accounts and inserting customer records in the IBuyAdventure database. This class implements the following methods:

- `Public Function InsertCustomer (ByVal objCustomer As Customer) As Customer`
  The `InsertCustomer()` method inserts a record into the `Customers` table using the data in the passed `Customer` business object. The updated `Customer` business object is returned to the caller.

- `Public Function CreateAccount (ByVal objCustomer As Customer) As Customer`
  The `CreateAccount()` method creates a new customer account by calling the `InsertCustomer()` method to insert a record into the `Customers` table and by calling the `InsertAddresses()` method of an `AddressesTx` object to insert all of the addresses associated with the customer.

E-mailConfirmations

The `E-mailConfirmations` class is a utility class that provides methods for sending e-mail confirmations to customers. E-mails are typically sent as a result of order status changes. This class implements the following methods:

- `Public Function SendOrderPlacedConfirmation (ByVal objOrder As Order, ByVal objCustomer As Customer) As Order`
  The `SendOrderPlacedConfirmation()` method sends an e-mail message to the customer confirming that their order has been received and is being processed. The customer's information including their e-mail address is included in the passed `Customer` business object (`objCustomer` parameter) and the order information is enclosed in the passed `Order` business object (`objOrder` parameter).

- `Public Function SendOrderStatusMessage(ByVal objOrder As Order, ByVal objCustomer As Customer) As Order`
  The `SendOrderStatusMessage()` method sends a generic e-mail message to the customer with the current status of the order passed in the `objOrder` parameter. The customer's e-mail address is included in the `Customer` business object passed in the `objCustomer` parameter.

OrdersTx

The `OrdersTx` class is a transactional data class that provides methods for inserting order header information into the IBuyAdventure database. This class implements the following methods:

- `Public Function InsertOrder(ByVal objOrder As Order) As Order`
  The `InsertOrder()` method inserts a single order record into the `Orders` table in the IBuyAdventure database using the data in the passed `Order` object.

- `Public Function UpdateOrder(ByVal objOrder As Order) As Order`
  The `UpdateOrder()` method updates a single order record into the `Orders` table in the IBuyAdventure database using the data in the passed `Order` object.

OrderItemsTx

The `OrderItemsTx` class is a transactional data class that provides methods for inserting items associated with an order. This class implements the following methods:

- `Public Function InsertOrderItems(ByVal objOrder As Order) As Order`
  The `InsertOrderItems()` method inserts a record into the `OrderItems` table for each line item in the `Order` business object passed in the `objOrder` parameter. The `Order` object containing the updated data is returned to the caller.

OrderAddressesTx

The `OrderAddressesTx` class is a transactional data class that provides methods for inserting addresses associated with an order. This class implements the following methods:

- `Public Function InsertOrderAddresses(ByVal objOrder As Order) As Order`
  The `InsertOrderAddresses()` method inserts order address records for each address in the `Order` business object passed in the `objOrder` parameter. The `Order` object containing the updated data is returned to the caller.

OrderCalculations

The `OrderCalculations` class is a business rule class that provides methods for calculating the extended price of each item on the order, and the subtotal, shipping, tax and grand totals. By isolating order calculations into a separate class, the IBuyAdventure system can easily adapt to changes in the business rules. The `OrderCalculations` class implements the following methods:

- `Public Function CalculateOrderTotal(ByVal objOrder As Order) As Order`
  The `CalculateOrderTotal()` method calculates the grand total of the order passed in the `objOrder` parameter. This method calls the other public methods of this class to independently calculate the subtotal, shipping, and tax totals and then simply summs the values together to derive the grand total, which is stored in the `Order.GrandTotal` property. An `Order` business object containing the updated order totals is returned to the caller.
- `Public Function CalculateShipping(ByVal objOrder As Order) As Order`
  The `CalculateShipping()` method calculates the shipping charges for the order passed in the `objOrder` parameter and stores the calculated costs in the `Order` business object's `ShippingTotal` property. The shipping charges for an order are calculated as one dollar per item on more than five items plus a base shipping charge. Orders with less than five items will always be charged the base shipping charge of $8.99. An `Order` business object containing the updated shipping total is returned to the caller.
- `Public Function CalculateTax(ByVal objOrder As Order) As Order`
  The `CalculateTax()` method calculates the tax for the order passed in the `objOrder` parameter and stores the calculated tax in the `Order` business object's `TaxTotal` property. Tax is only charged for orders with a shipping address located in the state of Florida. The tax is set to `0` in all other situations. An `Order` business object containing the updated tax total is returned to the caller.
- `Public Function CalculateSubTotal(ByVal objOrder As Order) As Order`
  The `CalculateSubTotal()` method calculates the subtotal for the order passed in the `objOrder` parameter and stores the calculated subtotal in the `Order` business object's `SubTotal` property. Before summarizing the items in the order, the `CalculateSubTotal()` method calculates and updates the `ExtendedPrice` by multiplying the `UnitPrice` times the quantity for each item. An `Order` business object containing the updated subtotal and item extended prices is returned to the caller.

OrderProcessingTx

The `OrderProcessingTx` class is a workflow class that provides methods for creating orders and processing order status updates from the fulfillment provider. As a workflow class, the `OrderProcessingTx` class coordinates the processing of other business service classes to perform these activities. This class implements the following methods:

- `Public Function CreateOrder(ByVal objOrder As Order, ByVal objCustomer As Customer) As Order`
  The `CreateOrder()` method creates an order in the IBuyAdventure system using the information stored in the `Order` business object for the `Customer` specified by the `Customer` business object. Creating an order involves performing several tasks by instantiating and calling methods of subordinate components, including the `OrdersTx`, `OrderItemsTx`, `OrderAddressesTx`, and `InventoryManagementTx` components, just to name a few.

- `Public Function UpdateOrderStatus(ByVal objOrder As Order, ByVal objCustomer As Customer) As Order`
  The `UpdateOrderStatus()` method updates the status for an order in the IBuyAdventure system using the information stored in the `Order` business object passed in the `objOrder` parameter. Updating the status of an order involves performing several tasks including decrementing inventory, releasing inventory allocations, sending an order status e-mail to the customer, and of course, updating the status of an order. Some of the subordinate components used to perform these tasks include the `OrdersTx`, `InventoryManagementTx`, and `E-mailConfirmations` components.

FulfillmentTx

The `FulfillmentTx` class is a transactional .NET Serviced Component that provides methods for integrating with the third-party fulfillment provider. This class doesn't fit any of the standard class types, since it doesn't manipulate data, apply business rules, or orchestrate a workflow. However, it is a transactional Serviced Component so it can be used as part of a larger transaction and vote on the transactions outcome. The `FulfillmentTx` class implements the following methods:

- `Public Function SubmitOrder(ByVal objOrder As Order) As Order`
  The `SubmitOrder()` method converts the passed `Order` object into an XML document and posts the XML document to a specified URL for the fulfillment provider.

ERPIntegrationTx

The `ERPIntegrationTx` class is a transactional .NET Serviced Component that provides methods for integrating with AdventureWorks internal ERP system. With this version the integration will be limited to sending orders to the ERP system using Microsoft Message Queue Server. However, additional functionality could easily be added to this class to facilitate additional integration points. Like the `FulfillmentTx` class, the `ERPIntegrationTx` class does not exactly fit one of the business service class categories we have defined. It is most like a data access class, in that it accesses a transactional resource, MSMQ. The `ERPIntegrationTx` class implements the following methods:

- `Public Function SendOrder(ByVal objOrder As Order) As Order`
  The `SendOrder()` method converts the passed `Order` object into an XML document and saves the XML document to a new MSMQ Message. IBuyAdventure ERP system automatically picks up messages from the queue and imports the contained order into the IBuyAdventure ERP system.

ReceiveOrderStatusUpdate HTTP Handler

In addition to the classes we've just discussed, the Business Services tier will also include a .NET HTTP Handler named `ReceiveOrderStatusUpdate`. A .NET HTTP Handler are the .NET equivalent of Internet Service API (ISAPI) DLLs commonly developed on the COM platform. A .NET HTTP Handler is a special class that can receive and respond to web requests. .NET HTTP Handlers are required to implement the `System.Web.IHttpHandler` or `System.Web.IHttpHandlerAsync` interfaces, which both provide a `ProcessRequest` method that is called when a web request is made.

.NET HTTP Handlers do not have the overhead of the ASP.NET Web Forms or Web Services engines, which makes them ideal for situations such as receiving an XML message where you only need to perform behind the scenes processing in response to an HTTP post or get web request. In fact, the ASP.NET Web Forms and Web Services engines are actually implemented as .NET HTTP Handlers and are designed to perform processing when a request for a file with the extension ASPX or ASMX is receive.

The `ReceiveOrderStatusUpdate` HTTP Handler is responsible for receiving and processing the `OrderStatusUpdate` XML messages posted by the fulfillment provider. The order status is updated by calling the `UpdateOrderStatus` method of the `OrderProcessingTx` business service class.

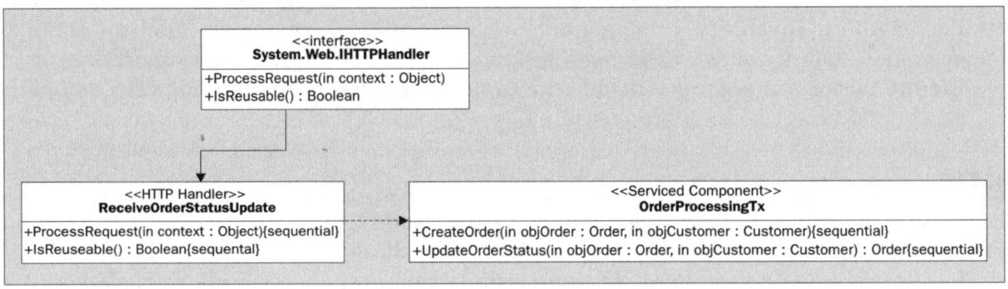

Data Services

The Data Services tier in the IBuyAdventure 2.0 system consists of a thin layer of stored procedures on top of the IBuyAdventure database. These stored procedures encapsulate the SQL statements for selecting, inserting, updating, and deleting data from individual tables in the database.

By encapsulating the data access logic, the stored procedures in the data services tier provide a layer of abstraction between the business services classes and the data store. The business services classes simply execute the stored procedures and pass in values for the required parameters. The business services classes are totally unaware of the processing that occurs within the stored procedure, nor do they care as long as the stored procedure returns the expected return value and/or resultset. This abstraction shields the business services classes from the database design and data storage details. It also provides additional flexibility and extensibility for implementing functionality such as data validation or data integrity rules, even after the business services classes have been created.

With prior versions of Microsoft SQL Server, the use of stored procedures could drastically benefit performance compared to executing dynamic SQL statements. Stored procedures were validated and partially compiled when they were created. When the stored procedure was first executed, the partially compiled execution plan was fully compiled and cached in memory by the SQL Query Engine before being executed. Subsequent executions of the stored procedure would use the fully compiled execution plan from memory, if available. Dynamically executed SQL statements, on the other hand, would have to be validated and fully compiled for each execution. As you can imagine this gave a significant performance difference especially in high volume, transactional applications. However, with Microsoft SQL Server 7.0 and 2000, the SQL Query Engine has been enhanced to cache and reuse execution plans for all SQL statements, not just stored procedures. Consequently, from a query engine standpoint there is no longer a performance benefit with stored procedures compared to dynamically issued SQL statements.

Despite the changes to the SQL Server query processor, stored procedures can still provide performance benefits when compared to dynamic SQL statements because they can reduce the number of necessary network roundtrips and reduce lock contention during transactions. Stored procedures can include `if` statements, `while` loops, and other Transact SQL (T-SQL) statements to execute simple data access logic by the query engine. Consequently, in situations where optimal performance is critical, it may make sense to apply certain business logic within stored procedures. The faster data can be accessed and manipulated, the faster transactions can complete and release valuable locks to shared data, allowing other transactions to execute.

The IBuyAdventure system does not use the transactional features of SQL Server from within stored procedures since we are using COM+ transactions in the business services classes. As we discussed earlier, COM+ transactions provide a number of advantages to SQL Server transactions including additional flexibility and extensibility, but they come at the cost of reduced performance.

Let's discuss each of the stored procedures that compose the Data Services tier of the IBuyAdventure system. Like the IBuyAdventure data model, the stored procedures have been organized into five logical categories: product catalog, customer account, order processing, and inventory management.

Product Catalog Stored Procedures

The product catalog stored procedures are responsible for retrieving and updating data in the `Products`, `ProductCategories`, and `Categories` tables in the IBuyAdventure database.

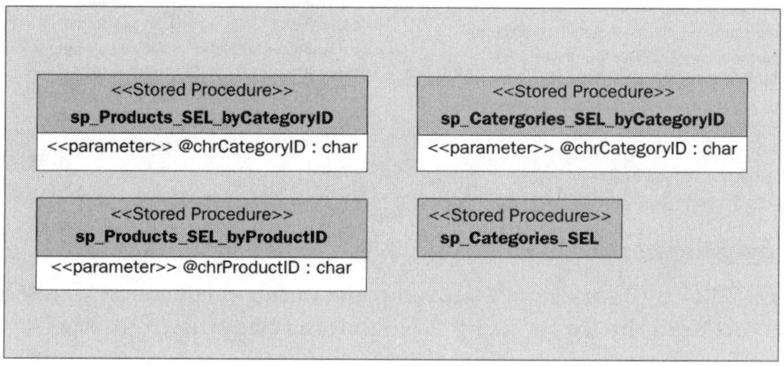

sp_Products_SEL_byProductID

The `sp_Products_SEL_byProductID` stored procedure executes a SQL `SELECT` statement to retrieve a single record from the `Products` table that matches the `ProductID` specified as an input parameter.

sp_Products_SEL_byCategoryID

The `sp_Products_SEL_byCategoryID` stored procedure executes a SQL `SELECT` statement to retrieve all the `Product` records that are associated with the `CategoryID` specified as an input parameter.

sp_Categories_SEL_byCategoryID

The `sp_Categories_SEL_byCategoryID` stored procedure executes a SQL `SELECT` statement to retrieve a single Category record that matches the `CategoryID` specified as an input parameter.

sp_Categories_SEL

The `sp_Categories_SEL` stored procedure executes a SQL `SELECT` statement to retrieve all of the columns and all of the records from the Categories table.

Customer Account Stored Procedures

The customer account stored procedures are responsible for selecting, inserting, and updating data in the `Customer` and `Addresses` tables in the IBuyAdventure database.

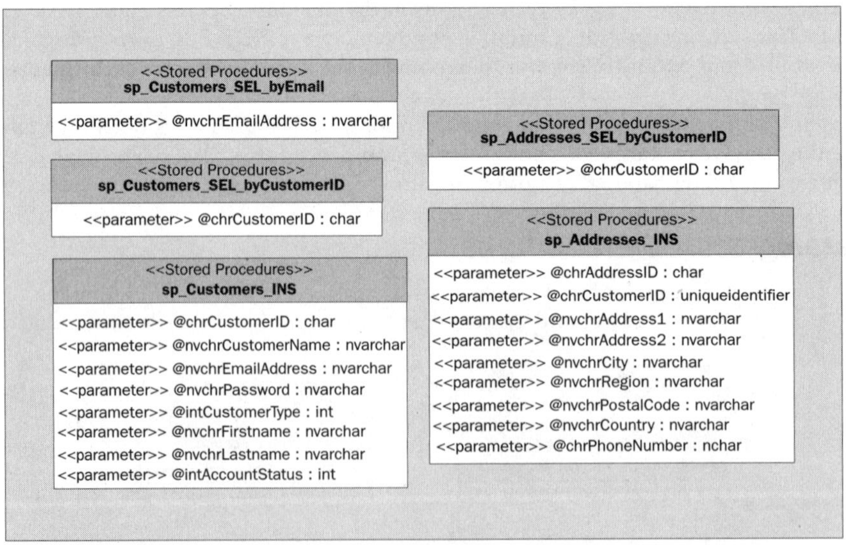

sp_Customers_SEL_byCustomerID

The `sp_Customers_SEL_byCustomerID` stored procedure executes a SQL `SELECT` statement to retrieve a single record from the `Customers` table that matches the `CustomerID` specified as an input parameter.

sp_Customers_SEL_byE-mail

The `sp_Customers_SEL_ByE-mail` stored procedure retrieves all of the data for a single record from the `Customers` table that matches the e-mail address specified as an input parameter.

sp_Customers_INS

The sp_Customers_INS stored procedure executes a SQL INSERT statement to insert a single record into the Customers table using the data passed in through input parameters as values for the new record. This stored procedure provides an input parameter for each column of the Customers table.

sp_Addresses_SEL_byCustomerID

The sp_Addresses_SEL_byCustomerID stored procedure executes a SQL SELECT statement to retrieve all of the records from the Addresses table that match the CustomerID specified as an input parameter.

sp_Addresses_INS

The sp_Addresses_INS stored procedure executes a SQL INSERT statement to insert a single record into the Addresses table using the data passed in through input parameters as values for the new record. This stored procedure provides an input parameter for each column of the Addresses table.

Order Processing Stored Procedures

The order processing stored procedures are responsible for selecting, inserting, and updating data in the Orders, OrderItems, OrderAddresses, and CreditCardPayments tables in the IBuyAdventure database.

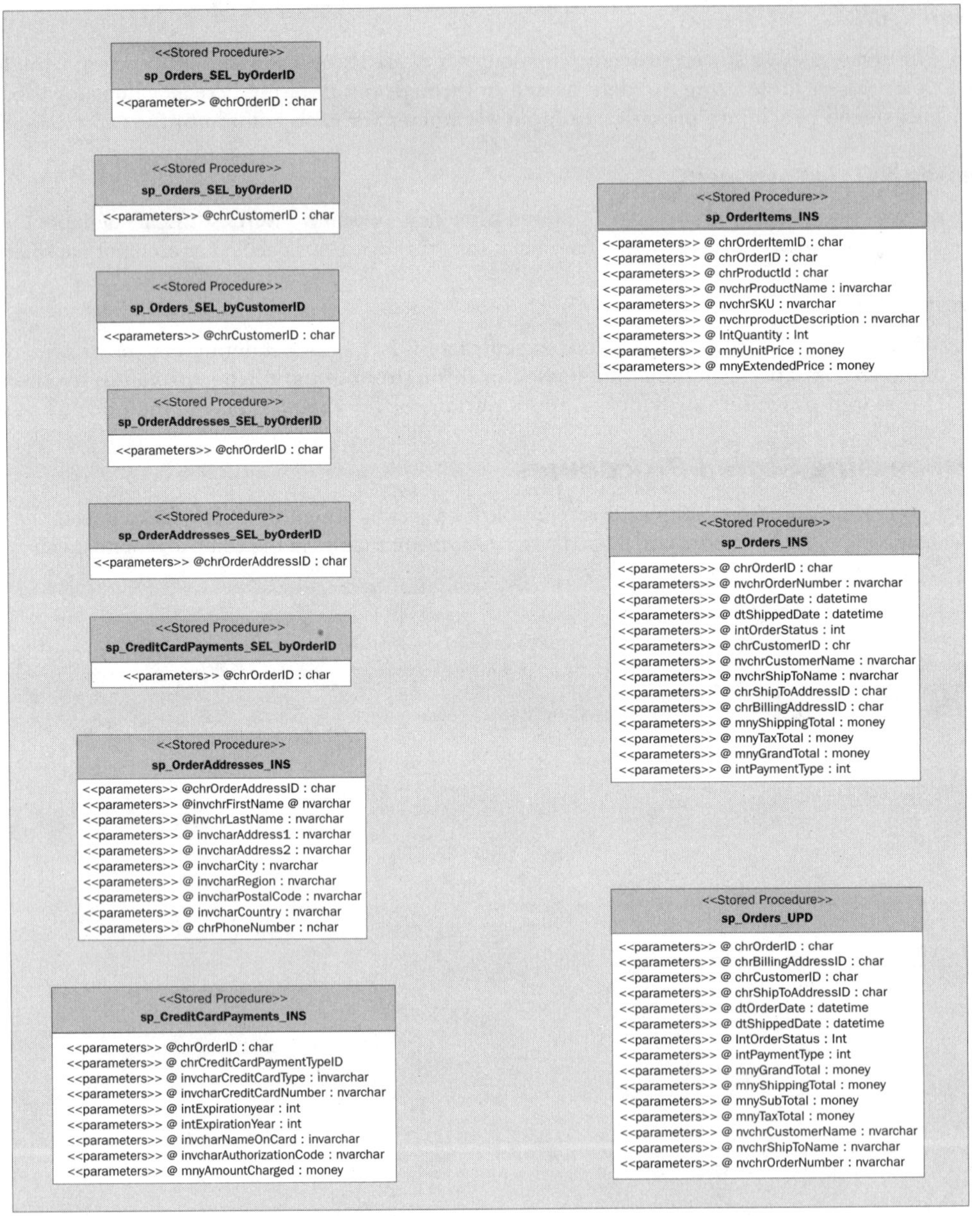

sp_Orders_INS

The `sp_Orders_INS` stored procedure executes a SQL `INSERT` statement to insert a single record into the `Orders` table using the data passed in through input parameters as values for the new record. This stored procedure provides an input parameter for each column of the `Orders` table.

sp_OrdersItems_INS

The sp_OrderItems_INS stored procedure executes a SQL INSERT statement to insert a single record into the OrderItems table using the data passed in through input parameters as values for the new record. This stored procedure provides an input parameter for each column of the OrderItems table.

sp_OrderAddresses_INS

The sp_OrderAddresses_INS stored procedure executes a SQL INSERT statement to insert a single record into the OrderAddresses table using the data passed in through input parameters as values for the new record. This stored procedure provides an input parameter for each column of the OrderAddresses table.

sp_CreditCardPayments_INS

The sp_CreditCardPayments_INS stored procedure executes a SQL INSERT statement to insert a single record into the CreditCardPayments table using the data passed in through input parameters as values for the new record. This stored procedure provides an input parameter for each column of the CreditCardPayments table.

sp_Orders_UPD

The sp_Orders_UPD stored procedure executes a SQL Update statement to update a single record in the Orders table using the data passed in through input parameters as values for the update. This stored procedure provides an input parameter for each column of the OrderItems table. The row that should be updated is specified by the OrderID, which is also passed in as an input parameter.

sp_Orders_SEL_byOrderID

The sp_Orders_SEL_byOrderID stored procedure executes a SQL SELECT statement to retrieve a single record from the Orders table that matches the OrderID specified as an input parameter.

sp_Orders_SEL_byCustomerID

The sp_Orders_SEL_byCustomerID stored procedure executes a SQL SELECT statement to retrieve all of the records from the Orders table that match the CustomerID specified as an input parameter.

sp_OrderItems_SEL_byOrderID

The sp_OrderItems_SEL_byOrderID stored procedure executes a SQL SELECT statement to retrieve the records from the OrderItems table associated with the order specified by the OrderID input parameter.

sp_CreditCardPayments_SEL_byOrderID

The sp_CreditCardPayments_SEL_byOrderID stored procedure executes a SQL SELECT statement to retrieve the records from the CreditCardPayments table matching the OrderID specified as an input parameter.

sp_OrderAddresses_SEL_byOrderAddressID

The sp_OrderAddresses_SEL_byOrderAddressID stored procedure executes a SQL SELECT statement to retrieve a single record from the OrderAddresses table matching the OrderAddressID specified as an input parameter.

sp_OrderAddresses_SEL_byOrderID

The `sp_OrderAddresses_SEL_byOrderID` stored procedure executes a SQL `SELECT` statement to retrieve the records from the `OrderAddresses` table associated with the order specified by the `OrderID` input parameter.

Inventory Management Stored Procedures

The inventory management stored procedures are responsible for selecting, inserting, and updating data in the `Inventory` and `InventoryAllocations` tables in the IBuyAdventure database.

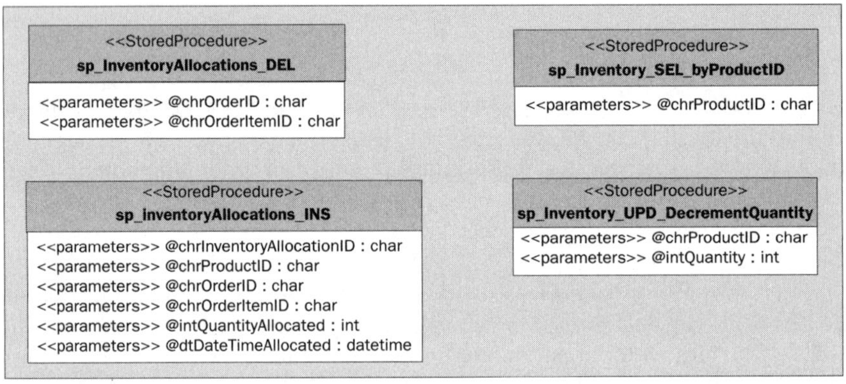

sp_Inventory_SEL_byProductID

The `sp_Inventory_SEL_byProductID` stored procedure executes a SQL `SELECT` statement to retrieve a single record from the `Inventory` table matching the `ProductID` specified as an input parameter. This stored procedure also calculates the available inventory for the specified product by summing of the `QuantityAllocated` for the product from the `InventoryAllocations` table and subtracting it from the `QuantityInStock` for the product from the `Inventory` table.

sp_Inventory_UPD_DecrementQuantity

The `sp_Inventory_UPD_DecrementQuantity` stored procedure executes a SQL `UPDATE` statement to update a single record in the `Inventory` table matching the `ProductID` specified as an input parameter. This stored procedure updates only the `QuantityInStock` column for the specified record by subtracting the current value in the `QuantityInStock` column by the amount specified in the `Quantity` input parameter.

sp_InventoryAllocations_INS

The `sp_InventoryAllocations_INS` stored procedure executes a SQL `INSERT` statement to insert a single record into the `InventoryAllocations` table using the data passed in through input parameters as values for the new record. This stored procedure provides an input parameter for each column of the `InventoryAllocations` table.

sp_InventoryAllocations_DEL

The `sp_InventoryAllocations_DEL` stored procedure executes a SQL `DELETE` statement to delete a single record in the `InventoryAllocations` table that matches the `OrderID` and `OrderItemID` specified as input parameters.

Physical Design

Now the conceptual and logical design of the IBuyAdventure system is complete. Before we begin the implementation itself, it is necessary to begin thinking about the physical aspects of the design, such as the assemblies, dependent technologies, and the physical architecture of the system. Although we won't go into a great amount of detail on these design aspects, some of tasks we performed during the physical design of the IBuyAdventure 2.0 system include:

- Choosing a programming language
- Organizing classes into namespaces
- Assigning classes to assemblies

Let's discuss each of these topics and learn about the decisions made for the IBuyAdventure system.

Choosing a Programming Language

With the .NET Framework and the Common Language Runtime, choosing a programming language is much easier than it was on the COM platform. In years past, choosing a programming language typically involved deciding between the core languages of Visual Basic, C++, Java, or Visual FoxPro. Each of these languages utilized a different programming model, making it difficult for developers to learn and be competent in multiple languages. In most situations the language's programming model had more to do with programming language selection rather than the actual syntax or constructs of the language itself. Each language also had its own benefits and drawbacks with respect to performance, developer productivity, and available tools.

With .NET we have a single, cross-language programming model consisting of thousands of classes. Each language provides its own unique syntax and techniques for performing common tasks, but the class library is consistent no matter which programming language is being utilized. Consequently, the programming language decision becomes less of an issue of developer familiarity, because most developers can quickly learn new programming languages by simply learning the syntax differences between the languages. Additionally, all languages are essentially treated as equals on the .NET platform, because all code is compiled to the Microsoft Intermediate Language (IL) before being executed by the Common Language Runtime. You can safely begin developing in one programming language and switch to another without having to rewrite all of your existing code.

The first version of the IBuyAdventure system was developed in C#; the new version will be developed entirely in Visual Basic .NET. There is no technical reason for using Visual Basic .NET exclusively, other than to be consistent with the rest of this book.

Organizing Classes in Namespaces

In the IBuyAdventure system, we'll simply define a namespace for each of the logical tiers with the exception of the Data Services tier, since it consists exclusively of SQL Server stored procedures. The following table details each namespace that we will define, and the classes and other types included in the namespace:

Namespace	Description	Classes/Types

`IBuyAdventure.Common`	The `IBuyAdventure.Common` namespace contains all of the classes that are common or shared across multiple tiers. These classes include the custom business objects, as well as typed dataset objects used to manage data in memory. These classes could have been further segmented into a `BusinessObjects` namespace and a `Datasets` namespace.	`Address`
		`Addresses`
		`CreditCardPayment`
		`Customer`
		`ExtensibleObjectBase`
		`Item`
		`Items`
		`Order`
		
		`AddressesDataset`
		`CategoriesDataset`
		`CreditCardPaymentsDataset`
		`CustomersDataset`
		`InventoryDataset`
		`OrderAddressesDataset`
		`OrderItemsDataset`
		`OrdersDataset`
		`ProductsDataset`

`IBuyAdventure.User Services`	The `IBuyAdventure.User Services` namespace contains the private classes, and all of the Web Form classes that compose the User Services tier of the IBuyAdventure system.	`AddItem`
		`Catalog`
		`Categories`
		`Checkout`
		`DefaultPage`
		`Footer`
		`Global`
		`Header`
		`Help`
		`Login`
		`NewAccount`
		`PaymentInfo`
		`Product`
		`Shopper`
		`ShoppingCard`
		`YourAccount`

Namespace	Description	Classes/Types

`IBuyAdventure.Business Services`	The `IBuyAdventure.Business Services` namespace contains the standard .NET classes and .NET Serviced Components that compose the business services tier of the IBuyAdventure system.	`Addresses`
		`AddressesTx`
		`Catalog`
		`CreditAuthorization`
		`CreditCardPaymentsTx`
		`Customers`
		`CustomersTx`
		`E-mailConfirmations`
		`ERPIntegrationTx`
		`FulfillmentTx`
		`InventoryManagement`
		`InventoryManagementTx`
		`OrderAddressesTx`
		`OrderCalculations`
		`OrderItemsTx`
		`OrderProcessingTx`
		`Orders`
		`OrdersTx`

`IBuyAdventure. WebServices`	The `IBuyAdventure.Web Services` namespace contains the `ReceiveOrderStatus Update` .NET HTTP Handler class.	`ReceiveOrderStatusUpdate`

Mapping Classes to Assemblies

Since we're using Visual Studio .NET to develop the IBuyAdventure system, the organization of classes to assemblies is dependent on the organization of classes within a project. In the IBuyAdventure system we'll simply create a Visual Studio .NET project, and thus an assembly, for each of the namespaces that we just defined. Although namespaces are not intrinsically tied to assemblies, this approach is used for simplicity. The following table details each assembly that we will define, and the classes and other types included in the namespace:

Assembly	Description	Classes/Types

`IBACommon.dll`	The `IBACommon.dll` assembly contains all of the common or shared classes that are defined in the `IBuyAdventure.Common` namespace.	`Address`
		`Addresses`
		`CreditCardPayment`
		`Customer`
		`ExtensibleObjectBase`
		`Item`
		`Items`
		`Order`
		
		`AddressesDataset`
		`CategoriesDataset`
		`CreditCardPaymentsDataset`
		`CustomersDataset`
		`InventoryDataset`
		`OrderAddressesDateset`
		`OrderItemsDataset`
		`OrdersDataset`
		`ProductsDataset`

`IBuyAdventure Web.dll`	The `IBuyAdventureWeb.dll` assembly contains all of the private classes and Web Forms that compose the User Services tier and are defined in the `IBuyAdventure.UserServices` namespace.	`AddItem`
		`Catalog`
		`Categories`
		`Checkout`
		`DefaultPage`
		`Footer`
		`Global`
		`Header`
		`Help`
		`Login`
		`NewAccount`
		`PaymentInfo`
		`Product`
		`Shopper`
		`ShoppingCard`
		`YourAccount`

Assembly	Description	Classes/Types
IBABS	The IBABS.dll assembly contains the standard .NET classes and .NET Serviced Components that compose the business services tier of the IBuyAdventure system. These classes are defined in the IBuyAdventure.BusinessServices namespace.	Addresses AddressesTx Catalog CreditAuthorization CreditCardPaymentsTx Customers CustomersTx E-mailConfirmations ERPIntegrationTx FulfillmentTx InventoryManagement InventoryManagementTx OrderAddressesTx OrderCalculations OrderItemsTx OrderProcessingTx Orders OrdersTx
IBuyAdventureWS	The IBuyAdventureWS.dll assembly contains the ReceiveOrderStatusUpdate .NET HTTP Handler.	ReceiveOrderStatusUpdate

Development Phase

Now that we have a clear understanding of the goals, functionality, and architecture of the IBuyAdventure system, let's take a look at some of the code and implementation details. Since we thoroughly discussed each Web Form, Business Services component, and stored procedure during the design phase of the system, we won't look at the code for each of these components. If we did so, this chapter would be a book in itself! Instead, for the sake of space, we'll focus on the core transactions of the IBuyAdventure system, including:

- Creating customer accounts
- Creating orders
- Receiving order status updates from the fulfillment provider

For each of these transactions we'll step through the code starting with the business services components, then the stored procedures that compose the data services tier, and finally with the ASP.NET Web Forms in the user services tier. But before we begin looking at the code for each of these transactions, let's examine the code for the IBuyAdventure common components, as they are central to each transaction and the entire system.

I just want to forewarn you that the amount of code to create the IBuyAdventure system is fairly sizable. I recommend downloading the entire IBuyAdventure system and browsing through the code on your local machine as you read along in this section.

Common Components

The `Common` components consist of the custom business objects and the typed datasets defined in the `IBuyAdventure.Common` namespace. As we discussed during the logical design, the IBuyAdventure common or shared components are used to pass structured data between tiers and components in the IBuyAdventure system. Before we begin developing the functionality for each of the three core transactions, we'll implement the following business objects contained in the `IBuyAdventure.Common` namespace:

- `ExtensibleObjectBase`
- `Order`
- `Items`

- `Item`
- `CreditCardPayment`
- `Address`
- `Addresses`
- `Customer`

Let's begin implementing each of these business objects, starting with the `ExtensibleObjectBase` class.

ExtensibleObjectBase

The `ExtensibleObjectBase` is a base (`MustInherit`) class that provides common functionality for the IBuyAdventure business objects. The `ExtensibleObjectBase` class maintains a private `StringDictionary` object that's used to store data as name/value pairs. Access to this data is provided by generic, public methods. Derived classes typically expose strongly typed property procedures on top of the data stored in the underlying `StringDictionary` object maintained by the `ExtensibleObjectBase` class. This class also provides manual serialization and deserialization of the data in the `StringDictionary`, since the `StringDictionary` class itself does not support serialzation.

We'll begin creating the `ExtensibleObjectBase` class by first importing the namespaces containing the types that are frequently used in the class file and define the namespace for this class.

```
'Import namespaces containing commonly used types
Imports System.Runtime.Serialization
Imports System.Collections.Specialized

Namespace IBuyAdventure.Common
```

Next we'll declare the `ExtensibleObjectBase` class as a `MustInherit` class, so it cannot be instantiated, but can only be used to derive new classes. We'll also implement the `System.Runtime.Serialization.ISerializable` interface so that classes that inherit from the `ExtensibleObjectBase` class can easily be serialized using the default serialization implementation in this base class.

```
    Public MustInherit Class ExtensibleObjectBase

        'Implement the System.RunTime.Serialization interface so this
        '...object can be serialized to the ASP.NET Session state
        '...and passed ByVal across boundaries
        Implements ISerializable
```

Now we'll declare a member-level instance variable to hold a reference to a `System.Collections.Specialized.StringDictionary` object. The `ExtensibleObjectBase` class (and its children) utilizes the `StringDictionary` object to maintain all of the data for the business object. By utilizing a dictionary instead of individual properties or fields, the `ExtensibleObjectBase` class and its children objects can easily store any amount of data.

```
        'declare a private variable to hold a reference to the
        '...StringDictionary object containing the Values for the base and
        '...derived classes.  Access to this StringDictionary object's
```

```
    '...contents is through the Value() property.
    Private m_dictValues As StringDictionary

    Protected Sub New()
        'Create an instance of the StringDictionary class to manage
        '...the dynamic values for this base class and derived classes
        m_dictValues = New StringDictionary()
    End Sub
```

Next let's create a protected method named `Deserialize`, which provides the ability to deserialize or recreate an object that derives from the `ExtensibleObjectBase` class. The `Deserialize` method simply populates our `StringDictionary` object with the values in the passed `SerializationInfo` object. This method is typically called by the deserialization constructor of an object that derives from the `ExtensibleObjectBase` class. We'll see an example of when this method is called later in this section.

```
    Public Sub Deserialize(ByVal info As SerializationInfo, _
                    ByVal context As StreamingContext)

        'Declare our procedure-level variables
        Dim objSerializationEntry As SerializationEntry

        'Iterate through each SerializationEntry in the passed
        '...SerializationInfo object and add the entry to our
        '...StringDictionary object
        For Each objSerializationEntry In info
            m_dictValues(objSerializationEntry.Name) = _
                                        objSerializationEntry.Value
        Next
    End Sub
```

The read-only XML public property builds and returns an XML-formatted string using the data in the `StringDictionary` object. First let's create an instance of the `System.IO.MemoryStream` class for managing the XML data in memory. Then let's create an instance of the `System.Xml.XmlWriter` class, and provide its constructor with a reference to the `MemoryStream` object for storing and managing the XML data.

```
    Public ReadOnly Property XML(ByVal strElementName As String) _
                                                        As String
        Get

            'declare the variables used in this property procedure
            Dim dictEntry As System.Collections.DictionaryEntry

            'Create an instance of the System.IO.MemoryStream class
            '...for managing the Address XML data in memory
            Dim objMemoryStream As New System.IO.MemoryStream()

            'Create an instance of the System.Xml.XmlTextWriter class
            '...and pass it a reference to the MemoryStream object for
            '...the underlying storage.
            Dim objXMLTextWriter As _
                New System.Xml.XmlTextWriter(objMemoryStream, _
                                    System.Text.Encoding.Default)
```

Using the new `XmlTextWriter` object, let's build an XML element with an attribute for each item in our `StringDictionary` object.

```
            'Build the XML document for this object, using the
            '...new XmlTextWriter object
            With objXMLTextWriter
                'Indent the XML we are building
                .Formatting = System.Xml.Formatting.Indented

                'Write the start tag with the specified element name
                .WriteStartElement(strElementName)

                'Iterate through each entry in the String Dictionary
                '...containing the data for this object and add an
                '...attribute for each entry.
                For Each dictEntry In m_dictValues
                    .WriteAttributeString(dictEntry.Key, _
                                             dictEntry.Value)
                Next

                'Write the closing tag for the specified element
                .WriteEndElement()

                'Write the XML to the MemoryStream object
                .Flush()
            End With
```

Finally, let's create an instance of the `System.IO.StreamReader` class for reading the contents of the `MemoryStream` and let's read and return the XML-formatted data from the `MemoryStream` object.

```
            'Move to the first position in the MemoryStream object
            '...containing the Address XML data.
            objMemoryStream.Position = 0

            'Create an instance of the System.IO.StreamReader class
            '...and load it with the contents of our MemoryStream
            Dim objStreamReader As _
                           New System.IO.StreamReader(objMemoryStream)

            'Return a string containing all of the XML data
            Return objStreamReader.ReadToEnd()
        End Get
    End Property
```

The `Value` public property simply sets and returns a string value for the specified key from the `StringDictionary` object. This property has the scope of `Public`, so it can be called by derived classes, as well as the clients using a derived class.

```
    'Provide public properties for retrieve and seting the value of
    '...our extensible properties for this class.
    Default Public Property Value(ByVal Key As String) As String
        Get
```

```
            'Simply return the value in our StringDictionary for the
            '...specified key
            Return m_dictValues(Key)
        End Get

        Set(ByVal strValue As String)
            'Set the value in our StringDictionary for the specified
            '...key name.
            m_dictValues(Key) = strValue
        End Set
    End Property
```

The `Values` property sets and returns the `StringDictionary` object that stores the data for the `ExtensibleObjectBase` class and it's derived classes. This property is declared with the scope of `Protected` so it can only be called by classes that inherit from this class.

```
    Protected Property Values() As StringDictionary
        Get
            'Return a reference to our StringDictionary object
            Return m_dictValues
        End Get

        Set(ByVal dictValues As StringDictionary)
            'Set our member-level String Dictionary object to the
            '...passed value
            m_dictValues = dictValues
        End Set
    End Property
```

Finally, the last method in the `ExtensibleObjectBase` base class is the implementation of the `GetObjectData` method that's defined by the `ISerializable` interface. The `GetObjectData` method is automatically called when an object whose class derived from the `ExtensibleObjectBase` class is being serialized. There are several situations when serialization occurs in .NET. In the IBuyAdventure system serialization occurs when an object is passed by value or when a business object is peristed to the ASP.NET Session State. We can serialize the `ExtensibleObject` base class by iterating through each entry in our `StringDictionary` and adding the value to the passed `SerializationInfo` object. This is just the opposite of the behavior implemented by the `Deserialize` method in this class.

```
    Public Overridable Sub GetObjectData( _
                              ByVal info As SerializationInfo, _
                              ByVal context As StreamingContext) _
                            Implements ISerializable.GetObjectData

        'Declare our procedure-level variables
        Dim dictEntry As System.Collections.DictionaryEntry

        'Iterate through each entry in the StringDictionary object
        '...containing the data for this class and add each entry to
        '...the passed SerializationInfo object.
        For Each dictEntry In m_dictValues
```

```
                    info.AddValue(dictEntry.Key, dictEntry.Value)
                Next
            End Sub
        End Class
    End Namespace
```

Order

The `Order` business object is used extensively in the IBuyAdventure system to store all of the information related to an order including the general order information, such as the `OrderID`, `OrderDate`, and `CustomerName`, the `CreditCardPayments` information, and the `Items` and `Addresses` assigned to the order. The `Order` business object inherits directly from the `ExtensibleObjectBase` class. Let's create the `Order` class now.

First let's import namespaces containing commonly used types, define the namespace for the `Order` class, and define the `Order` class itself. Notice that we apply the `Serializable` attribute to the `Order` class. This is required for the `Order` class to support serialization, including being passed by value between components and persisted to the ASP.NET Session State between page requests in the User Services tier.

```
    'Import namespaces containing commonly used types
    Imports System.Runtime.Serialization


    Namespace IBuyAdventure.Common

        'Mark this class as serializable so it can be passed by value between
        '...physical process boundaries and persisted to the session state
        <Serializable()> _
        Public Class Order
```

Next let's inherit from the `ExtensibleObjectBase` class that we created earlier.

```
            'Inherit from the custom ExtensibleObjectBase class so objects
            '...can easily be serialized and extensibly store data
            Inherits ExtensibleObjectBase
```

Then let's define public enumerations for the `Order Statuses` and `PaymentTypes` in the IBuyAdventure system.

```
            'Define a public enum to hold constants for the Order Statues that
            '...can take place in the IBuyAdventure system.
            Public Enum OrderStatusEnum
                OrderStatus_Received = 1
                OrderStatus_Processing = 2
                OrderStatus_Shipped = 3
            End Enum


            'Define a public enum to hold constants for the Payment Types
            '...in the IBuyAdventure system.
            Public Enum PaymentTypesEnum
```

```
        PaymentType_CreditCard = 1
        PaymentType_OnAccount = 2
    End Enum
```

Let's declare member-level variables to hold references to the other business objects used by the `Order` class. We'll also implement the default constructor for this class, which is responsible for creating instances of the child objects exposed by the `Order` business object.

```
    'Declare any member-level instance variables
    Private m_objItems As Items
    Private m_objAddresses As Addresses
    Private m_objCreditCardPayment As CreditCardPayment


    Public Sub New()

        'Create a new instance of the Items class for managing a
        '...collection of Item objects, representing the Items
        '...associated with this order.
        m_objItems = New Items()

        'Create a new instance of the Addresses class for managing a
        '...collection of Address objects, representing the Addresses
        '...associated with this order.
        m_objAddresses = New Addresses()

        'Create a new instance of the CreditCardPayment class
        m_objCreditCardPayment = New CreditCardPayment()


        'Create a new GUID value to be used as the unique OrderID.
        '...This value will be overriden during deserialization.
        MyBase.Values.Add("OrderID", System.Guid.NewGuid().ToString())
    End Sub
```

Next we'll implement the constructor required for creating instances of the `Order` class as the result of deserialization. Since the `Order` business object manages (and serializes) child objects such as the `Items` and `Addressses`, we can't utilize the simple deserialization provided by the `ExtensibleObjectBase` class. Instead we'll provide our own custom functionality in the deserializaton constructor for the `Order` business object.

```
    Public Sub New(ByVal info As SerializationInfo, _
                   ByVal context As StreamingContext)

        'Call our default constructor on this object to perform the
        '...default initialization for this object
        Me.New()


        'Declare our procedure-level variables
        Dim objSerializationEntry As SerializationEntry
```

```
        'Iterate through each SerializationEntry in the passed
        '...SerializationInfo object and Add the entry's value to our
        '...base class's data dictionary, if the entry is not the
        '...Items, Addresses, or CreditCardPayments objects
        For Each objSerializationEntry In info
            With objSerializationEntry
                If (.Name.Equals("Items") = False) _
                 And (.Name.Equals("Addresses") = False) _
                 And (.Name.Equals("CreditCardPayment") = False) Then

                    MyBase.Values(.Name) = .Value
                End If
            End With
        Next


        'Now deserialize the Items, Addresses, and CreditCardPayments
        '...objects into our member level variable.
        '
        'NOTE:  The actual deserialization of these subordinate
        '...objects will occur after this method completes.
        m_objItems = _
           info.GetValue("Items", GetType(IBuyAdventure.Common.Items))
        m_objAddresses = info.GetValue("Addresses", _
                              GetType(IBuyAdventure.Common.Addresses))
        m_objCreditCardPayment = info.GetValue("CreditCardPayment", _
                        GetType(IBuyAdventure.Common.CreditCardPayment))
    End Sub
```

Now let's define the public read-only property procedures for returning references to the subordinate objects associated with the `Order`. These objects include instances of the `CreditCardPayment` class, and the `Items` and `Addresses` collection classes.

```
    Public ReadOnly Property CreditCardPayment() As CreditCardPayment
        Get
            'Return a reference to the CreditCardPayment object
            '...containing all of the payment data for this order
            Return m_objCreditCardPayment
        End Get
    End Property


    Public ReadOnly Property Items() As Items
        Get
            'Return a reference to the Items collection object
            '...containing all of the Item object's for this Order.
            Return m_objItems
        End Get
    End Property


    Public ReadOnly Property Addresses() As Addresses
        Get
```

```
            'Return a reference to the Addresses collection object
            '...containing all of the Address object's for this Order.
            Return m_objAddresses
        End Get
    End Property
```

Now let's define public property procedures for the general order information. These property procedures are strongly typed, read and write properties that simply return or set the corresponding property value stored in the base class' `StringDictionary`, which is accessible through the base object's `Values` property. These methods are fairly simplistic.

```
    'Define public property procedures for common values so the data
    '...is read/written using strong types, which can also be used for
    '...data binding.
    Public Property OrderID() As String
        Get
            Return CType(MyBase.Values("OrderID"), String)
        End Get

        Set(ByVal Value As String)
            MyBase.Values("OrderID") = Value
        End Set
    End Property


    Public Property OrderNumber() As String
        Get
            'Return an emptystring if there isn't a value stored in
            '...the specified key.
            If MyBase.Values("OrderNumber") Is Nothing = False Then
                Return CType(MyBase.Values("OrderNumber"), String)
            Else
                Return ""
            End If
        End Get

        Set(ByVal Value As String)
            MyBase.Values("OrderNumber") = Value
        End Set
    End Property


    Public Property CustomerID() As String
        Get
            'Return an emptystring if there isn't a value stored in
            '...the specified key.
            If MyBase.Values("CustomerID") Is Nothing = False Then
                Return CType(MyBase.Values("CustomerID"), String)
            Else
                Return ""
            End If
        End Get
```

```
            Set(ByVal Value As String)
                MyBase.Values("CustomerID") = Value
            End Set
        End Property

        Public Property CustomerName() As String
            Get
                'Return an emptystring if there isn't a value stored in
                '...the specified key.
                If MyBase.Values("CustomerName") Is Nothing = False Then
                    Return CType(MyBase.Values("CustomerName"), String)
                Else
                    Return ""
                End If
            End Get

            Set(ByVal Value As String)
                MyBase.Values("CustomerName") = Value
            End Set
        End Property

        Public Property ShipToName() As String
            Get
                'Return an emptystring if there isn't a value stored in
                '...the specified key.
                If MyBase.Values("ShipToName") Is Nothing = False Then
                    Return CType(MyBase.Values("ShipToName"), String)
                Else
                    Return ""
                End If
            End Get

            Set(ByVal Value As String)
                MyBase.Values("ShipToName") = Value
            End Set
        End Property

        Public Property OrderDate() As String
            Get
                'Return an emptystring if there isn't a value stored in
                '...the specified key.
                If MyBase.Values("OrderDate") Is Nothing = False Then
                    Return CType(MyBase.Values("OrderDate"), String)
                Else
                    Return ""
                End If
            End Get

            Set(ByVal Value As String)
                MyBase.Values("OrderDate") = Value
            End Set
```

```
    End Property

    Public Property ShippedDate() As String
        Get
            'Return an emptystring if there isn't a value stored in
            '...the specified key.
            If MyBase.Values("ShippedDate") Is Nothing = False Then
                Return CType(MyBase.Values("ShippedDate"), String)
            Else
                Return ""
            End If
        End Get

        Set(ByVal Value As String)
            MyBase.Values("ShippedDate") = Value
        End Set
    End Property

    Public Property OrderStatus() As OrderStatusEnum
        Get
            'Return a default OrderStatus if there isn't a value
            '...stored in the specified key.
            If MyBase.Values("OrderStatus") Is Nothing = False Then
                Return CType(MyBase.Values("OrderStatus"), _
                                                       OrderStatusEnum)
            Else
                Return OrderStatusEnum.OrderStatus_Received
            End If
        End Get

        Set(ByVal Value As OrderStatusEnum)
            MyBase.Values("OrderStatus") = Value
        End Set
    End Property

    Public Property PaymentType() As PaymentTypesEnum
        Get
            'Return a default PaymentType if there isn't a value
            '...stored in the specified key.
            If MyBase.Values("PaymentType") Is Nothing = False Then
                Return CType(MyBase.Values("PaymentType"), _
                                                      PaymentTypesEnum)
            Else
                Return PaymentTypesEnum.PaymentType_CreditCard
            End If
        End Get

        Set(ByVal Value As PaymentTypesEnum)
            MyBase.Values("OrderStatus") = Value
        End Set
    End Property
```

```
        Public Property SubTotal() As Decimal
            Get
                Return CType(MyBase.Values("SubTotal"), Decimal)
            End Get

            Set(ByVal Value As Decimal)
                MyBase.Values("SubTotal") = Value
            End Set
        End Property


        Public Property ShippingTotal() As Decimal
            Get
                Return CType(MyBase.Values("ShippingTotal"), Decimal)
            End Get

            Set(ByVal Value As Decimal)
                MyBase.Values("ShippingTotal") = Value
            End Set
        End Property


        Public Property TaxTotal() As Decimal
            Get
                Return CType(MyBase.Values("TaxTotal"), Decimal)
            End Get

            Set(ByVal Value As Decimal)
                MyBase.Values("TaxTotal") = Value
            End Set
        End Property


        Public Property Total() As Decimal
            Get
                Return CType(MyBase.Values("Total"), Decimal)
            End Get

            Set(ByVal Value As Decimal)
                MyBase.Values("Total") = Value
            End Set
        End Property
```

The `ShippingAddress` property returns and sets the `Address` object that represents the shipping address for the order. The `AddressID` for the shipping address is stored in the `StringDictionary` managed by the base class. When the shipping address is being retrieved, this method simply gets the `AddressID` for the shipping address out of the base class' `StringDictionary` and returns the corresponding `Address` object from the private `Addresses` collection (instance of the `Addresses` class). When the shipping address is being set, this property procedure verifies that the `Address` already exists in the collection of `Addresses`, and if it doesn't then it is automatically added to the collection.

```
        Public Property ShippingAddress() As Address
            Get

                'Get the ShippingAddressID for this order out of our
                '...dictionary
                Dim strShippingAddressID As String = _
                                          MyBase.Values("ShippingAddressID")

                'Acquire and return a reference to the Address object from
                '...the Addresses Collection
                Return m_objAddresses(strShippingAddressID)
            End Get

            Set(ByVal Value As Address)

                'Get the AddressID for the passed Address object
                Dim strAddressID As String = Value.AddressID

                'Acquire a reference to the Address object from the
                '...Addresses collection
                Dim objExistingAddress = m_objAddresses(strAddressID)

                If objExistingAddress Is Nothing = True Then
                    'The passed Address object does not exist in our
                    '...collection of Addresses. Add it to the collection.
                    m_objAddresses.Add(Value)
                End If

                'Set the ShippingAddressID to the AddressID for the new or
                '...existing Address
                MyBase.Values("ShippingAddressID") = strAddressID
            End Set
        End Property
```

The `BillingAddress` property behaves exactly the same as the `ShippingAddress` property that we just discussed.

```
        Public Property BillingAddress() As Address
            Get

                'Get the BillingAddressID for this order out of our
                '...dictionary
                Dim strBillingAddressID As String = _
                                          MyBase.Values("BillingAddressID")

                'Acquire and return a reference to the Address object from
                '...the Addresses Collection
                Return m_objAddresses(strBillingAddressID)
            End Get

            Set(ByVal Value As Address)
```

```
                'Get the AddressID for the passed Address object
                Dim strAddressID As String = Value.AddressID

                'Acquire a reference to the Address object from the
                '...Addresses collection
                Dim objExistingAddress = m_objAddresses(strAddressID)

                If objExistingAddress Is Nothing = True Then
                    'The passed Address object does not exist in our
                    '...collection of Addresses. Add it to the collection.
                    m_objAddresses.Add(Value)
                End If

                'Set the BillingAddressID to the AddressID for the new or
                '...existing Address
                MyBase.Values("BillingAddressID") = strAddressID
            End Set
        End Property
```

The GetObjectData method, defined by the ISerializable interface, and implemented by the ExtensibleObjectBase class does not provide the desired behavior for serializing the Order business object. If you recall, this method is called when an object is serialized as a result of passing an object as a by value parameter or manually persisting the object, by saving the object to the ASP.NET Session State for example. The ExtensibleObjectBase class' implementation of this method only serializes the data in the StringDictionary. However, since the Order object also contains other objects that need to be serialized such as the Items, Addresses, and CreditCardPayments objects, it was necessary to override the base class's implementation of this method. We still perform the default serialization of the StringDictionary maintained by the base class by calling the GetObjectData method on the base, but we also append our instances of the Items, Addresses, and CreditCardPayments classes to the SerializationInfo dictionary passed into this method. It's important to understand that any objects added to the SerializationInfo dictionary must also support serialization. After the GetObjectData method completes, the Items, Addresses, and CreditCardPayment objects will automatically be serialized as well, because they were added to the SeralizationInfo dictionary by the Order object. This behavior, known as **Deep-Serialization**, allows us to serialize our entire object model, by simply serializing the Order object.

```
        Public Overrides Sub GetObjectData( _
                                ByVal info As SerializationInfo, _
                                ByVal context As StreamingContext)


            'Serialize this object by first performing the default
            '...Serialization procedures contained in the base class
            MyBase.GetObjectData(info, context)

            'Also, serialize the Items, Addresses, and CreditCardPayment
            '...objects by adding them to the SerializationInfo object
            info.AddValue("Items", m_objItems, GetType(Items))
            info.AddValue("Addresses", m_objAddresses, GetType(Addresses))
            info.AddValue("CreditCardPayment", m_objCreditCardPayment, _
                                         GetType(CreditCardPayment))
        End Sub
```

The XML property procedure provided by the `ExtensibleObjectBase` class is designed to return an XML-formatted string for the data stored in the underlying `StringDictionary` object. However, the XML data returned from the `ExtensibleObjectBase` class's XML property does not include the data for any child objects. With the `Orders` class, we need to return an XML document containing the data for the `Order` object, and the `Items` and `Addresses` associated with the order. So we'll create an overloaded version of the XML property that returns an XML-formatted string containing all of this data.

First we'll create an instance of the `System.IO.MemoryStream` class for managing the XML data in memory. Then we'll create an instance of the `System.Xml.XmlTextWriter` class using the new `MemoryStream` object as the underlying storage mechanism.

```
    Public Overloads ReadOnly Property XML() As String
        Get

            'declare the variables used in this property procedure
            Dim dictEntry As System.Collections.DictionaryEntry
            Dim objItem As Item
            Dim objAddress As Address


            'Create an instance of the System.IO.MemoryStream class
            '...for managing the Order XML data in memory
            Dim objMemoryStream As New System.IO.MemoryStream()

            'Create an instance of the System.Xml.XmlTextWriter class
            '...and pass it a reference to the MemoryStream object for
            '...the underlying storage.
            Dim objXMLTextWriter As _
                New System.Xml.XmlTextWriter(objMemoryStream, _
                                             System.Text.Encoding.Default)
```

Next we'll initialize our new `XmlTextWriter` object and write start tag for the root `Order` element. Then we'll iterate through each entry in the `StringDictionary` managed by the base class and write the value for each entry as an attribute of the `Order` element.

```
            'Build the XML document for this Order object, using the
            '...new XmlTextWriter object
            With objXMLTextWriter
                'Indent the XML we are building
                .Formatting = System.Xml.Formatting.Indented

                'Write the start of the document marker
                .WriteStartDocument()

                'Write the start tag for the <Order> element
                .WriteStartElement("Order")

                'Iterate through each entry in the String Dictionary
                '...containing the data for this class and add an
                '...attribute for each entry.
                For Each dictEntry In MyBase.Values
```

```
                .WriteAttributeString(dictEntry.Key, _
                                                   dictEntry.Value)
            Next
```

After the `Order` data has been written to the XML document we'll write the `Items` and `Addresses` by iterating through each collection and calling the `XML` property procedure provided by each object.

```
            'Write the start tag for the <Items> element
            .WriteStartElement("Items")

            'Iterate through each Item and get the Item's data
            '...formatted as XML and add the XML data to our
            '...current stream.
            For Each objItem In m_objItems
                .WriteRaw(objItem.XML)
            Next

            'Write the closing tag for the </Items> element
            .WriteEndElement()

            'Write the start tag for the <Addresses> element
            .WriteStartElement("Addresses")

            'Iterate through each Address and get the Address's
            '...data formatted as XML and add the XML data to
            '...our current stream.
            For Each objAddress In m_objAddresses
                .WriteRaw(objAddress.XML)
            Next

            'Write the closing tag for the </Addresses> element
            .WriteEndElement()
```

Then we'll write the XML data for the `CreditCardPayment` object associated with the `Order` by calling its `XML` property.

```
            'Write out the XML data for the CreditCardPayment
            .WriteRaw(m_objCreditCardPayment.XML)
```

We've included all of the `Order` data to the `MemoryStream` using the `XmlTextWriter` object. Now let's write the closing tag for the `Order` element and end the document.

```
            'Write the closing tag for the </Order> element
            .WriteEndElement()

            'Write the end of the document marker
            .WriteEndDocument()


            'Write the XML to the MemoryStream object
            .Flush()
        End With
```

Finally, we'll move to the first position in the MemoryStream object and create a new instance of the System.IO.StreamReader object for the MemoryStream. Using the new StreamReader object, we'll get and return a string for all of the XML data stored in the MemoryStream.

```
                'Move to the first position in the MemoryStream object
                '...containing the Order XML data.
                objMemoryStream.Position = 0

                'Create an instance of the System.IO.StreamReader class
                '...and load it with the contents of our MemoryStream
                Dim objStreamReader As _
                               New System.IO.StreamReader(objMemoryStream)

                'Return a string containing the XML formated Order
                Return objStreamReader.ReadToEnd()
            End Get
        End Property
    End Class
End Namespace
```

Items

The Items class is a strongly-typed collection class responsible for managing a collection of Item objects that represent the items on the order. This class inherits from the System.Collections.CollectionsBase base class, which provides generic methods and properties for managing a collection of objects.

We'll begin creating the Items class by importing the namespaces, declaring the Items class, and enclosing it in the IBuyAdventure.Common namespace. As I mentioned, this class will inherit from the CollectionsBase base class. The Items class also supports serialization by applying the Serializable attribute to the class declaration and by implementing the ISerializable interface.

```
'Import namespaces containing commonly used types
Imports System.Runtime.Serialization


Namespace IBuyAdventure.Common


    'Mark this class as serializable so it can be passed by value between
    '...physical process boundaries and persisted to the session state
    <Serializable()> _
    Public Class Items

        'Inherit from the System.Collections.CollectionBase class so this
        '...class can act as a strongly typed collection.
        Inherits System.Collections.CollectionBase

        'Implement the System.Runtime.Serialization.ISerializable interface
        '...so this class can manually serialize and deserialize itself.
        Implements ISerializable
```

The `Items` class exposes two constructors. The first constructor is a default constructor that does not provide any implementation. The second constructor is required for the `Items` class to support deserialization. In the deserialization constructor we will iterate through each of the entries in the passed `SerializationInfo` dictionary object and if the name of the entry is prefixed with the string `ItemID_`, we will acquire a reference to the `Item` object stored in the entry's value and add the new `Item` object to our collection. It's important to understand that by retrieving the `Item` object out of the `SerializationInfo` structure, the `Item` object itself will automatically be deserialized. After this constructor completes, the deserialization constructor for each `Item` object we loaded will be called. Since the deserialization constructor for the `Item` object is called after this constructor completes, the property values of the `Item` object are not available within this constructor. In other words, we can check the `ItemID` of the new `Item` object within this constructor because the `Item` object hasn't actually been deserialized yet.

```
        Public Sub New()
            'This constructor is provided so there is a default constructor
            '...for this class

        End Sub


        Public Sub New(ByVal info As SerializationInfo, _
                       ByVal context As StreamingContext)

            'declare our procedure-level variables
            Dim objSerializationEntry As SerializationEntry
            Dim objNewItem As Item

            'Acquire a reference to the IList interface for the passed
            '...object.
            Dim pIList As System.Collections.IList = MyBase.List

            'Iterate through each SerializationEntry in the passed
            '...SerializationInfo object
            For Each objSerializationEntry In info

                If objSerializationEntry.Name.IndexOf("ItemID_") <> -1 Then
                    'Deserialize this entry into an Item object because the
                    '...has a prefix "ItemID"
                    objNewItem = CType(objSerializationEntry.Value, _
                                       IBuyAdventure.Common.Item)

                    'Add the deserialized Item object to the base object's
                    '...underlying collection
                    pIList.Add(objNewItem)
                End If
            Next
        End Sub
```

Next we'll implement two Add methods, which add Item objects to the underlying collection provided by the CollectionBase base class. These Add methods are strongly typed to only manage instances of the Item class or instances of classes that derive from the Item class. The first Add method accepts parameters for the data associated with an item, creates an instance of the Item class passing the parameter values to the constructor, and then adds the new Item object to the collection, before returning it to the caller.

```
Public Function Add(ByVal strProductID As String, _
                    ByVal strSKU As String, _
                    ByVal strProductName As String, _
                    ByVal strListPrice As String, _
                    ByVal strDescription As String, _
                    ByVal intQuantity As Integer) As Item

    'Create a new instance of the Item class and pass the
    '...constructor the same values that were passed as parameters.
    Dim objNewItem As New Item(strProductID, strSKU, _
                   strProductName, strListPrice, strDescription, _
                                                     intQuantity)

    'Add the new Item object to the base collection
    MyBase.List.Add(objNewItem)

    'Return a reference to the new Item object
    Return objNewItem
End Function
```

The second Add method simply adds a passed Item object to the underlying collection and returns the added object to the caller. The purpose of returning the object to the caller is that we can optionally add additional processing for an Item when it is added to the collection, such as changing the ItemID, and then return the updated object to the caller to work with.

```
Public Function Add(ByVal objItem As Item) As Item

    'Add the passed Item object to the base class's collection
    MyBase.List.Add(objItem)

    'return the new Item object to the caller
    Return objItem
End Function
```

The Items class provides two read-only property procedures named Item, which return references to specific Item objects within the collection. The first Item property accepts the index of the Item object requested. The second Item property accepts the ItemID of the desired Item as a parameter and iterates through the collection of Item objects until an object with a matching ItemID is located. If a matching Item object is located, then a reference to the object is returned. Otherwise, a value of Nothing is returned.

```
Default Public ReadOnly Property Item(ByVal Index As Long) As Item
    Get
        'Get and return a reference to the Item object specified by
        '...the passed Index
```

```
            Return MyBase.List.Item(Index)
        End Get
    End Property

    Default Public ReadOnly Property Item( _
                                ByVal strItemID As String) As Item
        Get
            'declare our property-level variables
            Dim objItem As Item
            Dim objFoundItem As Item = Nothing

            'Iterate through each Item object in the base classes
            '...collection.  If the ItemID for the item matches the
            '...specified ItemID, we'll get a reference to the matching
            '...item.
            For Each objItem In MyBase.List
                If objItem.ItemID.Equals(strItemID) Then
                    objFoundItem = objItem
                    Exit For
                End If
            Next

            'Return the reference to the matching item or Nothing
            Return objFoundItem
        End Get
    End Property
```

The `Items` class provides two overloaded versions of a `Remove` method, which is used to remove an `Item` object from the collection. The first version accepts the `Item` object that should be removed as a parameter and then removes the object by calling the `Remove` method of the base class's `IList` interface. The second version accepts an `ItemID` indicating which `Item` should be removed. This method then acquires a reference to the `Item` object specified by the passed `ItemID` by calling the `Item` property implemented by this class and then removes the object from the collection using the acquired reference.

```
    Public Sub Remove(ByRef objItem As Item)
        'Remove the passed Item object from the collection, using the
        '...base object
        MyBase.List.Remove(objItem)
    End Sub


    Public Sub Remove(ByVal strItemID As String)

        'Acquire a reference to the Item object for the specified
        '... ItemID, by calling the default Item property on this class
        Dim objItem As Item = Me.Item(strItemID)

        'Remove the specified item by calling the other public Remove
        '...method of this class
        Me.Remove(objItem)
    End Sub
```

Finally, we need to implement the GetObjectData method defined by the ISerializable interface that we implemented earlier. When the GetObjectData method is called because the Items object is being serialized (by the GetObjectData method in the Orders class), then we'll iterate through the collection of Item objects and add each Item object to the passed SerializationInfo dictionary. Since the names of entries in the SerializationInfo dictionary must be unique, we'll construct a name by appending the prefix ItemID_ to the Item object's ItemID GUID value.

```
        Public Sub GetObjectData(ByVal info As SerializationInfo, _
                                 ByVal context As StreamingContext) _
                                    Implements ISerializable.GetObjectData

            'Declare our procedure-level variables
            Dim objItem As Item

            'Iterate through each Item object in the base Collection and add
            '...the Item to the passed SerializationInfo object with the key
            '...being the ItemID prefixed by "ItemID_"
            For Each objItem In MyBase.List
                info.AddValue("ItemID_" & objItem.ItemID, _
                                          objItem, GetType(Item))
            Next
        End Sub

    End Class
End Namespace
```

Item

The Item class represents an Item that is associated with an Order (through the Items collection class). The Item class provides read/write properties that can be used to access the data associated with an item.

Let's begin implementing the Item class by importing the commonly used namespaces, declaring our class with the Serializable Attribute, and inheriting from the ExtensibleObjectBase base class.

```
'Import namespaces containing commonly used types
Imports System.Runtime.Serialization


Namespace IBuyAdventure.Common

    'Mark this class as serializable so it can be passed by value between
    '...physical process boundaries and persisted to the session state
    <Serializable()> _
    Public Class Item

        'Inherit from the custom ExtensibleObjectBase class (also in this
        '...project) so this class's objects can easily be serialized and
        '...store data extensibly
        Inherits ExtensibleObjectBase
```

The `Item` class provides three constructors that can be used to create new instances. The first constructor is a default constructor that initializes the new `Item` object by creating a new GUID value for the `ItemID`. The second constructor provides several parameters that can be specified when creating a new instance of the `Item` class. After initializing the new object by calling the default constructor, the values of these parameters are loaded in to the base class's `StringDictionary` object. The third constructor is a deserialization constructor that, when called, initializes the new object and performs the default deserialization by calling the `Deserialize` method of the `EntensibleObjectBase` class.

```
    Public Sub New()

        'Create a new GUID value for the CreditCardPaymentID and store
        '...it in our dictionary
        MyBase.Values.Add("ItemID", System.Guid.NewGuid().ToString())
    End Sub


    Public Sub New(ByVal strProductID As String, _
                   ByVal strSKU As String, _
                   ByVal strProductName As String, _
                   ByVal strListPrice As String, _
                   ByVal strDescription As String, _
                   ByVal intQuantity As Integer)

        'Call our default constructor on this object to perform the
        '...default initialization
        Me.New()

        'Store the data in the passed parameters in the base object's
        '...dictionary object
        MyBase.Values("ProductID") = strProductID
        MyBase.Values("SKU") = strSKU
        MyBase.Values("ProductName") = strProductName
        MyBase.Values("ListPrice") = strListPrice
        MyBase.Values("Description") = strDescription
        MyBase.Values("Quantity") = intQuantity
    End Sub


    Public Sub New( _
         ByVal info As System.Runtime.Serialization.SerializationInfo, _
         ByVal context As System.Runtime.Serialization.StreamingContext)

        'Call our default constructor on this object to perform the
        '...default initialization for this object
        Me.New()

        'Deserialize this object by performing the default
        '...deserialization procedures contained in the base class
        MyBase.Deserialize(info, context)
    End Sub
```

Next, we'll define the strongly typed public property procedures that can be used to read and write the data for the `Item` object. These property procedures simply encapsulate access to the data managed in the base class's `StringDictionary` object.

```
'Define public property procedures for common values so the data is
'...read/written using strong types, which can also be used for data
'...binding.
Public Property ItemID() As String
    Get
        Return CType(MyBase.Values("ItemID"), String)
    End Get

    Set(ByVal Value As String)
        MyBase.Values("ItemID") = Value
    End Set
End Property


Public Property ProductID() As String
    Get
        Return CType(MyBase.Values("ProductID"), String)
    End Get

    Set(ByVal Value As String)
        MyBase.Values("ProductID") = Value
    End Set
End Property


Public Property SKU() As String
    Get
        Return CType(MyBase.Values("SKU"), String)
    End Get

    Set(ByVal Value As String)
        MyBase.Values("SKU") = Value
    End Set
End Property

Public Property ProductName() As String
    Get
        Return CType(MyBase.Values("ProductName"), String)
    End Get

    Set(ByVal Value As String)
        MyBase.Values("ProductName") = Value
    End Set
End Property


Public Property Description() As String
    Get
        Return CType(MyBase.Values("Description"), String)
    End Get
```

```
        Set(ByVal Value As String)
            MyBase.Values("Description") = Value
        End Set
    End Property

    Public Property ListPrice() As Decimal
        Get
            Return CType(MyBase.Values("ListPrice"), Decimal)
        End Get

        Set(ByVal Value As Decimal)
            MyBase.Values("ListPrice") = Value
        End Set
    End Property

    Public Property Quantity() As Integer
        Get
            Return CType(MyBase.Values("Quantity"), System.Int32)
        End Get

        Set(ByVal Value As Integer)
            MyBase.Values("Quantity") = Value
        End Set
    End Property


    Public Property UnitPrice() As Decimal
        Get
            Return CType(MyBase.Values("UnitPrice"), Decimal)
        End Get

        Set(ByVal Value As Decimal)
            MyBase.Values("UnitPrice") = Value
        End Set
    End Property

    Public Property ExtendedPrice() As Decimal
        Get
            Return CType(MyBase.Values("ExtendedPrice"), Decimal)
        End Get

        Set(ByVal Value As Decimal)
            MyBase.Values("ExtendedPrice") = Value
        End Set
    End Property
```

Finally, we'll create an overloaded version of the XML read-only property that returns the `Item` object's data as an XML-formatted string by calling the XML property provided by the `ExtensibleObjectBase` class. The XML data structure will have a root element name of `Item`. This property procedure is overloaded because the `ExtensibleObjectBase` class also provides an XML property, which we actually call here.

```
        Public Overloads ReadOnly Property XML() As String
            Get
                'Return the data for this object formatted as XML by using
                '...the default persistence mechanism built into the base
                '...class.  The root element should be named "Item".
                Return MyBase.XML("Item")
            End Get
        End Property
    End Class
End Namespace
```

CreditCardPayment

The `CreditCardPayment` class manages the credit card information for an order, such as the `CreditCardNumber`, the `ExpirationMonth`, the `ExpirationYear`, etc.

Let's begin creating the `CreditCardPayment` class by importing the namespaces containing commonly used types and declaring the class within the `IBuyAdventure.Common` namespace. The `CreditCardPayment` class also supports `Serialization` and inherits from the `ExtensibleObjectBase` class.

```
'Import namespaces containing commonly used types
Imports System.Runtime.Serialization


Namespace IBuyAdventure.Common

    'Mark this class as serializable so it can be passed by value between
    '...physical process boundaries and persisted to the session state
    <Serializable()> _
    Public Class CreditCardPayment

        'Inherit from the custom ExtensibleObjectBase class (also in this
        '...project) so this class's objects can easily be serialized and
        '...store data extensibly
        Inherits ExtensibleObjectBase
```

Next we'll implement the constructors for the `CreditCardPayment` class. In the default constructor we'll simply initialize the `CreditCardPaymentID` stored in the base object's `StringDictionary` with a new GUID value.

```
        Public Sub New()

            'Create a new GUID value for the CreditCardPaymentID and store
            '...it in our dictionary
            MyBase.Values.Add("CreditCardPaymentID", _
                                          System.Guid.NewGuid().ToString())
        End Sub
```

For the deserialization constructor, we'll initialize the object by calling the default constructor and then perform the default deserialization of the object's data by calling the `Deserialize` method provided by the base class.

```
        Public Sub New(ByVal info As SerializationInfo, _
                       ByVal context As StreamingContext)

            'Call our default constructor on this object to perform the
            '...default initialization
            Me.New()

            'Deserialize this object by performing the default
            '...deserialization procedures contained in the base class
            MyBase.Deserialize(info, context)
        End Sub
```

Next, we'll define the strongly typed public property procedures that simply provide read and write access to the credit card payment information, which is managed in the base class's `StringDictionary` object.

```
        'Define public property procedures for common values so the data is
        '...read/written using strong types, which can also be used for data
        '...binding.
        Public Property CreditCardPaymentID() As String
            Get
                Return CType(MyBase.Values("CreditCardPaymentID"), String)
            End Get

            Set(ByVal Value As String)
                MyBase.Values("CreditCardPaymentID") = Value
            End Set
        End Property

        Public Property CardNumber() As String
            Get
                Return CType(MyBase.Values("CardNumber"), String)
            End Get

            Set(ByVal Value As String)
                MyBase.Values("CardNumber") = Value
            End Set
        End Property

        Public Property CardType() As String
            Get
                Return CType(MyBase.Values("CardType"), String)
            End Get

            Set(ByVal Value As String)
                MyBase.Values("CardType") = Value
            End Set
        End Property

        Public Property NameOnCard() As String
            Get
                Return CType(MyBase.Values("NameOnCard"), String)
            End Get
```

```
        Set(ByVal Value As String)
            MyBase.Values("NameOnCard") = Value
        End Set
    End Property

    Public Property ExpirationMonth() As String
        Get
            Return CType(MyBase.Values("ExpirationMonth"), String)
        End Get

        Set(ByVal Value As String)
            MyBase.Values("ExpirationMonth") = Value
        End Set
    End Property

    Public Property ExpirationYear() As String
        Get
            Return CType(MyBase.Values("ExpirationYear"), String)
        End Get

        Set(ByVal Value As String)
            MyBase.Values("ExpirationYear") = Value
        End Set
    End Property

    Public Property AuthorizationCode() As String
        Get
            'Return an emptystring if there isn't a value stored in the
            '...specified key.
            If MyBase.Values("AuthorizationCode") Is Nothing _
                                                            = False Then
                Return CType(MyBase.Values("AuthorizationCode"), String)
            Else
                Return ""
            End If
        End Get

        Set(ByVal Value As String)
            MyBase.Values("AuthorizationCode") = Value
        End Set
    End Property

    Public Property AmountCharged() As Decimal
        Get
            'Return 0 if there isn't a value stored in the specified
            '...key.
            If MyBase.Values("AmountCharged") Is Nothing = False Then
                Return CType(MyBase.Values("AmountCharged"), Decimal)
            Else
                Return 0
            End If
        End Get
```

```
            Set(ByVal Value As Decimal)
                MyBase.Values("AmountCharged") = Value
            End Set
        End Property
```

Finally, we'll create an overloaded version of the XML read-only property that simply returns the `CreditCardPayment` object's data as XML by calling the XML property provided by the `ExtensibleObjectBase` class. The XML data structure will have a root element name of `Payment`.

```
        Public Overloads ReadOnly Property XML() As String
            Get
                'Return the data for this object formatted as XML by using
                '...the default persistence mechanism built into the base
                '...class. The root element should be named "Payment".
                Return MyBase.XML("Payment")
            End Get
        End Property
    End Class
End Namespace
```

Address

The `Address` business object represents a customer or order address in the IBuyAdventure system. This class inherits from the `ExtensibleObjectBase` class and simply provides strongly typed properties for each of the address-related fields stored in the system.

Let's begin implementing the `Address` class by defining the structure for the class file and inheriting from the `ExtensibleObjectBase` class. We'll also apply the `Serializable` attribute to the class declaration so the `Address` object can be serialized along with an order or a customer, when they, as parent objects, are serialized.

```
Imports System.Runtime.Serialization

Namespace IBuyAdventure.Common

    'Mark this class as serializable so it can be passed by value between
    '...physical process boundaries and persisted to the session state
    <Serializable()> _
    Public Class Address

        'Inherit from the custom ExtensibleObjectBase class (also in this
        '...project) so this class's objects can easily be serialized and
        '...store data extensibly
        Inherits ExtensibleObjectBase
```

Next we'll implement the default constructor for the `Address` class. For now we'll simply create a new GUID value to be used as the `AddressID` for the `Address` object.

```
        Public Sub New()

            'Create a new GUID value for the AddressID and store it in our
```

```
        '...dictionary
        MyBase.Values.Add("AddressID", System.Guid.NewGuid().ToString())
    End Sub
```

The Address business object also defines a public constructor that accepts parameters for each of the address-fields. When called, this constructor simply performs the default initialization by calling the default constructor and then maps the values in the passed parameters to their corresponding keys in the base class's string dictionary.

```
    Public Sub New(ByVal strAddress1 As String, _
                   ByVal strAddress2 As String, _
                   ByVal strCity As String, _
                   ByVal strRegion As String, _
                   ByVal strPostalCode As String, _
                   ByVal strCountry As String, _
                   ByVal strPhone As String)

        'Call our default constructor on this object to perform the
        '...default initialization
        Me.New()

        'Store the data in the passed parameters into our dictionary
        '...object
        MyBase.Value("Address1") = strAddress1
        MyBase.Value("Address2") = strAddress2
        MyBase.Value("City") = strCity
        MyBase.Value("Region") = strRegion
        MyBase.Value("PostalCode") = strPostalCode
        MyBase.Value("PhoneNumber") = strPhone
        MyBase.Value("Country") = strCountry
    End Sub
```

Next let's create the deserialization constructor for the Address business object. This constructor simply calls the default constructor to initialize the object and then calls the generic Deserialization method provided by the ExtensibleObjectBase class.

```
    Public Sub New(ByVal info As SerializationInfo, _
                   ByVal context As StreamingContext)

        'Call our default constructor on this object to perform the
        '...default initialization for this object
        Me.New()

        'Deserialize this object by performing the default
        '...deserialization procedures contained in the base class
        MyBase.Deserialize(info, context)
    End Sub
```

Now we'll create an overloaded version of the XML read-only property that returns the Address object's data as an XML-formatted string by calling the XML property provided by the ExtensibleObjectBase class. The XML data structure will have a root element name of Address.

```
        Public Overloads ReadOnly Property XML() As String
            Get
                'Return the data for this object formatted as XML by using
                '...the default persistence mechanism built into the base class.
                '...The root element should be named "Item".
                Return MyBase.XML("Address")
            End Get
        End Property
```

Finally, we'll define the strongly typed public property procedures that simply provide read and write access to the address data stored in the base class' `StringDictionary` object.

```
        'Define public property procedures for common values so the data is
        '...read/written using strong types, which can also be used for
        '...data binding.

        Public Property AddressID() As String
            Get
                Return CType(MyBase.Value("AddressID"), String)
            End Get

            Set(ByVal Value As String)
                MyBase.Value("AddressID") = Value
            End Set
        End Property

        Public Property Firstname() As String
            Get
                Return CType(MyBase.Value("Firstname"), String)
            End Get

            Set(ByVal Value As String)
                MyBase.Value("Firstname") = Value
            End Set
        End Property

        Public Property Lastname() As String
            Get
                Return CType(MyBase.Value("Lastname"), String)
            End Get

            Set(ByVal Value As String)
                MyBase.Value("Lastname") = Value
            End Set
        End Property

        Public Property Address1() As String
            Get
                Return CType(MyBase.Value("Address1"), String)
            End Get

            Set(ByVal Value As String)
                MyBase.Value("Address1") = Value
```

```
        End Set
    End Property

    Public Property Address2() As String
        Get
            Return CType(MyBase.Value("Address2"), String)
        End Get

        Set(ByVal Value As String)
            MyBase.Value("Address2") = Value
        End Set
    End Property

    Public Property City() As String
        Get
            Return CType(MyBase.Value("City"), String)
        End Get

        Set(ByVal Value As String)
            MyBase.Value("City") = Value
        End Set
    End Property

    Public Property Region() As String
        Get
            Return CType(MyBase.Value("Region"), String)
        End Get

        Set(ByVal Value As String)
            MyBase.Value("Region") = Value
        End Set
    End Property

    Public Property PostalCode() As String
        Get
            Return CType(MyBase.Value("PostalCode"), String)
        End Get

        Set(ByVal Value As String)
            MyBase.Value("PostalCode") = Value
        End Set
    End Property

    Public Property Country() As String
        Get
            Return CType(MyBase.Value("Country"), String)
        End Get

        Set(ByVal Value As String)
            MyBase.Value("Country") = Value
        End Set
    End Property

    Public Property PhoneNumber() As String
```

```
            Get
                Return CType(MyBase.Value("PhoneNumber"), String)
            End Get

            Set(ByVal Value As String)
                MyBase.Value("PhoneNumber") = Value
            End Set
        End Property
    End Class
End Namespace
```

Addresses

The Addresses class is a strongly typed collection class responsible for managing a collection of Address objects that represent the Addresses associated with an order or with a customer. This class is very similar to the Items class.

We'll begin creating the Addresses class by importing the namespaces, declaring the Addresses class, and enclosing it in the IBuyAdventure.Common namespace. This class inherits from the System.Collections.CollectionsBase base class, which provides the underlying collection. The Addresses class also supports serialization by applying the Serializable attribute to the class declaration and by implementing the ISerializable interface.

```
'Import namespaces containing commonly used types
Imports System.Runtime.Serialization


Namespace IBuyAdventure.Common

    'Mark this class as serializable so it can be passed by value between
    '...physical process boundaries and persisted to the session state
    <Serializable()> _
    Public Class Addresses

        'Inherit from the System.Collections.CollectionBase class so this
        '...class can act as a strongly typed collection.
        Inherits System.Collections.CollectionBase

        'Implement the System.Runtime.Serialization.ISerializable interface
        '...so this class can manually serialize and deserialize itself.
        Implements ISerializable
```

The Addresses class provides two constructors. The first constructor is simply a default constructor without any implementation and the second constructor is the deserialization constructor. The deserialization constructor iterates through the entries in the passed SerializationInfo dictionary and deserializes each Address object stored in the dictionary. We determine that an entry contains an Address object when the entry's name is prefixed with AddressID_. The Address object is then added to our collection.

```
        Public Sub New()
            'This constructor is provided so there is a default constructor
```

```
            '...for this class

        End Sub


        Public Sub New(ByVal info As SerializationInfo, _
                    ByVal context As StreamingContext)

            'declare our procedure-level variables
            Dim objSerializationEntry As SerializationEntry
            Dim objNewAddress As Address

            'Acquire a reference to the IList interface for the base object.
            Dim pIList As System.Collections.IList = MyBase.List

            'Iterate through each SerializationEntry in the passed
            '...SerializationInfo object
            For Each objSerializationEntry In info

                If objSerializationEntry.Name.IndexOf("AddressID_") _
                                                        <> -1 Then
                    'Deserialize this entry into an Address object because
                    '...the key has a prefix "AddressID"
                    objNewAddress = CType(objSerializationEntry.Value, _
                                                          Address)

                    'Add the deserialized Address object to the base
                    '...object's underlying(Collection)
                    pIList.Add(objNewAddress)
                End If
            Next
        End Sub
```

The Addresses class provides two overloaded versions of an Add method, used to add Address objects to the collection. The first version accepts all of the data for the Address as parameters and creates a new Address object using the passed data. The second version simply adds a passed Address object to the underlying collection.

```
        Public Function Add(ByVal strAddress1 As String, _
                            ByVal strAddress2 As String, _
                            ByVal strCity As String, _
                            ByVal strRegion As String, _
                            ByVal strPostalCode As String, _
                            ByVal strCountry As String, _
                            ByVal strPhone As String) As Address

            'Create a new instance of the Address class and forward the
            '...values passed to this method to the constructor
            Dim objAddress As New Address(strAddress1, strAddress2, _
                        strCity, strRegion, strPostalCode, _
                        strCountry, strPhone)

            'Add the passed Address object to the base class's collection
```

```
        MyBase.List.Add(objAddress)

        'return the new Address object to the caller
        Return objAddress
    End Function

    Public Function Add(ByVal objAddress As Address) As Address

        'Add the passed Address object to the base class's collection
        MyBase.List.Add(objAddress)

        'return the new Address object to the caller
        Return objAddress
    End Function
```

The Addresses class provides two read-only property procedures named Address, that return references to specific Address objects within the collection. The first Address property accepts the index of the Address object requested, based on its position in the collection. The second Address property accepts the AddressID of the requested Address as a parameter and iterates through the collection of Address objects until an object with a matching AddressID is found. If a matching Item object is found, then a reference to the object is returned. Otherwise, a value of Nothing will be returned.

```
    Default Public ReadOnly Property Address(ByVal Index As Long) _
                                                            As Address
        Get
            'Get and return a reference to the Address object specified
            '...by the passed Index
            Return MyBase.List.Item(Index)
        End Get
    End Property

    Default Public ReadOnly Property Address( _
                                ByVal strAddressID As String) As Address
        Get
            'declare our property-level variables
            Dim objAddress As Address
            Dim objFoundAddress As Address = Nothing

            'Iterate through each Item object in the base classes
            '...collection.  If the AddressID for the item matches the
            '...specified AddressID, we'll get a reference to the
            '...matching address object.
            For Each objAddress In MyBase.List
                If objAddress.AddressID.Equals(strAddressID) Then
                    objFoundAddress = objAddress
                    Exit For
                End If
            Next

            'Return the reference to the matching Address object or
```

```
                '...Nothing
                Return objFoundAddress
            End Get
        End Property
```

The Addresses class exposes two overloaded Remove methods used to remove Address objects from the collection. The first Remove method simply removes a specified Address object from the underlying collection. The second Remove method locates the Address specified by a passed AddressID by calling the Address property on this class and then removes the object using the acquired reference.

```
        Public Sub Remove(ByRef objAddress As Address)
            'Remove the passed Address object from the collection, using the
            '...base object
            MyBase.List.Remove(objAddress)
        End Sub

        Public Sub Remove(ByVal strAddressID As String)

            'Acquire a reference to the Address object for the specified
            '...AddressID, by calling the default Item property on this
            '...class
            Dim objAddress As Address = Me.Address(strAddressID)

            'Remove the specified Address by calling the other public Remove
            '...method of this class
            Me.Remove(objAddress)
        End Sub
```

Finally, the Addresses class must implement the GetObjectData method defined by the ISerializable interface in order to provide serialization. Within this method we'll simply iterate through each Address object in our underlying collection and add the Address object as an entry to the passed SerializationInfo dictionary. The literal string AddressID_ is appended to the AddressID for the object to facilitate deserialization and ensure that the name of the added entry is unique. Adding an Address object to the SerializationInfo structure will cause the GetObjectData method to be called on the Address class for each object that is added.

```
        Public Sub GetObjectData(ByVal info As SerializationInfo, _
                                 ByVal context As StreamingContext) _
                                Implements ISerializable.GetObjectData


            'Declare our procedure-level variables
            Dim objAddress As Address

            'Iterate through each Item object in the base Collection and add
            '...the Item to the passed SerializationInfo object with the key
            '...being the AddressID prefixed by "AddressID_"
            For Each objAddress In MyBase.List
                info.AddValue("AddressID_" & objAddress.AddressID, _
                                        objAddress, GetType(Address))
```

```
            Next
        End Sub
    End Class
End Namespace
```

Customer

The Customer class is responsible for encapsulating the data associated with a Customer and providing access to the data through read/write property procedures. This class inherits from the ExtensibleObjectBase class, which is used to manage all of the data in an underlying StringDictionary object.

Let's begin creating the Customer class by declaring it with the Serializable attribute and inheriting from the ExtensibleObjectBase class.

```
'Import namespaces containing commonly used types
Imports System.Runtime.Serialization


Namespace IBuyAdventure.Common


    'Mark this class as serializable so it can be passed by value between
    '...physical process boundaries and persisted to the session state
    <Serializable()> _
    Public Class Customer

        'Inherit from the custom ExtensibleObjectBase class (also in this
        '...project) so this class's objects can easily be serialized and
        '...store data extensibly
        Inherits ExtensibleObjectBase
```

Next we'll define some public enumerations for the possible Customer Types and the possible Account Statuses. We'll also declare the member-level instance variable used to hold a reference to an instance of the Addresses class.

```
        'Define a public enum with constants for the CustomerTypes supported
        '...in the system.
        Public Enum CustomerTypesEnum
            CustomerType_Unknown = 0
            CustomerType_Consumer = 1
            CustomerType_Business = 2
        End Enum

        'Define a public enum with constants for the possible Account
        '...Statuses
        Public Enum AccountStatusEnum
            AccountStatus_Enabled = 1
            AccountStatus_Disabled = 2
        End Enum
```

```
        'Declare any member-level instance variables
        Private m_objItems As Items
        Private m_objAddresses As Addresses
```

Like all of the other business objects in the `IBuyAdventure.Common` namespace, the `Customer` class provides two constructors. The first constructor is the default constructor, which simply initializes the `Customer` object by creating an instance of the `Addresses` class and by creating a new GUID value to be used for the `CustomerID`. The second constructor is the deserialization constructor, which initializes the object by calling the default constructor and then loads the data for the `Customer` object out of the passed `SerializationInfo` dictionary.

```
        Public Sub New()
            'Create a new instance of the Addresses class for managing a
            '...collection of Address objects, representing the Addresses
            '...associated with this order.
            m_objAddresses = New Addresses()

            'Create a new GUID value to be used as the unique CustomerID.
            'This value will be overriden if this object is deserialized.
            MyBase.Values.Add("CustomerID", _
                                            System.Guid.NewGuid().ToString())
        End Sub

        Public Sub New(ByVal info As SerializationInfo, _
                    ByVal context As StreamingContext)

            'Call our default constructor on this object to perform the
            '...default initialization
            Me.New()

            'Declare our procedure-level variables
            Dim objSerializationEntry As SerializationEntry

            'Iterate through each SerializationEntry in the passed
            '...SerializationInfo object and Add the entry's value to our
            '...base class's data dictionary, if the entry is not the
            '...Addresses object
            For Each objSerializationEntry In info
                If objSerializationEntry.Name.Equals("Addresses") _
                                                          = False Then
                    MyBase.Values(objSerializationEntry.Name) = _
                                                objSerializationEntry.Value
                End If
            Next

            'Now deserialize the Addresses object into our member level
            '...variable.
            '
            'NOTE:  The actual deserialization of this subordinate object
            '...will occur after this method completes.
            m_objAddresses = info.GetValue("Addresses", GetType(Addresses))
        End Sub
```

```
Next we'll define the strongly-typed public property procedures that can be used
to get and set the values for the Customer data fields.  These methods simply
encapsulate access to the data managed in the base class' StringDictionary object.

        Public Property CustomerID() As String
            Get
                'Return an emptystring if there isn't a value stored in the
                '...specified key.
                If MyBase.Values("CustomerID") Is Nothing = False Then
                    Return MyBase.Values("CustomerID")
                Else
                    Return ""
                End If
            End Get

            Set(ByVal Value As String)
                MyBase.Values("CustomerID") = Value
            End Set
        End Property

        Public Property CustomerName() As String
            Get
                'Return an emptystring if there isn't a value stored in the
                '...specified key.
                If MyBase.Values("CustomerName") Is Nothing = False Then
                    Return MyBase.Values("CustomerName")
                Else
                    Return ""
                End If
            End Get

            Set(ByVal Value As String)
                MyBase.Values("CustomerName") = Value
            End Set
        End Property

        Public Property E-mailAddress() As String
            Get
                Return MyBase.Values("E-mailAddress")
            End Get

            Set(ByVal Value As String)
                MyBase.Values("E-mailAddress") = Value
            End Set
        End Property

        Public Property FirstName() As String
            Get
                Return MyBase.Values("FirstName")
            End Get

            Set(ByVal Value As String)
```

```
            MyBase.Values("FirstName") = Value
        End Set
    End Property

    Public Property LastName() As String
        Get
            Return MyBase.Values("LastName")
        End Get

        Set(ByVal Value As String)
            MyBase.Values("LastName") = Value
        End Set
    End Property

    Public Property Password() As String
        Get
            Return MyBase.Values("Password")
        End Get

        Set(ByVal Value As String)
            MyBase.Values("Password") = Value
        End Set
    End Property

    Public Property AccountStatus() As AccountStatusEnum
        Get
            'Return a default value if there isn't a value stored in the
            '...specified key.
            If MyBase.Values("AccountStatus") Is Nothing = False Then
                Return CType(MyBase.Values("AccountStatus"), _
                                                        AccountStatusEnum)
            Else
                Return AccountStatusEnum.AccountStatus_Enabled
            End If
        End Get

        Set(ByVal Value As AccountStatusEnum)
            MyBase.Values("AccountStatus") = Value
        End Set
    End Property

    Public Property CustomerType() As CustomerTypesEnum
        Get
            'Return a default value if there isn't a value stored in the
            '...specified key.
            If MyBase.Values("CustomerType") Is Nothing = False Then
                Return CType(MyBase.Values("CustomerType"), _
                                                        CustomerTypesEnum)
            Else
                Return CustomerTypesEnum.CustomerType_Unknown
            End If
        End Get

        Set(ByVal Value As CustomerTypesEnum)
```

```
            MyBase.Values("CustomerType") = Value
        End Set
    End Property
```

The `Addresses` read-only property procedure simply returns a reference to the member-level instance of the `Addresses` class:

```
    Public ReadOnly Property Addresses() As Addresses
        Get
            'Return a reference to our instance of the Addresses
            '...collection class
            Return m_objAddresses
        End Get
    End Property
```

Finally, we must override the `GetObjectData` method defined by the `ISerializable` interface and implemented by the `ExtensibleObjectBase` class. Just as with the `Order` class, the `Customer` class must serialize additional objects that are not serialized by the default implementation of the `GetObjectData` method on the `ExtensibleObjectBase`. We'll still serialize the data stored in the base class's `StringDictionary` by calling the `GetObjectData` method on the base class, but we'll also serialize the collection of `Addresses` associated with the customer.

```
    Public Overrides Sub GetObjectData(ByVal info As SerializationInfo, _
                                      ByVal context As StreamingContext)


        'Serialize this object by first performing the default
        '...Serialization procedures contained in the base class
        MyBase.GetObjectData(info, context)

        'Also, serialize the Addresses collection by adding it to the
        '...passed SerializationInfo object
        info.AddValue("Addresses", m_objAddresses, GetType(Addresses))
    End Sub
  End Class
End Namespace
```

New Customer Account Transaction

The new customer account transaction is probably one of the simpler transactions in the IBuyAdventure system. Customer accounts can be created at any time in the IBuyAdventure site from the `NewAccount` Web Form. Users can simply navigate to the new account page in the IBuyAdventure web site and enter their contact and address information to create a new account. However, behind the scenes the process is more involved. The following UML static structure diagram illustrates the Web Forms, business services components, and stored procedures involved in the new customer account transaction:

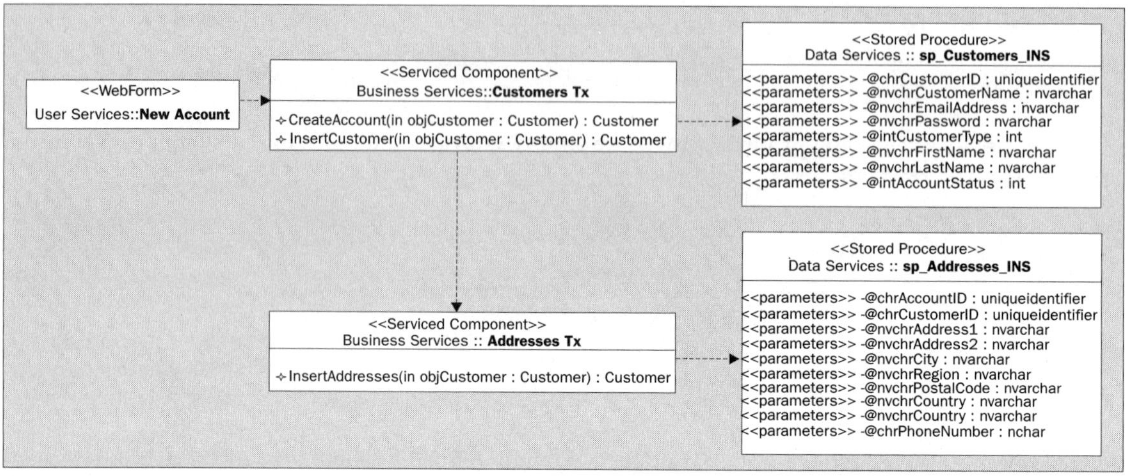

The following UML sequence diagram illustrates the interactions or method calls between the `NewAccount` Web Form, the Business Services components, and the SQL stored procedures involved in the new customer account transaction:

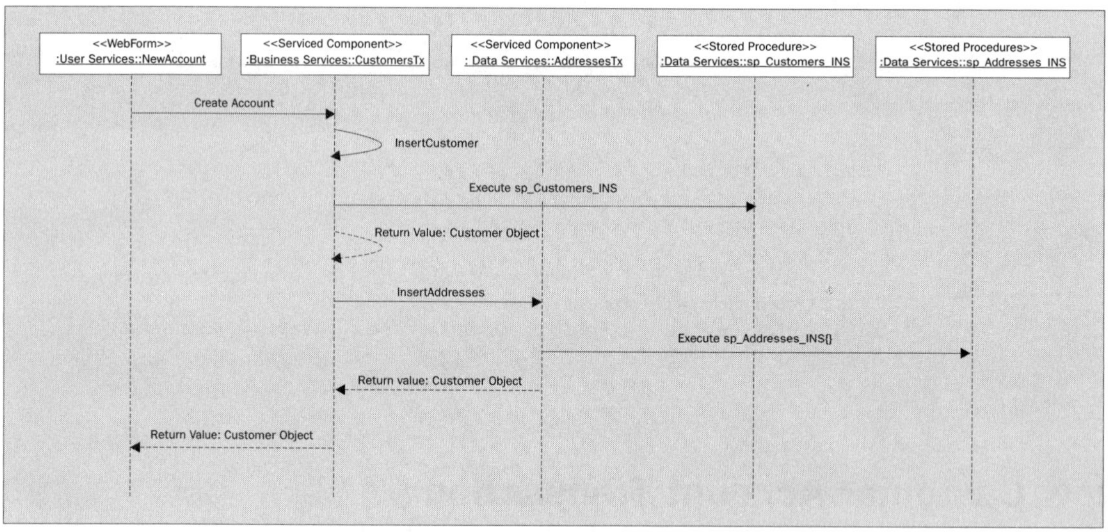

As you can see from this sequence diagram, the `NewAccount` Web Form interacts with the `CustomersTx` .NET Serviced Component, which orchestrates the new customer account transaction.

When the user initiates the process of creating a new customer account, the `NewAccount` Web Form instantiates the `CustomersTx` .NET Serviced Component and invokes the `CreateAccount()` method, passing the new `CustomerTx` object the user's account information packaged in a `Customer` business object. Since the `CustomersTx` component is a .NET Serviced Component configured to require transactions, behind the scenes COM+ automatically creates a new transaction and coordinates with MS DTC to ensure that all operations performed by the object are done so within the protection of a transaction. The `CustomersTx` object then calls its own `InsertCustomer()` method, forwarding the `Customer` object.

The InsertCustomer() method executes the sp_Customers_INS stored procedure in the Data Services tier to insert a single record into the Customers table. After the InsertCustomer() method call returns the updated Customer information, the CustomersTx object then creates an instance of the AddressesTx .NET ServicedComponent and calls its InsertAddresses() method. Since the AddressesTx .NET Serviced Component is also configured to require transactions, COM+ propagates the transaction information to the new object so that any operations it performs are included in the transaction started by the CustomersTx object.

The InsertAddresses() method iterates through the collection of addresses in the passed Customer object and executes the sp_Addresses_INS stored procedure to insert a record into the Addresses table for each Address object in the collection. Typically there will only be one or two addresses for a customer (a billing and shipping address); however, our business service and data services design is extensible to support multiple addresses per customer, should this feature be exposed to the user by the User Services tier. After the AddressesTx object completes and returns the Customer object with the updated data, the CustomersTx object votes to commit the transaction if no errors have occurred and returns the updated Customer object to the NewAccount Web Form. Should an exception occur in either the CustomersTx or AddressesTx object, they will vote to abort the transaction and throw the exception to the caller.

Business Services

The Business Services components involved in the customer account creation transaction include the CustomersTx and AddressesTx transactional .NET Serviced Components. Both of these components are configured with a transaction support attribute of Required, to indicate that they must be created within a transaction.

CustomersTx

The CustomersTx class is a transactional .NET Serviced Component that serves as the root of the new customer account transaction. It implements two methods, CreateAccount() and InsertCustomer(), both of which are called within the new customer account transaction.

Let's begin looking at the code for the CustomersTx class by first defining the structure for our class file, including the imports and namespace statements. You'll notice that this common code is repeated in every business services class:

```
'Import namespaces containing commonly used types
Imports System.Data
Imports System.Data.SqlClient
Imports System.EnterpriseServices
Imports IBuyAdventure.Common

Namespace IBuyAdventure.BusinessServices
```

Since the CustomersTx class is a .NET Serviced Component, we need to define a public interface containing the method signatures for the CreateAccount() and InsertCustomer() methods implemented by this class. As we learned in Chapter 7, with .NET Serviced Components it is necessary to define a public interface containing the signatures of public methods and implement the interface in order for the methods to be configured with COM+ when the Serviced Component is registered. Otherwise, only the component itself will be configured in COM+, not the interfaces and methods.

We'll simply name our interface the same name as the class prefixed with a capital "I". So for the `CustomersTx` class the public interface will be named `ICustomersTx`. This is a common naming convention carried over from the COM platform where the letter "I" stands for "interface".

```
'Define a public interface containing the signatures for members
'...of this class
Public Interface ICustomersTx
    Function CreateAccount(ByVal objCustomer As Customer) As Customer
    Function InsertCustomer(ByVal objCustomer As Customer) As Customer
End Interface
```

Next, let's define the `CustomersTx` class itself. We'll apply `Attributes` defined in the `System.EnterpriseServices` namespace to specify how the `CustomersTx` class should be configured in COM+. The `Transaction` attribute is used to specify that the `CustomersTx` class should be configured with a COM+ Transaction Support Attribute (TSA) of `Required`. Although not explicitly required, we'll also configure the `Synchronization` attribute to `Required` and the `JustInTimeActivation` attribute to `True`. These attributes are not necessary because COM+ defaults these services to the same values when a class is configured with a TSA of `Supported`, `Required`, or `Requires New`. However, by including a few lines of additional code to explicitly set these attributes we can easily improve the readability and maintainability of the code. This is a good practice to ensure that other developers that follow you can easily understand what is happing in the application.

```
    <Description("Contains methods for Creating Customers and inserting Customer
records in the IBuyAdventure system."), _
        Transaction(TransactionOption.Required), _
        Synchronization(SynchronizationOption.Required), _
        JustInTimeActivation(True)> _
    Public Class CustomersTx
```

In order for the `CustomersTx` class to support COM+ services including transactions, the `CustomersTx` class must inherit from the `System.EnterpriseServices.ServicedComponent` class. Let's also implement our custom `ICustomersTx` interface that we just defined.

```
'Inherit from the System.EnterpriseServices.ServicedComponent class
'...to allow this component to utilize COM+ services
Inherits ServicedComponent

'Implement the ICustomersTx interface and it's members
Implements ICustomersTx
```

Now let's define the member-level instance variables or member-level constant variables used by this class. In the `CustomersTx` class, as with most of the Business Services classes in the IBuyAdventure system, we'll define a member-level instance variable to hold the connection string for accessing the IBuyAdventure database. We'll see how this variable is assigned in just a moment:

```
'declare any member-level instance variables
Private m_strConnectionString As String
```

Next, we need to implement the default constructor for the CustomersTx class, which reads the Connection string for the IBuyAdventure database out of the application configuration file into the member-level instance variable we just defined. In this situation the value is being read from the Machine.Config file, which we'll configure later in this chapter. This code is common to all of the Business Services classes that access the IBuyAdventure database:

```
Public Sub New()

    'Load the configuration settings out of the either the
    '...Machine's global configuration file or the calling
    '...application's configuration file, into member-level
    '...variables.

    'Get the ConnectionString for the IBuyAdventure system
    m_strConnectionString = _
        System.Configuration.ConfigurationSettings.AppSettings( _
                "IBuyAdventure.BusinessServices.ConnectionString")
End Sub
```

After the general structure for the CustomersTx class is established and we've implemented the default constructor, let's implement the CreateAccount() method, which is responsible for coordinating the new customer account transaction. First, define the signature for the CreateAccount() method. This signature must exactly match the signature for the CreateAccount() method defined by the ICustomersTx interface. Since this method is the actual implementation of the ICustomersTx.CreateAccount() method, we must specify so using the Visual Basic .NET Implements keyword. Although not required, let's also apply the Description attribute defined in the System.EnterpriseServices namespace to specify a description for this method when it is configured in COM+.

```
<Description("Creates a new Customer Account in IBuyAdventure.")> _
Public Function CreateAccount(ByVal objCustomer As Customer) _
                                                   As Customer _
                                   Implements ICustomersTx.CreateAccount
```

Now we're ready to implement the logic for the CreateAccount() method. Let's enclose the code in this method in a Try block so we can catch exceptions and vote on the outcome of the transaction accordingly.

```
    Try
```

Next let's call the public InsertCustomer() method of the same object to insert the Customer record and pass it the Customer business object containing the new customer's data. We'll replace our Customer business object with the updated Customer business object returned from the InsertCustomer() method.

```
        'Insert the Customer record into the IBuyAdventure
        '...database by calling the public InsertCustomer method
        '...of this class. Get a reference to the updated Customer
        '...object returned from the method call.
        objCustomer = Me.InsertCustomer(objCustomer)
```

Next, let's create an instance of the AddressesTx .NET Serviced Component, which is also defined in the IBuyAdventure.BusinessServices namespace. Then we'll call the InsertAddresses() method on the new AddressesTx object to insert a record into the Addresses table in the IBuyAdventure database for each Address object contained in the passed Customer object.

```
            'Create an instance of the
            '...IBuyAdventure.BusinessServices.AddressesTx
            '...NET(ServicedComponent)
            Dim objAddressesTx As New AddressesTx()

            'Insert the Addresses included with the passed Customer
            '...object into the IBuyAdventure database
            objCustomer = objAddressesTx.InsertAddresses(objCustomer)
```

We've completed all of the processing logic for the CreateAccount() method, so now let's call the SetComplete() method of the System.EnterpriseServices.ContextUtil shared class to vote to commit the COM+ transaction. Since the CustomersTx class, and specifically the CreateOrder() method, is the root of the new customer account transaction, calling the SetComplete() method will cause COM+ to deactivate the CustomersTx object and attempt to commit the transaction when the CreateAccount() method completes. Before completing, let's also return the Customer business object, which contains the updated Customer data from our transaction.

```
            'We successfully created the Customer account, so tell
            '...COM+ that this object votes to commit the transaction
            '...and deactivate.
            ContextUtil.SetComplete()

            'Return the updated Customer object to the caller
            Return objCustomer
```

Should an exception occur in the CreateAccount() method, we'll call the SetAbort() method of the ContextUtil shared class in our Catch block to vote to abort the transaction and throw the exception that occurred back up the call stack to the immediate caller. In the new customer account transaction, the immediate caller is the NewAccount Web Form.

```
        Catch excp As system.Exception
            'An exception occured creating the Customer account.

            'Tell COM+ that this object votes to abort the transaction
            '...and deactivate
            ContextUtil.SetAbort()

            'Throw the exception to the caller of this method
            Throw excp
        End Try

    End Function
```

The CreateAccount() method is now complete. Now let's begin implementing the InsertCustomer(), by first defining the method signature. Just as with the CreateAccount() method, the InsertCustomer() method accepts an IBuyAdventure.Common.Customer business object containing the customer's data.

```
        <Description("Inserts a new Customer record in IBuyAdventure.")> _
        Public Function InsertCustomer(ByVal objCustomer As Customer) _
                                                         As Customer _
                                      Implements ICustomersTx.InsertCustomer
```

Next let's enclose the code in this method in a `Try` block and implement some validation logic that creates a new `CustomerID` if one was not supplied in the passed `Customer` business object. If created, the new `CustomerID` GUID value is stored in the `CustomerID` property of the passed `Customer` business object. As we discussed during the data model design, by using GUIDs for primary key values, we can easily create the primary key in our application logic instead of having to re-query the database after performing an insert.

```
            Try
                'If the CustomerID is empty, then create a new CustomerID
                '...and put it back in the Customer object
                If objCustomer.CustomerID.Length = 0 Then
                    objCustomer.CustomerID = _
                                            System.Guid.NewGuid.ToString()
                End If
```

Next let's create an instance of the `System.Data.SqlClient.SqlCommand` for executing the `sp_Customers_INS` stored procedure. Then let's add a new `SqlParameter` object to the `SqlCommand` for each input parameter supported by the `sp_Customers_INS` stored procedure. After initializing the `SqlCommand` object for the `sp_Customers_INS` stored procedure, let's copy the data in the passed `Customer` business object into the corresponding `SqlParameters`.

```
                Dim sqlcmdInsertCustomer As _
                                    New SqlCommand("sp_Customers_INS")

                With sqlcmdInsertCustomer
                    'Set the command type for the new SqlCommand object to
                    '...Stored Procedure
                    .CommandType = CommandType.StoredProcedure

                    With .Parameters
                        'Create and Append SqlParameter objects for
                        '...our SqlCommand
                        .Add("@chrCustomerID", SqlDbType.Char, 38)
                        .Add("@nvchrCustomerName", SqlDbType.NVarChar, 50)
                        .Add("@nvchrE-mailAddress", SqlDbType.NVarChar, 50)
                        .Add("@nvchrPassword", SqlDbType.NVarChar, 20)
                        .Add("@intCustomerType", SqlDbType.Int)
                        .Add("@nvchrFirstname", SqlDbType.NVarChar, 50)
                        .Add("@nvchrLastname", SqlDbType.NVarChar, 50)
                        .Add("@intAccountStatus", SqlDbType.Int)

                        'Set the values for each of the SqlParameter
                        '...objects to the values stored
                        '...in the passed Customer object
                        .Item("@chrCustomerID").Value = _
                                                objCustomer.CustomerID
                        .Item("@nvchrCustomerName").Value = _
```

```
                                              objCustomer.CustomerName
                    .Item("@nvchrE-mailAddress").Value = _
                                              objCustomer.E-mailAddress
                    .Item("@nvchrPassword").Value = _
                                                  objCustomer.Password
                    .Item("@intCustomerType").Value = _
                                              objCustomer.CustomerType
                    .Item("@nvchrFirstname").Value = _
                                                 objCustomer.FirstName
                    .Item("@nvchrLastname").Value = _
                                                  objCustomer.LastName

                    'Set the AccountStatus for the new customer
                    '...to Enabled
                    .Item("@intAccountStatus").Value = _
                      Customer.AccountStatusEnum.AccountStatus_Enabled
                End With
            End With
```

Next, let's create an instance of the `System.Data.SqlClient.SqlConnection` class and establish a connection to the IBuyAdventure database. We'll specify the connection information for the IBuyAdventure database by passing the `SqlConnection` class' constructor the connection string that we read out of the Application Configuration earlier. It's important to notice that we waited until after the `SqlCommand` object for the `sp_Customers_INS` stored procedure was created and initialized before we established a connection to the data store. To develop scalable and high performance transaction processing systems you should only acquire expensive resources, such as database connections, as late as possible and release them as soon as possible.

```
            'Create an instance of the
            '...System.Data.SqlClient.SqlConnection class
            Dim sqlconIBuyAdventure As New _
                                  SqlConnection(m_strConnectionString)

            'Establish a connection to the IBuyAdventure
            '...SQL Server 2000 database
            sqlconIBuyAdventure.Open()
```

Now, let's assign the new `SqlConnection` object to the `SqlCommand` object and execute the command, causing the `sp_Customers_INS` stored procedure to be executed with the parameter values we assigned. Notice that we execute the `SqlCommand` object by calling its `ExecuteNonQuery()` method. The `ExecuteNonQuery()` method is designed and optimized to execute SQL statements or stored procedures that do not return a Resultset.

```
            'Assign the SqlConnection object to the SqlCommand for
            '...executing the stored procedure
            sqlcmdInsertCustomer.Connection = sqlconIBuyAdventure


            'Execute the sp_Customers_INS stored procedure without
            '...returning a resultset
            sqlcmdInsertCustomer.ExecuteNonQuery()
```

Next let's explicitly close our connection to the IBuyAdventure database, vote to commit the transaction, and return the passed `Customer` business object to the caller.

```
                    'Explicitly close our open connection to the
                    '...IBuyAdventure database
                    sqlconIBuyAdventure.Close()

                    'We successfully inserted the Customer record, so tell
                    '...COM+ that this object votes to commit the transaction
                    '...and deactivate.
                    ContextUtil.SetComplete()

                    'Return the updated Customer object to the caller
                    Return objCustomer
```

If an exception occurrs in this method, we'll use the `Catch` block vote to abort the transaction and throw the exception to the caller, which is the `CreateAccount()` method. Since the `InsertCustomer()` method is not the root of the transaction, the transaction will not immediately be aborted if this method call votes to abort. Instead, the exception will be thrown to the `CreateAccount()` method, which will catch the exception and also vote to abort the transaction. Since the `CreateAccount()` method is the root method that caused the transaction to start, COM+ aborts or commits the transaction only when the `CreateAccount()` method has completed.

One other important issue to keep in mind is the fact that these methods are called on the same object. Each object has only one vote on the transaction's success, and the last vote cast before an object deactivates is the only vote that counts. Consequently, in this situation, if the `CreateAccount()` method were to call the `SetAbort()` method, it would override the vote made by the `InsertCustomer()` method. Considering this issue, it would be safer if the `CreateAccount()` method had created a new instance of the `CustomersTx` class when calling the `InsertCustomer()` method, instead of calling the method on itself.

```
                Catch excp As system.Exception
                    'An exception occured inserting the Customer record.

                    'Tell COM+ that this object votes to abort the
                    '...transaction and deactivate
                    ContextUtil.SetAbort()
                    'Throw the exception to the caller of this method
                    Throw excp
                End Try

            End Function
        End Class
    End Namespace
```

AddressesTx

The `AddressesTx` class is a transactional .NET Serviced Component that implements a single method named `InsertAddresses()`. The `InsertAddresses()` method is called by the `CreateAccount()` method of the `CustomersTx` class within a new customer account transaction to insert all of the addresses associated with the customer. Let's take a look at the code for this method now.

First, let's establish the structure for our class file by importing the namespaces containing the types frequently utilized by this class and by defining the namespace for the `AddressesTx` class.

```
'Import namespaces containing commonly used types
Imports System.Data
Imports System.Data.SqlClient
Imports System.EnterpriseServices
Imports IBuyAdventure.Common

Namespace IBuyAdventure.BusinessServices
```

Next we'll define a public interface named `IAddressesTx` and the signature for the `InsertAddresses()` method. Then we'll declare the `AddressesTx` class and implement the new `IAddressesTx` interface. Since the `AddressesTx` class is a transactional .NET Serviced Component, we'll apply the `System.EnterpriseServices` attributes, including the `Transaction` attribute, to the class declaration and we'll inherit from the Serviced Component base class.

```
    'Define a public interface containing the signatures for members of
    '...this class
    '
    'NOTE:  It is necessary to define a public interface with the
    '...signatures for methods that utilize COM+ method-level attributes.
    '...Otherwise the interface and methods will not be displayed and
    '...configured in COM+, although the component will be configured.
    Public Interface IAddressesTx
        Function InsertAddresses(ByVal objCustomer As Customer) _
                                                          As Customer
    End Interface

    <Description("Contains methods for inserting Address records."), _
        Transaction(TransactionOption.Required), _
        Synchronization(SynchronizationOption.Required), _
        JustInTimeActivation(True)> _
    Public Class AddressesTx

        'Inherit from the System.EnterpriseServices.ServicedComponent
        '...class to allow this component to utilize COM+ services
        Inherits ServicedComponent

        'Implement the IAddressesTx interface and its members
        Implements IAddressesTx
```

Let's declare our member-level instance variables and the default constructor for the `AddressesTx` class. Within the constructor we'll read in the `ConnectionString` from the application configuration settings into our member-level variable.

```
        'declare any member-level instance variables
        Private m_strConnectionString As String

        Public Sub New()

            'Load the configuration settings out of the either the
```

```
        '...Machine's global configuration
        '...file or the calling application's configuration file, into
        '...member-level variables.

        'Get the ConnectionString for the IBuyAdventure system
        m_strConnectionString = _
            System.Configuration.ConfigurationSettings.AppSettings( _
                    "IBuyAdventure.BusinessServices.ConnectionString")
    End Sub
```

Now let's implement the `InsertAddresses()` method, as it is defined by the `IAddressesTx` interface. First let's create and initialize an instance of the `SqlCommand` class for executing the `sp_Addresses_INS` stored procedure. Then we'll create and append `SqlParameter` objects to the `SqlCommand` for each of the `sp_Addresses_INS` stored procedure's parameters.

```
    <Description("Inserts new Address records in IBuyAdventure.")> _
    Public Function InsertAddresses(ByVal objCustomer As Customer) _
                                                     As Customer _
                                Implements IAddressesTx.InsertAddresses

        Try
            'declare any procedure-level variables
            Dim objAddress As IBuyAdventure.Common.Address

            'Create a new instance of the
            '...System.Data.SqlClient.SqlCommand
            '...class to use for executing sp_Addresses_INS
            Dim sqlcmdInsertCustomerAddress As _
                                 New SqlCommand("sp_Addresses_INS")

            With sqlcmdInsertCustomerAddress
                'Set the command type for the new SqlCommand object to
                '...Stored Procedure
                .CommandType = CommandType.StoredProcedure

                With .Parameters
                    'Create and append SqlParameter objects
                    .Add("@chrAddressID", SqlDbType.Char, 38)
                    .Add("@chrCustomerID", SqlDbType.Char, 38)
                    .Add("@nvchrAddress1", SqlDbType.NVarChar, 50)
                    .Add("@nvchrAddress2", SqlDbType.NVarChar, 30)
                    .Add("@nvchrCity", SqlDbType.NVarChar, 30)
                    .Add("@nvchrRegion", SqlDbType.NVarChar, 30)
                    .Add("@nvchrPostalCode", SqlDbType.NVarChar, 20)
                    .Add("@nvchrCountry", SqlDbType.NVarChar, 30)
                    .Add("@nchrPhoneNumber", SqlDbType.NChar, 15)
                End With
            End With
```

Create an instance of the `System.Data.SqlClient.SqlConnection` class and establish a connection to the IBuyAdventure SQL Server database using the `ConnectionString` we retrieved from the application configuration settings.

```
                'Create an instance of the
                '...System.Data.SqlClient.SqlConnection class
                Dim sqlconIBuyAdventure As _
                                  New SqlConnection(m_strConnectionString)

                'Establish a connection to the IBuyAdventure
                '...SQL Server 2000 database
                sqlconIBuyAdventure.Open()
```

Assign a reference to the new `SqlConnection` object to the `SqlCommand` object, so we can execute the `sp_Addresses_INS` stored procedure against the IBuyAdventure database.

```
                'Assign the SqlConnection object to the SqlCommand for
                '...executing the stored procedure
                sqlcmdInsertCustomerAddress.Connection = _
                                                    sqlconIBuyAdventure
```

Loop though each `Address` object in the passed `Customer` object's `Addresses` collection, load the data in each `Address` object into the corresponding `SqlParameter` objects associated with the `SqlCommand`, and execute the `SqlCommand`, causing the `sp_Addresses_INS` stored procedure to execute with the parameter values we loaded.

```
                'Iterate through each Address object in the passed
                '...Customer object's Addresses collection and insert a
                '...record into the Addresses table for each one
                For Each objAddress In objCustomer.Addresses

                    'Perform some light validation on the current Address

                    'If the AddressID is empty, then create a new
                    '...AddressID and put it back in the Address object
                    If objAddress.AddressID.Length = 0 Then
                        objAddress.AddressID = _
                                            System.Guid.NewGuid.ToString()
                    End If

                    'Set the values for each of the SqlParameters to the
                    '...values stored in the properties and fields for
                    '...the current Address object.
                    With sqlcmdInsertCustomerAddress.Parameters
                        .Item("@chrAddressID").Value = _
                                                   objAddress.AddressID
                        .Item("@nvchrAddress1").Value = _
                                                    objAddress.Address1
                        .Item("@nvchrAddress2").Value = _
                                                    objAddress.Address2
                        .Item("@nvchrCity").Value = objAddress.City
                        .Item("@nvchrCountry").Value = objAddress.Country
                        .Item("@nchrPhoneNumber").Value = _
                                                 objAddress.PhoneNumber
                        .Item("@nvchrPostalCode").Value = _
                                                  objAddress.PostalCode
```

```
                    .Item("@nvchrRegion").Value = objAddress.Region

                    'Set the value of the CustomerID parameter to the
                    '...value stored in the passed Customer object
                    .Item("@chrCustomerID").Value = _
                                       objCustomer.CustomerID
                End With

                'Execute the sp_Addresses_INS stored procedure
                '...without returning a resultset
                sqlcmdInsertCustomerAddress.ExecuteNonQuery()
            Next
```

After inserting the Address records we can close our open SqlConnection, vote to commit the transaction by calling the SetComplete() method of the ContextUtil class/object, and return the updated Customer business object, and its contained Address objects, to the caller:

```
            'Close our open connection to the IBuyAdventure database
            sqlconIBuyAdventure.Close()

            'We successfully inserted the Addresses record, so tell
            '...COM+ that this object votes to commit the transaction
            '...and deactivate.
            ContextUtil.SetComplete()

            'Return the updated Customer object and Addresses
            Return objCustomer
```

Finally, in the Catch block, we'll call the SetAbort() method of the ContextUtil class/object to vote to abort the transaction and throw the exception to the caller:

```
        Catch excp As system.Exception
            'An exception occured inserting the Address records.

            'Tell COM+ that this object votes to abort the transaction
            '...and deactivate
            ContextUtil.SetAbort()

            'Throw the exception to the caller of this method
            Throw excp
        End Try

    End Function
  End Class
End Namespace
```

That completes the code for the CustomersTx and AddressesTx transactional .NET Serviced Components, now let's look at the stored procedures in the Data Services tier that they execute.

Data Services

The stored procedures in the data services tier that are used in the create customer account transaction include sp_Customers_INS and sp_Addresses_INS. Let's create both of these stored procedures now.

sp_Customers_INS

The sp_Customers_INS stored procedure simply inserts a single record into the Customers table using the values passed as input parameters for the column values in the new record. Notice that the CustomerID parameter, @chrCustomerID, is defined with the data type char(38) instead of with the UniqueIdentifier data type. This type casting is used to avoid potential errors that can occur when executing stored procedures that use the UniqueIdentifier data type for an input parameter. Fortunately, when using ADO.NET we can use UniqueIdentifier data types for parameters without any significant challenges. We can simply convert a string into a System.GUID and assign the GUID to a parameter before executing a query. However, several tools have difficulty with UniqueIdentifiers as a data type, but they can accept character fields with the same value.

```
CREATE PROCEDURE sp_Customers_INS
      -----------------------------------------------------------
      -- Declare the parameters for this Stored Procedure
      -----------------------------------------------------------
      @chrCustomerID char(38),
      @nvchrCustomerName nvarchar(50),
      @nvchrE-mailAddress nvarchar(50),
      @nvchrPassword nvarchar(50),
      @intCustomerType int,
      @nvchrFirstname nvarchar(50),
      @nvchrLastname nvarchar(50),
      @intAccountStatus int

AS
```

After defining the input parameters, simply execute a SQL INSERT statement for the Customers table and use the values of the input parameters to fill the columns of the new record.

```
      -----------------------------------------------------------
      -- Perform the intended operation againist the Database
      -----------------------------------------------------------


      INSERT INTO Customers
                        (CustomerID,
                        CustomerName,
                        E-mailAddress,
                        Password,
                        CustomerType,
                        Firstname,
                        Lastname,
                        AccountStatus,
                        DateCreated)
      VALUES      (@chrCustomerID,
                        @nvchrCustomerName,
                        @nvchrE-mailAddress,
                        @nvchrPassword,
```

```
                        @intCustomerType,
                        @nvchrFirstname,
                        @nvchrLastname,
                        @intAccountStatus,
                        GetDate())

        -- Return 1 (true) to indicate success
        return 1

GO
```

sp_Addresses_INS

The sp_Addresses_INS stored procedure simply inserts a single record into the Addresses table using the values passed as input parameters for the column values in the new record. Let's define these input parameters with the same data types as the corresponding columns in the Addresses table:

```
CREATE PROCEDURE sp_Addresses_INS
        ---------------------------------------------------------
        -- Declare the parameters for this Stored Procedure
        ---------------------------------------------------------
        @chrAddressID char(38),
        @chrCustomerID char(38),
        @nvchrAddress1 nvarchar(50),
        @nvchrAddress2 nvarchar(30),
        @nvchrCity nvarchar(30),
        @nvchrRegion nvarchar(30),
        @nvchrPostalCode nvarchar(20),
        @nvchrCountry nvarchar(30),
        @nchrPhoneNumber nchar(15)

AS
```

Then let's execute the SQL INSERT statement to insert a record into the Addresses table using the values of the input parameters as the column values for the new record.

```
        ---------------------------------------------------------
        -- Perform the intended operation againist the Database
        ---------------------------------------------------------

        INSERT INTO Addresses
                        (AddressID,
                        CustomerID,
                        Address1,
                        Address2,
                        City,
                        Region,
                        PostalCode,
                        Country,
                        PhoneNumber)
        VALUES      (@chrAddressID,
                        @chrCustomerID,
                        @nvchrAddress1,
```

```
                        @nvchrAddress2,
                        @nvchrCity,
                        @nvchrRegion,
                        @nvchrPostalCode,
                        @nvchrCountry,
                        @nchrPhoneNumber)

        -- Return 1 (true) to indicate success
        return 1

GO
```

We've created both of the stored procedures that are used in the new customer account transaction, now let's look at the User Services tier.

Preparing Data Services for Code Example

If you wish to run the IBuyAdventure application, now would be a good time to prepare the data services.

First of all, you have to attach the supplied database (which we have downloaded from the Wrox site (www.wrox.com) to `C:\VBNETTrans\Chapter10\IBuyAdventure\Data\IbuyAdventure_Data.MDF`. Open the SQL Server Manager and right-click on Databases, then All Tasks, then Attach Database.... When the dialog box opens follow the instructions – attach the database (Attach as:) as `IBuyAdventure` and set the user to `sa`. Browse through to the above data file in the dialog box, and select it. It should also pick up the LDF log file too. Make sure the database is now included with the others in Enterprise Manager, and you can also run the Query Analyzer to flip through the tables to be sure.

User Services

The User Services tier includes the following classes that are involved in the new customer account transaction:

- `Shopper` Class
- `NewAccount` Web Form

Let's examine the code for each of these classes.

Shopper Class

Before we can implement the `NewAccount` Web Form for the User Services tier of the new customer account transaction, we need to discuss the `Shopper` class contained in the same assembly. The `Shopper` private class provides methods for common functionality needed by most ASP.NET Web Forms in the users services tier of the IBuyAdventure system. Most of these methods are responsible for saving, loading, and managing state between page requests.

First let's import some of the namespaces containing commonly used types:

```
'Import namespaces containing commonly used types
Imports System.Web
Imports Microsoft.VisualBasic
Imports IBuyAdventure.Common
```

Then let's define the Shopper class and declare the member-level instance variables used by the class. Notice that we declare member-level instance variables for holding references to the Customer and Order objects for the shopper. We also have a member-level instance variable for holding a reference to a System.Web.HttpContext object, which is used to load and persist data in the ASP.NET Session State:

```
Public Class Shopper

    'declare the member-level instance variables used by this class
    Private m_objCustomer As Customer
    Private m_objBasket As Order
    Private context As HttpContext
```

The single constructor for the Shopper class receives a reference to a System.Web.HttpContext object as a parameter and stores the reference in the member-level instance variable:

```
    Public Sub New(ByRef context As HttpContext)
        'Store a reference to the System.Web.HttpContext object that
        '...was passed to this constructor in a member-level variable
        Me.context = context
    End Sub
```

The Customer property procedure sets and returns an IBuyAdventure.Common.Customer object that contains the user's customer account information. In the Get procedure for this property, the Customer object is loaded or deserialized from the ASP.NET Session state if it has not already been loaded and stored in a member-level instance variable. If the Customer object cannot be loaded from the user's session state, then a new instance of the Customer class is created and returned to the caller. The Set procedure for the Customer property simply updates the member-level instance variable with a reference to the specified Customer object.

```
    Public Property Customer() As Customer
        Get

            If IsNothing(m_objCustomer) = True Then
                'We don't currently have a reference to a Customer object.

                'Load/deserialize the Customer object out of the Session
                m_objCustomer = context.Session.Item("Customer")

                'If the Customer object loaded out of the Session state is
                '...nothing then we'll simply create a new instance of
                '...the IBuyAdventure.Common.Customer class
                If IsNothing(m_objCustomer) = True Then
                    m_objCustomer = New Customer()
                End If
            End If

            'Return a reference to the Customer object
            Return m_objCustomer
        End Get

        Set(ByVal Value As Customer)
```

```
            'set the Customer object reference in our member-level
            '...variable to the value passed into this property.
            m_objCustomer = Value
        End Set
    End Property
```

The `Basket` property procedure functions exactly the same as the `Customer` property procedure, except it works with `IBuyAdventure.Common.Order` objects that represent the shopper's current basket.

```
    Public Property Basket() As Order
        Get

            If IsNothing(m_objBasket) = True Then
                'We don't currently have a reference to an Order object.

                'Load/deserialize the Customer object out of the Session
                m_objBasket = context.Session.Item("Basket")

                'If the Order object loaded out of the Session state is
                '...nothing then we'll simply create a new instance of the
                '...IBuyAdventure.Common.Order class
                If IsNothing(m_objBasket) = True Then
                    m_objBasket = New Order()
                End If
            End If

            'Return a reference to the Order object representing
            '...the shopper's basket
            Return m_objBasket
        End Get

        Set(ByVal Value As Order)
            'set the Basket/Order object reference in our member-level
            '...variable to the value passed into this property.
            m_objBasket = Value
        End Set
    End Property
```

The `SaveCustomer()` and `SaveBasket()` methods also function almost identically. The `SaveCustomer()` method saves or serializes the `Customer` object referenced in the member-level instance variable to the user's session state in the `Customer` key. The `SaveBasket()` method serializes the `Order` object representing the shopper's current basket to the session state in the `Basket` key.

```
    Public Sub SaveCustomer()

        'Save the customer data object by serializing it into the user's
        '...session state in the Customer key.
        context.Session.Item("Customer") = m_objCustomer
    End Sub


    Public Sub SaveBasket()
```

```
        'Save the Basket/Order data object by serializing it into the
        '...user's session state in the Basket key.
        context.Session.Item("Basket") = m_objBasket
    End Sub
```

The ResetBasket() method simply deletes the Order object stored in the Basket key in the user's session state and releases the member-level reference to the Order object for the user's basket. Consequently, the next time the Basket property is retrieved; a new Order object will be created.

```
    Public Sub ResetBasket()

        'Reset/Clear the shopper's basket by removing the data stored in
        '...the Session object for the Basket key.
        context.Session.Remove("Basket")

        'Release our reference to the IBuyAdventure.Common.Order object
        '...representing the user's Shopping basket
        m_objBasket = Nothing
    End Sub
```

The ResetShoppingSession() method completely resets the user's session by releasing the member-level references to the Order and Customer objects and by deleting the contents of the user's session state for the entries used to store the Customer and Order objects.

```
    Public Sub ResetShoppingSession()

        'The caller want's to reset the current shopper's shopping
        '...session, probably because the user logged out of the site.

        'release our Basket and Customer objects, if we have already
        '...loaded them from the session.
        m_objBasket = Nothing
        m_objCustomer = Nothing

        'Clear the values stored in the ASP.NET Session object for the
        '...Basket and Customer objects
        context.Session.Remove("Basket")
        context.Session.Remove("Customer")
    End Sub
```

The ShopperLoggedIn() method returns a Boolean value indicating whether or not the current user has logged into the IBuyAdventure site. Since the IBuyAdventure site is utilizing HTML Forms-based authentication, this is determined based on the value of the IsAuthenticated property of the User.Identity object.

```
    Public Function ShopperLoggedIn() As Boolean
        'return a boolean value indicating whether or not the shopper has
        '...been authenticated

        'NOTE:  The authentication status of the user can be determined
        '...using the HTML Forms authentication components.
        Return context.User.Identity.IsAuthenticated
    End Function
```

The `UpdateBasketSubTotal()` method is a utility procedure that simplifies the routine process of updating the subtotal calculation of the user's shopping basket. This method updates the subtotal for the current shopping basket by calling the `CalculateSubTotal()` method on an instance of the `OrderCalculations` business services component. After updating the subtotal, the shopping basket is saved by calling the public `SaveBasket()` method, which we just implemented. We'll implement the `OrderCalculations` component during our discussion of the `order` processing transaction.

```
    Public Sub UpdateBasketSubTotal()

        'Acquire a reference to the IBuyAdventure.Common.Order object
        '...representing the shopper's current basket by calling the
        '...public Basket property of this class, so the basket
        '...will be loaded if it hasn't already.
        Dim objCurrentBasket As IBuyAdventure.Common.Order = Me.Basket

        'Create an instance of the
        '...IBuyAdventure.BusinessServices.OrderCalculations class for
        '...calculating the subtotal and pricing information
        Dim objOrderCalculations As New _
                        IBuyAdventure.BusinessServices.OrderCalculations()

        'Update the ListPrice and Unitprice for each item and the subtotal
        '...for the entire order and this update this class with the most
        '...current basket.
        Me.Basket = _
                  objOrderCalculations.CalculateSubTotal(objCurrentBasket)

        'Save the changes to the shopper's basket by calling the public
        '...method on this class
        Me.SaveBasket()
    End Sub
End Class
```

Now that we have completed the `Shopper` class, let's look at the `NewAccount` Web Form.

NewAccount Web Form

The `NewAccount` Web Form allows the user to enter demographic information and their billing and shipping addresses to create a new customer account at the IBuyAdventure site. The following screenshot shows the `NewAccount` Web Form in design mode in Visual Studio .NET.

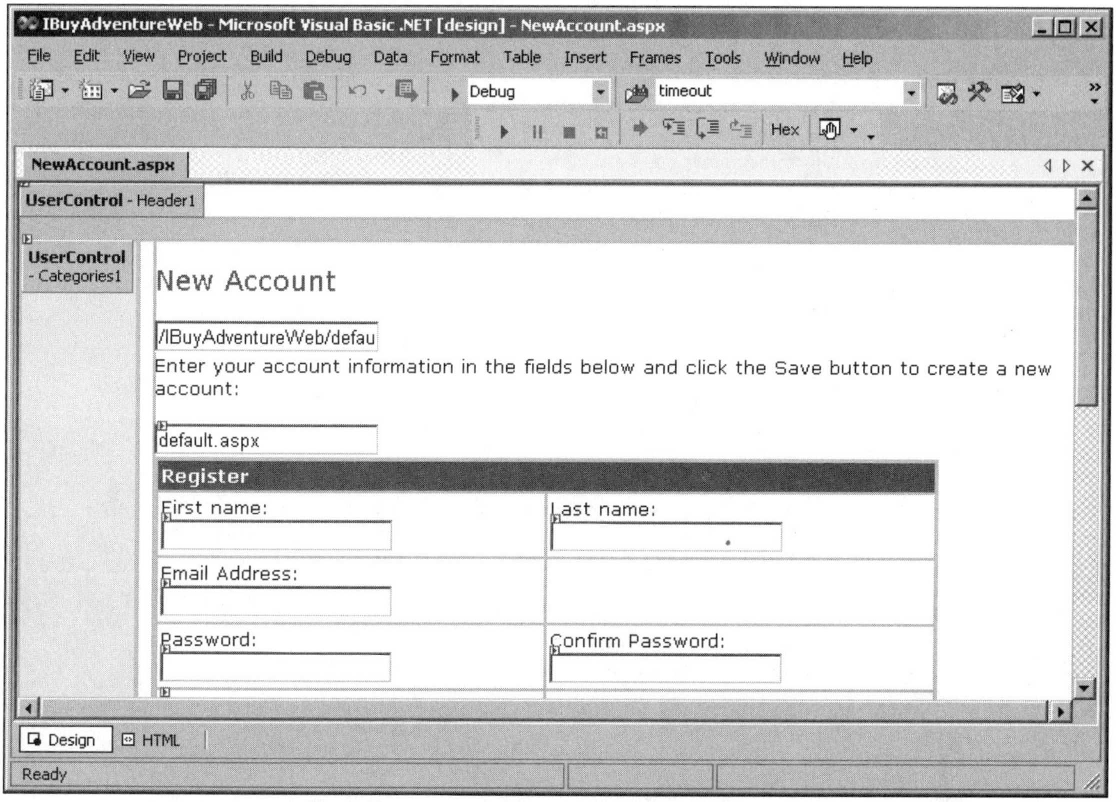

When the Same as Billing Address field is checked, the NewAccount Web Form performs a post-back and fills the Shipping Address fields with the corresponding values in the Billing Address fields. Although not visible in this screenshot, at the very bottom of the NewAccount Web Form are two ASP.NET Button Web Controls with the captions Save and Cancel. When the Cancel button is clicked the user is redirected to the DefaultPage Web Form in the IBuyAdventure site. When the Save button is clicked, the server-side event handler initiates the new customer account transaction. Let's take a look at the code behind the Save button's click event.

The first line of code in the Save button's click event handler creates an instance of the IBuyAdventure.Common.Customer business object for managing and storing the user's customer account information.

```
Sub btnSave_Click(ByVal sender As Object, ByVal e As System.EventArgs) Handles
btnSave.Click

    'Create a new instance of the IBuyAdventure.Common.Customer class
    Dim objCustomer As New IBuyAdventure.Common.Customer()
```

Next we'll load the new Customer business object with the values entered into the Web Controls on the Web Form. We'll also create and append two new Address objects and copy the values from the address fields into the corresponding properties provided by the new Address business objects.

```
'Load the new Customer object with the data from the WebControls
'...on this WebForm
With objCustomer
    .FirstName = txtFirstname.Text
    .LastName = txtLastname.Text
    .Password = txtPassword.Text
    .E-mailAddress = txtE-mailAddress.Text
    .CustomerName = .FirstName & " " & .LastName

    'This new Customer Account will be for a consumer customer
    .CustomerType = _
IBuyAdventure.Common.Customer.CustomerTypesEnum.CustomerType_Consumer

    'Add the Billing Address to the Customer object using the data
    '...entered by the user on this WebForm
    .Addresses.Add(txtBillingAddress_Address1.Text, _
                txtBillingAddress_Address2.Text, _
                txtBillingAddress_City.Text, _
                lstBillingAddress_State.SelectedItem.Value, _
                txtBillingAddress_PostalCode.Text, "United States", _
                txtBillingAddress_PhoneNumber.Text)

  'Add the Shipping Address to the Customer object using the data
    '... entered by the user on this WebForm
    .Addresses.Add(txtShippingAddress_Address1.Text, _
                txtShippingAddress_Address2.Text, _
                txtShippingAddress_City.Text, _
                lstShippingAddress_State.SelectedItem.Value, _
                txtShippingAddress_PostalCode.Text, "United States", _
                txtShippingAddress_PhoneNumber.Text)
End With
```

Let's create an instance of the CustomerTx transactional .NET Serviced Component. Notice that we instantiated this component just like any other .NET class, even though the CustomersTx class is a Serviced Component configured in COM+ and requires transactions.

```
'Create an instance of the IBuyAdventure.BusinessServices.CustomersTx
'...NET(ServicedComponent)
Dim objCustomersTx As New IBuyAdventure.BusinessServices.CustomersTx()
```

Now we're ready to actually create the new customer account. Call the CreateAccount() method of the new CustomersTx object and pass the IBuyAdventure.Common.Customer object that contains all of the new customer's information and addresses. Notice that this method will return a new Customer object, which we'll store in the same variable reference:

```
'Create the new Customer account using the data in our Customer object
'...and get a reference to a new Customer object updated by the
'...Business Service object
objCustomer = objCustomersTx.CreateAccount(objCustomer)
```

After the `Customer` account has been created, we need to save the `IBuyAdventure.Common.Customer` business object containing the updated customer data and addresses to the session state so it is available between page requests. The `Shopper` class in the User Services tier provides methods with this functionality. Let's create an instance of the `Shopper` class and pass a reference to the `NewAccount` Web Form's `HttpContext` object to the `Shopper` class' constructor. The `Shopper` class will use the `HttpContext` object for accessing and manipulating the Session data. Once we have created an instance of the `Shopper` class, let's give it a reference to our `Customer` business object using the `Customer` property and then save the `Customer` object to the session state by calling the `SaveCustomer()` method of the `Shopper` object:

```
        'Create an instance of the Shopper class and pass a reference to the
        '...HTTPContext object for this page to the constructor
        Dim objShopper As New Shopper(context)

        'Update the Customer object managed by the Shopper object
        objShopper.Customer = objCustomer

        'Save the Customer object in the user's session so it is available
        '...between page requests
        objShopper.SaveCustomer()
```

Finally, we have created a new customer account and cached the customer information locally, so we are ready to redirect the user to another Web Form. But first, since the user just created a new account, let's tell the ASP.NET Forms Authentication service that the user has been authenticated, so they're not asked to login again during this shopping session. Then let's redirect the user to the destination URL they were originally trying to access, which is stored in the `hdnReturnURL` hidden HTML input element on this Web Form:

```
        'Simulate a login for the new user by setting the Client
        '...Authentication Cookie and redirect to the destination page
        '
        'NOTE:  A persistent cookie is created if the user checked the Persist
        '...login checkbox.
        System.Web.Security.FormsAuthentication.RedirectFromLoginPage( _
                                 objCustomer.CustomerID, chkRemember.Checked)

        'Redirect user back to where they came from
        Response.Redirect(hdnReturnUrl.Value)
    End Sub
```

Order Processing Transaction

The order processing transaction occurs when an order is created in the IBuyAdventure system. A number of operations are performed during this transaction, including: calculating the order totals, validating and saving the order, authorizing the customer's credit card information or account status, and sending an order confirmation e-mail to the customer. The order processing transaction also involves submitting the order to the fulfillment provider for processing and sending the order information to the AdventureWorks ERP system through MSMQ.

This transaction is initiated in two different situations depending on the type of customer placing the order. For consumer customers, orders are created in the IBuyAdventure site and submitted by the `Checkout` Web Form in the User Services tier. In the case of business customers, orders are received and submitted by the `OrderReceiving` Web Service. The following UML Sequence diagram illustrates the ASP.NET Web Forms, Web Services, business services components, and stored procedures that are involved in the order processing transaction:

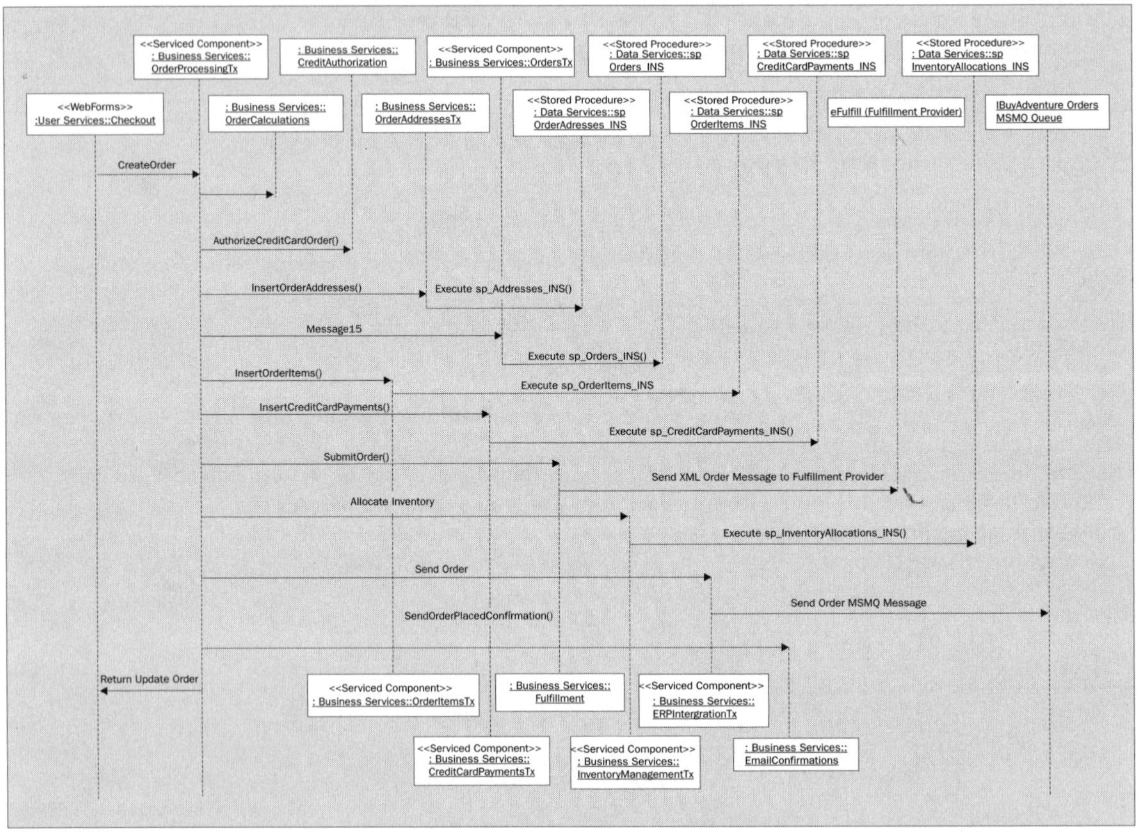

Business Services

The order processing transaction utilizes several business service components in the process of creating an order. Virtually every activity performed during the order processing transaction has been split into separate components to maximize the system's flexibility and extensibility. As we discussed during the design phase, by creating several very modular, specialized components we can easily reuse the component's functionality independently or to compose different transactions. These business services components include the following:

- `OrderProcessingTx`
- `OrdersTx`
- `OrderItemsTx`
- `OrderAddressesTx`

- CreditCardPaymentsTx
- ERPIntegrationTx
- FulfillmentTx
- InventoryManagementTx
- CreditAuthorization
- E-mailConfirmations

With the exception of the `OrderCalculations` and `E-mailConfirmations` components, each of these business service components are .NET Serviced Components configured to require COM+ transactions. Let's implement each of these components, starting with the transactional .NET Serviced Components.

OrderProcessingTx

The `OrderProcessingTx` component is a transactional .NET Serviced Component that acts as the coordinator of the process of creating an order. It implements two public methods: `CreateOrder()` and `UpdateOrderStatus()`. For the purposes of the order processing transaction, we'll focus on the `CreateOrder()` method. We'll implement the `UpdateOrderStatus()` method during our discussion of the order status update transaction later in this chapter.

First, let's import the namespaces containing commonly used types and define the namespace for the `OrderProcessingTx` component:

```
Imports System.Data
Imports System.Data.SqlClient
Imports System.EnterpriseServices
Imports IBuyAdventure.Common

Namespace IBuyAdventure.BusinessServices
```

Next let's define a public interface for the `OrderProcessingTx` class, named `IOrderProcessingTx`. Initially, this interface will only contain the signature for the `CreateOrder()` method. We'll add the `UpdateOrderStatus()` method when we discuss the order status update transaction.

```
    'Define a public interface containing the signatures for members of
    '...this class
    '
    'NOTE:  It is necessary to define a public interface with the
    '...signatures for methods that utilize COM+ method-level attributes.
    '...Otherwise the interface and methods will not be displayed and
    '...configured in COM+, although the component will be configured.
    Public Interface IOrderProcessingTx
        Function CreateOrder(ByVal objOrder As Order, _
                             ByVal objCustomer As Customer) As Order
    End Interface
```

Now let's declare the `OrderProcessingTx` class and apply the `System.EnterpriseServices` attributes to specify the configuration for this component when it is registered in COM+. Let's also implement the `IOrderProcessingTx` interface that we just defined and let's make this class a .NET Serviced Component by inheriting from the `System.EnterpriseServices.ServicedComponent` base class:

```
    <Description("Contains methods for creating and updating the status of Orders
in the IBuyAdventure system."), _
        Transaction(TransactionOption.Required), _
        Synchronization(SynchronizationOption.Required), _
        JustInTimeActivation(True)> _
    Public Class OrderProcessingTx

        'Inherit from the System.EnterpriseServices.ServicedComponent
        '...class to allow this component to utilize COM+ services
        Inherits ServicedComponent

        'Implement the IOrderProcessingTx interface and it's members
        Implements IOrderProcessingTx
```

Now we're ready to implement the `CreateOrder()` method. First let's define the method signature with the same parameters and return value that was defined for the `IOrderProcessingTx` interface.

```
        <Description("Creates a new Order in IBuyAdventure.")> _
        Public Function CreateOrder(ByVal objOrder As Order, _
                                    ByVal objCustomer As Customer) _
                                                          As Order _
                                 Implements IOrderProcessingTx.CreateOrder
```

Since we need to catch and properly handle exceptions, let's enclose all of the code in the `CreateOrder()` method within a `Try` block.

```
            Try
```

Before performing any transactional processing we should assign values to some of the properties in the passed `Order` and `Customer` business objects. If this was a production system we would also want to perform validation of the data contained in these business objects before performing any transactional operations.

It's important to consider the concepts we discussed in Chapter 6 about the differences between the logical transaction and the physical transaction when working with COM+ transaction services. If you recall, COM+ creates a logical or virtual transaction used to coordinate objects and propagate transaction information when the root object is created. However, COM+ does not call down to MS DTC to create the physical transaction until a connection is established to a transactional data store and is enlisted in the transaction. At that point MS DTC is involved and will be responsible for coordinating the commitment or rollback of the transaction with the enlisted resource managers (data stores).

By performing the data validation and applying business rules up front, before any transactional operations, we can maximize the performance and scalability of the system. If a rule is violated, before performing any transactional operations, only the logical transaction will be aborted and MS DTC does not have to coordinate a rollback with the resource managers. In fact, in this situation MS DTC is not even involved with the transaction.

```
                'Declare any procedure-level variables
                Dim objWorkingOrder As Order
```

```
                'Set the OrderDate on the order to today
                objOrder.OrderDate = Now()

                'Set the CustomerID for the order to the passed Customer
                '...object's CustomerID
                objOrder.CustomerID = objCustomer.CustomerID

                'Create a new GUID for the OrderNumber
                objOrder.OrderNumber = System.Guid.NewGuid.ToString()
```

After initializing the passed `Order` and `Customer` business objects, we need to calculate the totals for the `Order`, including the extended price for each item and the subtotal, tax, and shipping totals for the order. We'll perform these calculations by creating an instance of the `OrderCalculations` business services component and invoking the `CalculateOrderTotal()` method on the instance. We'll pass the `CalculateOrderTotal()` method our `Order` business object and store the returned `Order` business object containing the calculated totals in our working `Order` object.

```
                'Create a new instance of the OrderCalculations class
                '...defined in this namespace
                Dim objOrderCalculations As New OrderCalculations()

                'Calculate the entire Order Total and update the totals
                '...stored in the Order data object with the calculated
                '...values. The updated order object is returned.
                objWorkingOrder = _
                        objOrderCalculations.CalculateOrderTotal(objOrder)
```

If the customer placing the order is a consumer, then we need to authorize the credit card payment information for the order, which is contained in the passed `Order` business object's associated `CreditCardPayment` object. This task is accomplished by calling the `AuthorizeCreditCardOrder()` method of an instance of the `CreditAuthorization` class and passing the method our `Order` and `Customer` business objects.

```
                If objCustomer.CustomerType = _
                     Customer.CustomerTypesEnum.CustomerType_Consumer Then

                    'Create a new instance of the CreditAuthorization
                    '...class defined in this namespace
                    Dim objCreditAuthorization As New _
                                                CreditAuthorization()

                    'See if the user has the available credit to place
                    '...this order using the payment method they've
                    '...specified. Replace our Working Order object with
                    '...the one returned from this method call.
                    '
                    'NOTE:  If the CreditCardPayment information fails
                    '...authorization, this method call will throw an
                    '...exception.
                    objWorkingOrder = _
                        objCreditAuthorization.AuthorizeCreditCardOrder( _
                                          objWorkingOrder, objCustomer)
                End If
```

Now we're ready to begin saving the Order data contained in the Order business object to the IBuyAdventure database. First we'll save the Addresses associated with our Order by calling the InsertOrderAddresses() method on a new instance of the OrderAddressesTx transactional .NET ServicedComponent, and passing the working Order object as a parameter.

```
'Create a new instance of the OrderAddressesTx
'...transactional .NET ServicedComponent
Dim objOrderAddressesTx As New OrderAddressesTx()

'Insert a record into the OrdersAddresses table in the
'...IBuyAdventure database for each Address in the Orders
'...object. The updated Order object (and it's Addresses
'...collection) is returned.
'
'NOTE:  It is necessary to insert OrderAddresses prior to
'...record(s) in the Orders or OrderItems tables because
'...of the referential integrity rules of the
'...IBuyAdventure database.
objWorkingOrder = _
 objOrderAddressesTx.InsertOrderAddresses(objWorkingOrder)
```

Next let's save the general Order information by calling the InsertOrder() method on a new instance of the OrdersTx transactional .NET Serviced Component and passing the working Order object as a parameter.

```
'Create a new instance of the OrdersTx transactional
'....NET ServicedComponent
Dim objOrdersTx As New OrdersTx()

'Insert a record into the Orders table in the
'...IBuyAdventure database for the new order.
'...The updated Order object is returned.
objWorkingOrder = objOrdersTx.InsertOrder( _
                            objWorkingOrder, objCustomer)
```

Then let's save the Items associated with the Order by calling the InsertOrderItems() method on a new instance of the OrderItemsTx transactional .NET Serviced Component and passing the working Order object as a parameter.

```
'Create a new instance of the OrderItemsTx transactional
'....NET ServicedComponent
Dim objOrderItemsTx As New OrderItemsTx()

'Insert a record into the OrdersItems table in the
'...IBuyAdventure database for each Item in the Orders
'...object. The updated Order object (and Items
'...collection) is returned.
objWorkingOrder = _
          objOrderItemsTx.InsertOrderItems(objWorkingOrder)
```

If the customer placing the order is a consumer customer, then we need to save the credit card payment information associated with the order. Let's create an instance of the `CreditCardPaymentsTx` transactional .NET Serviced Component and call the `InsertCreditCardPayments()` method, passing the working `Order` object as a parameter.

```
If objCustomer.CustomerType = _
     Customer.CustomerTypesEnum.CustomerType_Consumer Then

    'Create a new instance of the CreditCardPaymentsTx
    '...transactional .NET ServicedComponent
    Dim objCreditCardPaymentsTx As _
                               New CreditCardPaymentsTx()

    'Insert a record into the Orders table in the
    '...IBuyAdventure database for the Credit Card
    '...Payments associated with the new order. The
    '...updated Order object is returned.
    objWorkingOrder = _
       objCreditCardPaymentsTx.InsertCreditCardPayments( _
                                      objWorkingOrder)
End If
```

Now we need to allocate inventory for each of the items on the order, so we can accurately calculate the available inventory of the products ordered. This is accomplished by creating an instance of the `InventoryManagementTx` transactional .NET Serviced Component and calling the `AllocateInventory()` method on the new object. We'll pass the `AllocateInventory()` method our working `Order` business object as a parameter and update our working `Order` object with the value returned from the method call.

```
'Create a new instance of the InventoryManagementTx
'...transactional .NET ServicedComponent
Dim objInventoryManagementTx As _
                           New InventoryManagementTx()

'Insert a record into the InventoryAllocations table in
'...the IBuyAdventure database for each Item in the Orders
'...object. The updated Order object (and Items
'...collection) is returned.
objWorkingOrder = _
            objInventoryManagementTx.AllocateInventory( _
                                      objWorkingOrder)
```

The `Order` has now been completely saved to the IBuyAdventure database and the `Inventory` information for the products ordered has been updated. Now we need to send the order information to the AdventureWorks ERP system. Let's create an instance of the `ERPIntegrationTx` transaction .NET Serviced Component and call the `SendOrder()` method passing the working `Order` business object as a parameter.

```
'Create a new instance of the ERPIntegrationTx
'...transactional .NET ServicedComponent
Dim objERPIntegrationTx As New ERPIntegrationTx()
```

```
'Send the new Order's data to the AdventureWorks ERP
'...system for accounting. Get a reference to the
'...returned Order object containg the updated Order and
'...Items data.
objWorkingOrder = _
        objERPIntegrationTx.SendOrder(objWorkingOrder)
```

Next we need to submit the new order to the fulfillment provider so they can package the order and ship it directly to the customer. Let's create an instance of the `FulfillmentTx` transactional .NET Serviced Component and call the `SubmitOrder()` method passing the working `Order` object.

```
'Create a new instance of the FulfillmentTx transactional
'....NET ServicedComponent
Dim objFulfillmentTx As New FulfillmentTx()

'Submit the new Order's data to the fulfillment partner so
'...they can pick, pack, and ship the Order to the
'...customer. Get a reference to the returned Order
'...object containg the updated Order and Items data.
objWorkingOrder = _
        objFulfillmentTx.SubmitOrder(objWorkingOrder)
```

If the customer placing the order is a consumer, then we also need to send an order confirmation e-mail to the customer's e-mail address indicating that we've received the order and it is being processed. This task is accomplished by calling the `SendOrderPlacedConfirmation()` method on a new instance of the `E-mailConfirmations` business services component, and passing the method call the working `Order` object and the `Customer` business object.

```
If objCustomer.CustomerType = _
     Customer.CustomerTypesEnum.CustomerType_Consumer Then

    'Create an instance of the E-mailConfirmations class
    '...for sending e-mail notifications to the customer.
    Dim objE-mailConfirmations As New E-mailConfirmations()

    'Send an Order Placed e-mail confirmation to the
    '...customer containing some of the order summary
    '...information, which is provided in our working
    '...Order object.
    objWorkingOrder = _
      objE-mailConfirmations.SendOrderPlacedConfirmation( _
                               objWorkingOrder, objCustomer)
End If
```

Finally, we've completed all of the processing in this method. Now all we need to do is call the `SetComplete()` method of the static `ContextUtil` object to notify COM+ that the `CreateOrder()` method has successfully completed its processing and the `OrderProcessingTx` object votes to commit the current transaction. We'll then return the working `Order` business object containing the updated information for the new order to the caller.

```
'We successfully created the Order, so tell COM+ that this
'...object votes to commit the transaction and deactivate.
ContextUtil.SetComplete()
```

```
            'Return the updated Order object to the caller
            Return objWorkingOrder
```

If an exception occurs in the `CreateOrder()` method, we'll simply call the `SetAbort()` method of the `ContextUtil` object to notify COM+ that the `CreateOrder()` method has failed for one reason or another and the `OrderProcessingTx` object votes to abort the current transaction. Since the `OrderProcessingTx` object is the root of the COM+ Transaction, when it is deactivated, as a result of calling the `SetComplete()` or `SetAbort()` methods, and it has concluded its processing, COM+ will evaluate the votes cast by each object involved in the transaction. If any object casts a vote to abort the transaction by calling the `SetAbort()` method or through any other means, COM+ will tell MS DTC to abort the entire transaction. However, if all objects voted to commit the transaction then COM+ will tell MS DTC to commit the transaction and MS DTC will initiate the two-phase commit protocol with the resource managers, which are SQL Server and the MSMQ Service in this situation.

```
        Catch excp As system.Exception
            'An exception occured creating the order.

            'Tell COM+ that this object votes to abort the transaction
            '...and deactivate
            ContextUtil.SetAbort()

            'Throw the exception to the caller of this method
            Throw excp
        End Try
    End Function

  End Class
End Namespace
```

OrdersTx

During our analysis of the `CreateOrder()` method in the `OrderProcessingTx` class we saw how the `CreateOrder()` method uses several business services components to perform the individual tasks in the order processing transaction. One of these components is the `OrdersTx` transactional .NET Serviced Component. The `OrdersTx` component implements two methods: `InsertOrder()` and `UpdateOrder()`. The `InsertOrder()` method is called within the order processing transaction so we'll implement it now.

First, let's define the structure for the `OrdersTx` class file. Let's also define a public interface named `IOrdersTx` that includes the signature for the `InsertOrder()` method.

```
'Import namespaces containing commonly used types
Imports System.Data
Imports System.Data.SqlClient
Imports System.EnterpriseServices
Imports IBuyAdventure.Common

Namespace IBuyAdventure.BusinessServices
  'Define a public interface containing the signatures for members of
  '...this class
  '
```

```
'NOTE:  It is necessary to define a public interface with the
'...signatures for methods that utilize COM+ method-level attributes.
'...Otherwise the interface and methods will not be displayed and
'...configured in COM+, although the component will be configured.
Public Interface IOrdersTx
    Function InsertOrder(ByVal objOrder As Order, _
                              ByVal objCustomer As Customer) As Order
End Interface
```

Next, let's define the `OrdersTx` class, apply the `System.EnterpriseServices` attributes, inherit from the Serviced Component base class, and implement the `IOrdersTx` interface:

```
<Description("Contains methods for inserting and updating Orders."), _
    Transaction(TransactionOption.Required), _
    Synchronization(SynchronizationOption.Required), _
    JustInTimeActivation(True)> _
Public Class OrdersTx

    'Inherit from the System.EnterpriseServices.ServicedComponent
    '...class to allow this component to utilize COM+ services
    Inherits ServicedComponent

    'Implement the IOrdersTx interface and it's members
    Implements IOrdersTx
```

Now, let's declare any member-level instance variables used by the class and implement the default constructor. Within the default constructor, we'll read the `ConnectionString` configured in the `Machine.Config` file into a member-level variable so it can later be used by the methods in this class.

```
    'declare any member-level instance variables
    Private m_strConnectionString As String

    Public Sub New()

        'Load the configuration settings out of the either the
        '...Machine's global configuration file or the calling
        '...application's configuration file, into member-level
        '...variables.

        'Get the ConnectionString for the IBuyAdventure system
        m_strConnectionString = _
            System.Configuration.ConfigurationSettings.AppSettings( _
                "IBuyAdventure.BusinessServices.ConnectionString")
    End Sub
```

Now let's implement the `InsertOrder()` method. First let's create the signature for the `InsertOrder()` method as defined by the `IOrdersTx` interface.

```
    <Description("Inserts a new Order record in IBuyAdventure.")> _
    Public Function InsertOrder(ByVal objOrder As Order, _
                              ByVal objCustomer As Customer) As Order _
```

```
                                Implements IOrdersTx.InsertOrder

        Try
```

Then let's create and initialize an instance of the `SqlCommand` class for executing the `sp_Orders_INS` stored procedure. We'll also create and append the `SqlParameter` objects to the `SqlCommand` for each of the parameters for the `sp_Orders_INS` stored procedure. We'll assign the `SqlParameter` objects the values out of the corresponding properties in the passed `Order` and `Customer` business objects.

```
            'Create a new instance of the SqlCommand class to use for
            '...executing the sp_Orders_INS Stored Procedure
            Dim sqlcmdInsertOrders As New SqlCommand("sp_Orders_INS")

            With sqlcmdInsertOrders
                'Set the command type for the new SqlCommand object to
                '...Stored Procedure
                .CommandType = CommandType.StoredProcedure

                With .Parameters
                    'Create and Append SqlParameters for our SqlCommand
                    .Add("@chrOrderID", SqlDbType.Char, 38)
                    .Add("@nvchrOrderNumber", SqlDbType.NVarChar, 40)
                    .Add("@dtOrderDate", SqlDbType.DateTime)
                    .Add("@dtShippedDate", SqlDbType.DateTime)
                    .Add("@intOrderStatus", SqlDbType.Int)
                    .Add("@chrCustomerID", SqlDbType.Char, 38)
                    .Add("@nvchrCustomerName", SqlDbType.NVarChar, 50)
                    .Add("@nvchrShipToName", SqlDbType.NVarChar, 40)
                    .Add("@chrShipToAddressID", SqlDbType.Char, 38)
                    .Add("@chrBillingAddressID", SqlDbType.Char, 38)
                    .Add("@mnySubTotal", SqlDbType.Money)
                    .Add("@mnyShippingTotal", SqlDbType.Money)
                    .Add("@mnyTaxTotal", SqlDbType.Money)
                    .Add("@mnyGrandTotal", SqlDbType.Money)
                    .Add("@intPaymentType", SqlDbType.Int)

                    'Set the values for each of the SqlParameter
                    '...objects to the values stored in the passed
                    '...Order and Customer objects
                    .Item("@chrOrderID").Value = objOrder.OrderID
                    .Item("@nvchrOrderNumber").Value = _
                                                 objOrder.OrderNumber
                    .Item("@dtOrderDate").Value = objOrder.OrderDate
                    .Item("@intOrderStatus").Value = _
                                                 objOrder.OrderStatus
                    .Item("@chrCustomerID").Value = _
                                               objCustomer.CustomerID
                    .Item("@nvchrCustomerName").Value = _
                                             objCustomer.CustomerName
                    .Item("@nvchrShipToName").Value = _
                                             objCustomer.CustomerName
                    .Item("@chrShipToAddressID").Value = _
                                   objOrder.ShippingAddress.AddressID
```

```
                    .Item("@chrBillingAddressID").Value = _
                                    objOrder.BillingAddress.AddressID
                    .Item("@mnySubTotal").Value = objOrder.SubTotal
                    .Item("@mnyShippingTotal").Value = _
                                          objOrder.ShippingTotal
                    .Item("@mnyTaxTotal").Value = objOrder.TaxTotal
                    .Item("@mnyGrandTotal").Value = objOrder.Total
                    .Item("@intPaymentType").Value = _
                                            objOrder.PaymentType

                    'Set the ShippedDate to null, since the order
                    '...hasn't shipped yet
                    .Item("@dtShippedDate").Value = _
                                             System.DBNull.Value
                End With
            End With
```

After the SqlCommand object for the sp_Orders_INS stored procedure has been created and initialized, let's create an instance of the SqlConnection class for establishing a connection to the IBuyAdventure database and execute the SqlCommand object. Since the sp_Orders_INS stored procedure does not return a Resultset, we'll execute the SqlCommand using the ExecuteNonQuery(), which is optimized for SQL statements that don't return Resultsets.

```
            'Create an instance of the
            '...System.Data.SqlClient.SqlConnection class
            Dim sqlconIBuyAdventure As _
                            New SqlConnection(m_strConnectionString)

            'Establish a connection to the IBuyAdventure database
            sqlconIBuyAdventure.Open()

            'Assign the SqlConnection object to the SqlCommand for
            '...executing the stored procedure
            sqlcmdInsertOrders.Connection = sqlconIBuyAdventure

            'Execute the sp_Orders_INS stored procedure without
            '...returning a resultset
            sqlcmdInsertOrders.ExecuteNonQuery()
```

Finally, we'll close the open connection to the IBuyAdventure SQL Server database, call the SetComplete() method of the static ContextUtil object to vote to commit the transaction, and return the Order object containing the updated data to the caller.

```
            'Close our open connection to the IBuyAdventure database
            sqlconIBuyAdventure.Close()

            'We successfully Inserted the Order record, so tell COM+
            '...that this object votes to commit the transaction
            '...and deactivate this object.
            ContextUtil.SetComplete()

            'Return the updated Order object (and Items collection)
```

```
                '...to the caller
                Return objOrder
```

If an exception is caught within the `InsertOrder()` method, we'll simply call the `SetAbort()` method of the static `ContextUtil` object to vote to roll back the transaction and throw the exception up the call stack to the immediate caller, which is the `CreateOrder()` method of `OrderProcessingTx` class for the order processing transaction.

```
            Catch excp As system.Exception
                'An exception occured inserting the order record.

                'Tell COM+ that this object votes to abort the transaction
                '...and deactivate
                ContextUtil.SetAbort()

                'Throw the exception to the caller of this method
                Throw excp
            End Try

        End Function

    End Class
End Namespace
```

OrderItemsTx

The `OrderItemsTx` class is a transactional .NET Serviced Component that implements a single method named `InsertOrderItems()`. The `InsertOrderItems()` method is called by the `CreateOrder()` method of the `OrderProcessingTx` component to insert all of the line items for the order into the `OrderItems` table in the IBuyAdventure database. Let's implement the `OrderItemsTx` component now.

First, let's import the namespaces containing some of the commonly used types, define the namespace for the `OrderItemsTx` component, and define a public interface named `IOrderItemsTx` containing the method signature for the `InsertOrderItems()` method.

```
'Import namespaces containing commonly used types
Imports System.Data
Imports System.Data.SqlClient
Imports System.EnterpriseServices
Imports IBuyAdventure.Common


Namespace IBuyAdventure.BusinessServices

    'Define a public interface containing the signatures for members of
    '...this class
    '
    'NOTE:  It is necessary to define a public interface with the
    '...signatures for methods that utilize COM+ method-level attributes.
    '...Otherwise the interface and methods will not be displayed and
    '...configured in COM+, although the component will be configured.
    Public Interface IOrderItemsTx
        Function InsertOrderItems(ByVal objOrder As Order) As Order
    End Interface
```

Next let's define the `OrderItemsTx` class, apply the necessary attributes from the `System.EnterpriseServices` namespace, and inherit from the `ServicedComponent` base class in order to make this component a transactional .NET Serviced Component. We'll also implement the `IOrderItemsTx` interface that we just defined, declare any member-level variables, and implement the default constructor for this class.

```
<Description("Contains methods for inserting OrderItem records."), _
    Transaction(TransactionOption.Required), _
    Synchronization(SynchronizationOption.Required), _
    JustInTimeActivation(True)> _
Public Class OrderItemsTx
    'Inherit from the System.EnterpriseServices.ServicedComponent
    '...class to allow this component to utilize COM+ services
    Inherits ServicedComponent

    'Implement the IOrdersItemsTx interface and it's members
    Implements IOrderItemsTx


    'declare any member-level instance variables
    Private m_strConnectionString As String

    Public Sub New()

        'Load the configuration settings out of the either the
        '...Machine's global configuration file or the calling
        '...application's configuration file, into member-level
        '...variables.

        'Get the ConnectionString for the IBuyAdventure system
        m_strConnectionString = _
            System.Configuration.ConfigurationSettings.AppSettings( _
                    "IBuyAdventure.BusinessServices.ConnectionString")
    End Sub
```

Now let's implement the `InsertOrderItems()` method as defined by the `IOrdersTx` interface.

```
    <Description("Inserts new OrderItem records in IBuyAdventure.")> _
    Public Function InsertOrderItems(ByVal objOrder As Order) _
                As Order Implements IOrderItemsTx.InsertOrderItems

        Try

            'declare any procedure-level variables
            Dim objItem As Item
```

Next, let's create an instance of the `SqlCommand` class and initialize it for executing the `sp_OrderItems_INS` stored procedure. We'll create and append a `SqlParameter` object to our `SqlCommand` for each of the parameters supported by the stored procedure. Then let's create a new `SqlConnection` object, and establish a connection to the IBuyAdventure database for executing the `SqlCommand`.

```
            'Create a new instance of the SqlCommand class to use for
            '...executing the sp_OrderItems_INS Stored Procedure
            Dim sqlcmdInsertOrderItems As _
                                   New SqlCommand("sp_OrderItems_INS")

            With sqlcmdInsertOrderItems
                'Set the command type for the new SqlCommand object to
                '...Stored Procedure
                .CommandType = CommandType.StoredProcedure

                With .Parameters
                   'Create and append SqlParameters for our SqlCommand
                    .Add("@chrOrderItemID", SqlDbType.Char, 38)
                    .Add("@chrOrderID", SqlDbType.Char, 38)
                    .Add("@chrProductID", SqlDbType.Char, 38)
                    .Add("@nvchrSKU", SqlDbType.NVarChar, 10)
                    .Add("@nvchrProductName", SqlDbType.NVarChar, 50)
                    .Add("@nvchrProductDescription", _
                                         SqlDbType.NVarChar, 255)
                    .Add("@intQuantity", SqlDbType.Int)
                    .Add("@mnyUnitPrice", SqlDbType.Money)
                    .Add("@mnyExtendedPrice", SqlDbType.Money)
                End With
            End With

            'Create an instance of the SqlConnection class
            Dim sqlconIBuyAdventure As _
                             New SqlConnection(m_strConnectionString)

            'Establish a connection to the IBuyAdventure database
            sqlconIBuyAdventure.Open()

            'Assign the SqlConnection object to the SqlCommand for
            '...executing the stored procedure
            sqlcmdInsertOrderItems.Connection = sqlconIBuyAdventure
```

Now let's iterate through each `Item` object in the passed `Order` object's `Items` collection, fill the `SqlParameter` objects with the corresponding data from the `Item` object, and execute a `SqlCommand` object for the `sp_OrderItems_INS` stored procedure to insert each item.

```
            'Iterate through each Item object in the passed Order's
            '...Items collection and insert a record into the Order
            '...Details table for each one
            For Each objItem In objOrder.Items

                'Set the values for each of the SqlParameters to the
                '...values stored in the properties and fields for the
                '...current Item object and Order object
                With sqlcmdInsertOrderItems.Parameters
                    .Item("@chrOrderItemID").Value = objItem.ItemID
                    .Item("@chrOrderID").Value = objOrder.OrderID
                    .Item("@chrProductID").Value = objItem.ProductID
                    .Item("@nvchrSKU").Value = objItem.SKU
```

```
                    .Item("@nvchrProductName").Value = _
                                            objItem.ProductName
                    .Item("@nvchrProductDescription").Value = _
                                            objItem.Description
                    .Item("@mnyUnitPrice").Value = objItem.UnitPrice
                    .Item("@intQuantity").Value = objItem.Quantity
                    .Item("@mnyExtendedPrice").Value = _
                                          objItem.ExtendedPrice
                End With

                'Execute the sp_OrderItems_INS stored procedure
                '...without returning a resultset
                sqlcmdInsertOrderItems.ExecuteNonQuery()
            Next
```

Finally, let's close our open connection to the IBuyAdventure database, return the `Order` object containing the updated `Order` and `Item` information, and call the `SetComplete()` method of the static `ContextUtil` object to vote to commit the transaction.

```
            'Close our open connection to the IBuyAdventure database
            sqlconIBuyAdventure.Close()

            'Return the updated Order object (and Items collection) to
            '...the caller
            Return objOrder

            'We successfully Inserted the OrderItem records, so tell
            '...COM+ that this object votes to commit the transaction
            '...and deactivate.
            ContextUtil.SetComplete()
```

If an exception occurs in the `InsertOrderItems()` method, the following `Catch` statement will trap the exception, call the `SetAbort()` method of the `ContextUtil` object to vote to abort the current transaction, and throw the exception up the call stack to the immediate caller.

```
        Catch excp As system.Exception
            'An exception occured inserting the OrderItem records.

            'Tell COM+ that this object votes to abort the transaction
            '...and deactivate
            ContextUtil.SetAbort()

            'Throw the exception to the caller of this method
            Throw excp
        End Try
    End Function
  End Class
End Namespace
```

OrderAddressesTx

The `OrderAddressesTx` is a transactional .NET Serviced Component that implements a single method named `InsertOrderAddresses()`. The `InsertOrderAddresses()` method is called by the `OrderProcessingTx` component's `CreateOrder()` method within an order processing transaction to save all of the addresses associated with the new `Order`. The `OrderAddressesTx` component and `InsertOrderAddresses()` method are very similar to the `InsertOrderItems()` method defined in the `OrderItemsTx` component. Let's implement the `InsertOrderAddresses()` method now.

First, let's establish the structure for the `OrderAddressesTx` class file, including the namespace and class definitions. We'll also define a public interface named `IOrderAddressesTx`, containing a single method signature for the `InsertOrderAddresses()` method, and implement this interface on the `OrderAddressesTx` class. Since the `OrderAddressesTx` class is a transactional Serviced Component, we'll also inherit from the `ServicedComponent` base class and apply the attributes defined in the `System.EnterpriseServices` to our class declaration.

```
'Import namespaces containing commonly used types
Imports System.Data
Imports System.Data.SqlClient
Imports System.EnterpriseServices
Imports IBuyAdventure.Common

Namespace IBuyAdventure.BusinessServices

    'Define a public interface containing the signatures for members of
    '...this class
    '
    'NOTE:  It is necessary to define a public interface with the
    '...signatures for methods that utilize COM+ method-level attributes.
    '...Otherwise the interface and methods will not be displayed and
    '...configured in COM+, although the component will be configured.
    Public Interface IOrderAddressesTx
        Function InsertOrderAddresses(ByVal objOrder As Order) As Order
    End Interface

   <Description("Contains methods for inserting OrderAddress records."), _
        Transaction(TransactionOption.Required), _
        Synchronization(SynchronizationOption.Required), _
        JustInTimeActivation(True)> _
    Public Class OrderAddressesTx

        'Inherit from the System.EnterpriseServices.ServicedComponent
        '...class to allow this component to utilize COM+ services
        Inherits ServicedComponent

        'Implement the IOrdersTx interface and its members
        Implements IOrderAddressesTx

        'declare any member-level instance variables
        Private m_strConnectionString As String

        Public Sub New()

            'Load the configuration settings out of the either the
```

```
        '...Machine's global configuration
        '...file or the calling application's configuration file, into
        '...member-level variables.

        'Get the ConnectionString for the IBuyAdventure system
        m_strConnectionString = _
            System.Configuration.ConfigurationSettings.AppSettings( _
                    "IBuyAdventure.BusinessServices.ConnectionString")
    End Sub
```

Now let's implement the `InsertOrderAddresses()` method as defined by the `IOrderAddressesTx` interface. Let's create and initialize an instance of the `SqlCommand` class for executing the `sp_OrderAddresses_INS` stored procedure. We'll also create and append a `SqlParameter` object for each of the stored procedure's parameters. Then we'll create an instance of the `SqlConnection` class, establish a connection to the IBuyAdventure database using the connection string stored in our member level variable, and associated the new `SqlConnection` object with the `SqlCommand` object for executing the `sp_OrderAddresses_INS` stored procedure.

```
    <Description("Inserts new OrderAddress records in IBuyAdventure.")> _
    Public Function InsertOrderAddresses(ByVal objOrder As Order) _
                                                      As Order _
                Implements IOrderAddressesTx.InsertOrderAddresses

        Try

            'declare any procedure-level variables
            Dim objAddress As IBuyAdventure.Common.Address

            'Create a new instance of the SqlCommand class to use for
            '...executing the sp_OrderAddresses_INS Stored Procedure
            Dim sqlcmdInsertOrderAddress As _
                                New SqlCommand("sp_OrderAddresses_INS")

            With sqlcmdInsertOrderAddress
                'Set the command type for the new SqlCommand object to
                '...Stored Procedure
                .CommandType = CommandType.StoredProcedure

                With .Parameters
                    'Create and append SqlParameters for the SqlCommand
                    .Add("@chrOrderAddressID", SqlDbType.Char, 38)
                    .Add("@nvchrFirstname", SqlDbType.NVarChar, 50)
                    .Add("@nvchrLastname", SqlDbType.NVarChar, 50)
                    .Add("@nvchrAddress1", SqlDbType.NVarChar, 50)
                    .Add("@nvchrAddress2", SqlDbType.NVarChar, 30)
                    .Add("@nvchrCity", SqlDbType.NVarChar, 30)
                    .Add("@nvchrRegion", SqlDbType.NVarChar, 30)
                    .Add("@nvchrPostalCode", SqlDbType.NVarChar, 20)
                    .Add("@nvchrCountry", SqlDbType.NVarChar, 50)
                    .Add("@nchrPhoneNumber", SqlDbType.NChar, 15)
                End With
            End With
```

```
                'Create an instance of the SqlConnection class
                Dim sqlconIBuyAdventure As _
                                  New SqlConnection(m_strConnectionString)

                'Establish a connection to the IBuyAdventure database
                sqlconIBuyAdventure.Open()

                'Assign the SqlConnection object to the SqlCommand for
                '...executing the stored procedure
                sqlcmdInsertOrderAddress.Connection = sqlconIBuyAdventure
```

Now, let's iterate through each `Address` object in the passed `Order` object's `Addresses` collection, fill the values of the `SqlParameter` objects with the data from the `Address` object, and execute the `SqlCommand` for the `sp_OrderAddresses_INS` stored procedure.

```
                'Iterate through each Address object in the passed Order's
                '...Addresses collection and insert a record into the
                '...Order Details table for each one
                For Each objAddress In objOrder.Addresses

                    'Set the values for each of the SqlParameters to the
                    '...values stored in the properties and fields for the
                    '...current Address object.
                    With sqlcmdInsertOrderAddress.Parameters
                        .Item("@chrOrderAddressID").Value = _
                                                     objAddress.AddressID
                        .Item("@nvchrFirstname").Value = _
                                                     objAddress.Firstname
                        .Item("@nvchrLastname").Value = _
                                                      objAddress.Lastname
                        .Item("@nvchrAddress1").Value = _
                                                      objAddress.Address1
                        .Item("@nvchrAddress2").Value = _
                                                      objAddress.Address2
                        .Item("@nvchrCity").Value = objAddress.City
                        .Item("@nvchrRegion").Value = objAddress.Region
                        .Item("@nvchrPostalCode").Value = _
                                                    objAddress.PostalCode
                        .Item("@nvchrCountry").Value = objAddress.Country
                        .Item("@nchrPhoneNumber").Value = _
                                                   objAddress.PhoneNumber
                    End With

                    'Execute the sp_OrderAddresses_INS stored procedure
                    '...without returning a resultset
                    sqlcmdInsertOrderAddress.ExecuteNonQuery()
                Next
```

Finally, let's close our open connection to the IBuyAdventure database, call the `SetComplete()` method to vote to commit the transaction, and return the `Order` object containing the updated `Order` and `Address` information. If an exception is caught, we'll simply call the `SetAbort()` method to vote to abort the current transaction and throw the exception to the caller.

```
                'Close our open connection to the IBuyAdventure database
                sqlconIBuyAdventure.Close()

                'We successfully Inserted the OrderAddress records, so
                '...tell COM+ that this object votes to commit the
                '...transaction and deactivate.
                ContextUtil.SetComplete()

                'Return the updated Order object and Items to the caller
                Return objOrder

            Catch excp As system.Exception
                'An exception occured inserting the OrderAddress records.

                'Tell COM+ that this object votes to abort the transaction
                '...and deactivate
                ContextUtil.SetAbort()

                'Throw the exception to the caller of this method
                Throw excp
            End Try
        End Function
    End Class
End Namespace
```

CreditCardPaymentsTx

The `CreditCardPaymentsTx` class is a transactional .NET Serviced Component that provides a single method named `InsertCreditCardPayments()`, which is called by the `CreateOrder()` method of the `OrderProcessingTx` component during an order processing transaction. The `InsertCreditCardPayments()` method inserts a `CreditCardPayment` record for the payment information associated with an order. Let's implement this method now.

First let's import the namespaces containing commonly used types and define the namespace for our class. We'll also define a public interface named `ICreditCardPaymentsTx`, which will include the method signature for the `InsertCreditCardPayments()` method.

```
'Import namespaces containing commonly used types
Imports System.Data
Imports System.Data.SqlClient
Imports System.EnterpriseServices
Imports IBuyAdventure.Common

Namespace IBuyAdventure.BusinessServices

    'Define a public interface containing the signatures for members of
    '...this class
    '
    'NOTE:  It is necessary to define a public interface with the
    '...signatures for methods that utilize COM+ method-level attributes.
    '...Otherwise the interface and methods will not be displayed and
    '...configured in COM+, although the component will be configured.
    Public Interface ICreditCardPaymentsTx
```

```
        Function InsertCreditCardPayments(ByVal objOrder As Order) _
                                                                As Order
    End Interface
```

Next, let's declare the CreditCardPaymentsTx class, inherit from the ServicedComponent base class, and implement our ICreditCardPaymentsTx interface. Let's also implement the default constructor for this class.

```
    <Description("Contains methods for inserting and updating Orders."), _
        Transaction(TransactionOption.Required), _
        Synchronization(SynchronizationOption.Required), _
        JustInTimeActivation(True)> _
    Public Class CreditCardPaymentsTx
        'Inherit from the System.EnterpriseServices.ServicedComponent
        '...class to allow this component to utilize COM+ services
        Inherits ServicedComponent

        'Implement the ICreditCardPaymentsTx interface and its members
        Implements ICreditCardPaymentsTx

        'declare any member-level instance variables
        Private m_strConnectionString As String

        Public Sub New()

            'Load the configuration settings out of the either the
            '...Machine's global configuration
            '...file or the calling application's configuration file, into
            '...member-level variables.

            'Get the ConnectionString for the IBuyAdventure system
            m_strConnectionString = _
                System.Configuration.ConfigurationSettings.AppSettings( _
                        "IBuyAdventure.BusinessServices.ConnectionString")
        End Sub
```

Now let's implement the InsertCreditCardPayments() method as defined by the ICreditCardPaymentsTx interface. Let's create and initialize an instance of the SqlCommand class for executing the sp_CreditCardPayments_INS stored procedure. We'll create and append a SqlParameter to our SqlCommand for each parameter supported by the sp_CreditCardPayments_INS stored procedure. The values for these parameters will be assigned using the data in the CreditCardPayment object associated with the passed Order business object.

```
        <Description("Inserts a new CreditCardPayment record.")> _
        Public Function InsertCreditCardPayments( _
                                    ByVal objOrder As Order) As Order _
                Implements ICreditCardPaymentsTx.InsertCreditCardPayments

            Try

                'Create a new instance of the SqlCommand class for
                '...executing the sp_CreditCardPayments_INS Stored Proc
```

```
Dim sqlcmdInsertCreditCardPayments As _
             New SqlCommand("sp_CreditCardPayments_INS")

With sqlcmdInsertCreditCardPayments
    'Set the command type for the new SqlCommand object to
    '...Stored Procedure
    .CommandType = CommandType.StoredProcedure

    With .Parameters
        'Create and Append SqlParameters for our SqlCommand
        .Add("@chrCreditCardPaymentID", _
                                    SqlDbType.Char, 38)
        .Add("@chrOrderID", SqlDbType.Char, 38)
        .Add("@nvchrCreditCardType", _
                                SqlDbType.NVarChar, 30)
        .Add("@nvchrCreditCardNumber", _
                                SqlDbType.NVarChar, 20)
        .Add("@intExpirationMonth", SqlDbType.Int)
        .Add("@intExpirationYear", SqlDbType.Int)
        .Add("@nvchrNameOnCard", SqlDbType.NVarChar, 50)
        .Add("@nvchrAuthorizationCode", _
                                SqlDbType.NVarChar, 50)
        .Add("@mnyAmountCharged", SqlDbType.Money)

        'Set the values for each of the SqlParameter
        '...objects to the values stored in the passed
        '...Order object and it's CreditCardPayment object
        .Item("@chrCreditCardPaymentID").Value = _
            objOrder.CreditCardPayment.CreditCardPaymentID
        .Item("@chrOrderID").Value = objOrder.OrderID
        .Item("@nvchrCreditCardType").Value = _
                        objOrder.CreditCardPayment.CardType
        .Item("@nvchrCreditCardNumber").Value = _
                      objOrder.CreditCardPayment.CardNumber
        .Item("@intExpirationMonth").Value = _
                objOrder.CreditCardPayment.ExpirationMonth
        .Item("@intExpirationYear").Value = _
                 objOrder.CreditCardPayment.ExpirationYear
        .Item("@nvchrNameOnCard").Value = _
                      objOrder.CreditCardPayment.NameOnCard
        .Item("@nvchrAuthorizationCode").Value = _
              objOrder.CreditCardPayment.AuthorizationCode
        .Item("@mnyAmountCharged").Value = _
                  objOrder.CreditCardPayment.AmountCharged
    End With
End With
```

Next, let's create an instance of the `SqlConnection` class, establish a connection to the IBuyAdventure SQL Server database, and execute the `SqlCommand` object for the `sp_CreditCardPayments_INS` stored procedure.

```
'Create an instance of the SqlConnection class
Dim sqlconIBuyAdventure As _
```

```
                                     New SqlConnection(m_strConnectionString)

                'Establish a connection to the IBuyAdventure database
                sqlconIBuyAdventure.Open()

                'Assign the SqlConnection object to the SqlCommand for
                '...executing the stored procedure
                sqlcmdInsertCreditCardPayments.Connection = _
                                                       sqlconIBuyAdventure

                'Execute the sp_CreditCardPayments_INS stored procedure
                '...without returning a resultset
                sqlcmdInsertCreditCardPayments.ExecuteNonQuery()
```

Finally, let's close our open SqlConnection to the IBuyAdventure database, call the SetComplete() method to vote to commit the transaction, and return the Order object containing the updated CreditCardPayment information. If an exception should occur, we'll simply call the SetAbort() method of the ContextUtil static class and throw the exception up the call stack to the immediate caller.

```
                'Close our open connection to the IBuyAdventure database
                sqlconIBuyAdventure.Close()

                'We successfully Inserted the CreditCardPaymet record, so
                '...tell COM+ that this object votes to commit the
                '...transaction and deactivate.
                ContextUtil.SetComplete()

                'Return the updated Order object (and Items collection) to
                '...the caller
                Return objOrder


            Catch excp As system.Exception
                'An exception occured inserting the CreditCardPayment

                'Tell COM+ that this object votes to abort the transaction
                '...and deactivate
                ContextUtil.SetAbort()

                'Throw the exception to the caller of this method
                Throw excp
            End Try

        End Function
    End Class
End Namespace
```

InventoryManagementTx

The InventoryManagementTx class is a transactional .NET Serviced Component that provides several methods for managing the inventory information for products in the IBuyAdventure system. This class implements three methods: AllocateInventory(), UnAllocateInventory(), and DecrementInventory(). However, only the AllocateInventory() method is called during the order processing transaction. We'll implement these other methods when we discuss the order status update transaction, but let's implement the AllocateInventory() method now.

Before creating the AllocateInventory() method, first we need to establish the InventoryManagementTx class file. Let's import the namespaces containing the commonly used types, define the namespace for this class, and define a public interface named IInventoryManagementTx. Initially, the IInventoryManagementTx interface will contain a single method signature for the AllocateInventory() method.

```
'Import namespaces containing commonly used types
Imports System.Data
Imports System.Data.SqlClient
Imports System.EnterpriseServices
Imports IBuyAdventure.Common

Namespace IBuyAdventure.BusinessServices

    'Define a public interface containing the signatures for members of
    '...this class
    '
    'NOTE:  It is necessary to define a public interface with the
    '...signatures for methods that utilize COM+ method-level attributes.
    '...Otherwise the interface and methods will not be displayed and
    '...configured in COM+, although the component will be configured.
    Public Interface IInventoryManagementTx
        Function AllocateInventory(ByVal objOrder As Order) As Order
    End Interface
```

Next let's declare the InventoryManagementTx class and implement the IInventoryManagementTx interface that we just defined. In order to make the InventoryManagementTx class a transactional .NET Serviced Component, we'll inherit from the ServicedComponent base class and apply the System.EnterpriseServices.Transaction attribute to the class definition.

```
    <Description("Contains methods for managing inventory."), _
        Transaction(TransactionOption.Required), _
        Synchronization(SynchronizationOption.Required), _
        JustInTimeActivation(True)> _
    Public Class InventoryManagementTx
        'Inherit from the System.EnterpriseServices.ServicedComponent
        '...class to allow this component to utilize COM+ services
        Inherits ServicedComponent

        'Implement the IInventoryManagementTx interface and it's members
        Implements IInventoryManagementTx

        'declare any member-level instance variables
```

```
        Private m_strConnectionString As String

        Public Sub New()

            'Load the configuration settings out of the either the
            '...Machine's global configuration
            '...file or the calling application's configuration file, into
            '...member-level variables.

            'Get the ConnectionString for the IBuyAdventure system
            m_strConnectionString = _
                System.Configuration.ConfigurationSettings.AppSettings( _
                        "IBuyAdventure.BusinessServices.ConnectionString")
        End Sub
```

Now let's implement the `AllocateInventory()` method. After declaring the method, let's create and initialize an instance of the `SqlCommand` for executing the `sp_InventoryAllocations_INS` stored procedure. We'll create and append `SqlParameter` objects to the `SqlCommand` for each of the stored procedure's parameters.

```
        <Description("Allocates product inventory in IBuyAdventure.")> _
        Public Function AllocateInventory(ByVal objOrder As Order) _
                                                                As Order _
                        Implements IInventoryManagementTx.AllocateInventory

            Try

                'declare any procedure-level variables
                Dim objItem As Item

                'Create a new instance of the SqlCommand class to use for
                '...executing the sp_InventoryAllocations_INS Stored Proc
                Dim sqlcmdInsertInventoryAllocations As _
                            New SqlCommand("sp_InventoryAllocations_INS")

                With sqlcmdInsertInventoryAllocations
                    'Set the command type for the new SqlCommand object to
                    '...Stored Procedure
                    .CommandType = CommandType.StoredProcedure

                    With .Parameters
                        'Create and Append SqlParameters for our SqlCommand
                        .Add("@chrInventoryAllocationID", _
                                                   SqlDbType.Char, 38)
                        .Add("@chrProductID", SqlDbType.Char, 38)
                        .Add("@chrOrderID", SqlDbType.Char, 38)
                        .Add("@chrOrderItemID", SqlDbType.Char, 38)
                        .Add("@intQuantityAllocated", SqlDbType.Int)
                        .Add("@dtDateTimeAllocated", SqlDbType.DateTime)
                    End With
                End With
```

After initializing our new SqlCommand object, let's create an instance of the SqlConnection class and establish a connection the IBuyAdventure SQL Server database.

```
'Create an instance of the SqlConnection class
Dim sqlconIBuyAdventure As _
                    New SqlConnection(m_strConnectionString)

'Establish a connection to the IBuyAdventure database
sqlconIBuyAdventure.Open()

'Assign the SqlConnection object to the SqlCommand for
'...executing the stored procedure
sqlcmdInsertInventoryAllocations.Connection = _
                                    sqlconIBuyAdventure
```

Next, let's iterate through each Item in the passed Order business object's Items collection, assign values to each of the SqlParameter s, and execute the SqlCommand for the sp_InventoryAllocations_INS stored procedure.

```
'Iterate through each Item object in the passed Order's
'...Items collection and insert a record into the Order
'...Details table for each one
For Each objItem In objOrder.Items

    'Set the values for each of the SqlParameters to the
    '...values stored in the properties and fields for the
    '...current Item object and Order object
    With sqlcmdInsertInventoryAllocations.Parameters
        .Item("@chrProductID").Value = objItem.ProductID
        .Item("@chrOrderID").Value = objOrder.OrderID
        .Item("@chrOrderItemID").Value = objItem.ItemID
        .Item("@intQuantityAllocated").Value = _
                                    objItem.Quantity
        .Item("@dtDateTimeAllocated").Value = _
                                  objOrder.OrderDate

        'Create a new GUID value for the
        '...InventoryAllocationID
        .Item("@chrInventoryAllocationID").Value = _
                            System.Guid.NewGuid.ToString()
    End With

    'Execute the sp_InventoryAllocations_INS stored
    '...procedure without returning a resultset
    sqlcmdInsertInventoryAllocations.ExecuteNonQuery()
Next
```

Finally, let's close our open connection to the IBuyAdventure database, call the SetComplete() method of the ContextUtil object, and return the updated Order object to the caller. If an error should occur, we'll simply call the SetAbort() method to vote to abort the current COM+ transaction and throw the exception to the caller.

```
                'Close our open connection to the IBuyAdventure database
                sqlconIBuyAdventure.Close()

                'We successfully Inserted the InventoryAllocation records,
                '...so tell COM+ that this object votes to commit the
                '...transaction and deactivate.
                ContextUtil.SetComplete()

                'Return the updated Order object (and Items collection) to
                '...the caller
                Return objOrder

            Catch excp As system.Exception
                'An exception occured inserting the InventoryAllocation

                'Tell COM+ that this object votes to abort the transaction
                '...and deactivate
                ContextUtil.SetAbort()

                'Throw the exception to the caller of this method
                Throw excp
            End Try
        End Function

    End Class
End Namespace
```

ERPIntegrationTx

The ERPIntegrationTx class is a transactional .NET Serviced Component that provides a single method named SendOrder, which is used to send an order to AdventureWorks internal Enterprise Resource Planning (ERP) system. The SendOrder method accomplishes this task by converting the Order business object representing the order being placed in the system to an XML formatted document and then sending an MSMQ message to a pre-determined queue named IBuyAdventure Orders. Since MSMQ is a Resource Manager that supports MS DTC and the OLE Transactions protocol, the operations performed against MSMQ by the ERPIntegrationTx object will automatically be performed within the order processing transaction.

The IBuyAdventure Orders queue must be created as a private, transactional queue on the local machine in order for this class to function properly. Let's create this queue before implementing the ERPIntegrationTx class. First, launch the Computer Management console by selecting the Computer Management option from Administrative Tools in Control Panel:

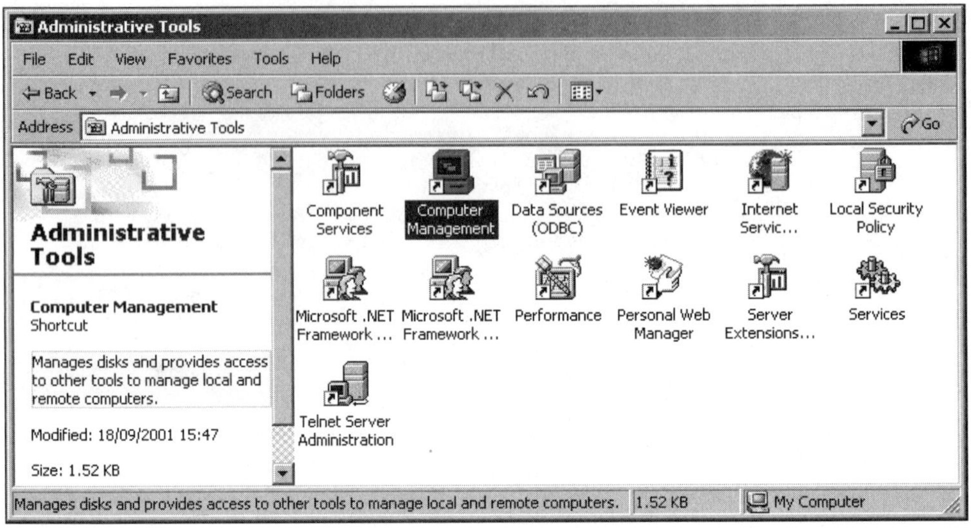

From the navigation tree in the left side of the Computer Management console, expand the Services and Applications group, then the Message Queuing node, and finally expand the Private Queues folder. Then right-click on the Private Queues folder, and select New | Private Queue from the context menu.

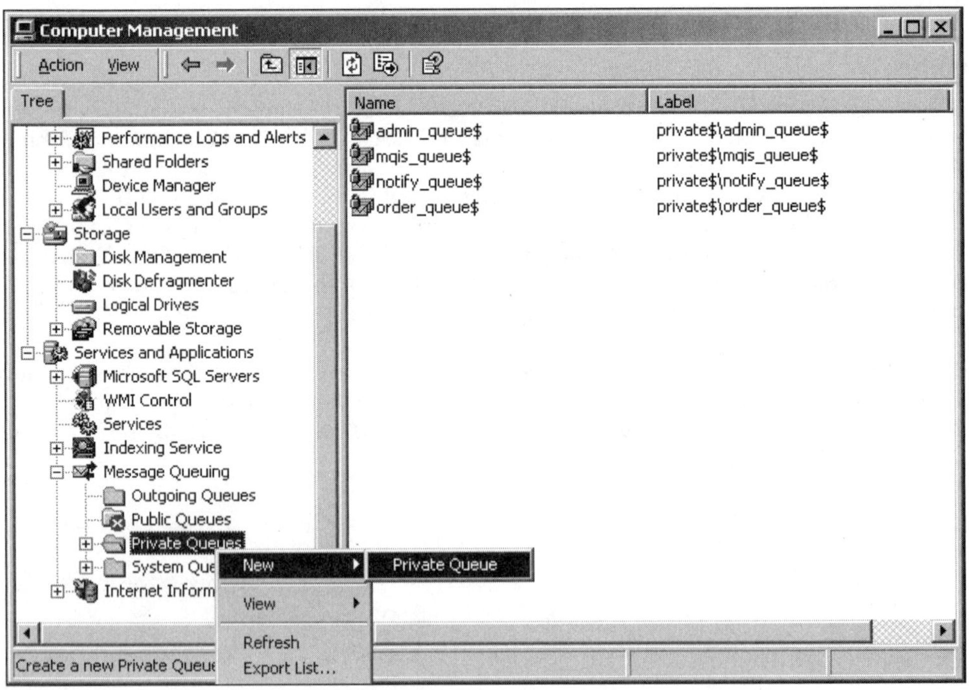

The **Computer Management** console will then display a small dialog window titled **Queue Name**. Simply enter the name of **IBuyAdventure Orders** for the private queue name and be sure to check the **Transactional** checkbox before clicking the **OK** button. You can use a different name for the queue if you like, but you're going need to modify the code for the `SendOrder` method in the `ERPIntegrationTx` component to reflect any changes.

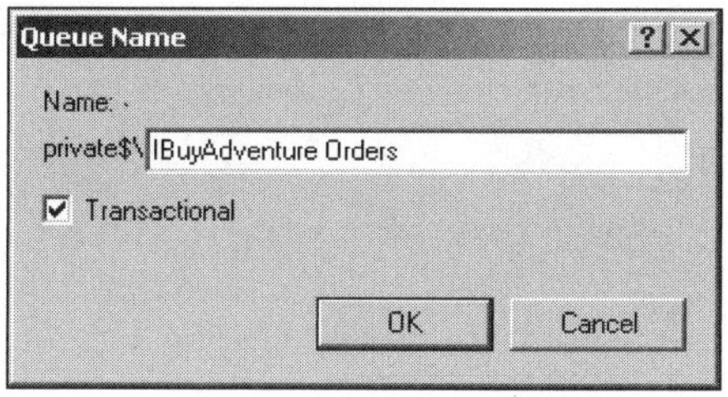

The private, transactional queue will now be created and added to the list of private queues in the **Computer Management** console application. But before we begin writing the code for the `ERPIntegrationTx` class let's first modify the configuration for the new queue. Simply right-click on the **IBuyAdventure Orders** queue from the list of private queues and select **Properties** from the context menu. The **Computer Management** console will then display a properties dialog window for the **IBuyAdventure Orders** queue. The only change we want to make to the default configuration for the new queue is to enable the **Journal**. In the **Journal** section on the **General** tab, simply check the **Enabled** checkbox and click the **OK** button to apply the changes and close the window.

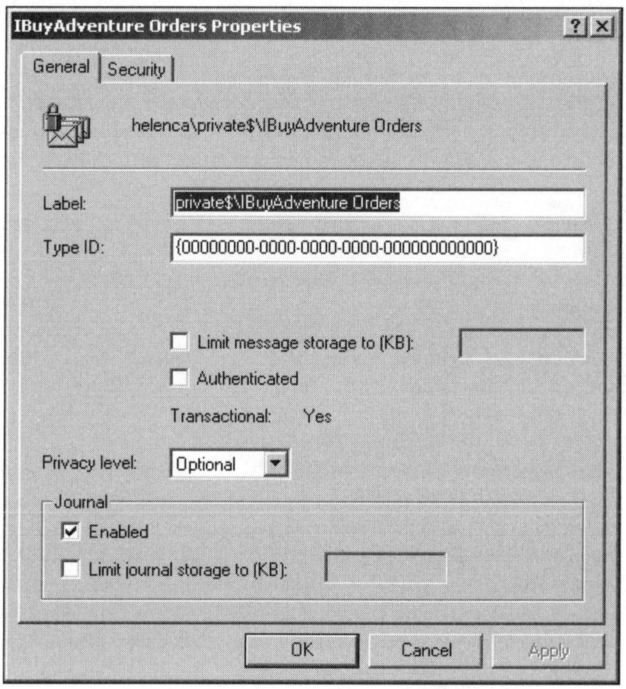

Now we're ready to create the ERPIntegrationTx class. Let's begin by first importing the namespaces containing commonly used types, defining the namespace for this class, and defining a public interface named IERPIntegrationTx. Notice that we also import the System.Messaging namespace in addition to the standard namespaces that we normally import for the other transactional Serviced Components. The System.Messaging namespace contains the types used for interacting with Microsoft Message Queue.

```
'Import namespaces containing commonly used types
Imports System.Data
Imports System.Data.SqlClient
Imports System.EnterpriseServices
Imports System.Messaging
Imports IBuyAdventure.Common


Namespace IBuyAdventure.BusinessServices

    'Define a public interface containing the signatures for members of
    '...this class
    '
    'NOTE:  It is necessary to define a public interface with the
    '...signatures for methods that utilize COM+ method-level attributes.
    '...Otherwise the interface and methods will not be displayed and
    '...configured in COM+, although the component will be configured.
    Public Interface IERPIntegrationTx
        Function SendOrder(ByVal objOrder As Order) As Order
    End Interface
```

Next let's declare the ERPIntegrationTx class, inherit from the ServicedComponent base class, and implement the IERPIntegrationTx class we just defined. Since this class accesses MSMQ during the order processing transaction, we'll specify a transaction support attribute of Required.

```
    <Description("Contains methods for integrating with the ERP system."), _
        Transaction(TransactionOption.Required), _
        Synchronization(SynchronizationOption.Required), _
        JustInTimeActivation(True)> _
    Public Class ERPIntegrationTx
        'Inherit from the System.EnterpriseServices.ServicedComponent
        '...class to allow this component to utilize COM+ services
        Inherits ServicedComponent

        'Implement the IERPIntegrationTx interface and it's members
        Implements IERPIntegrationTx
```

Now we're ready to implement the SendOrder method. Within a Try block we'll first get an XML-formatted string for the passed Order business object by calling its XML property. Then we'll create a new instance of the System.Messsaging.Message class, which represents a new MSMQ message, and pass the XML-formatted Order as a parameter to the Message class constructor:

```
        <Description("Sends an Order to the ERP system using MSMQ.")> _
        Public Function SendOrder(ByVal objOrder As Order) As Order _
```

```
                                    Implements IERPIntegrationTx.SendOrder

        Try
            'Get an XML string representing the passed Order object
            '
            'NOTE:  We could also use the XMLFormatter class here.
            Dim strOrderXML As String = objOrder.XML

            'Create a new System.Messaging.Message class representing a
            '...new MSMQ message
            Dim objMessage As New Message(strOrderXML)
```

Then we need to initialize our new `Message` object for sending the `Order` to the `IBuyAdventure Orders` queue. The message will be sent with a `Normal` priority and a standard `Label` of `"IBuyAdventure Order"`. We'll also set the `UseJournalQueue` property of the `Message` object so that a copy of the message will be kept in the Journal queue for debugging purposes.

```
            'Set the properties of the new MSMQ Message object
            With objMessage
                .Label = "IBuyAdventure Order"
                .Priority = MessagePriority.Normal
                .Recoverable = True
                .UseJournalQueue = True
            End With
```

Next we'll create an instance of the `System.Messaging.MessageQueue` object and specify the path to the `IBuyAdventure Orders` private queue located on the local machine. If you created the `IBuyAdventure Orders` queue with a different name or on another machine, then you will need to modify the path to the queue for your environment. Finally, we'll send the MSMQ Message by calling the `Send` method of the `MessageQueue` object and passing in a reference to the `Message` object that we created earlier in this method. Notice that we specify `MessageQueueTransactionType.Automatic` as the second parameter of the `Message` object's `Send` method. This parameter is required when accessing a transactional message queue from a transactional Serviced Component.

```
            'Create a new instance of the System.Messaging.MessageQueue
            '...class for sending the MSMQ Message
            Dim objMessageQueue As New MessageQueue()

            'Specify the path to the Queue for receiving orders
            '
            'NOTE:  The IBuyAdventure Orders queue must exist.
            '...It may be necessary to change this path for your
            '...environment.
            objMessageQueue.Path = ".\Private$\IBuyAdventure Orders"

            'Specify the path to the Queue for receiving orders
            '
            'NOTE:  The IBuyAdventure Orders queue must exist.
            '...It may be necessary to change this path for your
            '...environment.
```

```
                    objMessageQueue.Path = ".\Private$\IBuyAdventure Orders"

                    'Send the MSMQ Message object to the destination queue
                    '
                    'NOTE:  You must specify TransactionType of Automatic when
                    '...using COM+ Transactions.
                    objMessageQueue.Send(objMessage, _
                                          MessageQueueTransactionType.Automatic)
```

Although we're accessing an MSMQ in the SendOrder method instead of SQL Server as we have in all of the other examples, the process for voting on the transaction outcome is exactly the same. We'll simply call the SetComplete shared method of the ContextUtil class if the SendOrder method completes successfully, or we'll call the SetAbort method if an exception occurred.

```
                    'We successfully sent the Order message, so tell COM+ that
                    '...this object votes to commit the transaction and
                    '...deactivate.
                    ContextUtil.SetComplete()

                    'Return the updated Order object to the caller
                    Return objOrder


                Catch excp As system.Exception
                    'An exception occured sending the MSMQ message containing
                    '...the order.

                    'Tell COM+ that this object votes to abort the transaction
                    '...and deactivate
                    ContextUtil.SetAbort()

                    'Throw the exception to the caller of this method
                    Throw excp
                End Try

            End Function
        End Class
    End Namespace
```

FulfillmentTx

The FulfillmentTx class is a transactional .NET Serviced Component that provides a single method named SubmitOrder that is used to integrate AdventureWorks with their fulfillment provider. The SubmitOrder method is called during an order processing transaction to forward the order to the fulfillment provider so that it can be packed and shipped to the customer. The order is posted across HTTP to a pre-determined URL on the fulfillment provider's site.

It's important to understand that although we're creating the FulfillmentTx class as a transactional .NET Serviced Component, there is not a Resource Manager available for the HTTP protocol, and therefore the task of posting the order to the fulfillment provider's web site will not be performed within the COM+ transaction. As a result, if the order processing transaction were to abort after the order was posted to the fulfillment provider then there is no way to roll back the task.

Let's begin by implementing the FulfillmentTx class by first importing the namespaces containing commonly used types and by defining a public interface named IFulfillmentTx.

```
'Import namespaces containing commonly used types
Imports System.Data
Imports System.Data.SqlClient
Imports System.EnterpriseServices
Imports IBuyAdventure.Common


Namespace IBuyAdventure.BusinessServices

    'Define a public interface containing the signatures for members of
    '...this class
    '
    'NOTE:  It is necessary to define a public interface with the
    '...signatures for methods that utilize COM+ method-level attributes.
    '...Otherwise the interface and methods will not be displayed and
    '...configured in COM+, although the component will be configured.
    Public Interface IFulfillmentTx
        Function SubmitOrder(ByVal objOrder As Order) As Order
    End Interface
```

Next we'll declare the FulfillmentTx class, inherit from the ServicedComponent base class, and implement the IFulFillmentTx interface. We'll also define a member-level constant to hold the URL for the fulfilment provider. For testing, we'll specify the URL to a test .aspx file located on the local machine.

```
    <Description("Contains methods for integrating with eFulfill."), _
        Transaction(TransactionOption.Required), _
        Synchronization(SynchronizationOption.Required), _
        JustInTimeActivation(True)> _
    Public Class FulfillmentTx
        'Inherit from the System.EnterpriseServices.ServicedComponent class
        '...to allow this component to utilize COM+ services
        Inherits ServicedComponent

        'Implement the IFulfillmentTx interface and it's members
        Implements IFulfillmentTx

        'Define a constant for the minimum shipping charge
        Private Const m_con_strFulfillmentProviderURL As String _
                            = "http://localhost/eFulfill/FulfillOrder.aspx"
```

Now we'll implement the SubmitOrder method, as defined by the IFulFillmentTx interface. Within this method we'll convert the passed Order business object into XML by calling its XML property, and create and initialize an instance of the System.Net.HttpWebRequest class by calling the shared Create method of the System.Net.WebRequest class and specifying the URL to the fulfillment provider.

```
        <Description("Sends an Order to the Fulfillment provider.")> _
        Public Function SubmitOrder(ByVal objOrder As Order) As Order _
                                      Implements IFulfillmentTx.SubmitOrder
```

```
        Try
            'Declare our variables used in this procedure
            Dim objWebResponse As System.Net.WebResponse
            Dim objWebRequest As System.Net.HttpWebRequest

            'Get the passed order as an XML formatted string
            Dim strOrderXML As String = objOrder.XML

            'Create a new instance of the WebRequest class for
            '...the URL for the fulfill provider.
            objWebRequest = System.Net.WebRequest.Create( _
                                        m_con_strFulfillmentProviderURL)

            'Initialize the new WebRequest object for posting the Order
            '...XML data
            objWebRequest.Method = "POST"
            objWebRequest.ContentType = "text/xml"
```

Ater the `HttpWebRequest` object has been created and initialized, we'll get a reference to the `System.IO.Stream` for the `WebRequest` and use a `System.Xml.XmlTextWriter` object to fill the stream with the XML-formatted `Order`.

```
            'Acquire a reference to the Request Stream for the
            '...WebRequest
            Dim objStream As System.IO.Stream = _
                                        objWebRequest.GetRequestStream()

            'Create a new instance of the XmlTextWritter class for the
            '...WebRequest object's RequestStream.
            Dim objXMLTextWriter As New System.Xml.XmlTextWriter( _
                                        objStream, _
                                        System.Text.Encoding.Default)

            'Write the Order XML data to the RequestStream for the
            '...WebRequest
            objXMLTextWriter.WriteString(strOrderXML)

            'Flush the Order XML data before closing the stream
            objXMLTextWriter.Flush()

            'Close the Request stream
            objStream.Close()
```

Next, we'll set the timeout for the `HttpWebRequest` object and post the `Order` data by calling the `GetResponse` method, which returns an instance of the `System.Net.WebResponse` class.

```
            objWebRequest.Timeout = 500000

            'Post the document and get the response.
            objWebResponse = objWebRequest.GetResponse()
```

Finally, after the XML-formatted `Order` has been posted to the fulfillment provider, we can vote on the outcome of the transaction, and either return the passed `Order` object or throw an exception to the caller.

```
                'We successfully submitted the Order to the Fulfillment
                '...provider, so tell COM+ that this object votes to commit
                '...the transaction and deactivate.
                ContextUtil.SetComplete()

                'Return the updated Order object (and Items collection) to
                '...the caller
                Return objOrder


            Catch excp As system.Exception
                'An exception occured sending the order to the Fulfillment
                '...provider.

                'Tell COM+ that this object votes to abort the transaction
                '...and deactivate
                ContextUtil.SetAbort()

                'Throw the exception to the caller of this method
                Throw excp
            End Try
        End Function
    End Class
End Namespace
```

CreditAuthorization

The `CreditAuthorization` class is a basic class that implements simple business logic for authorizing a customer's order based on various business rules in the IBuyAdventure system. Unlike most of the other components involved in the order processing transaction, the `CreditAuthorization` component is not a .NET Serviced Component, and consequently, it does not utilize or support COM+ transactions.

The `CreditAuthorization` class implements two methods `AuthorizeOnAccountOrder()` and `AuthorizeCreditCardOrder()`. During our discussion of the `OrderProcessingTx` component we learned about the role of each of these methods in the order processing transaction. Now let's implement both of these methods, starting with the `AuthorizeOnAccountOrder()` method.

First, let's define the structure for the `CreditAuthorization` class file by importing namespaces containing commonly used types and by defining the namespace for the `CreditAuthorization` class. We'll also define the `CreditAuthorization` class itself. Notice that the `CreditAuthorization` class does not define and implement a public interface or apply any of the attributes defined in the `System.EnterpriseServices` namespace to the class definition. These tasks are not necessary since the `CreditAuthorization` class is not a .NET Serviced Component.

```
'Import namespaces containing commonly used types
Imports IBuyAdventure.Common

Namespace IBuyAdventure.BusinessServices
```

```
Public Class CreditAuthorization
```

Next, let's define our member-level instance variables and constants. Specifically, we'll define a member-level constant to hold the value for the maximum charge amount of $2500 for credit card purchases. We'll see how this constant is used when we discuss the `AuthorizeCreditCardOrder()` method.

```
'Define a member-level constant for the maximum charge amount
Private Const m_con_dcmMaximumChargeAmount As Decimal = 2500
```

Now let's implement the `AuthorizeOnAccountOrder()` method. First we'll get a reference to a `CustomersDataset` object containing all of the information for the specified customer from the IBuyAdventure database. If the `Customer`'s account status returned in the `CustomersDataset` object is set to `Disabled`, then we'll create a new instance of the `System.Exception` class and throw the exception up the call stack to the caller. Since the `CreditAuthorization` class is not a transactional Serviced Component, we don't have to notify COM+ to commit or abort the transaction. Instead the caller, which is the `CreateOrder()` method of the `OrderProcessingTx` component in this situation, will handle the exception and call vote to abort the transaction.

```
Public Function AuthorizeOnAccountOrder(ByVal objOrder As Order, _
                                  ByVal objCustomer As Customer) _
                                                         As Order

    'Create an instance of the Customers class in this namespace
    Dim objCustomers As _
                New IBuyAdventure.BusinessServices.Customers()

    'Get a typed DataSet object containing the Customer
    '...information for the customer specified by the passed
    '...Customer object
    Dim dsCustomers As CustomersDataset _
            = objCustomers.GetCustomer(objCustomer.CustomerID)

    If dsCustomers.Customers.Rows.Count = 0 Then
        'The DataSet does not contain any customer records, so
        '...return nothing and exit this function
        Return Nothing
        Exit Function
    End If

    If dsCustomers.Customers(0).AccountStatus = _
            Customer.AccountStatusEnum.AccountStatus_Disabled Then

        'An order from this customer is not authorized.
        '...Throw an exception to the caller.

        'Create a new exception for the Account Order
        '...Authorization failure
        Dim excpAccountOrderAuthorization As New _
        System.Exception("Customer Account Authorization failed!")

        'Throw the exception to the caller
        Throw (excpAccountOrderAuthorization)
```

```
        End If

        'Return the updated Order object
        Return objOrder
    End Function
```

Now let's implement the `AuthorizeCreditCardOrder()` method. In this method we'll first set the `AmountCharged` for the `CreditCardPayment` object to the total amount of the order and then verify that the `AmountCharged` is not greater than the maximum charge amount the site supports. If the `AmountCharged` is greater, then we'll create an instance of the `System.Exception` class and throw the exception to the caller.

```
    Public Function AuthorizeCreditCardOrder( _
                                        ByVal objOrder As Order, _
                                        ByVal objCustomer As Customer) _
                                                                As Order

       'Since the system only supports a single credit card
       '...authorization at this time, set the amount that supposed
       '...to be chared to the credit card to the amount of the order.
        objOrder.CreditCardPayment.AmountCharged = objOrder.Total

        If objOrder.CreditCardPayment.AmountCharged > _
                                       m_con_dcmMaximumChargeAmount Then
            'The Amount that is supposed to be chared to the Credit
            '...card is greater than the maximum amount the
            '...site supports.

            'Create a new exception for the authorization failure
            Dim excpCreditCardAuthorization As _
             New System.Exception("Credit card authorization failed!")

            'Throw the exception to the caller
            Throw (excpCreditCardAuthorization)
        End If
```

If the `AmountCharged` for the `CreditCardPayment` object is a valid amount, then we'll create a new GUID value for the authorization code and return the updated `Order` object, which contains the `CreditCardPayment` object. In a production e-commerce system we would want to pre-authorize the customer's credit card using a third party credit authorization service, and throw an exception to the caller if the credit authorization failed.

```
        'Create a credit card authorization code and store it with the
        '...Order's Credit Card Payment information.
        objOrder.CreditCardPayment.AuthorizationCode = _
                                         System.Guid.NewGuid.ToString()

        'Return the updated Order object to the caller
        Return objOrder
    End Function
End Class
End Namespace
```

E-mailConfirmations

The `E-mailConfirmations` component is also a base .NET class. It implements two methods `SendOrderPlacedConfirmation()` and `SendOrderStatusMessage()`. The `SendOrderPlacedConfirmation()` method is called within the order processing transaction to create and send an e-mail message to the customer indicating that their order has been received and is currently being processed. We'll implement the code for the `SendOrderStatusMessage()` method when we discuss the order status update transaction.

First let's define the structure for the `E-mailConfirmations` class including the namespace and class definition.

```
'Import namespaces containing commonly used types
Imports IBuyAdventure.Common

Namespace IBuyAdventure.BusinessServices

    Public Class E-mailConfirmations
```

Now we'll implement the `SendOrderPlacedConfirmation()` method. This method receives both an `Order` object containing the information for the order that was placed and a `Customer` object containing the data for the customer who placed the order.

```
        Public Function SendOrderPlacedConfirmation( _
                                          ByVal objOrder As Order, _
                                          ByVal objCustomer As Customer) _
                                                                   As Order

            Try
```

Next let's create and initialize an instance of the `MailMessage` class, which represents an e-mail message. We'll use the e-mail address of the passed `Customer` object as the `To` address of the `MailMessage` object and build a simple text message for the e-mail message body.

```
                'Create a new instance of the System.Web.Mail.MailMessage
                '...class for sending an e-mail message to the customer
                Dim objMailMessage As New System.Web.Mail.MailMessage()

                'Set the properties of the new MailMessage object
                With objMailMessage

                    'Set the From Address for the Message
                    .From = "Service@IBuyAdventure.com"

                    'Send the e-mail message to the customer
                    .To = objCustomer.E-mailAddress

                    'Set the message format to plain text
                    .BodyFormat = System.Web.Mail.MailFormat.Text

                    'Build the simple body for the e-mail message
                    .Body = "Your order # " & objOrder.OrderNumber _
```

```
                                                  & " has been placed."
                End With
```

Finally, let's send the e-mail message by calling the `Send()` method of the `System.Web.Mail.SmtpMail` static class and pass the new `MailMessage` object as a parameter. If an exception is caught in this method, then we'll simply throw the exception up the call stack to the immediate caller.

```
                'Send the new MailMessage now
                System.Web.Mail.SmtpMail.Send(objMailMessage)

                'Return the updated Order object to the caller
                Return objOrder

            Catch excp As System.Exception
                'An exception occured sending the Order Placed
                '...e-mail confirmation.

                'Throw the exception to the caller of this method
                Throw excp
            End Try
        End Function

    End Class
End Namespace
```

Data Services

The order processing transaction utilizes the following stored procedures in the Data Services tier:

- `sp_Orders_INS`
- `sp_OrderItems_INS`
- `sp_OrderAddresses_INS`
- `sp_InventoryAllocations_INS`
- `sp_CreditCardPayments_INS`

Let's look at the T-SQL that composes each of these stored procedures.

sp_Orders_INS

The `sp_Orders_INS` stored procedure simply executes a SQL `INSERT` statement to insert a single record into the `Orders` table in the IBuyAdventure database. The column values for the new record are passed to the stored procedure as input parameters. This stored procedure is called by the `InsertOrder()` method of the `OrdersTx` transactional Serviced Component during the order processing transaction. The following T-SQL `CREATE PROCEDURE` statement defines the `sp_Orders_INS` stored procedure:

```
CREATE PROCEDURE sp_Orders_INS
    -------------------------------------------------------
    -- Declare the parameters for this Stored Procedure
```

```
        -----------------------------------------------------
        @chrOrderID char(38),
        @nvchrOrderNumber nvarchar(40),
        @dtOrderDate datetime,
        @dtShippedDate datetime,
        @intOrderStatus int,
        @chrCustomerID char(38),
        @nvchrCustomerName nvarchar(50),
        @nvchrShipToName nvarchar(40),
        @chrShipToAddressID char(38),
        @chrBillingAddressID char(38),
        @mnySubTotal money,
        @mnyShippingTotal money,
        @mnyTaxTotal money,
        @mnyGrandTotal money,
        @intPaymentType int
AS
        -----------------------------------------------------
        -- Perform the intended operation againist the Database
        -----------------------------------------------------
        INSERT INTO Orders(
                        OrderID,
                        OrderNumber,
                        OrderDate,
                        OrderStatus,
                        CustomerID,
                        CustomerName,
                        ShipToName,
                        ShipToAddressID,
                        BillingAddressID,
                        SubTotal,
                        ShippingTotal,
                        TaxTotal,
                        GrandTotal,
                        PaymentType)
        VALUES          (@chrOrderID,
                        @nvchrOrderNumber,
                        @dtOrderDate,
                        @intOrderStatus,
                        @chrCustomerID,
                        @nvchrCustomerName,
                        @nvchrShipToName,
                        @chrShipToAddressID,
                        @chrBillingAddressID,
                        @mnySubTotal,
                        @mnyShippingTotal,
                        @mnyTaxTotal,
                        @mnyGrandTotal,
                        @intPaymentType)

        -- Return 1 (true) to indicate success
        return 1
GO
```

sp_OrderItems_INS

The sp_OrdersItems_INS stored procedure executes a SQL INSERT statement to insert a single record into the OrderItems table in the IBuyAdventure database. The column values for the new record are passed to the stored procedure as input parameters. This stored procedure is called by the InsertOrderItems() method of the OrderItemsTx transactional Serviced Component during the order processing transaction. The following T-SQL CREATE PROCEDURE statement defines the sp_OrderItems_INS stored procedure:

```
CREATE PROCEDURE sp_OrderItems_INS
      ---------------------------------------------------------
      -- Declare the parameters for this Stored Procedure
      ---------------------------------------------------------
      @chrOrderItemID char(38),
      @chrOrderID char(38),
      @chrProductID char(38),
      @nvchrProductName nvarchar(50),
      @nvchrSKU nvarchar(10),
      @nvchrProductDescription nvarchar(255),
      @intQuantity int,
      @mnyUnitPrice money,
      @mnyExtendedPrice money

AS
      ---------------------------------------------------------
      -- Perform the intended operation againist the Database
      ---------------------------------------------------------

      INSERT INTO OrderItems
                           (OrderItemID, OrderID, ProductID, ProductName,
ProductDescription, Quantity, UnitPrice, ExtendedPrice, SKU)
      VALUES     (@chrOrderItemID, @chrOrderID, @chrProductID, @nvchrProductName,
@nvchrProductDescription, @intQuantity, @mnyUnitPrice,
                           @mnyExtendedPrice, @nvchrSKU)

      -- Return 1 (true) to indicate success
      return 1
GO
```

sp_OrderAddresses_INS

The sp_OrdersAddresses_INS stored procedure simply executes a SQL INSERT statement to insert a single record into the OrderAddresses table in the IBuyAdventure database. The column values for the new record are passed to the stored procedure as input parameters. This stored procedure is called by the InsertOrderAddresses() method of the OrderAddressesTx transactional Serviced Component during the order processing transaction. The following T-SQL CREATE PROCEDURE statement defines the sp_OrderAddresses_INS stored procedure:

```
CREATE PROCEDURE sp_OrderAddresses_INS
      ---------------------------------------------------------
      -- Declare the parameters for this Stored Procedure
      ---------------------------------------------------------
      @chrOrderAddressID char(38),
```

```
        @nvchrFirstname nvarchar(50),
        @nvchrLastname nvarchar(50),
        @nvchrAddress1 nvarchar(50),
        @nvchrAddress2 nvarchar(50),
        @nvchrCity nvarchar(30),
        @nvchrRegion nvarchar(30),
        @nvchrPostalCode nvarchar(20),
        @nvchrCountry nvarchar(50),
        @nchrPhoneNumber nchar(15)

AS
        ---------------------------------------------------------
        -- Perform the intended operation againist the Database
        ---------------------------------------------------------
        INSERT INTO OrderAddresses
        (
                OrderAddressID,
                Firstname,
                Lastname,
                Address1,
                Address2,
                City,
                Region,
                PostalCode,
                Country,
                PhoneNumber
        )
        VALUES
        (
                @chrOrderAddressID,
                @nvchrFirstname,
                @nvchrLastname,
                @nvchrAddress1,
                @nvchrAddress2,
                @nvchrCity,
                @nvchrRegion,
                @nvchrPostalCode,
                @nvchrCountry,
                @nchrPhoneNumber
        )

        -- Return 1 (true) to indicate success
        return 1
GO
```

sp_InventoryAllocations_INS

The `sp_InventoryAllocations_INS` stored procedure simply executes a SQL `INSERT` statement to insert a single record into the `InventoryAllocations` table in the IBuyAdventure database. The column values for the new record are passed to the stored procedure as input parameters. This stored procedure is called one or more times by the `AllocateInventory()` method of the `InventoryAllocationsTx` transactional Serviced Component during the order processing transaction. The following T-SQL `CREATE PROCEDURE` statement defines the `sp_InventoryAllocations_INS` stored procedure:

```
CREATE PROCEDURE sp_InventoryAllocations_INS
      ------------------------------------------------------
      -- Declare the parameters for this Stored Procedure
      ------------------------------------------------------
      @chrInventoryAllocationID char(38),
      @chrProductID char(38),
      @chrOrderID char(38),
      @chrOrderItemID char(38),
      @intQuantityAllocated int,
      @dtDateTimeAllocated datetime
AS
      ------------------------------------------------------
      -- Perform the intended operation againist the Database
      ------------------------------------------------------
      INSERT INTO InventoryAllocations
                      (InventoryAllocationID, ProductID, OrderID,
                      OrderItemID, QuantityAllocated, DateTimeAllocated)
      VALUES      (@chrInventoryAllocationID, @chrProductID, @chrOrderID,
                  @chrOrderItemID, @intQuantityAllocated,
                  @dtDateTimeAllocated)

      -- Return 1 (true) to indicate success
      return 1
GO
```

sp_CreditCardPayments_INS

The `sp_CreditCardPayments_INS` stored procedure simply executes a SQL `INSERT` statement to insert a single record into the `CreditCardPayments` table in the IBuyAdventure database. The column values for the new record are passed to the stored procedure as input parameters. This stored procedure is called by the `InsertCreditCardPayments()` method of the `CreditCardPaymentsTx` transactional Serviced Component during the order processing transaction. The following T-SQL `CREATE PROCEDURE` statement defines the `sp_CreditCardPayments_INS` stored procedure:

```
CREATE PROCEDURE sp_CreditCardPayments_INS
      ------------------------------------------------------
      -- Declare the parameters for this Stored Procedure
      ------------------------------------------------------
      @chrOrderID char(38),
      @chrCreditCardPaymentID char(38),
      @nvchrCreditCardType nvarchar(30),
      @nvchrCreditCardNumber nvarchar(20),
      @intExpirationMonth int,
      @intExpirationYear int,
      @nvchrNameOnCard nvarchar(50),
      @nvchrAuthorizationCode nvarchar(50),
      @mnyAmountCharged money
AS
      ------------------------------------------------------
      -- Perform the intended operation againist the Database
      ------------------------------------------------------
      INSERT INTO CreditCardPayments(
                        CreditCardPaymentID,
```

```
                              OrderID,
                              CreditCardType,
                              CreditCardNumber,
                              ExpirationMonth,
                              ExpirationYear,
                              NameOnCard,
                              AuthorizationCode,
                         AmountCharged)
        VALUES          (@chrCreditCardPaymentID,
                              @chrOrderID,
                              @nvchrCreditCardType,
                              @nvchrCreditCardNumber,
                              @intExpirationMonth,
                              @intExpirationYear,
                         @nvchrNameOnCard,
                         @nvchrAuthorizationCode,
                         @mnyAmountCharged)

        -- Return 1 (true) to indicate success
        return 1
    GO
```

User Services

The following Web Forms in the User Services tier are involved with initiating the order processing transaction

- `ShoppingCart`
- `PaymentInfo`
- `Checkout`

Let's look at the user interface and functionality for each of these Web Forms.

ShoppingCart Web Form

The `ShoppingCart` Web Form, shown below in design mode, allows a consumer customer to view and manage the items in their virtual shopping basket. After reviewing the contents of their basket, the user can click on the button titled Go To Checkout, to begin a series of steps for placing an order for the items in their basket.

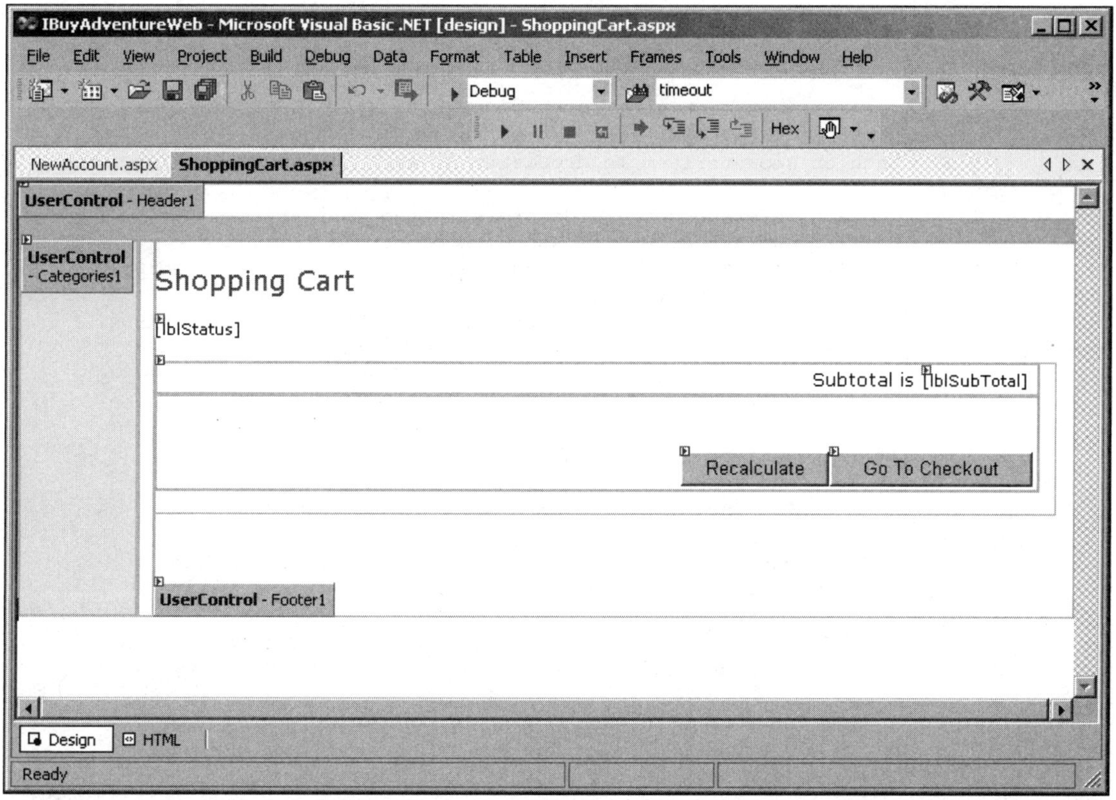

Let's take a look at the code for the Checkout button's Click event handler (btnCheckout_Click()) and a private method named UpdateBasketItems(), which updates the quantities of the items in the basket based on the user's input.

```
Private Sub btnCheckout_Click(ByVal sender As Object, _
                              ByVal e As EventArgs) _
                                          Handles btnCheckout.Click

    'Update the Items in the Shopper's basket to reflect any deletions
    '...or quantity changes
    UpdateBasketItems()

    'Update the Unit and Extended prices for each item and the
    '...subtotal for the basket and save the updated basket
    m_objShopper.UpdateBasketSubTotal()

    'Redirect the user to the secure checkout page
    Response.Redirect("secure/PaymentInfo.aspx")
End Sub

Private Sub UpdateBasketItems()

    Dim intListItemsCounter As Integer
```

```
        Dim objRepeaterItem As RepeaterItem

        'Iterate through each item in the Basket DataList and update the
        '...quantities for each item in the shopper's basket.
        For Each objRepeaterItem In drpBasket.Items

            'Obtain references to WebControls in the current row
            Dim txtQuantity As System.Web.UI.WebControls.TextBox = _
                CType(objRepeaterItem.FindControl("txtQuantity"), TextBox)
            Dim chkRemove As System.Web.UI.WebControls.CheckBox = _
                 CType(objRepeaterItem.FindControl("chkRemove"), CheckBox)
            Dim hdnItemID As System.Web.UI.HtmlControls.HtmlInputHidden _
                      = CType(objRepeaterItem.FindControl("hdnItemID"), _
                                                            HtmlInputHidden)

            If (txtQuantity Is Nothing = False) _
                    And (chkRemove Is Nothing = False) _
                    And (hdnItemID Is Nothing = False) Then

                'We have valid references to the WebControls for the
                '...current row

                'Convert the value in the txtQuantity field to an integer
                Dim intQuantity As Integer = Int32.Parse(txtQuantity.Text)

                If (chkRemove.Checked = True Or intQuantity = 0) Then
                    'The user checked the Remove checkbox for the current
                    '...item or they set the quantity to 0. Remove the
                    '...specified item from the shopper's basket.
                    m_objShopper.Basket.Items.Remove(hdnItemID.Value)
                Else
                    'Update the quantity for the item in the basket with
                    '...the quantity entered in the txtQuantity field
                    m_objShopper.Basket.Items( _
                                  hdnItemID.Value).Quantity = intQuantity
                End If

            End If

        Next

        'Save the changes to the shopper's basket
        m_objShopper.SaveBasket()

        'The contents of the basket could have changed, causing the
        '...subtotals to be incorrect. Tell the Header UserControl to
        '...update it's basket summary.
        Header1.UpdateBasketSummary()
    End Sub
```

PaymentInfo Web Form

After logging into the IBuyAdventure site or creating a new customer account, the user is required to enter credit card payment information before placing their order. The `PaymentInfo` Web Form contains fields for collecting the credit card information including the credit card number, expiration month and year, card type, and the full name on the card. After entering all of the credit card information, the user clicks the **Next** button to proceed to the next step in the checkout process. The following screenshot shows the `PaymentInfo` Web Form in design mode within Visual Studio .NET:

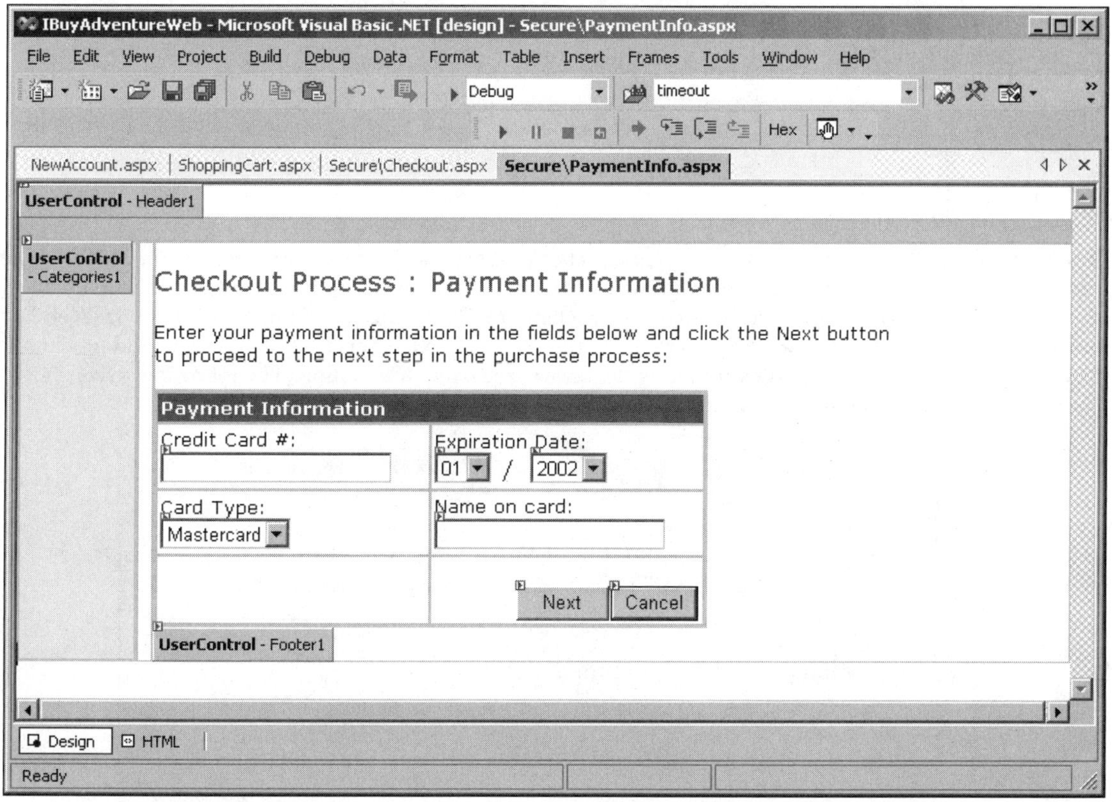

Now let's implement the code for the `PaymentInfo` Web Form. Specifically, let's focus on the code for the **Next** button's click event handler. In this event handler, the first thing we do is to create an instance of the `Shopper` class, which is also located in the User Services tier. If you recall, we implemented the `Shopper` class during our discussion of the new customer account transaction.

```
    Sub btnNext_Click(ByVal sender As Object, _
                      ByVal e As System.EventArgs) Handles btnNext.Click

        'Create an instance of the Shopper class and pass a reference to
        '...the HTTPContext object for this page to the constructor
        Dim objShopper As New Shopper(context)

        'Load the CreditCardPayment object associated with the user's
        '...basket data with the payment data from the WebControls on this
```

```
        '...WebForm
        With objShopper.Basket.CreditCardPayment
            .CardNumber = txtCardNumber.Text
            .CardType = lstCardType.SelectedItem.Value
            .ExpirationMonth = lstExpirationMonth.SelectedItem.Value
            .ExpirationYear = lstExpirationYear.SelectedItem.Value
            .NameOnCard = txtNameOnCard.Text
        End With

        'Save the changes to the shopper's basket
        objShopper.SaveBasket()

        'Redirect user to the Checkout page so they can confirm the order
        Response.Redirect("Checkout.aspx")
    End Sub
```

Checkout Web Form

The `Checkout` Web Form is the final step in the checkout process for a consumer purchase. This Web Form displays all of the information for the customer's order and allows the customer to either confirm or cancel the order. If the customer confirms the order by clicking the Place Order button, the `Checkout` Web Form creates an instance of the `OrderProcessingTx` transactional .NET Serviced Component and invokes the `CreateOrder()` method, thereby initiating the order processing transaction. The following screenshot shows the `Checkout` Web Form in design mode in Visual Studio .NET:

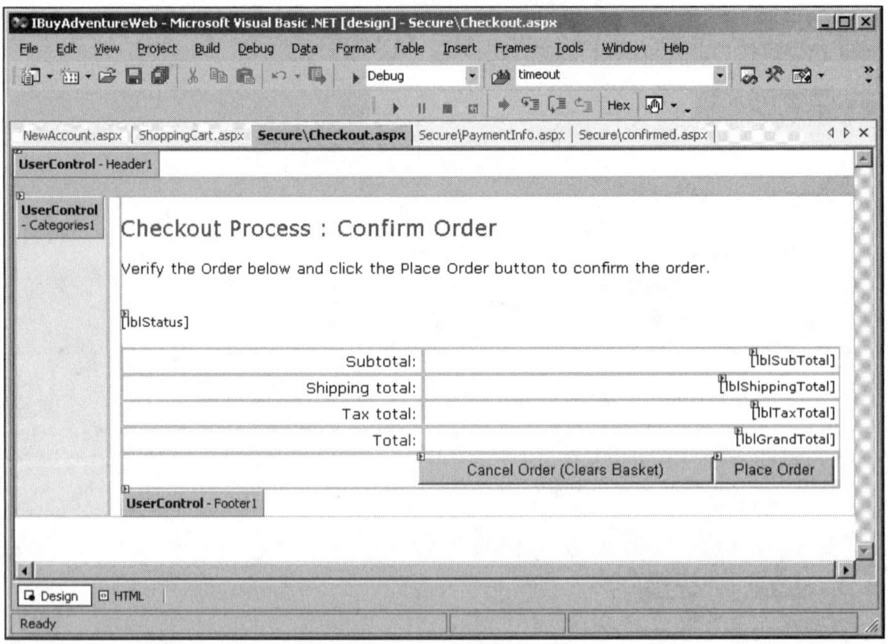

Let's examine the code for the `Checkout` Web Form. First we'll declare the `Checkout` class and inherit from the `Page` base class in order to make the `Checkout` class an ASP.NET Web Form. Then we'll declare variables for the fields and controls on the Web Form and perform the page initialization and loading procedures:

```
Public Class Checkout
    Inherits System.Web.UI.Page

    Protected WithEvents btnPlaceOrder As System.Web.UI.WebControls.Button
    Protected WithEvents btnCancelOrder As _
                                       System.Web.UI.WebControls.Button
    Protected drpBasket As System.Web.UI.WebControls.Repeater
    Protected lblStatus As System.Web.UI.WebControls.Label
    Protected lblSubTotal As System.Web.UI.WebControls.Label
    Protected lblTaxTotal As System.Web.UI.WebControls.Label
    Protected lblShippingTotal As System.Web.UI.WebControls.Label
    Protected lblGrandTotal As System.Web.UI.WebControls.Label

    'declare a member-level variable to hold a reference to an instance of
    '...the Shopper class
    Private m_objShopper As Shopper

#Region " Web Form Designer Generated Code "

    'This call is required by the Web Form Designer.
    <System.Diagnostics.DebuggerStepThrough()> _
    Private Sub InitializeComponent()

    End Sub

    Private Sub Page_Init(ByVal sender As System.Object, _
                      ByVal e As System.EventArgs) Handles MyBase.Init
        'CODEGEN: This method call is required by the Web Form Designer
        'Do not modify it using the code editor.
        InitializeComponent()
    End Sub

#End Region

    Private Sub Page_Load(ByVal sender As System.Object, _
                      ByVal e As System.EventArgs) Handles MyBase.Load
        'Put user code to initialize the page here

        'Create an instance of the Shopper class and pass a reference to
        '...the HTTPContext object for this page to the constructor
        m_objShopper = New Shopper(context)

        If (Page.IsPostBack = False) Then
            'This page is not being loaded in response to postback

            'Populate the WebControls on this page with the Shopper's
            '...Basket data
            PopulateDataFields()
        End If
    End Sub
```

In the Place Order button's `Click` event handler, we'll first get the `Order` object representing the shopper's current basket and `Customer` object containing the shopper's customer account information. Then we'll call the `SetAddresses()` private method in this class to set the billing and shipping addresses for the order using the addresses stored for the shopper's customer account.

```
Private Sub btnPlaceOrder_Click(ByVal sender As Object, _
                                ByVal e As EventArgs) _
                                           Handles btnPlaceOrder.Click

    'Get a reference to the Shopper's basket (Order object)
    Dim objOrder As IBuyAdventure.Common.Order = m_objShopper.Basket

    'Get a reference to the Customer object for the current shoppper
    Dim objCustomer As IBuyAdventure.Common.Customer = _
                                            m_objShopper.Customer

    'Set the Order's Addresses to the customer's billing and shipping
    '...addresses
    SetOrderAddresses(objOrder, objCustomer)
```

After preparing the order for processing, we'll create an instance of the `OrderProcessingTx` transactional Serviced Component and call its `CreateOrder()` method, passing the `Order` and `Customer` business objects as parameters. This method call will initiate the order processing transaction. When the `CreateOrder()` method call completes, we'll replace our `Order` object with the `Order` object returned from the method call, reset the shopper's basket to clear the order information, and redirect the user to the `Confirmed` Web Form passing the `OrderID` and `OrderNumber` for the new order as parameters on the URL.

```
    'Create an instance of the OrderProcessingTx
    '....NET ServicedComponent for creating a new order
    Dim objOrderProcessingTx As _
                New IBuyAdventure.BusinessServices.OrderProcessingTx()

    'Place the order in the IBuyAdventure system using the order data
    '...in the shopper's basket (IBuyAdventure.Common.Order) and pass
    '...the shopper's customer information
    objOrder = objOrderProcessingTx.CreateOrder(objOrder, objCustomer)

    'Reset and clear the shopper's basket
    m_objShopper.ResetBasket()

    'Redirect the user to the Order Confirmation page to display a
    '...confirmation for the order they just placed.
    Response.Redirect("Confirmed.aspx?OrderID=" & objOrder.OrderID _
                      & "&OrderNumber=" & objOrder.OrderNumber)
End Sub
```

If the user clicks the Cancel Order button, then we'll simply redirect them to the `DefaultPage` Web Form in our `Click` event handler:

```
Sub btnCancelOrder_Click(ByVal sender As Object, _
                         ByVal e As EventArgs) Handles btnCancelOrder.Click
```

```
        'The user want's to cancel the Ordering process.

        'Redirect the user to the Default page for the site
        Response.Redirect("/IBuyAdventureWeb/default.aspx")
    End Sub
```

The `UpdateBasketTotal()` private method updates all of the totals for the pending order by calling the `CalculateOrderTotal()` method on an instance of the `OrderCalculations` business services component and passing the user's current shopping basket:

```
    Private Sub UpdateBasketTotal()

        'Create an instance of the OrderCalculations class for
        '...calculating the basket Totals
        Dim objOrderCalculations As _
                    New IBuyAdventure.BusinessServices.OrderCalculations()

        'Update the ListPrice and Unitprice for each item and the subtotal
        '...for the entire order
        m_objShopper.Basket = _
             objOrderCalculations.CalculateOrderTotal(m_objShopper.Basket)

        'Save the changes to the shopper's basket
        m_objShopper.SaveBasket()
    End Sub
```

As I just mentioned, the `SetOrderAddresses()` method sets the billing and shipping addresses of the `Order` using the customer's stored addresses. This involves creating a new instance of the `Address` business object for both the billing and shipping address, copying the data from the Customer's `Addresses` into the new objects, and assigning the new `Address` objects to the `ShippingAddress` and `BillingAddress` properties of the passed `Order`.

```
    Private Sub SetOrderAddresses( _
                       ByRef objOrder As IBuyAdventure.Common.Order, _
                       ByRef objCustomer As IBuyAdventure.Common.Customer)

        'declare any procedure-level variables
        Dim objShippingAddress As IBuyAdventure.Common.Address
        Dim objBillingAddress As IBuyAdventure.Common.Address


        'Create a copy of the Customer's Shipping Address by copying the
        '...data into a new Address object which will be used for the
        '...Shipping Address for the order.
        With objCustomer.Addresses(0)
            objShippingAddress = _
                  New IBuyAdventure.Common.Address(.Address1, .Address2, _
                                                 .City, .Region, .PostalCode, _
                                                 .Country, .PhoneNumber)

        End With
```

```
        'Set the Firstname and Lastname for the Shipping Address to the
        '...Customer() 's First and Lastname
        objShippingAddress.Firstname = objCustomer.FirstName
        objShippingAddress.Lastname = objCustomer.LastName

        'Assign this new Address object to the Shipping Address of
        '...the Order
        objOrder.ShippingAddress = objShippingAddress

        'Create a copy of the Customer's Billing Address by copying the
        '...data into a new Address object which will be used for the
        '...Billing Address for the order.
        With objCustomer.Addresses(0)
            objBillingAddress = _
                  New IBuyAdventure.Common.Address(.Address1, .Address2, _
                                                   .City, .Region, .PostalCode, _
                                                          .Country, .PhoneNumber)

        End With

        'Set the Firstname and Lastname for the Billing Address to the
        '...Customer() 's First and Lastname
        objBillingAddress.Firstname = objCustomer.FirstName
        objBillingAddress.Lastname = objCustomer.LastName

        'Assign this new Address object to the Billing Address of
        '...the Order
        objOrder.BillingAddress = objBillingAddress
    End Sub
```

The `PopulateDataFields()` private method populates the fields and Web Controls on the `Checkout` Web Form with data by binding the `Items` collection from the `Order` object that represents the user's current shopping basket to a `DataRepeater` Web Control. We'll also set the text for individual label Web Controls on the `Checkout` Web Form with the totals for the order:

```
    Private Sub PopulateDataFields()

        'Populate the DataReader on this page with the Shopper's Basket

        If m_objShopper.Basket.Items.Count = 0 Then
            'The shopper's basket is empty.

            'Update the status message on this page
            lblStatus.Text = "Your shopping cart is empty."

            'Hide the Basket DataRepeater control
            drpBasket.Visible = False

            'Exit this procedure
            Exit Sub
        End If
```

```
        'Update the status message
        lblStatus.Text = _
                  "Please confirm you want to order the following items:"

        'Update the Unit and Extended prices for each item and the
        '...subtotal for the basket
        UpdateBasketTotal()

        'Bind the Items collection stored with the shopper's basket to the
        '...DataReader WebControl on this page.
        drpBasket.DataSource = m_objShopper.Basket.Items
        drpBasket.DataBind()

        'Display the Totals on the Checkout page
        lblSubTotal.Text = _
                      String.Format("{0:C}", m_objShopper.Basket.SubTotal)
        lblTaxTotal.Text = _
                      String.Format("{0:C}", m_objShopper.Basket.TaxTotal)
        lblShippingTotal.Text = _
                 String.Format("{0:C}", m_objShopper.Basket.ShippingTotal)
        lblGrandTotal.Text = _
                         String.Format("{0:C}", m_objShopper.Basket.Total)
    End Sub
End Class
```

Order Status Update Transaction

The order status update transaction involves updating the status of an existing order in the IBuyAdventure system, and decrementing the available inventory for products when an order status update XML message is received from the fulfillment services provider. The order status update XML message is sent by the fulfillment provider to the `ReceiveOrderStatusUpdate` .NET HTTP handler. The `ReceiveOrderStatusUpdate` HTTP handler is responsible for parsing the XML message and initiating the order status update transaction. The following UML sequence diagram illustrates the interactions between the `ReceiveOrderStatusUpdate` HTTP handler, the business services components, and the stored procedures that are involved in the order status update transaction:

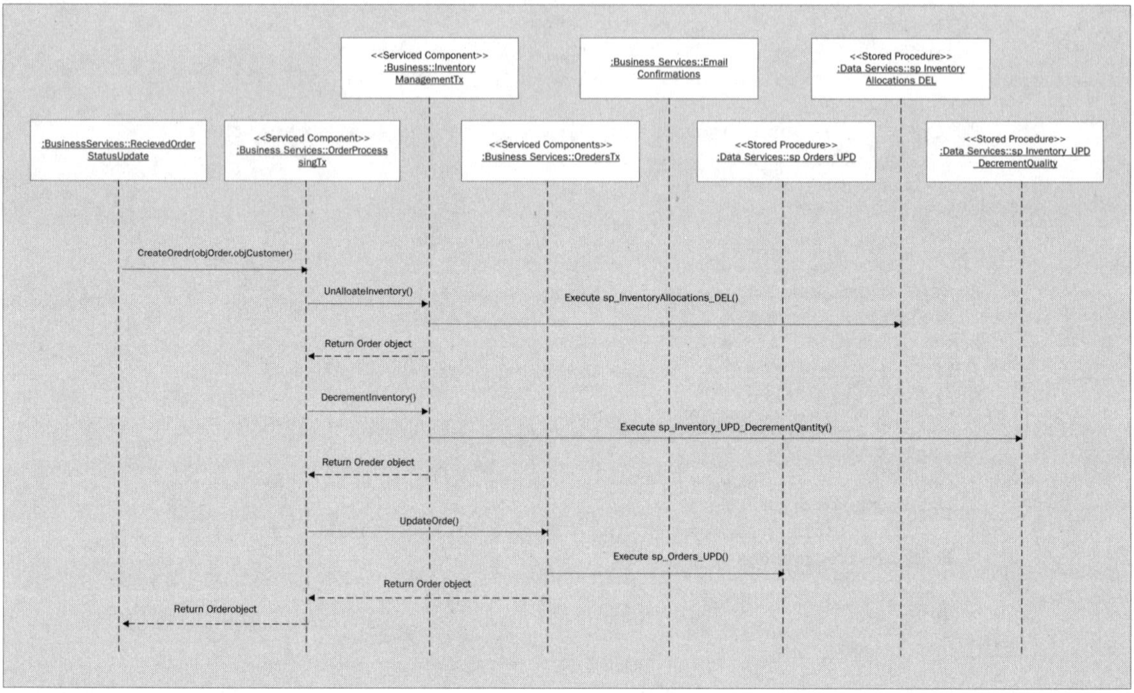

Business Services

The following business services components participate in the order status update transaction:

- `OrderProcessingTx`
- `OrdersTx`
- `InventoryManagementTx`
- `E-mailConfirmations`
- `ReceiveOrderStatusUpdate` HTTP handler

With the exception of the `ReceiveOrderStatusUpdate` HTTP handler, we've actually created all of these business service components for the order processing transaction. However, these components provide additional methods that are used for the order status update transaction. Let's implement these additional methods for each of these business services components now, and we'll create the `ReceiveOrderStatusUpdate` HTTP handler later in this section.

OrderProcessingTx

Just as with the order processing transaction, the `OrderProcessingTx` component also serves as the root of the COM+ transaction for the order status update transaction. In this situation the `OrderProcessingTx` component's `UpdateOrderStatus()` method is responsible for coordinating the entire order status update transaction, which includes updating an order's status, adjusting inventory, and sending order status update e-mail messages to the customer.

Let's begin by modifying the OrderProcessingTx component to support the order status update transaction by first adding the method signature for the UpdateOrderStatus() method to the IOrderProcessingTx interface that we created earlier.

```
'Import namespaces containing commonly used types
Imports System.Data
Imports System.Data.SqlClient
Imports System.EnterpriseServices
Imports IBuyAdventure.Common

Namespace IBuyAdventure.BusinessServices

    'Define a public interface containing the signatures for members
    '...of this class
    '
    'NOTE:  It is necessary to define a public interface with the
    '...signatures for methods that utilize COM+ method-level attributes.
    '...Otherwise the interface and methods will not be displayed and
    '...configured in COM+, although the component will be configured.
    Public Interface IOrderProcessingTx
        Function CreateOrder(ByVal objOrder As Order, _
                             ByVal objCustomer As Customer) As Order

        Function UpdateOrderStatus(ByVal objOrder As Order, _
                                   ByVal objCustomer As Customer) _
                                   As Order
    End Interface
```

Now let's add the UpdateOrderStatus() method implementation to the OrderProcessingTx component. First, let's declare the method as it is defined by the IOrderProcessingTx interface.

```
        <Description("Updates the status of an Order in IBuyAdventure")> _
        Public Function UpdateOrderStatus(ByVal objOrder As Order, _
                                   ByVal objCustomer As Customer) As Order _
                             Implements IOrderProcessingTx.UpdateOrderStatus
```

Next, let's create an instance of the InventoryManagementTx transactional Serviced Component and call the DecrementInventory() method to decrement the available inventory for the products on the order. After calling the DecrementInventory() method, we'll call the UnAllocateInventory() method on the same object.

The UnAllocateInventory() method releases all of the allocations or reservations for products, which were created during the order processing transaction. Both the DecrementInventory() and UnAllocateInventory() methods receive an Order business object containing the data for the Order being updated. Both methods also return an updated Order object containing any updated information for the order.

```
            Try

                'Declare any procedure-level variables
                Dim objWorkingOrder As Order
```

```
'Create a new instance of the InventoryManagementTx
'...transactional .NET ServicedComponent
Dim objInventoryManagementTx As _
                              New InventoryManagementTx()

'Decrement the available inventory for each item in the
'...updated order by the quantity of each item. The
'...updated Order object is returned.
objWorkingOrder = _
    objInventoryManagementTx.DecrementInventory(objOrder)

'Delete all of the inventory allocations for each item
'...in the updated order, which were created when the
'...order was placed. The updated Order object (and Items
'...collection) is returned.
objWorkingOrder = _
   objInventoryManagementTx.UnAllocateInventory(objOrder)
```

Now that the product inventory and inventory allocations have been adjusted to accurately reflect the available inventory, let's update the actual `Order`. Let's create an instance of the `OrdersTx` transactional Serviced Component and call the `UpdateOrder()` method on the new object, passing it our `Order` object containing the current order data and the `Customer` object representing the customer who placed the order.

```
'Create a new instance of the OrdersTx transactional
'....NET ServicedComponent
Dim objOrdersTx As New OrdersTx()

'Update the Order in the IBuyAdventure database for the
'...passed Order. The updated Order object is returned.
objWorkingOrder = objOrdersTx.UpdateOrder( _
                           objWorkingOrder, objCustomer)
```

If the customer who placed the order is a consumer customer, then we'll create an order status update e-mail confirmation and send it to the customer's e-mail address contained in the passed `Customer` object. To accomplish this, let's call the `SendOrderStatusMessage()` method on an instance of the `E-mailConfirmations` business services component and pass the method our `Order` and `Customer` business objects.

```
'Create an instance of the E-mailConfirmations class for
'...sending e-mail notifications to the customer.
Dim objE-mailConfirmations As New E-mailConfirmations()

'Send an Order Status Update e-mail confirmation to the
'...customer containing some of updated order information,
'...which is provided in our working Order object.
objWorkingOrder = _
         objE-mailConfirmations.SendOrderStatusMessage( _
                           objWorkingOrder, objCustomer)
```

Finally, we'll call the `SetComplete()` method of the `ContextUtil` object to notify COM+ that the `OrderProcessingTx` object can be deactivated and we vote to commit the current transaction. Since the `OrderProcessingTx` component is the root of the order status update transaction, when the `OrderStatusUpdate()` method completes, COM+ will attempt to commit or abort the transaction based on the total voted outcome of the objects. We'll also return the `Order` object containing the updated order data to the caller.

```
                'We successfully updated the Order status, so tell COM+
                '...that this object votes to commit the transaction
                '...and deactivate.
                ContextUtil.SetComplete()

                'Return the updated Order object to the caller
                Return objWorkingOrder
```

If an exception should occur in the `UpdateOrderStatus()` method, then we'll call the `SetAbort()` method of the `ContextUtil` object to notify COM+ that this object can be deactivated and it votes to abort the current transaction. After casting the transaction vote, we'll throw the exception to the immediate caller.

```
            Catch excp As system.Exception
                'An exception occured updating the order status.

                'Tell COM+ that this object votes to abort the transaction
                '...and deactivate
                ContextUtil.SetAbort()

                'Throw the exception to the caller of this method
                Throw excp
            End Try

        End Function
```

OrdersTx

The `UpdateOrder()` method of the `OrdersTx` transactional Serviced Component is called during an order status update transaction to update an existing order in the IBuyAdventure database.

Let's begin implementing the `UpdateOrder()` method by modifying the `IOrdersTx` interface to include the method signature.

```
'Import namespaces containing commonly used types
Imports System.Data
Imports System.Data.SqlClient
Imports System.EnterpriseServices
Imports IBuyAdventure.Common

Namespace IBuyAdventure.BusinessServices

    'Define a public interface containing the signatures for members
    '...of this class
    '
```

```
'NOTE:  It is necessary to define a public interface with the
'...signatures for methods that utilize COM+ method-level attributes.
'...Otherwise the interface and methods will not be displayed and
'...configured in COM+, although the component will be configured.
Public Interface IOrdersTx
    Function InsertOrder(ByVal objOrder As Order, _
                         ByVal objCustomer As Customer) As Order

    Function UpdateOrder(ByVal objOrder As Order, _
                         ByVal objCustomer As Customer) As Order
End Interface
```

Now let's add the `UpdateOrder()` method to the `OrdersTx` component. First we'll create and initialize an instance of the `SqlCommand` class for executing the `sp_Orders_UPD` stored procedure. Then we'll create and append a `SqlParameter` object to the `SqlCommand` for each of the `sp_Orders_UPD` stored procedure's parameters. We'll populate the values of the `SqlParameter` objects with the values from the corresponding properties in the passed `Order` and `Customer` business objects.

```
 <Description("Updates an existing Order record in IBuyAdventure.")> _
    Public Function UpdateOrder(ByVal objOrder As Order, _
                                ByVal objCustomer As Customer) _
                                                          As Order _
                                    Implements IOrdersTx.UpdateOrder

        Try

            'Create a new instance of the SqlCommand class to use for
            '...executing the sp_Orders_INS Stored Procedure
            Dim sqlcmdUpdateOrders As New SqlCommand("sp_Orders_UPD")

            With sqlcmdUpdateOrders
                'Set the command type for the new SqlCommand object to
                '...Stored Procedure
                .CommandType = CommandType.StoredProcedure

                With .Parameters
                   'Create and Append SqlParameters for our SqlCommand
                    .Add("@chrOrderID", SqlDbType.Char, 38)
                    .Add("@nvchrOrderNumber", SqlDbType.NVarChar, 40)
                    .Add("@dtOrderDate", SqlDbType.DateTime)
                    .Add("@dtShippedDate", SqlDbType.DateTime)
                    .Add("@intOrderStatus", SqlDbType.Int)
                    .Add("@chrCustomerID", SqlDbType.Char, 38)
                    .Add("@nvchrCustomerName", SqlDbType.NVarChar, 50)
                    .Add("@nvchrShipToName", SqlDbType.NVarChar, 40)
                    .Add("@chrShipToAddressID", SqlDbType.Char, 38)
                    .Add("@chrBillingAddressID", SqlDbType.Char, 38)
                    .Add("@mnySubTotal", SqlDbType.Money)
                    .Add("@mnyShippingTotal", SqlDbType.Money)
                    .Add("@mnyTaxTotal", SqlDbType.Money)
                    .Add("@mnyGrandTotal", SqlDbType.Money)
                    .Add("@intPaymentType", SqlDbType.Int)
```

```
                    'Set the values for each of the SqlParameter
                    '...objects to the values stored in the passed
                    '...Order and Customer objects
                    .Item("@chrOrderID").Value = objOrder.OrderID
                    .Item("@nvchrOrderNumber").Value = _
                                         objOrder.OrderNumber
                    .Item("@dtOrderDate").Value = objOrder.OrderDate
                    .Item("@intOrderStatus").Value = _
                                         objOrder.OrderStatus
                    .Item("@chrCustomerID").Value = _
                                       objCustomer.CustomerID
                    .Item("@nvchrCustomerName").Value = _
                                     objCustomer.CustomerName
                    .Item("@nvchrShipToName").Value = _
                                     objCustomer.CustomerName
                    .Item("@chrShipToAddressID").Value = _
                                objOrder.ShippingAddress.AddressID
                    .Item("@chrBillingAddressID").Value = _
                                 objOrder.BillingAddress.AddressID
                    .Item("@mnySubTotal").Value = objOrder.SubTotal
                    .Item("@mnyShippingTotal").Value = _
                                       objOrder.ShippingTotal
                    .Item("@mnyTaxTotal").Value = objOrder.TaxTotal
                    .Item("@mnyGrandTotal").Value = objOrder.Total
                    .Item("@intPaymentType").Value = _
                                         objOrder.PaymentType

                    'Set the ShippedDate parameter if the Order has a
                    '...shipped date.
                    If objOrder.ShippedDate.Length() > 0 Then
                        .Item("@dtShippedDate").Value = _
                                          objOrder.ShippedDate
                    End If
                End With
            End With
```

Next, let's create an instance of the `SqlConnection` class and establish a connection to the IBuyAdventure SQL Server database. Using the new `SqlConnection`, we'll then execute the `SqlCommand` object for the `sp_Orders_UPD` stored procedure.

```
            'Create an instance of the SqlConnection class
            Dim sqlconIBuyAdventure As _
                         New SqlConnection(m_strConnectionString)

            'Establish a connection to the IBuyAdventure database
            sqlconIBuyAdventure.Open()

            'Assign the SqlConnection object to the SqlCommand for
            '...executing the stored procedure
            sqlcmdUpdateOrders.Connection = sqlconIBuyAdventure


            'Execute the sp_Orders_UPD stored procedure without
```

```
                    '...returning a resultset
                    sqlcmdUpdateOrders.ExecuteNonQuery()
```

Finally, we can close our open connection to the IBuyAdventure database, call the `SetComplete()` method to vote to commit the current transaction, and return the `Order` object containing the updated `Order` information. In our `Catch` block we'll simply call the `SetAbort()` method to abort the current COM+ transaction and throw the exception to the caller.

```
                    'Close our open connection to the IBuyAdventure database
                    sqlconIBuyAdventure.Close()

                    'Return the updated Order object (and Items collection) to
                    '...the caller
                    Return objOrder

                    'We successfully updated the Order record, so tell COM+
                    '...that this object votes to commit the transaction and
                    '...deactivate the object
                    ContextUtil.SetComplete()

                Catch excp As system.Exception
                    'An exception occured updating the order record.

                    'Tell COM+ that this object votes to abort the transaction
                    '...and deactivate
                    ContextUtil.SetAbort()

                    'Throw the exception to the caller of this method
                    Throw excp
                End Try

            End Function
```

InventoryManagementTx

The `InventoryManagementTx` transactional Serviced Component implements two additional methods that are called during the order status update transaction: `UnAllocateInventory()` and `DecrementInventory()`. The `UnAllocateInventory()` method deletes the inventory allocations or reservations that were created for each item on the order when the order was placed for the customer. The `DecrementInventory()` method updates the available inventory for each product on the order to subtract the inventory that has shipped from the fulfillment provider's warehouse. Let's create both of these methods now.

First, we need to define the signatures for the `UnAllocateInventory()` and `DecrementInventory()` methods in the `IInventoryManagementTx` interface.

```
'Import namespaces containing commonly used types
Imports System.Data
Imports System.Data.SqlClient
Imports System.EnterpriseServices
Imports IBuyAdventure.Common
```

```
Namespace IBuyAdventure.BusinessServices

    'Define a public interface containing the signatures for members
    '...of this class
    '
    'NOTE:  It is necessary to define a public interface with the
    '...signatures for methods that utilize COM+ method-level attributes.
    '...Otherwise the interface and methods will not be displayed and
    '...configured in COM+, although the component will be configured.
    Public Interface IInventoryManagementTx
        Function AllocateInventory(ByVal objOrder As Order) As Order
        Function UnAllocateInventory(ByVal objOrder As Order) As Order
        Function DecrementInventory(ByVal objOrder As Order) As Order
    End Interface
```

Now let's implement the `UnAllocateInventory()` method. First we'll create and initialize an instance of the `System.Data.SqlClient.SqlCommand` object for executing the `sp_InventoryAllocations_DEL` stored procedure.

```
        <Description("UnAllocates product inventory in IBuyAdventure.")> _
        Public Function UnAllocateInventory(ByVal objOrder As Order) _
                                                        As Order _
                Implements IInventoryManagementTx.UnAllocateInventory

            Try
                'declare any procedure-level variables
                Dim objItem As Item

                'Create a new instance of the
                '...SqlCommand class to use for executing the
                '...sp_InventoryAllocations_DEL Stored Procedure
                Dim sqlcmdInsertInventoryAllocations As _
                        New SqlCommand("sp_InventoryAllocations_DEL")

                With sqlcmdInsertInventoryAllocations
                    'Set the command type for the new SqlCommand object to
                    '...Stored Procedure
                    .CommandType = CommandType.StoredProcedure

                    With .Parameters
                        'Create and append SqlParameter objects for
                        '...our SqlCommand
                        .Add("@chrOrderID", SqlDbType.Char, 38)
                        .Add("@chrOrderItemID", SqlDbType.Char, 38)
                    End With
                End With
```

Next we'll create and establish a connection to the IBuyAdventure SQL Server database and assign the new `SqlConnection` object to the `SqlCommand` we just created.

```
                'Create an instance of the SqlConnection class
                Dim sqlconIBuyAdventure As _
```

```
                                    New SqlConnection(m_strConnectionString)

                'Establish a connection to the IBuyAdventure database
                sqlconIBuyAdventure.Open()

                'Assign the SqlConnection object to the SqlCommand for
                '...executing the stored procedure
                sqlcmdInsertInventoryAllocations.Connection = _
                                                    sqlconIBuyAdventure
```

Then we'll iterate through each `Item` object in the passed `Order` object's `Items` collection and execute the `SqlCommand` object for the `sp_InventoryAllocations_DEL` stored procedure.

```
                'Iterate through each Item object in the passed Order's
                '...Items collection and insert a record into the Order
                '...Details table for each one
                For Each objItem In objOrder.Items

                    'Set the values for each of the SqlParameters to the
                    '...values stored in the properties and fields for the
                    '...current Item object and Order object
                    With sqlcmdInsertInventoryAllocations.Parameters
                        .Item("@chrOrderID").Value = objOrder.OrderID
                        .Item("@chrOrderItemID").Value = objItem.ItemID
                    End With

                    'Execute the sp_InventoryAllocations_DEL stored
                    '...procedure without returning a resultset
                    sqlcmdInsertInventoryAllocations.ExecuteNonQuery()
                Next
```

Finally, we'll close our open `SqlConnection` object and vote on the transaction outcome. If the `DecrementInventory` method completed successfully, we'll call the `SetComplete` method and return the passed `Order` business object. Otherwise, we'll call the `SetAbort` method and throw the exception to the caller.

```
                'Close our open connection to the IBuyAdventure database
                sqlconIBuyAdventure.Close()

                'We successfully Deleted the InventoryAllocation records,
                '...so tell COM+ that this object votes to commit the
                '...transaction and deactivate.
                ContextUtil.SetComplete()

                'Return the updated Order object (and Items collection) to
                '...the caller
                Return objOrder

            Catch excp As system.Exception
                'An exception occured deleting the records from the
                '...InventoryAllocation table.

                'Tell COM+ that this object votes to abort the transaction
```

```
                '...and deactivate this object.
                ContextUtil.SetAbort()

                'Throw the exception to the caller of this method
                Throw excp
            End Try
        End Function
```

Now let's implement the `DecrementInventory()` method. First we'll create an instance of the `System.Data.SqlClient.SqlCommand` class for executing the `sp_Inventory_UPD_DecrementQuantity` stored procedure and create and append the necessary `SqlParameter` objects.

```
        <Description("Decrements the available product inventory.")> _
        Public Function DecrementInventory(ByVal objOrder As Order) _
             As Order Implements IInventoryManagementTx.DecrementInventory

            Try
                'declare any procedure-level variables
                Dim objItem As Item

                'Create a new instance of the SqlCommand class to use for
                '...executing the sp_Inventory_UPD_DecrementQuantity
                '...Stored Procedure
                Dim sqlcmdUpdateInventory As _
                      New SqlCommand("sp_Inventory_UPD_DecrementQuantity")

                With sqlcmdUpdateInventory
                    'Set the command type for the new SqlCommand object to
                    '...Stored Procedure
                    .CommandType = CommandType.StoredProcedure

                    With .Parameters
                        'Create and append SqlParameter objects for our
                        '...SqlCommand object
                        .Add("@chrProductID", SqlDbType.Char, 38)
                        .Add("@intQuantity", SqlDbType.Int)
                    End With
                End With
```

After establishing a connection to the IBuyAdventure database, we'll iterate through each `Item` object in the passed `Order` business object's `Items` collection and execute the `SqlCommand` object for the `Item`.

```
                'Create an instance of the SqlConnection class
                Dim sqlconIBuyAdventure As _
                                  New SqlConnection(m_strConnectionString)

                'Establish a connection to the IBuyAdventure database
                sqlconIBuyAdventure.Open()

                'Assign the SqlConnection object to the SqlCommand for
                '...executing the stored procedure
```

```
            sqlcmdUpdateInventory.Connection = sqlconIBuyAdventure

            'Iterate through each Item object in the passed Order's
            '...Items collection and update the Inventory quantity
            '...for each one.
            For Each objItem In objOrder.Items

                'Set the values for each of the SqlParameters to the
                '...values stored in the properties and fields for the
                '...current Item object and Order object
                With sqlcmdUpdateInventory.Parameters
                    .Item("@chrProductID").Value = objItem.ProductID
                    .Item("@intQuantity").Value = objItem.Quantity
                End With

                'Execute the sp_Inventory_UPD_DecrementQuantity stored
                '...procedure without returning a resultset
                sqlcmdUpdateInventory.ExecuteNonQuery()
            Next
```

Finally, we'll close our `SqlConnection` object representing an established connection to the IBuyAdventure database and we'll vote on the transaction outcome.

```
            'Close our open connection to the IBuyAdventure database
            sqlconIBuyAdventure.Close()

            'We successfully Updated the Inventory records, so tell
            '...COM+ that this object votes to commit the transaction
            '...and deactivate.
            ContextUtil.SetComplete()

            'Return the updated Order object (and Items collection) to
            '...the caller
            Return objOrder

        Catch excp As system.Exception
            'An exception occured updating the Inventory records.

            'Tell COM+ that this object votes to abort the transaction
            '...and deactivate
            ContextUtil.SetAbort()

            'Throw the exception to the caller of this method
            Throw excp
        End Try
    End Function
```

E-mailConfirmations

In addition to the SendOrderPlacedConfirmation() method that we implemented for the order processing transaction, the E-mailConfirmations class also implements a method named SendOrderStatusMessage(). This method is very similar to the SendOrderPlacedConfirmation(). Currently, the only difference between these methods is the differences in the contents of the e-mail message body. However, by creating two separate methods, we can easily modify the e-mail format or extend the functionality of the e-mail confirmations for either transaction.

Let's create the SendOrderStatusMessage() method now. Since the E-mailConfirmations class is not a .NET Serviced Component, we don't have a public interface that defines the methods for this component, so we can move straight into the implementation. First let's create an instance of the MailMessage class and initialize the new object to send the e-mail message to the value specified in the E-mailAddress property for the passed Customer business object. We'll also build the e-mail message body to include the current order status.

```
Public Function SendOrderStatusMessage(ByVal objOrder As Order, _
                          ByVal objCustomer As Customer) As Order

    Try
        'Declare any procedure-level variables
        Dim strOrderStatusText As String

        'Create a new instance of the System.Web.Mail.MailMessage
        '...class for sending an e-mail message to the customer
        Dim objMailMessage As New System.Web.Mail.MailMessage()

        'Set the properties of the new MailMessage object
        With objMailMessage

            'Set the From Address for the Message
            .From = "Service@IBuyAdventure.com"

            'Send the e-mail message to the customer
            .To = objCustomer.E-mailAddress

            'Set the message format to plain text
            .BodyFormat = System.Web.Mail.MailFormat.Text

            Select Case objOrder.OrderStatus
                Case Order.OrderStatusEnum.OrderStatus_Received
                    strOrderStatusText = "Received"

                Case Order.OrderStatusEnum.OrderStatus_Processing
                    strOrderStatusText = "Processing"

                Case Order.OrderStatusEnum.OrderStatus_Shipped
                    strOrderStatusText = "Shipped"

            End Select

            'Build the simple body for the e-mail message
            .Body = "The status of your order is:  " _
                    & strOrderStatusText
        End With
```

Finally, let's send the order status update e-mail to the customer by calling the `Send()` method of the `SmtpMail` shared object and passing the method the `MailMessage` object that we just created and initialized. We'll return the `Order` object containing any updated information for the order.

```
                'Send the new MailMessage now
                System.Web.Mail.SmtpMail.Send(objMailMessage)

                'Return the updated Order object to the caller
                Return objOrder
```

If an exception occurs in this method, we'll simply catch the exception and throw it up the call stack to the immediate caller. Notice that we're not calling the `SetAbort()` method of the `ContextUtil` object, because this is a simple, non-transactional .NET class. However, by throwing the exception to the caller, this method can cause the transaction to be aborted, because the immediate caller will catch the exception and call the `SetAbort()` method to vote to abort the transaction.

```
            Catch excp As system.Exception
                'An exception occured sending the Order Status e-mail.

                'Throw the exception to the caller of this method
                Throw excp
            End Try
        End Function
```

Data Services

The order status update transaction utilizes the following three stored procedures:

- `sp_Orders_UPD`
- `sp_Inventory_UPD_DecrementQuantity`
- `sp_InventoryAllocations_DEL`

Let's implement each of these stored procedures.

sp_Orders_UPD

The `sp_Orders_UPD` stored procedure updates a single record in the `Orders` table using the data passed into the stored procedure as input parameters. An input parameter is defined for each column in the `Orders` table. The following T-SQL statement defines the `sp_Orders_UPD` stored procedure and its parameters:

```
CREATE PROCEDURE sp_Orders_UPD
    -------------------------------------------------------
    -- Declare the parameters for this Stored Procedure
    -------------------------------------------------------
    @chrOrderID char(38),
    @nvchrOrderNumber nvarchar(40),
    @dtOrderDate datetime,
    @dtShippedDate datetime,
    @intOrderStatus int,
    @chrCustomerID char(38),
    @nvchrCustomerName nvarchar(50),
```

```
        @nvchrShipToName nvarchar(40),
        @chrShipToAddressID char(38),
        @chrBillingAddressID char(38),
        @mnySubTotal money,
        @mnyShippingTotal money,
        @mnyTaxTotal money,
        @mnyGrandTotal money,
        @intPaymentType int
AS
```

Now, let's simply execute a SQL `UPDATE` statement against the `Orders` table using the values of the input parameters as the new values for the columns. We'll limit the update to the single `Order` record matching the `OrderID` specified in the `@chrOrderID` input parameter.

```
        ----------------------------------------------------------
        -- Perform the intended operation againist the Database
        ----------------------------------------------------------

        UPDATE     Orders
        SET        OrderID = @chrOrderID, OrderNumber = @nvchrOrderNumber,
                   OrderDate = @dtOrderDate, OrderStatus = @intOrderStatus,
                   CustomerID = @chrCustomerID,
                   CustomerName = @nvchrCustomerName,
                   ShipToName = @nvchrShipToName,
                   ShipToAddressID = @chrShipToAddressID,
                   BillingAddressID = @chrBillingAddressID,
                   SubTotal = @mnySubTotal,
                   ShippingTotal = @mnyShippingTotal,
                   TaxTotal = @mnyTaxTotal,
                   GrandTotal = @mnyGrandTotal,
                   PaymentType = @intPaymentType
        WHERE OrderID = @chrOrderID

        -- Return 1 (true) to indicate success
        return 1
GO
```

sp_Inventory_UPD_DecrementQuantity

The `sp_Inventory_UPD_DecrementQuantity` stored procedure updates the `QuantityInStock` column for a single record in the `Inventory` table by decrementing the current quantity in stock by the value specified in the `@intQuantity` input parameter. This SQL `UPDATE` statement is limited to a single record matching the `ProductID` specified in the `@chrProductID` input parameter. The following T-SQL `CREATE PROCEDURE` statement defines the `sp_Inventory_UPD_DecrementQuantity` stored procedure:

```
CREATE PROCEDURE sp_Inventory_UPD_DecrementQuantity
        ----------------------------------------------------------
        -- Declare the parameters for this Stored Procedure
        ----------------------------------------------------------
        @chrProductID char(38),
        @intQuantity char(38)
```

```
AS
     ------------------------------------------------------------
     -- Perform the intended operation againist the Database
     ------------------------------------------------------------
     UPDATE    Inventory
     SET       QuantityInStock = QuantityInStock - @intQuantity
     WHERE ProductID = @chrProductID

     -- Return 1 (true) to indicate success
     return 1

GO
```

sp_InventoryAllocations_DEL

The `sp_InventoryAllocations_DEL` stored product executes a SQL `DELETE` statement to delete all of the records from the `InventoryAllocations` table matching both the `OrderID` and `OrderItemID` specified in the `@chrOrderID` and `@chrOrderItemID` parameters, respectively. The following T-SQL script defines this stored procedure:

```
CREATE PROCEDURE sp_InventoryAllocations_DEL
     ------------------------------------------------------------
     -- Declare the parameters for this Stored Procedure
     ------------------------------------------------------------
     @chrOrderID char(38),
     @chrOrderItemID char(38)
AS
     ------------------------------------------------------------
     -- Perform the intended operation againist the Database
     ------------------------------------------------------------
     DELETE FROM InventoryAllocations
     WHERE     (OrderID = @chrOrderID) AND (OrderItemID = @chrOrderItemID)

     -- Return 1 (true) to indicate success
     return 1

GO
```

ReceiveOrderStatusUpdate HTTP Handler

As I mentioned earlier, the `ReceiveOrderStatusUpdate` HTTP Handler is responsible for receiving an order status update XML message sent by the fulfillment provider to the IBuyAdventure system across the HTTP or HTTPS protocols. The following XML document is an example of the `OrderStatusUpdate` XML document sent by the fulfillment provider to the IBuyAdventure system.

```
<?xml version="1.0" ?>
<OrderStatusUpdate>
     <Order OrderID="F0EA462E-AC02-4F95-B6C9-B91037736B0B"
               OrderNumber="1234" ShippedDate="01/17/2002"
               OrderStatus="Shipped">
          <Items>
               <Item ItemID="B8046194-D535-4E8F-945D-431B52788460"
```

```
                        ProductID="EE931DF1-8080-4215-9EAD-E3379A183F53"
                        SKU="AW310-12" ProductName="Polar Star"
                        Quantity="5" />
            </Items>
      </Order>
</OrderStatusUpdate>
```

An HTTP Handler is a component that can perform low-level processing of HTTP requests. HTTP Handlers are similar to ISAPI extensions, but they are much simpler to develop and they leverage the common ASP.NET classes. ASP.NET actually provides two HTTP Handlers, one for ASP.NET Web Forms with the extension `.aspx` and another for ASP.NET Web Services with the extension `.asmx`. There are two tasks involved with creating a .NET HTTP Handler.

- First, create a class that implements the `System.Web.IHttpHandler` interface
- Register the HTTP Handler in the `Web.Config` file

Let's perform each of these tasks for implementing the `ReceiveOrderStatusUpdate` HTTP Handler.

ReceiveOrderStatusUpdate

The `ReceiveOrderStatusUpdate` class is the implementation of our HTTP Handler. This class implements the `IHttpHandler` interface and is responsible for processing the `OrderStatusUpdate` XML messages posted by the fulfillment provider by initiating the order status update transaction.

Let's begin creating the `ReceiveOrderStatusUpdate` class by first importing the namespaces containing frequently used types and by defining the namespace for the `ReceiveOrderStatusUpdate` HTTP Handler. Notice that we've defined a namespace with the name `IBuyAdventure.WebServices` instead of the `IBuyAdventure.BusinessServices` namespace, to which most components in the business services tier belong.

```
'Import namespaces containing commonly used types
Imports System.Web
Imports System.Web.Handlers

Namespace IBuyAdventure.WebServices

Next let's declare the ReceiveOrderStatusUpdate class and implement the
IHttpHandler interface so this component can behave as a .NET HTTP Handler.

    Public Class ReceiveOrderStatusUpdate
        'Implement the System.Web.IHttpHandler interface so this class
        '...can be a .NET HTTP Handler.
        Implements IHttpHandler
```

Now, let's implement the `ProcessRequest()` method defined by the `IHttpHandler` interface. Let's enclose all of the code in this method within a `Try` block so we can catch and handle any exceptions. Then we'll declare some procedure-level variables to hold references to the `Order` and `Customer` objects for the order we will be updating.

```
    Public Sub ProcessRequest(ByVal context As HttpContext) _
                              Implements IHttpHandler.ProcessRequest
        Try

            'Declare any procedure-level variables
            Dim objOrder As IBuyAdventure.Common.Order
            Dim objCustomer As IBuyAdventure.Common.Customer
```

Next, let's create an instance of the `XmlDocument` class and load the `OrderStatusUpdate` XML message posted to the `ReceiveOrderStatusUpdate` HTTP Handler. This is easily accomplished by calling one of the overloaded `Load()` methods of the new `XmlDocument` object and passing the `Request` object's `InputStream` as a parameter. The `Load()` method will then load and parse the XML data contained in the input stream.

```
            'Create an instance of the System.Xml.XmlDocument class
            Dim xmldocOrder As New System.Xml.XmlDocument()

            'Load the passed OrderStatusUpdate message into our new
            '...XmlDocument object
            xmldocOrder.Load(context.Request.InputStream)
```

Next, let's get the `OrderID` value specified in the `OrderStatusUpdate` XML message using our new `XmlDocument` object, and acquire a reference to an `Order` business object containing all of the data for the specified `Order`. We can retrieve the loaded `Order` object by calling the `GetOrderData()` method on an instance of the `Orders` business services component and passing the `OrderID` from the `OrderStatusUpdate` XML message.

```
            'Acquire a reference to the <Order> element in the
            '...OrderStatusUpdate message
            Dim nodOrder As System.Xml.XmlNode =      _
              xmldocOrder.SelectSingleNode("/OrderStatusUpdate/Order")

            'Get the OrderID out of the OrderStatusUpdate XML document
            Dim strOrderID As String = _
                           nodOrder.SelectSingleNode("@OrderID").Value

            'Create an instance of the
            '...IBuyAdventure.BusinessServices.Orders class
            Dim objOrders As New _
                             IBuyAdventure.BusinessServices.Orders()

            'Get the Order object with the data from the database for
            '...the current order
            objOrder = objOrders.GetOrderData(strOrderID)
```

Next let's update the `Order` object with the `OrderStatus` and `ShippedDate` that was specified in the `OrderStatusUpdate` XML message.

```
            'Update the data in the Order object with some of the data
            '...in the OrderXML document
            Dim strOrderStatus As String = _
```

```
                        nodOrder.SelectSingleNode("@OrderStatus").Value()
                Dim strShippedDate As String = _
                        nodOrder.SelectSingleNode("@ShippedDate").Value()

                'Translate the Order Status text into the equivalent
                '...enum value.
                If strOrderStatus.Equals("Shipped") = True Then
                    objOrder.OrderStatus = _
                                Order.OrderStatusEnum.OrderStatus_Shipped
                End If

                'Set the ShippedDate for the Order to the value that was
                '...in the OrderStatusUpdate
                objOrder.ShippedDate = strShippedDate
```

Next, we need to acquire a reference to a `Customer` business object containing all of the data for the customer who placed the `Order`. We'll create an instance of the customer's business services component and call the `GetCustomerData()` method, passing the `Order`'s `CustomerID` as a parameter.

```
                'Create an instance of the
                '...IBuyAdventure.BusinessServices.Customers class
                Dim objCustomers As New _
                                IBuyAdventure.BusinessServices.Customers()

                'Get the Customer object for the customer who placed
                '...the order
                objCustomer = _
                        objCustomers.GetCustomerData(objOrder.CustomerID)
```

Finally, we'll create an instance of the `OrderProcessingTx` transactional .NET Serviced Component and call the new object's `UpdateOrderStatus()` method passing in the `Order` and `Customer` business objects as parameters. The `UpdateOrderStatus()` method will handle the entire process of saving the updated order to the IBuyAdventure database. Assuming everything completes successfully, we'll set the HTTP response status code to `200`, indicating that everything completed successfully.

```
                'Create a new instance of the
                '...IBuyAdventure.BusinessServices.OrderProcessingTx
                '...transactional .NET ServicedComponent
                Dim objOrderProcessingTx As New _
                        IBuyAdventure.BusinessServices.OrderProcessingTx()

                'Update the Order in the database with the updated
                '...information in the Order object
                objOrderProcessingTx.UpdateOrderStatus(objOrder, _
                                                       objCustomer)

                'Set the Status Code returned to 200 (OK), indicating
                '...an error occured.
                context.Response.StatusCode = 200
```

If an exception should occur in the `ProcessRequest()` method, we'll simply return an HTTP response status code of `500`, indicating that an application error occurred and write out the information for the exception.

```
            Catch excp As system.Exception
                'An exception occured processing the OrderStatusUpdate msg

                'Set the Status Code returned to 500, indicating an
                '...error occured.
                context.Response.StatusCode = 500

                'Also write out the Exception message
                context.Response.Write(excp)
            End Try

        End Sub
```

Before the ReceiveOrderStatusUpdate HTTP Handler is complete, we need to implement the IsReusable read-only property procedure defined by the IHttpHandler interface. When this property is called, we'll simply return a value of false, indicating that the ReceiveOrderStatusUpdate HTTP Handler does not support pooling and cannot be reused for multiple requests.

```
        Public ReadOnly Property IsReusable() As Boolean _
                                    Implements IHttpHandler.IsReusable
            Get
                'Return false indicating that this HTTP Handler cannot
                '...be reused.
                IsReusable = False
            End Get
        End Property
    End Class
End Namespace
```

Web.Config

Finally, we need to register the ReceiveOrderStatusUpdate HTTP Handler by creating an entry in the Web.Config file located in the same virtual directory as the bin directory containing IBuyAdventure.WebServices.dll assembly. We'll assign the ReceiveOrderStatusUpdate HTTP Handler a path of ReceiveOrderStatusUpdate.aspx, so it can be addressed with this "virtual" filename across HTTP. Although the .aspx extension is also used by the ASP.NET Web Form HTTP Handler, since we're explicating specifying a virtual filename and an extension, ASP.NET will automatically route HTTP requests for this address to our ReceiveOrderStatusUpdate class.

```
<?xml version="1.0" encoding="utf-8" ?>
<configuration>
     <system.web>
          <!--  DYNAMIC DEBUG COMPILATION
          Set compilation debug="true" to insert debugging symbols (.pdb
          information) into the compiled page. Because this creates a
          larger file that executes more slowly, you should set this
          value to true only when debugging and to false at all other
          times. For more information, refer to the documentation about
          debugging ASP.NET files.
          -->
          <compilation defaultLanguage="vb" debug="true" />
```

```
<!--  CUSTOM ERROR MESSAGES
Set customErrors mode="On" or "RemoteOnly" to enable custom
error messages, "Off" to disable. Add <error> tags for each of
the errors you want to handle.
-->
<customErrors mode="RemoteOnly" />
<!--  AUTHENTICATION
This section sets the authentication policies of the
application. Possible modes are "Windows",
"Forms", "Passport" and "None"
-->
<authentication mode="Windows" />
<!--  AUTHORIZATION
This section sets the authorization policies of the
application. You can allow or deny access
to application resources by user or role. Wildcards: "*" mean
everyone, "?" means anonymous
(unauthenticated) users.
-->
<authorization>
      <allow users="*" /> <!-- Allow all users -->
      <!--  <allow     users="[comma separated list of users]"
                  roles="[comma separated list of roles]"/>
       <deny      users="[comma separated list of users]"
                  roles="[comma separated list of roles]"/>
      -->
</authorization>
<!--  APPLICATION-LEVEL TRACE LOGGING
Application-level tracing enables trace log output for every
page within an application. Set trace enabled="true" to enable
application trace logging. If pageOutput="true", the trace
information will be displayed at the bottom of each page.
Otherwise, you can view the

application trace log by browsing the "trace.axd" page from
your web application root.
-->
<trace enabled="false" requestLimit="10" pageOutput="false"
      traceMode="SortByTime" localOnly="true" />
<!--  SESSION STATE SETTINGS
By default ASP.NET uses cookies to identify which requests
belong to a particular session.
If cookies are not available, a session can be tracked by
adding a session identifier to the URL. To disable cookies, set
sessionState cookieless="true".
-->
<sessionState mode="InProc"
    stateConnectionString="tcpip=127.0.0.1:42424"
    sqlConnectionString="data source=127.0.0.1;user
    id=sa;password=" cookieless="false" timeout="200000" />
<!--  PREVENT SOURCE CODE DOWNLOAD
This section sets the types of files that will not be
downloaded. As well as entering a httphandler for a file type,
you must also associate that file type with the xspisapi.dll in
```

```
             the App Mappings property of the web site, or the file can be
             downloaded. It is recommended that you use this section to
             prevent your sources being downloaded.
             -->
             <httpHandlers>
                    <add verb="*" path="*.vb"
                          type="System.Web.HttpNotFoundHandler,System.Web" />
                    <add verb="*" path="*.cs"
                          type="System.Web.HttpNotFoundHandler,System.Web" />
                    <add verb="*" path="*.vbproj"
                          type="System.Web.HttpNotFoundHandler,System.Web" />
                    <add verb="*" path="*.csproj"
                          type="System.Web.HttpNotFoundHandler,System.Web" />
                    <add verb="*" path="*.webinfo"
                          type="System.Web.HttpNotFoundHandler,System.Web" />
                    <add verb="*" path="ReceiveOrderStatusUpdate.aspx"
                    type="IBuyAdventure.WebServices.ReceiveOrderStatusUpdate,
                          IBuyAdventureWS" />
             </httpHandlers>
             <!--   GLOBALIZATION
             This section sets the globalization settings of the
             application.
             -->
             <globalization requestEncoding="utf-8"
                   responseEncoding="utf-8" />
       </system.web>
</configuration>
```

Next Steps

Now that we've completed the design and development of the IBuyAdventure 2.0 system, what are the next steps? We'll I'm glad you asked. There are actually a number of enhancements we could integrate into this solution to make it more robust, maintainable, and scalable using the .NET Framework, Enterprise Server Products and development tools. Some of these additional enhancements include the ability to:

- Expose additional functionality to business customers through Web Services, including the ability to check product availability and pricing
- Utilize BizTalk Server 2000 to support additional protocols and data formats for receiving orders from business customers
- Receive and process orders asynchronously by using MSMQ
- Utilize .NET Alerts to notify consumer customers of order status, product availability, etc. .NET Alerts allow users to be notified in a variety of ways, based on their established preferences

Maybe these will be the topics of another book! We'll have to wait and see. Stay tuned at Wrox Press web site at http://www.wrox.com for information about existing and future titles.

Summary

Wow! We're finally complete! In this chapter we've taken a detailed look at how to design and develop a 3-tier, transactional application using Visual Basic .NET and several other .NET technologies, including ADO.NET, ASP.NET, and .NET Serviced Components. We've learned several valuable techniques for developing distributed applications on the .NET platform. Specifically, in this chapter we:

- Discussed the business objectives, challenges, and requirements for IBuyAdventure's new e-commerce system
- Learned how to optimize data model design for transaction processing systems
- Utilized an *n*-tier architecture to segment the user interface, business logic, and data access logic into separate tiers
- Analyzed the benefits and drawbacks of the various transaction processing technologies
- Implemented three complex transactions: Customer Account Creation, Order Processing, and Order Status Receiving
- Developed several transactional .NET Serviced Components
- Manipulated data in a Microsoft SQL Server database and Microsoft Message Queue within a single transaction
- Created a .NET HTTP Handler that receives XML formatted documents
- Learned how to utilize custom business objects as intelligent data containers for passing and managing structured, in-memory data

I personally hope you have found this case study and this book beneficial for learning how to develop transactional applications using Visual Basic .NET.

Pro Visual Basic .NET Transactions

Index

A Guide to the Index

The ~ character is used to reduce the need to duplicate almost identical entries. For example, *Authorize*CreditCardOrder()/~OnAccountOrder() methods means AuthorizeCreditCardOrder() method/AuthorizeOnAccountOrder() method. Note that the common part of the entries is italicized.

.NET references are alphabetized as starting with an 'N'.

Symbols

A

D

J

K

L

O

P

T

U

Y